JOHN FITZGIBBON, EARL OF CLARE

John FitzGibbon, Earl of Clare

Protestant Reaction and English Authority in Late Eighteenth-Century Ireland

Ann C. Kavanaugh
PhD at Trinity College, Dublin

IRISH ACADEMIC PRESS

This book was set in 10.5 on 12.5 point Ehrhardt
by Woodcote Typesetters for
IRISH ACADEMIC PRESS
44 Northumberland Road, Ballsbridge, Dublin 4, Ireland
and in North America for
IRISH ACADEMIC PRESS
5804 NE Hassalo St, Portland, Oregon 97213.

A catalogue record for this title
is available from the British Library.

ISBN 0-7165-2605-0

Printed in Ireland
by ßetaprint Ltd, Dublin

Contents

To my parents, with eternal love and gratitude
and to Kevin, Sheila , Peter and Holly Anne, of course

Preface

No author ever writes a book alone. Behind my name on the title page are hundreds of people who have helped and supported me as I've struggled to understand FitzGibbon's complex, often appalling and, as often, admirable and heroic, character. Probably foremost in any list of acknowledgments would be my advisor at Trinity, Professor L.M. Cullen. If this manuscript is at all accurate and readable, it is due in great part to his vast knowledge, judicious editing and above all, patience through a long process. I also owe a great debt to Dr Anthony Malcomson, who generously shared his own extensive materials on FitzGibbon; I would never have had access to much of this material without his help. His keen sense of 18th-century social mores and his knowledge of art and collecting during this period also saved me from some egregious blunders.

I also need to acknowledge the support I received from other members of the Department of Modern History at Trinity, especially Professor Hammerstein and Professor David Dickson. Professor Hammerstein, as Dean of Graduate Studies, supported me through the terrors of departmental requirements and the miseries of lost financial aid checks, while Professor Dickson generously invited me to participate in the 1991 conference marking the bicentenary of the founding of the United Irishmen, which was probably one of the most exciting and stimulating conferences I have ever attended – and a graduate student attends a fair number of them when slouching toward commencement.

I also received some much needed financial help from Trinity College in the form of travel stipends which allowed me to do research in Belfast, and a generous grant from the Grace Lawless Lee Foundation, which made it possible for me to devote the summer of 1995 to revising and correcting the manuscript.

I also owe a special debt to Kevin Whelan, Daire Keogh and Tommy Graham who helped me publish portions of this work. Tommy very kindly accepted a version of the first chapter, on the historiography of Lord Clare, for publication in *History Ireland* (Vol. 1, No. 3, Autumn 1993). The American writer, Edith Wharton, a rather ceremonious grande dame, apparently danced up and down the stairs when she first appeared in print. While I wouldn't put myself in Edith Wharton's class as a writer, I certainly had the same reaction when I saw the beautiful presentation of the article and the sensitive editing it received. Kevin and Daire published a version of the second chapter, on FitzGibbon's family background in their anthology *The United*

Irishmen: Republicanism, Radicalism and Rebellion (Dublin: 1993). They made many insightful and thoughtful revisions that I have very happily incorporated in the final version of the book. They also shared their own extensive knowledge with me and gave me some very helpful guidance and encouragement about approaching publishers.

No writer or researcher can do a thing without the assistance of librarians and archivists. I worked most extensively with the National Library of Ireland, the Public Record Office of Northern Ireland and Trinity College Dublin. I can't begin to express my gratitude for the patience, efficiency and kindness I encountered from the librarians at all three of these institutions. I also need to acknowledge the librarians of the University of Keele, who provided me with copies of FitzGibbon's extensive – and absorbing – correspondence with Lord Auckland, and the excellent colleges and public libraries in my home city of Fargo, North Dakota.

I need to acknowledge the many friends and well wishers who lend time and resources to read the manuscript or to listen to my endless conversations about FitzGibbon's various foibles. I hope that if I forgot anyone, they will forgive the oversight and realize that I am at least as grateful as I am forgetful: my kind publishers at Four Courts, for their patience and flexibility, Nuala, Eva and Christine Cullen for their gracious hospitality and friendship, Larry Peterson and old colleagues at North Dakota State University, for their unfailing support and encouragement, Karlin Lillington, who believed in me and Lord Clare when I was about ready to give up on both, Jane Ohlmeyer and her wonderful mother, Shirley, for their hospitality and kindness when I was in Belfast, Eve Patton, Kevin Herlihy, Sheila Clancy, Troy Davis, Rosemary O'Connor, Laura Davis, Rebecca Gardner, for her superb critical sense *and* her laser printer, Evonne Vaplon, Chris Boyle and Jim White, Kim and Brian Melton, Sonja and Ray Berry, Judy Holzy, Solveig [*sic*] Haugland, Connie Sauer, Jeannette Larson, Karen and Doug Burgum, and my wonderful co-workers. Even though the subject couldn't be more remote from their interests, they have supported me faithfully by giving me access to the fax, the copy machine and the mysterious, non-billing long-distance service. I also have been very honored by the kind interest of the Knight of Glin, who has much of value to add about FitzGibbon's family background.

I can't forget to mention, with respect and gratitude, my advisor at the University of Minnesota, Dr. Josef Altholz, who first suggested the subject of FitzGibbon to me. As the descendent of Wexford rebels, I wasn't terribly thrilled at the prospect of researching "Black Jack". Initially, I planned to do a quick hatchet job to qualify for my MA and move on to bigger and better things. But revulsion soon turned to fascination, and ultimately to respect, and even a certain proprietary affection at times.

Finally, I owe a debt I can't possibly ever repay to my whole family. Above all, I want to acknowledge my parents and siblings. To them, in particular, I dedicate this book.

I

Historiographical Dilemmas

Few men in the 18th-century political world rose more rapidly or spectacularly than John FitzGibbon. He entered Parliament in 1778 as a young lawyer of thirty. Within five years, he was appointed Attorney General and in 1789, he attained the highest legal office in Ireland, that of Lord Chancellor. He then rose with celerity in the ranks of the peerage. The appointment as Lord Chancellor brought him the title Baron FitzGibbon of Lower Connello in Limerick, his native county. In 1794, he advanced to the rank of Viscount FitzGibbon of Limerick, and finally, in 1795, he attained the title by which he became most noted, or perhaps, most notorious, the Earldom of Clare. In his various official capacities, he gained an extraordinary influence over successive viceregal administrations in Ireland and became the dominant political figure of the 1790s. The hatred he aroused in his rise to power equaled, if it did not surpass, the honors he earned. The circumstances of the late 18th century and his particular reaction to them accounted for this antagonism.

During the period of FitzGibbon's career, the Irish political world collapsed into a state of entropy. The small body of Anglicans who maintained a precarious monopoly on political power, were bitterly divided on the question of what, if any, political and civil rights Catholics and, to a lesser extent, Presbyterians should receive. The equally vexed questions of the constitutional relationship between England and Ireland and of parliamentary reform created further fragmentation. Such noted figures as Charlemont, Flood and Sir Edward Newenham favored a high degree of Irish autonomy and reform, while opposing concessions to Catholics, with varying degrees of emphasis. Yet another faction, led by Grattan and the Ponsonby and Fitzgerald families, favored what later became known as Catholic Emancipation, as well as autonomy and reform. Still other Anglicans, mainly disillusioned members of the middle class, became convinced that the twin evils of parliamentary corruption and English domination would never end with piecemeal reforms from College Green and half-hearted concessions from Whitehall. Only a secular republic, based on French and American models, could save Ireland. The United Irishmen were devoted to this end virtually from their inception in 1791.

The United Irishmen also included numerous Presbyterians. Contrary to the fixed belief of the governing classes in Ireland, Ulster Presbyterians did not have a uniform predilection for republicanism. But sympathies for the American cause had run high enough in Ulster to give the Castle serious cause for concern in the 1770s. Moreover, Belfast, the chief city of the province, had become an established center of political radicalism by the end of the American conflict. Many of its citizens warmly welcomed the French Revolution, and the 14th of July was celebrated with *éclat* in Belfast. Not surprisingly, a group which included Wolfe Tone chose to inaugurate the United Irishmen in this like-minded city.

The highly politicized atmosphere of the late 18th century inevitably affected the Catholics. Far from enjoying a unity imposed by the Pope, their priests and French agents, a frequent claim of Castle informants, they were as divided as their Protestant rulers. They ranged from timid reactionaries like Lord Kenmare to violent radicals like Luke Teeling. The great mass of Catholic farmers and laborers, scorned by the upper classes of both religions as "barbarians" showed a considerable aptitude for political resistance. The Whiteboys and the Defenders were effective and formidable organizations which terrified their "betters".

FitzGibbon had the distinction of antagonizing all of these diverse and contending factions. In an era when nationalistic feelings were at a height, FitzGibbon bluntly insisted on the necessity of strengthening constitutional and economic ties with England. Toward the end of his career, this conviction prompt him to support the Act of Union, the measure which did the most to secure his infamous reputation. Earlier he had taken a similarly unpopular stand on the question of parliamentary reform by opposing even the most moderate proposals. At a time when Catholics were growing increasingly restive and aggressive and when many Protestants were encouraging their political aspirations, FitzGibbon resisted concessions with all his considerable ruthlessness and cunning. Nor did he soften his opposition with the tone of patronizing benevolence which late 18th-century Irish Protestants commonly adopted toward Catholics. On the contrary, he freely expressed his contempt for the Irish Catholics and for their Church. Although the danger of Catholics to the Protestant establishment in Church and State remained his dominant obsession, he had the conventional suspicions of the Presbyterians and their turbulent republican tendencies.

His violently reactionary stands on the major issues of the time inevitably aroused equally violent antagonism. The most vitriolic attacks on FitzGibbon appeared in the public press of Dublin, the chief stage of his career and with Belfast one of the two centers of radical and nationalistic opinion. Almost from the start of his career, he drew hostile comment for arrogance, effeminacy, drunkenness and debauchery, as well as for his objectionable political opinions. The newspapers also accused him of exerting a Mephistophelian influence over viceroys. The depictions of FitzGibbon as an evil seducer, at once epicene and ruthless, reached a culmination in a paragraph which appeared in 1784. It portrayed FitzGibbon as no more and no less than Lucifer incarnate:

> No sir, the Devil in hell is not quite as bad as the Devil in human form of whom

> I mean to speak [FitzGibbon];– and yet there is, I must confess, in some particulars, a marvelous similarity between the two.
>
> Pride and envy, we are told, were Lucifer's crimes and for those he justly forfeited eternal happiness – the ambition of our Devil is boundless – his envy sickens at the welfare of his neighbor; and to gratify these tormenting passions he would willingly forgo every earthly enjoyment.
>
> The Devil is a liar; so is our devil; the Devil is a sophister; our Devil is a lawyer, and a lawyer, it is said, can outwit the Devil himself. The Devil is a tempter; he first deceives unthinking mortals into the commission of wickedness, next abandons them to destruction and then mocks at their sufferings. Our Devil seduces the credulous innocent female, robs her of her honor, abandons her to infamy and ruin and then answers her reproaches with derision:– of this numberless living examples can be produced.[1]

Other squibs attributed his influence to carnal reasons; they accused FitzGibbon of ingratiating himself with his English masters by pimping for them.[2] Above all, his hostile critics in the press harped on the central paradox of his life: the most arrogant and obdurate champion of the Protestant oligarchy came from a comparatively obscure Irish Catholic background.

The hatred he aroused in life pursued him to his grave. His funeral in Dublin was a macabre saturnalia, and his standing in the popular imagination did not improve as the years passed. The sobriquet by which he is best known, "Black Jack", dates from the 19th century. In the words of an ordinary Dubliner interviewed by Madden in the 1840s, FitzGibbon was "so called for the nature and amount of his political crimes".[3] Most 19th-century memoir writers and historians perpetrated the Black Jack myth. His opponents on the issue of the Union and their descendants displayed particular bitterness. Sir Jonah Barrington continued the tradition of FitzGibbon as Lucifer in this sketch of his character:

> Authoritative and peremptory in his address, commanding, able and arrogant in his language, a daring contempt for public opinion was the fatal principle which misguided his conduct and Ireland became divided between the friends of his patronage – the slaves of his power – and the enemies of his tyranny.[4]

The son of Henry Grattan, FitzGibbon's greatest political opponent, piously continued his father's political feud. In his memoirs of his father, published between 1843 and 1849, the younger Grattan portrayed FitzGibbon as an overweening vulgarian of "Popish" extraction who destroyed the free constitution of Ireland.[5]

Even historians who had sincere intentions of judging FitzGibbon fairly could not avoid an antagonistic or critical tone. Lecky, the paradigm of the scrupulous and fair-minded historian, attempted to do credit to FitzGibbon's more amiable private qualities and to his abilities as a judge. But his adulation for Henry Grattan ultimately defeated him. In slightly more measured language, he confirmed the judgment of the younger Grattan: FitzGibbon was a sordid, cynical intrigante whose reactionary intransigence sparked the 1798 rebellion and led ultimately to the disaster of the Union.[6] A similar triumph of disgust over detachment afflicted the legal historian, O'Flanagan, whose study of the Irish lord chancellors appeared some years before Lecky's great history. Like Lecky, he expressed admiration for FitzGibbon's judicial policies, revulsion for his political actions, and a gentlemanly Victorian distaste for the coarser aspects of FitzGibbon's character and temper.[7]

C. Litton Falkiner took a more benign view of FitzGibbon in his *Studies in Irish History*, published in 1902. He went much further than Lecky in paying tribute to FitzGibbon's "legal intellect ... which constantly led him to take the most generous, most humane and most tolerant view open to him".[8] He also included an invaluable collection of letters in his essay on FitzGibbon with the intention of showing his "lighter and kindlier features". Yet even Falkiner was forced to admit that "in his public aspect [FitzGibbon] was a man of imperious, not to say despotic temperament, little tolerant of opposition and disposed at times to wield authority with Cromwellian sternness".[9]

FitzGibbon did have his defenders, and the strength of opinion against him made them especially ardent. Not surprisingly, the arch-loyalist historian Sir Richard Musgrave gave FitzGibbon a prominent and illustrious role in his *Memoirs of the Different Rebellions in Ireland.* In Sir Richard's view, FitzGibbon did not merely defend the British and Protestant constitution from assorted Popish rebels; he *was* the constitution in all its pristine glory:

> The exalted sphere to which he [FitzGibbon] has been raised, and the honors conferred on him by our gracious sovereign prove the superior excellence of a mixed government, where the monarch selects men like him distinguished for wisdom, abilities and virtue to fill the principle departments of state.[10]

An adulatory article published in the *Dublin University Magazine* in 1848 no doubt represented a reaction to the spate of anti-Union and anti-FitzGibbon memoirs that appeared during that nationalistic decade.[11] Undesirable contemporary events also inspired J.A. Froude's *History of the English in Ireland in the Eighteenth Century*. In Froude's case, his opposition to the disestablishment of the Irish Church prompted him to look to the past for polemical material.

Froude was perhaps the greatest devotee of the FitzGibbon cult. Unfortunately, like many true believers, he was sometimes ludicrously naive. Froude transformed FitzGibbon into a hero worthy of one of his own over-blown romances and made this prediction (as yet unfulfilled):

> If undaunted courage, if the power to recognize and the will to act upon unpalatable truth, if a resolution to oppose at all hazards those wild illusions which have lain at all times at the root of Ireland's unhappiness, be the

> constituents of greatness in an Irish statesman, Grattan and FitzGibbon were likely hereafter to change places in the final judgment of history.[12]

Unfortunately, Froude unwittingly did his hero a disservice. The "Black Jack" legend bestowed a certain evil glamour on FitzGibbon which Froude's tiresome eminent Victorian manifestly lacks. So intent was Froude on transforming FitzGibbon into an honest and upright pro-counsel of Empire that he ignored very strong evidence of a robust and pleasure-loving temperament in his hero:

> I believe FitzGibbon's private life to have been a simple one. Had it been stained by any vice, we should all have heard of it, for no other public man ever had more bitter or unscrupulous antagonists.[13]

In light of innumerable newspaper articles, even in government-controlled publications, and in light of the recollections even of favorable contemporaries, all of which attested to FitzGibbon's "gallantry", drinking and taste for luxury, Froude's claim is astonishing, to say the least.

A more creditable defense of FitzGibbon came from an unexpected source: James Roche, a devoutly Catholic member of a great merchant family with branches in Cork and Limerick. Roche had one powerful advantage over Froude or indeed, most of the historians who judged FitzGibbon. Roche could claim a personal acquaintance with the great man. Perhaps in consequence, Roche's reminiscences, published in 1851 under the title *Critical and Miscellaneous Essays by an Octogenarian*, offered the first recognizably human portrait of FitzGibbon. He emerged from Roche's pages neither as Lucifer nor as the apotheosis of the British Empire, but as a mere mortal, with an ordinary mixture of good and bad qualities. Roche acknowledged FitzGibbon's "overbearing temper and despotic authority". He also noted FitzGibbon's coarse language and demeanor (more evidence which seems to have escaped Froude's attention). At the same time, Roche paid what is perhaps the most deeply felt and affectionate tribute to FitzGibbon: "In private life ... I can affirm that he was a generous and indulgent landlord, a kind master and an attached friend."[14] He also refuted nationalist and popular myths of FitzGibbon's despotic cruelty. Roche not only acknowledged that FitzGibbon had "substantial grounds for several of his public measures", he added: "I could state many redeeming instances of persons whose legal guilt could not be gainsaid, saved by him from the lash and the halter."[15] Of all the 19th-century writers who addressed the enigma of John FitzGibbon, Roche probably deserves the most credence. Not only was he a Roman Catholic, he wrote at a time when FitzGibbon had few defenders. Under such circumstances, the tribute of a man who had every reason, religious and political, to dislike FitzGibbon, has infinitely more worth than the hagiography of Musgrave or Froude.

The 20th century has seen the appearance of many excellent historians of 18th-century Ireland. Their efforts have resulted in valuable reassessments of both nationalist and loyalist myths. In spite of these positive developments, FitzGibbon, the 18th-century figure most enshrouded in myth, has attracted comparatively little attention from historians. Full-length biographical studies do exist, but most of them continue the dubious tradition of hagiography. Eliot Fitzgibbon's odd little book *Earl of Clare: Mainspring of the Union*[16] is a case in point. He devotes half his book to proving FitzGibbon's impeccable descent from the Normans and the ancient Trojans and the other half to arguing that if proper heed had been paid to FitzGibbon, the British Empire would never have fallen and the world would not have fallen under the dominion of Papists, blacks, Americans, Communists and others deemed undesirable by the author.[17]

A direct descendent, Constantine FitzGibbon, merits mention for what is probably the most amazing claim in nearly 200 years of writing on the subject. In *Miss Finnegan's Fault*, a personal memoir of his family, and in other works, Constantine FitzGibbon argued that his ancestor was, all appearances to the contrary, a Roman Catholic, who went to Mass in his carriage every Sunday.[18] The notable lavishness, even gaudiness, of John FitzGibbon's equipages alone would refute such a claim. Whatever his secret religious yearnings, FitzGibbon probably did not advertise them by descending on country chapels in his gold embossed carriage. The man had many faults, but stupidity was not one of them. In a touching display of family loyalty, Constantine FitzGibbon, a prolific novelist, lapsed into fiction.[19]

The nature of the man usually has thwarted FitzGibbon's historians, not any lack of ability or distinction on their part.[20] On the contrary, the genius of a Froude or a Lecky transcends their problematic encounters with FitzGibbon. The brutal sectarian and nationalistic antagonism of his time probably scarred FitzGibbon more than any of his contemporaries. An 18th-century polish softens the edges of Charlemont, Grattan and Flood, while the glamour of youthful idealism and youthful death hover over his United Irish antagonists Tone, Teeling and McCracken. Because the same conflicts persist today, FitzGibbon, as both a victim and a perpetrator of them, remains a disturbing figure. Consequently, no historian can pretend to an unprejudiced view. By his very nature, FitzGibbon inspires instinctive admiration or instinctive antagonism. FitzGibbon will probably find justice from historians only when the tragic history he helped to create comes to an end.

2

Antecedents and Early Years 1600–1776

In spite of his notoriety, only the most fragmentary and doubtful information about FitzGibbon's antecedents exists. His numerous political enemies gleefully took advantage of the general obscurity to taunt him for his supposed lowly origins. FitzGibbon's family, or lack of it, provided fair game for every one from anti-Union memoir writers to opposition pamphleteers. Barrington made the sneering observation that "his ascertained pedigree was short".[1] Charlemont was more frankly abusive: FitzGibbon sprang from the "dregs" of the people.[2] In her satiric political verse, Henrietta Battier, alias Peter Pindar, portrayed FitzGibbon's grandfather as a humble purveyor of buttermilk, and his grandmother as a rapacious shrew who supplemented her gains from sharp dealing in livestock by hiring out as a wet-nurse.[3]

Even those with no particular animus against FitzGibbon, could find nothing notable or illustrious about his ancestry. The 19th-century Herald of Ulster, Sir William Betham, frankly admitted that he could only trace FitzGibbon's pedigree to his father John. (Betham mistakenly identified him as FitzGibbon's grandfather.)[4] His warm admirer, Richard Musgrave delicately alluded to FitzGibbon's *arriviste* origins by noting that he (FitzGibbon) owed his rise to royal favor. FitzGibbon's success, Musgrave observed, illustrated the benevolence of legitimate royal authority, which drew valuable servants from all ranks (and by implication from the most obscure).[5]

FitzGibbon himself never responded to the aspersions cast on his antecedents. It fell to his cousin, also named John FitzGibbon, to assert the family's claims to gentility. In 1810, he provided Sir William Betham with a romantic account of his family's descent from the Earls of Desmond and their loss of an estate allegedly worth "upwards of twenty thousand a year":

> My great-grandfather, Thomas FitzGibbon, lived at Ballylanders. The Earl of Kingston, who had the lower Manor of Mitchelstown, resided in the Castle in that town. A strong intimacy subsisted between them. The Earl wanted FitzGibbon to go with him to revise his patent, which at that time was necessary because of the new restrictive laws against Popery. FitzGibbon, a steady Roman Catholic, pleaded the gout as an excuse for not going. He would sooner forfeit his property than swerve from his religion. He begged the Earl to cover his

> estates under his patent and gave him £100, the expense of so doing. The Earl promised faithfully to declare his trust on his return. Some say Sir William Fenton was the person who covered the estates under his patent. He was connected with the family. Still, I cannot conceive how he could be the person entrusted from what follows.
>
> Before the Earl's return, FitzGibbon died and left an only son, John. The Earl took him to has castle and had him educated, then sent him to Paris to study Physic, at that time reckoned a very genteel profession. The Earl died without declaring the trust of leaving any document of it. Thus was my family most fraudulently thrown out of their property.[6]

This story, redolent of Lady Morgan, has a somewhat dubious chronology. The three generations enumerated by Cousin John FitzGibbon do not necessarily carry the family pedigree far enough back to the early 17th century. Nonetheless, his account neatly explains the family's glaring absence from the Civil Survey, and it has some pretensions to plausibility. A significant legal menace to Irish Catholic property did arise during the reign of James I, in the guise of his newly revived Court of Wards. Individuals claiming property under jurisdiction of this court were required to "sue out a livery" or receive confirmation of title. James hoped above all to raise income by charging fees for suing out livery. But ever the zealous Protestant, he imposed an additional burden on Irish Catholics, requiring them to take the oath of supremacy as well as paying the requisite fees.[7]

Unfortunately, no positive proof exists for Cousin John FitzGibbon's story. Moreover, the story has an element of anachronism. The practice of holding land in trust occurred more commonly in the 18th century. When confronted with such a fascinating, but unsubstantiated tale, a historian has no choice but to disregard it, however reluctantly.

The reality appears to have been neither wronged gentility nor melodramatic penury, but middling respectability. The Registry of Deeds offers the most reliable documentation of his family. In the will of one John Weekes of Knockstevenagh, County Limerick, dated 18 July 1708, John FitzGibbon, Doctor of Physic, appears as a witness.[8] This man undoubtedly was FitzGibbon's earliest known ancestor. While claims of a lost estate worth £20,000 can only be met with skepticism, there is no particular reason to doubt the assertions of FitzGibbon's cousin that their mutual great-grandfather practiced medicine.

According to Betham's correspondent, Dr FitzGibbon had one son, Thomas. Even less is known of him. The Betham letter offers no worthwhile information. John FitzGibbon the cousin reported only that his grandfather "lived at Ballyseeda in the Liberties of Limerick in a most respectable light".[9] Serious, well meaning biographers, such as the legal historian J.F. O'Flanagan, as well as Henrietta Battier and other detractors, made the assumption that Thomas sank into the ranks of the peasantry.[10] No proof exists to confirm the hopes and suspicions of FitzGibbon's enemies. Thomas's eldest son, John, later claimed the status of "gentleman" for his father.[11] Thomas could well have maintained some pretensions to gentility as a very minor freeholder. It seems unlikely that Dr FitzGibbon, the provincial physician, endowed Thomas with land or with much money. Nor is there any evidence that Thomas engaged in any lucrative pursuit, whether selling buttermilk or following in his father's medical footsteps. He seems to have made his gentlemanly fortune, such as it was, through a good marriage to one Honor Hayes. Whatever the truth of Henrietta Battier's claims of unscrupulousness and rapacity, Honor indisputably came from a comfortable, rising family. Her brother, Jeremiah Hayes, apparently either purchased land from John Weekes, Dr FitzGibbon's patient, or he married into the family. His will, dated 1732, lists him as the owner of a number of estates that had belonged to Weekes.[12] Honor provided Thomas FitzGibbon not only with a fortune, but with a large family as well. There were four sons, John, born in 1708, Patrick the father of Betham's correspondent, Thomas and Gibbon.

Whatever his religion at birth, Jeremiah Hayes was unquestionably a Protestant at the time of his death. He could not have come into such extensive property otherwise. Both of his daughters married into strongly Protestant families, the Blennerhassets and the Gradys. Yet his sisters all appear to have married Catholics.[13] Although Honor herself was probably a Catholic, her brother provided an early and constant example to her sons of the economic and social advantages of Protestantism.

Whatever the later social and religious influence of the Hayes family, the elder John FitzGibbon and his brothers began life as Catholics. At the age of sixteen, he went to the Irish College in Paris to study medicine, a circumstance that effectively refutes claims made of his family's penury. Nonetheless, the fact that he, the eldest son, had to take up a profession at all suggests that the family's resources were not quite sufficient to assure its claims to gentility, even with the help of Honor's *dot*. At the same time, the fact that two of Thomas's sons eventually enrolled in the Middle Temple suggests a degree of economic standing and lofty social pretensions, as the law was the most genteel of professions.

Roche's memoirs provide what information exists about the elder FitzGibbon's earliest years: a solitary anecdote of a boyish escapade. O'Flanagan repeated the story almost word for word:

> As usual for newcomers, he [the elder FitzGibbon] was allowed the first day to take a view of the city. John FitzGibbon on this occasion was accompanied by a student as companion and caretaker ... The youths, having transversed the metropolis in every direction, stopped at the cathedral of Notre Dame in the vicinity of the College; when exhausted with fatigue, they sought repose on the benches of the choir and fell so soundly asleep that they noticed not the closing of the church doors, while they were equally unobserved. It was past midnight when they awoke, and finding themselves thus immured, they groped about in the dark until they happened to reach the bell chains, which they vigorously

> pulled to the surprise and affright, not only of the sexton, but of the city at large, having made the great chimes –even the fearful TOCSIN— resound and spread alarm over the city. They were finally liberated, though not without a strong reprimand, followed by the severer and more impressive reproof of the President of the College.[14]

Unfortunately, while Roche's memoirs and O'Flanagan's paraphrase give an endearing portrait of old FitzGibbon as an innocent abroad, they offer no explanation for his momentous decision to desert the study of medicine for that of the law and in the process to "abandon his native creed", as Roche discreetly put it. John FitzGibbon entered the Middle Temple in 1726 and was called to the bar in Hilary term of 1731. He was enrolled as a convert on 23 November 1731.[15]

Of course, the explanation for old FitzGibbon's change of plans may have seemed so obvious Roche simply felt no need to mention it. The bar was, without question, the surest and most rapid way to wealth and social advancement. The fact that FitzGibbon's conversion closely followed his admission to the bar suggests that he was not in any zealous hurry to change his religion and he did so only when his professional life absolutely demanded it.

His brothers all converted as well. Again, professional or economic reasons offer the likeliest explanations for this circumstance, unusual in a convert family. Patrick, the second son, converted shortly after John, on 24 June 1732. His reasons for doing so are not apparent. Possibly some favorable property settlement offered an inducement. At any rate, whatever his reasons or his degree of sincerity, his descendants quickly reverted to Catholicism. Thomas, the third son, was enrolled in 1736. That same year, he followed his elder brother's example and entered the Middle Temple. Gibbon, the youngest, held out until 1763. He married soon afterward, which suggests the likeliest explanation for his change after so many years.[16] He may have hoped to make a more lucrative and advantageous match as a Protestant than as a Catholic.

According to O'Flanagan, FitzGibbon's law career experienced a shaky start, owing to a series of law reports which he published while enrolled in the Middle Temple. A debt to his landlord had evidently prompted this venture into print. In the process of meeting his obligation, FitzGibbon offended some of the judges, who found his reports unflatteringly accurate. One judge complained the FitzGibbon's reports made them "talk nonsense by wholesale".[17] The uproar died down with no lasting effects. The elder FitzGibbon returned to Ireland, where he quickly established himself as an active and skilled lawyer. A cousin, Daniel Hayes, himself a barrister, paid tribute to his ability to elucidate legal complexities: "Who like FitzGibbon clears Law's mystic spell?"[18] His mastery of the law's mystic spell brought him many clients and lucrative fees. O'Flanagan reported that at the time of his death, Old FitzGibbon left a fortune of over £100,000.[19]

FitzGibbon managed his own affairs as shrewdly as he managed those of his clients.

He invested some of his earnings in Mount Shannon, an estate encompassing land in both north Limerick and north Tipperary. He also owned property in the city of Limerick.[20] In 1738, he married Elinor Grove, the daughter of a Cork landowner. Miss Grove had an impeccable Protestant pedigree. One of her ancestors had been attainted by the Jacobite Parliament of 1689.[21] Apart from a conventional eulogy detailing her many virtues, published after her death in 1786, no account either favorable or unfavorable exists of her.[22] Presumably, she was a conventional dutiful wife, living quietly under her husband's domination and attending to her domestic responsibilities.

FitzGibbon had seven children by his wife, three daughters and four sons. The daughters all married advantageously. Arabella, the eldest girl, married St John Jeffereyes, a wealth Cork landowner whose demesne included Blarney Castle. Elizabeth married the Reverend William Beresford, a younger son of the Earl of Tyrone. This connection was to have particular significance in the younger FitzGibbon's career. Elinor, the youngest sister, became the second wife of Dominic Trant; like his father-in-law, he was an aspiring convert lawyer.[23] While his daughters creditably advanced the family fortunes, the elder FitzGibbon experienced tragedy of Greek proportions with his sons. His two eldest sons died in quick succession in childhood; a third, Ion fared somewhat better in the mortality stakes, reaching young adulthood. Like his mother, Ion left little impression on the world at large. Roche wrote kindly of his "mild and easy temper", but a letter of Edmund Malone's offers an acid portrait of a shallow, absurdly fastidious coxcomb:

> I met FitzGibbon at Bath on his way to Hotwells. His unparalleled effeminacy, I am now convinced, is unconquerable. Change of kingdoms has, I think, rather increased the unnatural delicacy of his manners. His *deshabille* was not by any means remarkable after a long journey from Oxford, but it gave him great concern that I should meet him in such undress.[24]

Malone may have been unduly harsh, mistaking the self-consciousness of adolescence for inveterate dandyism. At any rate Ion never had a chance to demonstrate greater maturity and development of character. He appears to have died in his early twenties. Only the youngest son and namesake, born in 1748, survived to maturity.[25]

Later commentators made much of the contrast between the virtuous patriotic father and the corrupt, power mad son. Ferrar's *History of Limerick*, published in 1787, portrayed him as an honest Roman, honorable, benevolent and disinterested:

> He [the elder FitzGibbon] died ... deservedly regretted as an able lawyer, a humane landlord, an honest man, who preferred the shade of retirement to the sunshine of a court.[26]

The son, who was at that time enjoying the sunshine of the lively Rutland viceregal court, did not merit so much as a passing mention. Ferrar evidently did not think him worthy of comparison with his father. In his memoirs of his own father, Henry Grattan Junior played on the same noble Roman theme:

> Mr John FitzGibbons [*sic*] ... was father to the earl of Clare, but a very different character, plain, straightforward and unostentatious. He lived retired and much respected [mistrusting] parade and grandeur, except for the true grandeur of simplicity.[27]

Years later, Edmund Burke proudly claimed him as a relation and praised him as a "good Irishman". He also portrayed old FitzGibbon as a man tragically torn between sympathy for his "blood" i.e., the Irish Catholics, and his ambition for his family.[28]

Nonetheless, other sources reveal a somewhat less edifying side to Old FitzGibbon. Henrietta Battier portrayed him as a true son of his rapacious mother.[29] Even some of the praise for old FitzGibbon inadvertently suggests rather miserly habits. In actuality, the "true grandeur of simplicity" may have been the true meanness of avarice.

An unabashed, single-minded, utterly a-moral opportunism seems to have been his master characteristic. In Lord Kenmare's manuscripts, he appears as a figure of infinite cunning, well versed in the complexities of the penal laws, and ably using his knowledge to enrich himself.[30] In effect the penal laws made old FitzGibbon; fees from such cases constituted the bulk of his massive legal earnings. It is true that William Gerard Hamilton accused him of crypto-Catholic sentiments. Hamilton had apparently won favor with FitzGibbon, "who is a Papist", by abusing King William.[31] In addition, Burke admired and respected old FitzGibbon, not only for his admirable character as an Irish patriot, but for his able defense of Burke's kinsman James Nagle, an accused Whiteboy.[32] It would have been perfectly logical for old FitzGibbon, a former Limerick Catholic, to have no great love for King William. And lingering family feeling, as well as skill and the prospect of a fee, undoubtedly made him an able advocate for James Nagle. He had, moreover, the capable support of impeccably Protestant colleagues, such as Scott and Yelverton. But the occasional displays of atavistic Jacobitism and of family loyalty do not by any means detract from the man's fundamental religious opportunism. According to James Roche, old FitzGibbon "refused all religious assistance on his deathbed".[33] In short, he appears to have lapsed into religious indifference or outright atheism. Unburdened by any inconvenient belief, he could exploit the penal laws to the great advantage of himself and of his new-made Protestant family. It would be difficult to blame him. An Irish Catholic of FitzGibbon's generation could easily have concluded that God was either non-existent or too indifferent to merit attention, much less devotion according to the forms of the Roman Catholic Church. Making the best of the world made by King William offered the only hope for a tolerable existence.

His Irish patriotism too was an uncertain quantity. He entered the new parliament of 1761 as a member for Newcastle in County Dublin, and he seems at first to have inclined toward government. William Gerard Hamilton, then acting as chief secretary of Lord Halifax, expressed satisfaction at an obscure service performed by FitzGibbon.[34] FitzGibbon does not seem to have received a suitably satisfactory return for his services, either in the form of money or in the form of power. By 1763, he had defected to the opposition benches, where he made thunderous speeches against the "Servile and Corrupt" and where he conveniently forgot his own connivance in friend Hamilton's quest for Irish office and Irish lucre.[35] Although there were fitful proposals to elevate FitzGibbon to the bench, nothing ever came of them, and by the 1770s he was still crying in the wilderness of the opposition. During Lord Harcourt's administration, he refused to vote in favor of a resolution supporting the "unjust" war against the Americans.[36] But old FitzGibbon was always ready to turn again, given encouragement. His most fundamental loyalties lay with himself, his family and their interests. His application for a bishopric for his son-in-law, William Beresford evoked this dry comment from Lord Harcourt's chief secretary: "... generally in opposition, yet will ask great Favors at the most critical time."[37]

This driven, amoral man's schemes for advancement centered around his youngest son and namesake. In him, old FitzGibbon instilled his vast store of legal knowledge and skill. Wolfe Tone, described FitzGibbon as a compendium of "Coke upon Lyttleton", as taught by "his papa".[38] To judge by his own public pronouncements, FitzGibbon adored his father, and willingly embraced the profession decreed for him. He referred to his "esteemed and honored father" several times in his will, and he spoke with particular affection of "the attachment" which "my most worthy and respected father manifested in every stage of his life to his children".[39]

The solitary anecdote of FitzGibbon's childhood, again provided by that indefatigable gossip Roche, portrays an indulgent father, helplessly charmed and amused by his precocious, if appallingly bratty, son:

> Having incurred his father's displeasure for some schoolboy fault, FitzGibbon senior sent his elder son to command young John's attendance. The message was authoritative: "Your father orders you to go to him, you must come instantly."
>
> "*Orders – must*", repeated the boy of thirteen. "Such language suits me not, nor will I stir an inch. DECRETUM EST" and proudly stamping his foot on the ground remained stationary.
>
> The messenger reported the reply. The old gentleman laughed heartily at this presumptuous bit of haughtiness and in a formal note, jocusely requested the honor of an interview with Mr John FitzGibbon, junior, when, after a few paternal words of admonition, no further notice was taken of the matter.[40]

If there is any truth to this slight tale, FitzGibbon did not carry these habits of rebellion into later life. On the contrary, the few certain facts about FitzGibbon's youth and early manhood give the impression of a dutiful son doing credit to a beloved father. After attending a school kept by one Dr Ball, FitzGibbon entered Trinity

College Dublin in 1762. There he distinguished himself by winning a prize for a translation of the *Georgics*. After receiving his BA in 1766, he proceeded to Christ Church Oxford, where he took an MA in 1769. He duly entered the Middle Temple in 1769, and he was called to the bar in 1772.[41] In spite of Barrington's claims that the younger FitzGibbon "at first attended but little to the duties of his profession", a fee book unearthed at an auction sale in the 19th century suggests instead a diligent young lawyer with a growing and lucrative practice.[42] When he returned to Ireland, he settled in his father's house on Stephen's Green. After the elder FitzGibbon's death in 1780, he continued to live with his widowed mother for another three years.[43] Not until he was in his middle thirties did FitzGibbon attain full independence from parental proximity. Never once does he appear to have displayed any restiveness at this situation, which must have been trying as his father grew older and declined in health.

This unrelenting sense of duty has a suspicious, forced quality. Perhaps old FitzGibbon did love his son as much as he was capable of loving anyone. Yet given the father's consuming ambition, it is difficult to believe that he was not also demanding and domineering. The sudden deaths of the elder brothers, and possibly, Ion's vacuous unpromising character, all could have increased the pressures on FitzGibbon to realize his father's aspirations. In the end, it is impossible to know whether FitzGibbon was the pride or the pawn of his father. In the terms that mattered to old FitzGibbon, however, their relationship was a clear and resounding success. The son not only adopted his father's profession, he imbibed all of his father's craving for status and power. If anything, the younger FitzGibbon was the more determined and the more single minded.

FitzGibbon also possessed his father's sharp intelligence. This trait, allied to his extensive experience on the Munster circuit, gave him an exceptionally keen insight into the realities of Irish society. He also seems to have learned from his father's mistakes. Old FitzGibbon had veered from government to opposition, with the result that no one trusted him and worse, no one gave him office. The younger FitzGibbon on the contrary, mapped out a clear, consistent strategy for advancement, which he followed unwaveringly to the end of his life.

An absolute rejection of his Catholic antecedents and a fierce identification with the Protestant interest lay at the heart of his strategy for advancement. FitzGibbon later made the claim that reason and sincere theological conviction lay at the heart of his abhorrence of Roman Catholicism. This claim is dubious. Given his worldly, sensual nature, FitzGibbon's religious vision was probably quite limited: God was a celestial lord-lieutenant and Jesus was his chief secretary. FitzGibbon rejected instead the powerlessness and the degradation attached to Catholicism in 18th century Ireland.

The Whiteboy *grande peur* that gripped Protestant Munster during his young manhood undoubtedly strengthened his impulse to move as far from his Catholic origins as he could. His encounters with Catholics in his legal practice also may have confirmed his sectarian snobbery. Contrary to the claims of nationalist mythology, Catholics did not inevitably display long-suffering incorruptibility in the face of the penal laws. On the contrary, it would have been surprising if they had not succumbed to the moral corruption such laws encouraged. In the case of *Redington v. Redington*, heard in Chancery in 1794, FitzGibbon encountered at least one instance of the chicanery to which Catholics could resort in evading the law. It involved a Catholic patriarch who encouraged his sons to convert so he could acquire property in their name.[44] In his long legal career, FitzGibbon undoubtedly handled countless similar, though now undocumented cases, all of which could have confirmed his notions of Popish untrustworthiness, cunning and obduracy.

His antagonism may have been exacerbated by a certain moral uneasiness. He was too perceptive not to recognize that the Papists, despicable as he may have considered them, did have legitimate grievances; the massive dispossessions of the 17th century in particular haunted his legal and his moral conscience, as his later public speeches frequently reveal.[45] The fact that he himself came from a Catholic background gave his political and social attitudes an inescapable taint of treachery. Perhaps to evade this unpalatable bit of self-knowledge, he occasionally adopted the role of a disinterested friend of the Catholics, anxious to protect "the respectable" and the "rational" (meaning a-political) among them.[46] In his capacity as Lord Chancellor, he usually behaved with exquisite fairness and propriety to Catholic claimants. And he inevitably prefaced any attacks on Catholics with elaborate disclaimers of esteem, respect and admiration.[47] At the same time he probably hated the Catholics all the more because their very presence cast so many troubling doubts on his painstakingly created identity.

No doubt in an attempt to justify himself, FitzGibbon later claimed his "esteemed and worthy father's" sanction for this act of renunciation. He informed Sir Lawrence Parsons that his father had frequently warned him of the innate evil of Irish Roman Catholics:

> My father was a popish recusant. He became a Protestant and was called to the bar, but he continued to live on terms of familiarity with his Roman Catholic relations and early friends and he knew the Catholics well. He has repeatedly told me that if ever they have the opportunity, they would overturn the established church and resume the Protestant estates.[48]

Of course his father may have said something of the sort, but the spirit of such remarks was probably different from that of similar ones made by the son. The younger constantly raised the specter of the "old inhabitants" brooding with "sullen indignation" over their wrongs to justify the Protestant oligarchy and to rally its frequently lax members.[49] The father probably was making a mere observation, with same chill-minded realism that allowed him to exploit the penal laws to such advantage.

In spite of his best efforts, the younger FitzGibbon remained an outsider to the

Protestant oligarchy which he so fiercely upheld. The obscurity of his family, their legendary lowliness and his father's education in France, the heart of international Popery, haunted and embarrassed him throughout his career. The Catholic origins of the FitzGibbons inspired numerous colorful myths. It was frequently claimed that old FitzGibbon had been "tonsured at St Omers", and perhaps in consequence, the younger FitzGibbon was sometimes mocked as "FitzJesuit" or "FitzFriar".[50] In response, FitzGibbon often expressed contempt for those he served. He reserved his severest comment for the Protestant patriotic party of Flood, Grattan, Charlemont, et. al. He took every opportunity of reminding them that in spite of their lofty pretensions to nationhood, they were the descendants of freebooters, dependent on English power to protect their ill-gotten gains.[51]

More than injured feelings accounted for these appeals to the might of England. He also came to recognize that the true fulcrum of power lay with the English government and not with the arrogant, quarrelsome Irish Protestant elite. This insight came at a particularly opportune time. The onset of FitzGibbon's political career came at a time when the English government was creating for the first time an effective control of Irish parliamentary life after the overthrow of the "undertakers". They were on the lookout for bright, hungry young men to fill the ranks of the new government party. In the earliest stages of his career, FitzGibbon of necessity identified himself as an Irish patriot. In the late 1770s, when FitzGibbon entered parliament, that party was in the truculent ascendant thanks to the unrest created by the American rebellion. But once the opportunity (and the promise of office) offered itself, FitzGibbon coolly shed his patriotic proclivities, and embraced the English government's interests. To his credit, he served the English interest steadfastly, and with fervor. As Lord Westmorland recognized, defending and promoting the English interest was his true religion: "... he has no god but English government."[52] Indeed, FitzGibbon found deep emotional satisfaction in his religion of imperialism. It offered the grace of power and office, and it offered the exquisite pleasure of domination, not only over the despised Irish Catholics, but over the Irish Protestants who despised him.

It would be immensely satisfying to dismiss FitzGibbon as a particularly unattractive careerist. But, however squalid his master motives, he did have many admirable, indeed likable, qualities. While FitzGibbon was not a particularly cultivated man, his letters, speeches, and legal opinions show no mean literary talent. His prose is terse, clear and often striking: in particular, his chancery opinion in the case of *Redington v. Redington* is a *tour de force* of social and psychological insight, and a letter recounting the dowager Duchess of Leinster's marital history is a racy, if cruel, comedy of manners.[53] In his private life, he seems to have demonstrated infinite kindness to his errant wife and to his sometimes lazy and feckless FitzGibbon relations.[54] His correspondence is full of acts of generosity and thoughtfulness: ordering Limerick gloves for English friends, praising an estate agent for a job well done, pleading for a stay of execution for the son of his shepherd. FitzGibbon had no illusions about the son: "I have strong grounds to believe that he is very criminal", but he pitied the father, "a very honest man".[55] If he fought hard and unscrupulously for power and place, he did try, however fitfully, to act with responsibility once he obtained them. Even his worst enemies had to acknowledge his integrity and ability as a judge.[56] Finally, he took his role as an improving landlord very seriously. To appeal once again to the evidence of his letters, they reveal generosity and fairness to his tenants and a good grasp of agriculture.[57]

To be sure, FitzGibbon's social grudges sometimes tainted his good qualities as a judge and as a landlord. In his court, he over-acted the role of avenging champion of the poor and oppressed, and in Parliament, he indulged in many and tedious lectures on the irresponsibility and neglect of his fellow landlords. In some respects, his displays of paternalistic virtue were a form of showing off, on a par with his gaudy carriage and his Epicurean dinner parties. They were meant to demonstrate that John FitzGibbon, the son of a former scholar at the Irish College, had a finer sense of aristocratic responsibility than those with more established pedigrees. But in light of the unrelenting condemnation FitzGibbon has suffered for more than two hundred years, it would be mean-spirited and unfair to over-emphasize his moral vanity or to deny his genuine impulses of compassion and honor.

Above all, FitzGibbon had an essentially sound grasp of Irish society and politics, in spite of his insecurities and prejudices. His constant harping on menace of the Catholic masses, "brooding in sullen indignation" on their historical wrongs, was far more than the ranting of a social and sectarian renegade. The Protestant elite did indeed depend for their political survival on a strong English presence and on a sectarian monopoly. Equally sound was his claim that wholesale enfranchisement of Catholics, reform, or grandiose claims of nationhood carried grave risks, given the paucity of Protestant numbers and the raw memories of conquest and dispossession. The bloodshed of the 1790s certainly proved FitzGibbon's point about the depths of sectarian hatred still lingering in Ireland, while the decline of Protestant political influence following the final grant of Catholic emancipation, bore out another frequently made prediction. No doubt on an abstract moral level, his political views were cynical and repugnant. He uncritically accepted a structure of power that many Irish, both Catholic and Protestant abhorred. But his experience as an outsider of Catholic descent unquestionably gave him a mordant clarity of mind possessed by few of his contemporaries.

Yet even when every allowance is made for his intelligence, and his many virtues and abilities, FitzGibbon's character remains disturbing, violent and repulsive. Throughout his life, he alternated between gracious kindness and sadistic bullying, between forthright warmth and terrifying rage, between courageous honesty and pathological dishonesty. Above all, he seems to have been consumed by a bitter dissatisfaction with others and still more with himself. Self-contempt drove him to a perpetual quest to remake himself in a more satisfactory image and likeness. His letters, even to intimates like Auckland, have the forced quality of a man continually acting a role. His loathing for the imperfections of the world drove him to impose perfect order and perfect submission to right as he saw it. Of course, he could never attain either. Perfect order is elusive in the nature of things, and many people disputed his notions of perfect right. Consequently, he existed in a perpetual state of seething rage and frustration. In a rare moment of self revelation, he summed up his usual state of mind to Auckland: "If it were not that at times I get relief from a volley of execrations, I do believe I should blow up."[58]

It would be tempting to attribute his darker qualities to the tyranny of expectation which his father exercised over him. But such an explanation would be both simplistic and inadequate. Plenty of sons of ambitious fathers manage to survive their upbringing while retaining a measure of sanity and stability. Even the brutal sectarian and social snobberies of 18th century Ireland cannot fully account for this side of FitzGibbon. Converts were sometimes taunted for their past religious loyalties; but most converts (or sons of converts) did not react with FitzGibbon's destructive and self-destructive fury.

The cruel and arbitrary misfortune of a bad genetic inheritance may have molded, or perhaps more accurately twisted, FitzGibbon's character. To put the matter bluntly, there does seem to have been a streak of eccentricity bordering on madness in the Hayes family. Acute alcoholism, another hereditary predisposition in the Hayes family, also may have played a part in the younger FitzGibbon's startling personality transformations. He was a notorious drinker and the symptoms of his final illness suggest death from cirrhosis. Of course, attributing FitzGibbon's inner demons exclusively to the malign genetic influence of his Hayes ancestors would be a dangerous over-simplification. Other unknowable circumstances and experiences, beyond the control of either father or son, undoubtedly played their part. Whatever the reasons for his conduct, FitzGibbon's harsh and disagreeable manner unquestionably crippled his public life. Repeatedly he created antagonism where there need not have been any, or he made a bad situation worse by violent, precipitous words and deeds. His unfortunate manner obscured his good sense and frequently defeated measures for which he labored diligently and faithfully. It would not be too much of an exaggeration to attribute much of the English government's growing lack of influence and disrepute to FitzGibbon's largely self-inflicted unpopularity.

3

Youthful Patriot 1776–80

I

As a matter of course, FitzGibbon not only took up his omnipresent father's profession, he followed him into the realm of politics. His own ravening ambition, as well as old FitzGibbon's expectations, made public life inevitable. The latter's setbacks and frustrations could only have impressed young FitzGibbon and instilled in him an ardent desire to do better and go farther than his father. Yet he started his career by adopting precisely the stance that had consigned his father to political oblivion: that of popular patriot. His lifelong docility and deference to his father, of course would have prevented him from adopting a radically different course, had he been so inclined. Moreover, when John FitzGibbon made his first incursions into politics in the mid-1770s, a young man intent on making a name for himself would have had little choice but to adopt such a stance.

Both the conflict with the American colonies and the unrest in Ireland had a common origin: attempts by the metropolitan government to establish a stronger, more consistent control over its colonies. In the case of Ireland, this movement toward centralization took the form of wresting power from the small clique of families, notably the Ponsonbys, the Fitzgeralds and the Boyles, who had "undertaken" the management of Ireland in return for a share of patronage. Under the controversial administration of Lord Townshend, which endured from 1767 to 1773, this process gathered pace, if only because he managed to retain office longer than his immediate predecessors. Although Townshend may not have refashioned the English administration in Ireland, he did unquestionably establish a pattern of aggressively reclaiming and using the government's powers of patronage to create a Castle interest. He did so by cultivating that elusive element of British politics, the independent country gentleman. Townshend himself later had to abandon this policy and to make an attempt to placate members of the old undertaker clique. But other families, most notably the Beresfords, rose to prominence because of the English government's desire for a counterweight to the great Irish aristocrats.

Despite the fact that they had developed patronage into a fine art, the interests displaced by Townshend denounced the government's use of it as "corruption". In particular, the opponents of (and sufferers from) a stronger Castle influence made use of that time-honored subject of quibble, government expenditure, and in particular, expenditures on pensions and sinecures. The Irish establishment was particularly vulnerable to attacks of this kind because it supported many foreign recipients of royal pensions. The subject of Ireland's contribution to the military establishment also served as a fruitful subject of contention. Townshend himself weathered a fierce battle over an increase in the number of troops Ireland contributed to the imperial military establishment.

The Irish opposition had another potent means of embarrassing the government unavailable to their English counterparts: the inflammatory question of the rights of the Irish nation. Two statutes from the Tudor era, Poynings' Act, which dated from the reign of Henry VII and the so-called "explanation" of Philip and Mary severely limited the powers of the Irish Parliament to draw up legislation. Strictly speaking, it did not draw up and debate bills, but proposals for or "heads" of bills. The heads of bills went first to the Irish Privy Council, which could alter them at will, and then to the English counterpart, which had the same power. The parliament in College Green could make no changes of its own on an objectionably altered bill. At the most, it could reject such bills and draw up new heads. Two other provisions of 18th-century origin further limited the power and autonomy of the Irish Parliament. In 1708, the Irish House of Lords lost its power of final appeal on cases tried in Ireland; the English bench assumed that jurisdiction. The so-called Declaratory Act, or the 6th of George I gave the English Parliament the power to legislate for Ireland. In spite of its cumbersome features, this process of legislation served its purpose well enough in the ordinary course of things. Nonetheless, when disagreements arose between the administration and Parliament, the matter of rights and restrictions could always provide plenty of fuel for rhetorical fires.

Ultimately, the English government could have maintained the political *status quo* in Ireland, in a stable world. The government had greater resources than the most princely Whig aristocrat, and thanks to Lord Townshend, it controlled the greater share of patronage. As old FitzGibbon discovered, lofty patriotism imposed the pains of insignificance as well as the pleasures of popularity. The well-known fact is that conditions in the 1770s did not remain stable. The revenues of government, in spite of complaints about high taxes and extravagance, shrank. The erratic economy of the 1770s, which fluctuated between boom and depression and the general administrative inadequacy accounted for lower revenue. Above all, the conflict in America ignited the long-smoldering issues of contention between the English government and the colonial oligarchy in Ireland. The government's need for troops aroused the usual rhetoric about excessive burdens on Ireland, and all the usual fears that Protestants would pay for new levies only to see them removed from the country, leaving them at the mercy of Papists, domestic and international.

At least in the early stages of the war, some members of the political class in Ireland also expressed sympathy for the Americans, regarding them as brother Englishmen struggling against the same evils of excessive taxation and ministerial high-handedness. In 1775, during debates on a government-sponsored resolutions against the American colonists, old FitzGibbon expressed a hope that "if Ireland refused her aid, the king would pause and proceed with greater caution, and thus Ireland would be the means of inducing him to put an end to so unjust a war".[1] In a gesture typical of the man, Sir Edward Newenham build a monument to George Washington on the grounds of his estate near Dublin.[2]

The difficulties with the rebellious colonies, combined with a business depression in Great Britain, had a severe impact on the Irish economy, circumstances which inevitably exacerbated political contention. These circumstances not only inspired menacing demonstrations from unemployed weavers and other workmen, it increased pressure on the English government to remove interdictions on trade with the British West Indies as compensation for lost markets. Associations to eschew English imports and to wear and to use products exclusively of Irish manufacture formed all over the country.[3]

These home consumption organizations, with their resemblance to similar associations formed in America, were unnerving enough, but the government faced a far more serious difficulty in the rise and growth of the so-called Volunteers. The ostensible purpose of the Volunteers was inoffensive enough. Because the demands of the war in North America had diminished the number of troops stationed in Ireland, a number of landed proprietors had taken it upon themselves to raise private forces at their own expense. Such organizations had existed in a rudimentary form during the Whiteboy disturbances of the early part of the decade.[4]

The government avoided the seemingly logical step of raising a militia to counter or to co-opt the Volunteers. While parliament had passed a militia bill, the government had acquiesced in it only because of powerful popular support for such a measure. Expense served as the ostensible plea, but in reality, Buckinghamshire and his fellow servants feared their ability to control a militia, given the discontents of Irish Protestants and the possibility that they might follow the example of the Americans. In the debate on the militia bill, the viceroy, Lord Buckinghamshire, argued that a militia was not only expensive, the sectarian peculiarities of Ireland seriously reduced the number of potential recruits to such a force. The companies raised would either fall short because of a lack of qualified Protestants or they would consist of Protestants of the wrong sort, i.e., Presbyterians. In a private dispatch to London, Buckinghamshire gave this convoluted explanation for his fears of the Presbyterians and specifically of Northern Presbyterians:

> ... the use intended by a Militia in the North being the Preservation of the Peace and good order among the People lest during the absence of his Majesty's forces that opposition to the payment of Rents, Tithes and Assessments which prevailed so strongly in some parts of the Northern Counties some years ago might be revived ... the Militia would be comprised of that body of the People which may be suspected of being inclined to enter into such riots, there could be no dependence upon their Acting in Suppression of them.[5]

He left unsaid a still greater fear: many of the rebels in America were the descendants of Ulster Presbyterians or recent emigrants from Ulster. He dreaded the possibility that their cousins yet remaining in Ireland, already restive and discontented, would follow their example, after the government had armed and arrayed them.[6] Buckinghamshire repeated the opinion of several "Lords in Council" that independent volunteer companies were "much better to be relied on than a militia" – presumably because landlords or influential gentlemen would control them and be accountable for their behavior.[7] In short, expense served as the ostensible excuse for ignoring the will of parliament by failing to embody a militia.

But having rejected a militia, the government had no legal means of bringing these independent companies under its regulation. Indeed, the Volunteers were effectively the units which would have made up a very independent minded militia, had commissions been issued. Left largely to their own devices, the Volunteers quickly expanded their role beyond the confines of a mere citizens' defense force. They spent as much, if not more, time framing resolutions calling for free trade and for a revision of Poynings' Act as they did drilling in their extravagant uniforms.[8] The government had no feasible way of reversing its policy of *laissez faire*. Buckinghamshire shrank from the obvious and forceful measure of seizing the arms of Volunteers and preventing them from assembling. Such an action on the part of the government only increased the risk of an American-style armed rebellion. Faced with his own powerlessness, Buckinghamshire made a legal virtue of necessity. As he pointed out to the Secretary of State, Lord Weymouth, a law of William and Mary allowed the subjects of Ireland to bear arms "suitable to their condition as allowed by law". Buckinghamshire added "... it would be a question of nice decision to determine whether they might not be justified at a time of declared Publick danger in learning the use of them."[9]

The same tone of frozen desperation pervaded most of the communications of Buckinghamshire, a nervous, conscientious man overwhelmed by the misfortune of presiding over the waning of government power and influence. Crises rocked his government at the very times when he felt least capable of dealing with them. Moreover, the treasury was temporarily in such bad straits that he was not only unable to co-opt the Volunteers, he could not meet the most minimal expenses of government.[10] He spent the greater part of his time and energy pleading with London for more money and more troops, for an easing of the trade embargo and for trade concessions.[11] Unfortunately, the government in London, negligent about Irish affairs in the best of times, was too preoccupied with the war to give its usual perfunctory attention. Buckinghamshire could rely only on a small body of government servants, notably Beresford and Foster, and even they blamed him for not acting more forcefully.[12]

II

In such an atmosphere, an ambitious young man entering politics in the 1770s could quickly make a name for himself by acting as the champion of the Irish nation against ministerial corruption and tyranny. FitzGibbon's classmate Henry Grattan had already discovered as much, and had begun a promising career as a parliamentary patriot under the patronage of Lord Charlemont.[13] A controversy at Trinity college gave FitzGibbon his opportunity to establish his own reputation as the scourge of ministerial tyranny and corruption and to win a visible and prestigious seat in parliament.

The turmoil wracking Trinity had nothing to do with great issues of trade or the rights of the Irish nation. Rather, it was of the particularly bitter kind originating in personality disputes. The personalities in question consisted of the provost, John Hely Hutchinson, on one side and the majority of the fellows and senior tutors on the other. Like John FitzGibbon the elder, Hely Hutchinson had formed an association early in his career with William Gerard Hamilton. Even when all due allowances are made for the proprietary and personal view of public office taken in the 18th century, the correspondence between Hutchinson and Hamilton is unedifying. Both had a consuming preoccupation with obtaining as many remunerative offices as possible.[14] Unlike the elder FitzGibbon, Hutchinson was remarkably successful in obtaining his various official demands. He served as prime serjeant from 1761 to 1774, and in 1778 he obtained the ceremonial, but lucrative office of secretary of state. In 1774, the administration of Lord Harcourt, which had dismissed old FitzGibbon's requests as exorbitant, bestowed on the far more exorbitant Hutchinson the post of provost of Trinity College.

Even before he took up residence in his predecessor's handsome house, Hutchinson's appointment aroused outrage. As he had not hitherto demonstrated a scholarly or intellectual bent, the lord-lieutenant's appointment of Hutchinson seemed an extraordinarily crass and blatant example of jobbing. The fact that Hutchinson was also a married man with a large family also grated. The statutes of the college as framed by the resolutely celibate Queen Elizabeth forbade fellows to marry. Of course, many of them did, but they were put in the absurd position of passing their wives off as housekeepers. Finally, and most important, Hutchinson did not treat his new office as a sinecure. From the start, he introduced major changes in the curriculum of Trinity. Many of his changes were astute and far-sighted. For example, he promoted the study of modern languages. But as is the case with many reformers, he offended those with an interest in the *status quo*, and he met with the usual retaliation, ridicule. His encouragement of such refinements as fencing and dancing lessons earned him the nickname "Jack Prancer".[15] Unfortunately, Hely Hutchinson soon had far more to worry about. In 1777, he became embroiled in a quarrel which endangered him both legally and politically. John FitzGibbon the younger was one of the subordinate antagonists.

Hutchinson's premier antagonist was Patrick Duigenan, a scholar who later became professor of feudal law at Trinity. Duigenan's career paralleled, or perhaps more accurately, parodied, FitzGibbon's. Baptized a Roman Catholic, he was taken in hand by a Protestant clergyman and educated in the Established Church. Like FitzGibbon, he emphatically rejected his Catholic past and, if possible, vented his anti-Popish sentiments more scurrilously. Like FitzGibbon, he rose rapidly in the legal profession. In addition to his position at Trinity, he later added the offices of advocate of the admiralty court and vicar general of the consistory court.[16] In 1777, Duigenan had no presentiment of his future success. On the contrary, he was convinced that Hely Hutchinson's deliberate slights had ruined his prospects for advancement. Duigenan retaliated with a series of anonymous attacks on the provost, culminating in a philippic entitled *Lachrymae Academiae*. Like most of Duigenan's literary exercises, it was a coarse and clumsy production, and Hutchinson, a hot-tempered man, soon responded in kind with a pamphlet attacking everything from Duigenan's intellectual abilities to those vulnerable points for every convert, his Popish origins and education.[17] The conflict soon raged out of control, fueled by the atmosphere of gossip and malice peculiar to academic and clerical communities.

It did not long remain confined within the stately walls of Trinity. The feud between Hutchinson and Duigenan soon involved no less a personage than Philip Tisdall, the attorney general. Although Hutchinson had reckoned Tisdall a friend and ally prior to the imbroglio with Duigenan, he suddenly seized on the notion that the attorney general was encouraging the attacks of his opponent. None of the various accounts, including Hutchinson's own voluminous and aggrieved correspondence gives a very clear idea of why he developed such a notion. It seems most likely that in his state of irritability, he assumed that everyone not for him was against him. Since Tisdall remained on friendly terms with Duigenan, Hutchinson came to the conclusion that he was, therefore, the attorney general's "creature". Acting on this belief, Hutchinson approached Tisdall with a request: "I am insulted by a person beneath my notice [to wit, Duigenan] – he is a retainer of yours, you must *answer* for him and I must expect satisfaction from you."[18] Allegedly, Hutchinson had also referred to Tisdall as an "old rascal" and an "old scoundrel", though he later made the rather disingenuous claim that he had not made use of *both* expressions and he had certainly not used either in the hearing of the attorney general.[19]

Whether or not it was accompanied by the epithets in question, Hutchinson's request was both rash and insulting. As might be expected, Tisdall retaliated by filing a complaint, which charged Hutchinson first with *lese majeste* for insulting one of the king's servants, secondly with insulting the Court of the King's Bench, and finally with setting a bad example for the impressionable youth of Trinity College. To press his suit, Tisdall retained no less than 17 counsel, among them young John FitzGibbon.[20]

Unlike his father, FitzGibbon had no association with Hutchinson, however casual, and Tisdall's case offered the perfect opportunity for a young lawyer to make an impression. He could appeal to the ascendent patriotic party by taking a stand against a notorious jobber; at the same time he could establish useful ties with the senior law officer of the country. Nothing came of this promising opening, as Tisdall died before the suit could proceed beyond preliminaries.[21]

FitzGibbon also served as Duigenan's counsel when Hutchinson filed suit against him for *Lachrymae Academiae*. In spite of his legal difficulties the provost was still spoiling for a fight. FitzGibbon not only defended Duigenan against Hutchinson, he filed a suit on Duigenan's behalf against two individuals by the name of Myers, for challenging him to a duel.[22] Duigenan of course could easily have offended a good many people besides Hutchinson, but the timing of the challenge suggests that they may have been acting on behalf of Hutchinson, who, thanks to his experiences with Tisdall, was leery of acting on his own.[23]

Hely Hutchinson's efforts to bestow one of Trinity's parliamentary seats on his son provided FitzGibbon with a far more important opportunity than any offered by Patrick Duigenan's troubles. According to Grattan the younger, FitzGibbon, thanks to his legal exertions against Hutchinson, became the favored candidate of those members of the University opposed to the provost's nepotism.[24] Unlike much of the filial memoir of the younger Grattan, this statement has a measure of likelihood, given FitzGibbon's ambition and the opportunities which the troubles at Trinity presented. He could present himself as the opponent of jobbery on the hustings as well as in the courts. Parliament received the petition against the younger Hutchinson's election in 1776, and in 1777, an unhappy year for the family, he was removed from his seat. In March of 1778, FitzGibbon carried the election by a margin of 45 to 22.[25]

Not surprisingly, FitzGibbon's persistent attacks on the Hutchinson family engendered the first of his many political enmities. Buckinghamshire later commented to Lord North that "the provost is disinclined to Mr FitzGibbon, who was elected for the college in opposition to the provost's son".[26] Yet the feud with Hutchinson does not appear to have taken on the operatic fury of his later antagonisms. At least he did not provoke in FitzGibbon the frenzied public rage and loathing which Curran later inspired.

III

He started his career with typical clat as the ardent young patriot. From March of 1778 until November of 1779, he supported the popular side uniformly on every issue. FitzGibbon first spoke in Parliament to champion the inhabitants of the city of Dublin against a turnpike bill, which, in his opinion, imposed exorbitant tolls.[27] He then turned his attention to the sheriff of Kilkenny, who had allegedly failed to submit election returns in a timely fashion, and thus had violated against the rights of the electors and the majesty of Parliament. In his speech against the sheriff, FitzGibbon displayed many of the characteristics that were to distinguish his later parliamentary demeanor. Already he saw himself as the scourge of incompetence, stupidity and wickedness. His naturally overheated emotions, as well as the desire of a young member to make an impression led him to elevate a minor and commonplace instance of official sloth into an act of *lese majeste* worthy of the most urgent attention and the most vigorous action: "I hope he [the offending sheriff of Kilkenny] will be ordered to attend at the bar, if they do not give a satisfactory account of the Return to their House, they will be made an example of."[28]

FitzGibbon took the popular side as emphatically on the question of the Catholic relief bill of 1778. At that time, popular meant Protestant. The belief that Popery inevitably went hand in hand with despotic government formed the foundation of British political mythology. The free British Constitution and, more important, the privileges and power of its Irish Protestant defenders depended on the penal code. In theory at least, the code interdicted Catholic worship, Catholic education, Catholic land ownership and above all, Catholic participation in public life. Any suggestion of significantly altering this code inevitably aroused horrified resistance.

In spite of the overall hostility the question of changing the penal laws was very much in the air in the 1760s and 1770s. In 1774, an oath was framed which disavowed such notorious doctrines as the supposed papal power to depose heretical kings. While such an oath probably did little or nothing to reassure hard line Protestants, it did give Catholics legal standing of a minor, grudging sort.[29]

The bill of 1778 went much further. It proposed to extend to Catholics full rights to buy and to sell property. It also proposed the repeal of the so-called "gavel" law, which compelled any Catholic still in possession of a landed estate to divide it equally among his heirs. The gavel law contained a humiliating provision allowing any child who converted to come into full possession of the estate at the expense of recusant siblings. The proposed relief bill removed yet another hated feature of the penal code which permitted a Catholic heir upon conversion to make his father a tenant for life. The English Parliament was in the process of extending similar privileges and immunities to Catholics in Great Britain.[30]

The liberalization of laws in England strengthened one of the chief arguments of the bill's opponents: that it was a sinister measure on the part of the ministry in London to weaken liberty-loving Irish Protestants by encouraging the Papists, with their predilection for despotism and unquestioning submission to authority. Henry Grattan, already one of the leading young patriot of the time, based his opposition on this premise.[31] Grattan was mistaken. When the Catholics presented a petition for relief in December of 1777, the English government, while sympathetic, was at first disinclined to the prospect of recruiting blindly obedient Catholic masses to its standard. When the petition arrived in England, Weymouth requested Buckinghamshire's advice on the prospects for liberalization of the penal laws and received this reply: "... the present time is unfavorable for such attempts, as it would probably occasion a flame in this country which it has been much my wishes to keep quiet."[32]

This initial reluctance quickly gave way to the exigencies of military defense. In a move both startling and shrewd, the Americans, the much adored champions of the rights of Protestant Englishmen, allied themselves with his Catholic Majesty of France. In addition to their anxieties about the American sympathies of the Protestants, Buckinghamshire and the English government now had to contend with the additional threat of French or Spanish ships landing in Ireland and receiving an eager welcome from their Irish co-religionists. Further affronting Irish Protestant opinion was no doubt a grave risk, but making no gesture to win the loyalty, or at least the quiescence of the Irish Catholics was a greater one, at least in terms of military defense.[33] Accordingly the government introduced a relief bill. Luke Gardiner, acting out of loyalty to the government and genuine sympathy, took on the unenviable task of marshaling the bill through parliament.

The bill was as detested by the majority of Irish Protestants as the government had expected. According to the *Dublin Evening Post*, Gardiner could not go out in the streets of Dublin without armed escorts because of the threats made against his life.[34] Within the more exalted sphere of Parliament, the debate on the bill offered an unedifying spectacle of hysteria and rancor. Members possessed of vast estates and vast rent rolls expressed dissatisfaction because the bill did nothing for poor Catholics. Most notably, George Ogle made the dubious claim that Catholic tenants preferred "benevolent" Protestant landlords to their allegedly harsher co-religionists.[35] Of course, opponents did not neglect to raise the usual claim that to allow any privileges to Roman Catholics would only encourage their tendency toward blood lust and rebellion.[36] The proposed bill suffered every possible kind of parliamentary delay, compromise and outright sabotage. Most notably, Ogle introduced an amendment which, instead of allowing Catholics the right to hold land in fee, substituted mere leasehold privileges for a maximum period of 999 years.[37]

The addition of a clause to repeal the Test Act further complicated matters and increased bad feeling. While some anti-Papists, notably Shannon and Ely, actively encouraged the clause to delay or embarrass the bill, far more than mere caprice or trouble making moved the proponents of this particular addition to the bill. The Presbyterians had mobilized with great effectiveness to obtain the repeal of the hated Vestry Act of 1774, which had deprived them of the power to vote in parish vestries. Many members felt it was politically dangerous to make wholesale concessions to the Catholics while ignoring a major Presbyterian grievance. Presbyterians, after all, had the power of the vote, and they had only recently demonstrated their willingness to use it to punish their opponents in the general election of 1776. Prudence, as much, if not more than, anti-Popery, dictated the inclusion of a measure to repeal the Test Act.[38]

A good deal of rhetorical outrage did indeed greet the bill when it returned from London without the repeal clause. Nonetheless, government managed to muster the necessary majority, in spite of its own diminished prestige and the bill's unpopularity. Fears of an invasion by French despotic hoards, aided and abetted by disappointed Irish Catholics, were already starting to outweigh fears of the despotic schemes of the English and Irish governments and fears of Presbyterian opinion.

In his memoir of his father, Henry Grattan the younger observed that the relief act of 1778 was "opposed by Mr FitzGibbon, who even at this early period discovered the sentiments which afterwards proved so fatal to his country".[39] Considering that the elder Grattan had also discovered such fatal sentiments, this remark demonstrates remarkable disingenuousness. It also does great injustice to FitzGibbon's reasons for opposing the bill. Unquestionably, he voted against the bill out of opportunism, but he did have solid legal and moral objections to the bill.

He displayed opportunism in his graceless and vulgar appeals to popular Protestant prejudice. The example of Luke Gardiner and his armed guard was evidently not lost on him. Moreover, his ever present impulses of self-hatred and self-reinvention compelled him to go to particular lengths to affirm his Protestantism. This remark in his final speech on the bill is a case in point: "... if a Papist can submit to the monstrous absurdities to which his religious teachers will oblige him to subscribe, it is his business not mine."[40] Nonetheless, FitzGibbon did make it his business to insist on retaining the law allowing a conformist heir to make his father a tenant for life. In the same vein, he opposed repeal of the gavel clause because, he argued, it encouraged conformity by compelling either a father or any of his heirs to convert to keep the estate intact.[41]

In the same guise of Protestant, as well as popular, champion, he expressed alarm at the rejection of the clause repealing the Test Act. Echoing Grattan, he claimed that this action revealed the government's sinister intentions to encourage Popish "implicit obedience" over Presbyterian "constitutional resistance".[42] His admiration for the latter (or more likely his need as a rising young popular politician for their good opinion) was fleeting. Later in his career, he would express a visceral contempt for "Puritans".[43]

George Ogle's frivolous legal fiction further aroused his concern for the popular interest. Exceedingly long leases in Catholic hands would "have so much of the landed property unrepresented", presumably because such lands would be out of the reach of voting Protestant tenants virtually forever. In consequence, FitzGibbon argued: "You will narrow the democracy of this country which is too much confined for the good of the country already."[44]

Yet FitzGibbon never could escape the awareness that his own family had until very recently suffered under the penal laws, a circumstance that aroused both shame and uneasy empathy. Such scruples compelled him to act as the sincere friend of the Catholic interest as well as the defender of free Protestants. In arguing for retention of the gavel clause, he noted that most Catholics wealthy enough to purchase land were in trade. As their assets consisted largely of cash and capital, a provision limiting the size of their estates would not harm their economic interests or detract from the advantages of acquiring land as an investment.[45] He was willing to go so far as to allow Catholics to make settlements of their own choosing on their children as part of their marriage contracts. Such prenuptial agreements would mitigate the effects of gaveling and at the same time protect the rights of any children who might choose to conform in adulthood.

Above all, he opposed the fiction of 999-year leases in lieu of freehold because he was convinced that it was bad law. He predicted that it would produce so many complications that "before the next session every Papist in the kingdom would cry out for a repeal of it".[46] Much of his opposition originated in his fixed idea that the gavel law was essential for the encouragement of Protestantism. Such a law could not apply to leases of the kind proposed by George Ogle. But he also argued against it on the grounds that it did not offer Catholics the security of freehold estates. Because the law regarded such leases as personal property, FitzGibbon argued, they were subject to forfeiture upon the smallest misdemeanor and the most minor debts. He also noted that the law had failed to repeal "several cruel and illiberal clauses of the old code".[47] A Catholic who fell under their provisions could suffer the same consequence. In particular FitzGibbon alluded to the laws which forbade Catholics to educate their children abroad yet denied them access to schools in their own country:

> those clauses in the old code inflict a forfeiture of this nature for suffering his sons to receive a liberal education.. the doors of our own University were shut against them ... what do you do? You confine them to the purchase of land which may be forfeited, you can't educate him at home, your laws prohibit that, if you send him abroad he is liable to forfeit the very interest you allow him to purchase.[48]

Like most of FitzGibbon's pronouncements on the subject of Catholics and Catholicism, his remarks were fraught with ambiguity. He was hardly in a position to complain about a failure to repeal "cruel and illiberal clauses" when throughout the debate he had insisted on retaining the two provisions of the penal code most abhorred by Catholics. Moreover, his anxiety about barriers to education did not originate in any desire to allow Catholics to instruct their children as they saw fit. Rather, he wanted them to remain in Protestant-ruled Ireland and to study in Protestant schools, which would presumably provide an added inducement to conformity. His preoccupation with education as indoctrination would find expression in later debates on Catholic relief. His ambiguous motives notwithstanding, FitzGibbon did make convincing arguments about the bill's legal defects. His proposed version of the bill appears to have offered solid, if severely limited, benefits to the Catholics. In spite of his limitations, personal and political, his actions were certainly superior to Grattan's partisan shallowness.

FitzGibbon pursued the same highly promising popular course when Dennis Daly drew up a petition to the king which complained of the economic distresses of Ireland and which requested redress in the form of an easing of the embargo and an extension of trading rights.[49] The government opposed the petition more in the interests of management than out of any particular disagreement with the points raised.

Buckinghamshire's own letters to the government in London were filled with similar pleas. The government objected to the petition first because it would raise jealousies in England, secondly because Daly had made his motion toward the end of a session, and finally, because Parliament proposed to forward the petition directly to the king, rather than submit it through the lord lieutenant, as was the usual practice.[50] In an ironic contrast with his later views of Anglo-Irish cooperation, FitzGibbon rejected any suggestion that the Irish parliament should consider the sensibilities of a "few boroughmongers in England".[51] FitzGibbon had even less sympathy for the prerogatives of the lord-lieutenant. He would not, he declared, sacrifice the interests of the people to a "point of ceremony and etiquette".[52] The government did manage to defeat the petition, though the economy was growing worse and its parliamentary luck was fast running out.

FitzGibbon reached the apogee of his popularity as a patriot in November of 1779, when he took a prominent part in the inquiry into debts owed by Sir William Cavendish, the deceased Teller of the Exchequer, to the Treasury. He had allegedly borrowed £20,000 from the Treasury, and FitzGibbon accused his son, Sir Henry Cavendish, of failing to pay the debt quickly enough. He also accused the government of condoning Sir Henry's defalcation and of preventing any serious inquiry into the matter.[53] The matter of Cavendish was the perfect vehicle for FitzGibbon to act the role of young patriot. Sir Henry was a prominent government member, and the Treasury's embarrassments in 1778 continued to provide useful rhetorical ammunition. FitzGibbon ably seized the opportunity to reiterate patriot convictions that ministerial corruption was sapping a distressed and weakened economy: "... it is an hardship that an individual should keep for three years in his pocket money which he is determined not to pay as long as he can avoid it."[54] Cavendish, of course, indignantly denied the charges, and claimed that on the contrary, he was making every effort to repay his father's debts, at great expense and hardship to himself.[55] Even Sir Frederick Flood, kinsman of yet another patriotic idol, Henry, ventured to defend Cavendish's honor against FitzGibbon's rhetorical onslaught: "I rejoice in the opportunity of vindicating the honor of the Rt Hon. baronet and to oppose a motion to ... establish a summary and oppressive mode of proceeding in times truly calamitous."[56] In the popular press, Cavendish received no such defense and FitzGibbon no such rebuke. A long paragraph in the *Hibernian Journal*, one of the many opposition papers in Dublin, paid tribute to FitzGibbon's patriotic zeal by making ironic pleas with him to restrain it:

> Pray consider also that by forcing him to pay or expelling him the House you will deprive the public of his taking an active part for them. You see his Gratitude has prompted him to take great pains about their accounts; and his keen Eye has discovered that it is to national bounty alone that you owe your national debt. Now, Sir, do you think he could ever have divulged that information if he did not find himself greatly interested in setting the people right about their money matters? I cannot conclude without telling you that you

> hazard the resentment of the People, by doing anything to distress a Gentleman so popular, so much beloved, so greatly admired for his Abilities, his Integrity and his Munificence. In short, he is a *pretty* lad; and is recommended to your tenderness.[57]

IV

Yet even as he was winning accolades for protecting the people of Ireland from ministerial peculation FitzGibbon was receiving approaches from the government. His very ardor in pursuing Henry Cavendish may have originated in a guilty patriotic conscience. He found the government's offers very attractive indeed, and he possibly hoped to soften the certain outrage at his defection with this final display of zeal.

The chronic misfortunes of the Buckinghamshire administration accounted for this sudden conciliatory attitude toward one of its more truculent opponents. Having survived the economic crisis of 1778, it experience the onset of a major political standoff in 1779. The opposition, then in full tide, planned to thwart the usual two-year grant of supplies to the government. They proposed instead to grant supplies for only six months as a means of putting pressure on government to grant "free trade", that is access to what remained of England's colonial markets.[58] Buckinghamshire's administration reacted with even more panic than usual. He and his few remaining supporters renewed their pleas to London to grant trade concessions while it still had the appearance of a freely given favor.[59] At the same time set about attempting to defeat the six-month money bill. The government needed able men to fill its depleted ranks and especially to speak on its behalf in the forthcoming debates. Support from erstwhile patriots would also steady the waverers, who grew in number as fervor mounted. The Government still had the ability to grant office, which remained a powerful inducement in spite of its tarnished prestige.

John Beresford took it upon himself to approach his young kinsman with an offer from Buckinghamshire. The lord-lieutenant was willing to appoint FitzGibbon to the first vacancy in the offices of prime serjeant, attorney or solicitor general, in return for support of the government during the impending debates on the short money bill. Beresford, an astute man of business, shrewdly played on FitzGibbon's fears as well as appealing to his ambition. He emphasized "how necessary it was for men of property to exert themselves to prevent mischief, which seemed to be the view of some people".[60] To a man newly risen from the despised Popish masses, Beresford's suggestions of impending social upheaval were very effective indeed. The prospect of obtaining high legal office less than two years after entering Parliament must have been irresistible to a man who had observed his father's 15-year career of frustration and failure. He agreed to Beresford's proposal.

Nearly 20 years later, Beresford, by then elevated into the archetype of ministerial corruption, was routinely accused of incorporating FitzGibbon into his empire of patronage.[61] His correspondence shows this claim to have been partisan nonsense. Though he clearly respected FitzGibbon and considered him a young man of promise, he had no particular proprietary interest in him. He made similar proposals to others. Moreover, John Scott, Tisdall's successor as attorney general, was just as active in recruiting FitzGibbon.[62]

Although FitzGibbon was agreeable to his kinsman's proposals, he expressed doubts about the good faith of Lord Buckinghamshire.[63] Events justified his darkest suspicions. When the money bill came up for final vote on 30 November 1779, the government abruptly changed course and conceded the six month version out of a belief that lacking the numbers to resist effectively, it could not in fairness expose its few supporters to popular attack.[64] Shortly after the government's retreat, the cabinet in London yielded to the inevitable and allowed Ireland to trade directly with the West Indies, on condition that the Irish parliament imposed the same duties and regulations as its English counterpart.[65]

FitzGibbon, understandably, did not care to sacrifice himself unnecessarily, and voted with the majority. He did not entirely abandon government even as he voted against it. During the debate, he denounced the measure as pernicious, although he did so on the solidly patriotic ground that a six -month's money bill would entail raising higher taxes to meet the inevitable shortfall.[66] In effect, he signaled to the ministry that while he would not fight their lost causes, he was available to protect property and order on future occasions.

In spite of his professed concern for the reputations and careers of government supporters, Buckinghamshire decided to hold FitzGibbon to a sterner standard. In retaliation for his perceived bad faith, Buckinghamshire bestowed the post of prime serjeant elsewhere, when that office became vacant upon the resignation of Hussey Burgh.[67] For their parts, FitzGibbon and his patron Beresford indignantly pointed out the unfairness of expecting him (FitzGibbon) to stand firm while the government succumbed to public pressure.[68] Beresford had this final comment on the business when Buckinghamshire, in anticipation of later opposition charges, accused him of promoting FitzGibbon's career to aggrandize his own and his family's interests: "I had no reason for mention him except that I knew him to be the most proper man in the country for His Majesty's service. They may now hunt for him themselves."[69] These negotiations, however abortive, left their mark on FitzGibbon. The glimpse of office tantalized him. Although his prospects with the Buckinghamshire administration were now dim, he could build a reputation as a government man that might possibly influence future administrations.

His opposition to the tenantry act of 1780 finally deprived him of his patriotic bloom. This act aimed at confirming the rights of tenants whose leases for lives had fallen into abeyance. Although its proponents claimed that the bill was intended to aid the struggling yeomanry of Ireland, it primarily affected more affluent, larger tenants. These individuals often held free-hold estates of their own in addition to leasing tracts of land, usually for a lifetime renewable forever. The life in question could be the landlord's, or it could be the lifetime of an agreed-upon, unrelated third-party, such as a member of the royal family. Since these leases covered such long periods of time, they frequently lapsed without either the landlord or the tenant recognizing the fact and formally making a renewal. A decision of the English Chancery Court jarred the easy-going habits of Irish land tenure. The case involved a rare instance when an Irish landlord did sue for ejection of a long-term tenant whose lease had expired. The Court decided in favor of the landlord, and thus prompted the bill.[70] In addition to heartrending rhetoric about the suffering yeomen driven from their holdings by unscrupulous landlords, the bill's supporters appealed to sectarian interest, which could always arouse emotion and compel votes. They argued that since such leases were held exclusively by Protestants, their rights particularly required protection, in light of the extensive leasehold privileges recently granted to Catholics.[71]

The bill not only commanded wide support, its sponsors included a key member of the Buckinghamshire administration, no less than John Scott, the Attorney General.[72] With unusual astuteness, the administration remained officially neutral, while allowing its chief law officer to act a popular part. It had a difficult enough time enforcing policy from Whitehall. It was not about to add to its difficulties by condoning or defending provocative decisions from the English Chancery Court as well.

FitzGibbon took the lonely and dangerous course of opposition in the first place because the bill offended his finely developed sense of legal propriety. It violated both the property rights of landlords, that pillar of 18th century jurisprudence, and the integrity of contracts. In his view, any tenant unjustly deprived of a lease already had ample means of seeking redress through the usual channels, without the addition of extraordinary and dubious legislation.[73]

In addition, he condemned the bill because it offered no benefits whatsoever to the small yeomanry. Rather, it confirmed the position of large land jobbers or middlemen, who had no proprietary interest in the soil, apart from making as high a profit as possible. Men such as these would inevitably "grind the faces of the poor".[74]

As usual with FitzGibbon, his habitual indulgence in righteous indignation tinged much of his attitude toward the bill. Middlemen were not inevitably the rapacious harpies he made them out to be. Most Irish estates were inordinately large and without the presence of such intermediate lessees, they would have been difficult to manage effectively. Middlemen frequently invested capital and brought a degree of innovation beyond the power of most landlords, who were indifferent, absent, pressed by debt, or again, unable to manage their oversized holdings.[75] His own family had very recently emerged from the ranks of the rural middle class, and they may possibly have held a subtenure of the kind he denounced. Consequently, he had a special need to defend the rights of landed gentlemen from grasping, arriviste jobbers.

Yet however wrongheaded his opposition may have been, however tainted with social pretentiousness, FitzGibbon displayed both integrity and, as always, cogent legal reasoning. He stood to gain nothing in the way of recognition from the government. Only a genuine desire to protect the smaller farmers and laborers, as well as a strong conviction that the bill violated fundamental principles of equity could account for his opposition.

Despite the laudable principles behind it, his stand immediately provoked a storm, particularly in the press. The *Hibernian Journal*, once his strongest advocate, turned against him all the more vehemently. In its edition of 20 June 1780, it accused FitzGibbon of callously disregarding the sufferings of the tenantry of Ireland:

> Regardless of the censure of every surrounding nation, which have long held up the Irish peasantry as starving objects of compassion, as the unhappy victims of Irish pride and Irish licentiousness, you, sir, in a scurvy minority, have been the Advocate for entailing a continuance of misery in the most injured body of Men that the Sun rolls his course over.

FitzGibbon also opposed the major patriotic initiative of 1780: Henry Grattan's resolution that the "King's most excellent majesty and the Lords and Commons of Ireland are the only power competent to make laws to bind Ireland". The aim of this resolution was, of course, the modification of Poynings' Act and the removal of other forms of British jurisdiction from the Parliament of Ireland. Barry Yelverton introduced the actual heads of bills for this purpose one week later. FitzGibbon, angling for the favor of future administrations, if not for a return to good graces of the Buckinghamshire administration, dismissed the resolution as the "production of a giddy faction".[77] According to Grattan the younger, FitzGibbon also appealed to Protestant insecurities. Specifically, he opposed the elder Grattan because "the result of his [Grattan's] plan would be to let loose an Irish army upon the country and they would seek to resume all forfeited lands".[78] In fairness to FitzGibbon, the newspaper accounts of his speeches do not contain any such blatant appeals to sectarian fears. In the published debates, he merely stated that such a resolution would "embroil both countries in a state of discord". Only an allusion to the fact that a similar resolution had appeared in the fatal year 1641 could be construed as an oblique reference to the Papist menace.[79] A fear that Catholics might take advantage of Protestant divisions could certainly have motivated him, in conjunction with a desire to establish his good standing with the government.

At the same time, FitzGibbon did not entirely break with his prior patriot stance. Although he had now come to respect the government's infinite powers of patronage, he could not afford entirely to alienate the patriots among his constituents. Without a seat in parliament, he had no hopes of office. Such considerations, as well as personal grievances, undoubtedly moved him to denounce the "imbecility and incapacity of government" in the same speech.[80] Such considerations also may have accounted for the more moderate stance he took toward the end of the debate. He supported a compromise proposed by Hussey Burgh, which called for an adjournment, as a resolution similar to Grattan's was already on the records of the House. In the words of the parliamentary reporter of the *Dublin Evening Post,* the leading patriotic newspaper of the capital:

> [This] gentleman [FitzGibbon] made amends for the warm and decided part he had taken in support of government by endeavoring to reconcile all parties in the House to concur in promoting the interest of this country.[81]

FitzGibbon reverted to the popular side on the issue of the Irish mutiny bill. Prior to 1780, the English Mutiny Act had applied to Ireland. Their resolution against Poynings' Act defeated, the popular party chose to assert the dignity and rights of the Irish Parliament by proposing its own mutiny bill. Lord Buckinghamshire's government was, once again, caught in an impossible situation. The ministry was determined to throw out any bill that specifically denied the authority of the English act. Yet Buckinghamshire did not want to exacerbate patriotic feeling further, especially in the wake of the defeat over Poynings' Act.[82] Moreover, as was usual with issues of Irish rights and prerogatives, no law positively forbade the Irish Parliament to pass a mutiny bill. As Buckinghamshire noted to the new Secretary of State, Hillsborough, the Irish Parliament had considered a mutiny bill in 1692, though for obscure reasons, this bill had been thrown out.[83] Finally, Buckinghamshire had good reason to fear that if the Irish mutiny bill failed to pass, many magistrates might refuse to enforce the English statute. He sent Lord Hillsborough a copy of a paragraph from the *Freeman's Journal* urging such a course.[84] Given these circumstances, Buckinghamshire pleaded with the English government not to compel him to take any extraordinary measures to suppress the bill:

> [It] cannot be advisable for a Lord Lieutenant scarcely, if ever, exerted to stifle a bill of universal Desire against the sense of the Commons, the Majority of Council and the gen'l sentiment of the Nation.[85]

The heads of the mutiny bill did pass in the Irish parliament, and the council duly forwarded them to London. The English cabinet returned the bill in August of 1780, with the inclusion of one provocative alteration: to prevent future displays of self-assertion, the English privy council had included a provision making an Irish mutiny act perpetual.[86]

As usual, the administration, after much dithering and hysteria, did manage to scrape together the majority necessary to pass the bill. But not surprisingly, its passage inspired yet another outburst of indignation both within and without Parliament. FitzGibbon had supported the original heads of the bill, when they were introduced in May of 1780, and in Buckinghamshire's account of the debates over the revised bill, his name appeared prominently with Grattan's as an opponent of the revised version. He took this stand on the grounds that bill, in effect, placed Ireland under a military government:

> It is an alarming attack upon the Constitution and the liberty of the British Empire that has ever been made. I think it tends directly to make this country a place of arms against this Empire.[89]

FitzGibbon continued to support the popular position on trade, when the issue of sugar duties came up for debate. Irish sugar bakers or refiners, had always operated at a disadvantage because, prior to the liberalization of trade laws, they had been compelled to import raw sugars via Great Britain and thus had been subject to two sets of duties, the English and the Irish. The opening of British West Indian trade to Ireland should have improved matters, but Irish refiners came to believe, in spite of reassurances to the contrary, that direct imports to Ireland would suffer delays, presumably because of the disturbed state of Atlantic trade. When the subject of new duties on sugar came up in Parliament, the Irish sugar manufacturers pressed for a prohibitory duty on British refined sugar, to protect themselves against further competition, and to put themselves in a better position to take advantage of direct imports on raw sugar, once they did begin.[90] With this aim in mind, Hussey Burgh proposed a positive prohibition on British refined sugars. Inevitably, the government, in the person of John Scott, pressed for a far lower duty. After much detailed and dull debate, Parliament settled on a compromise between the virtual embargo proposed by Burgh and the virtual open market proposed by Scott.[91] For his part, FitzGibbon declared, "I don't see the injustice of monopolizing the Trade for our own Market".[92]

His occasional votes for popular measures failed to restore his standing in public opinion, or at least that part of public opinion reflected in the press, by 1780 virtually monopolized by radicals. His opposition to Grattan's resolution exacerbated the ill-will aroused by his stand on the tenantry act. In the same editorial which denounced FitzGibbon for his supposed indifference to the suffering tenantry of Ireland, the *Hibernian Journal* made this comment on the subject: "On that memorable day, you rolled down the Tide with the Government as a Crab-Apple, you had little to boast of over the ball of Horse dung in the fable."[93] The *Dublin Evening Post* contented itself with listing FitzGibbon as a member of the Court party. On a scale of 0 to 25, his elocution and his powers of argument rated a mediocre 15, and his parliamentary influence was rated at 0.[94]

FitzGibbon was by no means the only public figure of the time to suffer bad press. The reputations of politicians rose and fell according to the fevered, often irrational fluctuation of public expectation and demand. In the overheated atmosphere of late eighteenth century Irish politics, public discourse reached unprecedented heights, or perhaps more accurately, depths of scurrility. But FitzGibbon arguably inspired a degree of malice unequaled by any other public figure of the time. His abrasive personality exacerbated the ill will aroused by his political views.

A brief squib appearing in the *Dublin Evening Post*[95] in March 1780 indicates that even before the introduction of the tenantry act, his demeanor was beginning to grate on some sensibilities. "Youth, Figure and Fortune do not make a man respectable", the *Dublin Evening Post* had admonished. By the end of 1780, comments on his arrogant, overbearing manner appeared regularly in all the Dublin newspapers. They inevitably referred to him by the sobriquet "Jack Petulant" or "Fitzpetulant" or by such variations as "Fitzarrogant" and "Fitzprig".[96] Occasionally, FitzGibbon did receive praise for his intelligence, for his legal knowledge and for the youthful beauty that Cosway later portrayed with such charm and delicacy. But the newspapers praised him only to lament that although "Nature" had given FitzGibbon "Person, Wealth and Talents ... [the] fair work was spoiled by Pride, Vanity and Petulance".[97] His erratic voting habits only increased the exasperation and the sense of promise betrayed which characterized press comment on him at this time. A paragraph which appeared in the *Dublin Evening Post* in May of 1781 brings into focus most clearly the popular image of FitzGibbon as a young man who was too pretty by half, too clever by half and wholly besotted by himself. Using one of the labored classical conceits common to the time, the author of the paragraph envisioned a visit to Ireland by Rhadamanthus, one of the judges of the underworld. Among the worthies summoned for judgment was a "handsome youth in a lawyer's gown". The author went on to give this account of his encounter with Rhadamanthus:

> A handsome youth in a lawyer's gown came confidently forward, who with a number of law phrases well put together and delivered with volubility made a long speech, the tendency of which it was impossible to divine; it was like a two edged sword, it cut every way. By one part of it, his hearers might imagine he was the advocate of the people, by his acrimonious invectives against the ministry, but by the other, one would think him the champion of Government; the instructions given by constituents to their representatives in Parliament, he stiled the clamours of a seditious mob; he was against the Irish Declaration of Right; he was for a Mutiny Bill and back and forward, sometimes on one side, sometimes on the other, even on the same question with a most ridiculous inconsistency ... After exhibiting in a strong manner a strange compound of pride, talents and ill-nature, he ended his strange harangue and cast his eyes around (and beautiful eyes they were) with a supercilious look, while his cheek dimpled with a smile of self-complacence. The Judge then touched his forehead with a dreadful wand; the culprit's size shrunk at the powerful touch to the diminutive form of a WASP![98]

He was soon to give the press no cause to complain of his inconsistency. By the autumn of 1781, he demonstrated emphatic and unvarying support for the government. The change in ministries accounted for this hardening of attitude.

4

The Making of a Government Man, 1776–83

I

The long crisis that was the Buckinghamshire administration came to a merciful end in December 1780. The Earl of Carlisle succeeded to the office of lord-lieutenant, and William Eden, later Lord Auckland, accompanied him in the capacity of chief secretary. The two had participated in abortive negotiations with the Americans in 1778. Presumably, their experience in dealing with recalcitrant colonials, however unsuccessfully, prompted North's government to send them to Ireland. Although Carlisle had offered generous terms to reconcile the Americans, his administration in Ireland adopted the same policy as that of his ill-fated predecessor: to resist as much as possible any major innovations in the political, economic or military relationship between England and Ireland. In a report to Hillsborough, dated 15 September 1781, shortly before the opening of Parliament, Carlisle listed the issues he expected to come up in debate and the stance his government would adopt on each. He intended to resist any renewed attempts to alter the mutiny act or to revive prohibitory duties on English refined sugar. On constitutional issues, Carlisle took an equally firm line:

> With respect to the whole class of what are called constitutional questions ... I conceive that I ought as much as possible to divert a line of disquisition which cannot at present be brought forward with any advantage to the true interest of this kingdom.[1]

Nonetheless, in discussing the possibility of "some Parliamentary applause" for the Volunteers, Carlisle took a far friendlier view than his predecessor who had, on the contrary pressed for Parliamentary condemnation. Carlisle acknowledged the dubious constitutional standing of "an armed Force not raised under the King's authority", yet he also acknowledged their good discipline, their loyalty and their valuable service enforcing "due Reverence to the Laws in a country where that Reverence is much less general than in any part of Europe".[2] Carlisle concluded that rather than resist a Parliamentary vote of thanks, the Administration itself should initiate such a measure:

> I think it my Duty to say that a decided and cordial acknowledgment from my administration of the loyal and becoming conduct which the Volunteer Corps have now manifested towards their King and Country would be the wisest measure with regard to them that can be acknowledged.[3]

In this same memorandum Carlisle expressed confidence that this combination of resistance couched in judicious flattery would effectively wear down any attempts to alter the structure of government in Ireland. He not only had what he believed to be an effective strategy, he had, unlike his predecessor, a reliable cadre of government members: "Nor am I without hope that the support which I have formed and in some degree consolidated for the measures of my administration will be fully equal to their task."[4]

Carlisle and Eden had built this support first by wooing and conciliating the great magnates and secondly by following more successfully Buckinghamshire's strategy of recruiting likely young men. FitzGibbon was prominent among those whom the new administration wanted to win over. In a letter to Lord Gower, Carlisle expressed hope that FitzGibbon, a man of "very considerable weight both in respect to property and ability" would not be "averse" to his administration.[5] FitzGibbon fully realized Carlisle's hopes. He supported the government not only because a new administration presented new opportunities to obtain office, but because of the attachment, bordering on infatuation, that he felt for William Eden.

The friendship undoubtedly originated in Eden's efforts to cultivate support for Carlisle through personal attentions to potential supporters. According to Charlemont, Eden's activities earned him the distasteful sobriquet "Manmonger".[6] FitzGibbon does not appear to have been at all troubled by any ulterior motives Eden might have had in seeking him out. He was literally smitten by Eden and remained devoted to him throughout his life. He inevitably visited Eden whenever he was in England and corresponded voluminously with him.

By any rational standard, Eden seems an unlikely object of adoration. He had his good points: he was a pleasant family man and a capable public servant. He also merited the friendship of Edward Gibbon, which suggests a high level of cultivation and intellect.[7] But a cool, ruthless cunning seems to have been his master characteristic.

Love gave FitzGibbon a more enchanted perspective. He saw only the suave, handsome English country gentleman, and he always tried to prove worthy of his idol. In his voluminous correspondence with Eden, he invariably assumed the persona of a man blessed with all the English virtues of common sense and plain speaking yet unhappily cursed with Irish ancestry and birth. The friendship with Eden holds interest not only because of the insight it gives into FitzGibbon's character, but because of its implications for his future political career. In spite of his later public emphasis on unquestioning co-operation with England and his denunciations of Irish and English Whigs for using each other to further their own interests, he and Eden habitually intrigued together to resist policies or ministries they opposed.

In 1781, FitzGibbon did not yet have this sort of influence or hardihood. He was a valued but very much a subordinate player in the making of English policy in Ireland. He revealed his sympathies most trenchantly and most clearly during the controversy which arose of the Portuguese government's confiscation of Irish woolen goods in August 1781. This controversy, like the dispute over sugar duties, originated in the trade concessions made by the English government in 1779. The Irish assumed that they had obtained access not only to the English West Indian markets, but to the markets of one of England's leading trading partners, Portugal. The so-called Methuen treaty of 1703 had established a very profitable trade between England and Portugal. The English imported Portuguese wines and exported fine grades of woolen cloth. Irish woolen manufacturers, no doubt attracted by the proximity of Portugal, quickly took advantage of what they thought were new trading privileges. The Portuguese, unfortunately, took a less generous view of this abrupt appearance of Irish textiles. Taking refuge in the legalistic argument that the Methuen treaty extended only to England, they seized the shipment from Ireland as contraband. But the true target of this action was not the Irish merchant community, but the British government. The Portuguese, unhappy with what they perceived as the unequal benefits of the Methuen treaty, hoped to force the English to renegotiate by creating difficulties over Irish imports.[8]

The Carlisle administration quickly recognized the potential political embarrassment of the Portuguese actions. Even before Parliament had opened Carlisle had received a petition from Comerford and O'Brien, the merchant firm involved in the shipment, and in response he had pressed the government to assert Irish trading rights as vigorously as possible.[9] The secretary of state, Lord Hillsborough, set forth the position that the British government was to maintain throughout the crisis. The Irish government could do nothing. Only the appropriate English ministers had the proper authority to negotiate with the Portuguese, and they, of course, would do everything in their power to promote and protect Irish trade and Irish merchandise. Hillsborough closed his communication by urging calm and moderation.[10]

Calm and moderation did not prevail during the parliamentary debates on the Portuguese actions in October and November 1781. The Portuguese action wounded both sensitive Irish national feeling and struggling Irish economic interests. Much ferocious rhetoric denouncing Portuguese perfidy and numerous uncomplimentary allusions to the mad, priest-ridden queen of Portugal circulated in Parliament. Hurt pride and outrage reached a culmination in a motion by Sir Lucius O'Brien for a committee to enquire into the provisions of the treaty of 1703, with the aim of drawing up resolutions protesting the actions of the Portuguese.[11] In keeping with his earlier instructions from Hillsborough and in keeping with his own determination to prevent any attempts to expand the constitutional powers of the Irish Parliament, Carlisle immediately set out to block any such inquiry:

With regard to the Impropriety of this inquiry, it is thought that the House of

> Commons in taking upon themselves the Interpretation of Treaties entered into by the Crown with foreign states would create a new and dangerous precedent.[12]

Initially, Carlisle hoped to avoid any debate on Portuguese trade. When such a debate inevitably did take place, Eden, in the role of chief spokesman for the government, reiterated first that the Irish parliament had no authority to intervene in the matter, and secondly that the proper authority, the English ministers, were doing everything in their power to persuade the Portuguese to accept Irish goods. FitzGibbon spoke in support of Eden with all his considerable powers of rhetorical excess. He repeated all the usual constitutional arguments against intervention by the Irish Parliament:

> ... that our goods had been detained in Lisbon we know, that they ought to be received we know, and that the King's ministers were doing their utmost to promote their reception we know, but the doubt remained whether their exertions would not be assisted by Parliamentary interference. For his part he thought not. All negotiations he thought by our constitutions should be ministerial though sometimes Parliament had interfered to ratify or reject.[14]

He added this effusive praise of Eden:

> He [FitzGibbon] thought that some confidence ought to be placed, some latitude of discretion given to a Minister (Mr Eden) who in so manly and liberal a way had come forward and assured the House of his determination to support this nation's rights with his utmost power; that for his part he would place a becoming confidence in him till he should do some act to forfeit it.[15]

The government did succeed in defeating Sir Lucius O'Brien's motion. Unfortunately, the English ministers exercised their proper constitutional powers to no avail. The Portuguese obdurately clung to their interpretation of the treaty of 1703. When Eden reported the outcome of the negotiations on 5 February 1782, he wisely made no further appeals to trust, moderation or patience and ostensibly, at least, he left the Irish Parliament with the power to act as it saw fit.[16] But Carlisle and Eden were not as indifferent as they claimed, as soon became apparent when FitzGibbon rose to speak.

He emphatically opposed any commercial retaliation against Portugal and suggested instead a petition to the king setting forth Irish complaints against the Court of Lisbon and pleading for his intervention:

> If by any bill of resentment we prohibit the import of Portuguese goods or load them with heavy duties, we provoke the Court of Lisbon to retaliate ... the trade with Portugal is of the highest importance to this kingdom, as it leaves a balance in our favor of £120,000 per annum and of the goods we get from thence, there are some with which we cannot be so well supplied from any other place. The only way I can think of to obtain relief is by addressing His Majesty and humbly

> requesting that he will be graciously pleased to assert the rights of his kingdom of Ireland, which in this instance have been grossly violated.[17]

Nonetheless, in the process of presenting these perfectly lucid and sensible arguments he made an extraordinary tactical blunder. Evidently forgetting the fact that not all of his colleagues shared his adoration for the chief secretary, he admitted freely that he had consulted with Eden on the matter:

> After having considered every circumstance of the negotiation I must observe that I communicated my intention of moving this address to the Right Honorable Secretary and he agrees in my opinion that it is the most proper method that can be taken.[18]

This revelation on FitzGibbon's part accounts for the prominent part he immediately assumed in the debate. In the guise of a moderate-minded, independent gentleman, he was proposing the course that the government, in spite of its official stance of neutrality, actually favored. This circumstance unavoidably raises the possibility that Eden approached FitzGibbon rather than the other way around. He and FitzGibbon may well have come to an agreement that the more moderate course of a petition would face a better reception from a member with some lingering claims to independence.

The suggestion of government influence, as well as anger and frustration inevitably led to sharp criticism of FitzGibbon's proposed petition. Lucius O'Brien, the aspiring scourge of the Portuguese, complained that the address lacked "sufficient spirit and nor will the Court of Portugal believe the Irish Parliament serious if we proceed in the languid manner proposed by the Hon. Gentleman (Mr FitzGibbon)"[19] Grattan was harsher and more explicit in his attacks:

> As to the address itself, it is languid, spiritless and undignified; ... and besides there is a ministerial poison through the whole of it which taints the purity of a national act.[20]

FitzGibbon responded by ridiculing the tendency of his former opposition colleagues to take issue with any act or proposal remotely sanctioned by the government: "... the minister has been consulted and therefore, it must be opposed." He also angrily asserted his independence, and he probably did so the more vehemently because he had been operating in collusion with Eden. In the process he made an unmistakable allusion to Grattan's close ties to the great opposition magnate Lord Charlemont:

> For my part Sir, as I am not brought into this House the *puppet of any man*, but stand here as a free agent, I shall do my duty, not regarding the judgments of men who are uniform in opposition or of those who uniformly support government; neither do I much regard the abusive terms that have been applied to the

> address – *vile, languid, undignified* – because they are words that may apply on any occasion.[21]

When the rhetorical dust had settled, FitzGibbon's petition passed unanimously and, apart from a few minor alterations proposed by Flood, with essentially the same wording. Indeed, however distorted by his partisan infatuation and his contempt for all things Irish, his judgments of the situation were unassailable: any hopes of military retaliation were indeed "idle" and Ireland depended far too much on the share of trade which Portugal did permit to engage in economic retaliation. However tainted by Eden's approbation, FitzGibbon's proposal represented the only reasonable course of action under the circumstances. Nor did the public expect much more, according to Lord Carlisle's report of the debate:

> The Gallery as on all days of Public Expectation was much crowded, but as soon as the Motion proposed by Mr FitzGibbon had been read by the Chairman, the greater Number of the Audience left the House without waiting as anxiety would have prompted them for the Conclusion.[22]

The issue of Irish trade to Portugal continued to create tripartite contention between Great Britain, Ireland and Portugal well into the 1780s. With the encouragement of the English government, which had shifted tactics, the Irish parliament did impose retaliatory duties on Portuguese wines and produce in 1785. But the duties, while indeed very damaging to Portuguese trade with Ireland, ultimately had little to do with the resolution of the dispute. Portuguese anxieties over the Anglo-French treaty, and the English desire not to undermine their traditional alliance with Portugal finally ended the standoff. The Portuguese agreed in 1787 to lift their embargo on Irish textiles in return for an English concession to admit Portuguese wines at a lower tariff than French wines. In short, the resolution of the dispute with Portugal confirmed FitzGibbon's unpalatable point, that the free and equal "sister kingdom" was still firmly subordinate to larger English concerns and policies, particularly in matters of trade.

FitzGibbon played a smaller role in the renewed debate over sugar duties, though of course, he could always be counted on to give a startling performance whatever the size of his part. He abruptly reversed his stand of the previous year and both spoke and voted against any further protective duties on English refined sugars. In response to higher bounties granted by the British Parliament to British sugar manufacturers, the opposition, notably Grattan and Flood, pressed again for higher duties on both raw and refined sugars imported from England. While the administration was willing to allow Parliament to raise duties to compensate for English bounties, Carlisle observed that "... this will not give satisfaction to those Gentlemen in the House of Commons of this Kingdom who contended in the last Session that a higher duty ought to have been imposed upon the importation of British refined sugar".[23] The gentlemen in question, in short, would have been satisfied with nothing less than a duty amounting to a prohibition on English sugars. The passage of a year and the arrival of a new administration had given FitzGibbon an entirely different view of the merits of monopolies. In 1780, he had seen nothing objectionable in them. In 1781, he contended that allowing Irish sugar bakers a monopoly of the market acted only to "raise the price of sugar beyond all reasonable bounds".[24] He also argued that British refined sugars commanded such a small share of the Irish market that prohibitory duties were unnecessary. Eliminating even this minor competition would deprive Irish sugar bakers of all inducement to reduce their costs by developing a direct trade with the West Indies. As matters currently stood, they deliberately continued to import via England, thus keeping their costs and prices high.[25] Finally FitzGibbon made this answer to the claim that Ireland's prospects of obtaining such a direct trade were slight:

> It has been said, though disproved by the fact that we should never be able to import our own sugars directly. But is it not idle to suppose, even if this were the case, that the British merchant would not import them here immediately from the islands and save the charges of double freight.[26]

In short, Irish interests and British interests need not always conflict. It was, he argued as much to the benefit of English merchants to develop a direct trade between Ireland and the West Indies as it was to the benefit of the Irish economy.

FitzGibbon's pronouncements on the intricacies of the sugar trade are not as important as the underlying meaning of his shift on the issue. Although he always spoke intelligently and clearly enough on such matters, the fact remained that he was not a particularly profound or original thinker on economic matters. His views on trade invariably reflect his political sympathies or intentions at a particular time. Prior to 1781, he had either shared or had attempted to conciliate nationalist sentiments, and in consequence, he took a defensive view of Irish economic rights. After 1781, when ambition and personal inclination made him a government man, he invariably took the stand that whatever benefited England of necessity benefited Ireland. Close economic ties inevitably strengthened political ties. Close political ties in turn were essential to the security of the Protestant colony on which his interest and his self-esteem depended.

In at least one instance, his public attitude toward the Volunteers, FitzGibbon took a more conservative stance than the government. In the opening session of Parliament in October 1781, he opposed a vote of thanks to that body, though he prudently appealed to parliamentary etiquette, and avoided allusions to the dubious constitutional and legal standing of the Volunteers. He observed that in the prior session the House had condemned resolutions passed by the more radical Volunteer corps in Dublin and in Ulster. A resolution of thanks in the subsequent session would create an impression of inconsistency detrimental to the dignity of the House.[27] His remarks provoked considerable indignation from his fellow members, many of whom were Volunteers and who consequently had imbibed the self-congratulatory attitude of that body. FitzGibbon quickly retreated before the hostility he had provoked. He assured his colleagues that "no man had a higher respect" for the Volunteers than he, and he joined in the final unanimous vote in favor of the resolution.[28] He had little choice. Quite apart from his own sympathies for the Volunteers, Carlisle had no intention of creating yet another grievance for the opposition:

> As it is unanimity has prevailed, the opposition have not had this opportunity of uniting and the first step (which is ever of great importance) has been as favorable to government as could be wished.[29]

Why FitzGibbon felt obliged to brave certain public outrage by opposing the popular patriotic idols is yet another mystery. He himself had served in the elite Dublin corps, and he appears in full splendid regalia in Francis Wheatley's painting of a Volunteer fete. He did, of course, develop a genuine disillusionment with the Volunteers and a genuine fear of the effects of popular agitation on the fragile equilibrium of the Irish social order. His tendency toward emotional excess may also have contributed to his isolated antagonism. Once he had committed himself to support the Carlisle administration, he undoubtedly was eager to show his devotion as early and as emphatically as possible, even on a matter where the government wished to avoid partisan conflict. Finally, an understandable weariness with patriotic exaltations and pretensions may have influenced him. He ridiculed a suggestion made in the same session to raise a Volunteer fleet to protect the coasts:

> Mr FitzGibbon thought this an improper time to enter on such a subject, and declared that if at present it was intended to be introduced, he would vote against it, and asked if the gentleman intended to pledge the House for the maintenance of an Irish navy.[30]

His denigration of Irish naval capabilities provoked this indignant riposte from Barry Yelverton: "An pray, why not of an Irish navy?"[31] On this matter FitzGibbon more closely matched the sentiments of Carlisle's administration. It was willing to take a tolerant view of a Volunteer army, but it did not want the same impulse to extend to naval defenses.

FitzGibbon did persevere in his opposition to the perpetual mutiny act when it again came up for debate in the session. Carlisle took a tolerant view of his stand. He observed to Lord Hillsborough that FitzGibbon had made a political commitment which his honor and his "Habits of intimacy" with members of the opposition (presumably Grattan and Yelverton) compelled him to maintain: "Mr FitzGibbon, tho' in principle disposed toward Government, was already committed on some of the popular points."[32] Carlisle could afford such generosity. He later reported to Hillsborough that "... my Government was supported by very great and respectable Majorities of both Houses in resisting Bills proposed with the Design of limiting the duration of that Act".[33]

On the matter of the rights and independence of the Irish parliament, the Carlisle administration adhered to its intention of opposing all efforts to abrogate the status quo. Initially the government was successful. Beginning in December 1781 and continuously throughout the months of February and March of the following year, Grattan and Flood alternately introduced resolutions declaring the sole and inviolable right of the Irish parliament to make laws for Ireland. In the same vein, they crowded the agenda with proposals to abrogate the powers of the Irish Privy Council to alter or throw out bills.[34] In every instance, Carlisle and Eden commanded the majorities to defeat Grattan and Flood in Parliament, and they could always rely on FitzGibbon to vote with them, and to speak for his vote in his usual fashion. For example, in the debate on Flood's first proposal for a committee to review and amend Poynings' act, FitzGibbon bluntly upheld the powers of the Irish Privy Council:

> I think that by law the Privy Council can either stop or alter bills in their passage to the throne. No words can be more express than those which give him that power.[35]

Yet even he was not entirely adamant. He was willing to concede that although the English Privy Council could stop bills, it could not alter them.[35]

II

Nonetheless, Carlisle and his supporters, including FitzGibbon, found it increasingly difficult to resist the agitation on constitutional questions. However adroitly Carlisle and Eden outmaneuvered Grattan and Flood, and however staunchly FitzGibbon supported them, they could not ignore or mollify the public agitation over Ireland's constitutional status. In December 1781, Carlisle observed to Hillsborough that "the Independence of the Irish Legislation is become the Creed of the Kingdom".[37] In the early months of 1782, his accounts of the public mood started to echo the grim and fretful tone of his predecessor. Reversing his initial benign attitude, he blamed the "restless and reasoning Disposition of the Volunteers ... and the Practice of frequent meetings and correspondence with each other" for the public mood.[38] Certainly both Grattan and Flood encouraged and received encouragement from Volunteer demonstrations.[39]

This restless and reasoning disposition most notably manifested itself in an assembly of Northern Volunteers held at Dungannon in February 1782 for the purpose of drawing up instructions to members of parliament on constitutional issues. In his dispatches on the subject, Carlisle dismissed the gathering as small and comprised mainly of troublemakers. He attributed the whole business to rumors of an impending election.[40] Yet however insignificant, the meeting at Dungannon set a dangerous precedent for large national gatherings claiming equal weight with Parliament as the representative of the people's will and attempting to control Parliamentary votes and proceedings. His successors were not as fortunate in their encounters with this new phenomenon.

Carlisle could not take a similarly belittling view of the elections that had supposedly promoted the meeting. The Volunteers' advocates in Parliament might be outvoted, their meetings might be insignificant, but Carlisle was well aware that Volunteer agitation could have a powerful and adverse effect for the government at the polls. Members who supported the government faced a significant risk of defeat, which in turn raised the possibility of a total breakdown of all English authority:

> ... I should be very short-sighted if I did not foresee that the due support and possibly the Existence of a permanent good government in this Kingdom depends much on maintaining the many respectable Friends of my administration in the fair opinion of their countrymen.[41]

Carlisle seized on a bill proposed by Barry Yelverton as a promising means of mollifying public opinion without fundamentally altering the status quo. His contact with Yelverton represented a volte face from his earlier estimations of the man. Carlisle had initially dismissed Yelverton as a "clever, pleasant man" who nonetheless "would not risk his popularity by any connection with us".[43] Yelverton's proposed bill simply confirmed, by independent fiat of the Irish Parliament, all English statues binding Ireland in the areas of trade and land title. As he himself frankly admitted, his bill strengthened the position of the popular party by removing one of the most potent objections to a declaration of Irish legislative independence: that it would invalidate land titles held by virtue of English acts of confiscation and forfeiture. Indeed, Flood later proposed a bill similar to Yelverton's for that very reason. Carlisle chose to overlook any popular benefits the bill may have and to see in it a creditable compromise for the government. On one hand, it allowed the Irish parliament to assert its rights and its dignity by confirming English statutes. On the other, it made no fundamental changes in the constitutional relationship between England and Ireland.[44]

In arguing for approval of this bill, Carlisle noted that it had the support of a "gentleman of so independent a character and so cordially disposed toward government as Mr. FitzGibbon".[45] No doubt FitzGibbon, like Carlisle, was looking for a creditable way to mollify popular opinion, with a view to upcoming elections. He had other, if possible more pressing, reasons. In seconding Yelverton's proposed bill when it came up for debate in Parliament, FitzGibbon declared that "Property in this Kingdom is not safe without some such bill". Irish juries were in many instances setting aside or ignoring English laws when deciding cases concerning property. Nothing could have been more calculated to unnerve FitzGibbon. The dread of chaos that had made him so suspicious of the Volunteers at the same time compelled him to take a popular course of action. The change of ministries in England in March 1782 ended Carlisle's administration before Yelverton's bill had completed the passage through Parliament. But given the general mood of the country, halfway measures from the government, from FitzGibbon and from Yelverton probably would have had little effect. Nothing less than an explicit acknowledgment of Irish parliamentary autonomy would have satisfied popular aspirations.

The Carlisle administration did experience something of a respite from the turmoil over constitutional issues. The once inflammatory issue of Catholic relief provided this respite. New legislation, again introduced by Luke Gardiner, completed the unfinished business of 1778 by extending to Catholics full rights to purchase land. It also made *de jure* the existing *de facto* tolerance of Catholic worship and it permitted Catholics to teach, though they could do so only in the capacity of private tutors. Gardiner's bill met FitzGibbon's criticisms of the 1778 act by removing all of the "insulting" and largely unenforced personal restrictions binding Catholics.[47]

The governments in both Dublin and in London, forming judgments from recent experience, again had doubts, not about the advisability of further Catholic relief, but about the reaction of Irish Protestants. Hillsborough expressed doubt that the Catholics would find such relief satisfactory and certainly that radical Protestants, particularly the "Independents" of Ulster, would follow the example of the Gordon agitators and use the bill as a pretext for a rebellion against a government which they already despised:

> In the present delicate state of Publick Affairs, it would be perhaps advisable not to stir any questions relative to Religion: Your Excellency will recollect the Disturbances occasioned not long ago in this country by the Act in favor of Roman Catholics; It certainly produced the dreadful conflagration and its consequences, which threatened the total Ruin and Destruction of this city ... I fear, if anything of that kind is attempted in the Parliament of Ireland, it will give an opportunity to the Independents and Disaffected in the North to raise Disturbances upon the Pretence of Religion, which may go further when once begun than it is easy to foresee.[48]

Carlisle took the hint. In the initial stages of the debate, the government adopted an attitude of cautious friendliness; it allowed Gardiner to proceed, and it provided reliable majorities, but it stood prepared to abridge or discourage his bill at the first sign of trouble.[49]

Hillsborough's chimera of a Gordon conflagration in Ireland never materialized. Gardiner's bill did of course meet with some opposition. Ogle remained verbosely hostile. Although he made mawkish protestations of his fraternal love for the Catholics, Flood stood on the traditional argument of Protestant patriotism, that they posed a menace to a free constitution. Consequently he felt obliged to oppose any privileges which tended to increase their political influence, particularly the privilege of land ownership.[50] They represented the exceptions. In marked contrast to 1778, the debates on the bill of 1782 were, according to Carlisle "carried on with good Humour".[51] The heads of the bill passed with few modifications and respectable margins, and received ready – and no doubt relieved – acquiescence from the English cabinet.

The conduct of the Catholics during the invasion scares of 1779 and 1780 accounted in the main for the startling shift in Protestant opinion. Contrary to traditional fears and suspicions, the Catholics had shown no inclination to welcome an invasion from their compatriots in despotism and superstition, the French. Instead they had contributed generously toward the expenses of coastal defenses and of various Volunteer units. Political interest as well as fellow feeling and gratitude accounted for this sudden change of heart. At the brief meeting at Dungannon, the majority of delegates supported a least a limited extension of Catholic rights. Indeed a Presbyterian had moved the resolution to that effect, *pace* Lord Hillsborough's assumptions about the obdurate antagonism of the "Independents" toward the Catholics.[53] In the midst of all the heady rhetoric about tolerance, love and peace between brother Christians and Irishmen, it could not have escaped the awareness of many delegates that Catholics, if welcomed as members of the proud and emerging Irish nation, could provide the weight of numbers to other popular causes. Within two years at least some Volunteer corps had moved beyond condescending expressions of good will; they openly recruited Catholics and appealed to them as allies against the government.

FitzGibbon showed his sympathies, if not as a friend of the Catholics as a friend of government: "... something he was certain ought to be done for the relief of so great a part of our fellow subjects whose dutiful and loyal behavior had rendered them deserving objects of attention."[54] His overall conduct during the debates on the bill continued in the same vein. He opposed a proposed version of the bill that would have required the recitation of all laws which the bill proposed to repeal. He pressed instead for the more expeditious method of declaring only those laws and restrictions that were to remain in force.[55] In conjunction with Yelverton and Gardiner, he drafted and refined the clause which restore to Catholics the right to purchase any kind of land in fee, with the exception of land bearing a right of advowson and lands within those boroughs possessing the right to return members of Parliament. He also took the liberal view that Protestant tenants holding under Catholic landlords in counties should have the right to vote.[56] Presumably FitzGibbon allowed this provision because he believed that Catholics were less likely to gain a prevailing interest in counties. Since the majority of Catholics were not in a position to purchase land on any great scale, most eligible county voters were likely to remain under the control of Protestant landlords. Their numbers could easily counter any Catholic interest that might develop. In contrast, the proprietor of a borough had a virtual vote in parliament. He determined who would sit for the borough and how his chosen member would vote in parliament.

Of course, given his particular psychological makeup, FitzGibbon could not get through the debate without displaying hostility and ambivalence. During the initial readings of the clause giving Catholics the right to purchase land, FitzGibbon threw the whole House into a panic with this declaration:

> ... till this morning, he had never considered the bill as dangerous; but on reading it over carefully the first clause had struck him as a repeal of the act of settlement, the act of forfeiture, and the act of reassumption; that if so, it must

> destroy the new titles under the Popery Laws and entangle the whole kingdom in a maze of confusion.[57]

FitzGibbon reiterated his support for the basic premise of the clause, but he recommended that the House take time to reconsider its wording:

> three or four days would not injure their [the Catholics] prospects of relief;... by allowing time to make the bill more perfect, it might save the nation from much distress.[58]

Some members failed to see any such danger. One Mr. Walsh in particular expressed his doubts with some acerbity:

> it was asserted pretty peremptorily and pretty self-sufficiently that property held under the new titles would be endangered, if this bill would pass into law. I have since looked over the penal statutes, but I do here stake any little reputation that I have as a lawyer that there is not the smallest danger whatever.[59]

FitzGibbon's morbid anti-Popery unquestionably played a part in this fear mongering. The original heads of the Gardiner's bill granted Catholics the right to acquire and to hold land, and to be "*exonerated and exempted from all Pains, Penalties, Forfeitures, Disabilities, Incapacities and Restraints, by any of the said former laws inflicted or imposed or intended to be inflicted or imposed on Papists or Persons professing the Popish religion.*"[60] Mr Walsh and others like him simply took this wording to mean that past statutes preventing Catholics from purchasing land were now repealed. FitzGibbon was incapable of such innocent literalism. Even at his most benevolent, he never could escape from his perception of the Irish Catholic as a creature of preternatural cunning and malice, always ready to grasp at any opportunity to seize Protestant possessions. According to his own fearful and labored reading, a Catholic bent on reclaiming an ancestral estate could argue that the clause in question effectively set aside all attainders and forfeitures dating from the Civil Wars and Restoration and opened all land to acquisition, either through purchase, or on the basis of a prior title or claim.

Alternatively, he may have been making a brief, panicked attempt to sabotage the bill under the guise of legal pedantry. By creating fundamental doubts about Gardiner's wording, he may have hoped that his fellow members would delay Catholic relief indefinitely, or better yet, that they would decide that the whole business was too risky to pursue further. If this indeed was his motive, FitzGibbon acted, not as a conscious hypocrite, but as a painfully ambivalent man. On one hand, he never lost his conviction that the dispossession of the Irish Catholics represented a fundamental injustice and a fundamental source of instability to the Protestant state. On the other hand, the penal laws affecting Catholic property had served as effective tools of Protestant dominance. The desire to preserve or to extend property had accounted for a good many conversions. Unlike his own proposals in 1778, Gardiner's bill swept away almost all inducements to conform. Always ready to fear the worst about the Catholics, FitzGibbon may have concluded that they would not rest content with the mere acquisition of property; they inevitably would demand its privileges, such as voting or holding office. His private scruples and his public standing as a loyal government man precluded the open opposition of Ogle or Flood; consequently, he resorted to legal hairsplitting to raise potentially destructive fears and doubts. Whatever the reasons for his panic, it passed as abruptly as it had come, and the side of him that pitied the dispossession of the "old inhabitants" regained control. He quickly agreed to a new version of the bill that presumably preserved the integrity of the Act of Settlement to his satisfaction.[61]

In the same restless spirit of fear and contention, FitzGibbon also pressed for a restriction preventing a Catholic from inheriting an estate from a Protestant unless he conformed. His reasoning was oddly inconsistent. Although he was happy enough to concede the vote to Protestant tenants holding under a Catholic purchaser , he did not want Catholics to acquire a possible electoral interest by inheritance. Why he took such a hard line on such a minor point eludes explanation. Few Catholics stood to inherit from Protestants, and moreover, a Catholic who purchased an estate was as likely to influence the votes of his tenants as a Catholic who inherited one. Possibly he hoped to retain at least one inducement to conformity. After some debate he eventually gave up the idea, perhaps out of a general sense of duty to a government bent on passing the bill with a minimum amount of trouble.[62]

In another manifestation of antagonism, he emphatically opposed any measures to give a legal standing to the common practice of Catholics going abroad to receive and education. Indeed, he threatened to oppose the entire relief bill if it incorporated such a provision. His speech on the matter was a *melange* of traditional patriot/Whig mythology and his own morbid perceptions of Papist obstinacy and ill-will:

> I declare that I will use every means in my power to prevent Roman Catholics from receiving a foreign education; and if there were not laws in force, I would propose new ones to that purpose. After what has been done for Roman Catholics, after we have gone more than halfway to meet them, will it be said that they should not come one step to meet us? Will they continue to send their children to France, to Spain, to Portugal to imbibe principles of freedom or attach them to the constitution of this country? Or will *you* suffer the Roman Catholics who make a considerable body of the people to resort to regions of bigotry and superstition, to imbibe principles of positive obedience and every idea hostile to liberty?[63]

He argued further that Catholics could not plead lack of opportunity as an excuse for sending their children abroad. He knew "to the honor of the present heads of the University" that Catholics attended Trinity "by connivance". Furthermore, he had "every reason to believe that His Majesty, if applied to [*sic*] would be graciously pleased to give his royal assent to a statue for granting them free admission". Based on these premises, FitzGibbon came to this conclusion about the Irish Catholic mentality:

> I think that if they persist in sending their children abroad, they are unworthy the great favors they have received. The University of Dublin is open to them, and if they decline the advantage it is not on account of religion for no religious conformity will be required but for fear their children should in early life imbibe the principles of a free constitution.[64]

At the very least, FitzGibbon's remarks revealed a willful obtuseness. It is highly unlikely that many Catholics would have been aware of Hely Hutchinson's liberality. Certainly the provost would not have been inclined to advertise his admissions policy too widely. Consequently, simple ignorance and not a predilection for positive obedience may have accounted for their failure to send their children to Trinity to "imbibe the principles of a free constitution". Moreover, many Catholics would have had understandable suspicions about sending their children to this pillar of the Protestant establishment. The notorious Charter schools, and indeed, every other public and licensed place of learning enforced conformity. FitzGibbon's disclaimers scarcely provided much reassurance. The principles of the "free constitution" which he was so anxious to instill of necessity meant indoctrination in Protestant biases and Protestant self-justifying myth. He more than anyone else would have known what effect exposure to the privileges and enlarged opportunities of Protestant classmates would have on young, ambitious Catholics.

Yet in typical fashion, he undermined and contradicted these fiercely expressed convictions about the insidious evils of a foreign education. FitzGibbon did not make any known effort to press for a revision of Trinity's charter to place Hely Hutchinson's *de facto* policy on a *de jure* basis. As a member for the College, he was the logical person to take up the matter. Having raised the possibility, he allowed it to slip into abeyance. Only in 1793, under the provisions of a relief act which FitzGibbon detested, did Catholics officially obtain the privilege of attending Trinity and receiving degrees. At the same time that he declared his unwavering opposition to permitting Catholics to study abroad, he deplored the very penal laws that he wanted to keep in place:

> He [FitzGibbon] said there was a law in being to punish Roman Catholic parents for sending their children to be educated in foreign countries; but it was such a law as no gentleman in that House would wish to see put in force; it was a disgrace to our statutes and would be a dishonour to the most uncivilized country in the world; it was a law wrote [*sic*] in blood and no court in this country would enforce it. This he knew from experience, as an attempt was made a few years ago to punish a gentleman of that persuasion for educating his children in France; but the charge was reprobated on account of the severity of the statute.[65]

Possibly a recollection that his own father might have been a sufferer under such laws made him retreat somewhat. Denunciations of foreign education from the son of a former scholar at the Irish College in Paris at best demonstrated a ludicrous lack of self-awareness and at worst had the taint of treachery to past ties and loyalties.

III

Although FitzGibbon's stand on the Catholic issue was fairly consistent with his past position and his psychological peculiarities, he showed a startling transformation when the matter of Ireland's constitutional status again came up for a vote in April 1782. His change of heart had nothing to do with any reasoned reassessment of the issue. Rather, it originated in partisan resentment that outweighed any of his prior fears about the dangers of renovation. To understand this resentment on FitzGibbon's part, some account of the circumstances behind the demise of Lord Carlisle's administration is necessary.

The fall of North's ministry in March 1782 restored the Whigs to power after a hiatus of over twenty years. As might be expected, they were anxious to re-distribute office to as many of their friends and adherents as they could, and, in the case of Lord Carlisle, they displayed a remarkable lack of tact or consideration. He was abruptly stripped of his rank as lord-lieutenant of the county of Yorkshire. His recall from Ireland would certainly have followed, had Lord Carlisle not evaded that insult by resigning.[66] With this action, the new Whig ministry effectively destroyed any hope the Duke of Portland may have had to gain control over the situation in Ireland. Contrary to the hopes of the opposition in Ireland, the new Whig lord-lieutenant had little more enthusiasm for Irish constitutional rights than his predecessors. The English opposition had willingly made use of the troubles in Ireland to embarrass North, but restoration to power had, inevitably, restored their sympathies for the claims of authority. Portland came to Ireland with the intention of adjourning Parliament, thus gaining time "to allay those heats and soothe those passions which I am sorry to tell you appear to me to have taken much stronger, fuller possession of the people here".[67] While heats were being allayed and passions soothed, Portland intended to consult with his colleagues in England to determine more fully what concessions they deemed safe and necessary. Portland quickly discovered that Grattan and his party had no intention of delaying his latest set of resolutions calling for a repeal of the declaratory act, an abridgment of Poynings' act and a repeal of the perpetual mutiny act.[68] Worse, many government regulars resented the new administration both on Lord Carlisle's behalf and on their own. As Portland reported to the new Home Secretary, Lord Sydney:

> I also had to apprehend the effects of disappointment, which operated upon the minds of those who supported Lord Carlisle upon condition of being recompensed at the end of the session.[69]

While not mentioned by name, FitzGibbon certainly belonged to this category. Had any legal office fallen vacant during Carlisle's administration, FitzGibbon would have received the appointment. The fact that after his return to England, Eden attempted to have FitzGibbon appointed prime serjeant certainly suggests a previous disposition in his favor.[70] Of course, having lost office himself, Eden had no power to obtain office for another. True to Portland's "apprehension", FitzGibbon acted in conjunction with Eden to undermine and embarrass the new administration. Outrage at the treatment meted out to his dear friend undoubtedly prompted him at least as much as disappointed ambition.

Eden made the first move. He still retained a seat in the English Parliament, and on 8 April, immediately after his return from Ireland, he rose to demand a repeal of the 6th of George I. He then returned to Ireland, where he circulated copies of a conciliatory speech made by Charles James Fox on the Irish question. His intention, of course, was to create further expectation and demand. According to Portland, he also raised doubts "respecting the effect of an appointment of new Lord-lieutenant, pending the session", a flimsy, not to say absurd pretext, as lords-lieutenant resigned, were recalled or were appointed without any reference to the meetings of the Irish Parliament.[71]

In justice to Eden, he acted out of more than mere pique. He was convinced that the new government, bent on pandering to public passions in Ireland, brought Carlisle's administration into disrepute and worse, disrupted a steady, cautious course of policy at a particularly dangerous time. As Eden himself stated the situation to Carlisle:

> After all, it is damned provoking. The language they [the new administration] hold is that by your immense majorities and steady management, you excited the jealousies of the people and gave birth to demands which must now be gratified and therefore, that it is wise to throw the odium of past refusal on you and the popularity of present gratification on your successor. There is an absolute fixed insensibility as to the personal inconveniences to which they expose us and as to the unjust principle of the whole transaction.[72]

However just his grievances, Eden's own behavior was scarcely more conducive to a moderate policy in Ireland, At the same time that he was blaming the Portland administration for succumbing to popular passions, he was doing his utmost to ensure that it had no chance to do otherwise.

Meanwhile, FitzGibbon was following Eden's irresponsible suit in the Irish parliament. He began with an exercise in petty humiliation. Portland had barely arrived in Ireland when FitzGibbon proposed a vote of thanks to Carlisle, and he apparently attempted to do the same for Eden.[73] While Portland was willing enough to allow such a courtesy to Carlisle, he adamantly opposed any recognition of a man whom he considered, with some justification, as a troublesome *intrigante*. Portland did succeed in confining the vote of thanks to Carlisle. He owed this success in part to Eden himself, who decided to request his friends not to press the matter.[74] He may have feared that as many, if not more, aspersions would be cast on him as on the Duke of Portland. With his usual intensity of purpose, FitzGibbon remained undeterred by Eden's professed wishes and he continued to make trouble over his friend's alleged due. Nearly two month's after Portland's arrival, he sounded out Carlisle about the possibility of persuading the administration in England "to obtain a mandate to the Duke of Portland" not to oppose a vote of thanks to Eden.[75]

In the same partisan spirit, he threw his support behind Grattan's resolutions, though they did not differ substantially from those he had opposed in 1780. His speech served more as an apologia for Carlisle's administration than as a vindication of Ireland's rights:

> I do confess that when the Declaration of Rights was moved, I voted with the administration on a decided conviction that it was then improper and inadequate to the end proposed ... I knew it was then improper for I had the most decided proofs that Lord Carlisle was at that time and had been from the very beginning of his government laboring with his utmost interest and influence to procure a repeal of the 6th of George I and to obtain whatever the friends of Ireland could wish. This is but justice to him. Knowing then that Lord Carlisle was laboring for the advantage of Ireland, I knew that it was then improper and inadequate to the end proposed. I did not chuse to commit the nation upon a question till it became necessary. It is now necessary...no man has said that the Duke of Portland has power to grant us redress for which the nation is now committed; but as the nation is committed, no man, I hope will recede, but go *through* HEART AND HAND for as I was *cautious* in committing the *nation*, so I will be firm in asserting the rights.[76]

In other words, he had not wished to make trouble for Lord Carlisle, but he had no such compunctions about the Duke of Portland's peace of mind. His claims that Carlisle was considering the repeal of the declaratory act from the very inception of his administration are exaggerated. Carlisle's own official correspondence reveals that at the most, he urged the English cabinet to avoid the exercise of the provisions of the 6th of George I, and he hinted, very gingerly, at the possibility of a repeal.[77] What is beyond doubt is that FitzGibbon, in making such claims, was attempting to maneuver Portland into making humiliating concessions and at the same time, to lessen any credit his administration might have taken in them. It was the very tactic which Eden had accused Portland of employing against Carlisle.

The demands of his constituents at Trinity, as well as personal disappointment and grievance at the wrongs of his friend contributed to his transformation into an Irish patriot. When requested to give his opinion of Grattan's proposed declaration of rights, his answer was uncharacteristically embarrassed and hedging. He made this thunderous denunciation of the 6th of George I:

> I have always been of opinion that the claims of the British Parliament to make laws for this country is a daring usurpation of the rights of a free people and have uniformly asserted the opinion in public and in private.[78]

He was less emphatic on the matter of Poynings' act. On one hand, he expressed some reluctance to tamper with the law as it stood, and he observed that the "University did, on a very recent occasion, experience that this law in its present form may operate beneficially". He added that "a total repeal of it will, I hope, on consideration appear to you to be by no means a desirable object". Yet he left his Trinity interlocutors with the impression that if pressed, he would give way to their views on the matter:

> You may rest assured that the best attention I can give the subject shall be exerted, and I trust, and doubt not, that upon a communication with you upon this topic, I shall be able to give you full satisfaction.[79]

When the vote did come up on Grattan's resolutions, he gave his best attention to his prospects in a future election and voted accordingly.

A letter to Lord Carlisle dating from May 1782 confirms that opportunism and pique moved him to support Grattan. In the letter he declared "... I cannot accuse myself of a very high veneration for the Commons of Ireland."[80] Any assessment of any given statement of FitzGibbon's must take into account his exquisite sense of his audience. He well knew that Lord Carlisle would hold such sentiments. Nonetheless, the contempt he expressed for the Irish parliament probably ranked, along with his abhorrence of Irish Catholicism, among his more sincere sentiments. His intellectual acuteness and his intellectual arrogance inclined him toward impatience with his colleague's rhetorical excesses, while his ambition inclined him to look upon it as a narrow and squalid base from which to pursue loftier things.

Events following Grattan's resolution served to give some basis to FitzGibbon's jaundiced view of the Irish parliament. The resolutions passed and a flood of English concessions followed. The British Parliament repealed the obnoxious 6th of George I and the Irish did likewise in the case of the equally obnoxious perpetual mutiny act. The Irish House of Lords regained its former status as the final court of appeal on all cases pertaining to Ireland. Finally, both the English and the Irish cabinets acceded to a revision of Poynings' act. The Irish Privy council was stripped of all power to alter or to abrogate bills. Although the English privy council retained the power to set aside bills, few ministers in London cared to risk certain trouble by exercising it.[81] Upon receiving these concessions, the Irish parliament made a generous, if utterly unrealistic offer to raise 20,000 men for the naval service and voted £100,000 toward that end.[82] There was one notable skeleton at the love feast, namely Henry Flood, who professed doubts about the good faith of the English government. In his letter to Carlisle, FitzGibbon gave this contemptuous account of Flood's response to the patriots' triumphs:

> Flood is outrageous ... He contrived to find out grounds of opposition to an Address [of thanks] moved by Grattan this day. He said that although the Act of the 6th of George I was repealed upon the principle for which we contended, he did reserve himself for the occasions which would necessarily occur hereafter for asserting the rights of Ireland with effect.[83]

Flood found such an occasion less than two weeks after the supposed restoration of eternal harmony and content. In the debates of 14 June 1782, he made the claim that the repeal of the declaratory act had not sufficiently secured Irish legislative autonomy. The English Parliament could, after all, easily re-assert its unlawful powers unless bound by an unequivocal renunciation of all right and power to legislate for Ireland.[84] With this remark, he launched what is probably the most absurd contretemps in 18th-century Irish history. His proposed renunciation offered no protection from the theoretical perfidy of the English. It was, after all, possible for the English Parliament to renounce its renunciation. In raising the matter in the first place, Flood displayed a passion to draw attention to himself that was nothing less than childish. Grattan had eclipsed him as a popular hero, having received a grant of £10,000 and a resolution of thanks for his successful promotion of the declaration of right.[85] By raising metaphysical doubts about the repeal of the declaratory act, Flood clearly wanted above all to reassert his position as the premier champion of Irish rights. FitzGibbon attributed Flood's discontent to a very familiar reason: disappointment over office: "He [Flood] has been passed by altogether."[86]

In spite of his dubious reasoning and more dubious motives, Flood succeeded in arousing once again the volatile political passions of his compatriots and in the process he regained his prominence. In contrast, Grattan, by venturing to argue that mere repeal was adequate, was abruptly transformed from the idol of the nation to demon and traitor in chief.

FitzGibbon supported Flood in the debates over renunciation. He observed that in the body of the act of repeal, the English House of Lords retained the right to decide any Irish cases pending on the current docket. Therefore, FitzGibbon argued "Could they retain these without retaining at the same time, the principle unimpeached? What could such a retention lead to, but for the purpose of a future reviving power?" He also observed that the Irish bill confirming all English acts concerning land titles had not as yet received certification from England. This piece of constitutional legislation was crucial, as it established the necessary security for the other concessions. The delay prompted FitzGibbon to conclude that: "It looked as if they would not return anything which wore the face of disclaiming their assumed rights over the kingdom. It were better to insist upon renunciation now, than when they would not be allowed a possibility of future discussion."[89]

In light of his prior comments to Carlisle, it would appear that FitzGibbon's behavior was at least as erratic as Flood's. Yet he was acting with perfect consistency in supporting renunciation. In so doing, he could both create more trouble for the

Portland administration. More important, an election was approaching, and he was obliged to demonstrate to his constituents his continuing devotion to the patriot cause.

Unfortunately, events in England conspired to keep the silly issue in the arena of public controversy. A resolution of an English peer, Lord Abington, seemed to confirm Flood's claims that the English parliament meant to reclaim its legislative authority. In this resolution, Abington set forth the premise that the trade concessions made in 1779 had diminished the English Parliament's rightful powers to legislate on external, imperial matters. The House of Lords quickly dismissed Abington's resolution, but not before he had created anxiety on the two most sensitive Irish issues, trade and autonomy.[90] The fall of the Whig ministry after Lord Rockingham's death, and with it the resignation of Portland, created further pretexts for mischief. Charles James Fox proceeded to create embarrassment for the new prime minister, Lord Shelburne and for the new viceroy, Lord Temple, by taking up the issue. Lord Beauchamp, one of Fox's allies and the scion of a family with extensive interests in Ireland, pursued the same line of conduct by publishing a pamphlet arguing in favor of renunciation.[91] In keeping with the established precedents of Irish intrigue, Flood kept in close contact with the English opposition and encouraged their efforts. Matters came to a head in November 1782, with the decision of Lord Mansfield to try an Irish case that had been entered into his court prior to the passage of the act granting all rights to hear appeal cases to the Irish House of Lords. Faced with the repercussions of this action, Temple acknowledged that Mansfield had been within his rights, but in exercising them, he had inadvertently undermined any efforts to persuade the public that the bill of repeal amounted to a renunciation: "... after having struggled with infinite difficulty in resisting ideal grievances, I have not had the smallest reason to imagine that I could be successful in endeavoring to explain away this Business." [92] The ministry in London, at first inclined to dismiss the matter, gave way to Temple's urging. Shelburne and Temple jointly drew up a bill which explicitly renounced all right on the part of the English parliament to legislate for Ireland. The bill duly passed and once again the vain hope stirred that all Irish issues and grievances were at last settled.[93]

FitzGibbon's actions during the session of 1782 were not entirely negative and adversarial. He supported the independence of the Irish judiciary, and he helped Grattan draft the bills establishing that independence. Professional interest and considerable professional ability rendered inevitable his participation in all matters affecting the judiciary.[94]

Nor did FitzGibbon inevitably vote against the government interest at this time. Most notably, he opposed a bill excluding all revenue officers from Parliament, an Irish imitation of similar measures introduced in England. He skillfully couched his opposition in rhetoric calculated to appeal to popular sentiments. The measure, so he maintained, was calculated to serve "only borough interests", though FitzGibbon gave no detailed explanations as to why it would have such effects.[95] Presumably, the wholesale statutory disenfranchisement of members by nature inclined toward government would leave the Irish parliament firmly in control of large aristocratic families with borough interests. FitzGibbon may have been alluding in particular to English Whig families and their allies in Ireland, who had such interests, and at Portland, who belonged to this particular familial and political coterie. Later in the debate, he made more explicit and hostile allusions to the Portland administration, though the lord-lieutenant had no particular favor for the bill either. FitzGibbon observed that the administration had agreed to the creation of two new offices, that of Solicitor and Attorney General to the Queen.[96] This Portland had done in acquiescence to the wishes of Lord Lifford, the chancellor, one of the few members of the old governing establishment who had remained loyal.[97] These two offices, FitzGibbon argued, were far more dangerous than the presence of government officers, as they were directly calculated to increase the influence of the Crown, and by implication the present, usurping lord-lieutenant.[98]

FitzGibbon had more interested and more reactionary reasons for opposing the bill. He must surely have recognized that his helpful kinsman, John Beresford, would surely suffer by this bill. He may also have sensed that an autonomous parliament, without a strong government interest to act as a check, would exist in a continual state of contention at best, and at worst, would completely destroy all British and Protestant control over Ireland. FitzGibbon may not have had much love for the English government as vested in the Duke of Portland, but he retained enough of his fear and his habitual caution to shrink at destroying the framework of his present security and his future power and favor.

FitzGibbon's commitment to close economic ties between Ireland and England also remained intact. He asserted this opinion during debates on the bill confirming all English statutes concerning trade. In return for constitutional concessions, the English government had insisted in particular on the passage of this facet of Yelverton's long-pending bill. What had once been a gesture of Irish independence became a necessary limitation of it and many of the more extreme patriots, led as usual by Flood, resisted. Flood had displayed no great Irish scruples about English acts confirming Protestant land titles, but he expended considerable rhetorical resentment on what he view as a confirmation of English economic dominance.[99] FitzGibbon, with greater clarity of mind recognized that English protection for Irish Protestants did of necessity entail economic dependency, and he reiterated what was to be his standard argument for the rest of his life:

> All the bill said, was merely that it would conduce to the benefit of the commerce of Ireland to adopt such acts, and nothing he conceived, but the adoption of such acts could strengthen the affection and harmony of both nations in the line of trade.[100]

IV

Portland prorogued Parliament on 27 July 1782.[101] Ministerial instability in England brought about his recall at the same time.[102] FitzGibbon later assured Portland's successor Temple that he would have "taken a warm and decided part in support of your government".[103] Undoubtedly the removal of the hated Portland administration would have restored FitzGibbon to his former course of supporting government. He did not have the opportunity to take any part on behalf of Temple. In June 1783, Temple resigned in the wake of yet another change of ministers in England.[104] Fox and his erstwhile rival North, thanks to their notorious coalition, brought down Shelburne's government. The new viceroy, Lord Northington, took advantage of the comparative quiet following the passage of the act of renunciation to dissolve Parliament, and to call an election.[105]

FitzGibbon did not fare particularly well in the elections which took place in the summer of 1783. His first disappointment occurred when he lost his seat for Trinity. As early as May 1782, the *Dublin Evening Post* was anticipating FitzGibbon's defeat in that contest:

> Among the electors of the college it is pretty generally said that their present representative MR FITZ [*sic*] will not again be returned---his amiable *cullibility* not having perfectly coincided with their ideas of Irish liberty and Irish rights.[106]

Presumably his equivocal conduct in Parliament and lingering resentments on the part of Hutchinson's partisans accounted for his failure to retain his seat for the College. No clear and explicit explanation appears either in FitzGibbon's correspondence or in the provost's.

FitzGibbon next turned his attention to the county of Limerick. His chances there appeared promising. He was one of its wealthiest landowners. He could draw on the capital of his father's excellent reputation, and he could undoubtedly count on his Hayes and FitzGibbon relations and their numerous collaterals. In addition to his family, he had the support of a former county member, Silver Oliver, with whom old FitzGibbon had extensive legal and business dealings.[107] FitzGibbon's brother-in-law, Dominic Trant also attempted to provide him with a Catholic interest in the person of Maurice O'Connell, the uncle of Daniel. When O'Connell was charged with smuggling, Trant, a warm personal friend, zealously took up his defense. In the process, Trant had solicited FitzGibbon's assistance and advice. FitzGibbon evidently complied, and Trant then called on O'Connell to return the favor by encouraging his tenants in Limerick to "vote for my brother-in-law, Mr FitzGibbon".[108] In this instance, FitzGibbon received recompense not only for his private but for his public generosity. He had, after all, championed the voting rights of Protestant tenants of Catholic proprietors in 1782. It is also very possible that he received financial help from his friends, the Roches. In 1783, relatively conservative Catholics like O'Connell and the Roches would have had no reason to have found FitzGibbon objectionable, apart from his occasional rhetorical exercises in Protestant zeal. For his part, he always took pride in maintaining friendly relations with duly submissive Catholics.

The election had a promising start for FitzGibbon. By 27 August 1783, he led the poll with 207 votes.[109] Sir Henry Hartstonge had 200 votes and Hugh Massey, one of the two incumbents, trailed with 192 votes. Notwithstanding, Massey eventually overtook FitzGibbon and was returned along with Hartstonge.[110] Given his narrow initial lead FitzGibbon depended on every possible vote and he worked with all of his accustomed energy to cultivate eligible individuals. In the disappointing aftermath of the election, he attributed his defeat exclusively to the treachery and unreliability of voters who could have made the difference between victory and defeat. His bitterness at those voters who had betrayed him led to a challenge to one such individual, an unprecedented action for FitzGibbon, who claimed to have a lofty scorn for men who were "too forward to fight".[111] He, of course, gave a full account of his disappointment to Eden with characteristic trenchancy:

> My dear Eden – It is now high time I should ... inform you of my defeat at the Election which was occasioned by the rashness of one man ... and by the treachery of another who broke faith with me. Fortunately for me, however, he was not so bigoted to the customs of the country as I was, for he refused to meet me when I sent to him.[112]

He adopted a more decorous tone in a letter to Charles Agar, the Archbishop of Cashel. Along with rather sententious remarks about the unspeakable abuse of his trust and good nature, FitzGibbon provided more specific information concerning at least one voter who disappointed him, though the man in question does not appear to have been the unnamed poltroon mentioned in the letter to Eden.[113]

FitzGibbon attributed his loss solely to individual vagaries. His actions in Parliament do not seem to have affected the outcome of the county election, at least in his own mind. Nonetheless, the return of Massey, who consistently supported the popular side on constitutional issues, suggests that at least some voters made judgments based on the events of the past four years.

Silver Oliver came to FitzGibbon's rescue after his defeat. He ensured his friend's return to Parliament by offering him the seat for Killmalock, a borough at his disposal.[114] Even then FitzGibbon could not rest easy. One of the more independent minded (or trouble making) voters for the borough questioned the legality of FitzGibbon's election. The exact identity of this voter remains uncertain. It is also unclear whether the dispute originated in resentment toward Oliver or toward FitzGibbon. FitzGibbon himself provided little illumination on the subject. When the petition was presented in November 1783, FitzGibbon contemptuously dismissed it as the plot of a faction comprised of "the parish curate, another was the parish clerk, another was the sexton, another the grave digger and two other old beggermen who received alms from the church" a striking, but not very informative declaration.[114] Fortunately, his fellow members threw out the petition, and Killmalock remained his base for the remainder of his career in the House of Commons. It is doubtful that even FitzGibbon's ferocious energy and ambition could have withstood yet another defeat and another contest.

V

He received ample consolation for his electoral miseries by gaining the desire of his heart since 1779, government office. Nor did he start with a modest probationary position: on the contrary, he was appointed attorney general, the most prominent and prestigious legal office short of a judgeship.

He owed his appointment to a viceroy serving under the great arch-Whig, Charles James Fox, another of the many ironies marking his career. In the autumn of 1783, Northington faced an array of vacancies in high legal office. Hussey Burgh, who had returned to the government fold and who had been serving as chief baron of the Exchequer, died suddenly. As part of his effort to woo and co-opt members of the popular party, Portland had appointed Barry Yelverton attorney general. Although Yelverton had held the office for little more than a year, Northington continued his Whig predecessor's policy and appointed him to the vacancy in Exchequer Court. FitzGibbon quickly emerged as the most likely candidate.[118] On 4 October, the *Dublin Evening Post* predicted his elevation, and one week later, FitzGibbon himself was announcing his new appointment to Eden.[119] Yet his position at this time was by no means as assured as he thought. He does not appear to have had any awareness that Northington was experiencing great difficulty in obtaining approval for the nomination from the English government.

Fox especially displayed reluctance, and understandably so. FitzGibbon after all had acted with notable hostility toward one of the premier members of his party, the Duke of Portland. But he seems above all to have been concerned that his political friends and allies in Ireland would resent the appointment. He also expressed doubts about their sudden new ally's ultimate loyalty to them:

> I hear many of our friends disapprove of the idea of advancing ... FitzGibbon: you know I am a friend of coalitions, but take care when you are giving them that you do not strengthen an enemy instead of gaining a friend.[120]

Northington's assurances that everyone whom he had consulted in Ireland approved of FitzGibbon and his praises of the latter's abilities dispelled whatever misgivings or ill-feelings Fox might have had.[121] Northington's letters to North had a similarly persuasive effect. On 30 November 1783, North informed the lord-lieutenant that FitzGibbon's appointment had at last received official approval from the cabinet in England.[122]

Henry Grattan later claimed that he had persuaded Northington to appoint

FitzGibbon attorney general. The son quoted the father's characteristically florid summary of the transaction: "I pressed for the appointment of FitzGibbon *and I have that sin to answer for*. I made him attorney general."[123] In his memoirs, Charlemont, Grattan's patron also credited, or perhaps more accurately, blamed Grattan for FitzGibbon's appointment. He claimed that pique over the issue of renunciation prompted him to support and promote a man known to be unfriendly toward the popular cause:

> He [Grattan] was not, perhaps, displeased that power should be lodged in the most unpopular hand and office bestowed on those whom the people most hated, pledged as he deemed himself, to require nothing more from England and inwardly vexed at what had lately been done to satisfy the cravings of the multitude in opposition to his judgment, he might possibly have been not unwilling to place power in the hands of those who would undoubtedly resist any further demands.[124]

Charlemont's falling out with Grattan renunciation led him to this bitter and unfair conclusion. He exaggerated Grattan's malice, and both he and Grattan exaggerated the latter's responsibility for FitzGibbon's appointment. Northington undoubtedly did consult Grattan about FitzGibbon. Grattan after all had been appointed to the privy council, and he had a long-standing acquaintance with FitzGibbon. Moreover, he would have had no reason to denigrate FitzGibbon at that time. Although Grattan and FitzGibbon had opposed each other on such matters as Portuguese trade and on the initial resolutions for constitutional autonomy, they had as often acted in concert. Most notably, they had taken the same position on the perpetual mutiny act; for reasons of his own, FitzGibbon had supported Grattan's resolution of 1782, and they had worked together on the bills establishing the independence of the Irish judiciary. Notwithstanding Northington's value for Grattan's opinion, he appears to have been influenced as much, if not more, by Yelverton's favorable view of FitzGibbon. FitzGibbon himself gave generous, if perhaps excessive, credit to Eden, who had evidently continued efforts on his behalf in England:

> The office [of attorney general] was offered to me by Lord Northington in very handsome and honorable terms indeed, for which I believe I am in great measure indebted to you, as he told me very fairly that he had first taken up his opinion of me from your representation.[125]

In the end, the recommendations of his various friends and colleagues accounted only in part for FitzGibbon's elevation. The fact remained that FitzGibbon, thanks to his abilities and his parliamentary skills, was beyond question the best candidate for the position. As Northington himself put it, FitzGibbon was "a gentleman of considerable Talents in the House of Commons, as well as of eminence and knowledge in his profession". Northington also gave Fox and North this assurance: "His appointment, I am persuaded, will give considerable satisfaction to the public."[126]

VI

Clearly Northington remained unaware of that part of the public whose radical views found expression in the popular press of Dublin. There the bad impression created by his opposition to the tenantry act and to the initial efforts toward constitutional autonomy had intensified. His arrogant and irritable manner continued to draw unfavorable comment, as this excerpt from the *Volunteers' Journal* indicates: "The ridiculous and insolent HAUTEUR which Jack Fitzpetulant assumes in the House of Commons merits a severe reprimand."[127]

In January 1784, soon after his elevation to office, a new charge against FitzGibbon, sexual incontinence, began to appear in the newspapers. Specifically, his alleged affair with one Mrs D provoked much salacious interest and much moral indignation. Again, the *Volunteer Journal* took the lead in drawing attention to the affair and denouncing it. On 16 January 1784, there appeared this breathless account of the corrupt and corrupting behavior of FitzGibbon and his paramour:

> The very pretty flirtation that passes between the delicate Mrs D and Jack Fitzpetulant almost every evening at the theatre must have a very strong tendency to do away all relics of *ungenteel mauvais honte* which disgraced our countrywomen heretofore. If a few more persons of consequence were to free themselves from the shackles of timidity and set a pattern equally laudable, we should soon become rival for the palm of confidence, with our Gallic neighbors. It is undoubtedly distressing to persons of fashion and figure, like these *billing doves* to be constrained by ties of matrimony, which were made only to confine vulgar folk who have not *spirit* enough to deviate from the paths chalked out for them by their *misty* grandees.

The newspapers continued to follow the affair avidly throughout the early months of 1784. Probably the elusive Mrs D, whose identity remains forever obscured in discreet blanks, suffered more than her lover. The newspapers may have concealed her name, but they did not spare her character. She was portrayed as a fickle and promiscuous woman who quickly cast aside FitzGibbon for a Scotsman in the lord-lieutenant's entourage.[128] Considering the latitude allowed to unattached young men in the 18th century, FitzGibbon almost certainly had some share of similar escapades to his credit, or discredit. The keen eye of partisan hatred had simply seized on this commonplace, squalid liaison to discredit him further. He also may have contributed to the unprecedented degree of hostile attention directed toward his sexual habits. Undoubtedly he was exhilarated by his success, and, as a result, he may have been unusually keen to enjoy himself and less discreet in doing so.

With a bland indifference to any inherent contradictions, the newspapers that accused him of bestial sexual excess also taunted him for priggish and effeminate over-refinement. The *Volunteers' Journal* sneered at him for displaying "the airs of a dancing master and the language of a coxcomb".[129] Yet another paragraph from the

Dublin Evening Post completed the picture of epicene narcissism. It gave an account of a supposed exhibition of pictures in the General Assembly room. They included:

> J—n F—zg—n in the character of Malvolio in the play of the Twelfth Night. The self-sufficiency of this coxcombical character is admirable well-expressed in the saucy and insignificant smirks which the artist has thrown into the countenance of this picture.[130]

Several paragraphs in the newspapers of this period showed an awareness that under his apparently frivolous manner, FitzGibbon was a fiercely ambitious young man. They also noted, with predictable contempt, the direction that ambition was taking. The *Dublin Evening Post* mockingly praised him for being "politically wise, for instead of attaching thyself to a party, which according to the changeability of state affairs might be turned out, you are at all times ready to be the pliant tool of any minister".[131] The *Volunteers' Journal* echoed this line: "It is evident that what Jack Fitzpetulant wants in ability, he is resolved to make up in zeal. No man can take [greater pains] to court the applause of administration."[132]

In reporting on the progress of his career, the press avidly noted setbacks, either real or imagined and made frequent predictions of his imminent political demise. The first issue of the *Dublin Evening Post* for the year 1784 predicted that "Jack Fitzpetulant would be very happy to ensure being Attorney General this day three months". The *Volunteers' Journal* took a more lofty moralizing tone, expressing a hope that his elevation would bring, if not immediate dismissal, at least the disappointment and unhappiness which ill-gotten office ought to bring: "Quere – will the virtues of an att–rn–y g——l's gown be sufficient to give the balm of peace to a corroded mind?"[134]

Along with attacks on his overweening and, it was hoped, his doomed ambition, the newspapers, shamelessly contradicting their vaunted popular principles, cast obloquy on his low birth. The *Dublin Evening Post* most clearly revealed this inconsistency in a series of article concerning a bill that FitzGibbon supposedly was framing to disarm the Volunteers. This report, like others of a similar nature, was highly exaggerated. His remarks in Parliament had merely displayed suspicion of the Volunteers' political role and a reluctance to bestow on them the effusive praise they regarded as their due. Notwithstanding, the *Dublin Evening Post* made this mournful prediction about the results of the disarming bill, which it "confidently" predicted:

> If the intended bill for disarming the Volunteers of Ireland should pass into a law (of which there can be little doubt) adieu to the liberties of this unhappy land. We shall become the slaves of an infamous aristocracy of a few men [including John FitzGibbon] not of Patrician birth but descended from the very dregs of the people.[135]

In other words, by daring to oppose the self-appointed guardians of the people, FitzGibbon met with contempt for allegedly being of the people. The *Volunteers' Journal* went even further. Displaying a curious sort of snobbish determinism for a newspaper championing the popular cause, it blamed his low origins for his private vices as well as for his public ones.

By appearing to threaten the Volunteers, FitzGibbon exposed himself to excoriation not only because of his plebeian origins but because of his Popish origins. The brutal sectarian snobbery of Irish society affected even those who made a point of their enlightened and tolerant opinions. The *Dublin Evening Post* was the first to make a stigma of FitzGibbon's convert background, in spite of the fact that by 1782, it had embraced the Catholic cause. On 4 December 1783, it reported that J—n FitzJesuit, Esq. "was skulking from the chastisement of several of the VOLUNTEERS" whose majesty he had offended. This sobriquet could have been a general attack on FitzGibbon's alleged arbitrary tendencies. The Jesuits, in the popular Protestant imagination, supposedly acted as the theorists, as well as the agents of despotism. Nonetheless, the mere fact that FitzGibbon was unfortunate enough to have a Catholic grandfather and a convert father made him, and not Yelverton or Grattan for example, vulnerable to slurs of this kind. Evidently, arbitrary Popish tendencies constituted a genetic doom that even the ardently Protestant FitzGibbon could not escape.

The persona established in the years from 1780 to 1784 – FitzGibbon the effeminate debauchee, FitzGibbon the upstart of Popish extraction, FitzGibbon the overweening and arrogant – grew more lurid and pronounced. Once established in an official position, FitzGibbon was to take the course most calculated to offend public opinion, or at least the radical opinion which found voice in the newspapers. With the lofty contempt that drew comparisons with Lucifer, he almost seemed to welcome every opportunity to demonstrate that whatever his opinions when he began his political career, and whatever past accommodations he had made to popular opinion, he was now a government man, wholly dedicated to upholding what remained of the English interest and resisting further demands for change in the ruling structures of the country.

5

Reformers, Sheriffs and Attachments

I

Given his peculiar temperament, FitzGibbon never experienced much happiness in his life. Nonetheless, while he was serving as attorney general, he probably came as close to happiness as he ever would. It was the happiness of rising power and influence, unrestrained by the irksome demands of popular opinion. Although he had acceded to and even encouraged patriot unrest to further his own ends, once he was firmly in office, he could freely indulge his natural propensities: ruthlessness toward the Volunteers and any other voices of popular discontent, profound suspicion of Roman Catholics, fervent devotion to the English government in Ireland and a corresponding impatience with any man or any party of men who remained in opposition to that government. To his mind, the concessions of 1782 and 1783 effectively satisfied all reasonable demands, and even a few unreasonable ones. Further demands for change in the constitutional relationship between England and Ireland manifested nothing less than madness or treason. FitzGibbon simply could not admit the concept of a loyal Irish opposition.

The English government during the 1780s pursued a program perfectly in keeping with FitzGibbon's own views, a circumstance which accounted in great part for his political felicity. By 1783 the English government was, not surprisingly, weary of new demands from Ireland. The rise of an Irish parliamentary reform movement particularly unnerved the officials in both Dublin and London. The proponents of reform, inspired by parallel movements in England, by American experiments in rational constitution-making or by local grievances and inequities, thought that they were completing the great work of 1782 by purifying the free Irish constitution. To the English government, reform threatened what remained of its authority in Ireland. The fact that the agitation for parliamentary reform came to the political forefront during the administration of Lord Northington, a Fox-North appointee, did not create a more favorable atmosphere to the idea. As the precept of the Duke of Portland showed, the English opposition, once in office, was as hostile toward radical Irish political aspirations as their opponents.

An eminently lucid memorandum by Charles Francis Sheridan, the private secretary of Lord Northington, best summed up the government's reasons for opposition. In common with many other opponents of parliamentary reform, Sheridan played on the common suspicion of any challenge to the established and congenial social order. Reform, he declared, was a "wild and extravagant notion" promoted by the low and the ignorant, who aimed at establishing a democratic tyranny.[1]

The peculiar situation of Ireland made any notions of reform especially unacceptable. Sheridan made note of the "licentious spirit which prevail[s] very generally among the People of this country at the present period". Like Carlisle before him, Sheridan blamed the Volunteers for introducing chaotic democratic notions among the people at large:

> ... the intimate communication it produced between the lower and higher classes of the People, excited the insolence of the former and sunk the consequence of the latter. The frequent meetings it produced, where Politicks were the constant and only topick, where men of the first Rank were obliged to associate with their lowest Tenants or Tradesmen ... weaken[ed] all habits of obedience.[2]

The reforming speculations of these political farmers, shopkeepers and tradesmen, were, in Sheridan's opinion, leading in a particularly dangerous direction: no less than the extension of voting rights to Catholics. Sheridan noted that prior to the American war, the Protestants of Ireland had been "unreasonably suspicious of their Roman Catholic brethren", and had willingly endured any and all British regulation to avoid being at their mercy. But the rage for abstract rights and for reform had even transformed the old reliable hatreds on which the government had depended for its stability:

> ... the change in the national temper and spirit has been as sudden as it is compleat ... no inconsiderable number of the Protestants of this country have now lost all attachment to England, all sense of their own weakness, if deprived of her support, all apprehension of embracing any illiberal or hostile measures toward her, and many of them all jealousy of Roman Catholics, with whom they are ready to share every political right and privilege, blind to the necessary consequence, the subversion of the Protestant government.[3]

Sheridan made the reassuring observation that not all advocates of parliamentary reform favored the extension of voting rights to Catholics, and that, for the time being, that issue divided and undermined the strength of the reform movement. Indeed, the Catholic question had aroused considerable contention at Dungannon. A largely Presbyterian party, influenced by the latest American and French notion of abstract universal rights, favored an end to any religious distinctions whatsoever. Their antagonists retained the traditional Protestant suspicions of Roman Catholics. In the end, the proposed plan of reform excluded all mention of extending voting privileges to the Catholics, thanks largely to the influence of Lord Charlemont, who acted out of the doctrinaire Whig's distrust of Roman Catholics as agents of tyranny.[4]

In spite of the rebuff at Dungannon, the notion of extending political as well as economic and civil rights to Catholics, did not fade away. Many Catholics, equally influenced by French and American thought, readily responded to favorable overtures from reform minded Presbyterians and sympathetic Anglicans. Indeed at least a few appear to have been so vociferous, that even their strongest journalistic advocate, the *Dublin Evening Post*, admonished them to act more discreetly; any undue demands could only endanger the cause of reform and thus any hopes of winning redress from an enlightened, uncorrupted Parliament.[5] Others, like this correspondent of Lord Kenmare, found their rapid transformation from political pariahs to sought after allies a source of bewilderment and uneasiness:

> Our situation strikes me as very difficult to manage between both parties to avoid offending the Presbyterians [presumably by rebuffing their offers of political friendship] and pleasing the others [by holding aloof from political activity, thus placating more suspicious Protestants, both Anglican and Presbyterian].[6]

The fact that Catholics were also serving in some Volunteer units increased the fears of those intent on preserving what remained of the ruling order. A letter from one Mr Vernon of Clontarf best expressed the sentiments which this phenomenon inspired. He assured the government that most Catholics in Volunteer units had joined at the behest of landlords who lacked Protestants to make up their units. Once the landlords withdrew their support, these Catholic peasant levies would return to "ye spade and ye cottage".[7] But even the more suave and liberal Sheridan found the presence of Catholics in Volunteer units ominous.[8]

New economic demands, this time for protective tariffs on English textile imports, were also challenging the government's efforts to assert its authority. This particular manifestation of chronic Irish discontent over trade first stirred during the administration of the Duke of Portland. In a dispatch dated 18 May 1782, at the height of the constitutional crisis, Portland reported to Shelburne on the disaffection of the silk and woolen weavers in Dublin. Portland acknowledged that their trade had fallen off, but he attributed the causes to a general decline in the quality of goods and to the "effects of the present time" by which he presumably meant the dislocations caused by war. The Dublin weavers, unfortunately, lacked his grace's breadth of vision and acumen in economics:

> Your Lordship [Shelburne] must know that the weavers in this place [Dublin] ... are a jealous, restless and impatient set of men, who feel the effects of the present time without recurring to the unavoidable causes of them and who are but too ready to attribute all their distress to the power and superiority of the English.[9]

According to Portland, the weavers had planned a meeting to organize yet another non-importation campaign, but Grattan, anxious not to jeopardize the constitutional negotiations with a trade war, intervened to propose a more moderate course. He suggested instead to "place by an open subscription, by which such as are willing to encourage the manufacturers are to engage to take goods made in this country to the amount [they] chuse to put down opposite their respective names". While grateful to Grattan for his intervention, Portland remained skeptical about the success of such an approach.[10] His doubts were justified. A harvest failure in 1782 followed by a harsh winter inevitably increased the price of provisions, and with it economic pressures on workers.[11] Yet another severe winter in 1783–4 increased the distress and political agitation of the working poor.[12] In response, Luke Gardiner introduced a bill to impose protective tariffs.[13] Some weavers, less willing to trust in the slow, doubtful outcome of such legislation, resorted to more forceful means of regulating trade: tarring and feathering merchants who sold English goods and destroying their shops.[14]

In response to these new agitations, the English government doggedly tried to salvage and uphold what remained of the status quo ante, a tack distinctly at odds with the wavering and conciliation of the past. Of course, as the chief law officer, FitzGibbon would have been expected to frame and support whatever measures the government found necessary to support its policies. Nonetheless he brought a particular zeal to the duties of his office because he could act on his own deepest convictions as well as on the wishes of the government. As the decade progressed, he inexorably progressed in favor, thanks to the perfect harmony between the policies of Whitehall and the Castle and the policies of FitzGibbon.

II

A new and powerful personal loyalty also bound FitzGibbon to the government. The defeat of the Fox-North coalition over the East India bill had elevated William Pitt the younger to power. In keeping with the established practice, the change of ministries required a change of viceroys. Given Pitt's own reputation for priggishness and high seriousness his choice of viceroy was curious. Charles Manners, Duke of Rutland epitomized the Georgian aristocracy at its most polished and glittering; he was handsome, pleasure loving, lively and affable. He also was a discriminating and knowledgeable collector of art who consulted with no less an authority than Joshua Reynolds. His own considerable personal attractions were enhanced by those of his beautiful, fashionable wife. FitzGibbon would have been prepared to revere anyone in the person of the lord-lieutenant. With Rutland, inclination became inevitability. The new lord-lieutenant not only represented the power and prestige of the British empire, he was a delightful young man who shared FitzGibbon's own luxurious tastes and pleasure loving temperament.

Rutland fully returned FitzGibbon's adoring regard. He never mentioned Fitz-Gibbon's name in his correspondence without some expression of gratitude and enthusiasm. More important, Rutland quickly became a warm advocate of FitzGibbon's claims and ambitions, often in the face of profound skepticism from London. FitzGibbon's relations with Rutland presaged the remarkable emotional and political hegemony he was to establish over later viceroys. While markedly less glamorous than Rutland, they were cast in the same general mold: modestly talented and inexperienced young aristocrats who quickly fell under the spell of FitzGibbon's personality and judgment. FitzGibbon's long reign of personality broke down only when Pitt finally appointed a viceroy of experience and maturity in the person of Lord Cornwallis.

FitzGibbon does not seem to have enjoyed the same sort of romantic friendship with Thomas Orde, which was not surprising, given Orde's singularly unromantic personality. Indeed, Orde did not have a personality as such; he had a worthy but exceedingly tiresome persona, that of the driven, over-conscientious civil servant. His voluminous memoranda on various subjects are remarkably detailed and well organized. No fact was too minor, no item of minutiae too inconsequential to escape his attention. His strong sense of duty and his desire to do well by his trust were also beyond question. Unfortunately, the protean complexities of Ireland often eluded his best administrative efforts, and left him baffled, irritated and exhausted. Anxiety and querulousness prevail throughout his papers and no doubt infused his day to day dealings with his colleagues. As will be noted, FitzGibbon may have suffered moments of irritation with Orde. Nevertheless, FitzGibbon's ambition imposed a rare emotional self-discipline on him, and in his direct dealings, he treated Orde with unfailing kindness and respect. For example, a letter to Orde concerning a plan for universal education in Ireland contained both legal advice and expressions of concern for Orde's always precarious health. Above all, FitzGibbon found the surest way to Orde's civil servant heart; he cooperated zealously and meticulously in Orde's Sisyphean schemes to render Ireland as orderly as his own memoranda. As a result, Orde joined with Rutland in promoting FitzGibbon's ambitions.

III

At least initially, FitzGibbon and his new patrons fared better than their luckless predecessors in Parliament. The government did not need to make any extraordinary effort to defeat Luke Gardiner's protectionist bill. The fact that protectionist demands drew the strongest support not from gentlemen but from the laborers and "mechanics" in the Liberties influenced many members to vote against it. "The people" deferentially applauding their patriot leaders as they entered Parliament was one pleasing thing. "The people" tarring and feathering recalcitrant merchants, calling for American-style separation from England, and forming their own Volunteer units independent of gentry control was quite another.

In one of his earliest appearances as the government spokesman, FitzGibbon was surprisingly moderate in his remarks. He expressed pity for the distresses of workers pressed by high prices and a fall off of trade, and he assured his auditors that he would have supported the bill if he thought it would do any good. He opposed the bill above all, because he wanted to avoid English retaliation against Ireland's most promising and prosperous industry, the manufacture of linen cloth.[15]

Although the new administration could, for the time being at least, count on a cowed majority in Parliament, Dublin remained in a state of rebellion. In their dispatches, both Rutland and Orde reported continuing violence sparked not only by demands for protective tariffs, but by proposed plans to widen the streets. This latter project aroused resentment because of the expense and the inconvenience, particularly to poorer citizens.[16] In response to these manifestations of violence from the lower orders the new government took the usual measure of increasing troop patrols in the Liberties and it introduced additional legislative repression, especially against the press, which the frightened reactionaries in the Castle identified as one of the chief fomenters of disaffection.[17]

Although himself one of the primary targets of the press, FitzGibbon played only a subordinate part in the act "to secure Liberty of the Press by preventing the Abuses arising from the publication of traitorous, seditious and scandalous libels". John Foster seems to have originated and drafted the bill.[18] He did so in reaction to a paragraph in the *Volunteers' Journal*, which purported to record the scaffold speech of "Jacky Finance", condemned to death for his alleged crimes against the people.[19] The bill faced some resistance, and not exclusively from those members of Parliament who believed that the bill menaced rather than secured liberty of the press. Lord Sydney, the Home Secretary, complained about the clumsy drafting and the unenforceable harshness of the bill.[20] Rutland in response defended the general principle of the bill, and assured Sydney that his ministers had made every effort to modify the more draconian provisions of the original draft. He cited both Foster and "Mr Attorney [General]" among those who had "shewed to [*sic*] much the wishes and yielded to the scruples of Gentlemen who would not venture to oppose the Principle or the general Provisions of the Bill, but endeavored to make out specious objections to some Parts of it". He also acknowledged the support of Grattan, who was clearly soured by his experiences with the public press.[21]

Even in its modified form the bill was formidable. It required publishers of newspapers to register with the government, thus creating a ready dossier of objects for prosecution. Stamp duties on newspapers were increased, as were penalties for allegedly libelous or seditious publications. Newspaper editors who published writings deemed offensive now faced prison sentences and crippling fines. Those newspapers which escaped statutory prosecution faced the more formidable, because undefined, menace of Parliamentary privilege. Members offended by a squib or a paragraph had the unlimited right to prosecute on the grounds that the writings in question impugned not only individuals but the authority and dignity of the whole legislative body.[22]

The government made some efforts to persuade as well as to coerce, by purchasing newspapers to reflect its point of view. In 1784, it gained control of the respected opposition newspaper, the *Freeman's Journal*, along with the short-lived *Volunteer Evening Post*. In 1788, it assumed editorial control of the eminently worthy and eminently moribund, *Faulkner's Dublin Journal*. These forays into journalism were, on the whole, unsuccessful. Once they recognized the government influence of these newspapers, Dublin readers quickly abandoned them. The prestige of government newspapers was not aided by the choice of editors. The new editor of the *Freeman's Journal*, Francis Higgins, supplemented his income by printing government proclamations and by acting as a part-time spy master. The government-sponsored editor of *Faulkner's*, John Gifford, never missed an opportunity to vent his virulent anti-Catholicism.[23]

The government quickly showed its determination to silence its boldest critics by arresting Matthew Carey, the proprietor of the *Volunteers' Journal*. In one of his many letters to Eden, FitzGibbon claimed a prominent role in Carey's prosecution. He also gleefully anticipated a guilty verdict on a charge of high treason and Carey's execution.[24] Contrary to FitzGibbon's hopes, the indictment for treason failed to materialize and Carey was released. Nonetheless, the experience of imprisonment, and the certainty of further harassment eventually compelled him to emigrate to Philadelphia.[25]

In spite of, or perhaps because of, the government's attempts at repression, the *Volunteers' Journal* defiantly continued to publish attacks on government, albeit under new management. The same held true for the other major Dublin newspapers. Rutland's debauchery, and Orde's sickly, unprepossessing appearance were favored subjects. FitzGibbon, of course, retained his pre-eminence as an object of hatred. His adventures with Mrs D his participation in disreputable revels at the Castle and his alleged cowardice and effeminacy continued to inspire bad lampoons and satires throughout 1784. Most notably the *Dublin Evening Post* reported on the progress of a fictional Castle Volunteer unit. According to this account, "Fitzpetulant was to have a command, but declined, for he abhors the report and detests the smell of gunpowder".[27]

In addition to placing curbs on the press, the Rutland administration also sponsored legislation for the easier apprehension of those suspected of houghing or cutting the Achilles tendons of soldiers, a common tactic of rioters.[28] In spite of these measures, and in spite of assurances that the disturbances would soon die down when confronted with the lofty firmness of government, episodes of violence continued unabated throughout the spring and summer of 1784. In August, a member of Rutland's own entourage was embroiled in an altercation with some members of a Dublin Volunteer corps. The flirtations of a Castle aide de camp with a tavern keeper's wife set off this squalid incident, which further diminished the reputations of Rutland and his intimates.[29] That same month, the public whipping of a man involved in a tarring and feathering led to a riot in which one person was killed by garrison soldiers.[30] In these highly inauspicious circumstances, a new campaign for Parliamentary reform began.

IV

In the spring of 1784, after the defeat of yet another of their bills, proponents of reform seized on the notion of mobilizing support through a national congress. Freeholders summoned by the sheriffs of each county and bailiwick were to elect this congress. The congress was to meet at Athlone, selected for its central location. There, delegates were to draw up yet another plan of reform to be presented to Parliament.[31] The intent was, of course, to introduce a bill which had the full weight of public opinion behind it, and which, consequently, could not, *pace* Charles Francis Sheridan, be dismissed as the product of an anarchic mob.

Nothing could have been more calculated to arouse the new government's fears and its repressive instincts. As has been noted, reform struck at the very heart of British policy, a return to the quiescence of the era of the Undertakers, with the government doing the undertaking. Moreover, in the view of the Rutland administration, this new wave of reform agitation seemed to confirm the bleakest forebodings of Charles Francis Sheridan: demagogues led it, and Papists willingly served as their tools of subversion.

Rutland and Orde responded with an all-encompassing hostility toward the Catholics that represented a startling departure from precedent. At least since the administration of Bedford, the English government in Ireland had assumed a conciliatory and protective attitude toward the Catholics, if only to counter Protestant defiance. Of course, given the nature and policy of English government in Ireland, Rutland and Orde inevitably would have discouraged further extension of Catholic civil or political rights. Nonetheless, the two went far beyond tactful evasion and vague promises for the always distant future, and adopted an attitude of blatant suspicion and contempt.

This attitude was apparent at the very onset of the Rutland and Orde administration. As early as April 1784, a Castle memorandum attributed the more inflammatory articles in the press to Catholics, both lay and clerical. Since neither the viceroy nor his very diligent secretary provided anything in the way of names or numbers, this claim necessarily must be regarded with caution. Most existing evidence suggests that the press was overwhelmingly in Protestant hands, albeit highly sympathetic Protestant hands.[32]

In addition, the government made much of the fact that a dozen Catholics in Dublin had signed a petition in support of the proposed reform congress. The intelligence service duly reported the names of those Catholics, along with their occupations. As most of them pursued relatively humble trades such as tailoring or small-scale shopkeeping, the report reinforced the government's perception that Parliamentary reform could only lead to the triumph of a Popish mobocracy.[33]

The government's hostility encompassed not only Catholics laborers and tradesmen, but the small body of gentry and aristocracy, hitherto remarkable for their conservatism and obsequiousness. Some indiscreet remarks calling for an eventual extension of voting rights to Catholics elevated Sir Patrick Bellew to the rank of Popish incendiary in chief.[34]

In response to this perceived Catholic menace, Rutland and Orde spent much of 1784 weighing various schemes to restore the cringing submissiveness which they clearly considered more suitable for a Papist. In his correspondence with Sydney, Rutland raised the possibility of suppressing Catholic political aspirations by threatening to revoke the rights and privileges granted in 1782.[35] Nothing came of this suggestion. The Rutland administration ultimately preferred orchestrated love in the form of loyal petitions, rather than fear, in the form of renewed penal laws. Government supporters and spies undertook a concerted campaign to persuade (or bully) Catholics into presenting loyal addresses asserting their perfect contentment with the benevolent order under which they lived and disavowing all claims to political equality.[36] A petition drive stirred briefly and died in the spring of 1784, then was resurrected in September and October as reform agitation reached a climax. Not surprisingly, the Catholics did not respond with any great enthusiasm. Lord Kenmare and James Butler, the Catholic archbishop of Cashel, did attempt to comply with government demands, but a deep sense of grievance tempered their habitual submissiveness.[37] In a letter to Sir Boyle Roche, Lord Kenmare expressed his mortification that he and other Catholics of his rank should be held accountable for the "Impudence" of "some insignificant individuals among us".[38] Lord Gormanston's correspondence from this period reveals a resentful awareness of government spies observing even the most eminent Catholics for indiscreet remarks or actions.[39] This same perception of the government's hostility led once reliable Catholics, notably Lord Fingall and the two partners in the great textile firm of Comerford and O'Brien, to refuse outright to promote such a petition.[40]

Nevertheless, it would be wrong to dismiss the anti-Catholicism of Rutland and Orde entirely as the panic of an inexperienced boy lord-lieutenant and his neurasthenic chief secretary. Anti-Catholicism wonderfully concentrated the policy, if not the mind, of their government. By intimidating the Papists, those time-honored and still eminently hated scapegoats, the administration also hoped to intimidate Protestants with unaccountable sympathies for Catholic political rights and parliamentary reform.[41] Of equal importance, by associating reform with Popery, the administration could effectively alienate those Protestants who were dubious about reform, about Catholics or about both. Rutland and Orde did succeed in creating a rift between the Protestant reformers and their Catholic allies. They benefited greatly from the strength of anti-Catholic feeling yet remaining among many Protestants who otherwise favored Parliamentary reform. For example, Sir Edward Newenham, one of the leading advocates of reform and the object of numerous hostile Castle memoranda, was notoriously anti-Catholic. He had earned the sobriquet "Knight of St Doulough" because he had allegedly defecated in a well dedicated to that saint.[42] But even Tandy, who had been foremost in encouraging Catholic political activity, backed off when he perceived that the issue of their participation was jeopardizing the unity and the appeal of the parliamentary reform movement.[43] Unfortunately, Tandy and his allies still could create reform trouble among Protestants. FitzGibbon's actions to crush all further reform activity, Protestant or otherwise, brought him, if possible, even greater measures of notoriety, favor and detestation.

V

FitzGibbon already was an experienced antagonist of the reformers. In November of 1783, he had taken the lead in opposing a reform bill introduced by Flood. The bill itself copied the moderate, firmly Protestant model that had emerged from Dungannon in 1782, but FitzGibbon, by then assured of the office of attorney-general, eagerly showed his mettle by treating it as a virtual act of revolution by an armed canaille:

> will gentlemen tell me the constitution is not invaded when any man shall dare to make a proposition by fifty thousand armed men, with fifty thousand more ready to join them? Gentlemen say it is dangerous to commit the parliament and the Volunteers; I know it is dangerous, I know the man that does it should answer the crime with his head; but I know the force of the laws is sufficient to crush them to atoms and for one I say that I do not think life worth holding at the will of an armed demagogue. If ever there was an occasion calling upon every man possessing one sentiment of liberty to exert in defense of the constitution, it is this, it is the present occasion which demands to spurn this bill away.[44]

His vows to crush the Volunteers and their reform movement to "atoms" proved superfluous. Flood's reform bill met with overwhelming defeat from members who feared the Volunteers, reform or both. FitzGibbon's sentiments were shared by no less a person than Barry Yelverton, the architect of the so-called constitution of 1782. He proposed a resolution for maintaining parliament's "Just Rights and Privileges against all Encroachment whatsoever."[45]

If he detested purely Protestant reform he anathematized proposals that included political rights for Catholics. Unquestionably, he encouraged Rutland and Orde in their anti-Catholicism. FitzGibbon was not the sole offender in this respect. Plenty of conservative Irish Protestants, angry at past concessions to the Catholics and fearful of future encroachments on their privileged position, flooded the Castle with minatory letters about the Popish menace.[46] But FitzGibbon's office and the favor he already enjoyed gave his pronouncements particular weight.

A comparison of a letter from Orde to Pitt and one from FitzGibbon to Eden, both written at the end of August 1784, display a similarity that could only result from mutual consultation leading to a mutual conviction of a Popish-radical Protestant conspiracy to overthrow the government. Orde gave this account of the Irish situation at the end of the summer of 1784:

> It is really provoking to think, that the Falsehood and misrepresentation of such a set of men should have the influence to put in hazard the very peace of the country and expose the Government to insult and revolution. There can hardly be a doubt that the direct intentions of the Faction are to sacrifice everything to the success of their schemes, which have in view not a mere non-importation agreement or a Parliamentary reform or even a dissolution of the present Parliament, but an entire dissolution of the subsisting connection with Great Britain, any change whatever must be of service to them who have nothing to lose, and if they would not scruple to use any Instruments by wch their success might be more easy and complete. It is on this account that I have never ceased to declare my opinion that they will seek to carry their purposes into execution by means of the Catholics and if it could be possible for so contemptible a crew to obtain the credit of any foreign encouragement, they would not hesitate to sue for it.[47]

FitzGibbon said the same, though characteristically, he was the more forceful and precise. He was also slightly more even-handed in his animosities. His early professions of admiration for their "constitutional resistance" long forgotten, FitzGibbon expressed as much contempt for trouble making Ulster Presbyterians as he did for Catholics with political notions. In addition, FitzGibbon, the Munster Protestant, happily circulated the old chestnut from the Whiteboy scares of the 1760s, of French gold circulating among the lower orders:

> As to a Parliamentary reform, as it is called in this country, if any alteration is made in the Constitution of the House of Commons in Ireland, there is an end of any connection with England, unless it can be sustained by the sword. I have very little doubt that French gold is in circulation amongst the lower class of people in this country. The Puritans of the North are become Advocates for Religious Tolerance and the Catholics profess a strong predilection for Republican government. The Puritans tell them if you will assist us in reforming the constitution we will assist you in shaking off every restraint with the laws of Ireland now impose upon you. If these worthy personages succeed in their projects, it does not require any great degree of sagacity to discover that we shall not very long have a Protestant government in this country.[48]

A passing remark by one of Orde's more active anti-Catholic correspondents, George Hamilton, a baron of the Exchequer Court, also suggests FitzGibbon's active participation in instilling hostility and fear in the new administration. Hamilton informed Orde that he would soon be receiving a visit from the attorney-general. The two may well have speculated together about the perfidious intentions of the Papists, and it is also likely that FitzGibbon served as a conduit for news that Hamilton could not or would not commit to paper.[49] Finally, FitzGibbon may have suggested the ploy of threatening the Catholics with the revocation of the privileges granted in 1782. As chief law officer, he had a powerful influence on the government's future legislative strategy; moreover, he was to suggest this approach to recalcitrant Papists at other stages of his career.[50]

Initially, FitzGibbon took no action against the reform activity that took place in the spring and summer of 1784. The government hoped that all or most sheriffs would reject the appeal from the reformers, thus sparing them the necessity of taking any action at all. While most made a gratifyingly negative response to the requisition, freeholder meetings did take place in some of the major counties and cities, not always with positive results for the government. The city of Belfast and the County of Antrim, of course, readily supported both reform and the requisition. By far the most liberal response came from Galway, which had a large and prosperous Catholic gentry and which was controlled politically by their sympathetic convert relations. The freeholders in that county quickly agreed to send delegates to the Congress and as quickly they resolved that "the prosperity of the nation depends on restoring the Democracy in Parliament [and] that the Roman Catholics should have the right of suffrage". None of the other freeholder meetings which agreed to send delegates were prepared to go as far. The freeholders of King's county, more typically, called for a strictly Protestant suffrage. The whims and quarrels of the local gentry, rather than the merits or demerits of Parliamentary reform, usually determined whether a county chose to respond to the requisition. Those counties where politics were successfully managed by a pro-Carlisle interest usually made loyal resolutions. In counties where disputed elections had taken place or where the gentry families were at odds over patronage and prestige, the requisition offered an opportunity to court popularity.[51]

The response of the county of Limerick to the requisition is of particular interest in determining FitzGibbon's local standing. It would appear that he did not exercise the same influence in Limerick that he did in government councils in Dublin. In response to the requisition a meeting convened in Limerick City. Speaker Pery, Hugh Massey and Sir Henry Hartstonge as well as FitzGibbon attended. The Limerick meeting did indeed condemn the Dublin requisition. At the same time, it passed resolutions in favor of protecting duties and in favor of "constitutional" reform, that is reform initiated by Parliament itself. The anonymous correspondent who reported on the county meetings for Orde's benefit commented that "All Parties united on this occasion, and concessions were made on both sides for the sake of unanimity". In agreeing to a resolution favoring his two professed aversions, protective duties and reform, FitzGibbon appears to have done most of the conceding. The popular interest, represented by Hartstonge and Massey, retained enough strength to impose on FitzGibbon a rare degree of restraint and flexibility. If he had acted with his Dublin high-handedness, he may well have suffered the humiliation of seeing the native county of the crown's chief law officer send delegates to the "congress".[52]

In spite of the general negative response to the requisition, the government could not rest easily until the county and the city of Dublin showed the same gratifying indifference. If either or both chose to send delegates, the Congress would gain in prestige and influence what it lacked in numbers. Also, a positive vote in the city or county of Dublin might influence as yet undecided cities and counties to send delegates. As Orde noted, Dublin "takes the lead of the Rest of the Country".

Initially, county Dublin took a lead that was highly unfavorable to the government. The sheriff of the county, Stephen Reilly, responded favorably to the reform requisition and summoned the county freeholders, who met on 31 July 1784. Luke Gardiner and General Luttrell appeared to articulate the government's disapproval: they questioned the legality of the meeting and protested at Reilly's casual definition of a freeholder. Theirs was a doomed mission, no doubt hampered further by the unsavory reputation of Luttrell, who earlier had distinguished himself as John Wilkes's opponent. The Dublin freeholders dismissed their protests and enthusiastically voted to send the requisite five delegates.[53] In the wake of this defeat, the government could only sponsor a petition protesting against the county meeting, duly signed by Luttrell and Gardiner, as well as by other noted government stalwarts, FitzGibbon of course prominent among them.[54]

Prospects looked no better in the city of Dublin, where the sheriffs had also agreed to convene a freeholders' meeting. Clearly, firmer measures than gentlemanly appeals and orchestrated protests were needed to stop the congressional contagion from spreading to a city already torn by riots. At this point FitzGibbon took visible command of the government's campaign against the reformers, with his usual ruthlessness and effectiveness. He resorted to verbal and physical intimidation ending in what can only be described as a show trial: a questionable proceeding that aimed not at trying a purported offense, but at asserting the power of the state.

FitzGibbon initiated his campaign with a letter to the sheriffs, addressed from his smart new home in Ely Place and couched in his usual tone of minatory arrogance:

> Gentlemen:
>
> I have read with great surprise a formal summons signed by you, as high sheriffs of the City of Dublin, calling upon the freeholders and freemen of your bailiwick to meet on Monday next, for the purpose of electing five persons to represent the City of Dublin in National Congress.
>
> I must inform you, that in summoning the freeholders and freemen of your bailiwick to meet for such a purpose, you have been guilty of a most outrageous breach of your duty; that if you proceed to hold such an election you are responsible for it to the laws of your country – and that I shall hold myself bound as the King's Attorney General, to prosecute you in the Court of King's Bench for your conduct, which I consider to be so highly criminal that I cannot overlook it.[55]

The sheriffs ignored the threats from Ely place, and the freeholders of Dublin city duly assembled on 21 September. As had occurred with the county Dublin meeting, a delegation of government supporters and beneficiaries made an appearance. This time, however, the government was represented by a far more vocal and formidable presence than the kindly Gardiner and the disreputable Luttrell. FitzGibbon himself appeared with an entourage that included the prime serjeant, Arthur Wolfe, John Beresford, Lodge Morres, Sir Boyle Roche and John Gifford, the future journalistic voice of the "Protestant ascendancy".[56] FitzGibbon quickly made it clear that he did not intend to debate the merits of parliamentary reform, he had attended to put an end to the proceedings altogether. First, his fire and brimstone letter to the sheriffs was read to the freeholders. He then declared the assembly illegal and ordered the participants to disperse. In spite of the predictable jeers and protests, one of the sheriffs, Kilpatrick, yielded to FitzGibbon and adjourned the meeting.[57] But he remained unconvinced by FitzGibbon's interpretation of the law, and expressed his determination to seek further advice on the content of the letter.

Kilpatrick's surrender, however conditional, exhilarated FitzGibbon. "The day is our own," he reportedly said in the wake of his performance.[58] As events turned out he had every reason for his exultation. At the beginning of October, the sheriffs of Dublin received two requisitions, one dated 1 October and a second dated 7 October, requesting them to convene a meeting of the freeholders to continue the business so ruthlessly and dramatically interrupted by FitzGibbon. Unfortunately for the reform party, a more amenable pair of sheriffs, Jenkin and Leet, had since assumed office and the new incumbents denied both requisitions.[59] The supporters of reform, on their own authority, then held an aggregate meeting at the Weaver's Hall and elected five delegates, Sir Edward Newenham notable among them. If he could not entirely thwart the election of delegates, FitzGibbon and the government he served succeeded in confining the election to the reform coterie. No wider agitation took place.

Not only did FitzGibbon stall reform activity, he enhanced the British government's good opinion of him, which also must have accounted for his euphoria. Such a motive surely prompted his performance as much as, if not more than, a desire to suppress the menace posed by rebellious sheriffs and disorderly public assemblies. The British government duly responded. Lord Sydney wrote: "The conduct of the attorney general ... does him the greatest credit, and your Grace will please to assure him that it has not escaped his majesty's notice."[60]

His conduct did not escape the notice of his old enemies in the press, though predictably, they took a less favorable view. Although the hired government newspapers dutifully praised FitzGibbon's forceful and manly actions, the more widely read radical press outdid itself in calumniating FitzGibbon. It would be impossible to do justice to the varied and highly inventive abuse that filled the newspapers following FitzGibbon's appearance at the aggregate meeting. This ingenious exercise in scatology, which purported to account for the fate of the warning missive sent by FitzGibbon, best represents the whole:

> The star chamber edict that our sheriffs received has amazed every man acquainted with the constitution – and it has amazed the city no less that they

> did not treat it with deserved contempt. Others of a similar nature were sent to such sheriffs in the country, as could not be flattered or bribed to destroy the public cause. One sheriff in particular treated it in a manner not certainly the most respectable to his majesty's attorney general. Having read Jacky Pert's letter, he hung it up in the grand jury room. When the grand jury were assembled, he handed it to them, and they unanimously expressed their indignation at such a daring attack on the inherent rights of the subject. The sheriff then with the consent of all present, quartered it, and immediately going to pay his devoirs in the Temple of Cloacina, he offered up the fragments on her alter as a peace offering to insulted liberty, after which he convened the county, to consider the most effectual means to promote a parliamentary reform.[61]

Nonetheless, FitzGibbon was not content with reducing the reform elections to comparative insignificance. He wanted to prevent any recurrence of this dangerous method of agitation. Toward this end, he chose to strike at the sheriffs, because their participation gave the freeholder meetings a measure of respectability and legal standing. Specifically, he chose to strike at Stephen Reilly, accusing Reilly of abusing his office by summoning an illegal and seditious assembly. The simple fairness, not to mention the legality, of the indictment were open to question. Other sheriffs had summoned meetings of freeholders, including the meeting for county Limerick that FitzGibbon himself had attended. Reilly's defiance of the known wishes of the government as expressed by Gardiner and Luttrell probably accounted for the indictment. The fact that he was sheriff of county Dublin, one of the premier centers of political power, also made him vulnerable to FitzGibbon's judicial revenge. Reilly's degree of guilt was secondary.

In spite of the favor FitzGibbon enjoyed, some members of the government had doubts about his action. Orde in particular sought out the opinions of Pitt and of Hugh Carleton, the solicitor general for Ireland, who was sojourning at Bath. If Orde had hoped for detailed instructions, to be executed with his habitual clerical meticulousness, he met with disappointment. Pitt looked upon the Congress as a contemptible affair and advocated lofty neglect. Carleton, while conceding that Reilly might have acted illegally, was similarly cautious in his judgment. Like Pitt, he noted that the congress could very well fade away of its own insignificant accord, thus depriving the government of any need to take definitive action. Carleton also observed that the restless circumstances of the times had created new forms of political organization and expression that did not fit traditional legal definitions of sedition and unlawful assembly:

> The Fashion of the Times, the use which has been made of Publick Meetings by members of Every Party in this Country: the acknowledged right of Petitioning, the modern practice of English opposition in availing themselves of the State of Irish Politicks to Embarrass the English Administration: the Novelty and Doubt attending the Legal Question and various other circumstances

> render it necessary to be peculiarly circumspect in every active measure which you may adopt.[63]

Orde's obligation to consult with England before taking any definitive step, as well as habitual fussiness, no doubt accounted for his correspondence with Pitt and with Carleton. Nonetheless, a short squib in the *Dublin Evening Post*, dated 5 October 1784, suggests yet another possible reason for the spate of correspondence. The paragraph in question reported on an alleged dispute between "Fitzprig" and "Aguecheek", on the course of action to be taken – or not taken – against Reilly and the Congress. FitzGibbon apparently strongly recommended prosecution, but "Aguecheek, however, thought proper for this time to differ with Prig, until he had better advice on the matter, lest the boy's rancour should lead him into error". Unlike most of the items reported about FitzGibbon at the time, this paragraph has some claims to plausibility. FitzGibbon, quick-witted and forceful, may well have found the plodding Orde irritating at times, while Orde, in return, may have found his devoted attorney general a bit too "decisive and manly", to borrow a common plaudit of the government newspapers.

If any disagreement did indeed arise, it abated quickly. Apparently, Orde wrote his nervous letters of inquiry without any noticeable signs of impatience or disapproval on FitzGibbon's part. Had he betrayed any such sentiments, Orde, given his oversensitivity, would have noted FitzGibbon's unsatisfactory behavior. The noncommittal answers of Pitt and Carleton and FitzGibbon's proximity eventually led to the triumph of his point of view.

In November 1784, FitzGibbon proceeded against Reilly through the legal device of "attachment". This procedure allowed the attorney general to lodge an "information" or complaint with the judges of the King's Bench. The judges then determined the merits of the case.[64] Unquestionably, FitzGibbon resorted to this mode of prosecution because it allowed him to avoid an almost certain dismissal of charges from a jury drawn from the populace of radical Dublin. He of course, claimed a loftier motive: preventing the delay of a jury trial and with it the spread of agitation.[65]

Once again, his actions aroused controversy. The radical newspapers, as a matter of course, heaped abuse on FitzGibbon's insolence, tyranny and ignorance of the law. He was, according to one paragraph, more conversant with lewd French novels than with Coke upon Lyttleton.[66] A dismal debate on the legality of attachments raged in both the press and in innumerable pamphlets. Those writers favoring reform and opposing the government denounced attachments as a violation of Reilly's right to a trial by a jury of his peers.[67] Those writers in government pay portrayed FitzGibbon's actions as a heroic attempt to curb the abuse of power by a public official.[68]

The paper war in the press held far less importance to the Rutland administration than the outcome in the courts. It faced a serious blow to its prestige if the judges decided that Reilly was merely presiding over a peaceable assembly of the King's subjects. The apprehensions of the government even embraced the judges, hitherto considered unquestionably loyal and compliant. In particular, the Recorder of Dublin, Sir Samuel Bradstreet, stirred official anxiety by publicly questioning the propriety of attachments.[69] In the end, when the verdict was finally pronounced on Reilly, the habitual docility of the Bench held true, even in the case of Bradstreet. To quote FitzGibbon's own inimitable turn of phrase, "Slippery Sam read his recantation handsomely", joining with his colleagues in finding the attorney general's complaint valid and Reilly guilty.[70] FitzGibbon requested a relatively mild penalty: one week in prison and a fine of one mark.[71] Having asserted the power of government and his own influence over that government, FitzGibbon undoubtedly felt free to act magnanimously. He also may have recognized that punishing Reilly with undue severity would give the reform party a new grievance, a new cause and a new initiative.

The preparations for the congress continued even as the legal proceedings against Reilly were grinding away. The impromptu Dublin city meeting passed resolutions praising Reilly's patriotism and condemning the "petulant peevishness of a placeman".[72] A straggling preliminary meeting of the delegates took place three weeks later, on 25 October. It ended with resolutions asserting the necessity of parliamentary reform and appealing to those counties with had chosen not to send delegates to reconsider. The congress then adjourned until January 1785. The second meeting was as bedraggled, and sparsely attended as the first. The resolutions adopted by the congress had all the futility and inconclusiveness of a lost cause and were distinguished mainly by an appeal to the public not to be intimidated and to continue the great struggle.[73] The specter of reform and with it the establishment of a Catholic dominated American style mobocracy, so terrifying in the summer of 1784, faded into anti-climax.

His triumphs in Dublin gave FitzGibbon the impetus to initiate yet another case, intended to drive home the lesson that the government would not tolerate reform activity of any kind on the part of anyone, no matter how exalted. He chose George Nugent Reynolds, a magistrate of County Leitrim, as the object of political edification. Although the sheriffs of Leitrim had rejected the requisition to elect delegates, Reynolds, on his own initiative, had organized a meeting for this purpose, which met in October 1784.[74] Once he had settled accounts with Reilly, FitzGibbon attached Reynolds, because he, as a magistrate, had defied the lawful authority of the sheriff. Reynolds and his like-minded colleagues on the bench appear to have anticipated such retaliation. They requested the noted Scottish Whig lawyer, Henry Erskine, to give an opinion of the legality of attachments. Not surprisingly, Erskine decided they were, on the whole, legal. Erskine's opinion was above all a gesture of partisan support, and had no weight in the case.[75] Certainly FitzGibbon would have held it in little regard. Nonetheless, in this instance, he did not enjoy the same success. Lord Earlsfort and the Chancellor, Lord Lifford, eventually dismissed the motion for attachment.[76] None of the accounts of the case give any coherent reasons for his failure in this instance. Presumably, by early 1786, when the case was eventually brought to judgment, the reform movement had to all appearances lapsed into moribundity.

Consequently, making an example of Reynolds was not a particularly pressing matter. FitzGibbon, engulfed as he was in legal and parliamentary business, may not have had the time to prepare the case with the same thoroughness. Finally, professional jealousy may have worked against FitzGibbon. Earlsfort, formerly John Scott, Buckinghamshire's attorney general, had turned against his former protégé, rightly seeing in him a superior rival. This sentiment may well have influenced his decision, if not that of the amiable, somnolent Lifford.[77]

FitzGibbon faced a far more immediate negative reaction in the aftermath of Reilly's trial. The writers in the radical press found their usual denunciations of mere mortal vices inadequate in the face of this most recent of his enormities. It was at this time that paragraphs comparing him to Lucifer appeared. His reaction suggests that the steady barrage of invective had wounded him, in spite of his professed contempt for anonymous hacks. In November 1784, he at last ended the amazing forbearance of four years and retaliated against the *Dublin Evening Post*, the most widely read of the radical newspapers. Curiously enough, he chose to prosecute, not for any its more recent offerings, but for a paragraph which had appeared almost six months before: the small item accusing him of preferring the smell of hair powder to that of gun powder. The reasons for his delay and for his choice of this comparatively mild gibe remain an unsolvable mystery. Possibly he had intended to ignore it, as he had ignored similar and worse squibs. As the tide of feeling against him rose and as the press, in spite of the recent law, grew more audacious, this paragraph simply served as a random flash point for his long accumulated and understandable anger. The *Dublin Evening Post* predictably ridiculed the suit:

> The most laughable matter yesterday before the King's Bench was an old paragraph in this paper, that a person called *Petulant* disliked the smell of any powder save powder prepared by the *friseur.* This was by innuendo made to allude to a gentleman of the law, but why any man should apply it to himself or what offense it could give, when applied is a matter of general astonishment and ridicule.
>
> Whether the *wanton boy* prizes gun-powder, hair powder or love powder most, we certainly must allow him to possess a fund of legal knowledge, as no hero that ever wriggled under a three tailed wig, or strutted under a silk gown diffused more *new information* among the people; but see what is to give encouragement to genius? If the benefit of the business were not so great, perhaps this gentleman's *great abilities* would never be known and J——the boy only fidget through life distinguished barely as the amorous barrister".[78]

Unfortunately, the *Dublin Evening Post's* legal troubles with FitzGibbon could not be laughed out of existence. On the contrary, this particular paragraph aggravated matters by exposing the paper's publisher, John Magee, to an equally serious charge of contempt of court. FitzGibbon again employed the procedure of attachment and again, he successfully prosecuted. In January 1785, Magee received a sentence imposing on him a £5 fine, a prison sentence of one month and sureties for good behavior for three years.[79] FitzGibbon's actions do not appear to have silenced his opponents in the press. They continued their attacks both personal and political. In particular, they seized on FitzGibbon's frequent use of attachments. For the rest of his life, allusions to his tyrannical contempt for the rights of trial by jury pursued him ad nauseam. FitzGibbon soon faced similar criticism, not merely from obscure journalists, but from his colleagues when Parliament opened in January 1785. The issue of attachments had given the opposition a new lease on life.

VI

By the end of 1783, many former enthusiasts for the people were growing as weary of change and upheaval as the government. Moreover, as has often been noted, many of them were enthusiastic about a very small and exclusive segment of the people. Their fraternal good will did not embrace radical Volunteers, Dublin workmen and Catholics. Most of the traditional pillars of the opposition maintained a firm distance from the reform activities of the summer of 1784. In Kildare, the Fitzgerald sphere of influence, no county meeting took place. Indeed, as early as February 1784, the Duke of Leinster had communicated to the government his opposition both to reform and to protectionist duties.[80] Grattan, it is true, had refused to sign a petition organized by government sympathizers to denounce the congress, but he did so out of habitual contrariness rather than out of any love for the principle of popular reform. Signing such a petition, he informed Orde, would compromise his dignity and his independence as a member of Parliament.[81] Grattan may well have avoided committing himself because he did not want to risk further public opprobrium. Whatever his reasons, nothing in his reply precluded further sympathetic overtures, had the government cared to make them. But no such overtures were made, either to Grattan or to any other major opposition figure.

Granted, Rutland's government, overwhelmed with immediate crises, had more pressing concerns than the placating the various factions of the Irish ruling elite. He and his ministers also may have assumed that in the face of the Catholic/reform menace, every self-respecting and self-interested Protestant gentleman would, as a matter of course, unite behind the government. In addition, the Castle was a bastion of former Carlisle men, while notable members of the opposition had past ties of loyalty or patronage to the Duke of Portland. The old Carlisle supporters surrounding Rutland had no interest in cooperating with the remnants of a party that they despised.

Certainly FitzGibbon would not have gone out of his way to make overtures to the remnants of Portland's party. He had never forgiven the Portland administration for the recall of Eden and Carlisle. Nor could he forgive the supposed pusillanimity which led to the constitution of 1782. As always, he confided his views most fully to Eden:

> The Fact is we now begin to feel the Effects of the Duke of Portland's government. You know the very wise part which he acted. He told the Volunteers of Ireland very explicitly that the government of the country was in their hands and that he depended for Support upon them. The Consequence was that they chuse a Parliament of their own which was to publish Edicts for the Assent of King, Lords and Commons.[82]

Edward Cooke, a witty and capable man who served in a variety of government positions, shared the same prejudices:

> Any late ferments are the natural results of the improper consequence and power to which the people were wrought in the Duke of Portland's government. All the gentlemen of rank, consequence and property left them and the present efforts are headed by a factious party in the city or electioneering candidates in the county.[83]

Nor were Rutland and Orde above partisan prejudice. As Pitt's men in Ireland, they probably needed no encouragement to look with disfavor on an Irish opposition so closely affiliated with the English Whigs.

For whatever reason the fragile rapprochement of 1784 had broken down by the time Parliament opened in January 1785. The opposition did not go so far as to advocate reform to spite the government. Most members of the opposition continued to shy away from reform, either because it threatened their own interests or because they had no love for the current leaders of the movement. Such was certainly the case with Grattan. In debates on the address to the king in 1785, he took the lead in condemning the Congress. Such ad hoc bodies, he claimed, prejudiced the "reform of parliament at the same time that they insult its authority".[84] Nonetheless the opposition did not want to surrender all claims to popularity. The use of attachments offered a convenient escape from their dilemma. The opposition could indulge in safe, but crowd pleasing accusations of arbitrary government while taking Rutland's line on reform. Lord Charles Fitzgerald, in conjunction with Brownlow, took the lead, introducing a resolution couched in the usual Whig pieties:

> That the proceedings of the Court of the King's Bench in attacking the Sheriff and punishing him in summary way as for a contempt, was contrary to the principles of the constitution as depriving him of his trial by jury and is a precedent of a dangerous tendency.[85]

FitzGibbon defended himself with his usual forcefulness and with his usual excess and acerbity. He also freely displayed his own and the government's anti-Popish paranoia. The meeting of Dublin freeholders was an "illegal assembly of Papists and men of all descriptions" bent on nothing less than the subversion of the constitution of church and state. Reilly, in summoning such a motley assemblage of undesirables was, therefore, guilty of misprision. Assuming the role of a lecturer in jurisprudence FitzGibbon offered his fellow members this definition of an illegal assembly:

> ... and that gentlemen may hereafter know what an unlawful assembly is, I will inform them. Serjeant Hawkins says, "An unlawful assembly is the meeting of a number of people with arms to demand the redress of any common grievance or the restoration of any common right, because no man can foresee what the event of such meetings may be."[86]

There were some small inconsistencies in his account. If Reilly was indeed guilty of inciting Papists and men of all descriptions to overthrow the constitution in church and state, he ought to have suffered a graver penalty than a brief imprisonment and an inconsequential fine. Also, there is no evidence that the assembly was armed.

Unfortunately, FitzGibbon's demeanor, barely within the bounds of acceptability when he was a struggling young backbencher, badly compromised the government's dignity and created needless antagonism when he spoke in the capacity of a high officer of state. Most notably, he engaged in a verbal brawl with John Philpot Curran, who was just beginning his career as a leading member of the radical wing of the opposition. Curran's criticism of Reilly's judges set off the imbroglio. In response FitzGibbon referred to him a "puny babbler", hardly a Ciceronian riposte.[87] Curran proved far superior in the art of malicious repartee, scoring points not only at the expense of FitzGibbon's character, but at the expense of the attorney general's recent electioneering troubles:

> He was not a man whose respect in person and character depended upon the importance of his office; he was not a young man who thrust himself into the foreground of a picture, which ought to be occupied by a better figure; he was not a man who replied with invective when sinking under the weight of an argument; he was not a man who denied the necessity of a Parliamentary reform at the time he proved the expediency of it by reviling his own constituents, the parish clerk, the sexton and the gravedigger.[88]

The final outcome of the debate no doubt offered some consolation to FitzGibbon. A satisfying majority overlooked the inconsistencies in his account of the Dublin meeting and accepted his central premise, that the government had acted with scrupulous legality to avert an act of subversion by a public official. The motion of Fitzgerald and Brownlow met with defeat by a margin of 143 to 73. A second attempt by Flood to reintroduce a measure condemning attachments was no more successful. Parliament rejected the measure by a still more resounding margin of 120 to 48.[89] As yet, the opposition could annoy, but it could not overcome the government's majority, bound by favor or the fear of further political disruption.

Even when a relative degree of unanimity and cooperation seemed attainable, the English government stepped in to undermine the government more effectively than the opposition ever could. Such was the case with the militia bill, introduced in February 1785. Rutland's fondest wish, or so he claimed, was to replace the Volunteers, which he perceived as dangerously Catholicized, with a safe, purely Protestant militia.[90] Moreover, he could claim a broad base of parliamentary support for such a measure: a resolution to array a militia had received overwhelming approval, the result of an improbable coalition of interests. The government, having opposed a militia in 1778, saw such a force as the lesser of two evils in 1785. The opposition saw the establishment of a militia as the achievement of a cherished ambition of the Patriots.[91]

The Volunteers, of course, still had vociferous supporters. Flood made the melodramatic claim that "A militia is to be raised, not that the people may learn the use of arms, but that they may be obliged to lay down their arms".[92] FitzGibbon, of course, took the opportunity to express his cherished sentiments; the Volunteers were a source of subversion and specifically of Papist subversion aided and abetted by Protestant infatuation. After making the characteristic disclaimer "I am not a bigot", he added "... I say the Irish Protestant who would admit Catholics to the use of arms, if he does not do it out of folly, is a most dangerous enemy to his country." He added, "Upon the whole, Sir, I do not think there can be a good government, while a body of men, independent of the state remains in arms. I would therefore wish to see them retire to cultivate the blessings of peace, for I think any man who does not array under lawful authority ought not to be trusted."[93] There could be no common ground between these points of view, and a resolution to thank the Volunteers, introduced by Brownlow, met with decisive defeat.

Nonetheless, for London, an Irish militia was anathema, which explains why, despite the protests of Orde and Rutland, Pitt and his ministers were determined to let the matter slip into abeyance.[94]

6

The Commerce of Empire, 1785–7

I

The opposition's increasing confidence, the English government's habits of maladroit interference and FitzGibbon's flaws as a spokesman became most apparent during the second round of debates on the so-called commercial propositions of 1785. This measure represented the Rutland administration's master plan to conciliate, once and for all, Irish grievances over trade. Sheridan had recommended as much early in 1784, convinced that such a course of action would eliminate Irish unrest and Irish addiction to such nonsensical notions as parliamentary reform, Catholic rights and protective tariffs aimed at English imports.[1]

The propositions took the form of a treaty between two ostensibly autonomous countries, which their respective parliaments were to debate and approve. They lifted all restrictions on trade and commerce between the two countries. The two countries were to impose uniform duties on colonial produce. Goods imported from Ireland were to be subject to the same regulations as goods passing from one British port to another, and neither country was to impose an additional or new duty or bounty on the products of the other. Furthermore, both countries were to discourage imports from the Continent and from America if either could supply similar or equivalent products to the other. This last provision, in effect, preserved the Irish monopoly on the British linen market from German and Russian competition. Some restrictions remained in force. The omnipotent East India Company retained its monopoly on trade to the East, though under the commercial propositions, its ships could stop at Irish ports for supplies. Thanks to the overwhelming interest of landlords in both countries, the propositions allowed for the occasional imposition of bounties and duties on cereal products. Above all, the Irish parliament was to duplicate all trade legislation passed by the English parliament. In addition, Ireland was to contribute all hereditary revenue over and above £600,000 to the maintenance of the Royal Navy.[2]

A great deal of lengthy and painstaking work, in both England and in Ireland, went into drafting these articles of trade. Given his lesser expertise in these matters, FitzGibbon appears to have played only a subordinate role in drafting the propositions. His kinsman, John Beresford, and John Foster bore the chief responsibility for negotiating on behalf of Ireland. Not surprisingly Orde was closely and busily involved as well. The minutiae of regulating the commerce in spotted linens, arrarack and meal well suited his particular mentality. On the English side William Pitt played a premier role in legislation that displayed his aims and abilities to best advantage, and FitzGibbon's cher ami Eden ably assisted.[3]

When the end result of this labor was submitted for consideration in Westminster and in London, it set off debates distinguished by length and by a partisan fury extraordinary even for that time. Charles James Fox and his followers fanned the general hostility and mistrust surrounding the treaty with the aim of embarrassing Pitt. The English Whigs played a skillful, if brazen double game, with a view to stirring bad feelings in both countries. They claimed at one and the same time that the propositions undermined the imperial authority of England and assaulted the independence, integrity and prosperity of Ireland. Rooted economic suspicions on both sides played an equal part in the hostile reception that greeted the commercial propositions. Irish manufacturers were convinced that they could not compete against their more advanced and sophisticated British counterparts. British manufacturers, notably Josiah Wedgwood, objected to the propositions because they feared that cheaper Irish labor would give goods from that country an unfair economic advantage in English markets.[4]

In spite of these suspicions, the Irish parliament did agree to an initial draft of the trade propositions. Having won this reluctant consent, Pitt then attempted to frame and to win acceptance for a final bill in England. He managed to overcome mercantile opposition and Foxite rhetoric, but the price was ultimately fatal: he had to make substantial alterations in the original draft of the propositions. In their final manifestation, the original ten propositions increased in number and in verbosity to accommodate every possible objection and suspicion on the English side. Most notably, the provision calling for the Irish parliament to duplicate English trade legislation was couched in more forceful language to answer any objections, real or partisanly spurious, that the propositions undermined English imperial authority.[5] Nothing could have been more calculated to inspire the Irish opposition, revitalized by the fight over attachments, encouraged by their English Whig counterparts, and spoiling for another attention-getting battle. Skillfully playing on ever-present fears and sensitivities, they denounced it as an attempt to undermine the autonomy granted in 1782. Of course, the Irish parliament had agreed in 1779 to a similar measure in return for the right to trade in the English West Indies. But a concession fairly requested and willingly made in 1779 became, by the peculiar partisan logic of 1785, an insidious plot against the freedom of the Irish nation.[6] The propositions did indeed pass, but by such a small margin and in such an atmosphere of rancour that the Rutland administration chose to abandon them. In an attempt to salvage lost dignity, government left all responsibility for initiating new Anglo-Irish trade arrangements to the Irish parliament.[7] Given enflamed nationalist sentiments, such an initiative was profoundly unlikely.

FitzGibbon later attributed the virtual defeat of the propositions to the stupidity and perversity of the Irish, a favorite theme.[8] Nonetheless his own inability, willful or constitutional, to move beyond the truculence of his backbench days to the calm, conciliation and astuteness required of statesmen, also bore a large share of responsibility for the bill's demise. FitzGibbon always spoke with impeccable logic and clarity:

> if England relaxes her navigation laws in our favor, she has a right to expect that we shall protect and cherish the ships and mariners of the empire as she has protected them. She has a right to expect that we will follow her in a code of laws, which have [*sic*] been the source of her commercial opulence, the prime origin of her maritime strength ... and it is as fact that our trade with England is a greater value than our trade with the rest of the world. If we were to lose it, in six months you would not have gold in circulation for the common occasions of life.[9]

Unfortunately, the situation in parliament required far more than mere appeals to reason. Only extraordinary patience, tact and grace under pressure could have carried the propositions over objections raised by honest doubt, partisan absurdity and misunderstanding. All these qualities FitzGibbon manifestly lacked. Acutely intelligent himself, he could not master his natural impatience with slower wits and dimmer perceptions. Consequently, he treated his colleagues as fools to be humiliated into common sense, rather than as equals to be persuaded. For example, when Flood ventured to express his fears for the autonomy of the Irish parliament, FitzGibbon cruelly parodied his opponent's own rhetoric on free trade during the debates of 1779:

> That I may not incur the hazard of contradiction when I state what was in 1779 considered perfect freedom of trade, I will recur to a gentleman now in my eye [Mr Flood] delivered in this assembly on the 20 December 1779. "What is a free trade? I was one of the first and most decided in using the term. It is a trade to the whole world subject to the restraints of our own legislature and that of the country with which you trade; consequently in Britain and the British colonies, subject to the restrictions of the British legislature, is a principle as clear as the sun which shines upon our reviving empire, and wide as the universe, if the Heavens were as wide as they are." This, Sir, is the Honourable Gentleman's definition of free trade, and upon his own principles, clear as the sun and wide as the universe, I meet him upon the present question.[10]

The virtual defeat of the propositions brought to the forefront FitzGibbon's most unattractive qualities: verbal bullying and an adolescent lack of emotional control. Flood once again offered the pretext for a squalid display of both. Intoxicated by the triumph of the opposition, Flood had proposed this resolution: "That Parliament ought not to enter into any engagement to give up the sole and exclusive right to legislate for Ireland as well externally as commercially and internally."[11] FitzGibbon's retort was at once supremely honest and supremely irresponsible:

> Let me tell gentlemen that it is not very prudent, upon every occasion, to come forward in terms of indignation against the sister kingdom. Let me tell them, that it will not be perfectly prudent to rouze Great Britain. She is not easily rouzed, but if rouzed, she is not very easily appeased. And in this, perhaps, lies the difference between the two nations. Ireland is easily roused but then she is easily appeased ... If you rouze the British lion, you may not easily lull him to rest.[12]

His remarks were exquisitely calculated to wound Irish nationalist sensibilities at their most tender point, perceived inferiority to England.

In the process, he effectively dispelled what faint hope remained that the Irish parliament would attempt to find an alternative arrangement for Anglo-Irish trade, once passions had calmed somewhat. His *de haute en bas* tone undermined the central premise (or fiction) of the propositions – that they represented a treaty between equals. He reminded them instead that England essentially held Ireland by force. While undoubtedly true, such bluntness scarcely encouraged a transition to a relationship based on cooperation and mutual interest. Finally, he shattered any lingering chance that the English government in Ireland would serve as a unifying force, rather than the first among factions. It was now unquestionably a party; worse, it was FitzGibbon's party, which brought it a still greater degree of disrepute and enmity.

In one instance, he went beyond mere words. His striking, if tactless phrase "besotted nation" led to yet another verbal imbroglio with Curran, which led in turn to a duel.[13] FitzGibbon acted curiously when the two met. He aimed with a care that suggested every intention of wounding or killing his antagonist. Yet the shot went wide, provoking Curran to remark, "It was not your fault, Mr. Attorney, if you missed me, for you were deliberate enough".[14] FitzGibbon reportedly left without responding. Once again FitzGibbon defies explanation. Froude, his Victorian devoté, later argued that FitzGibbon had, in his infinite good nature, avoided harming Curran, preferring instead to impress on him that he was not a man to be trifled with. From a less enchanted perspective, his deliberateness suggests petty sadism and his shot surprisingly bad marksmanship for such an avid sportsman. Rage may have spoiled his aim, or possibly the recollection that an indictment for murder or manslaughter scarcely befitted the chief law officer of the crown.

His reaction to the failure of the commercial propositions seems above all wildly disproportionate, even for a man given to extremes of emotion. He clearly regarded them as far more than a series of provisions regulating the commerce in meal, linen and liquor. They represented an opportunity to strengthen ties with England, dangerously loosened by the weakness of past administrations, particularly Portland's, and by the reckless self-assertion of the Irish ruling oligarchy. In one of his speeches, he reminded his fellow members that their very survival depended on maintaining that relationship. They were, after all, a small body of Protestants surrounded by an overwhelming and hostile Catholic population, and by all the power of Catholic Europe.[16] He was to repeat this theme in later confrontations with the Irish opposition.

II

The Rutland administration did succeed in passing another significant piece of commercial legislation highly desired by the English government, an Irish version of the Navigation Act. FitzGibbon conducted this business far more creditably. Thanks to his gift for grasping the English perspective on Irish matters, he framed the legislation with both speed and precision. He also seems to have learned from the fiasco of the commercial propositions. He went out of his way to avoid any possible pretext for opposition caviling. Although he could not entirely escape from opposition fault-finding, his conduct during debates on the bill displayed far more tact.

Early in 1787, Lord Hawkesbury, one of the Commissioners of the English Board of Trade, contacted the Irish government regarding a revision of the Navigation Acts. These acts, originally passed during the reign of Charles II, conferred on British-built ships a virtual monopoly on foreign and colonial trade. Initial versions of the Navigation Acts had extended the same rights to Irish ships, and the Dublin parliament, in the so-called "Act of Customs" had duly acknowledged its authority. Later English legislation considerably curtailed Irish trading privileges, particularly with the colonies. The patriot initiatives of the 1770s did succeed in removing most of these later restrictions from colonial trade, but prohibitions against shipping plantation produce from Ireland to England still remained in force.[17]

Hawkesbury's revisions aimed at strengthening the Navigation Acts by tightening the regulation of ship registration. Foreign ships often fraudulently registered as British or as Irish ships to evade the restrictions of the Navigation Acts. The Americans were particular offenders. To thwart them, Hawkesbury introduced in 1786 an elaborate system of ship registration covering every possible kind of commercial vessel. The act imposed heavy fines for failure to comply, and it explicitly excluded American ships from trade with the remaining British colonies. Hawkesbury's new modeled Navigation Acts aimed above all at undercutting American trade, just as the original had attempted to curtail Dutch competition. Ireland represented only a secondary concern. If anything, the act conferred a benefit, since it confirmed Ireland's share in the monopoly.[18]

Nonetheless, Hawkesbury needed parallel legislation from Ireland to complete his system, however beneficial. According to FitzGibbon, English judges had raised doubts about the Navigation Acts' authority in Ireland. Consequently, it was all the more important to obtain legislative confirmation of the Navigation Acts from the Irish parliament, thus preventing Ireland from serving as a safe haven for American, Irish and English shippers bent on flouting the act's restrictions. Although the question of suppressing the Whiteboys preoccupied him at the time, FitzGibbon acted as Hawkesbury's main liaison. In March 1787, he made a full and lucid response to Hawkesbury's inquiry. FitzGibbon began by apologizing for his delay in replying: "... the novelty of the question in this country, and the general diffidence entertained upon it at the first opening, by gentlemen whom it was necessary to consult, have necessarily induced delay".[19] The diffident gentlemen in question were probably Foster, Beresford and Parnell, the main authorities on trade legislation in the Irish government. After the drubbing which the commercial propositions had received in Parliament, they understandably shied away from any revival of the touchy question of Anglo-Irish trade. In spite of this reluctance, FitzGibbon, with their help, had managed to draw up and introduce an Irish navigation bill.

Although this legislation by and large reproduced the provisions of the English act, FitzGibbon reported to Hawkesbury some minor changes made to accommodate peculiarities in Irish legislative procedures and in the Irish political scene. Most of the changes concerned minor points of law or redundancies. FitzGibbon noted that the draft of the English statute made a general reference to duties passed by previous acts of parliament. He had omitted this reference, first because the "general reference to duties imposed by acts not named ... [is] ... not usual in our acts of parliament" and secondly because the duties in question were already levied through the Act of Navigation and the Act of Customs. Therefore, any mention of them was unnecessary. FitzGibbon also omitted the provision in the English statute restricting the stamp duty on bonds to one shilling. As he pointed out to Hawkesbury "... the stamp duty upon bonds of any description in this country does not exceed one shilling". The Irish navigation bill also omitted a clause which made it a capital offense to forge "Mediterranean passes", that is, permits granted by the bey of Algiers to navigate the territorial waters of the Barbary States. FitzGibbon believed that an entirely separate bill could more appropriately deal with this offense, as well as a "practice which I am afraid prevails too generally in both countries, of selling Mediterranean passes, particularly to the owners of American ships". He quickly grasped the essential anti-Americanism of Hawkesbury's revamped mercantile system.[20]

Hawkesbury's suggestions for the preamble of the bill gave FitzGibbon and his colleagues the greatest cause for concern. He acknowledged to Hawkesbury that some sort of declaration upholding the authority of the English Navigation Acts in Ireland was necessary. Nonetheless, an outright declaration declaring that such acts would apply to Ireland was likely to create "cavil and misrepresentation". While FitzGibbon attributed such fears to his unnamed colleagues, he too unquestionably shared them. In spite of his contempt for the opposition, he had enough astuteness to recognize the dangers of yet another brawl over trade. He therefore made oblique allusions to the authority of the English statutes in Ireland. His preamble simply noted that according to a provision in the Irish Act of Customs, the English Navigation Acts applied to Ireland.[21]

Hawkesbury gave complete approval to FitzGibbon's alterations:

> ... the alterations you have made in it appear to me to be judicious and to remove objections on your side of the water, and cannot, I am sure, be in the least degree disapproved of here.[22]

One month later, FitzGibbon reported to Hawkesbury that the parallel Irish legislation had passed through both Houses of the Irish parliament "without any alteration whatever". He acknowledged some difficulty from Grattan, who had "committed himself upon the subject before he had perfectly comprehended it". But ultimately even the most confirmed member of the opposition acknowledged the fundamental premise of the act, that Great Britain and Ireland should "always be united in maritime policy".[23]

In actuality, the debate over the proposed statute was somewhat brisker than FitzGibbon let on. Unplacated by FitzGibbon's tactful phrasing of the preamble, Grattan and his allies revived the uneasy ghost of the 1785 propositions. The Irish navigation bill, they claimed, was in fact a proposition, but unlike the unmourned predecessors of 1785, it did not even offer the pretext of equal trade. Hawkesbury's act did nothing to remove the unjust later constructions of the English Navigation Acts, especially the restriction on imports of plantation produce from Ireland to England. Such restrictions, or so Grattan and his various supporters argued, had made any access to the English colonies of virtually no value to Ireland. Unless the English government put an "equal construction" on the Navigation Act and removed this restriction, the Irish parliament should refuse to pass any parallel legislation confirming it. Grattan also questioned whether the Act of Customs did in actuality uphold the authority of the English Navigation Acts, and he claimed that this new and sweeping trade legislation might overturn other regulations confirmed by Yelverton's Act. He then introduced two resolutions calling for a complete equality of rights and privileges under the English Navigation Acts, which meant the freedom for Irish merchants to ship colonial and plantation products to England.[24]

FitzGibbon displayed a reasonable measure of calm in answering these points. He expressed an equal dislike for the English policy of excluding plantation produce shipped via Ireland. But the Irish parliament had no power to force the English to change their policies on their own colonies. He emphasized that the revised Navigation Act in and of itself conferred on Ireland as well as England a monopoly on colonial shipping. The restrictions so obnoxious to the opposition had nothing to do with the with the Navigation Act as it had originally been framed or the proposed Irish bill. FitzGibbon briefly trod on dangerous grounds when countering Grattan's trouble-mongering allusions to the infamous fourth proposition, the one requiring duplicate trade legislation. That proposition, he rather unfairly claimed, had originated with the English opposition. Once they had obtained this object, they promptly and cynically used it to stir up Irish fears and prejudices. FitzGibbon appealed to his fellow members to show that they were no longer the easy dupes of the Foxite opposition. They could recognize their true interest and adopt a piece of legislation confirming their own privileges and strengthening an all important tie with England, maritime policy.[25]

No great outrage in the form of rhetoric inside parliament or duels elsewhere resulted from this broadside. Grattan contented himself with reminding FitzGibbon that he owed his office to that same opposition.[26] But as FitzGibbon had observed, the opposition lacked the fuel to stoke partisan conflagrations like those that had consumed the commercial propositions. Hawkesbury's Navigation Act, as interpreted by FitzGibbon and his colleagues, did not represent a startling new departure from British policy. Even Grattan conceded that the Navigation Acts had a de facto, if not a de jure authority in Ireland and even Grattan claimed that he was for "British shipping".[27] Recognition of privileges that the English and Irish statutes did confer ultimately outweighed any opposition caviling over privileges that they withheld.

7

Police, Whiteboys and the Fitzgerald Trial

I

Following the failure of the commercial propositions, the Rutland Administration, with FitzGibbon in the lead, reverted to a legislative program of straightforward repression. In particular, the government turned its attention to the city of Dublin, long a source of trouble, and long unpacified, thanks to the legislative distractions of reform and propositions. As early as December of 1784, Orde was collecting information on the peacekeeping forces in Dublin. The information the government received confirmed that the provisions for preserving public order were so inadequate as to be nugatory.

According to the returns made by various parish officers, each parish contributed men to a watch which amounted to 368. But Richard G. Cadwell, the magistrate submitting the report, warned that some parishes had failed to submit returns. In addition "... the number of men employed in some parishes [is] imagined or overrated".[1] The watchmen were not only small in number, they performed their tasks with a palpable lack of zeal. Nor could their appearance have inspired much awe or respect. Cadwell reported that "Coats are generally given only every second year", which suggests that the parish watches were a woefully shabby as well as lackadaisical lot. They hardly posed a threat to vigorous young apprentices bent on tarring and feathering merchants who sold English goods; nor were they capable of protecting their fellow citizens from thieves, footpads, highway robbers, pickpockets and other assorted ordinary perils of 18th-century urban life. As Cadwell described the situation:

> On account of the Insecure state of the Parish by the inability or negligence of the Watchmen, the inhabitants of several parishes have been obliged to raise subscriptions to a very considerable amount for the support of Patrols.[2]

Presumably he meant private patrols composed of more trustworthy professional watchmen. In short, even without the formidable complications of rioting apprentices, the government would probably have been obliged to take measures to strengthen the machinery of public order. Nonetheless, the political and sectarian tensions of Dublin moved Rutland's government to draw up a bill far more comprehensive and severe than any that would have been considered for London, in spite of its equal degree of crime and violence.

According to the provisions of the bill, Dublin and its environs, were divided into six districts. The new law retained the custom of drawing watchmen from the various parishes; the vestries were to elect 167 men to serve in the patrols. Evidently, the lower requirement would be easier to meet and more difficult to inflate in an overly optimistic reply to a government inquiry. But the patrols were not to act under the direction of the aldermen, as was formerly the case. Five commissioners of police, appointed by the Lord lieutenant, and answerable to him, were to have jurisdiction over parish patrols. The proposed bill gave them the authority to levy an ease on the annual value of each house in every parish. The commissioners were to hold the moneys collected and to use them as they saw fit. They also obtained extraordinary powers to act as magistrates "any law, usage, custom or statutes to the contrary notwithstanding". In other words, the new officers would not be as subject to neighborhood prejudices and ties as ordinary magistrates.[3]

The law also included secondary provisions aimed at curbing the excessive drinking of the lower orders, the perceived root of most riot and disorder. "Ale and Porter Houses" were to close by a certain hour every night; recalcitrant tavern keepers were penalized with a fine for a first offense and the revocation of their license for a second.[4] Finally, and perhaps most provocatively, the bill included a provision to search houses and seize arms from those not authorized by law to carry them. This sweeping turn of phrase covered a multitude of political sinners, most notably workers of all religions and Catholic Volunteers.

Orde's correspondence contains no communication with FitzGibbon on the subject of the police bill, though in his usual methodical fashion, he collected opinions from "Slippery Sam" Bradstreet, among others.[5] Of course, their daily proximity made written memoranda unnecessary. Given the requirements of his office, FitzGibbon undoubtedly provided advice and suggestions, and he played a central role in drafting the bill. The harsh provisions against illegal arms in particular bear his stamp. Once again he had responsibility for defending the fruit of his labor in Parliament.

The opposition, triumphant after the virtual defeat of the commercial propositions, lost no time in acting against this latest assertion of authority by the government. Grattan and Curran, as usual, provided the impassioned lead; the Ponsonbys and the Fitzgeralds duly followed the party line, while Burroughs and Forbes offered more thoughtful and reasoned objections.[6] The bill offered pretexts aplenty for opposition. The provision for five commissioners appointed by the lord-lieutenant aroused objection because such additional offices increased the opportunities for corruption and extravagance on the part of Government, the old standards of opposition rhetoric. The imposition of five new city officials with extraordinary judicial powers, also violated the autonomy and charter rights of the city of Dublin, or so it was claimed. The FitzGibbonesque clause giving both the commissioners and the ordinary magistrates the power to enter suspicious dwelling and seize arms aroused inevitable accusations of a evil designs against the Volunteers

FitzGibbon made no apologies for the stringency of the bill. He reminded his colleagues of the scenes in 1784. He also answered objections to the disarming clause with blunt appeals to the class and sectarian prejudices of his auditors. In doing so, he alluded not only to the dangers of an armed laborers inflamed by resentment and drink, but to the growing agrarian unrest among the Catholic peasantry in the South.[9]

As for the Volunteers, whose rights were allegedly at stake, FitzGibbon dismissed them as insignificant, except as a vehicle for opposition troublemaking.[10] The bill by its very nature belied FitzGibbon's claims of the government's lofty indifference. Certainly the clause, if enforced to the letter, would have the effect of dispersing those remaining units comprised of Catholics or workmen or both. But even FitzGibbon, for once, had discretion enough not to admit to this intent.

The bill did pass, in spite of the rhetorical specters of tyranny, oppression and corruption raised by Grattan, Curran and their allies. FitzGibbon and the other speakers on the government side appealed to more palpable fears when they alluded to "drunken weavers" in the Liberties and armed Catholic peasants in Kerry. The reactionary fears and class interests that had prevailed in the votes on reform, protective tariffs and the press act, once again stood the Rutland administration in good stead. In most matters concerning public order, and especially public order in the sense of repressing undue political assertiveness on the part of the lower orders, most members followed the government lead quite docilely. The opposition thrived only when they could seize on an issue that could again revive the heady atmosphere of the early 1780s: national aggrievement and inflated national amour propre.

Notwithstanding, the opposition made the police act a perennial nuisance issue. In 1788 and again in 1789, the act again came up for debate. The debate of 1789 was particularly heated, owing to the peculiar political circumstances of that year. Much political capital was made of the fact that the offices of the police commissioners had been elaborately fitted up with, among other things, pier glasses.[11] FitzGibbon once again reminded his auditors of the public scenes that had necessitated the act, especially the "patriotic American discipline" of the "Tarring and Feathering Committees".[12] Once again class fear and class interest defeated opposition attempts to repeal the bill. Grattan and his colleagues finally did succeed in repealing the bill during their brief ascendancy during the Fitzwilliam administration in 1795.

II

Although the perils of the capital city, rebellious workmen and restless opposition politicians occupied the Rutland administration in its early stages, by 1786, official attention and anxiety shifted to the countryside. It had long been a given of Irish political discourse that the lower orders were ignorant, superstitious, contemptuous of the law and mired in poverty, while the gentry and aristocracy were absent, negligent or willing connivers in the crimes of the lower orders. Although many consciences had been troubled, and many improving pens had stirred to suggest solutions to the problem of Irish poverty and lawlessness, the government in Dublin had never undertaken any systematic effort to address the situation. By 1786, the Rutland administration could no longer afford the luxury of negligence, faced as it was with two instances, one private and one alarmingly public and widespread, which reflected this phenomenon of rural disorder perpetrated or connived at by the gentry. The first was the murder of Randall McDonnell by his neighbor George Fitzgerald. The second concerned an upsurge of Whiteboy activity, organized resistance by the peasantry to the payment of tithes to the Church of Ireland clergy. In both, FitzGibbon played a major role.

George Fitzgerald's brutality and recklessness went far beyond even the license allowed to 18th-century Irish gentlemen.[13] He first demonstrated his peculiarities within his family circle by holding his own father prisoner in the aftermath of a quarrel. He later went on to establish his reputation as the premier hair trigger Irish duelist of his time. Although he fitfully and unsuccessfully solicited the government for a baronetcy, his anarchic temper inclined him more strongly toward a vague radicalism.[14] After 1780, his consuming interest, above and beyond dabblings in radical politics and linen manufacturing, was plotting the murder of his neighbor and former boon companion Randall McDonnell.[15]

The origin of the quarrel seems to have been an unfortunate accident, rather than any deliberate wrongdoing: McDonnell had shot Fitzgerald's horse while the two were engaged in a bout of drunken roughhouse. Even the condoned form of murderous vengeance, the duel, could not satisfy Fitzgerald's outrage. Nothing less than McDonnell's certain death would suffice.[16]

Over the course of six odd years, Fitzgerald made several attempts to do away with McDonnell, all unsuccessful and all using various hired underlings. From the start of his project, Fitzgerald preferred to let menials do the hangable work. McDonnell apparently made no attempt to call on the authorities for protection, until one of Fitzgerald's bravos wounded him in the leg. He then made a complaint to a magistrate; unfortunately political rivalries, and general cowardice and irresponsibility on the part of the magistrates allowed Fitzgerald to evade imprisonment.

With Fitzgerald again at large, McDonnell sensibly took refuge in Castlebar. But reports that Fitzgerald's retainers had stolen arms from his house drew him out of hiding. Fitzgerald quickly took advantage of this lapse of judgment and seized McDonnell, along with two retainers, Hipson and Gallagher.

At this point Fitzgerald's intentions become murky. Ostensibly he intended to subject McDonnell and his servants to the same sort of brutal confinement he had inflicted on his father. Privately, however, he had instructed his retainers to fire on the prisoners at the first sign of any rescue attempt. The chief witness against Fitzgerald later claimed that this condition was a mere pretext. Fitzgerald planned to kill McDonnell and his companions whether or not an attempt was made to rescue them. Fitzgerald's retainers anticipated their master's wishes with brutal zeal. Some members of the party heard or pretended to hear a stray shot, which they duly interpreted an approaching rescue party. In the ensuing attack, Hipson died instantly; Gallagher was wounded slightly, but feigned death. McDonnell made one last attempt to escape. He was ridden down and shot by a retainer variously identified as McGregor, Craig or Creagh, but who was best known by his sobriquet "Scotch Andrew".

In spite of his monumental arrogance and stupidity, Fitzgerald soon realized that even the magistrates of Mayo could not ignore this latest outrage, and he went into hiding. The man who had terrorized Mayo proved remarkably easy to capture. A search party found him hiding under some blankets in a store room. Fitzgerald, McGregor and their associates were escorted to the jail in Castlebar.

There, he and his retainers became victims of the very sort of violence they had so casually inflicted on others. A mob attacked Fitzgerald's house and demolished it. Soon afterward, another mob chose not wait the law's delay and attacked the jail in Castlebar. Fitzgerald received horrible injuries. According to a report provided to the Duke of Rutland, Fitzgerald was clubbed with a candlestick, stabbed with small swords and the blade of a walking stick was broken in his arm. The report went on to add that the jailer's wife had also suffered injuries, as did another associate of Fitzgerald's described by Rutland's correspondent, with casual anti-Semitism, as "an English Jew solicitor of the name of Brecknock". Fitzgerald's assailants went undiscovered and unpunished, though there were justifiable suspicions that Gallagher had participated in the attack on the prison. Given the character of the victim and the number of his enemies, the officers of the law in county Mayo had neither the time nor the inclination to pursue the matter.[17]

Fitzgerald's trial took place in June 1786 during the summer assizes. Rutland's correspondence reveals an avid interest in the case and an equally avid intention of obtaining a conviction. The government saw in Fitzgerald a chance for another exercise in judicial theater, on the order of Reilly's trial. Both had challenged the government's authority, though obviously their motives differed profoundly: Fitzgerald acted out of brutish arrogance while Reilly acted out of popular sympathy and perhaps, a desire for popular adulation. But the Rutland administration hoped to use both trials to convey the same political moral: it would tolerate no further Irish disorder, either in the guise of reforming sheriffs or Mayo landlords acting as petty warlords.

Because of the great importance which the government attached to the case, FitzGibbon traveled to Mayo to lead the prosecution. In addition, the *Dublin Evening Post* reported that "So great is the impatience of the Duke of Rutland to know the issue of the trials at Castlebar, that his private secretary has been dispatched to attend in court and return express with the result."[18]

The case was in some respects not quite as simple as Fitzgerald's blatant degree of responsibility would have suggested. No doubt because of the tremendous hurry to pursue the case, the government's law officers had drawn up the indictment in such a way that Fitzgerald could have evaded prosecution for murder altogether. According to the arcane rules of judicial prose, the omission of the single word "feloniously" from the description of Fitzgerald's actions rendered the indictment invalid. Whatever FitzGibbon's degree of responsibility for the oversight he and the solicitor general quickly stepped in to correct the error. They rewrote the indictment to include the missing word, thus preventing the possibility of Fitzgerald's escape on a verbal technicality. In the words of the *Dublin Evening Post*, "... there is little room to expect that anything of that kind can be attempted with success".[19]

FitzGibbon was to encounter a far more serious legal issue as the trial proceeded. Fitzgerald's habit of leaving the actual acts of violence to his subordinates allowed him to plead that he was, at the most, merely an accessory to the act committed by Scotch Andrew. As Fitzgerald's counsel noted, common law had established that principals were to be tried before accessories. But convicting a commonplace brute like Scotch Andrew would have defeated the whole purpose of the trial. The government was anxious to convict and execute the perceived mastermind of the crime. Moreover, Scotch Andrew could not testify against Fitzgerald if he were tried and convicted first. Since his testimony was the foundation of the government's case, FitzGibbon faced the unnerving possibility of Fitzgerald's acquittal for lack of evidence.

FitzGibbon himself had doubts about the course he was taking, and at least initially he had thought he would have enough evidence to convict Fitzgerald without the dubious contribution of Scotch Andrew.[20] Apparently, this evidence was not adequate and he was compelled to rely on his tainted star witness. FitzGibbon, as always, rose to the legal occasion. First, he seized on the fact that Fitzgerald's counsel had raised the issue of accessories after the jury had been impaneled. FitzGibbon argued that by putting himself on his trial, by appearing before a sworn and impaneled jury, Fitzgerald had in effect "consented" to be tried first. More solidly, he argued that there was indeed a statute that would allow Fitzgerald to be tried before Scotch Andrew.[21] The statute in question dated from the reign of Henry VII and defined both murder and the incitement to murder as treason.[22] Under this definition, Fitzgerald was as guilty as Scotch Andrew; thus FitzGibbon, on behalf of the state, could try the two in whatever order he saw fit.

The presiding judge, Baron Power, remained dubious. According to Power, FitzGibbon should have discharged the jury and resolved whether Fitzgerald was an accessory or a principle before proceeding. Also, FitzGibbon had failed to make an adequate distinction between the nature of Fitzgerald's treasonable action and Scotch Andrew's. As Power put it, "... procuring a murder was a distinct, *substantive* and independent act of treason."[23] Whatever his personal doubts, Power allowed the trial to proceed. Like Bradstreet, he was not about to let his legal scruples stand in the way of the government's obvious desire to obtain a conviction.

The trial ended triumphantly for the FitzGibbon and the Rutland administration Thanks largely to Scotch Andrew's testimony, Fitzgerald was duly convicted and hanged, along with two associates, the maligned Brecknock and Fulton. In return for his services, Scotch Andrew escaped sharing the scaffold with his confederates.[24] In a letter to Rutland, Orde gave this exultant (and rather meanspirited) account of Fitzgerald's demeanor at the end:

> I cannot help sending you my congratulations upon the event of Fitzgerald's trial. I as yet know few of the circumstances but it would appear from what I have heard, that this arch-malefactor lost his constancy and hauteur at the last, and was thrust out of this world with ignominious impatience by the officers of justice.[25]

In actuality, Fitzgerald retained his constancy very well under the circumstances. His execution was a grisly botch job, the rope breaking at the first attempt to hang him. With remarkable presence of mind, he instructed the executioner to use a longer rope, which finally served the purpose. FitzGibbon, out of fastidiousness, pity or the demands of other business, did not stay to witness the execution.

Many years later, yet another victim of FitzGibbon's legal skill and relentlessness, Lord Aldborough, portrayed his prosecution of Fitzgerald as a monstrous exercise in tyranny and injustice. According to Aldborough: "[he] had a man convicted and executed as being the plotter of a murder on the bare testimony of a wretch who confessed himself the perpetrator of it."[26] In this judgment, Aldborough stood alone in retrospective malice. At the time, the opinion prevailed unanimously that Fitzgerald had met a richly deserved end. This opinion prevailed even among the members of his family. Orde observed that "His relations here had discontinued all intercession for mitigation of his punishment". The relatives in question included Fitzgerald's own mother, long since estranged from her son and established in England.[27] FitzGibbon's old enemies in the opposition press likewise freely admitted Fitzgerald's guilt and echoed the hopes of the government that his fate would strike a salutary fear in the multitudes of casual lawbreakers in Ireland. The *Dublin Evening Post* declared:

> It is sincerely to be hoped that the fate of this unfortunate gentleman will be of the greatest utility in suppressing the turbulent disposition and contempt of the laws which have too long disgraced many parts of this country.[28]

FitzGibbon himself also came in for a degree of unaccustomed praise from this same quarter. His unsuccessful effort to revive an inquiry into the assault on Fitzgerald drew this comment: "It would be ungenerous to pass over in silence the indefatigable industry of the Attorney General to bring them [the leaders of the mob] to condign punishment."[29]

The surviving accounts of the trial suggest why FitzGibbon drew such a high degree of admiration even from ordinarily hostile observers. He may have strained a legal point to establish Fitzgerald as the principle defendant but he conducted the trial itself with meticulous fairness. Most notably, he did everything possible to assure a reasonably impartial jury. He took it upon himself to disallow any jurors named McDonnell and he made a powerful plea to those impaneled to set aside everything they may have heard against Fitzgerald and to consider the evidence as though he were a total stranger.[30] He was undoubtedly asking the impossible from a Mayo jury, but his request did indeed bear out yet another observation by the *Dublin Evening Post* : "those who acted on behalf of the Crown [did so] with a firm impartiality and a regard to justice."[31]

Inevitably the radical press reverted to old habits of antagonism. Even so, the more disenchanted comments did not denigrate FitzGibbon and his conduct as a prosecutor. Blandly contradicting their earlier pronouncements about the salutary effects of the trial and the execution on public order, they instead suggested that Rutland's administration had exaggerated the importance of the Fitzgerald case, to detract from its own neglect of the more serious Whiteboy disturbances in Munster. The same paragraph that praised FitzGibbon's impartial conduct of Fitzgerald's trial added this qualification:

> But it [the trial] is by no means a matter of that national importance which it is so pompously represented to be, nor can it ever be supposed to dispel the tumults which disturb this country and which proceed from causes far different from that which gave rise to the melancholy event at Castlebar.[32]

Yet another paragraph stated the case more acerbically:

> One would imagine to read the fulsome puffs and heard the fulsome panegyrics uttered by the Castle laborers [i.e. government owned journalists] that in Fitzgerald a great Goliath was slain and now the champion was dead, all the Philistines would fly and peace be instantly restored – but alas! if they really think so they will find themselves fatally mistaken – there are other things to be done – grievances and burthens of a WRETCHED PEASANTRY lightened.[33]

III

The burthens of the wretched peasantry referred of course to tithes paid by farmers to the Church of Ireland clergy. After reaching a peak in the late 1760s and early 1770s agitation over tithes abated. The revival of the 1780s occurred mainly in the South. In a dispatch dated 28 December 1784, Rutland reported an attack on a tithe proctor or collector in Kilkenny.[34] He briefly noted that an unusually active magistrate had captured those responsible and that the lord chancellor would be sending a special commission to try them. This offhand tone did not continue in future dispatches. By 1786, Whiteboy disturbances had spread all over Munster.

Contemporary observers commented above all on the extraordinary discipline, organization of the Whiteboys. They used sophisticated and often ruthless tactics to infiltrate parishes. Emissaries from parishes already dominated by Whiteboys traveled to uninitiated areas and tendered an oath to the farmers and laborers. This oath required them to pay tithes according to rates agreed upon by the Whiteboys. Those who refused to comply suffered punishments, frequently of a highly inventive cruelty. One unfortunate man was stripped naked and thrown into a pit of thorns. Other resisters lost their ears or suffered horsewhipping. This combination of the genuinely committed and the terrorized effectively defied what authority held sway in the countryside. Nor did military force, either professional or gentry/amateur, prove as effective as it had in the past. The Whiteboys (or Rightboys, as they chose to call themselves) of the 1780s showed a considerable awareness of military discipline and tactics. In areas – and there were many – where they had established total and undisputed authority, they often staged parades and drills of considerable scale and finesse.[35]

The activities of the Whiteboys aroused fears among more conservative Protestants that altering the structure of tithes would lead to further changes in the penal laws. Such fears inevitably led to that commonplace of 18th-century political discourse, the pamphlet war. In spite of their varying degrees of style and quality, the defenders of the Church of Ireland made essentially the same argument: reducing tithes would inevitably destroy the Protestant cause and with it all civil order. An impoverished and weakened Church of Ireland would only lead to the triumph of the Church of Rome and its inevitable corollaries, persecution and despotism. Attempting to placate the lower orders by violating the property rights of the clergy would only encourage further rebellion and the ultimate subversion of all rank and property. They also uniformly portrayed the Church of Ireland clergy as paragons of benevolence and civility who never claimed more than their just due and who often graciously settled for less. Further undermining this already inadequate income would only reduce their numbers. Fewer Protestant clergy would in turn reduce the chances that their apostolic purity and meekness would convert the benighted Popish masses.[36]

The spate of high Church pamphlets provoked both Presbyterian pamphlets and an unprecedented display of Catholic indignation. Rather than endure the usual claims of despotic and disloyal inclinations in meek silence, Catholics, aided by sympathetic Protestants, indignantly asserted their love of and loyalty to the Constitution. A decade of rhetoric about (and tantalizing promises of) equality had increased Catholic assertiveness and decreased their tolerance for the old political myths.

In the midst of heated disputes over such matters as the meaning of Salvo Meo Ordine and the degree of authority exercised by papal nuncios, more secular and more mundane causes for the Whiteboy disturbances occasionally received attention. Some commentators noted a connection between the resistance to tithes and the harsh winters of the early 1780s. After successive seasons of dearth, the peasantry in Munster were just beginning to experience a modest prosperity, or at least a return to ordinary levels of subsistence. Tithes, whatever the Christian self-denial of the Church of Ireland clergy, seemed a particularly irksome barrier to recouping the losses of the first part of the decade.[37] Others reiterated the alleged connection between Irish drinking and Irish disorder.

Above all, the negligence, selfishness and bad judgment of the Irish gentry once again were identified as the chief cause of disorder. Even those inclined to cast suspicion on the Roman Catholic church acknowledged the role played by renegade Protestant gentry in encouraging the disturbances.[38] The Whiteboys certainly benefited from the apathy, the collusion or the absence of landed proprietors. Political opportunism also accounted for the atmosphere of indulgence, particularly in Cork. Colthurst and the other gentry opposed to the Shannon interest found in the Whiteboys a convenient tool for influence and intimidation.

FitzGibbon's sister Arabella Jefferyes played an embarrassingly prominent role in the pro-Whiteboy faction of the Cork gentry. Genuine compassion more than political opportunism probably accounted for her Whiteboy sympathies. Like her brother, she treated her tenants with great humanity and generosity, though like her brother, she had an overdeveloped sense of her own superiority. Imperious and obtuse, she could have provided Jane Austen with a ready model for Lady Catherine de Bourgh. In spite of her unfortunate demeanor, her impassioned paternalism (or perhaps more appropriately maternalism) earned her the adoration of her tenants, who bestowed on her the honorary title of "Lady" Jefferyes. Perhaps inevitably, her sense of pity and her sense of importance got her into trouble during the Whiteboy agitations. Her behavior bordered on megalomania and even outright complicity. She took it upon herself to set tithes for the incumbent of the Church of Ireland living at Blarney Castle as well as fees for all the Roman Catholic priests in her vicinity. She also encouraged church parades, and she allegedly condoned the gathering of Whiteboys on her estate.

Suspicion of Arabella reached a climax when Whiteboys openly participated in her scheme to drain a large lake near Blarney Castle. Arabella herself never made clear why she had undertaken this spectacular act of civil engineering. Her baffled neighbors ventured three possible reasons: she hoped to build a canal linking Blarney and the city of Cork, she hoped to create more arable (and rentable) land on her estate or, she hoped to reclaim a treasure supposedly concealed there by the previous occupants of Blarney, the McCarthys. According to the treasure hunt theory, Arabella shared her brother's morbid fears of the "old inhabitants" and got it into her head that the McCarthys would soon reclaim their ancestral demesne. (Perhaps her perpetual state of insolvency gave her the notion that a moneyed McCarthy might purchase the place.) She hoped to compensate herself for her loss with the McCarthys' ancestral jewelry and plate. Whatever her motives, Arabella ardently disclaimed any knowledge of Whiteboy activity and attributed the large gathering to the overflowing kindness of her neighbors. She was either deluded or disingenuous: in actuality, this project offered the pretext for extensive organization and oath-taking.[39] Moreover, to show their gratitude to "Lady Jefferyes" troops of Whiteboys commandeered both horses and men for service at Blarney.[40]

Arabella experienced a less flattering reception from her male peers. Her efforts to impose her own scale of fees on a local priest brought only the contemptuous response that "he knew of no person named Arabella Jefferyes". Father O'Leary, who made a tour of Munster to preach against the Whiteboys, privately ridiculed her *grande dame* mannerisms, which admittedly were as absurd as they were pathetic.[41] Her brother showed even less sympathy for Arabella. According to one commentator, she received a "very severe reprimand for her conduct" from FitzGibbon. Precisely what he said to this unhappy and thwarted woman, who so resembled him, remains unknown.[42]

Although FitzGibbon smartly put an end to Arabella's politicking, he and his colleagues proceeded more cautiously against her Whiteboy protégés. Embarrassment over the sheer complexity and extent of the Whiteboy disturbances undoubtedly accounted for this hesitation. The government may also have had trouble deciding whether repression or conciliation offered the best means of dissolving the formidable alliance of Whiteboys and opposition gentry in Cork. The progress of General Luttrell through Munster best exemplifies the initial ambivalence on the part of the government. Luttrell toured Munster, both to intimidate the Whiteboys with a show of force and to negotiate a mutually agreeable schedule of tithes. These efforts came to little; Luttrell and the peasantry, as might have been expected, could not agree on what constituted a fair and just system of tithes.[43]

FitzGibbon's reluctance to act against the Whiteboys was a distinct departure from his sadistic gusto in pursuing libelous publishers, rebellious Dublin sheriffs and "drunken weavers" in the Liberties. Like Orde, the complexity of the disorders and the demands of County Cork politicking undoubtedly constrained him. His habitual compassion for the rural poor also may have accounted for his reluctance, as this moving speech of February 1787 indicated:

> I know that it is impossible for human wretchedness to exceed that of the miserable peasantry in that province [Munster]. I know the unhappy tenantry are ground to powder by relentless landlords. I know that far from being able to give the clergy their just dues, they have not food or raiment for themselves, the landlord grasps the whole.[44]

FitzGibbon's public expressions of pity, both before and during the Whiteboy agitations, may have raised hopes that he would support tithe reform. In July 1786, an appeal appeared in the government-sponsored *Freeman's Journal*:

> Your humanity, abilities and rank in life give us hope that you will assist in shielding us from calumny and persecution. We have many very respectable protectors, and trust when *you* consider our motives and conduct, your feelings will raise us up another able advocate in the cause of distress and poverty.[45]

This item may have been inserted with the intention of portraying the attorney general, rather than the politically ambitious County Cork gentry, in the role of defender of the oppressed. Alternatively, it may have reflected genuine public expectation that as a well known enlightened landlord, he would naturally sympathize the Whiteboys.

In the end, the habitual answer of the Rutland administration to all Irish social problems, legal brute force, prevailed. To his credit, Orde showed some abatement in his terrors of the Roman Catholic Church. He could acknowledge that no discernible evidence existed of a systematic, large-scale plot embracing every Catholic in Ireland.[46] Nonetheless, in the end he remained in fundamental agreement with the high church party: responding to the menaces of Popish peasants by curtailing the rights and privileges of the Protestant clergy would only encourage further rebellion and the ultimate subversion of the establishment in Church and State.[47] As for FitzGibbon, his sectarian sensitivities would have made him see the dangers of conciliation at least as readily as Orde.

In February 1787, shortly after the opening of Parliament, FitzGibbon presented the bill he had drawn up to suppress the Whiteboy disturbances. The bill reflected none of the compassion he had expressed in the House. It offered two elegant solutions to the grievances of the peasantry, transportation or the gallows. Those who administered oaths or who interfered with the collection of tithes faced transportation. The death penalty was attached to such actions as seizing arms or using force to compel individuals to join combinations. In short, all the tactics which had made the Whiteboys formidable now carried terrifying penalties.[48] Notwithstanding its bloodthirstiness, the bill passed fairly quickly through Parliament. FitzGibbon's fears affected most members, however sympathetic to the Whiteboys. They came to recognize that attacks on the tithes of the established clergy inevitably undermined the security of gentlemen's rents. Indeed, the Whiteboys had already begun to press for a reduction in rents as well as a commutation of tithes.[49]

FitzGibbon's fellow members balked at one provision of the act, which aimed a preventing the Whiteboys from using Catholic chapels to organize their activities and to tender oaths to new initiates. FitzGibbon authorized magistrates to demolish any chapels used by the Whiteboys for such purposes. This measure disgusted even Sir Edward Newenham, a man not otherwise known for his respect for Catholic holy places. He spoke for all of his parliamentary colleagues when he denounced it as a "most insulting and oppressive clause".[50]

Initially, FitzGibbon made a shamefaced retreat before the outrage of his fellow members. He insisted that he had intended no insult to the Catholics. On the contrary, no one had "more respect for the worthy part of them". Furthermore, he claimed Catholic precedents for this exercise in architectural humiliation: "I have known this very punishment inflicted in catholic countries, and have actually seen churches shut up by order of the King of France for offenses of a political nature."[51] He also claimed no less than the authority of Jesus Christ to justify his pet clause. "As we are told from the highest authority that when the temple had become a den of thieves the doors were therefore shut."[52] FitzGibbon insisted that he had inserted the offending clause mainly to intimidate his old enemies the middlemen. They were inciting the Whiteboys to deprive the Protestant clergy of their tithes, with the intention of increasing their own rapacious exactions. FitzGibbon expressed the hope that once the middlemen recognized they could lose their chapels, they would stop stirring up trouble.

FitzGibbon's excuses, apologies and exercises in Biblical exegesis did not alter the fundamental nature of the clause directed against chapels: it was a naked act of sectarian terrorism. The clause reflected, not only FitzGibbon's perpetual and furious renunciation of his Irish Catholic ancestry, but his profound knowledge of the Irish Catholic mentality. Nothing could have been better calculated to terrify and humiliate that people, many of whom still had raw memories of the old penal code. FitzGibbon himself revealed his true motives later in debate. Irritated by the continued criticisms of the chapel clause, he allowed the Bible-quoting, Catholic-respecting mask to slip:

> The Attorney-General here explained that he by no means relinquished the principle of the clause particularly objected to. – He thought it extremely just if popish meeting houses were made places of combination to rob the protestant clergy, they ought to be prostrated. However, he would not press the clause, himself being desirous of unanimity; but he never would forgo the opinion he entertained of the justness of his principle.[53]

In spite of FitzGibbon's bravado, the clause continued to cause outrage. Even the government-sponsored *Freeman's Journal* expressed horror. A paragraph in the *Freeman's* declared that only the most stringent rules of evidence could justify this "obnoxious clause" and "protect the religious and civil liberties of at least one half the subjects" from an "interested or prejudiced informer".[54] More seriously, Orde may have had doubts about FitzGibbon's harshness, just as he had during the Reilly crisis. Orde never explicitly objected to the clause. On the contrary, in a letter to Pitt, he loyally supported FitzGibbon's avowed intention to revive the chapel wrecking clause if Whiteboy activity continued. At the same time, he went out of his way to emphasize the administration's humanity and moderation towards Catholics. He assured Pitt that the clause had been deleted out of respect for the Catholic nobility and gentry, many of whom had been active in repressing Whiteboys. Since neither Orde nor his government had ever displayed much respect for the sensibilities of Catholics of any rank, his claim is dubious. Possibly, he feared that Pitt and his colleagues might object to the chapel wrecking clause as vehemently as the Irish House of Commons did. By bringing attention to the purported humanity of the administration, he may have hoped to fend off a possible rebuke either to FitzGibbon or to the Rutland administration as a whole.[55]

Having effectively reinforced the machinery of state terror to suppress the rebellion of the Whiteboys, it now remained for FitzGibbon to keep his self-imposed promise to consider their grievances. He escaped any serious threat of honoring this promise during the session of 1787; however, in the ensuing session Grattan called his bluff by introducing a comprehensive series of proposals for reforming tithes. Ingrained habits of opposition and a still more ingrained fondness for the limelight prompted Grattan's undertaking, as did his most admirable qualities, passion for justice and generosity of mind. His ambitious, and probably unrealizable program, included the elimination of much hated tithe proctors, a septennial valuation of corn to arrive at rates more accurately reflecting current market values, the establishment of local committees to determine such rates, an exemption of hay, potatoes and other widely used commodities and the partial commutation of some tithes to cash payments. Grattan also included a provision exempting reclaimed barren lands from tithes for a period of seven years. Using all of his considerable rhetorical virtuosity, he drew on a formidable mass of information ranging from the tithing practices of the ancient Jews to the prices of provisions in Munster to bolster his central argument: the reform of tithes could only benefit the Protestant establishment by removing an endemic source of disaffection and by securing for its clergy a steady, reasonable income.[56]

FitzGibbon reacted with many cavils and warnings. Any meddling with tithes, he claimed, could only undermine the authority and prestige of the established church and worse, encourage a revival of Whiteboy disorders. Rejection of a bill based on Grattan's proposals would stir outrage and rebellion, while any reforms would fail to satisfy. Nothing less than the abolition of tithes altogether would settle the benighted peasantry. FitzGibbon tacked a highly unconvincing disclaimer to this speech of opposition: "However if they [Grattan's proposals] were reduced to a bill, he would examine them. If they were such as he approved, he should support, if not he should reject them."

This brief note to Orde, written in the autumn of 1787 anticipated the stance FitzGibbon was to take: "By the way, I am told that Grattan in busily employed in investigating the subject of Tythes, but if I know him, the deeper he goes there, the Faster will he stick."[58]

In effect, FitzGibbon's claim of an open mind on the subject of tithe reform was a sham from the start. As the letter to Orde indicates, he hardly believed in the pose himself.

Grattan's efforts to promote a more comprehensive reform of tithes in the winter of 1788 did indeed stick fast. A comfortable majority, bored with the subject or antagonistic to it, rejected Grattan's motion. The vote was 49 to 121.[59] By that time, Rutland had died of alcoholic excess and Orde had retired to England with his nerves and his various ailments. But the new government of the Marquis of Buckingham took the same line. This letter from Evan Nepean to Alleyne Fitzherbert, Buckingham's chief secretary, demonstrates the official view that had carried over from one administration to another:

> The motion made by Mr. Grattan upon the subject of Tythes ... would, had it been agreed to by the House, certainly have brought forward the discussion of

questions, which apart from their nature would again be likely to interrupt the publick tranquillity.[60]

While Grattan never lost interest in tithe reform, other issues claimed a greater share of his attention, his enthusiasm and his rhetorical virtuosity. As for the peasantry of Munster, the subject of so much pity and outrage, discouragement, as well as the threat of hanging or transportation effectively broke any further attempts at sustained, large scale resistance of tithes.

In addition to the riot act, which addressed the immediate uprisings in Munster, the Rutland administration introduced an ambitious system of law enforcement to prevent a recurrence of similar disorders. Once again Orde collected memoranda on the disorderly state of the Irish countryside.[61] Once again this flood of fact and impression was condensed into a bill, which in turn became the subject of further memoranda and analysis. The end result, introduced in the winter of 1787, amounted in effect to an extension of the Dublin police act to encompass the whole countryside.[62]

In essence, the proposed law addressed one of the greatest causes of complaint, absentee, negligent or partial magistrates, sheriffs and peace officers. In its initial draft stages, the bill provided for a wholesale purge of the magistracy, and a reissuing of new commissions. The bill next provided for the division of each county into baronial districts, bearing the name of one of the baronies, presumably the largest. Each of these districts was to have one peace officer and a constable along with "sixteen proper persons ... to act as subconstables". The proper persons were, of course, Protestants. They were to form armed bodies to patrol the countryside. The grand juries of the counties were to levy cesses to pay the salaries of the constables and peace officers. In addition, the proposed law required the convening of a general sessions of the peace in every county eight times a year rather than four, as was the custom. Finally and perhaps most controversially, the bill provided for the appointment of barristers to assist justices at these sessions of the peace. The provisions of the bill required the assistant barristers to have at least six years of experience, and it denied the post to any barrister who was also serving in Parliament. Presumably members of Parliament would have faced a conflict between enforcing impartial justice and maintaining their popularity with voters in their particular district. Yet another provision required judges to select a certain number of justices to attend at all sessions of the peace "having a due Regard to the Distance of the Residence of every such Justice from the Town, at which every session is to be holden". Nonetheless, justices not on the roster could attend if so inclined.

The bill also attempted to introduce some measure of system to two common areas of abuse: licensing and the taking of sureties. One provision gave chief constables and justices the power to check for and to verify the licenses of all vendors of "Beer, Ale or Spirituous Liquors". The magistrates were to take reasonable recognizances for offenses against the peace and they were to accept no surety until they had ascertained the parties in question were householders who could make good the promised sum.[63]

Such a systematic and comprehensive bill was of course doomed to failure. It offended every instinct of amour propre, sloth and public, as opposed to private, parsimony, that characterized too many country gentlemen. They saw and no doubt rightly, the barristers who purportedly were to advise them also infringed on their autonomy. The presence of a disinterested legal authority, with no local ties and no interest to maintain in a particular locality effectively prevented any favoritism or slackness in the interpretation or the enforcement of the law. The provisions imposing additional sessions and requiring attendance also offended those who looked upon the office of magistrate chiefly as an honorary and prestigious title. Above all, the bill was costly. The proposed salary for the chief constable was £50; the subconstables were to receive from £10–12 per annum and the assistant barristers were entitled to a compensation not exceeding £300. According to the proposed magistracy bill, fines levied by the magistrates were to defray these expenses, in addition to grand jury levies. While these salaries were, to be sure, comparatively modest, the status quo, that is inaction occasionally interrupted by military action, was cheaper. Finally, regional sensitivities contributed in large measure to the opposition to the bill. Members from Ulster in particular, the former hotbed of tithe agitation, resented the fact that their law abiding province should suffer tyranny and expense because of the misbehavior of Munster.[64]

Faced with so much resistance to expense, exertion and responsibility, the government adopted the same course it had taken toward the commercial propositions: it retreated, and left the implementation of the various rural policing proposals to the discretion of the individual counties. Only four eventually chose implementation: Kerry, Cork, Kilkenny and Tipperary.[65]

Limerick, the attorney general's home county, was conspicuously absent. He had provided information on the barony divisions of Limerick with an undoubted view to the bill's adoption there, and he had, in addition acted his usual part of advocate in Parliament. Nonetheless, he actively repudiated it at the county meetings on the subject.[66]

Possibly the newest direction of his ambition prompted his startling accommodation to the hostile country gentlemen of Limerick. As will be seen, both Rutland and Orde favored his promotion to Lord Chancellor. He may have repudiated the magistracy act either to create popular sympathy for his bid for the Seals, or to establish a foundation for another try at one of the county seats in case his appointment failed to materialize.

Whatever the motives for his action, FitzGibbon suffered no repercussions for this sacrifice of public responsibility for private politicking. Lord Shannon, who had established a reputation as a zealous Churchman and whose county had suffered considerable upheaval from the Whiteboys was, not surprisingly, angry with the attorney general and with the Rutland administration overall. However distressing Shannon's disapproval may have been, he did not influence the appointment of Lord Chancellor. Those who did, Rutland and Orde, do not appear to have expressed any disapprobation of FitzGibbon's actions. His past service, as well as the abatement of Whiteboy activity undoubtedly made them take a more tolerant view of FitzGibbon's efforts to woo the country gentlemen of Limerick at the expense of larger government policy.

8

Court Business

I

In addition to his legislative duties, FitzGibbon advised the government on legal matters and represented its interests in the courts. His cases touched on all facets of the law and involved all classes of people, from the wretched accomplices of George Fitzgerald to Roman Catholic peers. His decisions did not necessarily reflect his religious and political sympathies; he was of course obliged to observe and uphold legal precedent. Nonetheless, it is possible to discern FitzGibbon's qualities in these cases, notably his sheer relentlessness, particularly in prosecuting disturbers of the civil order.

Some cases concerned routine government business. One opinion of interest concerned an abortive exercise in educational social engineering on the part of Thomas Orde. Orde's plan involved a thoroughgoing reform of the local parish schools, the creation of collegiate schools to improve the caliber of candidates admitted to the university, and the establishment of four vocational/technical colleges to teach practical subjects such as accounting, surveying and agriculture. The scheme, and in particular the revamped parish schools and the technical schools, purported to transform the lower classes from Irish-speaking Whiteboys and general disturbers of the peace into dutiful, submissive English speakers with a smattering of useful skills and literacy. Yet Orde introduced provisions that contradicted this intention. While Catholic children could attend the parish schools at no cost to their purses or, at least in theory, to their consciences, they were obliged to take instruction from Protestant school masters under the direction of the resident Protestant clergyman. As for the higher levels of state-sponsored education, Orde limited the beneficiaries to Protestants of the Established Church or to Catholics willing to bring their children up in the state religion. The collegiate and the vocational schools were, in effect, the old Charter schools in a slightly more expensive and elaborate guise.[1] Orde believed that by providing Protestants, cradle or converted, with a superior, state-funded education the government could ensure their "Ascendancy". His baffling and mean-spirited myopia guaranteed that few if any Catholics would experience the alleged civilizing benefits of his school system. Certainly no self-respecting Whiteboy would have sent his children to schools run by tithe-exacting Protestant clergymen.

The question of funding involved FitzGibbon in the education scheme. Among many other sources of income, Orde considered drawing on profits from the sales of lands forfeited to the Crown in 1641 and in 1690. Evidently enough of these remained unsold to guarantee a fair source of cash. To judge from FitzGibbon's correspondence on the subject, Orde wanted to earmark the money for "publick schools", which could only have meant the great collegiate schools. Nonetheless, Orde had doubts about the Irish government's right to draw on the money coming from sales of forfeited lands. FitzGibbon gave him a favorable opinion on the question. The Irish government could freely draw on profits from land forfeited in 1641. Lands forfeited after 1690 fell under the provisions of an act passed by the English parliament; but FitzGibbon was optimistic that the English government would revise the act to transfer jurisdiction over such lands to its Irish equivalent.[2]

To repeat, FitzGibbon was deciding merely on a point of law. No record of his general opinion of the scheme survives, as he took no part in the first and only debate on the completed education bill. Nor is it possible to form much judgment based on his past pronouncements on the subject. In 1782, he had expressed his abhorrence for the Catholic practice of foreign education in "regions of bigotry and superstition". The sectarian exclusivity of Orde's scheme offered nothing in the way of an alternative, as FitzGibbon surely must have recognized. On the other hand, he may have favored Orde's scheme on the grounds that a superior Protestant school system offered an inducement to conformity, his own favored solution to the Catholic question. At any rate, FitzGibbon never had a chance to elucidate his opinions in subsequent debates. After an initial friendly reception, even from opposition stalwarts who mistakenly looked upon it as a promising step toward non-sectarian education, the scheme fell into abeyance. Orde's retirement deprived it of sponsorship, and no one else, least of all FitzGibbon, stepped forward to continue his work.

In other cases FitzGibbon to defend the commercial and industrial monopolies of the British Empire. He undertook several prosecutions of merchants for making false declarations to customs. FitzGibbon took judicial measures to limit American competition in another case involving of a group of men who had lured apprentices and journeymen to the United States. The *Freeman's Journal* gave this explanation for the government's and FitzGibbon's actions:

> In consequence of the praiseworthy and spirited attention of the Right Honorable Attorney General in commencing several late prosecutions against those who were seducing our artificers to emigrate, it is supposed very few emigrations will, in future, take place to America, which will tend to form the true and proper strength of a nation – its population. That population constitutes the riches of a country is evident not only from the consumption of things taxable, but for the supply of hands to arts, manufacture, war and commerce.[3]

The *Freeman's* correspondent displayed both pre-Malthusian innocence and considerable disingenuousness. It is doubtful that FitzGibbon would have been called upon to prosecute anyone for luring spalpíní to the United States. The fact that the young men in question had the skills to create an industrial base in a rival country concerned the Irish government and the attorney general. FitzGibbon's contempt for Americans as habitual rioters and smugglers undoubtedly enhanced his zeal in pursuing the case.

The social chaos of Ireland, and especially of its capital city, offered FitzGibbon considerable practice in criminal law. His greatest prosecutorial triumph, the Fitzgerald case had left some loose ends, in the form of lesser accomplices. One Foy in particular had been acquitted of complicity in the McDonnell murders, but FitzGibbon, convinced of his guilt, framed a new indictment naming him as an accessory before the fact. Foy's counsel took the position that FitzGibbon was attempting to try Foy for the same crime under a different title, and thus was violating the principle of autrefois acquit. In response, FitzGibbon claimed that this new bill of indictment represented an entirely different charge. In this instance, FitzGibbon failed to carry his point. Foy's claim of autrefois acquit was accepted.[4] Whatever the merits of his case, his actions against Foy reveal above all FitzGibbon's ruthless streak toward those whom he perceived as evil doers. To redress what he perceived as an unpunished wrong, he stretched the bounds of legal propriety, not to mention simple moderation.

The same morality and relentlessness characterized his prosecution of Richard Griffith, Sir John Freke, and Henry Hatton. This particular case concerned an incident in Merrion Square in the spring of 1788. Evidently that great Georgian showpiece was not always a scene of calm, fashionable elegance. On the contrary, servants from the surrounding houses habitually appropriated the square on Sunday evenings for wrestling matches and other boisterous pastimes. Although the inhabitants seem to have tolerated the Merrion Square holiday parties, one Sunday stroller took a less kindly (or less resigned) view: Alderman Exshaw, who was also serving as one of the police commissioners under terms of the act of 1786. He perceived the servants' recreation as little better than a riot, or at the very least, as a profanation of the Sabbath, and he ordered the Sunday revelers to disperse. Hatton, Freke and Griffith happened to observe Exshaw's actions while taking the air together. They took exception to what they regarded as Exshaw's arbitrary manner. Exshaw in response turned his prosecutorial attention from the servants to the gentlemen. He arrested them on the grounds that Griffith and his companions had gone beyond a reasonable questioning of a public official. On the contrary, they had created an equal danger to public order by actively and maliciously interfering with his reasonable efforts to disperse the crowds. On Exshaw's behalf, FitzGibbon filed an information against Griffith and his companions for obstructing justice, and he undertook the prosecution. He succeeded in obtaining the conviction of Griffith.[5]

Initially, the verdict and the attorney general enjoyed a brief measure of favor, if that popular bellwether, the *Dublin Evening Post* is any indication:

> By the late decision in the case of Alderman Exshaw against Sir John Freke, Mr

> Hatton and Mr Griffith, it is presumed that the respectable inhabitants of Merrion Square will be freed from the intolerable nuisance with which their ears and eyes were formerly offended, Sunday after Sunday. It evinces that the sanction of no rank, however high, nor the protection of any character, however respectable, will be sufficient to screen disturbers of the peace from justice.[6]

FitzGibbon's triumph was short-lived. Griffith succeeded in obtaining an arrest of judgment on the grounds that the original information had not defined clearly enough how he had obstructed Alderman Exshaw and justice.[7] FitzGibbon, again displaying his relentlessness toward perceived wrongdoers, as well as his constitutional inability to accept a situation that did not go as he wished, filed yet another, more clearly defined information one week later. As with the Fitzgerald case, the *Dublin Evening Post* reversed its initial positive judgment:

> The prosecution, or rather the persecution of Mr Griffith is not yet abandoned, for a great Law-Officer has filed another information against that gentleman, wherein it is said, he means to avoid those official blunders that caused an arrest of judgment on a recent occasion. Yet, so sure of their prey were the prosecutors, when they had once got a jury to convict Mr Griffith, that the extent of his punishment was, it is said, determined on, which as we hear was to have been a fine of £500 and a year's imprisonment.[8]

In spite of the *Dublin Evening Post*'s rather fulsome initial claims, it is difficult to believe that the prosecution of Griffith was purely a matter of a gentlemanly rioter receiving his just and impartially administered deserts. Griffith, a member of Parliament for Askeaton, had kept up a continual and active opposition to the police act from its very inception. Earlier in the year, he had presented a petition from the citizens of Dublin requesting a repeal of the act and the return of the old parish watches.[9] FitzGibbon, with the full support of the Castle and of the police commissioners, may have seen the prosecution as a golden opportunity to humiliate and silence a troublesome opponent. Exshaw's over-reaction and the harshness of the proposed sentence suggest that Griffith was not punished in spite of the fact that he was a gentleman, but because he was a gentleman in vocal opposition to sensitive government policy.

Yet it would be unfair to dismiss FitzGibbon as a hypocrite. He did have a genuine conviction that the law should protect the poor and punish the well-born lawbreaker with particular severity. No doubt his vision of justice had a certain naiveté. No doubt it had characteristic elements of self-dramatization, featuring FitzGibbon himself a little too prominently as the protector of the good and humble and the scourge of the wicked and disaffected. Above all, an obtuse self-righteousness flawed his vision of justice. FitzGibbon had an alarming tendency to confuse his political positions with absolute morality and absolute right. He believed that all gentlemen had an obligation to support measures of public order decreed by legitimate authority. Those who opposed measures like the police act necessarily were troublemakers furthering their own cynical political ends. That Griffith may have had perfectly legitimate objections to the police act, that he may not have been a well-born incendiary on the order of Lord George Gordon probably never occurred to FitzGibbon. A healthy dose of skepticism, indeed cynicism, would have done wonders for FitzGibbon's judgment and for his peace of mind.

A separate case involving the wealthy and the well born offers a slightly less tainted example of FitzGibbon's commitment to equal justice. It involved Lord Hillsborough, who unlike Griffith, shared FitzGibbon's political perspective. A protégé of Hillsborough's, one Knox, had embezzled £10,000 while serving as an officer of the revenue. Knox had offered to make good the loss if FitzGibbon would refrain from prosecution. FitzGibbon refused. He acknowledged that from a pecuniary standpoint, Knox's offer had advantages. But leniency would "in point of example ... be pernicious" to the government's reputation for probity and justice. At best, FitzGibbon agreed to warn Knox, through Hillsborough, of any pending prosecution. Knox could then discreetly leave the country. Perhaps in strictest justice, Knox should have paid the full penalty of the law, but exile in disgrace scarcely represented an act of grace and favor.[10]

The endemic crime in Dublin made a bizarre intrusion into FitzGibbon's own life. A casual charwoman was arrested for stealing some valuables from his house. The police took her to a holding cell in a jail near the Liffey. While in confinement, she pried open the window of her cell, which overlooked the river, and jumped. Unfortunately her skills in swimming did not equal her skills in prison breaking, and she drowned.[11] Since the woman so dramatically escaped prosecution, what role FitzGibbon would have played must remain unknown. Probably he would have taken a very active part: visiting the woman's cell and bombarding her with questions and with moral indignation. He dealt in the same way with the man accused of assaulting him in 1795 and with the household servants accused of murdering his steward in 1799.[12]

The sensitive subject of Catholics occupied FitzGibbon in the courts as well as in Parliament. In the 1780s several Roman Catholic peers, or in the case of Lord Trimelston, recently converted Roman Catholic peers, attempted to reverse decrees of attainder or outlawry dating from the troubled end of the Jacobite wars. Lord Trimelston hoped to regain his right to sit in the House of Lords, while a more general wish to erase a social and legal stigma prompted those peers who remained Roman Catholic. As one of his more unenviable duties, FitzGibbon was obliged to sift through a mindboggling assortment of genealogies, self-serving histories of the civil wars of the 17th century and parliamentary decrees. Lord Trimelston, the Protestant convert, enjoyed the quickest resolution. His legal encumbrances were lifted in 1788.[13] The Catholic peers endured a longer wait to clear their escutcheons. Lord Fingall was still struggling with the question of his legal status in 1794, while the Lords Gormanston, father and son, suffered greater vicissitudes.[14] In 1786, FitzGibbon denied the 11th Lord Gormanston's request for a reversal of outlawries on the grounds that he had not provided enough evidence of an alleged royal pardon.[15] Only in 1800 did his young son (or perhaps more accurately his young son's lawyers) provide documentation enough to satisfy the legal establishment and the soon to be defunct Irish House of Lords.

It is tempting to discern a pattern of sectarian prejudice in FitzGibbon's judgments. Many Protestants feared that restoring titles to Catholic peers could open the way to restoring lands to dispossessed Catholic proprietors of all ranks.[16] FitzGibbon himself, of course, always feared for the stability of Protestant tenure. In addition, he had never demonstrated any great love for the Catholic gentry and aristocracy. During the debates on the relief bill of 1778, his many arguments against the repeal of the gavel clause included a claim that such a repeal would only benefit Catholic peers bent on consolidating their estates.[17] In the decade following his attitude seems to have warmed to glacial indifference. Only in the 1790s did he adopt the role of friend and patron. Indeed, only in the 1790s did he have any social contact with Roman Catholic gentlemen and nobility. Hitherto he seems to have been exposed mainly to middle or lower class Catholics: remote relations, the Roches, tenants, and objects of charity. Yet FitzGibbon probably did act as fairly as he was capable. His veneration for the law would have prevented him from committing a deliberate injustice, even to Papists. Certainly neither the 11th Lord Gormanston, nor any member of his arch-Catholic family ever suggested that FitzGibbon had acted out of sectarian animosity.[18]

In another case involving the Gormanston family, FitzGibbon unmistakably displayed great sectarian animosity. The sudden death of Anthony Preston, the 11th Viscount Gormanston, in December of 1786, raised the awkward question of who would or could act as guardians for his twelve-year old son Jenico. In his will, the late lord had named as guardians an assortment of peers and gentlemen both English and Irish. They included his brother, Mr John Preston, Lord Killeen, Lord Kenmare, Sir Patrick Bellew, and the Duke of Portland. According to the terms of Lord Gormanston's will, John Preston was to raise the child at Gormanston Castle, the child was to be raised a Catholic and above all, his English Protestant mother was to have absolutely no contact with him. Shortly after Jenico's birth Lord Gormanston had separated from his wife. The reasons for the separation were obscure, but the husband's lingering death-bed antagonism was obvious.[19]

The law and the sectarian politics of Ireland and England brought these arrangements into immediate dispute. Lady Gormanston, the estranged wife, quickly emerged from fashionable exile to assert her rights as a mother, and the law as it stood, seemed to give her claims precedence. A statute from the reign of Charles II deprived not only Catholics but Dissenters of the right to appoint guardians for their children. Since the wholesale repeal of penal legislation in 1782 had never addressed the rights of guardianship, the law of Charles II conceivably remained in effect in Ireland as well as in England.[20]

The late Lord Gormanston's shrewd inclusion of the Protestant Duke of Portland in the collection of noble guardians added another element of ambiguity. No law barred Portland from acting as guardian, and, still more to his advantage, he had promised the late Lord Gormanston that he would acquiesce in the child's Catholic upbringing. Evidently greater familiarity with the laws regarding the guardianship of Catholic children forced Portland, or gave him a pretext, to retreat from this deathbed promise. He planned, if given custody of the child, to cajole Jenico into conformity with the help of various avuncular Anglican clergymen.[21]

As for the Catholic guardians, they tried as much as possible to keep their distance. Lord Kenmare, characteristically, was the most forward in shying away from the whole business. He affected great surprise at his appointment and claimed that he had barely known his fellow Roman Catholic peer. Lord Killeen and Sir Patrick Bellew made polite promises to treat little Jenico like their own son should they obtain custody. But they did not press the matter. By this time they knew the government of Thomas Orde and the Duke of Rutland all too well.[22]

Yet another faction in the matter of little Jenico, his Preston relations resident in Liege, chose not to wait passively for the decision of Protestant courts. This faction comprised the child's paternal grandmother and another uncle, also named Jenico, who was chancellor to the Prince Bishop of Liege. Acting under their energetic direction, Mr Dixon, a chaplain attached to the Gormanston household, secretly traveled with little Jenico from Gormanston to England. From there, the child sailed to the Continent and to the custody of his grandmother and his uncle.[23]

Predictably, a great legal and Parliamentary uproar ensued. The Prestons of Liege had deprived the Protestant Establishment in Church and State of a potential convert in the form of a small, impressionable child. All Catholics who had the remotest connection, real or suspected, with Jenico's flight to the Continent suffered some form of legal intimidation. The mother filed writs of habeas corpus demanding the return of little Jenico against half a dozen individuals. They included John Preston and one of his sisters, neither of whom had any advance knowledge of the scheme.[24] Sir Edward Newenham took up the cause of wronged Protestant motherhood in Parliament, and proposed a bill making it a crime to spirit a minor overseas. He claimed that would have done the same for a Roman Catholic child kidnapped to a Protestant seminary in Switzerland or Germany, a rather dubious claim, but one which showed signs of improvement in the Knight of St Doulough.[25] The most vociferous, not to say the most hysterical, of the Protestant/Lady Gormanston partisans was, not surprisingly, the attorney general. The Liege branch of the Preston family confirmed his darkest suspicions about Catholics: they were ruthless bigots who lurked in realms of despotism and superstition.

Although he agreed to help Sir Edward Newenham frame his proposed bill, FitzGibbon's Protestant outrage demanded even sterner measures. He also advocated a bill of outlawry against Jenico Preston the elder; this proposed outlawry would bar the elder Jenico from inheriting his nephew's estate in remainder. FitzGibbon, always one for the terrorizing example, included this act of legislative disinheritance "... in order to convince people that the laws could not be violated with impunity."[26] In spite of all the parliamentary sound and fury, both proposed bills slipped mysteriously into abeyance. The legislative records for the session of 1787 give no indication that Sir Edward's proposed bill ever passed into law. Toward the end of the session, on 7 May 1787, a bill was introduced "to vindicate the laws, which have been grossly violated by clandestinely conveying out of this kingdom, into parts beyond the seas, out of his Majesty's dominions, the person of Jenico Preston, commonly called Lord Viscount Gormanston, a minor under the age of twelve years ..."[27] Lord Chancellor Lifford's son, rather than FitzGibbon, introduced the bill. Again, nothing seems to have come of this bill, either in the form of further debate or in the form of a final act of parliament.

FitzGibbon may have put Lifford's son in charge of the parliamentary matters so that he could more effectively pursue the Prestons and their friends in the courts. He started with a familiar tactic, filing an information against Mr Dixon, who nonetheless managed to evade the rather bungling attempts of the police to entrap and arrest him.[28] A Catholic gentleman by the name of Dease was subjected to FitzGibbon's interrogation because little Jenico had spent the night at his house while en route from Gormanston Castle.[29] Nothing serious came of this encounter. Dease was a friend and relation of Lord Westmeath, who in his turn had just embarked on his disastrous marriage with FitzGibbon's niece. Family feeling, and more important, the fundamental fairness which never quite deserted him even at his worst inclined FitzGibbon to take a lenient view. He acknowledged that he could find no evidence that Dease had been aware of the plot when he offered his hospitality to little Jenico and Dixon.[30]

No individual was too peripheral to escape the attorney general's wrathful attention. William Cruise, an eminent conveyancer resident in London, received a letter from FitzGibbon, which was an extraordinary exerciser in rudeness, hysteria and futility. FitzGibbon regaled Cruise with hints of the murderous intentions of little Jenico's Popish relations. They had, he claimed, viciously and willfully risked the child's life by exposing him to the dangers of a sea voyage during the height of winter. (Had he succeeded in capturing and interrogating Mr Dixon, he might have learned that the voyage was, in fact, calm and uneventful.) FitzGibbon then peremptorily ordered Cruise to intervene and to bring the child back to Ireland.[31] Cruise's family connection with one of the men who had accompanied little Jenico on his life-threatening journey to the Continent seems to have prompted this communication.[32] Cruise's response, if indeed he made any, seems to have disappeared in the conflagration of FitzGibbon's personal correspondence. Presumably he told FitzGibbon the simple truth: he had had no concern in the matter in the first place, and he could do nothing about it now.

If Cruise took offense at FitzGibbon's manner, he was certainly in company with the other Catholic peers and gentlemen involved. In a letter to Sir Patrick Bellew, Lord Killeen articulated what was probably a general dislike and fear of FitzGibbon.

In discussing a possible meeting of Jenico's nominal Catholic guardians, Killeen suggested avoiding Dublin and the attorney general:

> I am afraid Dublin would be an improper place, we are so watched there, that our consultation might be deemed a Popish plot and some of us summoned before the Attorney General in half an hour afterwards.[33]

One Catholic gentleman, in the person of the elder Jenico Preston, remained perfectly unmoved by FitzGibbon's threats and indeed by the threats and appeals of the English and Irish governments. He contemptuously ignored all demands, official and unofficial for the child's return. In one instance, he allegedly referred to the seal on a Chancery document as a mere bit of wax. Preston had a staunch ally in the Prince Bishop of Liege. When a seedy confidential agent by the name of Miles made abortive efforts to re-abduct little Jenico, the Prince Bishop dispatched a guard to the Prestons' house. He too denied all official appeals to return the child to Ireland, though presumably he used more tact than the elder Jenico Preston.[35] FitzGibbon for once met his match in a man as ruthless and as fanatically committed to his conceptions of religious duty.

Four years of stalemate followed. Little Jenico remained quietly in Liege, though to judge from surviving correspondence, his life was not easy. The elder Jenico may have rescued his nephew from Protestant coercion in the guises of his mother, the Irish attorney general and the Duke of Portland; but he himself was something of a sacerdotal bully, at once querulous and sententious. He never missed an opportunity to remind little Jenico that his uncle had saved his immortal soul from certain destruction.[36]

The intervention of the Earl of Carhampton ended the impasse. Whatever his later brutalities against United Irishmen and Defenders, Carhampton behaved in this one instance with admirable sense and moderation, qualities singularly lacking in the other adults involved, Catholic or Protestant. In 1789, he sued for the guardianship of young Jenico on the grounds that he was the child's closest Protestant relation on the father's side of the family. He seems to have acted with reasonable disinterestedness. As he himself noted in his chancery brief, he had no financial concern whatsoever in the Gormanston estate. He wanted only to stop depredation and waste in the management of the child's property.[37] On the Protestant side, he alone seems to have had any sympathy for or understanding of the elder Jenico Preston's motives and feelings.[38] He finally accomplished what years of threats had failed to do, and brought little Jenico back to Ireland.[39] The increasingly agitated state of Europe as well as the passage of a law in 1790 permitting Catholics to act as guardians possibly made Preston more amenable.

The details of the agreement are not entirely clear, but it appears that Carhampton agreed to place little Jenico in the care of John Preston, as the 11th viscount had intended. Nonetheless, the child's mother was to have access to him. Lady Gormanston promptly wrote to Jenico with promises of an amusing evening at the Castle with the viceroy.[40] (Given Westmorland's gelid personality, this prospect seems rather dismal.) Her letter had all the pathetic desperation of a woman trying, without much hope, to overcome years of alienation and separation. Nothing came of her attempt, if such it was, to dazzle Jenico with the great Protestant world of power and fashion. Indeed, Jenico seems to have had no further contact with her whatsoever.[41] The long separation may have accounted for their continued alienation, or his uncle's constant warnings about Lady Gormanston's Protestant wiles. Possibly the son may have developed a dislike for his mother for the same reasons that had so alienated and embittered his father. In spite of the ordeal of his childhood, Jenico survived to a ripe old age, dying in 1860 at the age of 85.[42]

FitzGibbon's precise role in the peaceful resolution of the Gormanston case can only be conjectured. But it would appear that he succumbed to moderation. By this time he had been elevated to the office of Lord Chancellor and in his capacity as the guardian of widows and orphans, he at least acquiesced in Carhampton's sensible proposal. There were other, often startling, manifestations of benevolence and calm. During the debates on the guardianship bill, FitzGibbon implied that he had always been more concerned with little Jenico's political principles, not his religion.[43] Considering his past bloodcurdling, not to say defamatory, suggestions about the elder Jenico Preston, FitzGibbon's remarks constituted an astounding feat of amnesia. But it was a lapse of truth in the right direction. At least he had retreated from his insistence that a British and constitutional education necessarily entailed Protestant indoctrination. Moreover, great cordiality marked his later contacts with young Jenico and with his Irish guardian, John Preston. During a chance meeting with John Preston at Bath in 1800, FitzGibbon, apparently no longer troubled by the legal doubts of 1786, gave an encouraging report of the progress of the outlawry case.[44] In that same year, when Jenico appeared in the House of Lords to hear the decree reversing his outlawry, FitzGibbon treated him with great kindness and attention.[45]

Jenico Preston the elder offered the simplest and most plausible explanation for FitzGibbon's change of heart: he wanted to make amends for his past behavior.[46] FitzGibbon rarely admitted a mistake, and he certainly did not do so in this case. But he may have entertained the possibility, however briefly, that his intransigence had delayed a sensible resolution of the case. The French Revolution, with its alluring promises of equality, and the re-awakening of the Catholic political demands both in England and in Ireland also may have influenced FitzGibbon. He was an extraordinarily prescient man, and he may well have sensed that he would soon be facing more troublesome Catholic issues than the guardianship of little Jenico Preston.

Nonetheless, FitzGibbon's conciliatoriness did not extend to one member of the Preston family, namely, Jenico Preston the elder. He was on the contrary furiously vindictive; while conceding the principle of the guardianship bill, he insisted on including a special provision penalizing those relations who spirited children abroad. Under the provisions of this clause the estates of such children would be transferred to the custody of the court of Chancery.[47] The aim of this particular provision was blatant, as those two otherwise disparate characters Carhampton and Curran pointed out.[48] Ironically, the elder Jenico, having carried his point, developed a certain respect for FitzGibbon's character. Indeed they had a great deal in common, notably sectarian ruthlessness and reactionary politics. Preston's comments on the new Catholic leadership of the 1790s echo FitzGibbon's.[49] But he did not trust to a similar change of heart on FitzGibbon's part. When the invading French armies forced him to leave Liege, he prudently settled in Wales.[50]

II

Although his office gave FitzGibbon an outlet for his vast energy, a variety of challenges for his formidable legal skills, and numerous opportunities to satisfy his appetite for power and domination, he inevitably looked for advancement. In May of 1786, Earlsfort, the chief justice of the Common Pleas, had fallen ill, and FitzGibbon had discreetly raised the possibility of succeeding him. Rutland acknowledged the justice of the claim, but he had more exciting plans for his adored favorite. Lord Chancellor Lifford was languidly anticipating his retirement and FitzGibbon was to be his successor.[51] Rutland not only hoped to reward a good and faithful servant, he regarded FitzGibbon as the linchpin of a personal political interest which he planned to create in Ireland:

> For the interest of my Government, his succession is essential, and in truth, I am anxious to establish a powerful and permanent interest in this country which may serve me even when I quit the Government; and this can only be done by attaching with essential favors and by bringing into the most important offices the best abilities and the most powerful connexions in the country.[52]

Orde recognized FitzGibbon as an "honorable and steady friend", but chracteristically, he took a more cautious view of Rutland's scheme.[53] Taking note of the standard prejudice in favor of an Englishman, he suggested playing for time to create a more favorable atmosphere for FitzGibbon's claims. He proposed Lifford's retirement and the succession of Eyre, the Chief Baron of the English Exchequer Court for a term of six or seven years.[54] By then the English government's objections to FitzGibbon's unfortunate nationality would presumably have abated. Rutland responded to any suggestion of an English locum tenens with true ducal peremptoriness:

> I do not think it would be fair or equitable to consent to an arrangement in the first law department merely to accommodate English convenience ... Indeed I could not with satisfaction see FitzGibbon's pretensions even postponed. I love the man. He has stood by me and I must stand by him. This opinion is final.[55]

Rutland's dreams of an Irish chancellor and an Irish interest in the person of

FitzGibbon came to nothing. Lifford remained obstinately healthy and in place, while Rutland sickened and died the following year.

As for the object of all this anxious speculation, FitzGibbon probably needed no prompting from either Rutland or Orde to aspire to the Seals of Ireland. Given his consuming ambition, he may have considered the possibility from the moment he assumed his place as attorney general. Earlsfort's office was to serve mainly as a stage in his progression. He may even have raised the subject to discover what alternative plans, if any, Rutland and Orde had for his advancement. If the latter assessment of his motives is correct, Rutland certainly exceeded his most daring and cherished expectations.

FitzGibbon's headlong pursuit of the Seals did not take place exclusively in the public realm of the Castle, the Parliament and the Courts. It even touched on his private life. Political considerations seem to have played a prominent role in his marriage to Anne Whalley in 1786. That same year FitzGibbon had first broached the subject of succeeding Lifford. In spite of his general favor, Orde expressed some concern about FitzGibbon's private life, as well as his nationality:

> I am very glad to hear of FitzGibbon's disposition to marry and to withdraw himself by degrees from the society of young men, which has indeed been hardly consistent with his public situation, and certainly created prejudices against him which the vigor and zeal of his conduct toward government could scarce efface.

Orde, of course, did not mean to suggest any homoerotic tendencies. The fate of William Beckford and worse would certainly have befallen FitzGibbon had there been even the slightest hint of such proclivities. He was a far more public and far more hated figure than the unfortunate Beckford. Orde presumably meant that FitzGibbon associated with young men because he indulged in the favored pastimes of young men: drinking, womanizing and rough sporting events. His conduct must have been appalling indeed if the chief secretary of the Duke of Rutland took exception to it. Orde had a point. The behavior of a young buck about town hardly became a thirty-eight year old man who served as attorney general and who aspired to the lofty post of Lord Chancellor. FitzGibbon took the hint and duly married to save his reputation.

In choosing Miss Whalley, FitzGibbon again displayed his finely honed instincts for social and political advancement. She came from a staunchly Protestant family. Her father, who died when she was a very small child, had earned himself the sobriquet "Burn Chapel Whalley" for his virulent anti-Catholicism. She was also very beautiful, no doubt a highly important consideration to a man of gallantry embarking on a life of married chastity. Above all, she had exquisite taste in clothes and she knew how to cut an elegant figure at social gatherings, an equally important consideration to an ambitious man who made great use of entertaining to promote himself. FitzGibbon would have had no use for less fashionable, but intellectually superior women like Maria Edgeworth.

The radical press quickly caught on to the direction that FitzGibbon's ambition was taking. One of his journalistic nemeses, the *Dublin Evening Post*, saw a connection between his friendly cooperation with the English cabinet over the new Navigation Act and his ambition:

> Had the Rutland Administration lived to see the retirement of the Chancellor, little doubt exists as to the gentleman who would be named his successor. It was long the darling object of Mr F's honest ambition; and so unconditional a return did his unconditional service to that Administration demand that it was morally impossible he should experience a refusal of anything – even of the Chancellorship. – Some go so far as to assert that he made it a condition for passing the partial construction of the Navigation Act through the House of Commons – a measure which may be of much injury to this country, tho' assented to for the mere purpose of pleasing British merchants and confirming British monopoly.[56]

Yet another paragraph in the *Dublin Evening Post* in October of 1788 made the same connection between FitzGibbon's judicial aspirations and the Irish version of the Navigation Act: "... it was his engaging to pass the partial construction of the navigation act that induced the late Duke of Rutland to enter into a solemn promise, at the instance of the British minister, to bestow the place on him".[57] The claim was revived in the contentious year 1795, again by the *Dublin Evening Post*. The enormities attributed to FitzGibbon included "... the curious construction of the Navigation act, by which Ireland conceded a point of the last importance to Great Britain, for the mighty equivalent of appointing a native to high official situation".[58]

This tale of a quid pro quo is pure legend, and like most legends, it combined elements of truth with elements of flagrant absurdity. In the first place, the Navigation Act was not exclusively the malign brainchild of FitzGibbon. Hawkesbury acknowledged the equal assistance of Sir John Parnell and John Beresford in his letter of thanks. Secondly, as noted earlier, the passage of an Irish navigation act simply confirmed an existing colonial maritime system. FitzGibbon had no power to eliminate restrictions on colonial trade and particularly not in the context of Hawkesbury's act, which was mainly concerned with ship registrations. Finally, while FitzGibbon's steady service to the English interest had won him many friends, he was scarcely in a position to bargain for the Seals of Ireland. He was, at this point, still a subordinate, albeit a trusted and respected subordinate. Certainly Rutland and Orde favored his promotion. But their influence, however powerful, could not guarantee FitzGibbon's promotion. FitzGibbon himself knew as much, as evinced by his shrewd cultivation of Hawkesbury and by his trip to England in the spring of 1788. His new bride's health and recreation served as the pretext, but in between jaunts to Tunbridge and Brighton, he called on both Thurlow and Pitt to press his claims. Both were non-committal, particularly Pitt, who never seems to have warmed to FitzGibbon.[59] (The reasons for Pitt's coldness, even at this early stage in their relationship, are unclear. Pitt may have recognized and mistrusted FitzGibbon's evident ambition, or he may have recoiled from the effusive and sometimes fawning manner which his devoted servant in Ireland displayed toward his English superiors.) FitzGibbon, in short, was utterly dependent on the good pleasure of the English government, and *pace* the *Dublin Evening Post*, that good pleasure was by no means unanimous or certain.

9

The Regency Crisis

I

Rutland's successor, the Marquis of Buckingham, probably did the most to obtain for FitzGibbon his "darling wish". Ironically, in the initial stages of their relationship, Buckingham looked upon FitzGibbon and his claims to the seals with considerable hostility. The fault did not lie with FitzGibbon, who remained as dutiful, compliant and diligent as ever, but with Buckingham. His singularly difficult personality combined peevishness, suspiciousness and oversensitivity. In his characteristically prolix and querulous fashion, Buckingham blamed both Rutland and Orde for giving FitzGibbon notions about the Irish seals. He complained that FitzGibbon initially would have been satisfied with a more modest legal promotion, but the outrageous flattery of his predecessor and his predecessor's chief secretary created expectations which were now awkward if not dangerous to slight:

> ... notwithstanding his [FitzGibbon's] strength in this kingdom, I think that he might have been resisted originally, and might have been flattered and perhaps gratified elsewhere, but you remember the manner in which Orde stated his claim and the very strong encouragement which had been given to him by the Duke of Rutland ... and even in the course of the first conversation with him, I was convinced that Orde had stated this encouragement short of the fact. By subsequent conversations with him I am certain of the fact, and it was even originally proposed to him as his object by Orde ... you will find Fitzherbert [Buckingham's chief secretary] equally impressed with me with the idea of the strength with which he will be able to urge his claim whenever the vacancy occurs. His intrepidity, his influence and weight have, in fact, placed him at the head of the country. We all fear him.[1]

In short, FitzGibbon while at present an able and faithful servant of government could, if disappointed become a formidable antagonist. Buckingham could only hope that the aging and ailing Lord Lifford would somehow endure in office and when he did retire or die, a suitable English candidate would be available to take his place. He maintained the same stand when FitzGibbon went to England in 1788 to sound out Pitt and Thurlow. Buckingham said and did nothing to discourage FitzGibbon and he advised Pitt to do the same.[2] Meanwhile, he anxiously watched Lifford for any signs of flagging health.

Buckingham had to admit that FitzGibbon did not display any undue presumption:

> All the engagement to which he pressed me was and is, that if it was judged advisable to give the seals to an Irishman, he might be the man. To this I had no difficulty of acceding and there stands my engagement.[3]

FitzGibbon knew better than to trust to a late lord-lieutenant's enthusiastic schemes and to the incumbent's highly qualified "engagement": hence the travels to England with his smart new wife in tow.

At the same time that he was expressing his fear of FitzGibbon, Buckingham was forced to acknowledge his loyalty and steadiness:

> To this I must add my conviction that he is firmly attached to Great Britain and to the King's prerogative as opposed to the frenzy of Irish republicanism.[4]

FitzGibbon's performance during the parliamentary session of 1788 convinced even him of the attorney-general's fundamental soundness. That session consisted mainly of desultory re-enactments of past battles between government and opposition. Some sparks flew at the opening, when Lawrence Parsons, an aspiring Parliamentary firebrand, took exception to that part of the speech from the throne expressing grief at Rutland's untimely death. Parsons expressed himself as ready as anyone to pay tribute to Rutland's amiable personal qualities, but the corruption of his administration required acknowledgment and suitable retrenchment.[5] According to Buckingham, some talk circulated of a *duel à la Curran* between FitzGibbon and Parsons.[6] Nothing came of these rumors, as FitzGibbon remained satisfied with parliamentary expressions of contempt.[7] The session then settled into a steady succession of opposition proposals for reforming the bad old government, and bad old government's defeats of those same proposals.

As has been discussed more fully elsewhere, FitzGibbon handily deflated Grattan's extensive plans for tithe reform. In addition, FitzGibbon lent his support to yet another extensive bill for indemnifying the clergy, though he acknowledged that any lingering disturbances were confined to Cork.[8] All the while he expressed his love and tenderness for the peasantry of southern Ireland.[9]

The police act prompted yet another flurry of opposition activity. A protest against police corruption presented by the citizens of Dublin provoked one of FitzGibbon's rare (and characteristically sadistic) flashes of wit. The chairman of this particular petition initiative happened to be a ropemaker. FitzGibbon remarked that he "could not be perfectly disinterested", meaning that a repeal of the police act could only increase capital crimes and in consequence the ropemaker's business.[10] Notwithstanding, FitzGibbon had to admit to flaws in his statutory creation. Since the government was prepared to amend the act, the petition was superfluous:

> It was admitted by all that the Police Act wanted amendment. A bill was now brought in to explain and amend the act. Did the petitioners mean to petition against the bill for amending the act of which they so much complained?[11]

The reform measure finally proposed by Marcus Beresford amounted to a minor administrative adjustment. Beresford proposed increasing the number on constables on foot by 100 and reducing the number of mounted constables from 40 to 20. The savings from the reduction of the mounted force was to pay for increase in the foot patrols.[12]

Beresford's inoffensive amendment passed, but it inevitably failed to satisfy those members of the opposition and the public who wanted the new police force abolished, not merely adjusted. A second attempt to obtain a hearing for the signatories of the petition prevailed. A succession of Dublin worthies then aired their complaints about the stupidity, rudeness and brutality of the police and called for the restoration of old parish patrols. In spite of these entertaining anecdotes, the government majorities held firm and rejected the petition. FitzGibbon appears to have been absent from this particular session. At least, he made no recorded comments or witticisms.[13]

Forbes' annual motion for a limitation on pensions and for the disenfranchisement of pension holders met with its annual lopsided defeat. Undeterred he proposed an address on the subject with the same dismal result.[14] FitzGibbon was similarly silent on this subject, but he probably would have offered his usual arguments in opposition: such measures were the product of self-interest and disappointment, and they arbitrarily deprived otherwise qualified gentlemen of the right to serve in Parliament.

FitzGibbon had an inevitable hand in some minor legal reforms . He introduced a bill allowing the lord chancellor or his representatives to issue writs of appeal in the Archbishop's court.[15] This abstruse measure inspired no debates and probably little interest in the average county member. His attention and criticism also descended to the more mundane area of penology. Some of the clauses in Richard Griffith's bill to reform the New Prison, FitzGibbon believed, had the effect of punishing the jailers of the prison through an *ex post facto* parliamentary statute. He made no excuses for the abuses and corruption of the jailers, but even they should not suffer such a manifest injustice. In marked contrast to their later encounters, Griffith civilly acknowledged FitzGibbon's point and withdrew the bill for amendment.[16]

A tobacco bill gave FitzGibbon a pretext to vent once again his abiding contempt for Presbyterians and Americans. Some Northern members had hoped to preserve Derry's privileges to import tobacco. The city's services to the Protestant cause a century earlier constituted its main claim to consideration. In return for closing its gates against King James in 1689, Derry deserved to retain the right of admitting tobacco to its wharves. This sentimental appeal to the glorious past failed to move FitzGibbon. Whatever their past Protestant merits, the people of Derry were currently shameless cheats working in profitable cahoots with American smugglers:

> I am astonished to see the people of Derry have the presumption to desire to be included in the bill. Sir, it is notorious to everyone that not above nine hogsheads of tobacco have paid duty in the port of Derry last year; and it is notorious that twelve hundred have been smuggled. Perhaps gentlemen do not know the manner this is carried on. I will tell them. An American ship appears on the coast. Immediately boats go off to her laden with money by way of ballast —they bring in their cargoes of tobacco, which are paid for in hard guineas, every one of which are carried to America. Nay, so much do they hold the house in derision, that they have named the creek where this is chiefly carried on Beresford Creek.[17]

Mr Stewart assured the house that the inhabitants of Donegal and not Derry were guilty of this particular practice.[18] Notwithstanding his special pleading the other members, convinced or offended by FitzGibbon's version of events, voted to excluded Derry, in spite of its past stand against "tyranny and despotism".

The otherwise dull session of 1788 did feature the novelty of FitzGibbon opposing a government measure: Sir John Parnell's proposal to pay off the entire funded debt and float a new loan at a lower interest rate. Parnell argued that current higher rates encouraged those with money to place the greater part of their assets in government securities, thus depriving the commercial markets of much need funds. Lowering interest rates would discourage this practice and encourage investors, large and small, to put more of their assets in trade and other commercial ventures. In addition, the £98,000 that the government would pay out to liquidate the current debt would increase the supply of money for investment in the economy at large. The majority of the House favorably received the bill, but FitzGibbon questioned Parnell's premise that expanding commercial markets necessarily went hand in hand with lower interest rates. He argued that as trade and commerce expanded, the demand for money increased, and the market naturally drove up interest rates, in spite of the government's efforts to contrary:

> ... the more open and extended our trade is, the more money will it require to carry it on and consequently the more will the price ... of that money be raised; for otherwise it would differ from every commodity we know.[20]

Moreover, the lower rates of interest resulted not from the natural forces of the economy, but from artificial adjustments in the government's accounts. According to Parnell's plan, the government was to contract with lenders to discount the interest. The lenders in turn would make up the difference from the proceeds of two lotteries.[21] FitzGibbon objected to the plan above all because it undermined the central tenet of his political creed, Ireland's absolute dependence, financial and political, on England. Parnell's proposal, however well intentioned, threatened essential English investment in Ireland. Ireland had such a bad reputation for political and legal chaos that only the inducement of high interest rates could overcome English reluctance:

> There are many circumstances against this country which in the minds of English lenders are scarcely balanced by the one percent by which our interest exceeds theirs. Any opinion has gone abroad, I hope ill-founded, that in disputes of property, justice is not always done, that men presume to expound the law, who are utterly unacquainted with the practice of courts of justice, and who do not even understand the first principles of law or equity; that suits are not decided according to the merit of the question, but according to the merit of the parties; therefore, until this opinion is done away, we must pay the additional one percent, or Englishmen would not lend at all at the risk of law, the risk of exchange and the certain expense of agency. England gives one percent to Holland beyond the rate of interest in that country, and you, if you wish to see your trade increase, must give one to England.[22]

This argument irritated Foster, who joined with the majority in seeing great promise in Parnell's measure:

> It has been said the England keeps up her interest to five percent in order to get money for her merchants and manufacturers from Holland. This is the first time that ever I heard that England, in a state of prosperity, borrows for her traders. The English trade upon English capitals, and the country receives the full advantage. Is it wise then of us to forgo a general national benefit for the speculation of trading on British money? Surely no. That country is in a wretched state, whose trade depends on foreign capital which in a moment of convulsion or superior demand at home may all be drawn away ... Should we not rather endeavor to give this practice a quiet check, and promote a capital of our own amongst our merchants?[23]

This exchange foreshadowed the later division between Foster and FitzGibbon on the subject of the Union. FitzGibbon was prepared to accept even economic subordination to maintain the all-important political ties with England. Foster, the more knowledgeable in economic matters, saw more clearly the dangers of such subordination.

The government took no official stand, though Buckingham himself favored the measure. Consequently, FitzGibbon suffered no repercussions for his unaccustomed opposition. With supreme ingenuousness or ingenuity, he left Buckingham no reasonable pretext for criticism. He could scarcely take issue with FitzGibbon for showing more concern for the English moneyed interests than the English government in Ireland. Buckingham did express discontent at the policy of neutrality in general and in Fitzherbert's slack parliamentary management in particular:

> Neutrality on any question produces relaxation of discipline and Mr. Fitzherbert is a little too much inclined to slacken the reins.[24]

Nonetheless, Buckingham may have had the attorney general's rather embarrassing independence in mind when he expressed his intention to tighten discipline in the government ranks:

> ... all the rest of us are so much for a tight hand that I trust we shall open and go through the next campaign very well in that respect.[25]

FitzGibbon still knew how to submit to a clear directive from the government when required, as the case of Baron Hamilton showed. Orde's busy and imaginative anti-Catholic spy faced the prospect of a parliamentary inquiry and impeachment. While on circuit in Limerick, Hamilton had summarily dismissed the suit of a farmer by the name of David Fitzgerald, who was resisting an ejectment. According to Fitzgerald, he had been presenting evidence to support his case when Hamilton abruptly interrupted him and, citing a press of business, discharged the jurors. The fact that Baron Hamilton found the time to attend a civic banquet in Limerick later that evening aggravated Fitzgerald's resentment.[26] According the Buckingham, FitzGibbon was "(from provincial politics) violent upon the subject".[27] Provincial politics would have made FitzGibbon very violent indeed. In his petition, Fitzgerald emphasized that he was a Protestant, which meant that he had a vote to cast in the forthcoming election. FitzGibbon was in no position to ignore that fact. The Seals were uncertain, and he may have hoped, as a poor second best, to avenge his humiliating defeat in the Limerick county elections. But "provincial politics" cannot entirely account for FitzGibbon's being "violent on the subject". Among his many roles, he particularly favored that of champion and protector of the honest farmer. Hamilton's carelessness unquestionably offended FitzGibbon's passion for judicial efficiency as well.

Buckingham made no apologies for Hamilton: "His conduct has been grossly indefensible".[28] Nonetheless, he pressed for a deferral of Hamilton's case until the end of the Parliamentary session. However blameworthy Hamilton's conduct, "the remedy is worse than the disease", meaning the frenzy of a parliamentary impeachment, with members up for election outdoing each other to show their indignation against unjust judges and their devotion to voting Protestant farmers. FitzGibbon dutifully pursued the course Buckingham so obviously desired: a brief airing of Fitzgerald's complaint followed by a dismissal. He maintained that Baron Hamilton had indeed erred, but he had done so with good intention. According to Hamilton, Fitzgerald's evidence was both extensive and involved. At the time, he had not believed that he could do justice to the case and to accomplish a general gaol delivery, which was also pending.[29] FitzGibbon pressed parliament to accept Hamilton's plea and his apologies for his error. Although he had acted illegally in discharging the jury without the consent of the parties, "... it was an error in judgment, an error arising from a good motive, a wish to discharge the gaol; and it is not attempted to be justified, and as upon reflection, the learned judge had altered his opinion, I wish to have the matter buried in oblivion".[30] FitzGibbon's fellow members duly dismissed the inquiry against the Baron, and thus averted what Buckingham had most dreaded: "a great inclination to ape England in the article of impeachment".[31]

Buckingham drew extensively on FitzGibbon's legal expertise outside of Parliament, especially during deliberations on an Irish office for his brother, William Wyndham Grenville-Buckingham initially hoped to provide Grenville with the office of Master of the Rolls. This office was a particularly lucrative plum. In addition to receiving a handsome salary, the holder of this office could dispose of six subordinate positions worth up to £20,000.[32] FitzGibbon, as well as Earlsfort and the embattled Baron Hamilton, were called upon to sort out the legal complications surrounding the proposed grant to Grenville. Buckingham brooded endlessly over whether Grenville would enjoy more security of tenure if he held his office for life or during pleasure. Grenville himself had scruples about selling the offices attached to the mastership of the rolls and about holding the position as a non-resident. The Duke of Leinster's interest in the Rolls further muddied the situation. Buckingham gave him a suitably evasive answer and continued his desultory and excruciatingly tedious correspondence with Grenville on the subject.[33] His letters revealed all his more unappealing qualities of indecisiveness, oversensitivity and suspiciousness. Finally, after expending much time and much paper, he came to the conclusion that the business entailed too much political and legal trouble. According to statute and tradition, the mastership could only be held during pleasure. Consequently, he could not legally offer Grenville the security of a lifetime tenure. Grenville's persistent refusal to sell off the subordinate offices, in spite of reassurances of the perfect legality of this practice, substantially reduced its value. Above all, Buckingham recoiled from the unpopularity which the proposed grant had quickly inspired.[34] With many petulant expressions of disappointment, Buckingham resigned himself to offering his brother a mere reversion to the Lord Clanbrassil's office as Chief Remembrancer.[35] The less fastidious Leinster received the office after all. Buckingham reported that he was "delighted with his Rolls".[36]

FitzGibbon's involvement in this matter earned him another of those sporadic and startling accolades from his nemesis, the *Dublin Evening Post*. That journal claimed that FitzGibbon had transcended his habits of pliant corruption and had opposed Grenville's appointment:

> A report was current through town ... that a law officer of eminence had absolutely refused to sign his name to the fiat granting the place of Master of the Rolls for life to the Right Honorable Mr. Wyndham Grenville. No persuasion or entreaty was powerful enough to induce him to assist in a matter which he conceived of as unjust and improper ... and we think that Mr. F. is certainly entitled to the approbation of his countrymen for this act of integrity and independence.[37]

This accolade, like much of the *Dublin Evening Post's* criticism, was quite undeserved. Far from raising objections to Grenville's appointment, FitzGibbon went to work with a will on the wording of the patent. Nor did he make any recorded dissent from the opinion of Earlsfort and Hamilton that Grenville could sell subordinate offices. FitzGibbon did make the stipulation that Grenville could only hold the office at pleasure, but he spoke as a lawyer and not as an opponent of corruption. The politically pliant Lifford had expressed the same opinion. Nonetheless, in an especially peevish letter to Grenville, Buckingham implied that political interest as much as statutory precedent had dictated the opinion of "these legal authorities", meaning FitzGibbon and the Chancellor:

> you will see the difficulty of thinking of a grant for life in the teeth of the opinions of FitzGibbon and the Chancellor. I do not know how far the indecision which has produced this delay...has not brought forward this reluctance from these legal authorities; but you have seen too much not to know that the defense of such a grant must lose ground every hour it is attacked and that no one defends it for fear of committing unnecessarily his name and character. [38]

In making these accusations Buckingham willfully seems to have forgotten FitzGibbon's opposition to any efforts to curb the government's powers to grant pensions and offices, including the recent imbroglio with Parsons. Moreover, FitzGibbon had repeatedly sacrificed personal popularity to serve the political interests of government. The case of Baron Hamilton could have reassured Buckingham on this point, had he cared to recall it. As for his complaints of delay, the greatest share of blame lay with Buckingham's own crabbed wool-gathering on the subject . But Buckingham was too disappointed and too peevish in his disappointment to do FitzGibbon justice. Possibly this tacit and unfair perception that FitzGibbon had let him down contributed to Buckingham's reluctance to consider him for the seals.

In other matters of government business the two worked together in reasonable harmony. Buckingham concurred in FitzGibbon's proposal to give the attorney generals of England and of Ireland the power to sue in either kingdom for the recovery of royal debts. Commonly, dishonest or defalcating office holders from Ireland took refuge in England without impunity, while English miscreants used Ireland as a safe haven. With italicized indignation, Buckingham complained that Pepper Arden had "never answered" a proposal for mutual jurisdiction which FitzGibbon had sent to him in December of 1787.[39]

The demands of government business did not prevent FitzGibbon from sharing the general interest in Warren Hastings' impeachment. He seems to have looked upon the whole business as Whig troublemaking at the former governor's expense. According to Buckingham, he flirted with the idea of offering his services as counsel to Warren Hastings.[40] A legal and political duel between FitzGibbon and his kinsman Burke would unquestionably have added yet another element of melodrama to the flamboyant theatrics at Westminster. FitzGibbon soon abandoned the idea, no doubt out of the conviction that he could not do justice both to his duties and to Hastings' defense.

Notwithstanding the affronts and disappointments which he had experienced, Buckingham took an optimistic view of his position at the close of his first parliamentary session. He had unavoidably hurt some jobbers' feelings, and he could always expect the opposition to take advantage of this and of every other opening to make trouble. Yet he felt his government could easily withstand any attacks prompted by disappointment and by habitual opposition:

> In this country I meet with much discontent at the refusal of jobs, which will inevitably brew upon the opposition, but I still think it will not be very serious. I am, however, obliged to be much upon my guard.[41]

Buckingham's personal secretary, Bernard took the same view of the government's strength:

> We are very quiet, but are told by all the little men that the great men hate us, and are threatened with much opposition next winter; which we shall have but it cannot be to a degree which will be material or which has not been foreseen from the first.[42]

II

In November the unforeseen descended on Buckingham's government in the guise of the King's illness. His incapacity instantly shattered the political calm which Buckingham and Bernard had so confidently reported. The question of the rights and powers of the King's singularly unfilial son, the Prince of Wales, ignited conflict first in England, then in Ireland.

In keeping with the unfortunate Hanoverian tradition, the Prince had made the opposition party his own. Fox in particular was a boon companion. Common habits of profligacy far more than common political principles united the two. The Prince was interested in politics only to the extent that he could get money for his exponentially increasing expenses. The fact that his father detested Fox and refused to admit him to any government provided a still more compelling reason for the Prince's allegiance.

The King's sudden incapacity, physical and mental, offered Fox and the Whigs an irresistible opportunity. Their friend and patron was the logical choice as regent. The serious, indeed desperate, condition of the King boded either a very long regency or the Prince's accession to the throne. Either way the Whigs stood to gain the office and the power that had so humiliatingly eluded them since 1784.

Pitt's consummate nerve and parliamentary skill, aided in great measure by the limitless Whig capacity for self-destruction, quickly dashed these bright hopes. Pitt naturally pressed for limitations on the Prince's powers, especially the powers of patronage. The Whigs, under the rhetorical lead of Fox and Burke responded with the claim that the Prince, by virtue of his position as heir to the throne had an "inherent" right to exercise full regal powers while acting as regent. In making this claim, the Whigs were venturing on very uncertain constitutional and political ground. As J.W. Derry has pointed out in his excellent study of the Regency crisis, a long tradition existed of parliament placing restrictions on regents.[43] Moreover, the English political world witnessed the curious spectacle of the "Man of the People", Fox, championing the prerogatives of the monarchy (or at least its princely branch) and William Pitt, the ministerialist, defending the rights of the people's representatives in Parliament. The incongruity, not to mention the transparent self-interest of the Whig arguments, badly damaged the party. Pitt succeeded in obtaining restrictions on the powers of the regent, and the King's recovery soon afterwards rendered even these limited powers unnecessary.

Meanwhile, Buckingham was attempting to address the Irish implications of the crisis, in his usual fretful and obsessive fashion. Upon receiving word of the King's incapacity, he immediately assumed that Pitt's government would fall and that the Prince's new Whig government would request his resignation. Curiously, FitzGibbon, not a man prone to fits of optimism, initially believed that the Prince would retain both Pitt and Fox in coalition. While his wife had been going on excursions in the royal landau, FitzGibbon had cultivated a contact in the Prince's household, one Anthony St Leger. At that time, St Leger had assured FitzGibbon that the Pitt had risen in the Prince's estimation. The Prince's supposed gratitude to Pitt for paying off one batch of his debts and Mrs Fitzherbert's displeasure with Fox's parliamentary denials of her marriage formed the basis for this claim.[44] FitzGibbon in turn repeated this backstairs *on dit* to Buckingham. He was not reassured: "I own I do not think a coalition can take place."[45] Doubts that Fox would agree to such an arrangement inclined him toward pessimism.

Having resigned himself to the certainly of his own recall, Buckingham struggled with the legal riddle of what powers he could legitimately exercise in the interim. FitzGibbon, along with the other government legal authorities, Lifford, Earlsfort and the rehabilitated Hamilton, were subjected to another barrage of inquiries. Could he legitimately summon Parliament, and if need be prorogue or dissolve it? Buckingham received assurances that he could indeed do so:

> I am advised by Lord Earlsfort and the Attorney General that the incapacity of the King does not attach on my commission so as to vitiate any of the powers entrusted to me.[46]

Buckingham was as fretfully preoccupied with the question of royal assent to legislation. In addition to addressing the question of the regency, the Irish parliament urgently needed to renew the mutiny and money acts, which were due to expire on 25 March. How could this legislation receive the required royal assent during the King's indisposition? Buckingham found the solution to this particular dilemma in

Yelverton's act of 1782, which had established the legislative groundwork for the new constitutional arrangements between England and Ireland. According to Yelverton's act, the application of the great seal of England signified the royal assent to legislation. Therefore, Buckingham could, in the normal course of legislation, transmit legislation to whoever had custody of the great seal of England during the King's illness. Again, "our lawyers", including FitzGibbon, assured Buckingham that Yelverton's Act did indeed offer a solution to the question of the enacting power:

> ... they did not hesitate one moment in declaring that there was a complete and perfect enacting power in Great Britain, from the moment that the Great Seal could be put, in his majesty's name and behalf, to a commission authorizing me to give the Royal Assent to the Bill, to which such commission was to be attached.[47]

Buckingham's solution was not airtight. It left open the possibility that the Prince's new government would refuse assent to a bill limiting his power. This particular dilemma seems to have escaped Buckingham's attention, in spite of his habit of creating complication, then brooding over it. The simple knowledge that the basic forms of government could continue to function for once reassured him.

In addition, Buckingham endlessly rehearsed with FitzGibbon and his colleagues the circumstances under which he would surrender his commission as lord-lieutenant. He was determined to retain his powers until the money, the mutiny and the Irish regency bills had passed safely through Parliament. This intention of presenting his successor with a legislative *fait accompli* raised the vexed question of how, if at all, the new government could compel him to surrender power. FitzGibbon suggested that a commission, "*not reciting the Regency*, but authenticated by the King's greeting, teste and seal in the usual form might revoke my commission and might be universally admitted".[48] Nonetheless, FitzGibbon admitted to uncertainty on this point and proposed further consultation.

The resignation question never did get resolved to Buckingham's satisfaction. Indeed, he expressed profound discontent with the quality of advice that he received from FitzGibbon and from his other Irish advisors. In one of his earliest letters in response to the crisis, Buckingham complained "... you would be astonished at the difficulties which I have found in the want of information in either of the three, Lord Earlsfort, FitzGibbon, and Foster whom I have consulted".[49] When FitzGibbon proved unable to satisfy him on the question of his resignation, he requested Grenville to send him "a little of Lord Thurlow's and Lord Kenyon's law if you could get it for me".[50] Given the extraordinary nature of the crisis, Buckingham's expectation of immediate and clear answers was characteristically graceless and unreasonable. His habit of raising the same questions over and over again further complicated the work of FitzGibbon and his colleagues. FitzGibbon himself displayed the extraordinary self-mastery dictated by his ambition, by his deference to any and all English authority, and perhaps by his sense of the gravity of the occasion. He met Buckingham's fits of nerve and temper with unfailing patience. Buckingham himselfacknowledged FitzGibbon's steadiness, but he assigned it to the most narrow and partisan self-interest. FitzGibbon could expect nothing from the Prince's new government, as "his position was desperate with Mr Fox". He even suggested that FitzGibbon would throw in his lot with the new government if they offered him the seals.[52]

In the midst of his irritable tergiversations, Buckingham remained firm on the absolute necessity of passing a regency bill in Ireland. Toward this end, he constantly badgered his brother for details on the proposed English bill, which the Irish government needed for a model. The delay of this information maddened him. He dreaded equally the thought of opening Parliament without a suitable English bill in hand and the thought of continually proroguing it, thus threatening the timely enactment of the money and mutiny acts. In his characteristic melodramatic italics, he described his situation as "*hell*".[53]

Buckingham initially seemed to think that an Irish regency bill would be a popular measure. He emphasized to Grenville that the opposition would accept limitations on the Prince's powers only if their own Parliament imposed such limitations:

> I need only refer you to the restrictions now proposed, or to any of them, and I will ask how it is possible to enforce them here but by Irish laws? And how it would be possible to convince Mr Grattan that this is not a direct resumption of internal legislation if the restrictions under British law could be valid?[54]

Because he hoped to placate Irish national feelings with an Irish bill, Buckingham vehemently protested an evanescent proposal to settle the regency for both kingdoms by means of an English convention. Even FitzGibbon "would not for a moment support the legality of any Act, vote or measure of such a Convention as attaching on Ireland; nor the legality or propriety of naming Ireland in such a declaration".[55] Despite his fundamental contempt for the Irish Parliament, FitzGibbon of necessity respected an autonomy ratified by the laws of both countries. An English convention decreeing a regent for Ireland would grossly violate the constitutional arrangement of 1782, as well as provoke the agitation he so dreaded and detested. His colleagues Wolfe and Earlsfort took the same view.[56] This particular proposal for English interference came to nothing. English interference in the form of Anglo-Irish Whig intrigues proved more persistent and pernicious.

The English Whigs lost no time in proselytizing their opposition counterparts in Ireland. By 18 November, less than a week after Buckingham received official word of the King's incapacity, the premier Whig doctrine was circulating in Dublin. Buckingham reported:

> After all this detail, you will be surprised at an idea which is discussed here ... that no Bill and no provisions are necessary, for the Prince of Wales is *ipso facto* Regent with kingly power.[57]

It was, of course, readily embraced by "those who are most interested in seeing such an arrangement".[58] Buckingham also reported on the industrious circulation of rumor, and the consequent credulity and panic:

> I have traced to these quarters [the English opposition and their Irish allies] several assertions that the King has been insane several month that Mr Pitt concealed it, and would have kept it secret for the purpose of governing without control, and that all stories of lucid intervals are false, and only calculated to prevent the interference of Parliament; and that the limited Regency is part of the same system.[59]

Regular contacts between the English and the Irish opposition nurtured both faith in the Prince's inherent right and rumors of Mr Pitt's demonic villainy. The leading members of the Irish opposition made regular pilgrimages to England for inspiration and direction. Buckingham named Forbes in particular as one of the chief missionaries of English Whig doctrine.[60] Nonetheless, the other leading members of the Irish opposition were as well traveled and as well indoctrinated. On December 8, Buckingham wrote, "Grattan is to remain till the questions are over in England and Yelverton sails by the first mail. The former has (I hear) expressed himself in favor of a sole regent; the opinions of the latter are too well known to be whatever is suggested to him by the Duke of Portland."[61] Yelverton, it appeared, still clung to the old loyalties of his year of glory, 1782. These activities persisted until the opening of the Irish Parliament in February. On 5 February, Buckingham reported to Grenville that he did not as yet know the opposition plan of attack:

> ... they wait for the *Saint Esprit* which under the care of Messieurs Ogilvie, Forbes and *Pelham* was to be transmitted from Burlington House.[62]

The Irish opposition used the mails as adeptly. Within a week of the King's breakdown, W.B Ponsonby had established a system of intelligence as good, if not better, than that of the Castle.[63] In short, the opposition in England was skillfully playing a "back game". If the proposed limitations passed in England, the Irish Whigs would make up for the defeat by obtaining for the Prince and his friends an unlimited regency in Ireland.

Although he quickly dismissed Ponsonby as a confirmed troublemaker and opportunist, Buckingham initially hoped that other great magnates would remain firm for the government. In the case of the Duke of Leinster, Buckingham counted on his jealousy of Ponsonby.[64] Lord Ely had recently received the lavish patronage of the Post Office, which plum Buckingham hoped would secure his loyalties.[65] Lord Shannon was a more dubious prospect. Buckingham professed a "dread" of "his wife's influence".[66] Lady Shannon was a member of the treacherous Ponsonby clan. Moreover, Shannon himself had ties to the arch-Whig Duke of Devonshire. Apart from these pernicious family influences, he was a habitual trimmer, always ready to throw in his lot with the ascendant power:

> Lord Shannon is, *entre nous*, very much hampered by his persuasion that the King is irrecoverable, and told my informant (whom I can trust) that he owed his peerage to the Duke of Rutland and not to Mr Pitt and that his leaning was to the Duke of Devonshire and his friends.[67]

Buckingham made the best use he could of bribes and threats to keep the aristocracy in line:

> I have held out every possible intimidation which could be grounded upon the King's recovery and upon the reappointment of Mr Pitt and have even dropped the idea of my returning to Ireland with the determination of marking those who abandoned us.[68]

These threats and promises could not prevail against the uncertain prospects of the government during the King's illness, the lavish promises of the English Whigs, and above all, "the general system of treachery and venality which has pervaded this Government and has taught them an absolute disavowal of principle or political opinion".[69] Unfortunately, most members of the Irish parliament, even pensioners and placeholders, chose their loyalties according to the precepts of Lord Shannon: they followed whoever was in power and whoever could reward them. Since the majority of the Irish governing class expected a change in ministry, they forgot past obligations and abandoned Buckingham in favor of the apparent rising power, the Prince and the English Whigs.

The Irish disease of self-interest and treachery affected even hitherto reliable government stalwarts, notably Lord Earlsfort. He made threats of abandoning Buckingham unless his price was met: "an office of £800 in exchange for one of £500".[70] Fearful of the demoralizing example Earlsfort's desertion would set, Buckingham gave in.[71]

Worse was to follow. On 25 January 1789, Buckingham reported the defections not only of the doubtful Shannon, but of the lavishly flattered and remunerated Leinster and Ely. Their conduct was as unexpected as it was outrageous:

> I will not give you the low names and histories of obscure individuals, but I will name you the Duke of Leinster, whose declarations to Fitzherbert (whom I sent to Carton a fortnight since on purpose) were direct and explicit to the support of the restrictions. These declarations were repeated on Saturday the 17th to a person I employed to sound him on the report of his wavering, and were repeated in terms of the strongest regard to me, he not knowing that the person was so employed by me; and on Tuesday morning, he declared that if the House had not met, he would move the address to the Prince of Wales. On Wednesday, I directed Fitzherbert to see him again; he shuffled an excuse of illness, so that it was not until Friday morning that he could summon resolution enough to see Fitzherbert, and to announce his intention of supporting his Royal Highness's wishes to the fullest extent. Lord Ely, on receiving the Post Office, made to me

> the most explicit professions, and still continues to assure me of them, but I have *certain intelligence* that he has promised his support to Ponsonby, and I doubt much whether he will not carry on the force of treachery to the last moment.[72]

In his understandable aggrievement, Buckingham attributed the actions of the great magnates, and indeed the whole opposition, to pure selfishness and cynicism. But in a sense that Buckingham could not understand, Ponsonby, Leinster, Shannon and the others were being true to an older tradition. The occasional office or title cast their way by a mistrustful government could not erase the memory that they had once had the management of Ireland. The crisis in royal government offered an opportunity to restore a perfectly agreeable and workable arrangement that had existed before the advent of Townshend. Moreover, many members of the Irish opposition, especially Grattan, had a genuine political vision, quite apart from the dictates of Mr Fox or the coterie at Burlington House. Grattan and his followers interpreted the events of 1782 to mean that the Irish parliament had complete autonomy on questions, from trade to the disposition of the regency.[73] They saw policies like the Commercial Propositions and a limited regency, not as measures for strengthening necessary ties with England, but as corrupt attempts to undermine the "Constitution of 1782". Irish loyalty could be trusted without such legislative encroachments.

From the start of his administration, Buckingham had looked upon the opposition as little better than republicans. If they and their mad ideas prevailed, all royal authority, and with it, the connection between England and Ireland would collapse. In the face of epidemic treachery in the government ranks and the contagion of "republican" ideas, he made what efforts he could to promote the government's position. At his direction, FitzGibbon and Wolfe drew up a paper putting forth the claim, that under Yelverton's Act, the government had the plenitude of power to summon parliament and to enact laws, including, by implication, a limited regency. This paper was to "fall into the enemies' hands"; the "enemies", presumably, were those members of the opposition claiming that the King's incapacity rendered all government null, until the Prince of Wales assumed an unlimited regency. In a final effort to make the idea of a limited regency palatable, Buckingham recommended an idea for a constitutional change originally suggested by Beresford. According to this plan, the King's letters for money (or the letters of the King's representative as determined by a regency bill) would require the signature of "three out of seven officers to be named for that purpose". These officers included the Secretary of State, the Chief Secretary, and the chief officers of finance. According to Buckingham's reasoning, "The restriction could never operate against a good government, and it would reconcile the people here to the general idea of a limitation to the Regency, from the prospect it would hold out of enabling them to make this check perpetual."[74]

When neither the legal niceties of Yelverton's Act, nor the prospect of minor constitutional change deterred the opposition, Buckingham resorted to delaying tactics. With no English regency bill on the horizon, he reluctantly prorogued Parliament from 25 January to 5 February.[75] In the continued absence of the English bill, Buckingham submitted at last to the dreaded inevitable. As he himself stated the situation: "*Jacta est alea* and Parliament is opened".[76] Although he expressed faint hopes that the Irish opposition would not be so "wild", they appeared determined to offer the Prince an unrestricted Regency and to make this offer by the most precipitant means possible, an address. In defense of the government and of a limited regency bill, Buckingham could count only on a handful of supporters in either house. In the Commons, he had FitzGibbon, Parnell, Foster, Daly, Beresford, Wolfe, and his increasingly frail and failing chief secretary, Fitzherbert. Buckingham described his situation with his accustomed self-pity, but for once his feelings seem understandable:

> ... I do not complain, but I feel that everything I prophesied three months ago in my most gloomy moments is come to pass; and that all the affection of those for whom I suffer can hardly repay me a thousandth part of my misery.[77]

The session was indeed as grim as Buckingham expected. Every attempt by government to delay the address to the Prince by introducing the reports of the King's physicians or by calling for an immediate consideration of the money and the mutiny bills came to nothing. Grattan sounded the main opposition theme when the subject of the reports was introduced:

> Ireland waits not for a lesson from Britain nor for a model whereby to frame her proceedings.[78]

He showed some regard for parliamentary procedure in his willingness to consider the reports. But he was prepared to allow only the most cursory examination of this evidence:

> They ought to call for the evidence ... they ought to consider it, and if in a few days it should appear that his majesty was incapacitated, then it would be necessary for some resolutions to be proposed, to give life and animation to the executive government.[79]

Since the reports of the King's physicians ran to almost 800 pages, the "few days" which Grattan proposed were ludicrously inadequate. When Fitzherbert, in keeping with the government's policy of delay, proposed 16 February as the date for considering the documents, Grattan, adhering in equal measure to the opposition policy of haste, proposed the 11th.[80] The earlier date was carried.[81] Barnard later placed the blame squarely on the majority provided by the Shannon, Ponsonby, Ely and Leinster interests.[82] Parnell's proposal on the following day to consider the money bills met with a similar defeat. Grattan insisted that the issue of the King's health and the regency took precedence over any other business.[83] The majority, fortified again by the interests of the great magnates, agreed.

By 11 February, the majority of the House had lost any inclination to go through the motions of hearing the doctors' reports. When the clerk attempted to read the reports, the House, in the discreet words of the *Parliamentary Reports*, "became very inattentive and disorderly".[84] Peremptory and efficient as always, FitzGibbon soon tired of the charade and ordered it stopped: "... if gentlemen will not listen, I certainly will not insist upon the farce of reading."[85] Grattan immediately proceeded to the long-mediated purpose of the Irish opposition, the address to the Prince offering an unrestricted regency. While acknowledging the eventual necessity of a bill, Grattan insisted on establishing the executive by address first. The details could be legislated later. The bill, moreover, would simply confirm, *pro forma*, the offer of unrestricted royal power:

> His Royal Highness's acceptance of the Regency of this realm, at the influence and desire of the two Houses of the Irish Parliament, and further to declare and enact that he is and shall be Regent thereof during the continuation of His Majesty's present indisposition. The terms of the act are to describe the powers of the Regent and the Powers intended is [*sic*] the personal exercise of full regal authority and the reason why plenitude of regal power is intended by the address, and afterwards by the bill, is to be found in the nature of the prerogative; which was given, not for the sake of the King, but for the people, for whose use Kings and Regents and prerogatives were conceived. We know of no political reason why the prerogative in question should be destroyed or no personal reason why they should be suspended.[86]

With FitzGibbon as almost the sole exception, speaker after speaker rose to support the idea of a free, generous and immediate offer of full power through an address. The same overwhelming numbers approved the appointment of a committee to proceed with the business.[87]

Not even the arrival on the following day, 12 February, of the long awaited British resolutions on the Regency could stall the breakneck speed of the address's progress.[88] Thomas Conolly had already prepared the form of an address to the Prince, which he proposed submitting to the House of Lords that day.[89] He of course received leave to do so. By 18 February, the Lords finished their very perfunctory deliberations[90] and on the 19th the two Houses went in delegation to the Castle. There they presented Buckingham with their address:

> We therefore beg leave humbly to request that your Royal Highness will be pleased to take upon you the government of this realm during the continuation of His Majesty's present indisposition and no longer; and under the style and title of Prince Regent of Ireland, in the name and on behalf of his Majesty to exercise and administer, according to the laws and constitution of this kingdom, all regal powers, jurisdictions and prerogatives.[91]

Holding fast to his oft repeated intention, Buckingham refused to transmit the address. The first good news to come his way in over two months, the possibility of the King's recovery, had reached him the previous day and had fortified his own stubbornness and resentment.

The rumors of recovery and Buckingham's refusal only increased the bravado of the opposition. During the session on the following day, Grattan proposed entrusting the address to representatives of the Irish House of Commons.[92] Once he carried this proposal, he framed and offered for consideration a resolution asserting the right of the Irish Parliament to address the Prince:

> That in addressing his royal highness, the Prince of Wales, to take upon himself the government of this country on the behalf and in the name of his majesty, during his majesty's present indisposition and no longer, the lords and commons of Ireland have exercised an undoubted right and discharged an indispensable duty to which, in the present emergency, they alone are competent.[93]

Grattan's exercise in rhetorical indignation unmistakably implied that Buckingham had tyrannically interfered with the exercise of this "undoubted right". This resolution met with inevitable smooth sailing in the opposition dominated House. The same easy majorities settled on Conolly, W.B. Ponsonby, John O'Neil and James Stewart to carry the address to the Prince. In addition, the House of Lords sent a contingent in the persons of Leinster and Charlemont.[94]

Their mission ended in a humiliating anti-climax. The delegates from the Irish parliament arrived to find the King in full recovery and their address redundant. Buckingham lost no opportunity in inflicting further embarrassment on the delegation. Taking a leaf from the opposition, he purposely hurried the business of announcing the King's recovery and of receiving in return the grateful happy address of Parliament:

> The real object of this is to prevent the report of the embassy, with the Prince's answer (which is expected next tide) appearing in the Journals as a part of our Business. This I thought most essential in a constitutional view, and therefore ... I went down [to the House] having prepared all things, and seeing a manifest advantage in securing to the Irish Embassy the same ridiculous circumstance upon their arrival in London, that they came one day after the fair.[95]

The King's recovery and the humiliation of the opposition represented a triumph, not only for Buckingham, but for FitzGibbon. Buckingham's initial suspicions of FitzGibbon as a rather menacing opportunist gave way to unbounded trust and adoration. In the opening stages of the regency debates, Buckingham made this observation:

> ... the conduct of our supporters, with the exception of FitzGibbon, has been paltry in the extreme. Upon his conduct in every point, whether public or private, I cannot say enough.[96]

One week later he wrote on the same theme:

> The violence in the House of Commons could not be conceived and nothing but FitzGibbon's steadiness prevented the instantaneous vote, without even the shadow of an argument. To his firmness, to his steady friendship, and to his very superior powers, I am more indebted than to any man in this kingdom, and Great Britain is not the less indebted to him as the only Irishman who would fight her battles in such a moment.[97]

Buckingham pleaded with Pitt to show suitable gratitude to his new favorite: "I wish that Pitt would write him [FitzGibbon] three lines of flattery."[98] After some additional pleading, FitzGibbon did indeed receive his "three lines of flattery", which, not surprisingly, "delighted" him.[99] But Buckingham wanted more for him than polite notes. In early March 1789, Lifford once again fell ill, and Buckingham had no doubts about the proper successor:

> ... The Chancellor has been seriously ill and has claimed a pension at the end of the sessions. He has fairly earned it and FitzGibbon ought to have a specific promise of it. I have assured him of my best wishes.[100]

The crisis had purged any perception of FitzGibbon as the spoiled creature of Rutland and Orde and any belief in the necessity of an English candidate for the Irish seals.

Grattan later claimed that his great antagonist in the regency debate had struck a deal with Buckingham. FitzGibbon had agreed to defend the government's unconstitutional and untenable position in return for the seals.[101] Before the revolution in his perception of FitzGibbon, Buckingham had made similar suggestions of opportunism. FitzGibbon unquestionably had an opportunistic streak, and as his conduct in 1782 demonstrates, he knew how to trim when the political occasion required it. Nonetheless, during the regency crisis, FitzGibbon probably would have resisted Grattan and his party, even if he had stood to gain nothing. The address to the Prince of Wales struck him, not as the dignified and generous gesture of a free nation, but as an act of madness and illegality. Where Grattan and his party saw limitless room for autonomous action, FitzGibbon saw severe and absolute limitations: "one king, one law and one religion" united Ireland to England.[102] By deliberately ignoring English precedent and direction, Grattan and the Irish opposition threatened all three. In his various speeches during the crisis, FitzGibbon relentlessly pursued this grim logic.

In the case of the King, the indecent haste of the opposition to turn the government over to the Prince, not to mention the willful neglect of crucial bills, threatened to destroy the very foundation of royal authority in Ireland:

> He could not avoid ... condemning in the severest manner, the hurry and precipitation with which gentlemen were desirous of proceeding on the most momentous occasion that could possibly offer itself to the consideration of Parliament; the House was called upon to adopt measures with the most

> indecent haste, they were called upon to dissolve the single tie that connected them with Great Britain, to dethrone the King to whom they had all sworn allegiance.[103]

In the same vein, he attacked the claim that the necessary business of government must wait until the Irish nation finished its independent deliberations on the regency:

> The Attorney General said it was a new idea, that it would be respectful to his Majesty to dissolve the Government and not provide for the payment of the army ... and if the right honorable Gentleman [Grattan] will take it upon himself to risk the consequences that might result from such a delay, and from civil and military establishments falling to the ground he should only say [alluding to Mr. Grattan] on his head be it.[104]

As for the law, FitzGibbon argued that the actions of the opposition threatened the very constitutional framework that Grattan and his compeers had established in 1782. Recurring to what had become an unfailing source of rhetorical ammunition for the government's position, Yelverton's Act of 1782, he reminded his audience that all legislation originating in the Irish parliament required the authorization of the British great seal. In their determination to ignore proceedings on the other side of the Channel, the Irish opposition risked grave legal and constitutional difficulties should the British Parliament choose a regent other than the Prince of Wales:

> Let me now for a moment suppose that we, in the dignity of our independence, appoint a Regent for Ireland, being a different person from the Regent of England, a case not utterly impossible, if the gentlemen insist on our appointing the Prince of Wales before it shall be known whether he will accept the Regency of England; and suppose we should go further and desire him to give the royal assent to bills, he would say, "My good people of Ireland, you have by your own wish made the great seal of England absolutely and essentially necessary to be affixed to each bill before it passes in Ireland, that seal is in the hands of the Chancellor of England, who is a very sturdy fellow; that Chancellor is an officer under the Regent of England, I have no manner of authority over him, and so my very good people of Ireland, you had better apply to the Regent of England, and request that he will order the Chancellor of England to affix the great seal of England to your bills, otherwise, my very good people of Ireland, I cannot pass them.[105]

When Grattan made the claim that FitzGibbon was "playing tricks with signs and seals, and confounding the stamp of authority with authority itself", he opened himself to a penetrating rejoinder. FitzGibbon reminded Grattan that he himself had helped to frame that very law. Grattan was now raising the same objections to his own brainchild that his archenemy Flood had made in 1782:

> And now if the right honorable gentleman is founded in his objections to the

> manner of passing bills under his own law, I hope it will be a lesson to him not to precipitate great and important measures.[106]

Grattan could only respond with arguments that made up in vehemence and sentiment what they lacked in substance:

> The people have a pride in their King, and will not transfer their love; but on the contrary will kindle at the quibble that would set in his place the great seal as an object of their allegiance, and substitute as their monarch.[107]

The question of religion troubled FitzGibbon above all. When he called for "one religion" as a point of unity between England and Ireland, he referred of course, to the Protestant Establishment in church and state. His position as an outsider of obscure Catholic descent gave him a special insight into the dynamics of power in Ireland. He alone could have reminded his colleagues that far from being a free and proud nation, they belonged to a small alien Protestant caste living uneasily among a hostile and dispossessed Catholic population. As Protestants, they enjoyed property and privilege, but only insofar as they preserved their remaining ties to England. In an eerie presage of his great speech on the Act of Union, FitzGibbon reminded Grattan and his followers of the tragic and squalid origins of their great nation:

> And give me leave to tell the country gentlemen of Ireland that the only security by which they hold their property, the only security which they can have for the present establishment in Church and State, is the connection of the Irish crown with, and its dependence upon, the crown of England, a connection and dependence which has been sealed with the best blood of their country, and if they are now duped into idle and fantastical speculations, which are to shake that connection, under the specious pretense of asserting national dignity and independence, they will feel, to their sorrow, that they are duped into a surrender of the only security by which they can hope to retain their property or by which they can hope to retain the present establishment in Church and State. For give me leave to say sir that when we speak of the people of Ireland, it is a melancholy truth that we do not speak of the great body of the people. This is a subject on which it is extremely painful for me to be obliged to speak in this assembly, but when I see the right honorable member driving the gentlemen of Ireland to the verge of a precipice, it is necessary to speak out. Sir, the ancient nobility and gentry of this kingdom have been badly treated, that act by which most of us hold our estates, was an act of violence, an act palpably subverting the first principles of the common law of England and Ireland. I speak of the act of settlement, passed in this country immediately after the restoration, which vests the estate of every man who had been dispossessed during the rebellion of 1641, absolutely in the crown, and puts the old proprietors to the necessity of proving they had not been guilty of high treason in order to avoid the penalties of confiscation; which by the sacred and fundamental

> principles of common law, can be incurred only upon conviction and attainder. And that gentlemen may know the extent to which this summary confiscation is gone, I will tell them, that every acre of land in this country, which pays quit rent to the Crown, is held by title derived under the act of settlement, so that I trust the gentlemen whom I see upon the opposite benches will deem it a subject worthy of their consideration how it may be prudent to pursue the successive claims of dignified, unequivocal independence made for Ireland by the right honorable gentleman.[108]

In their madness, the Irish opposition threatened a revival of the civil wars of the 17th century or of the medieval period. FitzGibbon reminded them that the "civil commotions" of the Houses of Fitzgerald and Butler had their origins in "English faction" as well.[109] This remark was well calculated to make the descendants of the Fitzgeralds, at least, squirm in their seats. The conduct of the Irish opposition and of their English friends threatened yet another equally unpalatable outcome, that of a union, which he described in yet another weirdly prescient speech:

> certainly if it be the scheme to differ in all imperial questions, and if this be abetted by men of great authority, they mean to drive us to an union, and the method they take is certainly more effectual to sweep away opposition, than if all the sluices of corruption were opened together and deluged the country's representatives, for it is certain nothing less than the alternative of a separation could ever force an union.[110]

In effect, FitzGibbon was making the same accusation against the English Whigs that Grattan would later make against him: they were deliberately undermining Irish independence by encouraging civil upheaval and with it, a union.[111] FitzGibbon probably intended to make a grim joke at the expense of the English friends of Irish independence. He assuredly was not a crypto-Unionist who in the heat of the moment revealed his true colors. After all, he had been ready to resist the idea of an English convention imposing a regency on Ireland. Unquestionably he despised the Irish parliament for its many acts of folly, from the past rejection of the Commercial Propositions to the present address to the Prince. But FitzGibbon in 1789 still believed that the constitutional arrangement of 1782 could work, so long as the Irish Protestant ruling caste cultivated close harmonious ties with England, the indispensable source of their power and security:

> So long as we remain satisfied with the constitution of Ireland as settled in 1782, and avail ourselves of every opportunity which may offer to cement the union of the crown of Great Britain and Ireland and to cultivate the affection and confidence of the British nation, we shall continue to cultivate peace and good order, and prosperity in this country.[112]

FitzGibbon not only maintained his faith in the Irish Parliament, he was no dogmatist on the issue of the regency bill. In the interests of turning the opposition from the dangerous course of an address, he was willing to allow for an Irish bill that gave more privileges to the prince than the English:

> Sir I abominate the idea of restraining the Prince regent in the power of making Peers in this country, or in limiting him in the power of making grants on the narrow principles of suspicion and distrust.[113]

He could even allow for the possibility of granting the Prince of Wales the "plenitude of power". He stipulated only the most basic cooperation with England: "in God's name let it be done by a bill", a bill passed after the English parliament had confirmed the Prince as regent.[114] He pleaded for this minimal cooperation not because of personal loyalty to Buckingham, as the lord-lieutenant had assumed with characteristic egocentricity, and not even because he wanted the seals. He pleaded for a social structure that guaranteed his own hard fought identity as a Protestant and a gentleman of property.

III

By the end of February, the King was firmly on the road to recovery, and the "rats", as Buckingham termed them, grew both frightened and defiant. On 22 February, the leading members of the opposition, in both the Lords and the Commons, produced a "round robin" or circular. The signatories of the round robin dictated first, the no man was to be the "victim of his vote"; that is, no office holder was to suffer dismissal for his vote on the Regency. Secondly, the signatories pledged that they would oppose, as a body, any government that engaged in such dismissals. Finally, they would refuse to accept any office from such government.[115] The round robin in the Lords included "those four great rats", Ponsonby, Leinster, Shannon and Ely, as well as Lords Charlemont, Granard, Drogheda and Clifden.[116] In the Commons, it embraced Grattan, Forbes and Curran. Considering the rapidly sinking fortunes of the opposition, it was an extraordinary act of effrontery.

Buckingham and his by now inseparable confidante FitzGibbon responded with predictable contempt. Buckingham declaimed against the, "insolence of this aristocracy and the danger and indecency of such a combination. He also observed that the English Whigs encouraged their defiance, and if this second exercise in Anglo-Irish cooperation was allowed to persist, it would soon "convulse the kingdom".[117] FitzGibbon taunted the members of the round robin. They were, he declared, little better than a combination of Whiteboys or "journeymen pinmakers". He made the additional observation, both menacing and mocking, that by laws of their own devising, "the miserable Whiteboy would be whipped at the cart's end".[118] The framer of the sanguinary riot act and the would-be destroyer of chapels was in no position to blame the members of the round robin for cruelty to Whiteboys. Yet

Buckingham thought these ripostes brilliant, and he cited them as further proof of FitzGibbon's sterling worth.[119] Buckingham and FitzGibbon did not confine themselves to mere denunciation. Undeterred by the threats in the round robin, they immediately set about to break the combination and to punish the most notorious "rats" not with whipping at the cart's tail, perhaps, but with the uniquely aristocratic humiliation of loss of office. FitzGibbon worked closely with Buckingham in determining the degree of punishment and pardon. Alleyne Fitzherbert and Robert Hobart, his eventual successor as chief secretary, assisted in these negotiations.

The opposition newspapers suggested that Buckingham and FitzGibbon acted with indiscriminate vindictiveness:

> "No pardon for the transgressor" is to be the future motto of the [government] standard; this latter we understand by the advice of a certain Attorney who acts as Provost Marshal of the Forces.[120]

The reality, as always, was murkier. Overall, Buckingham and FitzGibbon took a tolerant view of "stragglers", the minor office holders who had erred and repented.[121] They concentrated on particularly egregious traitors in government service and on great aristocrats holding great office. Charles Francis Sheridan, Northington's able memorandum writer, allowed his loyalties to his famous brother to get the better of his loyalties to the government. In spite of the protests of the round robin, he lost the office of Secretary of War to Edward Cooke. The Sheridan knack for marrying attractive women allowed him to salvage something from the wreck of his fortunes. Buckingham granted a pension of £600 per annum to his "handsome and amiable" wife.[122] Toward Leinster and Ponsonby, who continued to act in defiant combination with their "kind friends" in England, Buckingham displayed the same obduracy. On 28 March, a month after the debut of the round robin, Buckingham notified them both of his intention to dismiss them from their offices.[123] One month later, Buckingham formally applied for their dismissal.[124]

Ponsonby, in particular, took the news badly. With breathtaking arrogance, he had not believed he would suffer any consequences and was "outrageous" (outraged).[125] Buckingham himself expressed delighted at Ponsonby's decision to remain in opposition. The government had always gone to far too much trouble to retain his precarious loyalties.[126]

Other aristocratic trimmers enjoyed a measure of mercy, thanks in large part to FitzGibbon's moderation. Buckingham was inclined to act with indiscreet vindictiveness. FitzGibbon, in contrast, saw that gratuitous humiliation would only encourage aristocratic discontent, and with it, partisan instability in the beleaguered Protestant elite. The case of Lord Ely most clearly demonstrated the difference in their approaches. Buckingham had wanted Lord Ely to resign the Post Office and to do a suitable period of penance in the political wilderness before re-assuming his place. FitzGibbon, enlisting Fitzherbert's aid, successfully pleaded with Buckingham to grant salvation upon mere repentance. FitzGibbon's shrewd clemency paid great dividends. Ely turned on his former associates with all the zeal of a reconverted apostate.[127]

Shannon initially was inclined to wear sackcloth and ashes, and both Buckingham and FitzGibbon stood ready to re-admit him to the government fold.[128] Less than a week after his submission, he abruptly reverted to the opposition. A domestic comedy of manners with Lady Shannon, *nee* Ponsonby, in the lead, provoked this sudden change of heart. According to Buckingham, Lady Shannon "raved like a madwoman" at her husband for deserting her brother.[129] The portrayal of Lord Shannon as a uxorious coward and his lady as a Whig virago seems too maliciously partisan and too amusing to be true. Nonetheless, Shannon admitted to Buckingham that he was obliged to stand by his brother-in-law for his "domestic peace".[130] Buckingham told his brother Grenville, "Everyone is loud in laughing at him [Shannon]".[131] The lord-lieutenant and the attorney general were less amused. Indeed, it was FitzGibbon's turn to be "outrageous". In this frame of mind, he lent his legal expertise to Buckingham's proposed revenge: depriving Lord Shannon of his vice-treasurership and dividing his salary between the two remaining holders of this office.[132] Nonetheless, FitzGibbon's instinct to let partisan bygones be bygones soon reasserted itself. In spite of their past differences FitzGibbon could not help but recognize that Shannon was a very reluctant Whig firebrand. Left to himself he was fundamentally a sound conservative in matters of Church and State. Buckingham noted the change not only in FitzGibbon, but in his other advisors; they "all now deprecate" any idea of Shannon's dismissal.[133] Buckingham remained adamant: "I must have the King's leave to dismiss Lord Shannon immediately for the sake of justice and example."[134] Eventually he carried his point. Shannon lost his office, and, in the election of 1790, control of County Cork. Government support for his antagonists Longfield and Kingsborough played a large part in the defeat of his interests. In 1793, Shannon enjoyed a slight measure of rehabilitation. Possibly through FitzGibbon's influence, he was appointed to the post of First Lord of the newly created Treasury Board. In that year of Catholic agitation, FitzGibbon was eager to encourage every like-minded Protestant, including the old apostate for whom he always had a soft spot.[135]

The opposition rebelled against the government's increasing ascendancy by introducing a series of what Buckingham termed "speculative measures". These speculative measures were of course, the standard lost causes: limiting pensions, disenfranchising revenue officers, and abolishing the police. In the euphoric beginnings of the session of 1789, Grattan seems to have believed that he could carry these oft-rejected measures under the auspices of a new Whig government. Buckingham sardonically observed, "Grattan evidently assumes the *role de ministre*; he pledged himself to the gallery to repeal the Police Bill [*sic*] and to intend to [*sic*] limit the Pension Bill to grants to addresses by Parliament".[136] As it became distressingly apparent that the bad old ways would remain in place, Grattan's various proposals took on the air of desperate and not very successful nuisance-making. Members of Grattan's own party balked at some of them, while his frequent tactical errors gave additional strength to his ministerial enemies. FitzGibbon, sardonic and assured, never failed to take advantage of the many opportunities provided by Grattan's blundering.

25 February marked not only the debut of the round robin, but the first salvo of their party. Grattan resorted to a short money bill, a venerable tactic from that year of glory, 1779. In response to Monk Mason's resolution in favor of supplies for the usual term of one year, Grattan proposed a limitation of two months. Nonetheless, he made an exception for those moneys necessary to maintain treaties and to meet immediate financial engagements.[137] The fear that Buckingham would dissolve Parliament after the passage of the money bill accounted in part for this measure.[138] Sheer partisan revanche played an even greater part. The opposition simply wanted to humiliate Buckingham for refusing to accept their address. FitzGibbon had to admit his own youthful support for the short money bill of 1779, but he denounced this latest manifestation as an exercise in factionalism, needless from a political standpoint and absurd from a legal one:

> See then the situation in which you place yourselves. You must form so much of your tax as is necessary for carrying the treaty into effect for twelve months, but that part which is applicable to the establishment, you must form out for two months; the same thing with regard to your colony trade; this I think impossible.[139]

Grattan's majorities held before this onslaught of ridicule and the short money bills passed. But it was an empty victory. Buckingham displayed an uncharacteristic, and disappointing, equanimity at this attempt to unnerve him. Six weeks later, the House extended the supplies for the usual period with no debate.[140]

An attempt to embarrass the government through William Grenville's *pis aller* reversion brought greater embarrassment on Grattan himself. Grattan proposed a resolution against the practice of giving any Irish office, including reversions, to absentees. This condemnation necessarily embraced Grenville, as the absentee claimant to a reversion.[141] It seemed a perfectly safe opposition exercise in troublemaking, but a devastating counterattack came from an unexpected quarter, Lawrence Parsons, the erstwhile critic of Rutland's corrupt legacy. Vehemently shifting course, he defended the incumbent viceroy's act of patronage. Raising the troubled ghosts of 1783, Parson's noted that Grenville had played a major part in obtaining an act of renunciation. For this singular service, he had obtained only the possibility of an office. Grattan, on the other hand, had manifestly blundered on the issue by adhering to a policy of simple repeal. Notwithstanding, he had received a lavish grant of £50,000 for incomplete services rendered.[142] FitzGibbon needed to do very little to complete Grattan's humiliation. He contented himself with the observation that deputies customarily fulfilled the duties of Chief Remembrancer. Since the office was relatively minor, no pressing reason existed to change this custom, and require Grenville to take up residence in Ireland. More discreetly, he reiterated Parson's point that the reversion had little value. Lord Clanbrassil, the present holder, continued hale and hearty. Consequently, Grenville probably would never succeed to the office, either as a resident or as an absentee.[143] A motion for adjournment allowed Grattan to drop the matter.[144]

Even the opposition's evanescent victory over the matter of pensions, long a favored nuisance issue, brought embarrassment to them and tactical advantage to the government. The bill limited pensions to £80,000, though Parliament by address, could approve additions over and above this amount. The bill also allowed the Crown to grant pensions from surpluses in the hereditary revenue.[145] In his various responses to the bill, FitzGibbon ingeniously combined the roles of high royalist, scourge of aristocratic corruption, and champion of the prerogatives of Parliament. He initially claimed that the bill insulted the king at the moment of his recovery, by attacking his unquestioned right to grant pensions. This ungracious ploy served only to increase the power of an aristocracy, "under whose baneful influence every bud of national prosperity was blasted".[146] Many illustrious members of the round robin could not help but recognize the allusion to their undertaker ancestors. Above all, FitzGibbon seized on the fact that the proposed bill placed a huge sum of money absolutely at the disposal of the Crown. Hitherto, Parliament had the right to review all pensions. Under the provisions of Forbes' bill, the Crown could grant a good many pensions without any Parliamentary intervention whatsoever.[147] Publicly, FitzGibbon gloated over the system of ministerial tyranny instituted by the men of the people. Privately, he urged Buckingham to assent to the bill. The government could increase its powers, enjoy the benefits of supporting a popular measure, and get rid of a perennial opposition nuisance issue.[148] The bill did pass the House of Commons, but only after considerable amendment. According the Buckingham, Ponsonby and Shannon in particular "took fright at the complexion of their own child".[149] He did not make clear whether Ponsonby and Shannon recoiled from the increase in the government's powers of patronage or from the decrease in their potential share of corrupt lucre. Their amendments proved unnecessary. The House of Lords, which was already resuming its accustomed role as a government bastion, ultimately threw out the bill. As Buckingham sardonically observed, "one half the Opposition would not vote as they do on these measures if they were not sure they would be thrown out in the House of Lords".[150]

An attempt to disenfranchise revenue officers met with similar defeat. According the Buckingham, this latter bill was "personally aimed at a borough interest belonging to Beresford", but Grattan, in his enthusiasm, once again gored some oxen in his own party.[151] Lord Shannon, a formidable boroughmonger and revenue officer in his own right, "disliked" the bill, though the "round robin" and his previous political commitments forced him to retain the galling, ill-fitting trappings of radicalism.[152] Fortunately, government majorities spared him from the nuisance of such a bill. The same convenient majorities defeated proposals to abolish the police, proposals which Shannon also constitutionally disliked.[153] By May, Grattan's campaign of radical intimidation had lost its momentum. When he proposed another place bill on 1 May, to "his utter amazement" he could find no seconders in the cowed or bored House of Commons.[154] His attempt to revive the issue of tithes met with equal indifference.[155] "In short", Buckingham wrote to Grenville, "we are triumphant and the King's government is completely re-established".[156]

In a sense, Buckingham was badly mistaken, and the battle had just begun. The embittered, unreconciled remnants of the opposition, including Grattan, Forbes, Ponsonby, Leinster and Charlemont, formed the so-called Whig Club in the disastrous wake of the session of 1789. This club aimed at creating and building on popular support for the standard opposition agenda of retrenchment and the abolition of the police.[157] FitzGibbon later contemptuously dismissed it as a convivial club for gentlemanly malcontents.[158]

Grattan's son, in filial indignation, later contrasted FitzGibbon's vulgar "popish extraction" with the impeccable Protestant, patrician and patriotic backgrounds of the Whig Club's founders.[159] From a less pious perspective, both the regency crisis and the Whig Club have an air of brittle aristocratic self-indulgence. Nonetheless, as FitzGibbon so clearly perceived, the regency crisis and its aftermath shook the Anglo-Irish government to its foundations. Grattan's arguments during the regency debates, carried to their logical extreme, reduced royal and English authority in Ireland to mere sentiment: "The people have a pride in their King and will not transfer their love." The Whig Club, however aristocratic and Protestant, revived the extra-parliamentary activity which had fallen into abeyance after the demise of the reform congress. Buckingham indulged in his habitual exaggeration when he termed the Irish opposition republicans. Yet Grattan's extreme notions of autonomy, tempered by sentimental royalism, were a small and logical step away from Irish republicanism, which rejected any monarchical or English authority whatsoever. Similarly, the aristocratic agitation of the Whig Club prepared the extra-Parliamentary way for the middle class militants of the Catholic Convention and for the United Irishmen. In short, the Irish opposition, driven by their own myopic partisan resentments, set an example of discontent.

IV

During the robin negotiations, Buckingham's demands that FitzGibbon be appointed to the seals continued. They reached their peremptory peak when Lifford died at the end of April. Buckingham threatened to force the government's hand by appointing his favorite Lord Keeper of the great seal. FitzGibbon once again tactfully intervened to curb Buckingham's emotional excesses. He urged his master to adhere to the usual practice of appointing several commissioners until the King's pleasure was known. Far from taking offense, Buckingham saw FitzGibbon's discretion as "an additional proof of the confidence he merits".[160] Continued silence on the part of the

English Government on the subject of Lifford's succession provoked yet another stream of high-strung threats. Buckingham once again raised the specter of a disappointed FitzGibbon going into opposition, and suggested in addition, that he himself would resign in protest:

> I conceive that you all know that if it is to be attempted to send an inferior man, or any of the King's Serjeants or counsel junior to FitzGibbon, he will fly out and the game will be irretrievable. Perhaps all this has been fully considered, but indeed, my mind is ill at ease till I know the result. You may, however, believe that I *cannot* join in any insult or outrage, *however recommended or supported.*[161]

Buckingham eventually learned from two separate communications that Thurlow's reservations stood in the way of FitzGibbon's appointment. First, Thurlow raised the issue of FitzGibbon's unpopularity, to which Buckingham indignantly replied, "Good God! Where could he have conceived this nonsense?"[162] Thurlow's perception was hardly nonsense. A glance at past issues of the *Dublin Evening Post* easily would have confirmed such an impression. Secondly, Thurlow held fast to the traditional prejudice in favor of an Englishman.[163] Finally, another outraged comment from Buckingham suggests that Thurlow had doubts about FitzGibbon's professional qualifications: "It is easy for Lord Thurlow to sit still in his chair and to consider this arrangement solely with a view to the *law* as the only point for consideration."[164] In other words, Thurlow had considered FitzGibbon as a lawyer and had found him wanting.

His judgment seems curious. FitzGibbon, a lawyer of almost 20 years' standing, could lay claim to a remarkable array of legal experience, both in parliament and in the courts. Thurlow may have concluded that FitzGibbon was merely a petty Irish courtroom brawler, incapable of grasping the subtleties of Equity. If so, he badly underestimated FitzGibbon. The mere fact that he had been a pleader on the Munster circuit gave him a surpassing insight into the intricacies of Irish property tenure, a frequent subject of Chancery cases.

Furthermore, as Buckingham was quick to point out, the Irish Lord Chancellor had a crucial role in the House of Lords. Since Lifford's accession, the Irish House of Lords had changed from a somnolent and thinly attended to an active and influential branch of government. Lifford had never acquired the vigor necessary to the new state of affairs in the Lords:

> I will not say how severely both kingdoms have paid for such a nomination, which has kept its ground for 22 years amidst so many changes of government, and with the strongest charges of constant misconduct and inefficiency as a political character; reprobated by almost every lord-lieutenant who has been in Ireland, who felt not only the want of assistance, but the actual mischief of his language and conduct in the official situation which the Irish lord chancellor must always hold.[165]

In his zeal to press FitzGibbon's claims, Buckingham did a cruel disservice to Lifford, who whatever his faults of indolence and neglect, had served the government with unfailing loyalty. But Buckingham did have a point. The office of Lord Chancellor of Ireland required a consummate political knowledge and skill that FitzGibbon unquestionably possessed.

Above all, there were simply no other suitable candidates. The two Englishmen and the Scotsman under consideration would only insult the Irish. Chief Baron Eyre, Orde's original nominee, was perhaps the "least exceptionable", but his manners were "unaccommodating" and he had no parliamentary experience. As for Buller, he was a notoriously corrupt and intemperate man, "not to be born [*sic*]" McDonald, the Scotsman, was junior to FitzGibbon at the Bar. Any one of them was guaranteed to arouse that dreaded and much to be avoided phenomenon, Irish political agitation:

> Any one of these persons is to be dropped from the clouds into the midst of a House of Lords who divided in this sessions, 84 members, and is told that he is their minister, to guide and direct a Machine so complicated, so entirely out of every rule, and with every unfavorable impression that can be conceived either from resentment, malice or to the general indisposition to an Englishman in that House.[166]

The last circumstance noted by Buckingham, the lack of a suitable alternative, probably accounted for the English government's final, grudging decision in FitzGibbon's favor. The news of his appointment reached Ireland on 13 June 1789. By then Buckingham, exhausted by the political, emotional and physical ordeal of the regency crisis, was preparing to retire to Bath. FitzGibbon's appointment, as much as the prospect of a leave of absence, had a therapeutic effect:

> I cannot say all that I feel for FitzGibbon's appointment; but I feel that this, and the leave of absence, has given me spirits beyond my present weak state of mind.[167]

The great drama of FitzGibbon's elevation to the Seals inevitably inspired reams of newsprint in the Dublin press. Lifford's death in April 1789 set the presses into speculative motion. The government newspapers, not unexpectedly, went into ecstasies at the prospect of FitzGibbon's nomination. "What a character must that man possess who is admired, esteemed and loved by all parties?" *Faulkner's Dublin Journal* asked rhetorically and inaccurately. The paragraph continued: "If his wisdom and integrity are now so conspicuous, what an ornament will he be to that Court, where the desire of the nation would have him preside? – His motto should be "unshaken, unseduced, unterrified".[168]

Such effusions were not surprising in a government newspaper. But the adulatory response of the opposition newspapers was perhaps the most startling outcome of FitzGibbon's possible elevation. It was as though Jack Petulant, the lewd, arrogant, effeminate coxcomb, the scourge of honest Whigs, and the Mephistopheles of viceroys, had never existed. The *Dublin Evening Post*, his most bitter journalistic enemy, took the lead in his rehabilitation. It did indeed touch on his "certain haughtiness of spirit", but it argued that his manner, far from making him objectionable, bespoke the honest pride, "which gives dignity to station and prevents a man from doing a mean---a base---an ignoble act". It further predicted, with sublime inaccuracy, that time and the dignity of office would soften "those asperities which shade the lustre of mental powers, however splendid".[169]

The other major popular newspaper in Dublin, the *Hibernian Journal*, was as hot and eager on FitzGibbon's behalf. It indignantly reacted to rumors that "the seals of this country have been refused to the A——y G——l on that most *illiberal principle of his being an Irishman!*"[170] Like the *Dublin Evening Post*, the *Hibernian* praised FitzGibbon's talents and ignored his faults on the liberal principle of his being an Irishman:

> ... it is acknowledged by every man in the nation, however, they differ in politics, that Mr F——n as a great and sound lawyer, is at least equal to any and superior to most gentlemen of his standing at the Bar in either kingdom – consequently, the chusing a foreigner at this time was totally unnecessary and must be considered an insult to our feelings and a dishonor to our country.[171]

The change of heart in these formerly antagonistic quarters may have provoked Buckingham's thunderous response to Thurlow's hints of FitzGibbon's unpopularity. In the spring of 1789, no one was more suddenly or more completely adored.

The same nationalistic fervor that had made FitzGibbon an object of loathing since 1780 now worked to his advantage. His Irishness, in effect, gave added radiance to the qualities with the opposition press had hitherto slighted, and softened those qualities which had hitherto aroused such intense detestation.

This curious combination of fulsome praise and reluctant criticism reached a climax in June, when FitzGibbon finally received the appointment for which he, his friends and his erstwhile enemies so devoutly wished. The *Dublin Evening Post's* announcement of his appointment in its edition of 13 June 1789 is worth quoting in full, if only to show the remarkable transformation of his image in the popular press:

> In this young man's progress through life – there has certainly been a consistency – a uniformity – a chastity of conduct – that has never even once stooped to those mean arts by which others have forced their way to station – and when there placed rendering dignity despicable, power oppressive, justice a phantom.
>
> There are some traits in the outline of his character that should be immediately softened – that warmth of disposition – that *hauteur* of manner, that peevish pettiness of temper so insulting to feeling, so disgraceful to sound argument, so disgustful to sense – that should and *ought* to be changed and that immediately.

By the end of the year even mild criticism had disappeared and a tone of uniform fawning adulation characterized accounts of FitzGibbon in the major Dublin newspapers. The *Hibernian* exulted over the improvements he was making in the Court of Chancery and rejoiced that "Irish talents and integrity" at last filled all the high judicial offices.[172] As for the government newspapers, this stray paragraph in the *Freeman's Journal* probably best sums up the absurd excesses into which they fell when writing of the new chancellor. In June of 1789, shortly after his elevation, FitzGibbon caught a summer cold, which prevented him from attending an official levee. The *Freeman's* elevated a minor case of the sniffles into a major crisis of state. FitzGibbon's condition:

> gave general concern and alarm to the town. From his Lordship's known integrity, firmness, and ability and being in the very prime and vigor of life, the nation look up to him for that dispatch of business in the Court which can be alone effected by those preeminent endowments and that vigorous application which a character like his lordship possesses. The warm and sincere wishes therefore of the public must be for his immediate recovery.[173]

10

Lord Chancellor

I

As Chancellor, FitzGibbon had a formidable array of responsibilities. His court administered trusts, wills in probate, and the property of widows, orphans and lunatics. As a matter of course, any disputes over wills and trusts came before him. In addition, the assets, if any, of bankrupts came under the jurisdiction of the Court of Chancery. FitzGibbon determined which creditors were to receive satisfaction and the priority of the various claims. In yet another capacity, the Lord Chancellor was in a position to rule on the propriety and correctness of judgments referred from other courts, both lay and ecclesiastical. These cases usually involved property or testamentary disputes of one kind or another. In his judicial capacity, the Lord Chancellor made no determinations on criminal cases. Nonetheless, as a Privy Councilor, FitzGibbon had a powerful influence on the issue of pardons in cases of murder and rebellion. Moreover, in 1798, he did play a prominent role in one of the more spectacular murder trials of the time. As Lord High Steward, he presided over Lord Kingston's trial in the House of Lords. Other responsibilities combined both politics and law. Buckingham noted the Chancellor's crucial role as speaker of the House of Lords. In this capacity, FitzGibbon not only directed debate on political matters, he presided over appeals from the courts, his own included. Finally, FitzGibbon had a profound influence on the character of the Irish judiciary. He appointed magistrates on the advice of county magnates, and he himself advised the lord-lieutenant on candidates for judicial promotion.

Assessments of FitzGibbon the Chancellor varied as sharply as assessments of FitzGibbon the politician. At one extreme stood Jerome Alley, a clergyman cum versifier. Shortly after FitzGibbon's death, Alley produced a long poem of tribute. As this excerpt shows, FitzGibbon inspired intense admiration, if not immortal verse:

> Clare is no more! The statesman and the sage,
> Whose mighty mind explored each depth of law,
> And by whose voice determined Justice spoke
> Her chaste decree ...[1]

Yet many of FitzGibbon's most bitter detractors admitted, with various degrees of reluctance, his ability and his integrity as a judge. In 1792, during the deliberations of the Wexford freeholders, Edward Sweetman denounced FitzGibbon's sectarian politics while paying this convoluted and grudging tribute to his administration of justice:

> If such a man as I have here portrayed, had not carried the audacious impurities of the senate to the judgment seat, but administered law in justice and in mercy as became his great abilities, the circumstance should be a drawback on the detestation of his countrymen, it should take but little from the distrust of the character.[2]

The *Morning Post*, an avowedly pro-Catholic, radical and hence short-lived newspaper, not unexpectedly took a highly unfavorable view of FitzGibbon overall. Nonetheless, the same paper published a spirited defense of him as a judge and as a statesman. He was "a high judicial character of eminent talents, of vigorous, investigating mind, of firm and independent spirit and unimpeached integrity". This writer, in the aftermath of the Convention Act and of the various other measures of repression against Catholic agrarian rebels and middle class radicals, still could praise FitzGibbon for displaying a "mixture of firmness in the public cause, together with lenity to the deluded instruments of the secret mischief of others ... rigour of justice with that mercy becoming a man who feels for human frailty and with the liberality of a gentleman".[3] The presumably pro-Catholic and liberal readers of the *Morning Post* took such a liking to this particular essay that they requested a reprint.[4] Shortly before Fitzwilliam's arrival, the *Morning Post* expressed satisfaction that FitzGibbon would remain as Chancellor, in spite of the change in administration:

> The Lord Chancellor certainly retains the Seals amidst the approaching change of men and measures – a continuation much to the public satisfaction, and highly conducive to an impartial dispensation of equity.[5]

The *Dublin Evening Post*, throughout FitzGibbon's life an unrelenting critic, nonetheless published a posthumous tribute to his judicial ability, though it could not rival Alley's fervor:

> On the judgment seat, his integrity stands [unimpeached?] His facility lay in a quick discernment and the utility of it in a familiar acquaintance with the modes of common life, and particularly with such of our habits as more especially national than others ... The practice of his court he improved by his exactness, and its reputation by the alacrity with which its business was transacted.[6]

During the 19th century, a similar reluctant admiration emerged from the most critical monographs. The urbane J.F. O'Flanagan recoiled from FitzGibbon's arrogant manner and his political antagonism toward Catholics. At the same time he acknowledged, with gentlemanly good grace, that FitzGibbon "did much to establish equity practice in Ireland on a solid basis". In particular, O'Flanagan continued, "he reformed abuses with no niggard hand and purged the court of much that called for reform. Fraud fled before him, for when grasped, he punished it with relentless vigour."[7] In a similar vein, C.L. Falkiner deprecated his "Cromwellian sternness" while paying tribute to his liberality as a judge, and particularly his protection of the poor and the dispossessed, the tenant and the Catholic.[8]

Chancellor FitzGibbon's detractors were as numerous and as vocal as his adherents. The arrogance and arbitrariness that inspired hatred in the political realm had the same effect in the judicial. The *Morning Post* published the ______ of FitzGibbon's critics as well as his partisans. One "Somers", in particular, contrasted FitzGibbon unfavorably with his predecessor Lifford:

> He was courteous to one profession without *partiality* and made the other respectable without *persecution*. His slowness was deliberation, his deliberation wisdom and he held a middle course between the flippancy of precipitate judgment and the dilatoriness of protracted decision, saw when the infirmity of exhausted nature occasioned reluctant procrastination. Conscious of the imperfection of human intellect, he courted the revision of his opinions and free from the vanity of fastidious infallibility, he could admit error and assent to the reversal of his own decrees. He had honour without insolence – dignity without ostentation – pride without arrogance – in a word possessing every good quality that could adorn the administration of justice.[9]

In another word, FitzGibbon possessed all the opposite qualities. He displayed the "flippancy of precipitant judgment", and he had besides insolence without honour, ostentation without dignity and arrogance rather than honest pride.

Lord Aldborough made perhaps the strongest attacks on FitzGibbon during his lifetime, for which he paid the harsh and degrading price of a prison term. In the draft of an address to the House of Lords, he not only made the usual accusations of haste and arrogance, he questioned FitzGibbon's competence as a judge by noting the large number of appeals from his decrees. He made the still more serious charge that FitzGibbon used the Court of Chancery to further his own political and personal ends. In this particular literary effort, one of many, Aldborough framed his accusations with elaborate and ironic disclaimers:

> Let us now, my Lords, attend to his conduct as Chancellor, where vindictiveness, rancour, partiality and revenge have no sway on the bench. He is courteous and attentive to every barrister. No marked distinctions or prejudices warp his complacent demeanor on the bench. He don't [*sic*] create rotten foundations to erect unstable structures on ... Thus my Lords, I have given our present speaker all the tribute due to his merit. But ... sometimes Homer nods; for we find numberless appeals from his decrees, justified by the opinions and signatures of the best and ablest counsel at the bar, to what cause owing, I am not competent to conjecture. I will not say, like some in his situation, that he prejudges cases

> before they are heard, because one party is his neighbor or rector of his parish, or subservient to his intrigues, county interests or politics or that he wishes to convert the House of Lords into a court of Chancery and domineer and dictate in both. No, my lords, this chancellor is superior to such paltry base acts.[10]

Sir Jonah Barrington made equally damning condemnations of FitzGibbon's conduct as a judge, though he made them many years after the Chancellor's death, and thus he evaded Lord Aldborough's unhappy fate. Like Aldborough, Barrington accused FitzGibbon of using the office of Lord Chancellor, not to dispense justice, but to intimidate his political opponents, to promote his own creatures, and to extend his powers of patronage wherever and whenever possible:

> He commenced his office with a splendor far exceeding all precedent. He expended four thousand guineas for a state carriage; his establishment was splendid and his entertainments magnificent. His family connections absorbed the patronage of the state and he became the most absolute subject that modern times had seen in the British Islands. His only check was the Bar, which he resolved to corrupt. He doubled the number of bankrupt commissioners; he revived some offices – created others – and under pretense of furnishing each country with a local judge, in two months he established 32 new offices of about six or seven hundred pounds per annum each. His arrogance in court intimidated many whom his patronage could not corrupt and he had no doubt of overpowering the whole profession.[11]

Barrington himself claimed to be one of the brotherhood of the Bar whom FitzGibbon had attempted to corrupt. Supposedly he had been offered the place of solicitor general on condition of supporting the union. Barrington refused the condition and with it, the office.

In addition to these general claims of political corruption, Barrington accused FitzGibbon of conniving at a gross miscarriage of justice. The victim, James Fitzpatrick Knaresborough, had been convicted and sentenced to death for the attempted abduction of a Miss Barton. Although Barrington had acted as counsel for Miss Barton, he became convinced of his client's mendacity and of Knaresborough's innocence. Under the conviction that Knaresborough had been unjustly convicted, he went first to the Lord Lieutenant, Westmorland, and to Chief Secretary Hobart. They in turn referred him to FitzGibbon. After setting forth his case, Barrington received this bloodcurdling response from FitzGibbon:

> That may be all very true, Barrington! but he is a rascal and if he does not deserve to be hanged for this, he does for a former affair right well![12]

FitzGibbon then presented Barrington with "affidavits and evidence on a former accusation (from which Knaresborough had escaped by lenity) for snapping a pistol at the father of a girl he had seduced".[13] In relating this damning anecdote, Barrington admitted that FitzGibbon agreed to commute the sentence to transportation. Knaresborough himself regarded transportation as no mercy. He begged to be hanged instead, but this favor was refused.

Finally even Roche, who genuinely loved FitzGibbon, tempered praise for his intellect with criticism of his general demeanor on the bench:

> ... he possessed a commanding energy and great intellectual powers; but ... this energy too often betrayed, in its official appliance both on the bench and in executive rule, a deep tinge of overbearing temper and despotic authority, and ... his intellectual powers were not always regulated in their direction or action, by prudence or considerate reflection.[14]

The more outrageous allegations, particularly on the part of Barrington and Aldborough, call for a large measure of skepticism. Both had bitter personal grudges against him: Barrington because FitzGibbon had allegedly stalled his advancement and Aldborough because FitzGibbon had decided against him in two Chancery suits. Indeed, some of Barrington's harshest criticism inadvertently reflect credit on FitzGibbon. The appointment of additional judges, which Barrington regarded as evidence of deep-dyed corruption, to a less prejudiced and embittered observer, seems like an enlightened effort to increase the accessibility and effectiveness of justice. Even the grisly tale about Mr Knaresborough has a more creditable aspect. FitzGibbon could well have made the comments which Barrington attributed to him. He had a cruel streak, and as attorney general he had already demonstrated his relentlessness toward perceived wrong-doers. Nonetheless, under the circumstances, a commutation to transportation was perhaps the only recourse open to FitzGibbon. A jury, with the aid, it must be mentioned, of Sir Jonah's eloquent pleading, had freely and openly found Knaresborough guilty. FitzGibbon could not overturn a legitimate verdict simply because of intimations on the part of the former prosecuting counsel. His comments to Barrington were as brutal as they were ill-advised, but he took the most merciful course of action possible.

This varied and conflicting evidence suggests only that FitzGibbon, in exercising the duties of his office, displayed many of his best qualities and a few of his worst. On the positive side, he dedicated himself to his work with an almost mystical fervor. He allowed neither the press of political business, nor his own frequent bad health to interfere with the efficient, speedy dispatch of the causes that came before him. His decisions displayed remarkable intellectual clarity, precision, and legal learning. Unfortunately, his foul temper and his moral and intellectual arrogance blighted his judicial, as well as his political, dealings.

First and foremost, FitzGibbon displayed a maniacal diligence. By his own account, he heard 700 to 800 cases a year.[15] While the *Freeman's* was admittedly a hired government newspaper, and thus particularly prone to fawning exaggeration, its account of FitzGibbon's fierce concentration has an unusual element of accuracy:

> Monday, the Right Honorable, the Lord Chancellor, attended at so early an hour as ten o'clock in the court of chancery; his lordship proceeded to the hearing of such cases as were ready – and what has not taken place for many years past in that court was, at this sitting accomplished – vis, the discharge of peremptories – a species of rule motion and proceeding which prevented suitors, however just their claim, from receiving redress of remedy for years together. This conduct must reflect high honour and credit on Lord FitzGibbon.[16]

FitzGibbon himself revealed his intensive dedication to Chancery business in a letter to a friend of Hamilton Rowan's. This gentleman had requested FitzGibbon to consider a petition for a pardon, which Rowan hoped to present to the King. FitzGibbon was certainly sympathetic. He was already acting as an unofficial financial and legal counselor to Rowan's wife. But his business in Chancery necessarily took precedence over any other concern, however worthy of attention:

> My dear sir – the weight of business which presses upon me in the Court of Chancery at this time renders it impracticable for me to attend to any other subject. I can readily conjecture the object of the petition which you wish to show to me, and [I] do not hesitate to say that patience under his most unpleasant situation, for a few months, will be the best policy on the part of Mr H. Rowan.[17]

Lord Redesdale, FitzGibbon's successor, suggested that his ferocious application to business not only led to some mistaken decisions; it cost him his life. In the case of *Chamley v. Lord Dunsany*, which involved a maddeningly complicated series of judgment debts, and which finally ended up in the English House of Lords, Redesdale took issue with FitzGibbon's sweeping refusal to consider some exceptions to a Chancery report on the matter. Redesdale attributed this faulty ruling to exhaustion and illness brought on by overwork:

> It was probably a misfortune to him and to the public that he persisted in transacting the business of the court during the term in which he made that order; perhaps a valuable life would have been saved to the country if he had not done so. It was the last term in which he sat and the state of his health at that time rendered it impossible for him to examine any difficult or entangled case. It was one of the last orders he made and in a day or two after it was made, he became unable to leave his house.[18]

Dispatch, along with dedication, characterized FitzGibbon as Chancellor. In a speech to the corporation of Drogheda, he himself declared his overmastering intention to eliminate the "law's delay" from his court:

> ... my best exertions shall be made speedily to extend the protection of the law to those who are suitors for it; and to correct the spirit of vexatious and oppressive litigation which has too long impeded the course of justice in this country.[19]

His decrees and rules demonstrated his determination to make the procedures of the Chancery court simpler and speedier. In June 1799, for example, he ruled that a suit which had been in abeyance for over twenty years could not be revived without special leave from the Court of Chancery.[20] In yet another ruling, FitzGibbon placed stringent limitations on crossbills or countersuits filed by defendants against the plaintiffs. FitzGibbon required affidavits that such crossbills did not originate in gratuitous attempts at delay. He also required the counsel submitting a crossbill to sign a certificate that "in his opinion it is necessary for the attainment of justice in the cause".[21]

Nonetheless, dispatch sometimes became an end in itself. The otherwise favorable obituary in the *Dublin Evening Post* tempered its praise of his "alacrity" with the observation: "... he sometimes seemed as if he valued himself not much less on a quick dispatch of the cause than on the merit of the decree."[22] Lord Redesdale found it necessary to clarify some of his predecessor's exercises in judicial efficiency. In the case of *Browne v. O'Dea*, Redesdale simply reworded a decree more precisely. This case concerned a disputed lease. FitzGibbon had decreed that the lease claimed by the tenant was fraudulent, but he directed the Master of the Rolls to take an account of any improvements made by the lessee and to balance the cost of such improvements against any outstanding rents or debts owed to the lessor.[23] Redesdale affirmed FitzGibbon's' decree in its essentials, but he directed the Master first to investigate whether any alleged improvements had lasting benefits to the landlord's property. Only then should the Master take them into account.[24]

In the matter of John Roche and the widow of Crosbie Morgell, Redesdale reversed FitzGibbon's decision altogether. In this cause, Mrs Morgell claimed that in a series of transactions with took place between 1788 and 1794, Roche had systematically defrauded her husband of large sums of money and an estate, Clonmeen. In her original suit, Mrs Morgell had requested a full account of all transactions between her late husband and Roche, and the setting aside of the sale of Clonmeen. In response, Roche submitted a bill of release dated 21 May 1791. In this document, Morgell had acknowledged two debts to Roche of £4500 and £4437 and two bonds to secure those debts. Apart from these sums, the two men agreed to waive any other outstanding claims. Roche insisted that Morgell had freely signed the release. In December 1798, FitzGibbon accepted the validity of the release and Roche's plea. The widow then appealed to Redesdale, who immediately reversed FitzGibbon's decree in favor of Roche. Redesdale based his judgment on the fact that the deed of release only covered transactions *up to* 27 May 1791; it did not include the day itself, a point overlooked by FitzGibbon in his original ruling. Therefore, a transaction made on that day was subject to discovery, and such discovery would necessarily encompass past transactions covered by the deed of release. Furthermore, accusations of fraud *required* investigation, notwithstanding the release. If fraud had indeed taken place, it necessarily impeached the whole transaction. Roche in his turn appealed to the House of Lords in 1809, whereupon Redesdale reiterated his original arguments. In so doing, he generously attributed FitzGibbon's error to the haste of a busy, hard-pressed man acting during a time of crisis. As tactfully as he could, Redesdale also suggested that even under the best of circumstances, FitzGibbon perhaps lacked the necessary knowledge to make an appropriate judgment:

> When he [Redesdale] looked at the date of the order which he had reversed, he felt that the mind of Lord Clare must have been at that time so occupied with the extraordinary events which had recently passed and were then passing in *Ireland*; that it was scarcely at leisure to attend to such a subject, and indeed it was a subject upon which the mind of Lord Clare had never been very attentively employed, and it was, on the contrary, a subject on which his own mind had been most attentively employed from his first entrance in the profession.[25]

His fellow peers took Lord Redesdale at his word and upheld the decision in favor of Mrs Morgell.

The less charitable Lord Aldborough implied that FitzGibbon decided cases quickly because he prejudged them according to his own selfish interests or passions. Consequently, the Lords heard more appeals from his court than from Lifford's.[26] Probably the fact that FitzGibbon decided more cases than Lifford, and consequently increased the number of potential appellants, accounted for this alleged increase in appeals. But there was perhaps a small glimmer of truth in Aldborough's dark malice. FitzGibbon was prone to error, but through an excess of virtue, rather than vice in the form of arrogance and corruption. His laudable desire to cut through obfuscation and chicanery, and indeed his superb ability to grasp the essentials of complex matters, do appear to have caused him to disregard subtle but important points. To his credit, FitzGibbon took reversals of his decrees with considerable good grace.[27] He declared to Aldborough in his own defense:

> I am no egotist. God knows that if I was sensible of having erred in the judgment seat, I could not sleep until such judgment had been corrected.[28]

FitzGibbon may have been somewhat mistaken about his lack of egotism, but he indeed deserved credit for the scrupulousness that made him both quick in judgment and quick to accept reversals of his judgments if legitimately founded.

Not surprisingly given his own precision of mind, FitzGibbon maintained exacting standards in his court. No item, however minute, escaped his attention. He established a rigid dress code for barristers who argued in his court. The *Dublin Evening Post* described the new sartorial rule:

> The Lord Chancellor, with a most laudable tenacity for the respect due to his Court, has signified his desire that no practitioner should appear therein in colored clothes, or without his professional gown, thus maintaining as well the respectability of professional conduct, the violation of which his Lordship has on so many occasions marked his upright determination to punish.[29]

His moral indignation and reforming zeal extended to the custom of putting money into a box on motion days; this money was later distributed to the poor. Evidently many individuals used the box to dispose of bad coinage, which offended both FitzGibbon's scrupulous sense of honour and his equally scrupulous sense of what was due to the poor:

> Lord FitzGibbon took notice of a wicked and improper practice used, his Lordship supposed, by some young men to cheat the poor, who received the money paid into the box on motion days. It had become a trick to put down bad money and in the course of the last term, his Lordship remarked that the sum collected in this way amounted to seventeen guineas, of which, on examination, not less than ten were found to consist of bad shillings – purchased as his lordship imagined, for the purpose of imposing on the poor. His Lordship was justly severe on such abominable conduct and humanely gave orders for the prevention of the like cheat being practiced in the future.[30]

In a further effort to improve the tone of the Court, FitzGibbon banished casual visitors and mere curiosity seekers from his court, as the *Hibernian Journal* reported:

> The regulations at present going forward in our High court of Chancery under the auspices of the Lord Chancellor add ornament and dignity to that venerable seat of Justice, at the same time that the restrictions on persons not immediately interested in the proceedings in that court, from being admitted, will prevent the intrusion of troublesome persons, on the serious proceedings of those immediately concerned.[31]

The *Hibernian* did raise one, self-interested objection to this otherwise laudable attempt to raise the tone of the Court:

> The only disagreeable consequence is that intelligence and legal information is to be withheld from those whose situations in life are such as ought not to be precluded from these advantages.

In other words, journalists could no longer observe proceedings in Chancery, under this new rule. Considering his past relations with the press, FitzGibbon probably would have seen no particular "disagreeable consequence" in their absence.

FitzGibbon did not confine himself to minor administrative reforms. He made sweeping efforts to improve the caliber of lawyers who prepared and who argued causes in Chancery. He had a bitter enmity towards attorneys who victimized their clients through unnecessary delay or through simple professional ignorance and incompetence. The *Dublin Evening Post* took due note of this aversion:

> The brotherhood of attorneys must particularly call for purgation; for the pettifoggers in this branch of the law are really a curse to society and a pest to common honesty. The Chancellor holds a vigilant eye on the conduct of certain

> fortunate knaves of this class and the first that is caught tripping in Court may expect to be held up to view, for the good example of his brethren.[32]

FitzGibbon himself spoke contemptuously of solicitors "versed in the science of collecting costs".[33] On 1 January 1791, he introduced an ambitious and stringent set of regulations binding on those solicitors practicing in Chancery. No solicitor could practice in Chancery who was not also enrolled in the King's Bench, the Common Pleas or the Exchequer. FitzGibbon also required aspiring solicitors in Chancery to have a fixed residence in Dublin. They were to obtain a certificate attesting both to residence in Dublin and to general professional fitness. The certificate was to be signed by the senior Master in Chancery, and the registrar of the court or his deputy. All solicitors thus admitted to Chancery practice were next to sign a roll kept by the Master or his deputies. Alphabetical lists of the solicitors who had signed the roll were to be posted in the offices of the Registrar and the Master of Keeper of the Rolls "for the inspection of every person who shall desire to inspect the same". FitzGibbon took measures not only to impose stricter registration of solicitors who practiced in Chancery, but to increase their accountability. They were obliged to sign all pleas and their names were entered on all writs. Finally, he took measures to instill his own standards of diligence in the attorneys who enrolled in his court. Every solicitor in Chancery, according to this decree, "shall regularly attend the Court from the first day of the Seal before each term to the last day in every year respectively, on pain of being suspended or struck off from the roll of solicitors".[34]

The rules were as clear-sighted as they were exacting. FitzGibbon's characteristic empathy for the situation of poorer, more ignorant suitors marks each one of them. He wanted to ensure that any solicitor pleading a suitor's case would be readily accessible to the supervision of the Chancellor or his deputies, hence the requirement of residence in Dublin. A solicitor in the depths of the countryside could presumably get away with chicanery or ignorance more easily. The required enrollment in other courts ensured at least a measure of legal experience while the certificates and roll of qualified solicitors gave some measure of protection against incompetents or impostors. The required attendance in court served to prevent solicitors from neglecting their cases.

The Act of Union required FitzGibbon to institute further reforms in the Court of Chancery to ensure that the business of the Court would continue during his anticipated absences in England. The Office of Master of the Rolls, which had long served as a sop to great aristocrats or to the relations of lords-lieutenant, became under FitzGibbon's capable direction, a fully functioning deputyship. In consultation with Pepper Arden, who held the equivalent office in England, FitzGibbon endowed the Mastership with all the effective powers of the Chancellor, including the hitherto reserved powers of presiding over commissions of bankruptcy and lunacy.[35] In keeping with the greater responsibilities of the position, FitzGibbon also improved the methods of remuneration. In a letter to Castlereagh, he revealed that practices which he had tacitly accepted as Buckingham's dutiful attorney general, he abhorred as Chancellor:

> There has, however, been a shabby perquisite of the office, arising from an open sale of the situations of six clerks and examiners of the Court of Chancery which certainly ought to be abolished.[36]

Grenville, it will be recalled, made this same objection, with no known support from FitzGibbon. Apparently, he knew too well Lord Buckingham's quite opposite views. Securely established in his desired office, FitzGibbon now recommended, in lieu of this "shabby practice", an annual remuneration of £3,000, including fees.[37] In short, FitzGibbon made every effort to ensure that suitors would not suffer delays for want of an effective, suitably remunerated deputy. This particular arrangement, in FitzGibbon's case, was short-lived. His English parliamentary career consisted of one very unsatisfactory session.

His efforts to improve the order, propriety and integrity of the Court of Chancery were praiseworthy indeed. Nonetheless, FitzGibbon himself, while always demonstrating the highest integrity, failed to show an equal order or propriety in his behavior. He terrorized the diffident, the unprepared or the honestly mistaken barristers who appeared before him. The editorial in the *Morning Post* suggested that during FitzGibbon's term as Chancellor, his detractors looked back longingly to the easy-going, amiable Lifford. An editorial in the *Dublin Evening Post*, published after his death, eagerly anticipated the return of civility and *politesse* under Redesdale:

> ... from the specimen which the Irish Bar has received of Lord Redesdale's manners, it is evident that while stern justice may govern his conduct with regard to the public, they may always expect to be treated with respectful indulgence and courteous affability. The man of modest merit will not be depressed by hauteur or caprice.[38]

If political enemies appeared in his court FitzGibbon lapsed from mere bad manners to childish sadism. Curran, not surprisingly, was a favored target. In one instance, while his great antagonist was making a plea, FitzGibbon ostentatiously played with a favorite Newfoundland dog, no doubt brought to court especially for this insulting purpose. Curran, no mean master of spite himself, did get the better of FitzGibbon. He abruptly paused in his argument, and when FitzGibbon asked the reason, Curran responded, "I thought your Lordships might have been in consultation". Curran also claimed that FitzGibbon's known hatred for him deprived him of clients and of Chancery briefs worth £30,000.[39] This accusation is somewhat dubious. Curran's forte was courtroom forensics, not the dry intricacies of Chancery law. But if FitzGibbon did not actively conspire against Curran, he did behave with extraordinary impropriety in dragging the antagonisms of College Green into the Court of Chancery. His conduct toward Curran and toward other, lesser lights who got into his bad graces presents a mournful contrast with his legal knowledge, his devotion to his office and his reforming zeal.

II

Although he often behaved shamefully when hearing cases, he as often displayed his finest qualities when deciding them. Catholic suitors did indeed find a fair and frequently favorable hearing from him, as Falkiner claimed. In cases concerning tenures he was not as inevitably favorable to tenants as Falkiner believed. But he always strove to impose order and regularity on the surreal confusion of land title and tenure in Ireland. A passion to protect the rights of individuals and an unfailing compassion for the poor and hard pressed also characterized his decisions. Moreover, the anonymous editorialist of the *Dublin Evening Post* rightly noted his remarkable insight into human, and specifically Irish human nature.

As a rule, FitzGibbon seems to have given Catholic claimants every possible benefit of the doubt, often at the expense of Protestants. His protectiveness and his generosity undoubtedly arose from that sense of past wrong that always haunted him. By offering them strict and certain justice in his courts, he tried to offer some redress for the violence and dispossession of the past, and to reconcile them to present English and Protestant rule.

For example, he dismissed the Protestant Lord Trimelston's attempt to repudiate two judgment debts on the grounds of religion. Trimelston had argued that the parties concerned, his father, another kinsman, and a merchant named Dillon, were all Catholics. FitzGibbon agreed that the religion of the parties may have affected the validity of the judgments; but he required stringent proofs that the parties were indeed Catholic and in this respect, Trimelston had manifestly failed to establish his case. As FitzGibbon tartly put it: "Not a tittle of proof of the religion of either [parties to the debt] was made in that cause, or suggested at the hearing of it in the Court of Chancery."[40] Because of this lack of crucial proof, and because of other absurdities and inconsistencies in Trimelston's case, FitzGibbon ordered him to pay the debts, amounting to nearly £4,500, to the Catholic relation claiming them.[41]

Shortly after his elevation to the seals in 1789, FitzGibbon dismissed a motion calling for the removal of a Catholic as guardian of a ward of the court. Although the Preston case remained in a state of tense deadlock, FitzGibbon dismissed the objection to this particular Catholic guardian as "groundless and frivolous."[42]

James Roche may have found FitzGibbon's manner on the bench a little too imperious for his taste, but his father Stephen certainly benefited from the judgment of their family friend. A Protestant discoverer had claimed an estate bequeathed to Stephen Roche by a brother. The brother had spent most of his life in Holland and had died in that country. Consequently, he had never taken the oaths of loyalty which in theory, if not in practice, were required of Catholics before they could benefit from the relief acts of 1778 and 1782. On this basis, the discoverer argued that the bequest to Stephen had no legal standing. FitzGibbon gave his decision in favour of Stephen. He had taken the required oaths and therefore had every right to inherit the property, regardless of his brother's negligence or simple incapacity.[43]

In the case of *Cockburne v. Hussey*, his scrupulousness in providing impartial justice to Catholic and Protestant alike led him to rule against a Protestant who certainly had a powerful moral, if not legal, claim. The case originated in the business transactions of one James Hussey. James, a resident of Drogheda, had conformed in Dublin in 1751. His father Stafford, consequently, became a tenant for life on the two family estates, Rathkenny and Galtrim. In 1767, James sold the reversion of Rathkenny to George Cockburne; six years later Cockburne purchased the reversion of the second estate, Galtrim. After James' death, Stafford took issue with the legitimacy of these sales. He argued that the certificate of conformity supposedly issued to his son gave his name as "James Hussey of Drogheda". Hussey maintained that his son had never gone by that name. Therefore, the certificate of conformity belonged to some other James Hussey. Since there was no proof of his son's conformity, Stafford claimed to be the rightful owner of the property, and not a tenant for life. Cockburne, and after his death, trustees acting for his son, set out to prove that James Hussey was indeed of Drogheda, and therefore, was the individual named in the certificate of conformity. No sooner had they established this fact, when they learned that if James Hussey was in fact of Drogheda, his conformity in Dublin had no validity. Conformity could take place only in the diocese of residence. James had clearly anticipated such a difficulty. He established residence in Dublin, and in 1762 he conformed again. Unfortunately, when the suit to eject Stafford Hussey finally came before Justice Henn in 1790, he refused to admit the evidence of James' second conformity. According to the case as it stood, James Hussey was of Drogheda and he had conformed, invalidly, in Dublin. Consequently, the flaw in his conversion invalidated the sales to Cockburne. The Husseys remained in possession.[44]

Cockburne the younger then applied to FitzGibbon to allow a new trial, thus giving him a chance to establish James Hussey's residence in Dublin and the validity of his second conversion. FitzGibbon refused two such applications and in 1792 Cockburne appealed to the House of Lords. In accounting for his decision, FitzGibbon expressed great sympathy for Cockburne's situation:

> This case has certainly been attended with considerable loss and hardship for the appellant. His father had purchased the estate in question from James Hussey at considerable price as now appears, upon a bad title.[45]

Although he never said as much, FitzGibbon probably regarded old Stafford Hussey as a particularly loathsome example of a rapacious Popish father. But he could not allow Cockburne to disprove his old case and prove another which would support his title. To do so would impeach the integrity of all judicial evidence:

> This application, I will venture to say, stands unexampled in a court of Equity; it struck me as monstrous, and I refused it with costs – However, it was renewed in the next term, when I again rejected it with costs, conceiving it to be a most dangerous and unprecedented experiment; and that compliance with it must have subverted the first principles of justice. I cannot suppose, that the appellant's object is to fabricate evidence to meet the objection to his title which has prevailed in the Court of Law; but if I were to make the precedent for *him* it must be plain to every man of common reason that it would open the door to gross perjury and injustice.[46]

To preserve the "first principles of justice", to maintain inviolate the rule of law for everyone, regardless of religion, FitzGibbon was willing to allow even such as Stafford Hussey to prevail.

Nonetheless, there were some notable exceptions to FitzGibbon's favorable judicial demeanor towards Roman Catholics. In the case of *Fauconberg v. Birch*, heard on appeal in the Irish House of Lords in 1790, the law as it stood did not allow him to make a more favorable ruling. In the matter of a disputed estate claimed by the Hovenden family, which was Roman Catholic, FitzGibbon's fears and antagonism, in this instance got the better of him. Even his successor, himself no friend of the Catholics, found FitzGibbon's ruling highly dubious.

The case of *Fauconberg v. Birch* concerned the validity of a judgment debt between two Catholics, contracted in 1745, when the penal laws were in full force. FitzGibbon ruled that the judgments represented an attempt to evade what were legitimate laws. No money had changed hands; the debt was simply a ploy to allow one of the parties to claim an estate which he could not legally purchase outright. In short, a transaction which in 1790 may have been perfectly legal was, in 1745, a fraud. Although FitzGibbon himself, with varying degrees of enthusiasm had supported the repeal of the penal laws affecting property, the circumstances of the case obliged him to uphold such laws after the fact. Even the impeccably pro-Catholic Yelverton was of this opinion.

However much it rested on a strict point of law, FitzGibbon's opinion had curious echoes of his truculent, anti-Popery speeches of 1778. He raised once again the specter of the ruthless, bigoted Catholic father preying on his convert son:

> ... by the act of passing judgments to the amount of £40,000 conformity to the established church was struck at, as it might be in the power of a father to cut off a son from his inherent right, insomuch that instead of a large estate, by such conveyance, he might not find himself worth ten pounds a year on the day of his conformity.[47]

None of the parties concerned in the case seem to have entered into the judgment out of paternal spite, at least according to published reports of the matter.[48] It would appear that FitzGibbon's visceral dread of Popish fathers made an irrational incursion on his legal reasoning.

His equal dread of dispossessed Catholics, waiting in "sullen indignation" to seize their lost estates, led in the Hovenden case to outright bad law, at least in the opinion of Lord Redesdale. This case involved estates claimed by three separate parties, the Hovendens, Lord Annesley, and Annesley's ter-tenants, the Saunders family. The Hovendens based their claim to the property on a decree of innocence awarded to an ancestor under the Act of Settlement. This decree, they argued, gave them precedence over Annesley, who claimed under a parallel grant of lands made, with extraordinary carelessness, by Charles II, and over the Saunders, who claimed on the basis of an alleged conveyance made by Annesley. In spite of his past attacks on the innate injustice of the Act of Settlement, FitzGibbon saw fit to deny those benefits of the act claimed by the Hovendens. A mere decree of innocence could not establish their claim. It merely left them at liberty to establish their title in a court of law: "... without such a prosecution of his right at law or such a patent, the claimant could never have gotten possession under the decree."[49] In effect FitzGibbon, who had in the past denounced the act for compelling Catholics to prove their innocence, increased the burden of proof. According to his ruling, Catholics were obliged to prove title to lands that himself admitted should never have been taken from them without conclusive evidence of treason or rebellion. A compelling fear of rapacious Catholics appearing in droves to claim lands under such decrees prompted this ruling: "... if his Lordship [FitzGibbon] were to decree title merely on the decree of innocence, he would shake to the foundation almost all the estates in the Kingdom."[50] In addition, he made this ruling in 1799, a year after a major Popish rebellion. No doubt he was particularly sensitive about the security of Protestant property. In a later appeal, Redesdale also dismissed the Hovendens' claim, but in so doing, he dismissed FitzGibbon's reasoning: "The ground on which he [FitzGibbon] is stated to have dismissed it is one which ... did not appear to me as clearly tenable."[51] Redesdale himself ruled against the Hovendens on the more straightforward grounds that the innocent Papist of 1661 was outlawed in 1690 and that his descendants moreover had long allowed other parties to remain in possession of their alleged property.[52]

His decisions in suits involving tenants do not appear to fall into any particular pattern of favor, *pace* Falkiner. In a laudable effort to give FitzGibbon his due, Falkiner seemed to suggest that he unfailingly championed small, struggling farmers. Yet in most of the reported cases, the suitors were wealthy holders of long leases. FitzGibbon tended in such cases to emphasize strict adherence to fair, freely entered, and open agreements on the part of tenant and landlord alike. No doubt he was reacting to the entropy of Irish land tenure, where leases frequently lapsed without due renewal and where tenants frequently assumed the rights of owners.

For example, he refused a renewal claimed by lessees of an Irish estate held by the Duchess of Chandos, because the agreement in question lacked the consent of one of the parties. The original owner of the estate, George Brydges, had granted these leases in 1729. The previous year, he had sold the reversion of the estate to the Duke of Chandos. When the leases came up for renewal, the Duke refused to renew on the grounds of *laches* (neglect) and fraud. The lessees claimed that the original covenant with Brydges had stipulated a renewal. When Chandos died, the tenants revived the suit against the Dowager Duchess and her young daughter, Lady Anne Eliza Brydges. (By the time the case was heard, first in Chancery and then on appeal in the Irish House of Lords, the Duchess had gone mad. It is uncertain whether the confused state of her Irish affairs contributed to her mental collapse.) FitzGibbon maintained that Brydges had never informed Chandos of this particular encumbrance on the Irish estate. Since he had never acted as a party to the original agreement, neither he nor his descendants had any obligation to carry it out.[53]

This same preoccupation with the integrity of agreements appears to have shaped another decision against a tenant. The suitor, George Berney, actually was a small sublessor of 15 acres. Berney claimed that his head landlord, owing to an election grudge, had conspired with Berney's father and uncle to eject him from his lease for supposed non-payment of rent. The father and the uncle failed to pass on rent that Berney had paid for his share of the leasehold. Notwithstanding this allegation of fraud, Berney entered into an agreement with the head landlord, one Moore, to pay fines and arrears by a certain date, in return for reinstatement to his tenure. Moore then claimed that Berney had failed to pay the agreed upon sum at the agreed upon time and again revoked his lease. The case as reported by Ridgeway, is singularly confusing and contradictory; to make matters worse, the report includes no comment by FitzGibbon, who had a genius for elucidating obscurity that Ridgeway was sometimes content to leave unplumbed. FitzGibbon simply may have concluded that Berney had failed to keep his end of the bargain to which he had freely agreed; whatever injustices and oppressions he had suffered in the past, he therefore lost his right to the tenure.[54]

As the matter of the Blundell estate reveals, FitzGibbon could rule as readily in the tenant's favor, if he believed the landlord was reneging on a just claim. The landlord, or rather the landlords, were the heirs of Lord Blundell. They comprised Anna Maria Blundell, Mary, Lady Robert Bertie and the Earl and Countess of Hillsborough. The tenant in question, one MacCartney, had leased the manor of Dundrum from Lord Blundell for £700 per annum. Landlord and tenant soon fell out. MacCartney failed to keep up on his rent, and in spite of a covenant to renew in the original lease, Blundell's heirs denied a second lease. MacCartney, in response, refused to give up possession of Dundrum. After a long, tedious series of suits and countersuits, Anna Maria Blundell and her co-heirs made an offer to FitzGibbon, who had inherited the suit from Lifford. They would take the suit to the Court of Common Pleas. That court could them weigh MacCartney's claims for damages for the broken lease against theirs for "tortious possession" of Dundrum. This comparison was to result in an equitable settlement of all outstanding damages. FitzGibbon agreed and the issue was tried. The verdict proved highly disappointing, not to say shocking, to Anna Maria Blundell and her co-suiters MacCartney's award far exceeded not only their own for "tortious possession", but the total assets of Lord

Blundell's estate. Claiming that their lawyers had misled them, they appealed to FitzGibbon to set aside the agreement. FitzGibbon refused and the Blundell heirs took the matter to the Irish House of Lords. In defending his judgment, FitzGibbon once again appealed to the inviolability of agreements, his guiding theme in determining all property and tenure suits:

> ... if your Lordships should establish such a precedent and reverse a leading order made by consent, upon the appeal of one of the parties to that consent, in my opinion, you will establish a most dangerous and unwarrantable precedent, more particularly as no objection has been made or can be made in this case to the leading order of the Court of Chancery as injurious in itself to the appellants – No; the injury of which they complain, if it exists, has arisen from their own deliberate act in another court – an act which was altogether their own, as the order of the Court of Chancery left it wholly in their option whether the make the set off or not in the Court of Law.[55]

His fellow peers upheld the contract and the decree.

If FitzGibbon the politician gained a reputation for a tyrannical contempt for individual rights, his conduct as chancellor gives exactly the opposite impression. In his judicial conduct, he spared no effort to uphold political, civil and legal rights to their fullest extent. In *Page in Error v. the King*, heard before the Irish House of Lords in 1792, FitzGibbon disallowed the admission of two freemen to the borough of Dundalk, because, among other irregularities, the bailiff had failed to notify one qualified voter of the impending election. According to FitzGibbon, the bailiff's negligence not only deprived one man of his right to vote, it deprived his fellow electors of opinions and insights that might have influenced the election in another direction: "... though his vote could not make a majority, yet his reasons might have influenced a majority."[56] Again, FitzGibbon's eloquence and his scrupulous notions of the rights of electors prevailed. The election was disallowed.

During Lord Kingston's trial for murder in May 1798, FitzGibbon showed an equal scrupulousness for the rights of the lordly defendant. The circumstances of the murder were deliciously corrupt and thunderously melodramatic, in the finest tradition of Irish aristocratic scandal. Colonel FitzGerald, an illegitimate relation, had seduced and eloped with Lord Kingston's daughter, Lady Mary King. Kingston and his son Robert duly tracked down the erring daughter and her seducer. Robert King defended his sister's honour in an inconclusive duel with FitzGerald. Lord Kingston, meanwhile, brought Lady Mary back to the virtuous seclusion of Mitchelstown. Kingston soon discovered that Colonel FitzGerald, unchastened by duel and disgrace, had followed Lady Mary to inveigle her into a second elopement. Kingston, again accompanied by an avenging brother, tracked FitzGerald down to a nearby inn. In the angry confusion that followed, FitzGerald aimed a pistol at young King, and Kingston, to defend his son, shot and killed FitzGerald. In the capacity of Lord High Steward, FitzGibbon presided over the trial in the House of Lords. His address to

Lord Kingston generously set forth several possible defenses and offered tactful and kindly reassurances:

> Robert, Earl of Kingston, you are brought here to answer one of the most serious charges that can be made against any man – the murder of a fellow subject. The solemnity and awful appearance of this judicature must materially discompose and embarrass your lordship. It may therefore not be improper for me to remind your lordship that you are to be tried by the laws of a free country, framed for the protection of innocence and the punishment of guilt alone, and it must be a great consolation to you that you are to receive a trial before the supreme judicature of this nation, that you are to be tried by your Peers, upon whose unbiased judgment and candour you can have the firmest reliance...It will also be a consolation to you to know that the benignity of our law has distinguished the crime of homicide into different classes. If it arise from accident, from inevitable necessity, or without malice, it does not fall within the crime of murder, and of these distinctions, warranted by evidence, you will be at liberty to take advantage.[57]

Lord Kingston had no need to make use of the elaborate defenses FitzGibbon offered to him. His fellow peers quickly came to the conclusion that regardless of accident, necessity or malice, Lord Kingston had acted as became any wronged father, and they accepted his plea of "not guilty".

FitzGibbon's loveliest quality, his compassion for the poor and hard-done by graced many of his decisions. The *Hibernian Journal* reported one instance of both pity and promptness of decision:

> The humanity and attention of his Excellency the Lord Chancellor was exemplified a few days in a very extraordinary manner. A trader who by various misfortunes in trade had been reduced to a state of bankruptcy, and against whom a commission had issued and who had complied with every requisite specified in the act for the relief of bankrupts, was arrested at the suit of an unrelenting and severe creditor (the debt by no means originating with the bankrupt) and thrown in jail. Under these circumstances, together with his having a summons from the commissioners named in the Commission which had issued against him, to attend them on a future day, the bankrupt was advised to petition the Lord Chancellor, which he did, and verified his petition by affidavits. The Lord Chancellor on reading the petition and the affidavit, instantly made an order in his own handwriting, that the bankrupt should be immediately discharged out of custody, and he was discharged accordingly.[58]

The matter of the dreadful Redington family offered yet another conspicuous example of FitzGibbon's compassion, as well as his penetrating common sense. The parties in the suit comprised the widow and children of one Michael Redington, a bankrupt merchant, Michael's brothers Nicholas and Thomas, and Thomas's son and namesake. The hard dealing of old Thomas Redington, father of Michael, Nicholas and Thomas, was the root of the case. Redington, apparently a Protestant himself, had married a Catholic lady and had reared his children in their mother's religion. Therefore, he was a Catholic, to all intents and purposes, under the penal laws. Redington, who emerged from the reports of the case as an extraordinarily mean-spirited, rapacious and unscrupulous individual, undertook an elaborate serious of schemes to evade the consequences of his legal status. He encouraged two sons, Nicholas and Michael, to convert to the established church. Through the agency of Nicholas, who acted as the nominal buyer, Old Redington acquired the estates of Lisinalla and Kilcornan. He bestowed Lisinalla on Nicholas and Kilcornan on Thomas, his remaining Catholic son. Michael set up as a merchant in Cork, and soon he too was purchasing property on his father's behalf. Through his agency, Old Redington acquired two additional estates, Cahirowen and Reyhill.

In 1775, Michael started having financial difficulties. His father refused to give him any assistance. Instead, he compelled Michael to enter into an enormous judgment debt that would have made his father his premier creditor in the event of a bankruptcy. Old Redington, of course, did not give Michael a penny of this supposed loan. He aimed above all at protecting his investment in the two estates which Michael had allegedly bought. Michael eventually did go bankrupt. He fled the country, and by the time the case came before FitzGibbon, he was presumed dead. Old Redington then came into possession of Michael's estates as chief creditor. His callousness toward the son fortunately did not extend to the son's widow and children. They lived with old Redington until his death in 1780.[59]

Old Redington's second son and namesake then paid Mrs Michael a maintenance of £93 6s. 8d., which amounted to one third of the rents of Cahirowen and Reyhill. Mrs Michael accepted this money under the impression that she was receiving her legal share from property that old Thomas had left to her husband and to her children. Thomas Redington II, who seems to have inherited many of his father's more unlovely traits, later claimed he had paid this odd sum strictly out of friendship for his unfortunate sister-in-law.[60] In 1788, Michael's oldest son, also named Thomas, came of age and claimed the two estates of Reyhill and Cahirowen. Like his mother, this Thomas Redington assumed that his grandfather had rescued the estates from bankruptcy for the benefit of Michael's widow and children. His uncle and namesake and his uncle Nicholas opposed this claim. They declared that Michael in fact had purchased the estates in trust for his brother and for his nephew. It was a particularly hard claim, since Thomas the son of Michael had nothing, while his uncle Thomas possessed a tidy estate of his own, and his cousin had inherited the bulk of old Redington's huge personal fortune.[61]

The suit went first to Chancery and then to the Irish House of Lords in 1794. In both his court and in the Lords, FitzGibbon upheld the claims of Michael's family. In his superb elucidation of this squalid and confusing case, FitzGibbon appealed to the principle of *Fauconberg v. Birch*. If Michael had indeed purchased the properties in trust for his Catholic father and brother, he had violated the laws of the time. Thus the whole transaction was therefore void.[62]

Apart from the limitations of the penal laws, Thomas, as the supposed beneficiary, had a compelling obligation to offer proof of any trust. He had manifestly failed to support his bare assertion of the trust's existence. On the contrary, his public actions all suggested that he, in fact, was acting as trustee for Michael and his family. For example, he had given a bid for the property on his brother's behalf, since Michael could not attend the auction in person. Michael, in return had given Thomas £100 for his services as agent. Whatever his claims of friendship, Thomas had paid his sister-in-law the precise sum of her dower right to the property, another indication that he knew perfectly well that Michael and his family were the rightful owners. FitzGibbon dismissed as "wild and fantastical" any claim that Thomas was pretending to act as trustee for his own trustee.[63]

Above all, the claims against Michael's hapless family simply violated all notions of sense and decency. Even a man as crabbed and selfish as old Redington would not have consigned Michael's wife and children to beggary, after having received them in his house.[64] Moreover, his will strongly suggested a settlement of some kind.[65] FitzGibbon contemptuously brushed aside the claim of the Redington brothers that their father had been referring to money advanced to Michael when he set up as a merchant. To suggest that old Redington would have considered this lost money a provision was ridiculous.[66] Moreover, in his account book, he had indicated that the advances to Michael were "on account," which surely meant that he intended to make a further provision.[67] In addition, old Redington had suggested that Michael and Nicholas had received equivalent settlements. Since Nicholas had received an estate from his father, however dubiously, then the same held true for Michael.[68]

FitzGibbon's statement of the case is striking, not only for the clarity and power of his statement of the facts, but for his obvious pity for the hapless Michael. In one particularly felicitous and stinging turn of phrase, FitzGibbon noted old Redington's displeasure at Michael for "the crimes of poverty and misfortune".[69] FitzGibbon brought this wretched tale of penal law corruption to the most satisfying possible conclusion. The House of Lords upheld his ruling and confirmed Michael's son in the ownership of Cahirowen and Reyhill.[70]

His rule of the 2 December 1800 seems out of FitzGibbon's usual compassionate character. It declared that if a pauper plaintiff failed to appear for the hearing of his cause, "in such case the defendant in such cause shall be entitled to have his costs of the day against such plaintiff, notwithstanding such plaintiff being a pauper".[71] FitzGibbon undoubtedly reasoned that poor suitors ultimately benefited the most from the swift determination of causes. Therefore, he had to discourage any kind of delay, even if that delay came from pauper plaintiffs who otherwise merited his compassion.

FitzGibbon had a remarkable gift, not only for making cogent summaries of confused facts, but for penetrating the darker mysteries of human motivation. The sharp, cynical observations which enliven his opinions suggest that he could have made a very fine novelist, had he cared to pursue the literary life. His opinions often read like a bleakly humorous novel of high life and low life in Georgian Dublin. In dismissing the will of Dorothea Napper, FitzGibbon executed an acute pen portrait of a half-crazed alcoholic spinster, vulnerable to every kind of trickery and undue influence:

> Upon inspecting the proofs in this cause, it appears to me that the said Dorothea Napper had been for some years before her death of a very capricious and extravagant turn of mind, and much addicted to the excessive and intemperate use of spirits. Considering her, therefore to have been a probable subject for imposition, I am humbly of opinion that there is sufficient ground for the objection, inasmuch as the evidence of her original instructions for this will is extremely defective and suspicious and the will does not correspond with the instructions which are alleged to have been given by the deceased for preparing it.[72]

The matter of *Kiely v. Monck* gave FitzGibbon a pretext to denounce paternal tyranny and to elucidate at length on the financial plight of marriageable men in Ireland. The father of Ann Kiely, the plaintiff, had bequeathed her £1,800 on two conditions: she was to receive permission for any marriage from both her mother and her uncle, and she was to confine her choice to a man who had a freehold estate of £500 per annum, clear of encumbrances. If she failed to meet either or both of these requirements, she could not inherit. Ann married the Reverend Mr Kiely after obtaining her mother's and her uncle's permission, as specified. Unfortunately, she apparently failed to ascertain his financial position carefully enough. When she applied to her brother for her legacy, he refused, on the grounds that Mr Kiely, whatever his other charms and graces, did not meet their late father's financial criterion. To FitzGibbon's mind, the old man's conditions were so unreasonable as to prevent Ann from marrying altogether. Few, if indeed any, men could claim an estate of £500 per annum, free and clear of encumbrances. His account of the economic situation of young middle-class bachelors has the social realism of a Trollope or a Balzac:

> How many particular professions are virtually excluded by that condition? What man of the profession of law has set out with a clear, unencumbered real estate of £500 a year, or has acquired such an estate for years after his entry into the profession? How many men of the other learned professions can come within this condition? It will in effect exclude 99 men in 100 of every profession, whether civil, military or ecclesiastical. It in effect excludes nearly every mercantile man in the kingdom, for let his *personal* estate be never so great, unless he is seized of *real* estate of the ascertained description, he is excluded. Every man who has an estate in remainder only, be the value what it may, is excluded.[73]

In short, this "weak old man" [Ann's father] had gone far beyond the legitimate authority of a parent and had virtually condemned Ann to spinsterhood. His action clearly violated legal precedent which prohibited unreasonable conditions in restraint of marriage. Ann's father had moreover, left a miserable legacy of family discord, which FitzGibbon described with his wonted moral indignation and novelistic power:

> And I cannot but say that the scenes of enmity and discord and disunion which has now prevailed for years in this family, ought to teach any man who hears me the mischievous folly of attempting to judge his narrowness, and caprice, even after he has sunk in the ground.[74]

FitzGibbon's powers of observation sometimes failed him. In the case of John Magee, publisher of the *Dublin Evening Post*, FitzGibbon possibly allowed his own personal enmities to affect his judgment. In the autumn of 1789, Magee had become embroiled in feud with Francis Higgins, the government's hired hack, and with Lord Clonmell, the Lord Chief Justice of the King's Bench. His two formidable adversaries retaliated with a libel suit, which they won. Clonmell, flush with legal victory, subjected Magee to a succession of imprisonments and fines. Magee faced additional legal anxiety when his brother, appalled at his reckless defiance of authority and at other instances of mental instability, sued to commit him as a lunatic. FitzGibbon dismissed the brother's suit. Magee, he argued, had undoubtedly shown extraordinary folly in many of his actions, but such behavior hardly constituted grounds for a claim of lunacy:

> ... there was no occasion – there was not a shadow of a ground for his issuing a commission, supposing all the charges true – they only amounted to acts of extravagance and indiscretion – but that was no ground for a Commission of Lunacy – if he was to grant one against every man who was to do an extravagant, an unwise, or even a bad thing, he was afraid he would have a great many wards of the court.[75]

For a brief period after this judgment, the *Dublin Evening Post* surpassed even *Faulkner's Dublin Journal* and Francis Higgins' *Freeman's Journal* for fawning, both in prose and in verse:

> Long mayst thou reign upon the judgment seat
> Long mayst thou be the guardian of the land
> Long mayst thou live to keep thy country great
> Esteem'd, entrusted with its chief command.[76]

FitzGibbon may have dismissed the lunacy suit , not because of his wisdom and benevolence, but because he saw an opportunity to snub his enemy Clonmell, who was in hot legal pursuit of Magee. Whatever FitzGibbon's motives, his decision proved disastrously mistaken. By 1797, Magee had lapsed into unmistakable madness and his newspaper came under the jurisdiction of the Court of Chancery.[77]

FitzGibbon's precision and pride of intellect made him sharply critical of his peers when they erred. At various times in his career as Chancellor, he directed his wrath toward a Judge of the Prerogative Court, the already sullied Baron Hamilton, Baron Power, and his old associate Patrick Duigenan. Their respective faults of judicial error, carelessness, financial impropriety and simple undignified mischief-making provoked his anger and his judicial intervention.

In the case of the judge of the Prerogative Court, FitzGibbon took issue with his handling of the disputed will of one James Goodwin, and he petitioned the King at length to grant a commission of review. Goodwin's nephew William had originally petitioned the Prerogative Court, an ecclesiastical tribunal which shared jurisdiction over wills and testaments. He requested this court to set aside a will disinheriting him and benefiting instead one Theodore Giesler. Shortly before his death, in August of 1788, Goodwin had abruptly left the home which he had long shared with relatives, and took up residence in the house of Giesler, "a native of Germany and an utter stranger to him". Giesler first prevailed on the ailing and confused old man to grant him a loan, on a very questionable security. Then, on the day before his death, Goodwin hastily drew up a will in Giesler's favor. FitzGibbon account of the case gives an unmistakable impression of psychological pressure, not to say intimidation: Goodwin was "surrounded by Giesler and his immediate friends and connections."[78] To complete the suspicious picture, FitzGibbon observed that Esther Patrickson, "who is nearly related to the wife of Giesler", acted as the old man's amanuensis. William Godwin's counsel noted the contradictions between the evidence of Patrickson and of the two witnesses to the alleged will, and called for its condemnation as a fraud. Instead of making a ruling on the proofs as they had already been presented, the judge, whom FitzGibbon discreetly left unnamed in his petition to the King, took "a most unwarrantable course of proceeding".[79]

The anonymous judge permitted Giesler's counsel to subject Patrickson to a *viva voce* examination, with a view to clarifying the contradictions in her earlier testimony. He then called for an examination of the two subscribing witnesses, again by Giesler's counsel. In his legitimate desire to establish the facts and to clear up inconsistencies, the judge in effect gave Patrickson and the other witnesses an opportunity to re-frame more convincing stories with appropriate guidance by sympathetic counsel. As FitzGibbon noted, Esther Patrickson could have been present in court to hear the objections presented by William Goodwin's counsel. By implication the two witnesses of the will as easily could have heard Patrickson's public *viva voce* examination and adjusted their testimony accordingly. FitzGibbon allowed that the judge could rightly examine the witnesses privately to "inform his conscience". But advocates in the cause were totally unsuited to do so; their examinations inevitably would "be influenced by their zeal for the interests of their client". In short the judge had badly undermined the integrity of the evidence with this unwarranted procedure. It was enough to madden FitzGibbon, who was a stickler for both rules of evidence and for correct procedure, and his appeal to the King clearly shows his irritation:

> From every inquiry which I have been able to make, this proceeding stands unexampled in this county and in my humble opinion, if it shall be drawn into precedent, must have the most dangerous consequences to the jurisprudence of your majesty's ecclesiastical courts in this kingdom. To re-examine the witness *viva voce* at the hearing, to supply a defect or to explain a contradiction in the testimony originally given which may bear directly upon the merits of the cause is a proceeding in my humble opinion, subversive of the first principles of justice.[80]

In addition to allowing impeached evidence, the judge had overlooked a significant item of information in the testimony of Charlotte Higgenbottam, with whom the old man had lived before he fell in with Giesler. She declared that the signature, J. Goodwin, was a forgery. According to Mrs. Higgenbottam, Goodwin had always signed either his full Christian name or he had used the abbreviation "Jas". The judge, nonetheless, gave more weight to the testimony of Patrickson and her confederates and had upheld the validity of the will. In a separate letter to Loughborough, FitzGibbon all but declared that the Judge of the Prerogative Court had behaved like a senile old fool and had put to shame the entire system of Irish ecclesiastical courts:

> Your Lordship will, I trust, upon reading my report, be of opinion that I could not in justice have done otherwise. But as it contains a statement which I am sorry to say does not reflect much credit upon that particular branch of jurisprudence in this country, I wish to apprise your Lordship that the late Judge of the Court of Prerogative, at the time he heard this cause, was considerably impaired in his faculties and that he retired from his situation very soon after he had pronounced sentence in it.[81]

He made a still harsher indictment of the Court of Delegates, whither Goodwin had carried an appeal. FitzGibbon faulted the judges for refusing Goodwin's request for a delay of one day to examine the record of past proceedings and to prepare his plea. Consequently, Goodwin was unable to present his case adequately, and the Court of Delegates re-affirmed Giesler's claim. To FitzGibbon, this decision weighed particularly harshly on Goodwin, whose "extreme state of poverty" prevented him from consistently pursuing his case. Goodwin, in fact, was entitled to more time than he had actually requested:

> When a record is removed from any of your Majesty's Courts of Law by writ of error, the plaintiff in error has four days allowed to him to assign errors, to the end that he may have an opportunity of inspecting the record, and if it has not been faithfully certified to the court of error, of alleging diminution.[82]

The Court of Delegates not only willfully prevented Goodwin from examining the record of the earlier trial, they themselves carelessly disregarded that same record.

FitzGibbon implied that any reasonably careful examination of the "transmiss" would have revealed flaws in the evidence and in the proceedings:

> ... as they had determined to pronounce final judgment upon the appeal submitted to them, without affording to the appellant an opportunity of being heard by his advocates and counsel upon the merits of his cause, in my humble opinion, it was their duty minutely to have inspected the whole transmiss and to have weighed attentively all the proofs which had been made in the cause and were certified to them, before they ventured to pronounce a sentence which must ultimately conclude the rights of the parties.[83]

In short, the conduct of the Court of Delegates offended not only his strict sense of judicial propriety, but his sense of the courts as a certain refuge for the poor. FitzGibbon laid the greatest share of blame on Baron Hamilton, who had acted as one of the delegates; he "was at times induced to expedite the decision of a court somewhat more than as perfectly consistent with due attention to its merits."[84] Apparently, Hamilton had learned nothing from the affair of David FitzGerald in 1788. His old slapdash habits of business persisted. The existing records do not indicate whether Goodwin obtained a re-examination of his cause. It is clear that FitzGibbon made a powerful case both for Goodwin's rights and for the weaknesses of the judges' decisions.

Baron Power literally preferred to die rather than face censure from FitzGibbon. In addition to serving as a judge of the Exchequer Court, Power held the position of Usher of the Court of Chancery. Traditionally, the Usher had the right to claim the interest from all moneys held in trust by the Court of Chancery. Power exceeded the limits of this perquisite when he appropriated the interest on the Irish rents of the Duchess of Chandos, who was not only a suitor but a ward in Chancery. According to the agreement made with her tenants and with her trustees, both rent and interest were to remain in trust. When the Chandos tenants and trustees learned that Power had made the interest over to himself, they complained to FitzGibbon. He promptly issued a characteristically peremptory order for Baron Power to appear in the Court of Chancery to account for the appropriated money. To Power, a haughty man who, in company with many others, detested FitzGibbon, this order constituted the worst humiliation. He did humble himself enough to plead his rank as a fellow judge and the long-standing practice of his office. Powers' rank had little weight with FitzGibbon, who prided himself on upholding the law without fear or favor. Nor did FitzGibbon, with his fastidious standards of judicial integrity, find Powers' claims of long-standing usage convincing. He had appropriated money in violation of a clear decree in Chancery, and he was obliged to account for it, as ordered. Power evaded his relentless colleague by the only means possible. The Sunday before his decreed appearance in Chancery, Power rode his horse to a pier near Ringsend. He dismounted, turned the horse over to the keeping of his servant, and walked off the pier. His body was washed ashore several days later.[85] In one of his few acts of patronage to a family member, FitzGibbon later bestowed the office of Usher in Chancery on his son Richard, the profits of which were to provide him with a portion of £20,000.[86]

Patrick Duigenan's antics as King's Advocate in the Court of Admiralty aroused the displeasure of his former counselor. The case which set them at odds originated in events occurring before and during the naval war with Spain in 1796–7. A captured Spanish vessel, the *Descada.* was the source of contention. Sir William Scott, the eminent judge of the English Admiralty, had condemned the *Descada* as a prize of war, which made all merchandise on board royal property. Duigenan, from the venue of the Irish Admiralty Court in Dublin, intervened in the case on behalf of two Irish merchants resident in Havana, René and Edward Payne. They had insured goods belonging to one Allwood, another merchant, presumably Irish as well, resident in Havana. In so insuring Allwood's merchandise, they paid the rates demanded for neutral shipping. In return for payment of the insurance and in satisfaction of debts which Allwood owed to them, the Paynes were to receive the proceeds from the sale of the goods in Hamburg. Unfortunately, while the *Descada* was en route to Hamburg, hostilities again resumed between Spain and England. Evidently, Duigenan had instituted a suit on behalf of René and Edward Payne to declare the ship and its cargo *British* and not Spanish property. In so doing, according to FitzGibbon, Duigenan acted "not only without authority from the Irish government, but against the strong remonstrances of Lord Camden [then lord lieutenant] from the first moment he heard of them". In response FitzGibbon again wrote to Loughborough and promised to put a curb on Duigenan's proceedings. He again indulged himself in castigating the indiscretion and foolishness of another of his colleagues in the Irish judiciary: "It seems necessary for me to state that his Majesty's Advocate is not a very right headed nor yet a very practicable man".[87] FitzGibbon would make every effort to "bring him to reason". But if Duigenan persisted in his trouble-making, FitzGibbon expressed perfect willingness to see him removed from office.[88] In passing, he also had some unkind words for Jonah Barrington, who, in spite of his patriotic principles, had managed to secure an appointment as admiralty judge. Barrington "shelters himself under the proceedings carried on by Dr Duigenan and alleges with some appearance of reason that so far as the suit has gone, he could not but entertain it, when prosecuted by the King's Advocate in the name and on behalf of His Majesty." Yet Barrington knew perfectly well that the suit was frivolous and spurious. Clearly FitzGibbon more than reciprocated Barrington's contempt. Duigenan apparently allowed himself to be brought to reason. Six months after these proceedings, he and FitzGibbon purged Trinity College of United Irishmen, with every appearance of harmony.

III

Above all, FitzGibbon displayed an absolute intolerance toward any aspersions on his conduct as a judge. He condemned the Redington family not only for callous greed but for publishing their own version of the suit, including highly critical comments on the Lord Chancellor's decision of it. In their case, he merely threatened prosecution if they, or any other suitor repeated the offense. Others were not so lucky. In 1799, FitzGibbon brought suit against one Parry, the proprietor and editor of an English radical newspaper called the *Courier*. Parry's accusations of corruption on the bench distressed FitzGibbon as much, if not more, than the alleged editorial calls for his assassination.[90] He refused all offers of a mere apology and requested damages of £2,000. The English jury placed a somewhat lower valuation of £1,000 on FitzGibbon's reputation.[91] Nonetheless, he pursued Lord Aldborough, a fellow peer, far more relentlessly than he did semi-convert gentry or English journalists.

The business started on 16 January 1797, when Aldborough, an eccentric as well as a hot-tempered man, introduced an address to the King. It was an odd, rambling production recommending, among many other things, the increased manufacture of rope and sailcloth, the improvement of Irish coinage and the maintenance of a fleet off the Irish as well as the English coast.[92] FitzGibbon refused to received the address, because Aldborough had presented it out of the usual order of business. All of the other peers who spoke on the matter, notably Dillon and Clonmell, supported FitzGibbon. Piqued, Aldborough entered the rejected address on the Journals as a protest.[93]

Four days later, Aldborough presented another address, thanking the yeomanry of Ireland for their loyal good service. This composition too his fellow peers rejected, first because it duplicated portions of the Speech from the Throne, and secondly because it made invidious distinctions between the yeomanry on one hand and the regular forces and the militia on the other. Aldborough's pride, already sore from the first rejection, rebelled at this second. He made the curious rejoinder that he had the "highest respect" for the regular forces and the militia, but "they are composed of the very refuse of society". Quite apart from militiamen and regulars of low degree, a "noble lord, high in station" provoked Aldborough. FitzGibbon, he claimed, had "beckoned to one or two other noble lords, his friends, to oppose me." Aldborough proceeded to attack FitzGibbon for this perceived insult to a fellow peer:

> The learned lord and I are at issue; he is not my friend and I am not his friend; and however high the ministerial situation of the learned lord, it was unparliamentary to treat a Peer of this realm with disrespect or set his face against this motion, for all he may be carried about in ever so much state.[94]

In his response, FitzGibbon cast ridicule on Aldborough's addresses on his claims that he had resorted to a "*beckoned* opposition": "Did any possible cause exist why I should be afraid to stand up in my place and express with freedom my sentiments on any motion of his?"[95] FitzGibbon then suggested the true reason for Aldborough's anger: he had previously decided two suits in Chancery against Aldborough himself. One of the suits involved actions taken against Aldborough's sister, Lady Elizabeth Tynte. The second concerned a sale of property, which had adversely affected

Aldborough. FitzGibbon claimed further that Aldborough, while the matter of the Tynte estates was pending in Chancery, had tried to influence his judgment:

> ... I will beg leave to set the noble Earl right in this respect, and probably he will agree in the correction if his memory leaves him relative to a correspondence with which his lordship was pleased to honor me about two sessions ago – a cause was then pending in the Court of Chancery in which a near relation of the noble earl was concerned. [Lady E. Tynte] On this subject the noble earl wrote me a letter of such a nature that when I perceived its tendency, I committed it to the flames.
>
> I received another letter on the same subject, and he even attempted to press it on me in the street. I took no other notice then of such an indignity offered to me and to justice, then merely telling the noble earl that many men were induced to acts of impropriety by female influence. – Notwithstanding, the solicitations were renewed by letter, and I was obliged to order my porter to write the noble earl a card, prohibiting the further honor of his correspondence; and had he persisted, I will now tell the noble earl, that I would have laid his estates under sequestration and made him feel the indignation and integrity of justice.[96]

Aldborough made no recorded public reply to these remarks. Instead, he resorted to a printed vindication of his own conduct and a ferocious attack on FitzGibbon's public and private character. He accused FitzGibbon of willful corruption in judging suits in Chancery, of arrogance and impropriety in presiding over the House of Lords, and of the arbitrary removal of perfectly honest magistrates from their commissions in Wicklow. In particular, he gave his own highly charged version of the causes to which FitzGibbon had alluded. In the matter of Lady Elizabeth Tynte, FitzGibbon had abruptly changed the receiver of the rents of her late son's estate; this action he took without any consultation with Aldborough, a trustee of Sir James Tynte. In addition, FitzGibbon had seized Lady Tynte's jointure and personal property out of mere personal, arbitrary spite. This last action, as Aldborough noted in another of his many commentaries on the case, "reduced a widow lady of respectability to beggary". As for the second suit, Aldborough accused FitzGibbon of deliberately preventing him from purchasing an estate and of favoring instead the claims of his relation, Marcus Beresford. He crowned these accusations with an anecdote about an extortionate Dutch skipper whom Aldborough had allegedly encountered in his travels. According to this tale, Aldborough had brought suit against the skipper for his various frauds, only to find, when he arrived in court, that the skipper himself was acting as judge. The skipper of course decided in his own favor. Aldborough then expressed a determination to appeal, but he soon dropped the matter when he learned that the skipper would preside over that suit as well. Of course, the tale had nothing to do with the perils of Dutch jurisprudence, and everything to do with the Court of Chancery in Ireland.[97]

According to Aldborough's own characteristically muddled and self-serving account, he had intended to distribute these printed copies privately to his friends. One of them, whom Aldborough never named, betrayed him and showed a copy to FitzGibbon. FitzGibbon then dispatched Marcus Beresford to the printer to purchase a copy. The printer informed Beresford that "he had none to sell". The printer unfortunately committed the indiscretion of leaving copies not only in full view but within reach of Beresford, who peremptorily seized one. The day following this transaction, FitzGibbon rose, appropriated pamphlet in hand, to denounce "one of the most infamous and daring libels ever uttered either against any individual or legislative Assembly".[98] FitzGibbon made an elaborate pretense of attributing the infamous and daring libel in question to the hapless printer, who, he pretended to believe, had misappropriated Aldborough's name. But he knew full well the true identity of the "reptile of a libeler." His supposed misapprehension gave him the liberty to indulge his fury to the full.

FitzGibbon adverted first to the charge that he had cheated Lord Aldborough out of an estate which was being sold to settle the claims of a suit in Chancery. In response, he read records of the Court indicating that had in fact, kept the sale open at Lord Aldborough's request, even after three other men had made bids and deposits on it. Lord Aldborough had promised to come forward, within two weeks with £280 more than the other bidders. Although he failed to keep his part of the bargain, he nonetheless applied again to FitzGibbon to keep the sale open. The fact that the estate adjoined his own accounted for Aldborough's persistence in the matter. As FitzGibbon explained to the Lords:

> "[he] urged as a principle inducement to my holding open the sale that the possession of the estate would give him considerable influence at the next general election and materially preponderate against that of a noble Lord his neighbor, in possession, but not residing in this kingdom; he urged in excuse for not coming forward agreeable to the condition [by] which I had made the order for keeping open the sale, that he was building a great house near Dublin, which employed all his money and where he hoped he should frequently have the pleasure of seeing me, with much more matter to this effect."[99]

In justice to the other parties, who were anxious to settle the business, FitzGibbon decreed the estate to the highest of the original bidders, Dominic McCausland, who "paid the full purchase money and was put in consequent possession".

As for the claims about wholesale and unjust dismissals of magistrates, FitzGibbon offered this explanation:

> I do recollect that there was a period when the legislature of this country thought it expedient to issue afresh the Commissions of the Peace; in doing so, and I am sure, adhering to the intention of such regulation, I remember having omitted the name of a distiller in Baltinglass, and mainly because I did not think any

> man in his situation sufficiently independent of all influence to be entrusted with so very important a function as that of magistrate. I am not sensible of any other instance of this kind with could affect the noble earl.[100]

FitzGibbon's account of the matter of Lady Elizabeth Tynte suggested not a wronged woman arbitrarily deprived of her just maintenance, but an incompetent and a dishonest spendthrift:

> On the demise the late Sir James Tynte's father, Lady Elizabeth Tynte was appointed executor; that the birth of Sir James having been posthumous, a minority of 21 years consequently ensued; that certain heavy encumbrances affected the estate, none of which were removed, that he dying and some circumstances occurring added to the suits instituted in the Court of Chancery for recovery of these encumbrances, his Lordship [FitzGibbon] had appointed receivers to the estates, and the consequence was, by the prudent and judicious management of the receivers, the incumbrances were nearly all discharged and that by the time the children of Sir James shall have arrived at age, their ... possessions will devolve to them undiminished instead of being wasted away ... as they would have been were they suffered to remain in the hands from which the libeler [calls] their act of removal an injustice. To state the foundation in truth of this opinion, his Lordship said that during all the time of Sir J.'s minority and since his death to this very day, Lady E. Tynte could not by any means be brought to account for the receipt of the estates for that period ... and were it not for the indulgence of the opposite party, he must have been obliged by the rules of his court to enforce her compliance by ordering her ladyship to prison.

FitzGibbon played the charade to the end by moving that the printer of the libel be ordered to the bar of the House of Lords. Aldborough, in response, asserted both his own authorship, and the truth of what he had written:

> The Earl of Aldborough said he would prove every word in what the noble earl called a libel to be founded in fact and to contain nothing but the most literal truth.

Halpern, the printer, did make a token appearance before the Lords, to confirm Aldborough's self-incriminating statements. Lord Aldborough, he informed the Lords, had indeed given him the material in question. With a supreme lack of curiosity, Halpern had never examined the original manuscript; he simply passed it on to his workmen. In answer to an inquiry from Clonmell, he stated that he had never sold any copies of Aldborough's work. Aldborough had intended them exclusively for the reading pleasure of his friends and supporters. In response to these statements, FitzGibbon declared his conviction of Halpern's innocence and requested his discharge without fees. The Lords agreed and Halpern was discharged.[101]

Next, they requested Aldborough to withdraw. In response, Aldborough reiterated his complaints about the sale of the estate and the dismissal of magistrates. Although his complaint on the latter business had originally concerned the Wicklow magistracy, his field of indignation had, within a day, widened to Kildare, where he also had an estate. He produced a list of magistrates in that county who had lost their commissions. He apparently did not mention this fact in the House, but in his later self-justifying writings, he emphasized that FitzGibbon had replaced these men, good Protestants all, with a pack of Roman Catholics. FitzGibbon replied that he had stricken their names from the roll of magistrates because of non-residence. The Duke of Leinster came to the defense of his long-time political antagonist by volunteering that he himself had identified them to FitzGibbon as non-resident. Aldborough's appeals to his own wrongs and the wrongs of the magistrates failed to save him. Nor were his pleas for mutual Christian forgiveness and forbearance any more effective. He was obliged to retire.[102]

In his absence, FitzGibbon moved for Aldborough's prosecution for a libel on the House of Lords. He assured the House that were he alone concerned, he "never should have though it [the libel] worth his notice. But Aldborough had impugned, not only FitzGibbon's integrity, but that of his fellow peers:

> It [Aldborough's writing] represented their lordships as ready to ratify unjust decrees made in the Courts below, which was an imputation as base and undeserved as could possibly be made.[103]

In an abrupt contradiction of his earlier expressions of lofty contempt, FitzGibbon closed by declaring his intention to take additional action against Aldborough for the insults to himself:

> ... I have no objection to commit myself to the noble Lord with a jury of my country. I shall in the first instance bring a civil action against him for the libel so far as it respects myself and I am not sure that I will not also proceed criminally against him for the libel which charges me with the foulest crime, that of prostituting the authority which I hold in the scale of justice and making unjust decrees for my own personal emolument.[104]

A prolonged and highly undignified game of legal and parliamentary cat and mouse ensued between FitzGibbon and Aldborough. Aldborough made a frivolous effort to prosecute the editor of a minor Dublin newspaper for misrepresenting the charge against him as "seditious libel" rather than mere libel. When FitzGibbon accepted the wretched man's plea of innocent error and dismissed him with a mild reprimand, Aldborough once again resorted to the Journals. There, he expressed his displeasure at FitzGibbon's leniency to a lying hack and unaccountable harshness to a fellow peer.[105] Two weeks later, on 27 February, he entered a second protest against FitzGibbon's refusal to drop the prosecution.[106] He then withdrew the protest, when several more discreet fellow peers hinted that he was only causing further, potentially prosecutable, offense.[107]

Wolfe, the attorney general, duly filed an information against Aldborough in Easter term of 1797. The matter then descended into a confused stalemate. FitzGibbon was preoccupied with disarming the rebels in Ulster and in the general business of repression. Aldborough seems to have absented himself discreetly for the remainder of that fatal session. On its last day, 3 July 1797, he made a final ineffectual attempt to resolve the quarrel with a general apology to the House of Lords and to FitzGibbon for any offense given by his writing or his other protests. He later claimed that FitzGibbon purposely prolonged the business of the House until the lord-lieutenant appeared to close the session. Thus, Aldborough had no chance to appeal to the mercy of his fellow peers.[108] The newspaper accounts suggest that Aldborough, on the contrary, did have an opportunity to speak, but whatever apology he offered failed to satisfy FitzGibbon: "... he had not heard anything from the Noble Lord (Aldborough) inclining to or that could be construed into contrition for the libel."[109]

FitzGibbon later made his own position brutally clear. No mere apology could appease him. He demanded nothing less than a full public recantation in the House of Lords or a written one "signed by his Lordship to the same effect, which I may if I think fit, make public in Great Britain and Ireland."[110] FitzGibbon admitted that no man of "Lord Aldborough's rank and station" could accept such conditions: "On the contrary, I think that no earthly consideration ought to induce him to submit to such a degradation."[111] In short, Aldborough's honor, as well as FitzGibbon's, compelled a trial and whatever consequences ensued.

From July 1797 to January 1798, Aldborough struggled desperately to avoid this prospect. He appealed variously to Lords Dillon, Yelverton, Powerscourt, Somerton (Agar) and Pery to mediate with FitzGibbon. He met with varying responses. Dillon was sympathetic and expressed his private opinion that Aldborough had made a perfectly adequate apology for any offense to the House of Lords. But he shied away from entanglement in the business. He chose to believe that any dispute between FitzGibbon and Aldborough was " a business of a private nature for an alleged libel on the Chancellor". Dillon added "... this being a matter of a private nature, I am not warranted by any intimacy with the Chancellor to interfere on so delicate a subject."[112] Yelverton also pleaded a lack of influence with FitzGibbon.[113] Powerscourt, Agar and Pery showed more hardihood and did try to mediate, but they had no success.

At the same time that he was recruiting his fellow peers to make his peace with FitzGibbon, Aldborough eased his feelings and amused himself with additional, private attacks on his enemy. FitzGibbon's private coach was "much finer than the viceroy's" and was moreover, purchased "at the public expense, thereby adding a very unnecessary onus on the people". (Luckily Aldborough did not publish this particular claim, as it appears that FitzGibbon, on the contrary, paid for his ostentatious coach himself.)[114] Although FitzGibbon spared himself no personal indulgence, he was stingy in his official hospitality to his fellow Lords. Unlike Lifford, who "hospitably and convivially" entertained his fellow peers "frequently each session" , FitzGibbon, in mean contrast, "[knocked] them off with one official dinner, two or three of which serves for all". FitzGibbon himself had libeled the House far more blatantly than Aldborough. Specifically, FitzGibbon had delivered a "most virulent Philippic against a committee's report of that House on the conduct and mismanagement and partial letting of the Board of Commissioners of the Public Streets and Ways". For the virulent philippic in question, Lord Farnham, the chairman of the committee demanded and received an apology. Aldborough also amassed a collection of choice FitzGibboniana contributed by other enemies of the Chancellor. They included a copy of George Nugent Reynold's famous letter, which alluded to the St Omers education of FitzGibbon *pere* and the horns of FitzGibbon *fils*, and a repulsive, clumsy poem about Anne FitzGibbon's alleged adultery with Lord Ormonde. Above all, Aldborough maintained the perfect truth of his claims of FitzGibbon's corruption.

Meanwhile, the suit followed a desultory course through the courts. The trial met with two delays. Aldborough later claimed that FitzGibbon engineered these delays to prevent any merciful intervention by the House of Lords. In his aggrieved egotism, Aldborough never considered the possibility that the court dockets were already overburdened with the trials of suspected rebels.

When the trial finally came up for the 21 November 1797, Aldborough himself lost his preference for dispatch and pressed for another delay. He hoped to present Agar, who was in England, as a favorable witness. In his unsuccessful attempts at mediation, Agar had obtained from Aldborough two formal apologies, both to FitzGibbon and to the House of Lords. Presumably, Agar was to present this favorable evidence on Aldborough's behalf. Aldborough received a postponement until November 30, but unfortunately, Agar sent word that he would not be returning to Ireland until after the Christmas holidays. His second application for a delay, in Aldborough's own aggrieved words, "was refused, while those of felons and traitors were admitted and trial put off for two terms on their affidavit of the absence of a witness".[119]

Aldborough made no defense at his trial. In keeping with the general tenor of his writing, his own account of his reasons is maddeningly confusing. Apparently, he first agreed to make no defense on the advice of John Dwyer, FitzGibbon's secretary. Why Dwyer intervened Aldborough never deigned to explain with any clarity. Whatever his motives, he gave Aldborough the impression that no defense, in addition to a suitably humble letter, would finally placate FitzGibbon. Dwyer either misled Aldborough, or FitzGibbon, if he did indeed initiate this meeting, abruptly recovered from his fit of magnanimity. The effect of Dwyer's advice "was the reverse" of what Aldborough had expected. FitzGibbon took advantage of Aldborough's compliance to hasten the trial and the desired guilty verdict.[120]

In spite of this failure to conciliate FitzGibbon, Aldborough persisted in making no defense, on the grounds that the charges against him were framed incorrectly.

Nothing in his publication, he believed, could be construed as a "libel against the House of Lords, in whose name the information was brought". He also took issue with the words, "seditious libel" which appeared in the information against him. The original order from the House of Lords had never contained that particular charge. Aldborough bolstered his case further with a rather confused memory of his own actions against a newspaper which had incorrectly reported that he was to be tried for seditious libel . The House of Lords had reprimanded not only this printer, but two others who had copied the same story. Aldborough came to the hopeful, if dubious conclusion that these reprimands amounted to a dismissal of any charge of seditious libel against Aldborough.[121] His memory was weak on this point. Not only was the reprimand very mild, FitzGibbon had maintained that the story was fundamentally correct and that Aldborough's writings were very seditious indeed.[122] The King's Bench placed no weight on Aldborough's interpretation of his own writings or on his interpretation of the transactions with the printers. The court found him guilty as charged. His failure to appear at his own trial was taken, not as a sign of meek innocence, as Aldborough had intended, but of assent to the charge.[123]

The events following the verdict were murkier, if that could be possible. Early in January 1798, FitzGibbon gave a second sign of relenting. He declared his willingness to drop the whole matter, if the Lords themselves chose to address the lord lieutenant for a *nolle prosequi.* Initially, Aldborough had the extraordinary notion that FitzGibbon himself would propose such an address. FitzGibbon quickly disclaimed any such intention, but Aldborough got the impression that "he would make no opposition to such a motion and that he had no obloquy to me."[124] FitzGibbon's reasons for this and for the earlier overture through Dwyer are, like so much else in the business, utterly obscure. He may very briefly have wavered because of the scandal which the prosecution of a fellow peer would cause at a time of revolutionary unrest. If so, his sense of the worse scandal of Aldborough's claims prevailed in both cases. On 10 January 1798, FitzGibbon accosted Aldborough in a shop on Dame Street and informed him that he did not intent to "relax one tittle, or such effect, that I [Aldborough] was very much deceived and so indeed I was, as far as I can understand words spoken to me".[125] FitzGibbon brushed aside all attempts by Aldborough's latest set of mediators, Powerscourt and Pery, to revert to his original merciful intentions. He informed Powerscourt that only a public admission of falsehood from Lord Aldborough would suffice.[126] He made a still more abrupt reply to Pery. Aldborough's note to Pery received the following endorsement:

> Under all the circumstances which have passed, the Chancellor feels it impossible on his part to say anything upon the subject of Lord Aldborough's message.[127]

Either FitzGibbon himself scribbled this peremptory message on the note, or Pery recorded his verbal remarks.

Aldborough himself made threats and appeals of his own. He again reverted to the alleged flaws in the information and argued that such injustice to a fellow peer justified a counter-suit for breach of privilege. His threat left FitzGibbon sublimely unmoved. He coolly referred Aldborough to the King's Bench to rectify any alleged flaws in the original information. In addition, he reminded Aldborough that he was in no position to menace him legally. He had not forgotten his earlier public promise to bring another suit for personal damages:

> ... he [FitzGibbon] said he intended bringing an action against the Noble Earl, on the trial of which he would have an opportunity of proving and thereby justifying the several charges in the printed paper, and the Earl of Clare said he would stake his reputation as Chancellor, as a Lord of Parliament and as a Gentleman that he would prove each and every of the charges to be groundless and false.[128]

His last chance of settlement gone, Aldborough had no choice but to suffer the consequences of the verdict. On 12 February, he received sentence of a year's imprisonment in Newgate, to commence that same day.

Aldborough remained in prison until 29 March 1798, when he received a pardon. The material circumstances of his imprisonment were perfectly comfortable. Lady Aldborough loyally joined him in prison, and he even had the diversion of a light domestic comedy. Lady Aldborough's companion formed an attachment to none other than young Knaresborough, whom FitzGibbon had wanted so badly to hang.[129] But comfort, conjugal companionship and occasional amusement hardly compensated for his humiliation at the hands of a "vindictive reptile".[130] In his journal, he could barely write of the experience:

> Let from the 12th of February to the 29 of March be blotted from my calendar unless to humble myself before my God and gracious deliverer.[131]

He emerged from prison to face the prospect of still more law suits: FitzGibbon's potential one for personal and punitive damages and another affecting his elaborate and elegant new Dublin town house. The circumstances of this latter suit, are, like everything else connected to Aldborough's affairs, a nightmare of confusion. Both Barrington and Aldborough's 20th-century biographer, Ethel M. Richardson, claims that in building this spendid new house, he became embroiled in a boundary dispute with Marcus Beresford.[132] FitzGibbon's decision in Beresford's favor provoked the fatal pamphlet. Yet all accounts of the dispute, both in Aldborough's personal writing and in the newspaper, contain not the slightest allusion to this particular case. To add to the confusion, Marcus Beresford had died in 1797, so he could not possibly have been party to a suit originating in 1798. The best that can be made of this curious development in Aldborough's affairs is that he got into a second, later dispute with another party. Barrington and Richardson possibly confused this suit with the other *causus belli* involving Marcus Beresford.

Aldborough at first reacted to this new FitzGibbon trouble with his accustomed pugnacity. In May 1798, he dashed off a letter to Lord Fitzwilliam, long his bitter rival in County Wicklow politics; he suggested an alliance against FitzGibbon, based on their past wrongs at his hands. Aldborough even suggested calling in Grattan:

> I am assured Mr Grattan can point out various abuses of this upstart, under whose implacable malice, insolence, oppression and influence in every department of the state and constitution I have already smarted. If he succeeds in this, his second attack, which I am told aims at possession of the house I have lately erected in this metropolis, and if a mere officer of the Crown be permitted to direct and influence the Bar, the courts below, the legislature and the executive power, he may then be considered as perpetual viceroy of this kingdom and will render it no residence for any man of mirth, freedom, loyalty or independence.[133]

But sheer weariness, and possibly the dread of another stay in the "enchanted castle" of Newgate finally broke even Aldborough's fighting spirit.[134] In November 1798, he finally made a painful disavowal of all his accusations regarding the disputed estate in Wicklow and the Tynte business. He closed with this weary and syntactically obscure remark:

> I hope I have now fully met Lord Clare's desire in being ready to withdraw the plea of justification and to acknowledge my present opinion from his Lordship's assertion that any matter in the paper complained of reflecting on him is unfounded.[135]

FitzGibbon appears to have been either satisfied at last or equally weary of the matter, since he took no further proceedings against Aldborough.

How much truth was there to the claims that Aldborough so obstinately maintained? The existing information on the two cases is incomplete and moreover comes from two highly irascible, arrogant men, each intent on serving their own personal purposes. Nonetheless, the weight of proof, slight as it is, does seem to favor FitzGibbon. In the matter of Tynte, Aldborough waxed at length about Lady Elizabeth Tynte's poverty and about FitzGibbon's arbitrary cruelty in depriving her of her personal property. But he never offers an explanation beyond mere tyranny and spite on FitzGibbon's part. Any familiarity with FitzGibbon's other dealings in the court of Chancery makes nonsense of Aldborough's claims. No one was more rule-bound, no one less likely to deprive a genteel widowed lady of her money and personal property for no good reason. The missing accounts of rents, to which FitzGibbon alluded in his speech, possibly offer a key to his conduct toward Lady Elizabeth Tynte. He may have sequestered her jointure to compel her to produce the accounts. Aldborough's one surviving letter to FitzGibbon about the Tynte affair never touches on this important matter. His silence suggests an uneasy realization that she was not entirely blameless.

Aldborough's own surviving correspondence on the disputed estate sale also bears out FitzGibbon's version of events. So far as matters can be comprehended, a certain

Francis Eardley needed to sell an estate to pay off a mortgage. One Dominic McCausland offered the highest bid, but Eardley found him an undesirable purchaser. He disdainfully described McCausland as a "beltmaker" or a "saddler". In October 1795, Eardley opened negotiations with Aldborough in the hope that he would purchase the estate instead of the socially objectionable McCausland.[136] FitzGibbon agreed to open the sale again, as he declared in his own statement in Parliament, and as Aldborough's own personal correspondence confirms. Nonetheless, he insisted that Aldborough pay the entire purchase price of £9,000 by February of 1796. Aldborough was unable to come up with £9,000 in ready money. He proposed instead making a partial payment of the purchase price and deferring payment of the balance for 10 or 12 months. This request FitzGibbon refused. In his later, self-justifying accounts of the transaction, Aldborough gave the impression that his habits of paternalistic generosity to his tenants left him strapped for ready cash:

> I prayed time till my March rents falling due would enable me to call in the Michaelmas one, my custom being to leave a back half-year in my tenants' hands.

In a letter of appeal to FitzGibbon, written on 30 December 1795, Aldborough gave quite a different reason for his lack of money. He was "engaged in building a very expensive town house ... and which I pay weekly for, as it rises and have but £3,000 I can at present spare from it".[138] Again, his own correspondence supported FitzGibbon's version of events. Aldborough couched this confession in appeals to the Protestant cause:

> I know not whether you will permit me to regard you as my friend, but I know you to be a staunch Protestant, and I believe not well inclined to let our late, short-lived viceroy [Lord Fitzwilliam] put the Co. Wicklow in his pocket, which I am told is his intention, by bringing in Mr. Grattan and another gentleman who are known only by name but have no property in it, to represent that county in Parliament on the ensuing general election.
>
> I am the second interest to his Lordship's and hope with little aid to be able to frustrate his designs. I opened a sale of Eardley's estate by your Lordship's permission last term, on which I think 18, and I would increase to 50 registered freeholders by next election which would bring me within four score of his Lordship's.[139]

He also resorted to simple flattery, also recalled with accuracy by FitzGibbon: he hoped he would often "be favored with your Lordship's company" at his splendid and expensive new Dublin town house. It was a singularly ill-advised appeal to FitzGibbon, who had a fine house of his own and who, moreover, resolutely tried to keep sectarian politics out of his court. He closed the sale to Dominic McCausland, the purveyor of fine leather goods.[140]

Aldborough's accusation of corruption rested on the fact that McCausland seems to have been acting as a broker or agent for Marcus Beresford, FitzGibbon's kinsman. While McCausland was closing the sale, Beresford was requesting the deeds to the estate to conclude the negotiations on his marriage settlement; six months after the sale was concluded with McCausland, Beresford took possession of the estate.[141]

Aldborough immediately concluded that FitzGibbon made a corrupt and partial decision in favor of his kinsman. FitzGibbon himself felt some delicacy about this circumstance. He avoided mentioning the connection between McCausland and Beresford in the version of events which he gave to the House of Lords.[142] Yet FitzGibbon had no need to be coy and Aldborough had no firm foundation on which to build a case of corruption. McCausland, whatever his connection with Marcus Beresford, had offered the highest bid, and more important, had the ready cash to back it up. FitzGibbon had given Aldborough an opportunity to purchase the estate instead of McCausland. Aldborough's own extravagance, not FitzGibbon's favor for Marcus Beresford or his agent, lost him the estate.

FitzGibbon's very tender sense of his own importance no doubt compelled him to pursue Aldborough so relentlessly. But Aldborough's claims went beyond mere personal insult. They struck at the mystique which he had tried to create for his court. He expected, and indeed he often brutally compelled the submission and deference of Catholics and of the lower orders in general. But he tried in return to offer unfailing, compassionate and above all disinterested justice to them. In suggesting that FitzGibbon's justice was, on the contrary, fraudulent and tainted, Aldborough threatened his authority as surely as any United Irishman. The very fact that he was a peer and a Protestant of the Established Church made his claims all the more dangerous and FitzGibbon's retaliation all the more relentless.

11

The Pride of Power

FitzGibbon was as preoccupied with the external trappings of power as he was with its exercise. His overmastering desire to create an elegant and aristocratic impression on the world at large affected even the most personal aspects of his life, from the paintings he commissioned to the entertainments of his leisure hours. This same impulse of self-reinvention also affected his behavior toward his family, determining which relations he cultivated, and which he kept at a discreet distance.

Focusing on such subjects as FitzGibbon's dinner parties, carriages, clothes and interior decor may seem like a descent from serious history into the realm of antiquarian gossip. But a political biography of FitzGibbon must necessarily look at this aspect of his life, since he himself placed such importance on the external elegances of life. His splendid displays at Mount Shannon or Ely Place played as much of a part in his quest for power as his actions in Parliament or the Four Courts.

The famous, or perhaps more accurately, notorious state carriage that FitzGibbon commissioned in 1790 epitomizes his obsession with his own public appearance. FitzGibbon had an established reputation as a connoisseur of smart equipages and good horseflesh.[1] Shortly after his appointment as chancellor, a trait that had once served as another object of mockery became, in the general FitzGibbon *manie*, another virtue. The *Dublin Evening Post* expressed a hope that FitzGibbon would replace Lifford's seedy carriage with one in keeping with the dignity of the "speaker of the House of Lords". The paragraph went on to declare:

> As his [FitzGibbon's] horses are remarkably handsome and well-appointed, the fashion and display of his carriage will be suited to them [state processions] and the whole correspond to his liberal spirit and exalted station.[2]

FitzGibbon fulfilled the fond expectation of the *Dublin Evening Post*. His new equipage, which was completed and delivered in September 1790, was a massive, gaudy contraption, encrusted with gilt.[3] It epitomized FitzGibbon's own exalted sense of his station and his appetite for luxury.

Unfortunately, FitzGibbon again offended sensitive national feelings by ordering his new carriage from England. Suspicion and resentment of England's commercial superiority and a belief that every Irishman ought to patronize home manufactures had long been essential articles of the patriot/opposition creed. These articles

FitzGibbon had flaunted on a grand scale. As a result, he brought on himself and on his carriage a month's worth of hostile comment in the two main opposition papers, the *Dublin Evening Post* and the *Hibernian Journal*. The *Dublin Evening Post* claimed that the population in general was bored with it. (To judge from the volume of commentary, the contributors to the *Dublin Evening Post* were less *blasé*).[4] The same paper sneered at the fact that the carriage was so large that it could not pass through the narrow streets surrounding the Four Courts. This circumstance, it noted, defeated the purpose of the carriage, which was to convey the Lord Chancellor to his court.[5] Both the *Dublin Evening Post* and the *Hibernian Journal* compared it unfavorably to the quality and the elegance of the Lord Mayor's Irish-made carriage.[6]

In the eyes of the government press, of course, FitzGibbon could do not wrong, either as a politician or as a patron of the decorative arts. Both the *Freeman's* and *Faulkner's* praised the beauty and workmanship of his carriage.[7] The *Freeman's* even tried to suggest that FitzGibbon was promoting Irish manufactures with his English-made carriage. Its workmanship would serve as a standard of emulation for Irish craftsmen.[8]

Compared with the high melodrama of FitzGibbon's past political career and compared with those in which he was to appear, the matter of the state carriage was a minor farce. FitzGibbon probably came to the very proper conclusion that the *Dublin Evening Post* and the *Hibernian Journal* had no business dictating where and how he should purchase his own personal carriage. He could therefore drive to his court in great state and in good conscience.

As a patron of arts, other than carriage-making, he inclined more toward the decorative than the fine. Curiously, his adoration for England and for English civilization did not extend to his taste in china and in interior decor. In this one respect, he was enthusiastically French. The prevailing style at Mount Shannon was Louis Quatorze.[9] He immediately took advantage of the treaty of trade with France to order a large set of "Seve". Whatever his deficiencies as a French linguist, he seems to have had considerable practice in purchasing and in importing French luxuries. Certainly he gave authoritative directions to Eden on methods of payment and methods of shipment.[10] He had, in addition to the "Seve", a splendid silver service. The food and wine at his dinners fully matched the superb settings. According to Lord Shannon, Lord Clare's cellar was worth £2,100 when he died, proof of both the high quality of his vintages and of the great quantity he and his guests drank.[11]

As for painting or sculpture, unlike the Duke of Rutland or his own eldest son, FitzGibbon does not appear to have collected original art on a large scale. Most of the art at Mount Shannon and at Ely Place consisted of copies of various European masterworks. Nevertheless, the presence of copies on his elegant walls does not necessarily mean that he had second rate taste or no taste at all. There was no stigma attached to copies of paintings at the time. On the contrary, for untraveled gentlemen like FitzGibbon, copies perhaps offered their only contact with the great masterworks of Rome, Venice or Paris. Existing evidence suggests that FitzGibbon had perfectly respectable, if rather conventional, taste. Copies of paintings by that great eighteenth century favorite, Raphael, as well as by Giulio Romano, graced the morning room at Mount Shannon, while copies from the elector of Saxony's superb collection appeared elsewhere in the house.[12] His only recorded commissions of original art consisted of portraits of himself. He listed these in critical detail for Eden's benefit:

> I sat to Mr Hoppner for a picture of which Hobart's is a copy, and Boydell desires my leave to make an engraving of it. This I gave him, of course, and desired that when the prints were engraved, he would give you a proof impression from me ... in the meantime, I will send you a print taken from a miniature by Cosway, for which I sat in the days of my youth. There is a vile bad one extant from a full length drawn by Stewart, which I shd be ashamed to sent you.[13]

It is not surprising that his sole recorded commissions in painting were portraits. His personal appearance pre-occupied him as much as his physical surroundings. His enemies in the press savagely teased the "pretty prig" for being a "man of dress".[14] In the 1790s some newspaper paragraphs taunted FitzGibbon for looking more like a groom than a gentleman, but they may have confused a daring sense of style with slovenliness.[15] FitzGibbon may have anticipated Brummel's emphasis on simplicity of dress. The sole surviving spontaneous picture of FitzGibbon, a sketch by James Gillray, shows a dapper, if badly debauched, man in neat, well-cut riding attire. Brummel probably would have approved of the coat, though he would have balked at FitzGibbon's hair, which was elaborately curled in the fashion of his youth.

As for his physical, as opposed to his sartorial, attributes, he was a slight man, fine-boned and not very tall. He had a pale complexion, black or very dark brown hair and large, penetrating gray eyes. His earliest portrait, a Cosway miniature done in 1781, bears out the contemporary description in the *Dublin Evening Post*. FitzGibbon was indeed a "handsome youth" with "beautiful eyes".[16] His delicate, almost feminine good looks did not long withstand his habits of hard drinking and high living. Neither Hoppner nor Hamilton could conceal the obvious deterioration of FitzGibbon's middle age, however valiantly they surrounded him with the pompous trappings of official 18th-century British portraiture. Perhaps the artist of *Los Caprichos* was more suited to portray that coarse and brutal face.

His preoccupation with dress and with the more superficial decorative arts may have reflected a certain shallowness and narcissism in his private character, but they unquestionably served FitzGibbon well in his public career. He instinctively knew how to create a splendid and intimidating appearance. In spite of the physical ravages of age and debauchery, he must have cut a magnificent figure at Mount Shannon and Ely Place, as he presided over his ornate French rooms, his elegant table, his beautiful, fashionable wife and his company.

As for literary, philosophical or philanthropic pursuits, these too were subservient to the demands of his career. The college prize for his translation of the *Georgics* marked the pinnacle of his achievement as a scholar. As an adult, he appears to have had no significant intellectual, literary or artistic interests. His apparent lack of interest in cultural matters set him apart. Most of FitzGibbon's contemporaries had at least some interest in the fine arts or sciences. Foster promoted a national gallery of art, and served on numerous civic and charitable boards. Gardiner and Beresford left a splendid, if now neglected architectural legacy. Charlemont not only built the exquisite Casino, his architectural studies of the Parthenon still command the respect of scholars.

The existing evidence of cultural exertion is highly dubious. Prior's *Life of Malone* records activity as a member of the Royal Irish Academy. One letter reprinted in this memoir portrays FitzGibbon in a characteristic pose: attempting to dampen the ardent Irish cultural, as well as political, patriotism of Charlemont:

> Our amiable friend the president [Lord Charlemont] is more wild and boisterous on the subject of Ireland than you can conceive. Many a warm dispute we have. I told him not long ago that my motto was "Nil Admirari" and that I was determined to combat all their cloud capped notions about their country and shake every idea that tends to set one race above another or promote national distinctions.[17]

Unfortunately, the original of this letter has never been located in any of the collections of Malone's papers.[18] Moreover, it has a spurious quality. FitzGibbon gave precious little evidence, either in words or deeds, that he believed in the universal brotherhood of all races. On the contrary, his attitude toward his own people and culture originated in a contempt born of self-hatred, certainly not in broadminded distaste for nationalist excesses. More important, FitzGibbon's name does not appear on any of the membership lists of the Royal Irish Academy, a curious omission. Surely the patronage of so illustrious a figure would have received notice. He is also absent from the membership list of the Royal Dublin Society. Nor does he appear to have participated in any of the other major charitable or cultural societies of the time.[19] He may have preferred the role of an anonymous benefactor, but this explanation seems unlikely. He had no reason to show such absurd coyness about his participation in public and institutional acts of patronage.

To be sure, as chancellor, he did serve on the boards of a number of institutions which included him by statute. Knowing his conscientious attention to all duties attached to his office, he probably was reasonably conversant with the affairs of the Royal Hibernian Marine Academy or St Patrick's Hospital, to name just two of the institutions in question. But it must be emphasized that he did nothing on his own initiative. His single-minded interest in promoting his own career, and possibly, a fundamentally pessimistic and contemptuous view of all types of Irish self-improvement may account for his absence from civic and philanthropic endeavors.

FitzGibbon's purchases from Denis Daly's library in 1792 confirm the impression of a man who read more for business than for pleasure or intellectual curiosity. A large proportion of the books he purchased, 15 titles out of 42, concerned English legal and constitutional history. He had a particular interest in the civil wars of the 17th century. There were fillips of interest in non-English countries and peoples: a history of the Gypsies, of Naples, and of Spain attracted his attention. He also purchased a number of titles in Latin, which suggests that his classical learning had not entirely deserted him. Some of his choices ran to the bizarre. They included Albertus Magnus's *Secrets of Women*, which probably had little to do with that great divine's usual theological aridities, two books on celibacy or virginity, and one on the right and wrong uses of flagellation among Christians.[20]

Of course, this single list of purchases is an incomplete, and perhaps unfair, criterion for judging FitzGibbon's tastes in reading. He was after all, supplementing his library. He may have displayed other, wider interests on unrecorded and uncatalogued visits to shops and sales. Indeed, credit must be given for the fact that he possessed a library at all and took pains to add new titles to it. He also cared enough about his books to make special mention of them in his will, and to express a hope that they would end up at Mount Shannon. But an overwhelming impression remains of a man who purchased books mainly to meet immediate practical concerns. The Catholic issue loomed large in 1792, and in FitzGibbon's mind, Popish discontent and assertiveness, if unchecked, could only lead to a revival of the civil contention and bloodshed of 1641. The 17th-century histories may well have provided him with ammunition for the terrifying rhetorical broadsides of 1793, and he may have intended to cull suitable illustrations of the horrors of Popish despotism from the histories of Naples and Spain. Even the odd books on celibacy and flagellation may have provided useful examples of Popish superstition, as well as pleasurable titillation. The quaint customs of the Gypsies meanwhile diverted his few idle hours.

Apart from Latin, FitzGibbon had a smattering of French. His level of skill in this language remains open to question. In his letters to Eden, he made blatant errors in spelling: "Hotch" for Hoche and "Seve" for Sevres.[21] He may have been genuinely maladroit. In yet another letter, to Lord Camden, FitzGibbon described his difficulties in communicating with an itinerant French priest whom he suspected of spying:

> I met an old Frenchman about a Mile on this side of Nenagh in the garb of a miserable beggar. I asked him a few questions in his own language, which the Keeper of a Turnpike Gate overhearing informed me that the Man could speak both the English and Irish languages. This circumstance induced me to interrogate the gentleman somewhat particularly. He said that he was a native of St Maloer [*sic*] and had come over in a smuggling vessel from thence to Belfast three years since. He would not say where he had lived during that time, nor how or by what route he had come from Belfast to Nenagh. I asked him whether he was a Republican, to which he said he did not know what a Republican meant.[22]

The man may have been too frightened to respond to FitzGibbon coherently, or he may have had difficulties with *l'accent de Limerick*.

As for Irish, FitzGibbon probably looked upon it solely as the language of the lower orders. He spoke enough to communicate with his dependents and other objects of dominance or of charity, but it is unlikely that he took any interest in Irish as a literary language.[23]

As sole surviving male heir and as a wealthy and powerful landowner and politician, FitzGibbon naturally dominated a family circle that comprised his sisters, their spouses and children, and remote relations in Limerick. His political aspirations and prejudices inevitably affected his dealings with them as well.

There were, nonetheless, some notable exceptions, which show a very loving, and often long-suffering side to FitzGibbon. His beautiful wife, for example, could sometimes be more of an embarrassment than an asset, but he never ceased to treat her with tenderness, compassion and admirable tolerance.

Anne FitzGibbon's conduct sometimes did display a lack of judgment and a self-absorption bordering on moral idiocy. She had a reputation as an adulteress. George Nugent Reynolds' famous philippic against FitzGibbon alluded to his wife's lack of chastity.[24] Henrietta Battier hinted at marital discord that may have originated in Anne Whalley FitzGibbon's sexual misadventures.[25] Imputations of unfaithfulness were not confined to political enemies like George Nugent Reynolds, or Henrietta Battier, who may possibly have had a personal as well as a political grudge against FitzGibbon.[26] Lord Glenbervie and Lord Shannon, who both esteemed FitzGibbon, took the same uncomplimentary view of his wife. According to Lord Glenbervie, FitzGibbon had forgiven his wife for one indiscretion, only to see her entangled in other extramarital affairs.[27] Lord Shannon identified the young Earl of Ormonde as at least one of the lady's lovers. After FitzGibbon's death, Shannon made the grimly jocular comment that Ormonde could now safely attend meetings of the Privy Council.[28] Evidently, Ormonde had discreetly avoided FitzGibbon by shirking his state duties.

Anne FitzGibbon also seems to have had a tendency to get into embarrassing, even ridiculous, social situations. Her friendship with the Prince of Wales was particularly marked by *faux pas*. She first attracted the attention of the Prince of Wales in 1788; FitzGibbon's enemies in the press hinted at impropriety by protesting too much:

> The lady of a great law officer now in England is, we understand, a principal favorite at the court of the Prince of Wales, frequently participating in his private parties and of a seat in his phaeton. She has indeed, beauty sufficient to attract all attention, but "chaste as the icicle hanging from Dian's temple" her virtue can suffer no imputation, not even from the influence of that warm region.[29]

Their relations probably did remain within the bounds of flirtatious propriety. Anne FitzGibbon was also on good terms with Mrs. Fitzherbert, never one to brook a serious rival.[30] However proper and chaste her relationship with the Prince, she often took undue advantage of it. In 1798, she obtained a private tour of Carlton House, though apparently the Prince had never given her formal permission.[31] Her tactics and her timing were, to say the least, maladroit. Her husband's allusions to the Prince in his famous reply to Lord Moira had caused considerable awkwardness earlier in the year. In 1806, the Prince was drawn into a feud between Anne FitzGibbon and Lord Westmorland's second wife. The new Lady Westmorland had taken offense at rumors that Anne FitzGibbon had impugned her character. Anne FitzGibbon made a panicked request to the Prince, as one of the supposed auditors of her remarks, to deny the story. He gamely did so, out of friendship, or out of sheer dread of her cajolery.[32]

Anne FitzGibbon's brother "Buck" Whalley provided yet another element of social embarrassment. FitzGibbon probably never had much love for his brother-in-law, who single-handedly perpetrated every undesirable stereotype of the insanely irresponsible, recklessly self-indulgent Anglo-Irish gentleman. Reportedly, FitzGibbon tried to dissuade Whalley from undertaking his most notorious feat, the successful bet to travel from Dublin to Jerusalem and back within one year. Whalley quickly went through the winnings from his pilgrimage to the Holy Land and in 1793, FitzGibbon was obliged to rescue him from a spunging house in London. Buck Whalley probably made many other unrecorded demands on his brother-in-law's time, patience and purse.[33]

In spite of her various indiscretions, personal and familial, FitzGibbon unquestionably loved his wife. He spoke of her with great tenderness in his will, and he entrusted the guardianship of their children to her.[34] He would not have taken this actions had she demonstrated extraordinary depravity. FitzGibbon seems to have taken a far more charitable view of his wife's lapses than either his friends or his enemies. In commenting on a pending divorce bill to Lord Auckland, he shared what was undoubtedly the rueful fruit of his own experience:

> My opinion is ... that you are to look for the root of the evil which must alarm every sober man to the dissolute habits of the higher ranks of men, who consider marriage as a mere traffick for private or political purposes, and that they are therefore at liberty to treat their wives with the most contemptuous neglect at best. I am quite satisfied it is the nature of womankind to behave well to every husband who treats his wife as becomes him.[35]

The insights offered in this letter may explain the forbearance that Shannon and Glenbervie found so extraordinary. If Anne FitzGibbon was indeed unfaithful, her husband generously attributed her affairs to loneliness and neglect rather than sexual incontinence. He also may have recognized that he had his own share of infidelities. Lord Glenbervie after all had emphasized that he was a "man of gallantry" as well as a cuckold. Although in private he took a tolerant view of her lapses, he proceeded ruthlessly against any public print that was impudent enough to publicize them. In 1792, one Perry, the publisher of an English radical newspaper called the *Argus*, served six months in the King's Bench prison and paid a fine of £200 for libeling Anne FitzGibbon.[37]

Her occasional lapses of moral judgment aside, she had a sweet and generous nature. Her name appeared on numerous charitable and cultural subscription lists. Anne FitzGibbon's comments on Lady Pamela Fitzgerald to the Duchess of Leinster show a kindly generosity that still endears and enchants:

> I have known few people that I have upon so short an acquaintance taken such a fancy to as her [Lady Pamela]. Her head and her heart are both what they should be.[38]

And in her turn, Anne FitzGibbon had ardent defenders, most notably Lady Sarah Napier, the Duchess of Leinster's sister. Lady Sarah indignantly refuted some of the more lurid stories about Anne FitzGibbon's infidelities, most notably the reports that she had taken no less than Lord Westmorland for a lover.[39]

For the most part, Anne FitzGibbon remained aloof from politics, which doubtless suited her husband. He probably preferred pretty passivity to active politicking in his women. Pragmatism and family interest determined Anne FitzGibbon's few recorded political actions. While her husband lived, she dutifully echoed his sentiments. In one instance, she suffered a taste of the bitter contempt he had inspired. At a soiree in London after the Act of Union, she repeated her husband's by then very low opinion of Lord Cornwallis. An English Whig lady present responded with a crushing allusion to FitzGibbon's public justification of the torture known as "half-hanging".[40] Yet the same sense of family loyalty led Anne FitzGibbon to intervene on behalf of the United Irishman, Lord Cloncurry. Toward the end of his worthless life, her brother had married Cloncurry's sister, which accounted for Anne FitzGibbon's interest in the case.[41] In the same spirit, the widow of the Earl of Clare and the daughter of Burn Chapel Whalley threw her support behind the pro-Emancipation candidate Windham Henry Quin, who was standing for County Limerick in 1807.[42] She had two promising young sons, and she seems to have come to the realization that the 40s. freeholders offered the surest source of popularity and influence. Her husband probably would not have shown the same flexibility.

A deep and troubled emotional attachment, rather than his accustomed calculation, also dictated FitzGibbon's actions toward his eldest sister, Mrs Jefferyes. They had in common acute intelligence and acute emotional instability. Unfortunately for Arabella Jefferyes, she had no outlet for her intellectual energy. She took refuge from the chronic boredom of her life in bullying benevolence. When she was not offering what might be construed as favor and encouragement to Whiteboys, she acted as a patroness of the arts, both fine and theatrical. An English actress, Mrs Frances Abdington, was one beneficiary of her patronage. At Mrs Jefferyes' suggestion, she wrote to FitzGibbon to request his protection from "the insult and imposition which she has been too often made to experience from managers of the English as well as the Irish theaters". What kind of protection FitzGibbon afforded remains an intriguing question and one possibly without very edifying answers.[43] The journals of the Cork Historical Society offer an amusing account of Arabella's patronage of an itinerant aspiring artist by the name of J.D. Herbert. Mrs Jefferyes overwhelmed him with domineering hospitality and commissions. She refused nonetheless to sit herself. Although Herbert considered her a striking woman, she displayed a strange and touching shyness about her appearance:

> ... she found by experience she was not a good subject for a picture, and she said I [Herbert] had quite enough in what I had done.[44]

When the young man expressed a desire to abandon painting for the stage, Mrs. Jefferyes promptly obtained a place for him in a London company, no less. Herbert never took advantage of this munificence. He himself gave the slight and unsatisfactory reasons that his mother did not approve. In truth, he may have come to feel like a prisoner of patronage in Blarney Castle.[45]

Initially, Arabella's similarities to her brother appear to have created a very close bond between them. She did at least some of the offices of a wife for him during his bachelor days. During a time when she was resident in London, FitzGibbon commissioned her to deliver some Limerick gloves which he had ordered for the Edens.[46] Even after her misadventures with the Whiteboys, FitzGibbon continued to provide patronage and assistance, often at considerable embarrassment to himself.

For a woman who so confidently ordered the lives of others, she displayed a remarkable incompetence in managing her own affairs. The scheme to drain the lake by Blarney Castle was above all a desperate financial gamble. Demands from her Whiteboy protgs for lower rents, rather than stern letters from her brother probably accounted for her abrupt withdrawal of favor. Her ghastly financial position did not permit that kind of self-sacrifice. She preferred the second hand benevolence of limiting clerical income. Apparently as a measure of economy, she had rented a house, but even in retrenchment, she ran into disaster. By 1790, her landlord threatened to evict her for non-payment of rent. FitzGibbon promptly paid up the arrears.[47]

He also attempted to obtain the post of adjutant general for Colonel Fremantle, who was married to Arabella's daughter Albinia. Abruptly, and considering FitzGibbon's extraordinary services in 1789, unaccountably, George III refused his consent. Possibly he felt that the Seals were honor enough for an Irishman, even an Irishman as loyal and self-abnegating as FitzGibbon. In keeping with his usual bearing, FitzGibbon swallowed his mortification and dropped the matter:

> ... he [FitzGibbon] was sorry His Majesty did not see his nephew in the same light, that if his Majesty continued disinclined to ye appointment, he should certainly not press ye point.[48]

In undertaking these singularly unrewarding actions for Arabella and her family, FitzGibbon was unquestionably acting out of a general sense of what was due to his office. The Lord Chancellor of Ireland could not be subjected to the embarrassment of seeing his sister publicly and unceremoniously evicted from her home, while the military promotion of his nephew would have enhanced his own position and influence. At the same time, the dark logic of FitzGibbon's character as easily could have dictated a break with Arabella as a result of her escapades in 1786 and 1787. As Grattan, Curran and Tone all learned, FitzGibbon's political quarrels could take on a terrifying personal malevolence. Lingering, grudging affection must have played at least a part in these two instances of patronage.

Undaunted, Arabella continued to engage in compromising and risky activities. She had a particular taste for dabbling in the law. According to her protégé Herbert, she pursued and won a case that her brother had given up as hopeless.[49] The matter of the Cahir estate and title constituted her greatest legal triumph. Dorothea Herbert gives the most complete and certainly the most romantic account of the story. The 10th Baron Cahir died in 1788 without immediate heirs. The closest claimant was the young son of a woman who earned a living grinding flour and occasionally begging. Other relations of the late lord tried to prevent the child from coming into possession of the title and estate by spiriting him and his siblings off to France. Who they were, when they removed the children, and how they persuaded the mother to part with them are all questions Dorothea Herbert's narrative leaves unanswered. Her story has the fairy tale's blissful lack of motivation and chronology, and she quickly skips to the happy ending. Mrs Jefferyes found the children in a garret in Paris, and brought them back to Ireland. She then successfully established the boy's claim to the barony and estate of Cahir. Her benevolence was not entirely self-interested. In 1793, the newly discovered Lord Cahir married her youngest daughter Emily, a great coup for the financially straightened mother.[50]

At the probable insistence of his mother-in-law, who notwithstanding her predilection for Whiteboys, was a militant Protestant, young Lord Cahir dutifully renounced Catholicism and conformed to the established church.[51] He probably needed little persuasion. Catholicism equaled conniving relatives, a penurious mother and Paris garrets. Protestantism equaled rescue by a great lady, a fortune, a title and a pretty wife. The same uxoriousness and gratitude may have accounted for his later opposition to emancipation.[52] His elevation to Protestant wealth and nobility was not entirely blissful. Pretty Emily, like her mother, was a busy dominatrix.[53] Nonetheless, she does not seem to have inherited her mother's eccentric but touching social compassion. On the contrary Emily Cahir occupied herself with squalid domestic intrigue, breathtakingly tactless electioneering and general attention-getting histrionics. Emily the domestic intrigante arranged a public wedding for an obviously pregnant, obviously unmarried daughter, complete with cleverly designed corsets for the bridal attire. (Lord Belfast was the lucky groom.) Emily the election agent wrote to the wealthy, grandmother of a favored candidate, without any knowledge or consent on his part, and demanded a donation of £2,000. Emily the enfant terrible chose, in her later years, to take up the cause of Queen Caroline. When the late queen's very unloving and unbereaved widower visited Ireland in 1821, Lady Cahir, by then elevated to the distinction of Countess of Glengall, ostentatiously appeared in black. Why such an enthusiast for the establishment in church and state would espouse a major Whig/radical cause defies all ordinary logic. But then, ordinary logic does not seem to have governed Emily to any significant extent.[54] According to local legend, her compliant husband rebelled against her sexually, if not religiously and politically. The charming little Swiss cottage in the grounds of Cahir Castle was supposedly built by him for a mistress.[55]

According to Dorothea Herbert, Arabella's disposal of Lord Cahir's hand in marriage infuriated FitzGibbon; although Miss Herbert's elliptical prose is sometimes difficult to interpret, FitzGibbon may have objected because Lord Cahir was still a minor and in the custody of his court. At one point, or so Miss Herbert claimed, he even threatened to imprison Arabella and Emily for their dubious manipulation of a ward of Chancery. He also may have resented his sister's rather naked financial interest in the marriage.[56] Indeed, the trips to Paris and her other legal investigations must have cost Arabella Jefferyes some badly needed money, though whatever investment she made paid off very handsomely.[57]

In her desperate craving for money, Arabella may have dabbled in activities that were frankly illegal. In his memoirs, Lord Cloncurry described the attempts of certain "Mrs J——" to obtain money from him under false pretenses. In company with one Mrs P——, the lady approached him during his imprisonment, and tried to prevail on him to give her £500. According to the proposal which she made to Lord Cloncurry, the two ladies were to turn the money over to a third, an unnamed *"chere amie"* (Cloncurry's words) of the Duke of Portland. This small consideration would presumably incline the *chere amie* to prevail on her lover to intervene in Cloncurry's case.[57] Cloncurry readily perceived this offer as a transparent ploy to rob him, and he refused.[58] The two women were desperate enough to go to one of Cloncurry's sisters with the same offer, and presented a forged note of permission from Cloncurry himself. The girl demonstrated the same astuteness as her brother and refused. Cloncurry's discretion or coyness renders it impossible to establish for certain whether the nefarious Mrs J—— was indeed Arabella Jefferyes. Nonetheless, Cloncurry gives a very damning hint: she was "nearly related to a learned and still more notorious lord."[59] It would be a remarkable coincidence if another woman had those initials and those family connections. Moreover, the boldness of the scheme and the financial desperation behind it are characteristic of Arabella Jefferyes. Whether FitzGibbon ever learned of this attempt to cheat Cloncurry remains uncertain. Probably Cloncurry remained discreetly silent. An accused United Irishman had little chance of proving charges against the sister of the Lord Chancellor. If so, Arabella was fortunate. FitzGibbon's rage would have known no bounds had he discovered these attempts to defraud a relation by marriage, however disreputable and steeped in treason. Given her powerful sense of family, Anne FitzGibbon would no doubt have encouraged her husband's mighty indignation.

His relations with his two other sisters, Elizabeth and Elinor, were far more placid.

Elizabeth provided her brother with his all-important connection to the Beresford family, but she was an obscure figure in a family of vivid public personalities. Presumably she was like her mother, dutifully domestic, quiet and retired. For the most part Elinor followed suit. Her account book reveals a tidy, careful and busy household manager. She chronicled toys for her children, salaries for the nurse, black silk breeches for Mr Trant, and losses at cards by Mr Trant.[60]

Elinor also seems to have looked after old Mrs FitzGibbon in her later life.[61] Why this responsibility devolved on her is unclear. At least in the case of her brother and her eldest sister, their political and public concerns may have occupied them too much to look after a failing old woman. On the other hand, old Mrs FitzGibbon may have preferred *not* to live in her son's lively bachelor establishment or in Blarney Castle, with its itinerant artists and Whiteboys.

Yet Elinor had her share of the FitzGibbon-Hayes *esprit*. She was a talented amateur actress who seems to have specialized in tragic roles. Even newspapers that regularly castigated her brother praised her splendid voice and fine figure.[62] That merciless satirist Henrietta Battier, among others, made suggestions of shrewishness and of immorality.[63] Mrs Battier may have made such insinuations not merely because Elinor was the sister of the despicable "Lord Jacky", but because she acted, an activity which, in spite of the ultra-respectable Mrs Siddons and Mrs Inchbald, still had overtones of sexual laxity.

In his will, FitzGibbon treated "dear" Elizabeth and "dear" Elinor equally. He placed them and their children in the defensive line of succession, and he left them both £50 for mourning. Their families also stood to inherit some of FitzGibbon's superb dishes.[64] Nonetheless, in his lifetime, he does not appear to have displayed the same evenhandedness. When he became lord chancellor, FitzGibbon bestowed one of the more lucrative sinecures at his disposal on the patronage-glutted Beresfords. His nephew John Beresford became his purse bearer at a salary of £700 per annum.[65] FitzGibbon, it is true, was on close and affectionate terms with William Beresford, Elizabeth's husband. At least in the final weeks of FitzGibbon's life, Beresford acted as a spiritual advisor, he was a principal mourner at the funeral and a principal beneficiary of FitzGibbon's estate.[66] But FitzGibbon's snobbish distaste for Elinor's husband, Dominic Trant, probably played as great a role in these grace and favor decisions.

After assisting Trant with the Maurice O'Connell's case, FitzGibbon seems to have had very little, if any contact with his brother-in-law. According an anonymous but sharp-tongued correspondent of Vere Hunt, FitzGibbon despised and neglected Trant until Trant fought a fatal duel with Sir John Colthurst. The two fought because Trant, a defender of the prerogatives of the Established Church, had accused Colthurst of actively encouraging the Whiteboys in Cork. According to Hunt's informant, this murder by *code duello* gave FitzGibbon an unaccustomed respect for this brother-in-law. Allegedly, FitzGibbon declared that he "never knew that there had been so much in him [Trant]". The destruction of a fellow human being, Hunt's correspondent observed tartly, was evidently the surest road to favor with the honorable attorney general. Trant took considerably less pride in his accomplishment; he was "very much shocked".[67]

For his pamphlet, if not for his marksmanship, Trant received the office of assistant barrister for County Tipperary.[68] His brother-in-law's role in this promotion is doubtful. FitzGibbon may have put in a casual good word, but having sacrificed the Magistracy Act to his own ambition, he may have had little further interest in the business. Trant probably owed far more to the Archbishop of Cashel, Charles Agar.[69] Trant had worked closely with Agar on church and political business since the 1780s.[70]

Trant died suddenly in 1790; consequently, it is impossible to know whether his relations with FitzGibbon would have improved further.[71] Probably FitzGibbon would have returned to his habits of contemptuous neglect. Trant by his very nature antagonized FitzGibbon. His surviving letters reveal a man of great kindliness, charm and literary skill.[72] His sunny good nature must have grated on the saturnine FitzGibbon's nerves. Nor would this polished and cultivated man have cut much of a figure in FitzGibbon's social circle of expensive and debauched young men. FitzGibbon probably hated Trant most for what they had in common. Like FitzGibbon, Trant was the son of a convert, who pursued law as a means to social advancement. Unlike FitzGibbon, his lineage was somewhat more illustrious, as he could claim Jacobite relations of some property and distinction.[73] Trant never posed the slightest political or professional threat to his brother-in-law, and he made his own way quietly and diligently. He simply reminded FitzGibbon too much of the past he was trying to escape. FitzGibbon preferred the power and glamour of William Beresford's family, as much if not more than his spiritual counsels.

Trant made matters worse by maintaining ties not only with Catholic laymen, like the O'Connells, but with Catholic priests. While a devout and sincere adherent of the Established Church, Trant was never infected with FitzGibbon's malevolent sectarianism. Shortly before his death, he was busily recruiting Catholic priests for secret service duty in Spain. His assessments of the candidates were models of astuteness.[74]

To his credit, FitzGibbon obtained a position in the East India Company for one of Trant's sons. He was acting at "dear" Elinor's behest, but possibly he was also trying to expiate past unkindness and neglect.76 A curious passage in a letter to Richard Wellesley, the vigorous governor-general of the Bengal Presidency, raises this possibility:

> This letter will be delivered to you by a young man who goes out a Cadet in the company service in consequence of my recommendation of him to Lord Cornwallis ... If he resembles the older branches of his family, I am quite certain he will not disgrace my introduction of him to your notice.[76]

FitzGibbon's language is obscure, but he was probably referring to young Trant. He does not appear to have had any other protégés in the East India service. If so, FitzGibbon may have been paying a posthumous tribute, however obliquely, to his late, despised brother-in-law in addition to recommending the nephew. The uncharacteristic and muddy metaphor "elder branches" could have applied to Trant as well as to his wife. FitzGibbon was perfectly capable of remorse, albeit of a furtive and veiled kind.

Of his relations in Limerick, he was probably closest to Thomas FitzGibbon, the son of FitzGibbon's uncle of the same name. FitzGibbon took over from his father in the capacity of guardian, and he discharged his responsibilities with his usual efficiency. Young Thomas received good medical care for his various childhood ailments, a watch for his birthday, and a smart new suit and a horse when he attained his majority.[77] Nonetheless, FitzGibbon made one entry in the list of accounts which suggests he was a distant as well as a kindly guardian:

> It is possible that payments may have been made to me for him, which in the Hurry of business I may have omitted to enter – This may easily be ascertained by him when he settles accounts with his tenants.[78]

When his great cousin's interest demanded it, young Thomas provided dutiful support in County Limerick politics. Most notably, he signed a Limerick county petition in favor of the Union which was initiated by FitzGibbon in the autumn of 1799.[79] The fact that Cousin Thomas played a part in his grand relation's political initiatives in County Limerick suggests that FitzGibbon wanted him to cut a respectable figure in the county

FitzGibbon unquestionably showed kindness and generosity to his one surviving uncle, Gibbon FitzGibbon. He seems to have been a luckless and pathetic man. FitzGibbon himself referred to him as "poor Gibbon FitzGibbon."[80] In 1787, Gibbon FitzGibbon appears to have lost a suit, and costs of £5,000 were decreed against him. FitzGibbon "entered into the judgment", that is, he paid off the debt on Gibbon's behalf.[81] FitzGibbon does not appear to have pressed for re-payment during Gibbon's own lifetime, and Gibbon's son, Thomas Gibbon, willfully ignored the obligation. So successful was he in evading repayment, that the second earl of Clare's lawyers were still trying to obtain at least minimal payments on the debt as late as 1842.[82]

FitzGibbon's relations with Thomas Gibbon FitzGibbon appear to have been more tenuous. He took no part in this cousin's upbringing. Gibbon's widow and an attorney by the name of Heffernan acted as guardians and trustees for his estate, such as it was. He too took his required supporting part in county Limerick politics. In company with his cousin and namesake, he signed the petition favoring the Union.[83] Unlike cousin Thomas, he showed a degree of energy and initiative, possibly because his financial circumstances were narrower. He matriculated at TCD, and he enrolled in the King's Inn in 1799, though it is unclear whether he practiced law to any significant extent.[84] He did, nonetheless, act as sheriff of County Limerick in 1803.[85] He also married decently: his wife was the daughter of Sir Thomas Osborne.[86] Thomas Gibbon was on good enough terms with his powerful cousin the Chancellor to be named in his will. Moreover, his grand marriage almost certainly must have sprung from a wider world made more accessible by cousin. In short, he seems to have been a rising and respectable young man, and his contacts with FitzGibbon were probably perfectly cordial, if infrequent.

FitzGibbon's relations with the descendants of his uncle Patrick are still more obscure. Patrick's son John, Betham's informant, had only one recorded contact with his more famous cousin and namesake. FitzGibbon's father had left John the nephew a legacy of £200; according to an entry in a surviving account book, the son doled this sum out in increments of £100.[87] If he had any contact with Patrick's side of the family, FitzGibbon probably showed them reasonable kindness and civility. Had he behaved otherwise, his cousin and namesake probably would not have tried so valiantly to defend the FitzGibbon escutcheon. Injured personal feeling would almost certainly have outweighed general claims of family honor. Nonetheless, any contact was probably even more brief and cursory than his contacts with Dominic Trant or with Thomas and Thomas Gibbon FitzGibbon. Patrick's descendants labored under a worse social stigma than poor Dominic Trant: they had reverted to Catholicism.

The evidence is fragmentary, but tantalizing. In 1792, a John FitzGibbon began practice in Dublin as a solicitor.[88] This John may have been Betham's correspondent, but if so, he would have been well advanced in middle age when he entered his profession. It is more likely that he had a son named John who practiced law. Although this John FitzGibbon started practice in the year Catholics were granted access to the legal profession, he probably was, at this time, a Protestant. He enrolled in the King's Inn in 1790, two years before the relief bill, and that institution strictly excluded Catholics.[89] John FitzGibbon the attorney subsequently had two sons, yet another John and Gibbon. John entered his father's profession, while Gibbon attended Trinity. Gibbon is identified as a Roman Catholic in the *Alumni Dublinesis*.[90] This circumstance suggests that John FitzGibbon the attorney either converted to Roman Catholicism at some point after 1790, or he married a Catholic and agreed to raise his children in their mother's religion.

John FitzGibbon the attorney and his two Catholic sons may have had no relation whatsoever to John FitzGibbon the Chancellor. Yet the names Gibbon and John were monotonously prevalent in the lord chancellor's family. More significantly, FitzGibbon completely excluded Patrick's descendants from his will.[91] FitzGibbon possibly had some obscure quarrel with Patrick's family as well, but if so, he surely would have made some dishonorable mention of their perfidious behavior. FitzGibbon was not one to suffer in dignified silence, either in his life or in his will. It seems more likely that the religion of Patrick's descendants rather than their individual demerits accounted for their absence. FitzGibbon was the son of a man well versed in the penal laws. He would have known that Protestants who reverted to Catholicism forfeited all civil, political, property and inheritance rights. This legal provision was for the most part a dead letter. If John the attorney did indeed revert to Catholicism, he suffered no apparent consequences in his professional life. Nonetheless, the presence of an apostate in the defensive line of legatees would have given Arabella, who was contesting the will, for reasons of her own, a powerful argument for breaking it.[92] If such was his motive for bypassing Patrick FitzGibbon's descendants, FitzGibbon showed great astuteness indeed. Lord Dunboyne's sister later seized on this lingering penal law to make devastating trouble.

The prolific Hayes family provided FitzGibbon with an extensive network of cousins in County Limerick. He maintained the closest contacts with the Furnells, descendants of Honor FitzGibbon's sister.[93] The Furnells, like the FitzGibbon, conformed in the 1730s, and they seem to have maintained a decent standard of gentility.[94] In 1784, FitzGibbon requested Vere Hunt to impanel one of his Furnell cousins, Michael, as a grand juror. He described Furnell as one of "my near relations and very particular friends." Michael Furnell was clearly placed on the Grand Jury to express his own (and his cousin's) opposition to the Dublin requisition.[95] The Furnells also turned out in force to sign the Limerick petition in favor of the Act of Union.

Some branches of the Hayes family either remained Catholic or reverted to that religion. Mary, another sister of Honor FitzGibbon, had married a yeoman farmer bearing the unmistakably Catholic name of Ignatius Terry.[96] No Terry appears on the convert rolls; if any descendants of the family survived, they presumably continued to practice their ancestral religion and to farm in a modest way. It would be unfair, in the absence of evidence, to assume FitzGibbon disowned any distant Catholic relatives altogether. As with the Furnells, he may have done minor friendly services.

Lecky made the magisterial statement that FitzGibbon himself was not corrupt, though he was a "most cynical corrupter of others".[97] FitzGibbon himself declared with injured pride that he hated jobbery.[98] He was indeed uncorrupt in the sense that he did not pack the Irish government and civil list with his relations. What backing his relatives received from him was confined to County Limerick and in terms of political office, was limited to the small, though not inconsiderable, post of collector of Limerick. In addition, FitzGibbon gave his relatives access to much coveted service on the grand juries that were impaneled twice a year. Grand jury service bestowed considerable influence and prestige because the jurors allocated county funds and because their resolutions on various public matters carried great weight. But FitzGibbon avoided pressing the claims of his relations too much. His own anti-jobbing principles or their own lack of ambition or drive may have accounted for his reticence. He also may have acted out of a fear that undue elevation of his country cousins would capital for his political enemies, always ready to comment on and indeed, to exaggerate his obscure, much despised origins. The 23 places were ardently sought by anyone with social standings (or social pretensions). FitzGibbon's relations, while decent enough, could claim only a modest social position. As for his apparent failure to promote them to more visible and prestigious offices in Dublin, FitzGibbon may have acted out of a single-minded but calculating readiness to advance them in the one area, County Limerick, where they could be of use to him.

As for his private friendships and social ties, they too, seem to have been dictated above all by the demands of power. His closest intimates generally were the people most useful to him or the people most likely to confer glamour and prestige. He was, not surprisingly, particularly hospitable to viceroys and chief secretaries.[99] His glittering entertainments strengthened the bonds created by his loyal and able service. As chancellor, if not before, he also seems to have socialized quite frequently with the great opposition families, notably the Ponsonbys, the Fitzgeralds and their Conolly relations. He remained on visiting terms with the dowager Duchess and her family, if Anne FitzGibbon's chatty correspondence is any indication.[100] FitzGibbon may have been engaging in some prudent political fence mending with these contacts, but he clearly valued the glamour which the Ponsonbys, the Conollys and the Fitzgeralds added to his elegant interiors and opulent festive boards. Nor were his motives entirely political and snobbish. He genuinely loved Lady Louisa Conolly, quite apart from her lineage and connections.

At least when Anne FitzGibbon, Lady Louisa and other fashionable ladies were present, these affairs were far more decorous than his bachelor entertainments for his coterie of young boon companions. Nonetheless, some evidence suggests when he chose, he could revert to the habits that had so shocked Thomas Orde. One particularly gamy charge surfaced during and after Lord Westmorland's administration: FitzGibbon had consoled Westmorland for the sudden death of his wife by providing him with pliant and attractive bed mates. In a poem that seems to have circulated widely even among FitzGibbon's political allies, this charge is bluntly put:

> And Westmorland was a good boy
> In making my Jacky an Earl
> And when he comes back here again
> My Jacky will get him a girl.[101]

An editorial celebrating the arrival of Fitzwilliam informed FitzGibbon that these particular services would no longer be required:

> The unfashionable virtues of Lord Fitzwilliam will not extract from you, my lord, those very gentle and very honorable submissions and hospitable attentions which your noble spirit was flattered in stooping to pay to the tender frailties of his gallant predecessor.[102]

FitzGibbon has suffered so much outright slander that this claim must necessarily be treated with a good deal of caution. His notable lack of chastity probably encouraged such suspicions. Even the super-obsequious *Volunteer Evening Post* conceded that the honorable attorney general did not number continence among his many virtues:

> he is known to be of a very libidinous constitution, a circumstance, although not absolutely criminal, is evidently dangerous to the chastity of his Majesty's liege subjects and manifestly unbecoming to the dignity of his situation.[103]

The comments of the very sympathetic Lord Glenbervie have already received notice. FitzGibbon himself confirms the impression that he was a hardened and adept seducer. In discussing the merits of a divorce bill with Auckland in 1801, he offered this very useful and fascinating insight into the mechanics of adultery, no doubt the hard won wisdom of his past adventures with Mrs D:

> I am decidedly of opinion that nothing would stagger the wiles of cuckold makers so much as the probable prospect of the intrigue ending in the marriage of the parties ... If I were to embark on such a pursuit, I do very truly assure you that I should consider such a penalty much more seriously than I could consider any other that could be inflicted on me. The prevention of marriage surely will never in any instance be considered by the gentlemen as a misfortune.[104]

But coarse talk and an over-active libido do not necessarily make FitzGibbon a pimp. Moreover, he had plenty of claims on Lord Westmorland's loyalty without resorting to procuring. Given the dubious nature of the evidence, even the most critical and antagonistic biographer must conclude that there were limits to what FitzGibbon would do to further his career.

12

Convicts, Whigs and Mayors 1789–90

I

Buckingham made his escape from Ireland and the Irish in June 1789. FitzGibbon, in company with Foster and the Archbishop of Dublin, served as Lord Justice until the arrival of the new lord-lieutenant, Westmorland, the following January.[1] His appointment as one of the lords justices, effectively one of the three governors of an interim administration, reflected both his standing and the administration's confidence in him. This seven-month interval saw a major war of wills between the English and the Irish governments. FitzGibbon in particular showed an unaccustomed, though short-lived and reluctant, assertiveness. A transport of Irish convicts to Newfoundland ignited this particular Anglo-Irish conflict.

The notorious police act of 1786 permitted the shipment of convicts to English plantations in America, or more generally, to any place outside of Europe.[2] This provision failed to take into account the policy of the English government, which had ceased to regard America as a penal settlement after the treaty with the United States in 1783, and which had been shipping convicts to Australia since 1788. The Irish government acted on the assumption that since the act in question had received the approval of the British Privy Council, convict shipments to America were still permissible. At a cost of appalling suffering to the unfortunate convicts, the Irish government learned differently.

The shipmaster acted callously and brutally, even for a man engaged in the transportation of human cargoes. He left the convicts in Newfoundland without making the most minimal provisions for food, clothing or shelter from the climate, which even in summer was inclement. Not surprisingly, some of the convicts, already weakened by the hard conditions of their Dublin imprisonment and of the voyage, died.[3]

The Dublin government eventually received word of the cruel and inadvertent death sentence suffered by some of the convicts. To his credit, FitzGibbon investigated the possibility of prosecuting the captain of the ship. He reluctantly came to the conclusion that government could not take any legal action against the shipmaster, however reprehensible his actions.[4] Neither he nor any of his colleagues seem to have inquired whether conditions for the survivors had improved. They apparently assumed that the remaining convicts would somehow fend for themselves; therefore, the Irish government could safely forget the whole unpleasant affair.

The surviving Irish convicts lingered miserably in Newfoundland until October, when the governor of the colony, Admiral Milbanke, loaded them on another ship bound for Spithead. He then informed the English Privy Council of his actions, and cited as justification the fears of the settlers and their inability to support this unwelcome and unconventional batch of Irish immigrants.[5]

Once he received this troubling news, William Wyndam Grenville immediately consulted the English Chancellor, Lord Thurlow. He suggested re-directing the ship to Ireland. Thurlow showed a rather careless grasp of the situation by adding that the convicts, once in Ireland, could "be dealt with according to the law, as their sentence seems not to have been executed".[6] Grenville was obliged to remind Thurlow that the convicts already had been tried, and the abortive journey to Newfoundland had constituted their sentence. He did acknowledge the "novelty and peculiarity of this case" and recommended a special meeting of the British Privy Council to consider it.[7] Thurlow, who still took a very dismissive view of the whole matter reluctantly agreed, though he recommended a small gathering, "for it would elevate the thing too much to make it the subject of *éclat*".[8]

On 25 November 1789, Grenville informed Chief Secretary Hobart of the decision of this small discreet meeting of the Privy Council. The Irish government was about to receive custody of those convicts, 80 in number, who had been shipped to England, courtesy of Admiral Milbanke. Grenville recommended confining the convicts until the Irish Parliament could make provisions to ship them to the new penal colony in New South Wales. He blandly accompanied his dictates with an estimate of costs. The Irish government should expect to pay £17 a head for the privilege of shipping convicts to New South Wales; in addition, they were to share the costs of the garrison stationed in Australia.[9]

If Thurlow had hoped to avoid "*éclat*" he badly underestimated Lord Justice FitzGibbon and his colleagues in the Irish government. The news of the English Privy Council's decision elicited vehement protests, both legal and political. In keeping with his habitual demeanor toward his masters in London, FitzGibbon adopted a conciliatory, if faintly reproachful tone in his letter of reply dated 28 November 1789. He acknowledged that the English government certainly had every right to bar the Irish from sending convicts to the American colonies. But he reminded Grenville that convicts from Ireland had been dispatched to America "for time immemorial."[10] [*sic*] With studied respect and implied rebuke, he added that if the English government had objections to penal convoys going to America, they ought to have indicated as much during the parliamentary session, when appropriate legislative action could have been taken:

> ... if an objection had been stated whilst our Parliament was sitting, certainly

> we should have been bound to make some provision for the disposal of our convicts which could not be deemed injurious to Great Britain or her colonies.[11]

He also pointed out to Grenville the terrible legal dilemma raised by the convicts' return. In one respect the English Government had placed the convicts in grave legal jeopardy: if they set foot in Ireland before their sentences expired, they faced death, whatever the circumstances of their return. The action of the English Government had raised a worse possibility, as their return of the convicts could be construed as a virtual pardon:

> If they [the convicts] are sent back to us by order of the British government, I do not know of any law which will warrant our magistrates to detain them in custody.[12]

Moreover, not only the convicts, but the shipmaster bringing them back to Ireland, could face prosecution and a possible death sentence. He closed by begging Grenville to keep the convicts in England until the Irish government could decide what to do about them.

Hobart, writing three days later, had no compunction about showing his anger. He reminded Grenville that the British Privy Council had approved the act of 1786, and this approval extended to the provision for sending convicts to America, or so the Irish Government had believed. He added sarcastically, "... it is presumed [the Act] was considered by his Majesty's ministers in England previous to the Great Seal being put to it." Hobart's allusion to the reaction of the Irish Parliament accounts for his extraordinary degree of rage:

> As the matter now stands, Admiral Milbanke has superseded an Irish Act of Parliament and you may will imagine what a ferment that will create in the Irish House of Commons.[13]

As a bruised veteran of the great battle over the Regency, Hobart had good reason to dread another outburst of wounded national pride.

FitzGibbon followed immediately on Hobart's epistolary heels with a second letter. He put forth the same arguments, though again, he did not feel at liberty to assume the same peremptory tone of voice. He began by pointing out that neither he nor any other member of the Irish government was aware of a prohibition against the transport of convicts to America. Like Hobart, he complained of the apparent contradiction of the Privy Council's actions. By returning the convicts to Ireland, the British government was over-riding a law which it had supposedly examined and approved:

> This whole proceeding [shipment of the convicts to America] was had under the authority of a law which was passed with the approbation of the British Ministry so late as the year 1786, and now they are to be returned to us in body by an act of that very Government which had assented to the law under which they were transported.[14]

He also touched on the political turmoil which the action could cause, though he was careful to lay the onus on Milbanke, rather than FitzGibbon's own masters and friends in the Privy Council. However justified he may have been in expelling the "wretches", Milbanke had committed a grave indiscretion by sending them to England. Had he sent them anywhere else; indeed had he sent them directly to Ireland, "we could easily have managed matters so as to prevent any serious difficulties to Irish government". By superseding the authority of the Irish government, and appealing instead to the English, Milbanke had raised again the volatile issue of Irish sovereignty. FitzGibbon had as compelling reason as Hobart to remember the horrors of the Regency Crisis and to dread their repetition:

> "if we are driven to the necessity of defending their return to us under all these circumstances, I freely own to you that it appears to me to be as difficult a task as could be assigned to the friends of Government in this Country."[15]

FitzGibbon begged Grenville, if possible, not to return the convicts under the authority of the British government. He suggested instead using Milbanke as the scapegoat. The broils of Irish politics could not affect him, secure in the fastness of Newfoundland:

> Let the act of returning them to us, if they must be sent here, be the act of Governor Milbanke. Probably he will never come to Ireland, and I do not suppose that he will very much feel any comments which our worthy Whigs may make upon him.[16]

He closed on a characteristically obsequious note:

> I should ask you a thousand pardons for troubling you with this very long letter; but I really feel very strongly the difficulties which must necessarily occur if these rogues are to be landed here in custody of one of your messengers by your warrant.[17]

Grenville's response to FitzGibbon's initial communication was very much in a tone of *de haute en bas*. He countered FitzGibbon's legal qualms with the higher authority of Lord Thurlow and the English judges of the King's Bench. The English judiciary held the opinion that the Privy Council had no other recourse but to ship the convicts to Ireland. The Irish judges of the King's Bench could have no difficulty in remitting the convicts to the various county prisons until Parliament or the courts of gaol delivery could dispose of them. Furthermore, Grenville informed FitzGibbon, America had ceased to served as a penal colony since the peace treaty with the United States in 1783. The remaining British colonies in North America "had all expressed a decided resolution not to receive them [shipments of convicts]". The Irish government had behaved with particular impropriety in sending convicts to Newfoundland, which was, strictly speaking, a fishing depot, not a colony. The "uniform tenor of our laws" and the King's instructions, restricted settlement, apart from the temporary residence of fishermen. Finally, Grenville pointed out that whatever the dangers and dilemmas of sending convicts to Ireland, the English authorities faced a far greater share of both. The convicts, in the eyes of English law, "have committed no crime and incurred no sentence". They had only one other course of action, aside from sending the convicts to Ireland, and that was "letting loose upon the people of this country a set of desperate ruffians who could have no recourse here but that of depredations upon the property of others".[18]

Before Grenville's rather schoolmasterish letter reached Dublin the Irish government sent a revenue cruiser to intercept the convict ship and to prevent its landing in Ireland.[19] This action had a quality of boldness and defiance utterly unlike FitzGibbon's past conduct toward the English government, and more important, utterly unlike the cautious tone of his communications with Grenville. Possibly his recent elevation to long-desired office, in addition to a fear of another political crisis, gave him an unusual degree of mastery. But it seems more likely that Hobart and Foster took the initiative, and FitzGibbon very reluctantly went along. Hobart and Foster would have borne the brunt of any parliamentary uproar over the matter. Consequently, they would have been more resentful of the English government's action and the more forceful in trying to thwart it. Foster may have had an additional motive. He always had a far more finely developed sense of Irish consequence than FitzGibbon.

Whatever the origins and motives of this action, it aroused predictable outrage in England. Grenville wrote to Westmorland, the viceroy in the wings, "I cannot enough lament the precipitation of this ill-advised step. It is however, now to be considered what are the measures which must be taken in consequence of it".[20] Thurlow was the more vehement: sending out the revenue cruiser was an "impertinent order" given by a "foolish Government".[21]

The show of independence by the Irish cabinet was fleeting. According to his own account, FitzGibbon immediately ordered the recall of the revenue cruiser when he received Grenville's letter of explanation.[22] In spite of its rather self-serving taint, his account seems likely. He probably was the last to agree to the order and the first to insist on its withdrawal. Hobart too fell in line, though his tone remained surly and defiant:

> If, notwithstanding the representations made from here, you persevere in your intention of sending the convicts, they will of course be received; we must get out of the scrape as well as we can.[23]

Grenville and FitzGibbon engaged in further desultory correspondence on the legal niceties of the business. Grenville attempted to close any discussion of Milbanke's actions. At this point, he argued, the questions about the propriety of Admiral Milbanke's actions were simply irrelevant. It sufficed that the English statutes uniformly pointed to a policy of forbidding settlement in Newfoundland. He reiterated again that the English government could have sent the convicts to no other place but Ireland. They had no legal right to hold the convicts in custody in England. Nor could Grenville see any grounds for prosecuting the convicts for returning to Ireland or for prosecuting the ship's captain and the Privy Council's messenger for cooperating in their return. The convicts, in fact had never begun to serve their sentences, and thus they could not in logic or in fairness be considered illegal returnees. They were in exactly the same position as any convict committed to gaol prior to transportation. As for the individuals who had carried out the Privy Council's order, the King's pardon could easily correct matters "if any magistrate of Dublin was so absurd as to commit them."[24]

FitzGibbon the legal purist could not take Grenville's cavalier view of Milbanke's judgment:

> You will not, I trust, be offended that I cannot agree in opinion with you that in this business it is not material whether Governor Milbanke was right or wrong ... If I can but satisfy myself that he was right in sending these convicts to England, I should feel no difficulty whatever upon the subject.[25]

In the same letter, FitzGibbon, the rather piqued legal authority, corrected Grenville on the point of Newfoundland settlement:

> I have looked into the statute of the 10th, 11th William III for encouraging the trade to Newfoundland, and I observe that advantages with respect to a temporary property in the stage at Newfoundland is given to the ships which shall first arrive there in order to fish; but I have not been able to find any Act passed in 1773 [*sic*] on the subject.[26]

He also held fast to the point that the convicts and the persons concerned with returning them could have faced unmerited legal dangers:

> With respect to what I mentioned to you that the person landing them here might be prosecuted for a capital felony, you will see that I stated that to be one objection against others to proceeding against the convicts as felons returned from transportation within the times limited by their sentence. If they were to be proceeded against in that way, I mentioned to you that the messenger and the captain might be prosecuted as accessories to the felony should any person be so mischievous as to swear information against them.[27]

Apart from these assertions of judicial authority, FitzGibbon made clear to Grenville that the Irish government would receive the convicts and that he himself would take the lead in defending the action of the English Privy Council. Indeed, he was prepared to go to fantastic lengths to present an act of bureaucratic browbeating as an act of grace and favour:

> ... if they do come back, you may be assured, whenever the matter may become the subject of public discussion , I shall be very anxious to prove their return to be a mark of high respect on your part to the people of Ireland.[28]

The business ended with unexpected calm. The revenge-minded Whig opposition showed more interest in re-fighting the battles of the Regency crisis than in investigating the subtleties of criminal law or of colonial jurisdiction. Parliament quickly passed a law authorizing transport to New South Wales.

The fate of the survivors of the Newfoundland voyage remains unknown. Presumably they were among the first to make the journey from Ireland to Australia. Of course, no one, FitzGibbon included, spared much thought for these "rogues" and "wretches" as they wrangled over their bounds of authority. The English and the Irish governments could just as well have been arguing over a disputed shipment of American tobacco or East India muslin.

Apart from its intrinsic tragedy, the affair of the convicts again exposed the fragile and uneasy relationship between the English and the Irish governments. In forbidding shipments of convicts to Newfoundland, and in preventing their arrival in England, Grenville, Thurlow and their colleagues acted out of broad imperial interests. Unfortunately, they rode roughshod over the fears and sensibilities of their Irish servants. In a sense, the business of the convict transports prefigured the far larger conflict over Catholic emancipation.

II

With the arrival of Westmorland in January 1790, FitzGibbon surrendered his role as Lord Justice. Westmorland quickly became an initiate into the great viceregal cult of FitzGibbon. It was perhaps inevitable that Westmorland would succumb to FitzGibbon's influence. He was a slightly duller version of the Duke of Rutland: young and amiable, unintellectual and unimaginative, and above all, utterly ignorant of Ireland. FitzGibbon did not need to go through a political crisis to win Westmorland's confidence, as he did with the prickly Buckingham. On the contrary he established his hegemony almost immediately. By 1791, Westmorland took the King's refusal to promote Colonel Fremantle as an insult to himself as well as to FitzGibbon.[29] By 1793, in the wake of the Catholic issue, Westmorland's correspondence bore the unmistakable stamp of long and frequent conversations with FitzGibbon. In his first accounts of the militia riots, he wrote to Dundas:

> In truth ye people of property and lower order here are as distinct sects as ye gentoos and Mahomedan, ye lower order of Irish consider themselves as plundered and kept out of their property by English settlers and on every occasion are ready for riot and revenge.[30]

The dark drama of the Popish dispossessed waiting to take their bloody revenge on English Protestant settlers was, of course, FitzGibbon's political leitmotif. His sybaritic hospitality (and his political opponents claimed, his adroit pimping), secured his hold over Westmorland. The bond did not break when Westmorland retired from Ireland. He, like Eden, became a recipient of FitzGibbon's sniping gossip and doom-ridden reports on the state of Ireland.[31]

As easily, the chief secretary, Robert Hobart, became a warm personal friend. They had already established a close working relationship during the Regency Crisis, and Hobart too became a frequent recipient of FitzGibbon's hospitality at Ely Place and at Mount Shannon.[32] If FitzGibbon found another pliable, amiable Rutland in Westmorland, he found in Hobart another romantic, glamorous William Eden. Like Eden, Hobart was polished, handsome, and English, and he had the additional luster of a military commission. FitzGibbon carried his admiration to the point of naming his younger son for Hobart.

FitzGibbon found it as easy to establish hegemony in the House of Lords. The practice of awarding peerages to government supporters made it a relatively tame body. The opposition peers, led by Charlemont and Leinster, were few in number and they were no match for FitzGibbon's intellectual and rhetorical powers. Consequently, the House of Lords was a quieter, if duller place. FitzGibbon had every intention of maintaining quiescence in his new parliamentary venue. Not for him the independence of the last Irish lord chancellor, Alan Broderick, Lord Midleton, who held office from 1715–25. Midleton had shown an embarrassing tendency to favor Irish interests over cherished imperial policies. Most notably, he opposed the notorious patent granted to Wood, though he looked with equally strong disfavor on the *Drapier's Letters* and refused to accept the dedication of this work to him. This stand so badly damaged relations between Midleton and the imperial government that he resigned. FitzGibbon, in contrast, almost always deferred to the dictates of English government, however reluctantly. He had done so in the case of the convicts and he was to do so again in the case of Catholic relief.[33]

During the session of 1790, FitzGibbon enjoyed a peaceful initiation into his new duties as speaker of the House of Lords. In the House of Commons, the opposition battled the government over the same tired issues of pensions, places and police. Grudges from the Regency Crisis enhanced the vindictiveness of these battles. Nonetheless, because newly restored government majorities quashed these issues in the House of Commons, the turmoil barely touched the House of Lords. Leinster raised some protest over Lord Strangeford's loss of a pension for voting against the government during the Regency Crisis. FitzGibbon handily replied that Strangeford, as a beneficiary of the Crown, had, very properly received a request to support it "on that great emergency". If he found the request of the Government offensive, "it did not follow that he had a right to complain at any wound offered to the delicacy of his feelings on this head or publicly to complain of a matter which was in his own power to remedy by resigning his pension." The votes followed FitzGibbon. Leinster's motion to censure the government for Strangeford's loss was defeated by a margin of 33 to 13.[34]

FitzGibbon had as easy a time with the only other major opposition issue to obtrude on the House of Lords. During the session of 1790, the Government introduced a bill to place the entire country under the jurisdiction of the "Act for the Better Execution of the Laws", better known as the Magistracy Act. This time Lord Portarlington took up the opposition standard. He reiterated all the complaints and all the accusations of 1787: the measure represented an attempt by the government to increase its tyrannical power by imposing an armed police force on the countryside. It also strengthened the government's corrupt powers of patronage in the guise of assistant barristers. In 1790, FitzGibbon personally had no county election to face and no outraged Limerick gentlemen to placate. Secure in his long-sought office, he could support the extension of the act, with the same arguments he had used in 1787. The bill entrusted peacekeeping to constables under the direction of the local magistrates, surely a far milder and more humane practice than the standard one of calling out the military. FitzGibbon indulged in rather murky antiquarian romanticism to support his argument. The freest government in English history, the Saxon had relied on a similar type of peacekeeping force. In short, the act represented no more and no less than an effort to police the countryside more effectively and more mildly. It was above all an Irish matter in which the English government could have no concern or interest. As for the barristers, they provided a useful service at a minimal salary. £300 a year hardly increased the government's expenses or its power to corrupt. Very few barristers with a reasonably good practice would find that salary tempting. Above all, he insisted on the key amendment to the act, which extended its jurisdiction to the entire country. To make exceptions would only encourage lawlessness in areas where the act did not apply. Once again, his arguments or the government's majority in the Lords prevailed.[35]

The remainder of FitzGibbon's parliamentary business in his first session in the Lords was desultory and mundane. Such matters as the regulation of charity schools and the licensing of the internal carriage trade took up the bulk of FitzGibbon's time. The session was as short as it was dull; parliament adjourned on 4 April, within four months of opening.

III

The quiet of his first parliamentary session as Lord Chancellor was illusory and brief. He may have missed out on the post-Regency crisis duels with the opposition in the House of Commons; but he soon received the dubious compensation of a central role in an extra-parliamentary dispute over the mayoral election of 1790. On one level, the dispute represented another skirmish in the desultory war over the police act. On another, it represented a naked attempt by both radical and government factions to control the outcome of the approaching general election. The mayor, along with the sheriffs, judged the qualification of voters, and they presided over the tally of votes.[39] In short, whichever party controlled the chief municipal offices controlled the outcome of the election for city members. Unfortunately, FitzGibbon's intervention exacerbated rather than resolved the crisis and brought him considerable discredit, not only with the usual political opponents, but with the English government.

Ordinarily each alderman served as Lord Mayor in rotation. The term of office was one year. Nonetheless, a law of 1759 permitted the popular branch of city government, the Common Council or Commons, to refuse a particular candidate.[40] On 16 April 1790, the Dublin Commons, under the leadership of that perennial radical Napper Tandy, denied the election of Alderman James. The fact that he was a commissioner of the hated police accounted for his rejection. The Commons expected the next in rotation, James' brother-in-law Howison, to received appointment instead. But the Aldermen, resentful over the high-handed treatment meted out to James, proposed every other alderman *but* Howison.[41] Not unexpectedly the Commons rejected every alternative *but* Howison. Howison's virtues appear to have been entirely negative. He was *not* a police commissioner and he did *not* have the approbation of the Board of Aldermen. Therefore he became the paladin of a Commons determined to assert its power and to control the outcome of the parliamentary elections.

Three days later, in keeping with another provision of the act of 1759, the Commons met at the Thosel to elect their own candidate. In spite of the isolated opposition of John Gifford, the government's hired newsman, the Commons stood by Howison. John Binns, Tandy's ally in the great initiative against James, then proposed laying the dispute before the Privy Council for a final judgment. He also suggested the inevitable side effect of all protracted disputes, a report. The Commons agreed to both proposals.[42]

The hearing took place on 26 April. Two leading luminaries of the Whig Club, George Ponsonby and John Philpot Curran, took the part of Howison. James retained Counselors Smith and Downes, both of whom later received appointments to the Bench. Already a municipal dispute had become a factional dispute among national parties. The Privy Council, with FitzGibbon in the lead, threw out Howison's election and called for a new one.[43] FitzGibbon's motives were obvious. He saw the election dispute as a partisan troublemaking at its most absurd, and he hoped that sense, calm, and order would prevail at a new election.

In the meantime, the parliamentary elections, the true *raison d'etre* for the whole contretemps, took place. In spite of their frustrations, the radical faction could take satisfaction in the results of the election: Henry Grattan and Lord Henry FitzGerald were duly returned as members for the city.[44] But the quarrel over the municipal elections raged on, with bad consequences for FitzGibbon. During a riot following the parliamentary elections his house suffered damage.[45] In a public advertisement, he gave an indignant account of the evil work done by this "riotous and tumultuous mob". They "broke down the windows and window shutters and poured showers of bricks and paving stones into every part of it they could reach". He offered a reward of £100 "for the discovery of persons concerned in the said outrage, or any of them as I may be enabled to prosecute him or them to conviction".[46] The reward was handsome, and FitzGibbon's determination strong, but he never seems to have discovered, much less "prosecuted to conviction" the culprits. What connection the attack had to FitzGibbon's Privy Council decision is unclear. The attack may simply have arisen from sheer mischief-making, drunken euphoria, and a popular dislike that persisted in spite of the nationalistic satisfaction with his elevation.

If the mob had indeed intended to express dissatisfaction over the decision of the Privy Council, FitzGibbon was unshaken. The new mayoral election ended in the same stalemate. The Aldermen proposed James and the Commons rejected him. When the frustrated Board of Aldermen asked for an explanation, the Commons gave an answer both laconic and shamelessly partisan: "they [the Commons] had acted according to the law, and did not think it incumbent on them to assign any cause".[47] The Commons then called for the nomination of another candidates, but the Aldermen withdrew from the farce. Left to their own triumphant devices, the Commons elected Howison a second time.[48]

For a second time the parties appeared before the Privy Council, with one minor change in the *dramatis personae*: Patrick Duigenan replaced Downs as one of James' advocates. FitzGibbon repeated his earlier action by dismissing the election and calling for another.[49]

The subsequent election followed its inevitable and childish course: the Aldermen proposed James, the Commons rejected him in favour of Howison, and the dispute was brought before the Privy Council for a third time.[50] The ever unreliable memoir of Grattan *fils* gives a full account of this particular hearing. Curran distinguished himself by a florid billingsgate which even the pious younger Grattan had to admit was self-defeating. His speech, blithely ignored the main legal question raised by the election, to wit, whether the Commons had a limitless right to reject candidates proposed by the Board of Aldermen. Instead, he indulged in a harangue against government in general and FitzGibbon in particular. When FitzGibbon interrupted a history of past Privy Council iniquities, Curran launched into this barely concealed assault on his old enemy's character:

> Alas, my lords, by what argument could any man hope to reclaim or dissuade a mean, *illiberal* and unprincipled minion of authority, induced by his profligacy to undertake and bound by his avarice and vanity to persevere.[51]

Upon hearing this forensic production, FitzGibbon no doubt regretted his poor marksmanship during the duel of 1785. Nonetheless, he showed an admirable, and uncharacteristic forbearance in his response; he simply asked Curran to stick to the legal point:

> Surely Mr Curran, a gentleman of your eminence in your profession must see that the conduct of former Privy Councils has nothing to do with the question before us. The question lies in the narrowest compass, whether the Commons have a right of arbitrary and capricious rejection or are obliged to assign a

> reasonable cause for their disapprobation. To that point you have a right to be heard, but I hope you do not mean to lecture the Council.[52]

Curran failed to take the hint and responded with more personal invective:

> I mean, my Lords, to speak to the case of my client, and to avail myself of every topic of defense which I conceive applicable to the case. I am not speaking to a dry point of law, to a single judge on a mere forensic subject. I am addressing a very large auditory consisting of co-ordinate members, of whom the far greater are not versed in law ... I am aware, my lords, that truth is to be sought only by slow painful progress; I know also that error is in its nature flippant and compendious; it hops with airy and fastidious levity over proofs and arguments and perches upon assertion which it calls conclusion.[53]

Grattan the younger gloatingly recorded that FitzGibbon ordered the Council Chamber cleared of spectators, once he realized the drift of Curran's speech.[54] Curran may well have succeeded in scoring a petty personal point, but he failed his client. FitzGibbon upheld James' claim and he informed the Commons that if they still were dissatisfied, they could take their case to the King's Bench. He added "... by the time that the Commons *had amused themselves there for three or four years, it was probable they would be tired of it and wish themselves out of the dispute.*"[55]

Young Grattan inferred from these comments that FitzGibbon had acted out of mere arbitrary caprice: "Such was the solemnity of his judicial decisions."[56] But FitzGibbon's decision was perfectly solemn and perfectly in character. He loathed party and judicial wrangling, particularly if aided and abetted by the Whigs. To his mind, James was a perfectly suitable candidate, and whatever rights of election the Commons might claim, they had no right to deny him an office to which he was otherwise entitled out of sheer partisan perversity. In short, his biases in favour of order and established procedure prompted him more that strict judicial reasoning. Anger at Curran and habits of irritable haste may have played no small part as well. Whatever his motives, FitzGibbon undoubtedly believed or hoped that if confronted with a firm decision against them and the prospect of a long lawsuit if they pursued the matter, the anti-James, anti-police partisans would back down.

Once again he miscalculated. Retaliation for his decision was swift. Three days after the meeting of the Privy Council, the Guild of Merchants met, with none other than Napper Tandy in the chair. The members voted to withdraw the congratulatory address and the freedom granted to FitzGibbon in the happy, heady days following his appointment as Chancellor.[57] The following day, 14 July, the Commons proposed a long list of resolutions, attacking both Alderman James and FitzGibbon's decision in his favour.

Among other things, they asserted that since the Aldermen had failed to provide a suitable alternative to James (in the person of Howison), the law of 1759 vested the right of an election exclusively in the Commons. The Privy Council, by over-riding this right and by upholding James' election "did as far as their power extended, *dispense with the law of the land*". Since James had assumed office illegally, the Commons declared themselves under no obligation to recognize him as mayor. On the contrary, they would "by every legal means oppose him in the execution of the office of Chief Magistrate". To drive home its point, the Commons barred James from the use of the Mansion House, they resolved to deny him any public funds, and they threatened to turn civic ceremonies into humiliating farces by refusing their attendance.[58] Finally, and most ominously, the Commons resolved to turn a municipal squabble into a drive for the purge of national government, and especially for the purge of FitzGibbon:

> That as Alderman James had by the Privy Council been declared Lord Mayor for the ensuing year, we do hereby direct an application to be made to all corporate cities and towns, to concur with us in an humble address to His Majesty, laying before His Majesty that whereas there had been a *violent infringement of our right* by the illegal exercise of the powers vested in the Lord Lieutenant and Privy Council, and praying that His Majesty will *remove from his Councils* those who advised that measure.[59]

The resolutions passed overwhelmingly. A certain Mr Wilson raised the sole voice of dissent by suggesting that the call for a petition to the King might create "injurious alarm".[60] No fears of injurious alarms intruded on the enthusiastic support given to the resolutions by a subsequent meeting of the freeholders and freemen of Dublin. The irrepressible Sir Edward Newenham was in his prime, as he denounced the "infringements made on the rights of the Commons of the City of Dublin".[61] The future United Irishman, Hamilton Rowan, made one of his first public appearances as chairman of the freeholders' meeting.[62] Inevitably, the Whig Club took advantage of the uproar to add polemical as well as legal assistance to the Common Council:

> That the Whig Club cannot possibly have witnessed what has lately passed respecting the election of a Lord Mayor without expressing the deepest concern and declaring that they will, both individually and as a body, co-operate with their fellow citizens in every legal and constitutional measure which may tend to vindicate the law and to support the rights of the metropolis.[63]

The Whig Club later published this resolution. Grattan's signature, as pro-secretary, appeared on it, as did the gilt-edged Whig names of Charlemont and Moira.[64]

FitzGibbon probably would have responded to the resolutions of the Commons and the Dublin freeholders with the contemptuous indifference he had displayed in 1784, during the great uproar over attachments. But the resolution of the Whig Club, and especially the participation of Moira and Charlemont, exacerbated his ever present resentment against the propertied and the well-born, who gratuitously disturbed public order for party purposes. An emergency meeting of Parliament, prompted by an impending war with Spain, gave FitzGibbon an opportunity to express his displeasure and to defend his actions. The speech was a typical FitzGibbon production, forceful, closely reasoned, and liberally laced with brutal invective. While making an elaborate pretext of disbelief that Moira and Charlemont would lend their names to such a proceeding, FitzGibbon cruelly and strikingly ridiculed their closest political associates:

> Now my Lords, if this resolution had appeared only under the authority of the Whig Club, signed by their secretary or pro-secretary, I would have treated it as I would any other resolution of any other eating or drinking club; but when a charge is made, or strongly insinuated, when that charge is, that an act to which my name is signed, an attack has been made on the rights of this metropolis, and an invasion of the law of the land – when it appears authenticated by the names of two of the Hereditary Councilors of the Crown, two of the Hereditary Judges of the land, it becomes necessary to know whether they have really submitted to have their names placed to it?[65]

When Moira and Charlemont affirmed that they had indeed signed the resolution of this particular "eating and drinking club", FitzGibbon launched into an elaborate history of the city government of Dublin, beginning with the reign of Richard III no less; in essence his history made the rather irrelevant point that the Commons had not always had the power of approbation and that traditionally the Aldermen alone had selected the mayor. This historical groundwork established, he offered an equally elaborate defense of himself. In essence, he maintained that his supposed act of arbitrary partisan illegality had in fact been an act of the most scrupulous judicial neutrality. He had simply referred the dispute to its proper sphere, the Court of King's Bench, which alone had the authority to decide on the merits of the election. If that decision came into dispute, it could, like any other, be appealed to the House of Lords. To set this judicial process in motion, the Privy Council chose that candidate who was "well-affected to Church and State" (in other words a suitably qualified Protestant) and who moreover appeared to have the best *prima facie* title. This practice "has been always considered as almost a matter of course in cases of double returns". On no account was this power of approbation a judicial power. FitzGibbon lambasted his present and absent auditors in the Whig Club for their legal ignorance on this point:

> It was preserved for the peculiar sagacity of the Irish Whigs to transform this right of approbation into a judicial power, which indeed, is such a perversion of sense and meaning as could only arise from the greatest confusion of ideas that ever distracted the brain of man.

Although he himself was of opinion that Alderman James had the best claim, FitzGibbon maintained his fundamental open-mindedness on the matter:

> I have spent the greater part of my life in endeavoring to acquire a knowledge

> of the law, and this is the opinion which I have formed upon the best consideration of the subject; yet when it comes to the Bar of this House of decision, if anything appears in argument sufficient to change that opinion, I shall not be ashamed to retract it.

After reiterating that the Courts alone could determine the validity of the election FitzGibbon closed with another warning against the danger and the folly of partisanship. Order and the rule of law existed only precariously in Ireland; the Whig Club and their allies in the Dublin Common Council were acting with criminal irresponsibility by subverting both in their selfish pursuit of power:

> Suppose the law other than as I conceive it; is the question to be decided by clamour and noise? Are they, the hereditary judges of the land, instead of appealing to the Court of King's Bench in the first instance, and to this House in the *dernier resort*, are they, I say, to appeal to the Whig Club, or to the Aggregate Body, or to men with National Cockades in their hats? If so, what is to become of property? My Lords, this country is, I am afraid, driven upon the verge of a precipice, and I am well aware there is a set of discontented men who would push her on to ruin. Good God! Is it not manifest? Who are the men who would invade the laws, the Lord Lieutenant and the Council who send the Question of right to a legal decision, or those who would shut up the Courts of Justice and appeal to the Whig Clubs, Aggregate Meetings or men with arms in their hands and national cockades in their hats? It has been much the fashion to decide questions by clamour, you may shut the Courts indeed and leave every peaceable honest man without redress; for every question that ever came before the King's Bench, the Exchequer, the Common Pleas or the Chancery may as well be decided by clamour as that between the contending parts of the Corporation of Dublin, and if so, what becomes of the law?

The government newspapers were predictably lavish in their praises of FitzGibbon's performance. *Faulkner's Dublin Journal* reprinted the speech at length, and the *Freeman's Journal* declared that FitzGibbon's arguments were so forceful and so sound that his Whig opponents, in and out of Parliament, "were struck dumb by the assertion of truth and the most uncommon strength of legal argument. Nothing was returned but silence and the admissibility of error."[66]

In actuality, FitzGibbon may have laboring under an uneasy sense of his own admissibility of error. For all his taunts at the "peculiar sagacity" of the Whigs, FitzGibbon, like Curran before him, evaded the central legal issue of the conflict, the interpretation of the statute of 1759. He retreated into claims of uncertainty: "... there are amongst wise and able men a variety of opinions on the subject – some adhering to the strict letter of the statue of the 33rd of George II, others construing the statute by general known principles of common law".[67] His claims of lofty neutrality and his appeals to the orderly procedure of the law amounted to *ex post facto* rationalizations.

With characteristic haste and irritability, he had decided the Commons was abusing its right of approbation. However right he may have been and however absurd the Commons, his interpretation of the law was dubious. The plain wording of the statute in question gave the Commons the right to refuse a candidate without any qualification whatsoever, as he himself had to admit.[68] By the time he delivered this speech, FitzGibbon may have recognized that he had overstepped the mark; he could never of course admit as much, so he transformed his flawed judgment on a clear point of law into a mere opinion on a doubtful point.

Worse, his speech, far from silencing anyone, needlessly prolonged the whole miserable business. Five days after he delivered it, Alderman James, notwithstanding his strong *prima facie* case, resigned the mayoralty in favour of Howison.[69] Ostensibly, he resigned to restore harmony to the city, but he undoubtedly did so out of sheer weariness. His opponents on the Common Council failed to show a similar magnanimity. At another meeting of the freeholders held on 4 August, Sir Edward Newenham criticized James for not admitting the illegality of his election when he resigned. "Mr McNally" (probably the future government spy cum United Irish defense counsel) compared Alderman James with King James: "the latter having given up a Crown under as contemptible circumstances as the other resigned his crown."[70] The Commons might have been sated with this public display of mean-spirited exultation, had FitzGibbon's speech not offered a new pretext for outrage and agitation.

Again, Sir Edward took the rhetorical lead. Borrowing a device from FitzGibbon himself, he made an elaborate pretext of disbelieving printed versions of the speech in the House of Lords. His remarks alluded to old grievances over attachments, to renewed grievances over the police and the mayoral election, and to FitzGibbon's supposed paternal connection to the Jesuits, a persistent and perhaps willful delusion of Sir Edward's:

> This pamphlet is said by the printer to contain the speech of Lord FitzGibbon, Lord High Chancellor of Ireland ... so far the printer put his Lordship's imprimatur to it – it may not, it cannot be genuine, but as it has been printed, reprinted and most assiduously circulated, and as no printer has been taken up, no information filed, no attachment issued in consequence of the publication, every man is at full liberty to answer it ... Nothing can be more trifling or partial than curtailing so material a clause of an act of Parliament – it might answer the scholastic chicanery of a disciple of Ignatius Loyola, the artful founder of the Society of the Jesuits, who skimmed the surface of truth, but never adhered to the substance, it must, however, be an error of the press, or a false conception of the parliamentary reporter, for it is impossible that the Lord High Chancellor could sink or curtail the essence of an act of Parliament to answer the degrading views of a police junto.[71]

The Whigs did their part to sustain the great uproar against FitzGibbon. Far from lapsing into silent consternation, they met, they drew up a predictable list of resolutions denouncing FitzGibbon, and they published their resolutions in the form of a pamphlet.[72] They too adopted the well-worn ruse of assuming FitzGibbon was not in fact the author of the speech in question. The Whigs declared that they would have ignored the publication "if [the] empty paper did not affect to call itself the speech of the Chancellor".[73] They then defended the actions of Charlemont and Moira for acting, not as mere hereditary judges but as "hereditary freemen – bound by interest – bound by affection ... and now by the offenses of His Majesty's ministers and their contumely – bound more than ever to make common cause with their countrymen".[74] Gleefully, the pamphlet seized on the irrelevancies and inconsistencies in FitzGibbon's argument. FitzGibbon was dryly informed that the history of Dublin corporation was perfectly well known. The Whigs, and indeed, the people of Dublin, asked for no more than their *current* chartered rights, permitted by an express act of Parliament.[75] As for his claims that the Privy Council had made no judicial decision, the Whig Club pamphlet observed that FitzGibbon had certainly given that impression. He had limited Curran to the discussion of a point of law, and he had inquired into the circumstances of the election in an exceedingly judicial manner. Simply by declaring that Alderman James had the best *prima facie* case FitzGibbon had made a judicial decision.[76] FitzGibbon's referral of the matter to the Court of King's Bench, and his unhappy turn of phrase in doing so also came under attack. Far from offering any redress, the decision was maliciously calculated to thwart opposition:

> But though the author informs us there is redress at law, yet the person whose name he assumes also informs us that "such redress would be a grievance and that the city after amusing itself for three years in the courts of justice would be heartily sick of the experiment". Our respect for decency prevents us from going so far as to cast a damp and despondency on appealing to the law of the land, yet we do agree that the forcing the city to that appeal was a very great injury, because the redress might be very tedious, the interim might be very disturbed and the period of the mayoralty expire before the point could be settled.[77]

FitzGibbon's rhetorical excess in general inspired indignant prose. His remark about the Whigs' "peculiar sagacity" in confusing a judicial power and a power of approbation provoked as merciless a rejoinder: he had displayed "gross and manifest presumption in making in so gross a manner so unfounded a clause".[78] The pamphlet alluded as well to FitzGibbon's past verbal bad manners and in particular to his infamous remarks following the rejection of the commercial propositions:

> We cannot avoid expressing our disapprobation of such a malapert way of addressing the people, a disregard for whom, under any government is unwise, under a free government graceless, and in a minister disqualification to hold the reins of power. We have not forgotten the gross language once before offered to

> the people; it was when they defended their country against the famous propositions. We flattered ourselves that we should never again be witness to the like froward discussions.[79]

Above all, the Whig Club pamphlet ridiculed FitzGibbon's interpretation, or rather his failure to interpret the Act of 1759. The Whigs had no such compunction:

> ... as from the speech under consideration, no trace whatever of the merits of the question appears, we think it proper to state from the act of the 33rd George II the following obvious inference – that by the Act no man can be mayor of the city who is rejected by the Commons; that the right of rejection in the Commons is co-extensive with the right of election in the board, both being limited by one and the same proviso, which only requires that the Board shall elect and the Commons approve of some one of the Board.[80]

It was a devastating and fundamentally sound critique of FitzGibbon's action. It also caused him profound offense. Grattan, who had the main responsibility for drafting the pamphlet, commented, "The Chancellor is, I believe, vexed, but could he expect to abuse us as a pack of blockheads and not to meet retaliation?"[81] Grattan's son later made the rather melodramatic claim that the pamphlet ended his father's boyhood friendship with FitzGibbon.[82] The Regency Crisis and its aftermath already had created a rift between the two. FitzGibbon's dismissive comments about the pro-secretary of the Whig Club, who was none other than Grattan himself, suggest as much. Moreover, Curran may have contributed as much, if not more to the offending pamphlet.[83] But the pamphlet was unquestionably harsh, and FitzGibbon may well have looked upon Grattan's collaboration in such a bitter personal attack as a betrayal which no political difference could justify. It may not have been the sole cause for the end of their friendship, but it was perhaps the inevitable *coup de grace*.

FitzGibbon's actions in the mayoral election of 1790 appear to have had other, and to him, more serious consequences than a broken friendship and some ugly verbal dueling in Parliament and in print. Grattan was ultimately unimportant, and FitzGibbon was well used to political brawls. But his reputation with the English government, and especially with Pitt, seems to have suffered. Lord Donoughmore hinted at a loss of favour:

> ... The Chancellor will certainly wish to be sole Minister as long as he can. But how far his Dublin stretches of power and consequent retreat may have increase the premier's confidence in him, I can only judge from what things ought to be.[84]

Admittedly, Donoughmore may have been displaying an element of partisan *schadenfreude* in these remarks. But rumors of a rift between FitzGibbon and Pitt over the former's conduct were so persistent that the Irish government felt compelled to issue a disclaimer through its mouthpiece, the *Freeman's Journal*:

> By the last accounts from London, we read that so far from any misunderstanding existing between the Lord Chancellor and the British Minister, both these exalted characters had in the greatest harmony waited on our Royal Sovereign with whom they had a private audience. This strengthens the caution which we have *already given* not to place any credit on those *political lies* with which the factious prints continually team.[85]

Nonetheless, there may have more to the rumors than Whiggish malice or the mendacity of factious prints. Even the Bishop of Ferns, who was neither a Whig nor a radical journalist, thought FitzGibbon's decision faulty, and he communicated his opinion to no less a personage than Lord Kenyon, the English Lord Chief Justice:

> No unlearned man who reads the 33rd of George II which regulates the election of a Chief Magistrate can suppose it possible that Alderman James could be duly elected.[86]

Kenyon may have passed this opinion on to the English ministers, including Pitt. Pitt, never favorably disposed to FitzGibbon, may have resented him for engaging in an embarrassing political brawl for no good legal reason. He longed above all to restore the equilibrium of *Hibernia non movere*. His premier Irish servant on the other hand, seemed more inclined to create a state of *Hibernia agire*. Nonetheless, FitzGibbon appears to have suffered nothing beyond some chilly interviews at Downing street. He no doubt employed his considerable powers of blandishment to smooth things over. More important, whatever his personal flaws and errors of judgment, he was simply too experienced, too knowledgeable and too reliable to be dismissed. The English government was to endure a great deal more for a very long time, before deciding that FitzGibbon was more trouble than he was worth.

13

Catholic Relief and Protestant Reaction 1790–2

I

FitzGibbon's initial reaction to the French Revolution was characteristically acerbic:

> By the way, our good neighbor the French King is now reaping the full fruits of his attachment to American liberty. If there exists anything in the shape of political gratitude, surely America will now send General Washington to the assistance of their great and good ally.[1]

By 1790, he surely must have recognized that the French-American disease of revolution was arousing a fever of euphoria and expectation in Ireland. The controversy over the mayoral election may have originated in electoral intrigues and old grievances over the police, but that same controversy saw the introduction of novel, French-inspired methods of protest and mobilization. The adherents of the Commons and of Howison took to wearing a national cockade in imitation of the French. At the meeting of the freeholders which followed the Privy Council's final decision in favour of James, someone, in jest or in earnest, pinned one of these cockades on a statue of the King.[2]

The government immediately responded to the provocation with menaces from the *Freeman's Journal,* though the *Freeman's* chose to rattle the old skeletons of the Gordon Riots rather than allude to the more current disturbances in France:

> In the present situation of affairs, it [wearing the cockade] is nearly an overt act of high treason. They will recollect that a display of a few blue ribbands under Lord George Gordon in London kindled a flame which threatened destruction to the metropolis and which after the ruin of men of property could not be extinguished but in the blood of the people.[3]

The French fever showed far graver manifestations than green tin party favors. The Volunteers, the bellwethers of radical political sentiment, emerged from their post-Rutland moribundity to drill and parade again. Many of them added the new national cockade to their uniforms.[4] The massive, frenzied political changes in France gave a new lease on life to thwarted demands in Ireland for parliamentary and tithe reform, and the Volunteers took their accustomed and long vacant place at the forefront of radical agitation. On 29th September, a so-called Volunteer Association met in secret committee and raised the old call for constitutional reform. The Association also resolved "... that the unlawful Exactions of Tithes are a national disgrace and grievance and ought to stand foremost for Redress and that we will to the utmost of our Power use every Exertion and act in conjunction with our fellow citizens to procure a total abolition thereof."[5] The ubiquitous names of Tandy and Newenham appeared on this set of resolutions.

Belfast took its accustomed place in the political *avant garde*. The so-called "Constitutional Compact" of 1 October 1790, drawn up by the Belfast Constitutional Society, praised the French for adopting the "wise system of Republican Government," and for "abrogating that enormous power and abused influence which the Clergy of that Kingdom had for years past usurped". The compact called on the people of Ireland to imitate the "bright example" of the French.[6]

French-inspired radical agitation did not show any sighs of letting up in 1791. On the contrary, the publication of Paine's *Rights of Man* provided a new tool for mobilization of public opinion. The *Freeman's Journal* took due and doom ridden note of the active dissemination of Paine's "King Killing" doctrines in Dublin.[7] According to the *Freeman's*, Paine's insidious doctrines were also spreading into the countryside. A correspondent from Kilkenny complained that the lower orders had lost all their former deference and peaceableness, thanks to the spread of Paineite ideas through the medium of "parish clerks, schoolmasters, poor scholars and others".[8] But the Defenders above all manifested the spread of revolutionary ideas throughout the countryside.

Probably no force for unrest more baffled and unnerved the government. The Defenders originated in Armagh in the 1780s and specifically in one of the consequences of Armagh Volunteer politics in 1784: Catholic attempts to carry arms, in spite of laws to the contrary.[9] The inflammatory nature of this issue cannot be over-estimated or over-emphasized. The furor which the prospect of armed Catholics aroused in Rutland, in Orde and in FitzGibbon himself has already received attention. For their part the Catholics bitterly resented restrictions on what was considered a premier right of every freeborn man. By asserting the right to bear arms, they brought into question the remaining civil and political restrictions against them, as well as inspiring the old fears of their capacity for massacre. The Armagh manifestation of this political conflict at first took the form of faction fighting; the Protestants adopted the name of Peep Day boys, while the Catholics assumed the name of Defenders. As the fighting grew more violent, more widespread and more elaborately orchestrated, the government was forced to take notice. Not surprisingly, FitzGibbon took the lead, and not surprisingly, he expressed particular concern about presence of armed gatherings of Catholics. Nonetheless, even he was not inclined to take immediate action, preferring to cling to the hope (or more accurately the delusion) that the magistrates would take suitable action to quell disorders.[10] The fact that the conflict took place in Ulster, never a region close to his heart, may account for his unaccustomed apathy. The perennial government hope that the trouble would simply die away again proved vain. Defenderism spread first to Down, Meath and Louth, and later beyond. It acquired in the process an elaborate Masonic-style organization, complete with the baroque mummery of code words and rituals, as well as a distinctly revolutionary program, which promised not only the abolition of petty restrictions on firearms, but and end to tithes and taxes and a reversal of the order created by the plantations.

The French Revolution also re-animated the political aspirations of the Catholic elite, dashed by the hostile Rutland administration and buried in oblivion during the brittle, self-indulgent wrangling of the Regency Crisis. It was a badly needed political *deus ex machina*. An item which appeared in the *Freeman's Journal* on 31 March 1789 epitomized their plight. In the Rutland-Orde tradition of captious bullying, the *Freeman's* criticized the Catholics for tardiness in presenting an address of congratulations to the King for his recovery. The *Freeman's* attributed this unbecoming delay to "certain ambitious individuals amongst themselves, who direct their counsels and who prevent this great body of people coming forward in due time to testify their loyalty and dutiful attachments to the Representatives of the Illustrious House of Brunswick". This particular correspondent certainly demanded an extraordinary alacrity and zeal from the Catholics. The King's recovery had received official confirmation scarcely three weeks before, and most Protestant corporations and grand juries had not yet presented addresses of congratulation. Presumably the elaborate *Te Deum* offered by Bishop Troy (and attended by two of FitzGibbon's sisters, Arabella Jefferyes and Elinor Trant) satisfied this particular correspondent.[11]

Nor could the Catholics hope for much from a Whig Club comprised of Shannon, Charlemont and the Ponsonbys. Like the much over-quoted Chancellor Bowes, the Whig Club, in its various manifestos, did not acknowledge that such a thing as an Irish Catholic existed. Grattan's great cause, tithe reform, had no place on the Whig agenda, out of consideration for Lord Shannon's high church sympathies. With the shameless flexibility of political polemic, the *Freeman's* taunted the Whigs for their rather discomfited attitude toward tithes, and for the presence of notorious anti-Catholics in their midst.[12]

The Catholics did receive approaches from someone in the anti-James camp, approaches which probably came from their old fair-weather friend of 1784, Napper Tandy. Whatever its origin, Bishop Troy was alarmed enough by the attempted alliance to issue a pastoral calling on the Catholics of Dublin to stay out of the dispute between the Commons and the Aldermen.[13] The *Freeman's* expressed its approbation of this sentiment with a banner headline. In so doing, the *Freeman's* alluded to the new tactics and rhetoric that the Revolution had introduced into Irish politics. Such tactics and rhetoric had a potentially dangerous appeal to Catholics, hence the official flattery:

LOYALTY OF THE ROMAN CATHOLICS

> Great hopes were formed by seditious characters on a late occasion, of cooperation in their schemes against the government on the part of the great Roman Catholic body. The example of France was repeatedly mentioned, in order to impress the idea of *revolution* –but the known zeal and loyalty of that numerous and respectably body were not to be temporized with or shaken and the expectation ended as it should, in disappointment.[14]

More radical reformers, particularly the Presbyterians of Belfast, showed more interest and more astuteness than the Whigs. The secular and republican Revolution in France gave new hope that Catholics were not uniformly bigots and slaves. The members of the Belfast Constitutional Society declared that "Protestant Dissenters" were "fully convinced of the Constitutional Principles of the Brethren the Roman Catholics and of their zeal to support and defend the liberty of their country".[15] The gentlemen of the Constitutional Society, in company with other radicals, were probably as fully convinced that without the support of Catholic numbers, their hopes of reform were doomed from the start. The Revolution gave new validity to the political mathematics of 1783–4, and revived thwarted hopes for an alliance. Resolutions for an abolition of tithes were obviously an appeal to the Catholics. But the Belfast Constitutional Society, in keeping with the traditions of its native city, shattered the usual reticence and hesitation on the subject and declared its intention to support "their [the Catholics] just claim to the Enjoyment of the Rights and Privileges of freeborn citizens entitled to fill every office and serve in whatever situation their country may think proper to call them".[16]

Radical reform aspirations reached their culmination in November 1791 with the formation of the Society of United Irishmen. The Society's manifesto powerfully articulated a new vision of Ireland that challenged the exclusively Protestant radicalism of the Dungannon tradition, the tired reformism of the Whig Club, and above all, the establishment in Church and State which FitzGibbon had so long and so vigorously defended. It also articulated, with unprecedented forcefulness, the old resentments of English domination:

> ... as the weight of English influence in the government is so great as to require a cordial union among all the people of Ireland, to maintain that balance which is essential to the preservation of our liberties and the extension of our commerce
>
> ... the sole constitutional end by which this influence can be opposed is by a complete and radical reform of the representation of the people in Parliament
>
> ... no reform is just which does not include Irishmen of every religious persuasion.[17]

II

In October of that year, Westmorland reported that the Catholics were planning to present a petition for the repeal of some penal laws during the upcoming session of Parliament. In his comments to Pitt, he noted the overtures being made to the Catholics by "ye dissenters and ye lower order of Whigs." But he expressed confidence both in the Catholic's fundamental loyalty and in the government's ability to fend off any untoward claims:

> There can be no question that ye spirit of change and disaffection prevails amongst ye dissenters and ye lower order of Whigs and that a desire to obtain further privileges might induce ye Catholics to cooperate with any party that gave them reason to expect further concessions, but at present I believe ye Committee of ye Catholics are resolved peaceably to give their aid to ye government, but mean, if my intelligence does not mislead me, to make application to Parliament for further privileges in ye next session...In what context any of these schemes may be proposed or pressed, I cannot yet ascertain, but I shall of course know in due time and shd hope we may be able to get rid of them without much trouble as ye business of government here seems to be to keep everything as quiet as possible.[18]

It was the old Rutland strategy of blocking any Catholic progress beyond the concessions of 1782. Westmorland differed only in the comparative lack of paranoia which he displayed at this stage.

Pitt's decision to support a relief bill on behalf of the very small, ultra-obsequious body of English Catholics made it very difficult for Westmorland to "get rid" of the Catholic issue in Ireland. The introduction of the English bill, which granted the rights to plead at the bar, sit on juries and bear arms, inevitably raised expectations among Irish Catholics that they could expect similar concessions from their own government. Indeed, it is hard to imagine that a bill was introduced without Cabinet discoveries of the implications for Ireland. This circumstance would in turn explain why the British government in late 1791 responded to promptings in the direction of Ireland.

On 18 February 1791, the Catholics of Dublin, who were the political voice for the Catholics of Ireland, resolved to petition for further relief. The post-Rutland mood of timidity prevailed and the resolution left the question of how much and what relief to the "wisdom and justice of parliament".[19] In response to the renewed Catholic political activity, Westmorland tentatively sounded out leading Irish Protestants on the possibility of granting further concessions. He met with an exceedingly discouraging response. In spite of the meek demeanor of the Dublin Catholic Committee, in spite of Westmorland's own conviction that "as far as I know the Catholics are good loyal subjects", he found that "ye Protestants here are much afraid of the Catholics".[20]

FitzGibbon stood foremost as an opponent of further relief. According to Westmorland, he made a blunt and emphatic answer when the subject came up: "he told me that ... ye Catholics must not be given further priviledges."[21] His answer was perfectly in character. The Catholics had every possible privilege and benefit as things stood: security of property and the protection of his court. FitzGibbon undoubtedly believed that granting even minor concessions would only create a demand for rights and privileges incompatible with the Protestant Establishment in Church and State. He probably reasoned as well that raising the subject during a time of unrest and revolution was especially dangerous. FitzGibbon's sensitivity to Catholic violence also may have played a part in his reluctance. He seems to have impressed his grim perceptions on Westmorland. On 5 March 1791, only two days before his conversation with FitzGibbon, Westmorland had declared for a second time his faith in the fundamental peaceableness and loyalty of the Catholics. He emerged from his *tête a tête* with FitzGibbon to write "There has been a great deal of private meeting ... and some cruelty from ye lower Catholics during ye year both North and South. There is nothing serious or alarming at ye same time that it is unpleasant and it is not easy to know how far ye contagion extends".[22] The cruelty in the North clearly was the work of the Defenders. That in the South is less easy to identify, but the cruelties in question were probably commonplace, isolated acts of agrarian violence. FitzGibbon would naturally have feared that Catholic political agitation would encourage unrest in the lower orders and as naturally, he would have instilled his fears into Westmorland.

FitzGibbon not only tried to discourage any actions in favour of the Catholics in Ireland, he may have tried even earlier to thwart concessions to the English Catholics, through the medium of his old friend Eden, recently elevated to the peerage as Lord Auckland. On 7 January 1790, Auckland wrote an urgent letter to Pitt, begging him to postpone any new legislation on behalf of English Dissenters and Catholics. He made the usual disclaimers made by every adherent of the Establishment, however virulent: "I trust I have neither a narrow or prejudiced mind on this subject." As proof of his broad and unprejudiced mind, he cited his past services on behalf of the Catholics in Ireland: "... I went to great lengths respecting it [Catholic relief] in 1781 [*sic*]" But he urged Pitt to resist "in gentle expressions but in the firmest and most decided manner every part of this business in the ensuing session".[23] Of course, it is always a temptation in a biographer to see the fine hand of the beloved subject in everything. Auckland remained a diehard champion of the Establishment throughout his political career and only altered his opinion before his death in 1814. He could have written this letter solely of his own volition. At the same time, he corresponded closely with FitzGibbon, who was his chief source of information on Irish affairs. FitzGibbon would have seen very early and very clearly the Irish implications of any concessions to English Catholics or English Dissenters. There is at least a possibility that he suggested to Auckland the need to discourage Pitt on the subject or that he strongly encouraged Auckland's own impulse.

If he acted in secret against the English Catholics, FitzGibbon initially seems to have wanted to keep his opposition to Irish Catholic claims a secret as well. In reporting FitzGibbon's answer on the subject, Westmorland added, "... you will take care not to mention his name, as perhaps he would not wish that the Catholics shd know how decided his opinion was on that subject." Westmorland's phrasing is somewhat ambiguous. He may have been assuming a discretion on FitzGibbon's part that he did not in fact possess. On the other hand, FitzGibbon may have had genuine scruples about making known his opposition to further concessions. Political calculation probably accounted for this unusual discretion. FitzGibbon may have recognized his notorious reputation in Catholic circles, and feared that if word of his own opposition got out, they would grow all the more intransigent and violent in pressing for concessions

The private warnings and discouragement from FitzGibbon and from other frightened Irish Protestants had their effect. When a Catholic delegation met with Chief Secretary Hobart on 24 March 1791, they received nothing beyond polished evasions and commonplaces. Hobart, a suave, adroit man, showed far more skill at this sort of operation than the charmless Orde. Any petition, he told the Catholics, should consist of a general request for relief and not of a list of specific requests. The government would then "reflect on the situation of the Catholics and how far they merit relief". The Catholics in response seem to have shown a satisfactory servility. According to a memorandum of the meeting with Hobart, they declared "... they do not approach to demand or to press government, but to supplicate humbly that *some part* of their present inconvenience may be removed".[25] Much to the government's relief, the Catholics presented no petition, however general and obsequious, during the parliamentary session of 1791.

Westmorland and Hobart also received satisfactory reassurances from England that the government there did not expect the Irish parliament to produce a duplicate Catholic bill. They were free to act as circumstances in Ireland dictated. In spite of Hobart's blandishments, in spite of their own initial timidity, the Catholics remained active and hopeful throughout the summer of 1791. Westmorland testily remarked to Dundas "I am sorry to say that ye indulgence to ye English Catholics will produce very serious difficulty here". He criticized Pitt and even the indulgent Grenville for failing "to consider us at ye time ye Bill passed", and he made the gloomy and accurate prediction, "I am afraid we shall have much correspondence on that subject hereafter."[26]

The Catholics meanwhile were tentatively considering other alliances and other strategies, having met with so little encouragement from the government. In July 1791, they approached Grattan in the hopes that the hitherto aloof Whigs might add their cause to the standard one of pensions, placemen and police. According to young Grattan, his father expressed great sympathy and interest, albeit through a third party.[27] Indeed, Grattan would have had every reason to do so. His interest in the question of tithes naturally would have inclined him to consider other Catholic grievances. Moreover, Grattan had a true crowd pleaser's instincts, and he must have sensed that the Whigs were being left behind in the post-revolution political arena. A handbill distributed in Belfast during the previous month had denounced the Whigs as little more than a selfish aristocratic faction, and while he may not have seen this particular production, Grattan may well have received other indications of growing indifference and contempt.[28] In addition, the English party leader, Fox, had already seen the potential in the Catholic issue and had tried to exploit it. During debates on the English Catholic bill, Fox had made the provocative suggestion that the same privileges ought to be extended to Catholics throughout the British Empire.[29] In the end, Grattan suggested to the Catholics that they continue to press their claims through the government.[30] It was the best and the only advice he could have given. His own party was simply too ineffectual and too divided on the subject to act as an effective advocate.

The old fear of a Catholic-Presbyterian alliance continued to haunt Westmorland during the summer of 1791. On 26 August, he informed Dundas, "The language and Bent of ye Conduct of these dissenters [in Belfast and in Newry] is to unite with ye Catholics and their union wd be very formidable". He remained hopeful that the "union is not made" and that "it never wd be".[31] But Catholics in Ulster and as far afield as County Roscommon seem to have picked up the prevailing radical spirit and responded.[32]

III

The breakthrough for the Catholics came when the Dublin Committee opened communication, not with temporizing Whigs, or with enthusiastic but marginal Presbyterians, but with the English government itself. In October 1791, Edmund Burke's son Richard contacted Dundas and Pitt and showed them a letter "from a body of Roman Catholics empowering him to converse with government and to communicate through him on their wishes and the views of the government to them".[33] As an agent Burke had definite drawbacks, not the least of which was his unfailing ability to incur the loathing of everyone he met. Only his adoring father seems to have seen any good in the unfortunate Richard. Even his Catholic clients wearied of him and discreetly replaced him with the more astute and personable Wolfe Tone.[34] But in spite of his difficult personality, Burke was diligent and devoted to his clients' cause, and he was by no means ineffective. Although Dundas summarily refused to have any independent contact with Burke and referred him to the Irish government, the magic of his father's name certainly made an impression. In Dundas's view, the mere fact that the Catholics had hired Edmund Burke's son suggested a fundamental conservatism and loyalty which, if properly cultivated, could strengthen government and prevent a much dreaded alliance with the Presbyterians.[35]

From his vantage point, Westmorland saw more to fear from Anglican jealousy of the Catholics than from Presbyterian fraternalism. He made vague promises of devising "some plan for proceeding" on the Catholic issue.[36] But rather peremptorily, he demanded that Dundas play the informant and supply him with the names of the Catholics who had hired Burke. He also requested him not to have any further communications with the Catholics, either directly or through agents. Above all, he instructed Dundas, "... you must be as quiet as possible...ye Subject is of ye utmost difficulty here and opinions are divided".[37]

In spite of Westmorland's admonition, the tension increased between a British government strongly inclined to encourage Catholic loyalty by granting concessions and an Irish government struggling to placate hostile and suspicious Anglicans who feared encroachments on their power and privileges. By December, the pressure on the Irish government to grant concessions was well nigh irresistible. Pitt, who had hitherto remained aloof, personally urged Westmorland to grant the Irish Catholics at least the same privileges as those granted in England, on the grounds that such concessions were "not liable to any real objection in Ireland more than in England"[38] But Dundas, consistently the most favorable, consistently the most fearful of an alliance between Catholics and Presbyterians, had become positively radical on the subject. In a lengthy memorandum dated 26 December, Dundas suggested giving suitably qualified Catholics the franchise in addition to the rights to practice law, sit on juries and to bear arms. He also called upon Westmorland to consider the repeal of any and all laws which discriminated against Catholics in the areas of education and intermarriage.[39]

Westmorland, in response, emphasized his own difficulties and embarrassments. He repeatedly pointed out that the Protestants felt betrayed and abandoned by this sudden show of favour for the Catholics. They felt that the English government was playing "ye Catholic Game" to intimidate them and to punish them for past acts of defiance on the part of the Irish Parliament. He insisted that he himself had no objection to reasonable conciliation of the Catholics. But concessions would not benefit the English government if in the process the Protestants, the mainstays of the Empire in Ireland, were alienated.[40]

The increasingly strident and radical tone taken by some Catholics and by their Protestant advocates added to Westmorland's reluctance. The Burkes, father and son, were particular *bêtes noirs*. If Dundas saw the involvement of Burke as proof of Catholic conservatism, Westmorland, on the contrary blamed them both for encouraging radical expectations.[41] It was certainly a startling view of Burke, and indicative of the extraordinary siege mentality articulated by Westmorland. To his fearful Castle advisors, advocacy of Catholic political enfranchisement or the advocacy of any Catholic political rights amounted to an incitement to revolution. This maxim extended even to the author of *Reflections on the French Revolution*.

The purge of that familiar government reliable, Lord Kenmare, exacerbated the government's sense that the Catholics were beyond conciliation and beyond control. Kenmare had single-handedly tried to dissociate the Catholics from the radicals and to restore the old public demeanor of utter abasement by means of a petition which he circulated in his territory, County Kerry. The language of the petition followed the servile tradition of the past; it assured the government of the perfect loyalty of the Catholics, their perfect abhorrence for agitation and disorder and their perfect willingness to accept whatever concessions the Irish parliament saw fit to grant, however insignificant or minor.[42] This language was no longer acceptable to the more assertive wing of the Catholic Committee, led by John Keogh and other substantial businessmen. Many of them, including Keogh, found the language of the United Irishman, not abhorrent, but very appealing. Moreover, Kenmare-style obsequiousness had brought nothing but smooth prevarication from Chief Secretary Hobart. In Westmorland's words, a "terrible battle" resulted, ending in a rout for Lord Kenmare: he was expelled from the Catholic Committee, and subjected to a humiliating public denunciation. 68 other members of the committee, including Lord Fingall and the great incendiary of the Rutland years, Sir Patrick Bellew, also withdrew, earning for themselves and their party the name "Seceders".[43]

Westmorland fretted over the ascendancy of the "violent and daring" Catholics and the *Freeman's Journal* scolded "... we warn them [the Catholics] against becoming instruments in the hands of faction. We warn them against submitting to be the dupes of designing men".[44] But in a sense the coup against Lord Kenmare was as much the fault of the government as of "ye Brotherhood" and "ye Democratic Catholics".[45] Since the time of the Rutland administration, the English government in Ireland had treated moderate, compliant Catholics with studied neglect at best and contemptuous bullying at worst. For nine years, they made no concessions which might have given the moderates credit and standing. Finally and too late, Westmorland recognized the urgency of concessions to gratify "ye better sort of Catholics".[46]

By 14 January 1792, Westmorland could report that his closest advisors had agreed to consider a relief bill. Only the egregious Charles Agar, Archbishop of Cashel, remained "unwilling to relax at all".[47] As for FitzGibbon, he almost certainly played a part in fueling fears and suspicions about the abandonment of the Protestants. He in fact may have been the first to suggest that Pitt was taking revenge against the Protestants for their fractious behavior since 1782. Vindictive himself, FitzGibbon naturally would have assumed that similar impulses moved Dundas and Pitt. Nonetheless, whatever his own private doubts, FitzGibbon was among the first to agree to grant Irish Catholics "ye English concession". However ill-advised, "ye English concession" as yet posed no fundamental threat to the Establishment. And FitzGibbon was undoubtedly anxious to avoid provoking his English masters in the wake of the election fiasco of 1790. In a curious foreshadowing of the emancipation activities preceding the act of Union, Westmorland concealed from FitzGibbon the more extreme ideas entertained in England. A suggestion from Dundas that FitzGibbon travel to London to consult in person on Catholic claims, prompted this response from Westmorland: "he [FitzGibbon] is much better here."[48]

"Ye English concessions" as agreed upon by FitzGibbon and his equally reluctant colleagues, did not include the unlimited right to carry weapons or to serve on juries.

The habitual lawlessness of the "lower orders", the bulk of whom were Catholics, precluded any relaxation of laws relating to arms: "The Point of conceding the Roman Catholicks an unlimited right to carry arms was considered *in itself dangerous*". Moreover, any respectable Roman Catholic could receive a license to keep a weapon, upon applying to the Privy Council and taking the prescribed oaths. Westmorland's faithful advisors made more dubious and desperate claims in support of their position. They claimed an equal dislike of "Roman Catholic gentlemen of Property" for the widespread use of arms among their poorer co-religionists, and they claimed Catholics had never placed much emphasis on this particular concession.[49] In light of the events in Armagh, this last claim was startling, to say the least. As for serving on juries, and in particular on grand juries, "it was admitted to be a point which considered by itself [abstractly] might be ... proper and becoming to be granted". At the same time, Westmorland noted that Grand Juries raised "great sums of money for various county purposes," and Protestants derived considerable prestige and power from controlling and allocating this money. A provision requiring them to share this power with numerically superior Catholics could well stir up so much jealousy as to jeopardize the entire bill.[50] As for the suggestion about the right of suffrage, Westmorland reported that "it seemed to cause much apprehension and discontent that such a proposal should have been listened to at all by the British Cabinet".[51] In effect, granting Catholics the right to vote would "give them a complete command in counties with a few Exceptions to Northern Counties where the Dissenting Interest prevails and thus put them in possession of the pure and popular part of the Representation".[52] In the view of the Irish Cabinet, the Catholics would inevitably use their votes to promote subversive ends with the help of equally disaffected Presbyterians. They would "soon be enabled to make a successful attack on the Tythes and established clergy so odious to themselves and the Presbyterians; if they should not *indeed* be enabled to go further as their Power gradually increased and with it their hopes and their ambitions". Their hopes and their ambitions ultimately encompassed the complete overthrow of the Act of Settlement.[53]

Westmorland did receive assent to a proposed bill that would open the Bar to Catholics, and remove any restrictions on education and intermarriage.[54] Even this comparatively innocuous bill inspired intense anxiety and extravagant ploys to make is passage as smooth and unobtrusive as possible. To avoid any preliminary debate or controversy, Westmorland and the Irish Cabinet decided to avoid any mention of Catholic concessions in the speech from the throne.[55] Dundas found this decision extremely dubious: "To whatever interest it may be thought right to go in point of concession, it seems proper that the grace of the suggestion should belong to Government".[56]

He added somewhat sourly, "This however I must leave to your Excellency's determination aided by the local opinions of those with whom you are to consult."[57] Sir Hercules Langrishe was to have the responsibility of springing the bill on the Commons, once the preliminary business of opening Parliament was complete. The "respectable" Catholics trusted him, and he was an experienced and adroit member, capable of seeing the bill through Parliament with the desired minimum of fuss.[58]

In his account of the consultations on the bill, Westmorland presented the collective opinions of his Irish advisors. He did not attribute insights or ideas to any one individual. Nonetheless, FitzGibbon undoubtedly took an active and vigorous part in a subject near, if not particularly dear, to his heart. In particular, the emphatic rejection of the unlimited right to bear arms and of the right of suffrage bear his stamp, as does the allusion to the Act of Settlement, always a sensitive point with him. Although Westmorland himself hoped to avoid any explicit declaration that this bill marked the end of all concessions, FitzGibbon labored under that impression. In an effort to reassure his worried fellow Protestants, and in an effort to make certain that the English government would never again propose mad, bad Catholic schemes, FitzGibbon, in company with Westmorland, met with the "friends of government" shortly before the meeting of Parliament. At this gathering, "... the Chancellor acquainted them that it was the Resolution of Government to resist the demand for arms and suffrage".[59] It never entered FitzGibbon's mind that the English government would ever put him in the terrible and humiliating position of going back on his word.

IV

The bill itself passed through the Commons with comparatively little opposition. Certainly Westmorland expressed considerable relief both at the successful completion of the business and at the fact that there had been no explicit resolution against further claims on the part of the Catholics.[60] Westmorland himself certainly had no desire to press for further claims; but he wanted to avoid rankling or provoking the Catholics as much as wanted to ease the feelings of the Protestants.

Unfortunately, Westmorland, with typical obtuseness, overlooked the full, insulting implications of the one dramatic incident arising from debates on the bill. During the proceedings, the rump of the Catholic Committee presented a petition requesting an extension of the franchise. They met with a humiliating response. David La Touche made an unprecedented motion to reject the petition out of hand, since the request could never meet with compliance. A ferocious debate then ensued, with many angry comments on the presumption of the Catholics and the dangers of allowing them even to entertain such a notion. Even those who spoke against La Touche's motion did so, not because they favored the petition, but because they felt that rejecting it out of hand was violated the right of any subject, however wrong-headed, to receive a full and fair hearing. The vote was cruelly lopsided: 208 votes in favour of outright rejection and 28 against. The numbers in favour of rejection included prominent government members, including Hobart, Wolfe, and Toler.[61]

Westmorland took the view that La Touche's rejection of the petition had fortunately prevented debates on its actual merits and a possible resolution barring Catholics from the suffrage forever. He also labored under the impression that the Catholics had been well and properly taught a lesson about where their true interest lay: with the government, and not with ill-judging hot-heads like Richard Burke and the Keogh-dominated Catholic committee:

> Last night's proceedings must convince all Catholics that they are indebted to Government for what they obtain; that by the Strength and moderate Management of Government only the Bill was carried and that the Rub they have received is to be attributed to the indiscretion of some of their body and their advisor, Mr Burke.[62]

The idea never penetrated Westmorland's mind that the Catholics, and specifically the wine dealers and poplin merchants of the Catholic Committee, would look upon this "Rub" as a goad for further activity. Nor did he entertain the possibility that some Catholics would not see "moderate management" in Mr Secretary Hobart's speeches against their petition.

Thanks to FitzGibbon's moderate management, the bill passed quickly and with virtually no debate through the House of Lords. The only hint of acrimony came from his Grace of Cashel, who made his memorable claim that Roman Catholicism was a religion fit only for fools and knaves.[63] While he could not impose a vow of silence on Cashel, FitzGibbon successfully thwarted any lengthy speeches and amendments, both favorable and unfavorable. He stopped the pro-Catholic Lord Donoughmore from opening a discussion on the philosophical desirability of emancipation, and he thwarted a minor mutiny by the decidedly anti Lord Aldborough.[64] Aldborough took issue with a subordinate feature of the bill which relieved Catholic schoolmasters from the necessity of obtaining a license from the local Protestant bishop. He felt that Protestant schoolmasters should have a similar freedom. FitzGibbon's response reveals his near desperate attempts to maintain a benevolent demeanor and to convince the Catholics that the bill was a willing, unanimously agreed upon act of generosity by the government, in keeping with the mild traditions of English law:

> For his part, he was, and always had been ready to concur in the repeal of the penal statutes as far as was consistent with the safety of the Establishments in Church and State. The removal of this hardship, he was convinced, would be productive of no danger to either, and therefore, he most heartily agreed to it. In the packets of this day, he said, he had observed an action had been brought against a Popish schoolmaster in England for teaching school without a license – but the prosecutor had been coldly treated by the court, and the Judge, with a liberality that did him honour had laid hold of an informality in the proceedings to non-suit the plaintiffs. – This circumstance indicated the liberal sentiments of the people of England on this point – he though this country ought

> to imitate them, especially as the Catholics had this indulgence much at heart, and there was none that could be granted them with more safety.[65]

He had agreed to the bill with the greatest reluctance. He fully intended it to be the last of its kind. At the same time, he hoped to placate once and for all, the English government and the Catholics whom that government had so ill-advisedly encouraged.

Nonetheless, signs of the old FitzGibbon emerged, in spite of his heroic restraint. During debates on a separate bill pertaining to loyalty oaths, he had menacing words for any Catholic who presumed to make further demands on the generosity of government:

> he could not help ... expressing his astonishment that after a bill, bestowing on the Catholics very considerable favours, had so recently passed both Houses of Parliament without a single dissentient voice, some members of that body had come forward in the public prints and, instead of gratitude for these indulgencies, had spoken of the legislation in terms of indignation for not having gone further – and had not scrupled even to assert that the right of suffrage was the inalienable right of every Irishman. The enemies of that body could not take any means more effectual to injure them than to hold such language. He sincerely hoped they would no longer make use of any such declarations, for if they did, they would assuredly do that body very essential disservice, by affording to their fellow subjects just grounds for doubt and suspicion.[66]

His actions against Graydon's combination bill may even have been a subtle exercise in sectarian politics. This particular bill represented a response to a spate of frequently violent combinations which had occurred in 1790 and 1791. Most notably, the bill required a journeyman leaving his master to produce a certificate of good conduct, and it decreed fines and whippings for runaway apprentices. FitzGibbon denounced the bill as a system of vasselage which was more likely to drive apprentices to crime than to discourage them from combining against their masters. Thanks to his influence, the House of Lords threw out the bill.[67]

His opposition to the combination bill bewildered many of his political colleagues and outraged those newspapers which ordinarily held advanced views on parliamentary reform and Catholic rights. The *Dublin Evening Post* expressed an ironic hope that FitzGibbon's sudden concern with constitutional liberty would extend to other issues:

> It was not unpleasant to observe the *beginning* of a regard for constitutional liberty which was yesterday evening manifested by a great Law Lord on the Combination Bill. We most sincerely hope he may "grow in grace and in knowledge and love of constitutional liberty" – and that a speedy falling off may not evince his having commenced the champion of freedom from party motives.[68]

The *Hibernian Journal*, while willing to give FitzGibbon credit for good intentions, took an equally dubious view. On paragraph went so far as to accuse FitzGibbon of disturbing the public peace, a novel charge:

> I do mean to insult your Lordship by accusing you of having been *willfully* the patron of the most dangerous combinations ever before known to this kingdom. No, my Lord, I can readily distinguish an error committed with a good intent, from one originating in an evil one. I am certain your Lordship is by this time fully aware of the prejudice which has arisen to the manufacture of this kingdom from the interest you lately took in its welfare and hope you will be in the future directed by your late acquired experience to use your utmost endeavors to suppress that spirit of combination which your Lordship has unintentionally sanctioned.[69]

Even the government papers expressed reservation. *Faulkner's Dublin Journal* made this ambiguous statement:

> Had Mr Graydon's Combination Bill or (in the words of the Lord Chancellor) "and Act for the encouragement of Outlawries and Highway Robberies" passed into a law, the measure *might* have produced consequences which though not immediately tending to the peace and happiness of the country would however have served the cause to which no doubt it was intended.[70]

In many respects, FitzGibbon's actions in throwing out the bill were perfectly consistent. He never missed a chance to step into the well-beloved and well-worn role of champion of the oppressed. As the *Dublin Evening Post* hinted, he may also have been taking advantage of an irresistible opportunity to score points against the Whig Club.[71] Mr Graydon, the originator of this particular system of vasselage, was a member.[72]

But FitzGibbon's action also had an ugly sectarian undertone. He may have been trying to win favour with Protestant workmen and apprentices, particularly in the Liberties. By throwing out the bill, he could win their support for the Protestant Establishment and diminish the seductive allure of radical appeals for a union of all religions against "oligarchy". A fugitive piece in the *Morning Post/Dublin Courant* suggests that FitzGibbon did enjoy a measure of popularity as the champion of Protestant workmen:

> The combining shoe blacks of Dublin who now insist for a double price, call themselves "de Prodistin Iscendancy". Their corporation assembles at a *whiskey forge* in Essex Street after morning service. The test of union to tip off de Prodistin Iscendancy in a full facer of de native stans pede in uno. They have changed their favourite oath from "the holy Saint Peter" to the "jolly St. George" to obviate all symptoms of Popery and crying out for de L—d Ch—r by *de holy* and the rights of *de people* swear they will work no longer for half price *like the bloody paphishes*.[73]

The author may have been engaging in a piece of Swiftian satire, suggesting first, that anyone however lowly, could play at the game of Protestant ascendancy and secondly that FitzGibbon had encouraged combination and rebellion. But a spy's report also confirms that there were strong anti-Popish, anti-republican sympathies among Protestant workmen in the Liberties. Writing in December 1792, he reported to Edward Cooke that the "Protestants almost to a man in the Earl of Meath's Liberties breath nothing but perfect loyalty". Of course, FitzGibbon may well have acted solely to protect the poor and dish the Whigs. But he was certainly clever enough and ruthless enough to recognize the Protestant sympathies in the Liberties and to exploit them.

14

Catholic Relief and Protestant Reaction, 1793

I

The notorious circular of Edward Byrne and the subsequent Catholic Convention destroyed any hope that the Catholics could be cajoled or menaced into silence. The circular, dated 26 May 1792, called upon Catholics to assemble in chapels and to select two "respectable" electors. The electors would in turn choose delegates to a an expanded general committee. This new committee was to petition for the rights denied in the recent act, and in particular for the right to vote and the right to serve on juries.[1] The exact origins of this plan remain unclear. Edward Byrne suffered months of public condemnation for merely signing the thing, though it was generally assumed that he and his fellow members of the Catholic Committee had acted under the direction of their renegade Protestant agents. Richard Burke and Wolfe Tone received credit, or rather blame, depending on which of them was the target of government attention or loathing.[2] In fact, the members of the Catholic Committee may not have needed inspiration from either Burke or Tone. They could have drawn on their own precedents and traditions. As early as 1760, Catholics in Dublin especially had held meetings in chapels and elected delegates to the committee. Thomas Orde had received a copy of an announcement of one such meeting in 1784. While he preserved it with his usual meticulousness among his papers, he paid curiously little attention.[3] The circular simply suggested transforming a Dublin practice into a national one.

The motives behind the circular were shrewd and practical. By expanding membership of the committee and by promoting the use of elections as a means of selection, Byrne and his fellow Committee members hoped the make their organization more accountable to more of the Catholic population and to prevent it from again falling under the domination of a single, self-interested faction like that of the discredited Lord Kenmare.[4]

The dissatisfaction of the more active Committee members with the Act of 1792, and above all the feeling that Westmorland and his minions at the Castle had cheated the Catholics of concessions that the English government had wanted to give, prompted this upsurge of activity. Westmorland had alluded to this last sentiment in a letter to Dundas written three weeks before the appearance of Byrne's circular.

The perceived unfairness and the blindness of the Catholic Committee radicals rankled:

> My public letter conveys to you an address from ye Roman Catholics signed by almost all ye [principle] people of ye country; Mr. Burke's tools ye committee are very much dejected at their expression of thanks, particularly as they endeavor as much as possible to represent that the English government wish to give them everything and that they were only stopped by my misrepresentations. The principle people are sensible that to govt. only are they indebted for what has passed but after Burke's conduct, it is not easy to satisfy ye others as they do not or will not see ye inveteracy, jealousy and obstinacy of Parliament on that subject.[5]

Byrne's circular indeed gave the distinct impression of powerful friends and sympathizers in the English government, waiting only for the united voice of the Irish Catholics to take up their claims:

> We have the FIRST AUTHORITY for asserting that this application will have infinite weight with our gracious sovereign and with Parliament if our friends are qualified to declare that it is the universal wish of EVERY CATHOLIC in the nation.[6]

The emphatically capitalized first authority was probably Richard Burke. Far from making tools of "ye committee", he was under considerable pressure from his clients to produce results, and in spite of the determined distance of Pitt and Dundas, he could easily have learned of the split between London and Dublin.[7] In desperation, he made promises of a more favorable hearing in England, and his clients in the Catholic committee, bitter over Castle reluctance and College Green "Rubs", readily believed him.

II

The prospect of a "Popish Congress" inevitably aroused Pandemonium among Westmorland's advisors. Most of them remembered the fearful days of 1784, when an exclusively Protestant reform congress had shaken the Rutland administration. FitzGibbon, the scourge of the 1784 reformers, naturally took the lead in advocating a similarly forceful approach to the proposed Catholic convention. Along with the attorney general, he urged that government "take some notice". Westmorland, as always terrified of confrontation, pressed him to hold back for the time being: "... I thought it very possible little or no attention might be paid by ye body of Catholics and that any proceeding wd only bring ye Committee more notice."[8] FitzGibbon reluctantly agreed, possibly regretting the opportunity to make a dramatic appearance at Derham's Chop-house, in the tradition of his grand entrance at the freeholders' meeting of 1784. With his usual incisiveness, he immediately seized on the underlying cause of the Committee's activity, and he strongly recommended immediate public discouragement of further Catholic claims from England:

> The Chancellor in ye most anxious manner desired I wd be prepared from you to assume support against these innovators. He stated that a great deal of their agitation was owing to misrepresentations of Mr Rd. Burke and others of English opinion and he was convinced that of these agitators understood they had no hope from that quarter their agitations would cease.[9]

Westmorland, FitzGibbon and the Attorney General considered possible measures to take if the planned convention proceeded. FitzGibbon and Wolfe suggested a proclamation, similar to one recently issued in England against seditious meetings, "with words hinting at this delegation". They also agreed on the possible uses of personal as well as public intimidation: "... we talked of private information to ye Roman Catholic body that by concerning in such election or assembly, ye Roman Catholics wd forfeit ye favour of government to whom they were indebted for every privilidge [*sic*] they had acquired."[10] Unfortunately neither studied neglect nor private information had the desired effect. Elections started taking place early in the summer of 1792, in response to Byrne's circular.

If Westmorland was incorrect in predicting Catholic indifference to the circular, he was perfectly accurate in his predictions of the Protestant response: "Whenever these papers become public, the Protestants will ... take alarm and we shall learn of them from ye grand juries and assizes."[11] During the months of July and August 1792, resolutions from grand juries all over Ireland crammed the columns of the newspapers. As a whole, they followed the same dismal pattern, combining patently insincere expressions of love and well wishes for "our Catholic fellow subjects" with deadly earnest denunciations of Edward Byrne, his circular and any proposed innovations in the constitution in Church and State.

Inevitably, a requisition denouncing Byrne and any further concessions came from County Limerick. Ostensibly it expressed the sentiments of a meeting of Protestant freeholders summoned by the high sheriff, one John Waller. The resolutions themselves differed little from similar productions of outraged Protestants in other counties. The effort of the Limerick Protestant freeholders made invidious comparisons between the proposed "Popish Congress" and the French National Assembly. It warned of dire threats to the present "happy establishment in Church and State" from this "Popish Democracy" proposed by "turbulent and seditious men." After assuring their "fellow subjects of the Catholic religion" of their "best wishes", the freeholders warned them against participating in "any such illegal and unconstitutional association as has been recommended by the said Edward Byrne and the said Sub-committee". The same resolution implied that they risked violent retaliation if they participated in the so-called "Popish Congress": any such activity "must lead to a renewal of those religious animosities which so long and so unhappily disturbed this country". Finally, the Limerick freeholders made it clear that they would instruct their representatives in Parliament to oppose any further relaxation of the "Popery Laws" if such a congress was elected or met, and they would , under all circumstances, "oppose any proposition which may be made for extending to Catholics the right of voting for Representatives in Parliament, a franchise which in the present situation of the Country, we are decidedly of opinion, cannot be extended to them with safety to the Protestant Establishment of Ireland in Church and State".[12]

This supposed spontaneous expression of local Protestant gentlemen in Limerick was, of course, nothing of the kind. It was unquestionably FitzGibbon's production from beginning to end. The meeting was packed with his friends and relatives, including his private secretary, John Dwyer, Valentine Quin and Vere Hunt. According to newspaper accounts, he appeared in his most elegant country *dishabille* –" a brown bob-Beresford, [buckboots], Carlow spurs, and a cutting horsewhip" –and prompted Waller.[13] Whatever the truth of this story, the resolutions were redolent of FitzGibbon's peculiar turns of phrase and of his *idees fixes*. Considering his visible office, he showed considerable indiscretion in taking so public and so extreme a stand on a sensitive and by no means settled issue. But his action, however unwise, was inevitable, given FitzGibbon's innate fears and given the amazing self-control he had displayed for almost two years. Edward Byrne had given him a much-desired pretext to revert to character.

FitzGibbon and the various Protestant grand jurors and freeholders who met and resolved during the summer of 1792 were all acting on an assumption articulated by Sir John Parnell: "... there was nothing to fear from the Catholics;... they always receded when met."[14] The Catholics did not recede. According to Westmorland, the members of the Committee were, initially taken aback by the great Protestant wind of grand jury and requisitioned sentiment.[15] But a legal opinion provided by Richard Burke's discreet successor Wolfe Tone, that Byrne's plan violated no known law, steadied the Committee's shaken resolve.[16] A particularly arrogant and insulting resolution from the Dublin Corporation, declaring the eternal primacy of Protestant King and Protestant Parliament, provided an added spark of defiance.[17] By November, Westmorland was reporting to Dundas that 28 counties had already elected delegates. He also gave an overheated account of the efficiency, relentlessness and vast hegemony of the Committee:

> But whatever may be the conduct of this assembly, the Circumstances of its formation, existence and continuance are in my mind highly alarming, as it tends to create a Government of Roman Catholics entirely distinct from the Protestant Government, totally unconnected with it, and completely republican. The General Catholic Committee have already exercised most of the functions of a Government; they have levied contributions, they have issued orders for the preservation of the peace, a circumstance perhaps more dangerous than if they direct the Breach of it, they maintain the Cause of Individuals

> accused of public crimes – their mandates are considered by the lower orders as laws, their Correspondences and Communications with different parts of the kingdom are rapid, carried on not by the post, but by secret channels and Agents.[18]

Westmorland saw only one logical conclusion to the efficient defiance of the Catholics. Their secret government within a government, taxing, keeping the peace, exercising judicial activity on behalf of the Defenders, would, if unchecked, subvert English and Protestant rule in Ireland:

> If their General Committee have acquired this degree of power, what may not be apprehended from the Power of the Convention, if their existence shall be long suffered and if their peaceable demeanor in the outset should afford them the means of continuing a Regular Progress towards acquiring a complete Dominion over the whole Roman Catholic body, more especially if any objects should be attained by their means. There is nothing which may not be ultimately demanded from their influence.[19]

Westmorland had to admit that hitherto, the Catholic Committee had not assumed one of the premier functions of government, raising an army. Westmorland had heard rumors that the Catholics were importing arms, but "I have made the strictest Inquiry upon this subject and particularly in the North, but do not find the rumors founded".[20]

In response to this activity, Westmorland did the inevitable: "I have fully consulted with the Chancellor and the other confidential servants of his Majesty with respect to the different measures which it would be advisable to pursue."[21] The response of FitzGibbon and his colleagues was as inevitable: they recommended intimidation, repressive legislation and, as a last resort, physical force should the Convention prove as violent and revolutionary as its French equivalent.

Specifically, they recommended a stern affirmation in the Speech from the Throne that the King's government in both England and in Ireland "was determined to support the Protestant Establishment in Church and State".[22] Contrary to FitzGibbon's hopes earlier that summer, the English government still had made no explicit refusal of further claims. The declaration in the Speech from the Throne, it was hoped, could serve as a belated, but still effective damper on Catholic expectations.

They also recommended backing up this declaration with armed intimidation in two guises: an augmentation of the regular army, and the formation of a Protestant militia.[23] Westmorland observed that volunteering was continuing to grow worrisomely. Radical sentiment drew recruits to some bands. Other bands drew reactionary Protestants who feared abandonment by the British government. The master obsession of the Rutland administration now gripped Westmorland: increased volunteering, for whatever reason, increased the possibility that arms would fall into the hands of the Catholics. A militia would put an end to this dangerous development by reassuring frightened conservatives and by thwarting radicals, both Catholic and Protestant.

As for the legal loopholes pointed out by Wolfe Tone and ably exploited by the Catholic Committee, Westmorland's Irish advisors "were of opinion that some new law should be prepared for ye consideration of Parliament to meet the point", that is to prevent any similar conventions for Catholic or for other disaffected groups.[24] In addition to an act specifically banning conventions of elected delegates, 17th century English jurisprudence offered a precedent of a second, reinforcing law: "it might be advisable to pass an Act here similar to the Act of Charles II for preventing tumultuous Petitioning."[25] FitzGibbon's contribution shows with particular clarity here. He was the chief law advisor, and he had been reading up on 17th century English history during the summer.

A more drastic solution to restore stability in Ireland appeared in the correspondence between Westmorland and the English government. On 18 November 1792, Pitt raised the possibility that the violent sectarian antagonism aroused by the Catholic issue could have a fortunate outcome:

> The Idea of the present fermentation gradually bringing both parties to think of a Union with this country has long been in my mind.[26]

A union would remove any objections to granting the vote to Catholics since they would become a minority in an empire governed by a Parliament, the "decided majority" of which would necessarily be Protestant. Catholics, in short, could have their desired rights and privileges, and Protestants could enjoy the security of numerical superiority. Pitt was under no illusions that such an idea could be carried easily, even in the "present fermentation":

> I hardly dare flatter myself with the hope of its taking place, but I believe it, tho' itself not easy to be accomplished, to be the only solution for other and greater difficulties.[27]

The other and greater difficulties presumably were those created by the fractious and unreliable Irish parliament, troublesome in the best of times and positively dangerous at a time of crisis.

Westmorland's mind had apparently been running along a similar track, to judge by Pitt's comments: "I am heartily glad that it [a union] is at least in your thoughts." Pitt had left it to Westmorland's discretion to "judge where and to whom the Idea can be confided".[28] He wrote back to Pitt with an encouraging response:

> An Union is certainly at present not looked to or talked of with disapprobation [amongst?] ye leading people.[29]

The Catholics would probably favour the idea since it would "put them on a Line with ye Protestants and open to them ye State".[30] (At this point apparently both Westmorland and Pitt envisioned that full political rights for Catholics would accompany a union.) As for the Protestants, the "great men dread very much ye Ruin of themselves and ye Establishment" and were therefore "not impracticable".[31] But he warned about the dangers of raising the subject prematurely. Rumor was already circulating that the English government was encouraging the Catholics with an eye to a union:

> Such an Idea [may] be suspected for it took a wrong turn, one cannot tell what mischief it might produce – as it is generally considered here that this Catholic question is of English making, the Irish have imagined that the English government wd not have raised such a Flame but to serve their own purposes, this being one has now and then been charged and therefore we must be particularly cautious.[32]

If an excess of religious jealousy and suspicion could destroy the hopes of a union, their absence would have the same effect: "...if the Protestants shd get over their Catholic prejudices, adiew to that cure for this country."[33] Evidently, the trick was to manage religious hatreds to the best advantage of British government.

This correspondence exonerates FitzGibbon from the grandiose accusations of his enemies that the union was exclusively his evil brainchild. Presumably, Westmorland regarded him as a reliable person to whom he could broach the subject and presumably, FitzGibbon was one of "ye great men" who found the idea of a union preferable to "ye Ruin of themselves and of ye establishment". But he does not seem to have demonstrated any overwhelming urgency or enthusiasm, or Westmorland would surely have made note of it. At this point, he seems to have thought of a union, at best, as a desperate last resort. At worst, talk of a union may have confirmed his own earlier fears that the English government was bent on punishing the Irish Protestants, by destroying the framework of their power. The sentiments which he had revealed to Lord Carlisle years before probably still held: he had no great love for the Irish Parliament, much less for the Irish nation. But he may have looked upon its abolition as a reflection on his skills as a political manager. He still believed that if left to his own devices, he could eventually bully the Protestant parliament into submission and the Catholics into their former silence and passivity. To prove as much he redoubled his efforts to preserve the existing structure of government, by redoubling his menaces against the Catholics. At the same time, he undertook in an extraordinary campaign of subtle intimidation against the very English government he wanted to preserve. FitzGibbon was willing to risk even renewed alienation from Pitt and Dundas, rather than accept the failure in the guises of Catholic power and the humiliating refuge of a union.

He made a studious, and in the wake of the Limerick resolutions, unconvincing display of neutrality and moderation on the subject:

> The Chancellor professes himself indifferent on the subject except as a servant of English government, to which he considers himself bound, and to his Mind,

> the concession under the present circumstances is so fatal to the English connection that every risk shd be run rather than yield.[34]

Every risk included sectarian warfare. When Westmorland asked him "in very strong terms" whether he was prepared to risk a rebellion "in the North and the South at the same instant" from disappointed Catholics, FitzGibbon, the raging prophet of Popish insurrection, was inclined to dismiss such a threat:

> he said (in which I suspect he was right) that he did not apprehend there was much Danger of either, that Gentlemen were very bold on paper, but very shy of risking either their Lives or their Fortunes.[35]

Nonetheless, he remained coolly prepared for violent retaliation against the Catholics. Indeed, he suggested to Westmorland that "England had better undertake a war in Ireland whilst the Protestants were her friends that when she had no friends in this country, which could be the case after the repeal of the Popery Code".[36] This cryptic comment had two possible interpretations: either the Protestants would stand back in sullen spite while the Catholics established a "Popish Democracy" in Ireland, or they would take matters into their own hands and resist both the Catholics and the English government. FitzGibbon probably never seriously entertained either possibility; he was merely trying to frighten the English government out of their unsuitable Catholic schemes. He not the first unionist; he was not a unionist at this time. But he had discovered the uses of that ploy of later unionists, conditional loyalty.

III

The Catholics, meanwhile, continued to be very bold and not at all shy. The convention met early in December of 1792, and the debates often took a strident, defiant tone. Luke Teeling, the delegate from Antrim, went to the extremes desired by his circle of Presbyterian/United Irish friends in Belfast. He objected to any limitation on Catholic demands and to any petition "which might sanction by anything which could be construed into acquiescence on their part, to one fragment of that unjust and abominable system, the penal code". He then moved for a paragraph "praying that the Catholics might be restored to the equal enjoyment of the blessings of the constitution".[37]

His fellow delegates showed somewhat more caution. They refused for example to receive a delegation from the United Irishmen, although that organization included many members of the Committee and many delegates to the convention, including Teeling and Keogh.[38] Avoiding public association with the United Irishmen was a prudent tactic. If the convention had received the delegation, the government would have had a powerful pretext for linking further Catholic relief with radicalism and disorder. In their debates, the members Convention instead chose to emphasize their long-suffering and deserving loyalty and their impeccable devotion to the constitution. Nonetheless, their proposed petition took the radical direction proposed by Teeling. They called, not only for the rights denied in the act of 1792, but for full political equality.[39]

The presentation of the petition was as provocative as its substance. It was undertaken in a way deliberately calculated to insult Westmorland and the government of Ireland, including FitzGibbon, the inciter of county freeholders. The delegates of the Catholic convention chose to present their petition directly to the King rather than through the Lord-Lieutenant, as was the usual practice. They took additional revenge for the humiliations of the past summer by choosing the notorious Edward Byrne to lead the delegation to London. He traveled in company with John Keogh, another figure of dread in Castle reports, and James Edward Devereaux, noted both for his outspokenness and for his libertinism. The presence of two solid members of the Catholic gentry, Bellew and French, hardly compensated for the deliberate offensiveness of their colleagues. As a final gesture of defiance, they traveled, in company with their United Irish secretary, via quasi-republican Belfast.[40]

Westmorland's response to Catholic "Rubs" was typically dense. He claimed that the delay in making him a Knight of the Garter, and not his supineness before Protestant reaction, was at the bottom of the Catholics' action. He wrote petulantly, "... you now probably see ye consequence of having so long delayed ye garter".[41] Only Westmorland know through what alchemy the garter would have restored the respect of the Catholics.

The Convention did not merely express its displeasure with Westmorland. It gave its approval to a pamphlet written by Wolfe Tone entitled *A Vindication of the Catholics of Ireland.* With his characteristic force and elegance, Tone not only vindicated the Catholics, he condemned their most notable opponents, especially FitzGibbon. The attacks on FitzGibbon in particular concerned a few of the more conservative delegates. They had no love for FitzGibbon himself, but they wanted to avoid open disrespect to a high official, and possible retaliation. Edward Sweetman, who had already made a bold attack on FitzGibbon in his native Wexford, dismissed these lingering traces of Kenmare-style timidity. In the process he denounced FitzGibbon as a bully and a coward:

> What ... are we to spare [this man] who made it his public and profligate boast that he would prostrate the chapels of the Catholics? We know that man [FitzGibbon] the road to his favour is through his fears. Let us become formidable to him and we shall be respected. He is the calumniator of the people, and therefore, he has our hatred and contempt. Loyalty itself becomes stupidity and vice where there is no protection, and are we to tender a gratuitous submission to men who have held us in fetters and in mockery and in scorn?[43]

J.E. Devereaux, Sweetman's kinsman and fellow delegate from Wexford, supported him, and the convention came to a unanimous opinion to adopt the pamphlet as it was, without sparing the lord high chancellor's feelings.[44]

Such criticism in an official Catholic publication was a remarkable sign of assertiveness. Hitherto, FitzGibbon had never met with any open criticism from the Catholics. Like Lord Killeen, they had vented privately any resentment aroused by his insulting remarks and conduct. At the most, FitzGibbon's outrageous chapel wrecking clause provoked a very obsequious and very general petition of protest from Kenmare and servile company.[45] Some public demonstrations against FitzGibbon did take place in Limerick following the freeholder resolutions, but a mixed crowd of Protestants as well as Catholics participated.[46] Tone's pamphlet, and the debates which it sparked in the convention revealed publicly and officially that the Catholics, at least the politically assertive Catholics of the Convention, hated FitzGibbon as bitterly as he hated them.

Far more shattering to FitzGibbon was the reaction of the English government to the delegation from the Catholic Convention. Dundas and Pitt not only received the delegates, they agreed to lend their support to another relief bill, granting the rights denied in 1792; only seats in parliament and high government and judicial office remained proscribed. The communication of this decision on the part of the British government was as abrupt as its formation. On 3 January 1793, Dundas sent Westmorland two dispatches containing, not a ringing declaration of support for the Protestant establishment in Church and State, but a recommendation for the further relief of His Majesty's subjects professing the Roman Catholic religion. In this and in a subsequent dispatch written the following day, Dundas also sent justifications, old and new, for the English government's decision. First of all, he dismissed Westmorland's lurid reports about the members of the delegation; to Dundas, they were not wild-eyed Jacobins, but respectable subjects with a perfectly respectful petition. Therefore, the English government had no legitimate reason to refuse their petition or to deny them access to the King. He acknowledged that the English ministers should have made their decision in conjunction with their Irish colleagues. According to Dundas, the delegates had expressed their own willingness to consult with any Irish ministers who cared to make the journey to England. But, Dundas noted, there was no probability of representatives of the Irish government arriving in good time, and the delegates "expressed a considerable degree of uneasiness at the apparent delay". Moreover, the Irish government itself had shown no particular willingness to engage in such a conference. The lack of response, in addition to the decision to open the Irish parliament at the earliest possible opportunity, left "no alternative but to form our own decision". He repeatedly assured Westmorland that the King's ministers had made no definite promises to the delegates. They could not dismiss Keogh and the rest of the Catholic delegation with "a sullen silence, calculated to aggrieve the jealousy which unfortunately seized on the minds of the Catholics of Ireland". Nonetheless, in making their polite answer, the English government had tried to show "every attention ... to the Government of

Ireland by referring the Catholics to the wisdom and liberality of the Irish Parliament."[47]

Dundas's explanations were flimsy, to say the least. Both he and the delegates must have recognized the futility of any discussions with the Irish ministers. Certainly if the Catholic delegates had expressed any such desire, they did so out of mere politeness or as a further show of moderation. It is difficult to imagine Devereaux or Keogh having any serious resolution of meeting with FitzGibbon. Moreover, although he claimed that the Irish government was free to act as it saw fit, Dundas left little room for choice. In spite of Westmorland's dispatches, filled with reports of Protestant defiance and Catholic rebellion, grand jury resolutions and secret republiçs, Dundas and his fellow ministers remained firm on the necessity for further concessions to restore peace and to stem the tide of revolutionary sentiment. Indeed, the impending war with France made them all the more anxious to lay to rest a troublesome distracting issue. Dundas even went so far as to declare that he had been wrong to acquiesce in the limited Irish act of 1792, and that the belated and grudging concessions were already doomed to failure:

> I must refer your Excellency to the reasoning contained in my letter of the 29th of December 1791, in every word of which I am confirmed by events which have since taken place. I there stated for the consideration of His Majesty's government in Ireland, the grounds which induced me to be of opinion that the Roman Catholics of Ireland were less likely to concur in disturbing the existing frame of Irish Government, where they were permitted to participate in the Franchise of that Government, than they were when compelled to live under a total seclusion from those essential benefits which must be most dear to men living in a country where the Powers of an Independent Parliament have been distinctly recognized. My reasoning did not satisfy the Government of Ireland, and of course the experiment was not made, and not having been made, it is perhaps idle to express any conviction that if it had, it would have succeeded. I pretend not to say that it now will. I am rather of opinion that the same concessions which would have quieted the question are not now likely to do it.[48]

Notwithstanding his personal doubts, Dundas made it impossible for the Irish government to refuse or to neglect a new Catholic bill without suffering grievous humiliation. His bland, official prose carried an implicit threat: frame a bill and support it in good faith or leave the King's Government in Ireland in a false, ridiculous position:

> If it is the determination of the Irish Parliament to refuse all further concession, I admit that the recommendation from the Throne must be embarrassing, as it must exhibit to the public view a difference of feeling in His Majesty and His Irish Parliament on a subject of such momentous concern. But if, as I trust there is, a universal sentiment prevalent both in the British and Irish Government,

> to connect all lovers of order and good Government in a union of resistance to all abettors of anarchy and misrule, I cannot discover any embarrassment that can arise from that sentiment being universally known.[49]

Even Westmorland had to take the hint. Hobart dutifully cobbled together a bill giving Catholics the right to vote, to serve on juries, to serve in the army and in the navy, to hold commissions up to the rank of general, to take degrees at Trinity College, and to be admitted as freeholders and as members of corporations. In keeping with Dundas's own guidelines, they remained excluded from Parliament, from the Bench and from the position of King's Counsel and from the higher Revenue offices.[50]

It is difficult not to sympathize with Westmorland as he struggled to reconcile a British government bent on settling a bothersome issue before undertaking a war, and the Irish Protestants, who felt betrayed and abandoned. As he himself declared with great poignancy: "My situation is most difficult and unpleasant every leader displeased with English government, what cabals will be made I cannot prophesy."[51] He pleaded for the complete support of English government as he tried to carry out what he considered a risky and ill-advised policy: "... we shall probably pay dear for what you have put on me and therefore you must give me ye strongest support." He could not resist a flash of anger: "... of you had left me alone, I cd have carried ye Measures with much less difficulty."[52] In light of his own voluminous accounts of recalcitrant Irish ministers, it was an extraordinary statement. In light of FitzGibbon's sentiments in particular, it was sheer fantasy.

He fought a desperate rearguard action up to the bitter end. On 26 December, Westmorland reported, "I had a long conversation with him [FitzGibbon] this morning; he admits that if concession of the two points [arms and suffrage] would bring content, he would readily give them up, but he is convinced of the contrary."[53] Given his views of Catholic treason and triumphalism, he would indeed have been convinced of the contrary. Given his frequently lonely and always courageous battle to maintain English Protestant authority in Ireland, he inevitably would have felt rage bordering on madness when that very authority stooped to negotiations with its most inveterate enemies.

IV

His remarks on the speech from the throne, made at the opening of Parliament on 10 January, offered a foretaste of the rhetorical wrath to come. He set the tone by denouncing the petition of grievance which the Catholics had presented to the King as "a gross and malignant deception on the father of his people".[54] The grievances in the petition were spurious and the demands outrageous. Most notably, he warned publicly, as he had warned in private counsel, of the dangers of allowing Catholics to bear arms, one of the main points of the petition. Still more impertinent, objectionable and dangerous was the petition's call for the right of suffrage. FitzGibbon made the obligatory disclaimers of personal prejudice against the Catholics, disclaimers which were doubly obligatory in his case:

> I do most solemnly protest that as an individual I never have, nor will I ever enquire what may be the religion of any man – if he be an honest man, whatever his religion may be, it shall never influence me in my private dealings and the more zealously any man is attached to any religion which he professes, the greater confidence I shall always be inclined to place in him.[55]

Furthermore, if the Catholics had any genuine grievances affecting their persons or their property, no one was more anxious than he to redress them:

> If there be a clause in the statute book which renders their characters, their persons or their property less secure than the characters, the persons or the properties of the Protestants, let it be repealed.[56]

But Catholics, given their fanatical devotion to their own religion, and their overwhelming numbers, could never exercise "efficient power" in a "free Protestant government". Nor could they be trusted to maintain the connection with the "Protestant Empire of Great Britain". They would inevitably attempt to subvert British and Protestant rule and to establish the dominion of their own church. The result could only be a recurrence of the sectarian wars of the 17th century:

> If unfortunately for this country we shall ever be induced to make so fatal an experiment, we may rest assured that the maintenance of a Protestant establishment and of our connection with Great Britain must once more be put to the issue of the sword.[57]

Above all, he declared his own determination to resist the fatal experiment, and his confidence that his fellow peers would do the same:

> ... whenever the subject recommended to us from the Throne shall come into debate, I will state without reserve, the grounds upon which I have framed that opinion. I trust, however, that no degree of lenity, rashness or timidity will ever induce the Parliament of Ireland to yield her best security for the peace and prosperity of the country committed to their care, whatever events may arise, I will persevere in defending the present Constitution of this country and transmitting it to posterity.[58]

It was an unprecedented act of defiance on the part of FitzGibbon. Not since he was a young opposition backbencher had he so vehemently opposed a government measure. Nonetheless, he opposed, not to gain notice or to make gratuitous trouble, as in the past, but out of a sincere, if headlong, desire to protect the English government from its own fatal self-deception. There were, nonetheless, dangerous measures of wounded pride and vainglory in FitzGibbon's action as well. Already he had come to believe that he alone truly understood Ireland, particularly benighted Popish Ireland. It was his duty to remind the English government that Ireland was an integral part of the British Empire, but a precarious and easily jeopardized part. The fact that Pitt in particular would so completely discard his opinion, and the fact that Pitt in particular would allow his views on Ireland to be influenced by rebellious Papists like Keogh or fatuous instigators like Richard Burke hurt FitzGibbon deeply.

FitzGibbon did not long maintain his stance of wounded defiance. In spite of his habitual mental dimness, Westmorland predicted as much and in the process, he delivered what is probably the most complete and striking summation of FitzGibbon's master motives ever made:

> The Chancellor spoke yesterday; he confined himself not to giving ye RC's; however he is violent for ye moment, but I am sure he has no other God but English government and will not distress us.[59]

Fear as well as reverence may have restored FitzGibbon to submission. Naked defiance brought with it a risk that he would lose either his office or indeed his remaining influence with the English government. Without his guidance, worse Popish follies might ensue. He may also have submitted because he had received assurances that a union would eventually accompany these concessions to Catholics. Dundas's private papers contain this cryptic statement in a memorandum of a conversation with Edward Cooke, one of FitzGibbon's confidantes: "Mr. Cooke Stated Ld. FitzGibbon's readiness to grant everything short of seats in Parliament, Corporations, and Sheriffs and to give a qualified right of carrying arms if such concessions should be blended with the system of final settlement."[60] The phrase "final settlement" can have no other meaning. If he had been comparatively indifferent, even reluctant, before, he was now in frantic earnest. In the end, FitzGibbon had no interest in contesting the form of Irish government. That was best which protected the Protestants best. With justice, he saw that an independent Irish Parliament could no longer guarantee Protestant privilege and power, and Pitt and Dundas were perfectly ready to accept his conversion and his terms.

Nonetheless, while the English government could now count on his vote and his cooperation in the House of lords, his anger and his sense of betrayal remained unabated. He seized the opportunity to rage and to warn again when the bill emerged from Commons, aided in its stormy course by bandwagon-hopping Whigs, reluctant government members, and members in the interest of Lord Abercorn, self-appointed patron of the Catholics and Keogh's favored shadow viceroy. When the bill came up for committal in the House of Lords on 13 March 1793, the initial reaction was, on the whole, compliant and even, in the case of the Bishop of Killala, enthusiastic. He welcomed the repeal of the penal laws which were the product of a "bigoted and persecuting age", and which had been imposed with equal "impolicy and injustice to a loyal body of subjects, whose conduct for that period was a full refutation of every argument that could be offered in support of that code". Killala proceeded to praise the bill as sound Christianity and as sound policy:

> He felt it his duty to declare fully his sentiments on these points, because he looked upon his Roman Catholic brethren as fellow subjects and fellow Christians, believers in the same God and partners in the same redemption. Speculative differences in some points of faith were with him of no account. They and he had but *one* religion, the religion of CHRISTIANITY. Therefore, as children of the same father, as travellers on the same road – and seekers of the same salvation, why not love each other as brothers? It was no part of Protestantism to persecute the Catholics and without justice to the Catholics, there could be no security for the Protestant Establishment. As a friend, therefore, to the permanency of this establishment, to the prosperity of the country, and the justice due his Catholic brethren, he should chearfully give his vote that the bill be committed.[62]

This speech, full of kindly 18th century platitudes, re-opened FitzGibbon's mental wounds. The speech was not only delivered by a Bishop of the Established Church, but by an Englishman. Poor good-natured Killala became the personification of what FitzGibbon perceived as the fatuous naiveté and irresponsibility of the English. He became, consequently, the convenient target for the rage FitzGibbon dared not direct toward the treacherous, but still adored Pitt. He held fire while Glandore, Portarlington and Waterford delivered their dutiful remarks in support of the bill.[63] He then delivered an extraordinary, and in many ways a masterful philippic against the Roman Catholics of Ireland and against his Grace of Killala's notion that they both deserved and could be trusted with political rights.

It was, arguably, his greatest speech. It is impossible not to admire the comprehensive array of arguments which he marshaled against the claims of the Catholics. The speech abounded in striking, forceful, and eminently quotable turns of phrase. Indeed, in terms of anti-Popish propaganda points, the speech offered such an *embarras de richesses* that adherents of the constitution in church and state reprinted the speech in 1813.

First and foremost, his politics were his religion. FitzGibbon paid a great deal of lip service to Christianity as taught by the Church of Ireland. In his will, for example, he dutifully parroted the standard Protestant formula for redemption:

> I earnestly entreat for the pardon of my sins from the mercy of Almighty God. I am truly sensible of, and grateful for, the many blessings which through his mercy and goodness I have enjoyed in this world and bow with resignation as becomes me to such difficulties as have been visited upon me, hoping through the mercy and mediation of my redeemer, his most blessed son, for salvation in the next world.[64]

In his visitation at Trinity in 1798, he warned, not only against the political unorthodoxies of the United Irishmen, but of religious unorthodoxy in the guise of necessitarianism: "... it [necessitarianism] must lead not only to deism, but atheism and must have the worst effects, particularly on weak minds."[65] No doubt he had as comprehensive a knowledge of the Book of Common Prayer as he did of the Common Law. But he was fundamentally a hard, sensual, practical and thoroughly unimaginative man. He had no patience with the spiritual exultations of Methodism. He later characterized one unfortunate general who had earned his disfavor as a "mad Methodist".[66] Still more objectionable were the extremes of private judgment exercised by dissenting Protestants, and especially by the detested Presbyterians. A "restless and republican spirit" tainted that religion.[67] In his great speech on the Act of Union, he described with compendious loathing the various religious unorthodoxies of the Cromwellian settlers, whom he detested as much as any "old Irish Catholic":

> And thus a new Colony of new Settlers, composed of all the various sects which then infested England, Independents, Anabaptists, Seceders, Brownists, Socinians, Millenarians and Dissenters of every description, many of them infected with the leaven of democracy, poured into Ireland and were put in possession of the ancient inheritance of its inhabitants.[68]

Oddly enough, in his uninquiring dogmatism, he resembled his own caricature of an Irish Roman Catholic. It is doubtful whether he engaged in any theological speculation or contemplation outside the decreed orthodoxies of the state church. Indeed, the speech of 1793 suggests that FitzGibbon adhered less to Anglicanism and more to a sort of imperialist Manicheanism.

The British Empire was for FitzGibbon a Kingdom of Light offering law and civilization to a benighted world and especially to benighted Ireland. The prop of Empire was the Church as by Law Established. Submission to the Empire necessarily entailed submission to its state religion. In short, religion was less a theological and ritualistic system purportedly revealing great universal truths than the premier instrument of conquest and subjugation. But FitzGibbon, as always, expresses himself best:

> I consider civil allegiance to my Sovereign to consist in an explicit acknowledgment of the powers which the constitution has entrusted to him, and in prompt and implicit obedience to the laws, civil and ecclesiastical by which he governs his subjects.[69]

Unfortunately a formidable and extensive Kingdom of Darkness perpetually threatened the authority of the Empire and the authority of its Church. That was, of course, the "Court of Rome" and its multitudes of savage, superstitious adherents in Ireland. FitzGibbon spared no effort to paint as dark and as grim a picture as he could of Roman Catholicism and its rival dominion in Ireland. He allowed no room for nuance, for exceptions to the rule, and even less for the possibility that Irish Roman Catholics may have had legitimate grievances. They always had been, were now and always would be, fanatical and superstitious in their devotion to the Roman Catholic religion and vicious and perverse in their resistance to the benevolent authority of England:

> ... I am sorry to say, and my opinion is formed from general and promiscuous habits of intercourse with the people for more than twenty years, that religious bigotry is as rank in Ireland as it was at any one period ... Nay more, I am satisfied that a very great majority of the inhabitants of Ireland are as zealously and superstitiously devoted to the Popish faith as the people of Spain, or Portugal or any [*sic*] the most bigotted [*sic*] districts of the German Empire.[70]

It was the sole, overriding wish of the Catholics of Ireland, whatever their professions of loyalty, to overthrow the rule of the British Empire, to destroy the established church and to "restore the ancient pomp and splendour of their religion". Their past record clearly demonstrated their evil intentions. Acting at the behest and the direction of the Court of Rome they had rebelled in 1641;[72] during the brief domination of the Catholic Jacobite parliament, Protestants had suffered attainder and confiscation, while their churches were converted to barracks and prisons.[73] In light of their past behavior, "hard necessity" (a frequent FitzGibbonism) compelled the Irish parliament to impose the penal code, "to abridge the power and influence of the old Irish Catholics".[74] In short, it was a just retribution for their crimes of rebellion and bigotry, and the Irish Catholics owed any mitigation of it, not to any inherent right, but solely to the mercy and magnanimity of the Protestants. What concession was granted was "but ill-requited by that body of men who had profited by it".[75]

Indeed, FitzGibbon suggested, the authority of the Protestant Empire existed only precariously. The Roman Catholic church in fact exercised a judicial and political authority over its subjects that frequently over-rode or defied the Protestant Government. Its priests and bishops acted as the omnipotent and domineering agents of that authority. Particularly abhorrent to FitzGibbon, who adored the Common Law as ardently as he adored the British Empire, was the rival jurisdiction of canon law. He indignantly cited some anecdotal evidence showing the extent of the legal usurpation exercised by the Catholic clergy:

> ... A Popish priest who acts as judge in the Consistorial Court of Elphin in the month of December 1791, cited parties who had lived together as man and wife to appear in his court in a cause of nullity of marriage; they had been married by a priest and had co-habited – however, the marriage contract was pronounced null and void, and the woman was turned loose upon the world. On her complaint to a neighboring gentleman, one of the representatives of the county, he remonstrated against this proceeding – but in vain: the consistorial judge persisted in enforcing his sentence, and in justification of himself enclosed to this gentleman a decree of the Council of Trent under which he had proceeded

> and in the course of his correspondence upon this subject, which is now in my possession, he very gravely stated that an attack upon the laws of their church would be an attack upon the whole body of Roman Catholics. This being a clear case, he had full and final jurisdiction.[76]

The Pope reigned supreme over this alternative empire of domineering clergy and savage, superstitious laity. FitzGibbon did not take the rather patronizing and complacent 18th century view of the Pope as a decayed, and rather ludicrous, Italian potentate. He took a grimmer, but at the same time more respectful view of His Holiness's powers. It had always been and was still the aim of the Holy See to impose a secular as well as a religious tyranny over all the world. Toward this end, the Court of Rome had continually disrupted the peace of society and had plunged Europe into religious warfare.[77] So long as Irish Catholics remained in thrall to this ecclesiastical tyrant, and to his minions the priests and bishops, their claims of loyalty meant nothing:

> ... I know that canonical obedience to the Pope as enjoined by the Court of Rome is utterly inconsistent with the duties of civil allegiance to my sovereign as enjoined by the laws and constitution of the British Empire.[78]

And since Catholics could not be truly loyal, if followed that they had no right to any power and privilege in a Protestant state. They existed in the British Empire only on sufferance, and for the safety of the empire, they must necessarily remain, like the Beast of the Apocalypse, permanently bound by the adamantine chains of exclusionary laws.

In spite of his claims to right and reason, FitzGibbon's religion rested on a foundation of gross intellectual dishonesty. His claim that the "Court of Rome" fomented the rebellion of 1641 was, to put it mildly, a highly imaginative fabrication. He was as unscrupulous in his use of contemporary sources. His treatment of John Troy's pastoral, *On the Duties of a Christian*, was a case in point. Troy had attempted to show that papal authority in no way interfered with secular authority. His weighty and pedantic tome was notably unsuccessful. Liberals, Protestant and Catholic alike, found its dogmatic tone embarrassing, while FitzGibbon found proof for his own contrary claim that papal authority posed an insidious threat to British imperial authority. In describing the procedure by which Irish bishops were selected, Troy stated that the bishops and selected priests nominated candidates and the Pope and College of Cardinals approved them. FitzGibbon seized on this incidental thread of information and wove from it a Jacobite plot. The cardinals' exercise of approbation became a "Cabinet of Cardinals at Rome for the ecclesiastical government of Ireland". In this cabinet there could be only one overriding influence and voice:

> I presume Cardinal York is at the head of it and therefore there can be no doubt that the mild, superintending spiritual influence of this Cabinet upon the Irish Catholics will have the best effects in cultivating their hereditary attachment to

> the British government and the British nation and their natural affection for the established constitution in Church and State.[80]

Like many reactionary propagandists he made much of a fancied division between rich and poor Catholics. Assumed the well-worn rhetorical cloak of indignant paternalism, he painted a lurid picture of the financial exactions which the Catholic Committee and its Convention levied on the peasantry: "... the taxes repeatedly levied upon the poor under the authority of this convention have in many districts reduced them to very great distress."[81] In fact, the Catholic Committee and the Catholic Convention were funded less by pennies extorted from the peasantry and more by the pounds of its wealthy mercantile members. Moreover, John Sweetman's attempts to address the concerns of poorer Catholics in Louth belied these claims of cynical exploitation. (FitzGibbon was to make his own use of Sweetman's activities, as shall be seen.) The division between poor exploited Catholics and the Jacobin Catholic elite remained a favorite rhetorical trope of FitzGibbon's. He articulated it more cynically and precisely during his examination of Dr MacNeven in 1798, when he questioned whether the Irish people cared "the value of this pen or the drop of ink it contains for Parliamentary Reform or Catholic emancipation?"[82]

In spite of his all-encompassing hatred for Irish Catholics, FitzGibbon did not blame them entirely. Protestant political irresponsibility had encouraged the innate rebelliousness of the Catholics. Repeating again his premier and very accurate observation of 1789, he warned that their divisions and their quarrels with England had set a bad and dangerous example:

> Till modern Irish patriots had succeeded in foment party heat and rancour and in dividing the Protestants of Ireland into opposite and inveterate factions, contending with each other, we never heard of any claim of political power advanced by the Irish Papist.[83]

He also played on an old theme from 1784, the dangers of a political alliance between the Papists, and those no less obnoxious religious rebels, the Presbyterians. If allowed to unite and gain control of Parliament, Catholics and "Puritans" would "join in sacrificing the established church; I have very little doubt that to one other point they will also agree, and that they will join in fomenting a quarrel with Great Britain". The result, FitzGibbon noted with sardonic *schadenfreude*, would not be to the advantage of the Presbyterians:

> And if they shall succeed in the ultimate object of both, which I know to be separation, these wise Puritanical reformers will then find themselves precisely in the situation of the horse in the fable; they will be obliged to carry their new allies; and when they are once fairly mounted, they will have to lament in vain their restless levity and infatuation.[84]

His observations on the effects of opposition political agitation and on the fundamental instability of a Catholic-Presbyterian alliance had large elements of truth. And he was certainly correct in recognizing that the bill would not satisfy Catholic demands. FitzGibbon rightly pointed out the fundamental illogic of granting the power of suffrage and at the same time, withholding the contingent power of holding office:

> Should the Parliament of Ireland once admit the claims of the Irish Papists to political power on the ground of right, I desire to know where else to draw the line? If the Papists have a right to vote for representatives in a Protestant Parliament, they have a right to sit in Parliament; they have a right to fill every office in the state, they have a right to pay tithes exclusively to their own clergy, they have a right to restore the ancient pomp and splendor of their religion, they have a right to be governed exclusively by the laws of their own church, they have a right to seat their Bishops in this House, they have a right to seat a Popish prince on this Throne, they have a right to subvert the established government and to make this a Popish country, which I have little doubt is their ultimate object.[85]

Wolfe Tone had much the same opinion of the bill, though of course, his language was less highly colored and he had different reasons for disliking it: "If the Catholics deserved what had been granted, they deserved what has been withheld."[86]

FitzGibbon was also very right in perceiving the rooted inveteracy of religious antagonism in Ireland. The Defenders, who were at the height of their activity, proved his point. Revanche against the Protestants was, or became, an element in their sometimes millenarian political creed.

Nor did FitzGibbon hold his ideas in solitary malevolence. Many honorable and well-intentioned Protestants believed that any grant of political power to Catholics would endanger their own rights, property and lives. The Swiftian rage of his convictions set FitzGibbon apart. Ironically, in his ardent feelings on the subject of Irish Catholics, FitzGibbon had much in common with Edmund Burke. Both were Irish outsiders who held a quasi-mystical reverence for the British Empire and the British Constitution. Unlike FitzGibbon, of course, Burke's vision of Empire incorporated the Catholics, whom he never ceased to perceive as inherently inclined to monarchy, aristocracy and hierarchy. His warm and fast ties with his Catholic relations, the Nagles, also certainly influenced his views. FitzGibbon, in his way, had as intimate a knowledge of Irish political realities, but he had no such ties of intimacy or affection with Catholics. At best, he was the lordly, domineering patron. Hence he could the more readily see Catholics as a force for instability, and he could the more easily demonize and detest them.

V

The speech itself had little effect on its principal target, Killala, and indeed, on those Lords who favored the bill, out of conviction or out of expediency. Killala made perhaps the most devastating response, given FitzGibbon's supreme self-importance and utter lack of a sense of humor: he made a joke of the speech and a joke of its deliverer:

> Much has been asserted as to the Romish belief, of the Pope's infallibility; but he saw it was not impossible men might in argument become *Popes* themselves and assert an infallibility of their own.[87]

Dunsany "most chearfully supported the bill", and Lord Westmeath gave his "hearty support." Leinster both declared his support and ventured to put FitzGibbon right on a point of religious history:

> The noble Lord had said there was no instance in any state where Protestants and Catholics agreed in any one system of government; an instance of the contrary was the Electorate of Saxony ... where the Prince was a Catholic and his Administration Protestant ... and in other Principalities of Germany there were many similar instances ...[88]

Only the egregious Cashel spoke on FitzGibbon's side.[89]

FitzGibbon was proud enough of his production to submit it for publication. The response outside of parliament was predictable. The *Freeman's Journal* praised FitzGibbon for his intellectual versatility and for his talents as an amateur theologian, a novel species of flattery:

> The Lord Chancellor's speech, just published, is as close and powerful a piece of reasoning as ever came from that exalted character, and does equal credit to the ingenuity of his mind and the depth of his research. His acquaintance with the Canonists seems profound and much more extensive than could be expected from a modern Judge; but the versatility of his talents is as striking as the perseverance of his application is to be admired.

Grattan, who had fervently and openly embraced the Catholic cause, and who as fervently and as openly detested FitzGibbon, wrote to Burke: "The Bishop was the statesman and the lawyer was the bigot."

As one opposition newspaper put it, FitzGibbon himself "condescended to vote against his own speech".[92] Even as he warned against the danger and the futility of the bill, he too voted for its committal. His god demanded submission to the heresy of Catholic emancipation, and he would therefore recant for the time being. Once the bill was committed, he worked steadily and honorably to steer it through the Lords. Westmorland wrote of his conduct in a rapture of praise and gratitude:

> I cannot do full justice to his conduct during ye present session, thinking what was proposed injurious to ye English connection in ye first instance, he acquiesced in ye wishes of government, discountenanced ye innumerable cabals that were at work, encouraged ye timourous and to his spirit and decision may in great degree be attributed ye successful stand we have made.[93]

He also recommended a promotion in the peerage for FitzGibbon as a reward for his meritorious actions.

FitzGibbon did press for one major revision to the bill. The Commons had limited the right to bear arms to those Catholics possessing property worth £100. FitzGibbon successfully pressed for a higher qualification of £300:

> The Lord Chancellor opposed this arrangement and though willing to put arms into the hands of £10 freeholders, his Lordship thought that a man's personal property of £100 did not put him on the same footing and the qualification of personal property should be at least £300. To give a man arms who hold a real property was but reasonable, but to put arms in the hands of men who had no property would be only to induce them to murder each other and to rob their neighbors; consequences which his Lordship felt were to be apprehended in the county where he resided, where year after year, merely on account of what were called *old grudges* from one town or family to another, and who instead of cudgelling each other very well, as they now usually do, if firearms were put into their hands would proceed to murder.[94]

With an eye to Peep O' Day troublemaking in Armagh, he later declared his own belief that the same qualification ought to apply to the lower order of Protestants, though he never displayed the courage of this particular conviction and attempted to put it into legal effect.[95]

However compliant his behavior with respect to the relief bill itself, FitzGibbon spared no effort to get revenge on the Catholics, and particularly the members of the Catholic Committee who had outmaneuvered him. Even before the bill had passed into law, FitzGibbon fired the first salvo in his campaign of revanche. The report of the Secret Committee of the House of Lords of February 1793, which was largely FitzGibbon's creation, implied, if it did not prove, a link between the Catholic Committee and the Defenders. He made his intentions amply clear in his speech in support of the formation of such a committee:

> The perpetrators of these outrages act upon system and under order; They proceed day after day in the accomplishment of their work and they are day after day enforced; they have been opposed and numbers have fallen before the military, yet the growth of this evil has not stopped; no man can shut his eyes against the fact; it is vain to butcher these deluded persons unless we can come at their advisors. My lords, I approve of a Secret Committee, and I would have it vested with powers to send for and examine all persons capable of furnishing

> any information by which we may trace the authors of this mischief to their lurking places whence I would rather drag one of them to the bar of a Court of Justice than sacrifice twenty of the wretches whom they have deluded; for though culpable, they are so in a secondary degree.[96]

A Louth grain merchant by the name of Coleman was one of the persons called upon to trace the authors of Defender mischief to their lurking place. Coleman implicated a very influential and radical Catholic indeed: John Sweetman, a wealthy brewer and a pillar of the Catholic Committee. Sweetman had written to Coleman the previous August inquiring whether a man accused of Defenderism was entitled to bail. The letter itself was perfectly straightforward; but FitzGibbon, displaying the same ruthless ingenuity which he had used against Dr Troy, presented it in such a way as to imply that Sweetman was one of the lurking authors of mischief:

> Several seditious and Inflammatory papers published in Dublin and dispersed through the country seem to have countenanced and encouraged the Defenders in their proceedings, and it appears that the Letters were written by a Member of the Committee of the Roman Catholics at Dublin previous to the last summer assizes to a person resident at Dundalk, in one of which the said person in the name of the Roman Catholic Committee directed Enquiries to be made touching the offenses of which the Defenders then in confinement were accused.[97]

FitzGibbon added a final demonic touch to the portrait of John Sweetman, aider and abettor of the Defenders, by adding, "... it does appear that the said person to whom the letter was addressed at Dundalk, did employ at considerable expense an Agent and Counsel to act for several persons who were accused of being Defenders, and were indicted for offenses committed by them in the County of Louth ..."

FitzGibbon used the same method of guilt by association to implicate the entire Catholic Committee. In his account of the rise of Defenderism, FitzGibbon stated his *a priori* conclusion about their leadership:

> Their [the Defenders'] Measures appear to have been concerted and conducted with the utmost secresy and a degree of regularity and system not usual in People of such mean condition and as if directed by Men of a superior rank.[99]

The report then abruptly shifted to a discussion of the Catholic Committee's methods of raising funds:

> Sums of money to a considerable amount have been levied and still continue to be levied upon the Roman Catholics in all parts of the Kingdom by Subscriptions and Collections at their Chappels [*sic*] and elsewhere.[100]

The report re-printed a prosaic circular from the Catholic Committee, submitting a plan for a general subscription "for defraying the many and growing Expenses incurred by the General Committee in Conducting the affairs of the Catholics of

Ireland."[101] Although FitzGibbon never made any explicit declaration to that effect, he obviously intended to suggest that the many and growing expenses included the expense of arming and inciting the Defenders.

In his recommendations for restoring peace and order, FitzGibbon again emphasized this supposed link between the Catholic Committee's subscriptions and the Defenders. He made relatively mild and indeed hackneyed recommendations for the appointment of "a sufficient number of active, resolute and steady magistrates." These gentlemen would not only "exert themselves to maintain the public peace", they would "cut off from these Deluded People all hope or Expectation of support of Defense arising from a Common Fund to be levied on persons of their Communion".[102]

FitzGibbon made rather perfunctory expressions of faith in the innocence and peaceableness of the generality of the Catholics, but even when making this verbal gesture of moderation he cast further aspersions on his true target, the Dublin-based Catholic Committee:

> The Committee think it their duty to state that nothing appeared before them which would lead them to believe that the Body of the Roman Catholics in this Kingdom were concerned in promoting or countenancing such disturbances, or that they were privy to this Application of any part of the money which had been levied upon them, however suspicious the conduct of Ill-Disposed Individuals of their Persuasion resident in Dublin may have been.[103]

Some of FitzGibbon's fellow peers expressed indignation at the patent unfairness of the Secret Committee and its report. During a later debate on quite a different matter, Lord Dunsany, who had the traditional sympathies of a convert, offered a more benign explanation for the collections: they were intended to benefit emigré French clergy. He also added indignantly, "He had heard much of the Secret Committee; he knew that the Committee was intended to injure the Roman Catholics."[104] FitzGibbon, as indignantly, defended his committee and his report:

> It had never been the intention of the committee to affect the Roman Catholics' interest, on the contrary, the Committee in its report had distinguished between the acts of the few and the many. It appeared to a demonstration that the Defenders had been encouraged and maintained by certain members of the Roman Catholic Committee.[105]

Indeed, the *Catholic*, as opposed to the Secret, Committee had injured the whole body of their co-religionists by committing illegal and seditious acts in their name. The Secret Committee had magnanimously chosen to disregard such claims, "though it had the authority of the Roman Catholics to justify it".[106]

FitzGibbon clearly hoped that Sweetman and his colleagues on the Catholic Committee would respond to the report with the terror and supineness of the Catholics of his youth or of the 1780s. He was wrong, particularly about John

Sweetman, a man of great intrepidity and intelligence. Sweetman and the Committee shrewdly waited until the Catholic bill was securely passed before mounting an attack on FitzGibbon and a defense against his charges.

On 2 April, the Catholic Committee published a public denial that it had ever raised money "for improper purposes and among others for the purpose of assisting the insurgents".[107] The Committee maintained that they had indeed communicated with the Defenders, but they had done so only after consultation with a group of Protestant gentlemen in County Down and they had confined themselves to appeals to keep the peace so as not to endanger the prospects of the relief bill.[108] Furthermore, the Committee had offered to assist only those Catholics who had suffered attack from the Peep O Day boys and who would "dutifully appeal to the law of the land for redress".[109] The Committee made clear that it would "in no case undertake the defense of any man who shall assist in any riotous or disorderly meeting or who shall not behave himself soberly, peaceably and honestly".[110]

The Committee also publicly came to the defense of John Sweetman and of his dealings with the Defenders. At the suggestion of Coleman, his Dundalk correspondent, Sweetman had indeed met with one Nugent, the brother of an accused Defender. As it turned out, since Nugent had questions about the legality of bail, which Sweetman did not feel qualified to answerHe referred to Nugent to an unnamed "professional gentleman".[111] This unnamed professional gentleman declared himself unable to offer any advice "the examinations in which the offense was specified not appearing".[112] Sweetman soon became convinced that Nugent was not a desirable object of assistance, however ineffectual:

> and with regard to Nugent himself, on examining him closely, good reason was found to doubt his being a person of the description mentioned in the Address of the General Committee dated 25 July, that is "one who if attacked in his house, property or person, should dutifully appeal to the law of the land for redress and who never assisted in any riotous or disorderly meeting.[113]

Having decide Nugent was a bad lot, Sweetman and those he consulted dismissed him "without advice or assistance or promise of either".[114]

As for the calls for subscriptions and the extraordinary expenses which FitzGibbon had found so suspicious, the Committee maintained that the Catholics had always been in the practice of subscribing money to defray the costs of lobbying and of presenting their cause in England. They had done so at least since the great dispute over quarterage fees.[115] The Committee then cited some of the extraordinary additional expenses which they had incurred. They had, for example, paid £2,000 to a "professional gentleman of great respectability" for his services as an agent in England.[116] This professional gentleman was presumably Richard Burke, who had not yet lost his position, either formally or informally. With the most implicit of sarcasm, the Committee suggested that FitzGibbon himself had known about this particular application of money:

> ... this expenditure happened with the knowledge of a noble lord high in legal situation and a member of the present Committee of Secresy.[117]

The Committee had incurred heavy advertising and printing expenses as well. They had been obliged to publish responses to an "Address presented in 1791, striking at the existence of the general committee" (in other words Lord Kenmare's address) and to "attacks on the public press ... by a variety of bodies of men and individuals." (including the Limerick resolutions framed by Lord FitzGibbon.)[118] The expense of the delegation to the King constituted another extraordinary burden requiring extraordinary donations. The Committee gave an account of its disbursement procedures to prove that neither Sweetman, nor any other member could have made an unauthorized, illegal use of common funds, even had they been so inclined. The nature of their procedures precluded any such abuse:

> But not to rest on the reason of the case, if they were so foolish or so wicked as to endeavor to misapply this money, they have not the power. No man nor body of men has dominion over the funds of the General Committee, but the General Committee itself; not a shilling can be drawn from the treasurer but by their order, except in particular cases, when they authorise the Sub-Committee to a limited amount and for a special purpose.[119]

Moreover, John Comerford, of the great mercantile house, currently managed the funds of the Committee, and his predecessor had been another commercial magnate, Mr McDermott. Their names, the Committee declared, "it is sufficient hereby to mention to satisfy the nation that they would not be concerned in so base a misapplication of the public contribution as that which is affected to be at present apprehended."[120] In short, the Committee owed its success to the business acumen of its members – not to secret rabbleraisings in the wilds of Ulster.

John Sweetman published his own personal vindication at the same time. He gave a similar account of his dealings with Nugent, and he emphatically denied an further involvement, financial or otherwise, with the Defenders:

> ... I never sent any money nor ordered any money to be paid to the Defenders, nor to any person for their use, directly or indirectly, either in my individual or official capacity. That I never corresponded or communicated with any Defender nor with any person for the purpose of holding such correspondence or communication with any of them. Nor did I in any manner whatsoever abet or encourage or take any part in abetting or encouraging the Defenders or their proceedings but on the contrary have used every means in my power both publicly and privately to express my abhorrence of their proceedings. I never employed either an attorney or barrister to oppose any prosecution carried on against them, nor did I ever order any person, whether professional or otherwise, to be employed in their behalf.[121]

Sweetman as emphatically denounced the Secret Committee's report, with considerable accuracy as "nothing more than a chain of ingenious insinuations founded upon surmise and supposition, for the sole purpose of attempting to prove one proposition, namely that certain Catholics in Dublin did take measures to disturb the peace and happiness of the country".[122] Sweetman also expressed his contempt for the chain's master-forger, though he prudently avoided mentioning FitzGibbon's name. He simply declared his lofty intent not to follow FitzGibbon's shoddy example:

> I hope I shall not forget myself, nor being hurried away by the force of imitation ascribe to others those opprobrious motives which have been so unhandsomely imputed to me.[123]

FitzGibbon took no notice of these defenses and denunciations. On the contrary, he repeated the same charges against John Sweetman and against the Catholic Committee in 1798.[124] No doubt the fact that Sweetman and many other members of the Committee had indeed become rebels convinced FitzGibbon of the fundamental rightness of his original claim.

In justice to FitzGibbon, he did have some grounds for his accusations. Sweetman's response, however brave and spirited, was fraught with prevarication. For example, the Rathfriland meeting to which he had alluded was scarcely the spontaneous act of concerned County Down squires. It was, in fact orchestrated and heavily attended by Belfast United Irishmen. Certainly Sweetman was a radical, committed United Irishman, even at this stage, and scarcely the injured, peaceable trader he made himself out to be. In addition, the Catholic Committee's contacts with Defenders probably were far more extensive occasional legal consultations. In short, FitzGibbon's instincts and perceptions were quite sound, but his methods blatantly violated the rules of evidence. He relied instead on innuendo and on the systematic and broad exaggeration which characterized much of his conduct on law and order issues. In consequence, he brought further discredit on himself and gave John Sweetman an opportunity to make a clever and effective *ad hominem* counterattack.

VI

FitzGibbon took more effective revenge against the Committee later that summer with the passage of the so-called "Act to prevent the Election or appointment of unlawful Assemblies under pretence of preparing or presenting public petitions or other Addresses to his Majesty or the Parliament".[125] The bill made the election of delegates "for the pretended purpose of petitioning" illegal. Magistrates had full powers to dissolve any such elected bodies and to arrest those who refused to comply. Following the precedent of the chapel-wrecking clause, FitzGibbon introduced draconian provisions, only to withdraw them in a show of moderation. The original draft of the bill had included a provision imposing a penalty of transportation on any such illegal delegates who refused to disperse within a half hour after being so ordered by a magistrate.[126] No doubt FitzGibbon would have relished the thought of shipping Devereaux, Sweetman, and Keogh off to the new colony of Botany Bay. But he settled instead for mere terror. He also asserted his fundamental respect for the "legal right of the subject to petition in a mild becoming manner for the redress of grievances"; along with this assurance, he made the ingenious argument that his act in fact enhanced rather than limited liberty by preserving the aristocratic independence of Parliament from tyrannical "multitudes" like those who dominated the "newfangled Government in a neighboring Kingdom."[127] This tired apologia for the blessings of oligarchy was fundamentally a sham. FitzGibbon was less concerned with preserving the liberty of the people than with depriving the people of the Catholic Committee of a potent political tool. He had long detested this particular form of agitation. He had intended to take this particular legislative action since November 1792.[128] A revival of the reform congress proposed by the United Irishmen gave him an additional, if entirely superfluous, reason to press for the bill. It certainly served its purpose well. In 1812, William Saurin, who held FitzGibbon's old office of attorney general as well as his fervent anti-Catholic views, applied the act precisely as its late framer would have wished. He prosecuted members of the revived Catholic Committee for holding illegal and seditious meetings as defined by the convention act. It remained a chilly menace until Daniel O'Connell devised a method of organization that evaded its restrictions and destroyed at last FitzGibbon's cherished sectarian oligarchy.

FitzGibbon showed his displeasure over the Catholic act in other, more petty ways. During debates on the militia bill, for example, he supported an abortive provision confining militia commissions to Protestants. In justification, he reiterated his *idee fixe* that the Catholics were still collecting funds for nefarious purposes, and he, for one, did not want to extend further privileges until they had ceased this practice. He also argued that the constitution had gone through too many drastic changes already: "... it would be wise to go no further until the Legislature had an experience of so great an alteration in the Constitution".[129] He fought his rearguard action in his capacity as vice chancellor of TCD as well. During commencement in the summer of 1793, he apparently objected when a college official tried to dispense with the oaths which had hitherto prevented Catholics from taking degrees. According to the *Dublin Evening Post*, FitzGibbon finally gave in to a combination of persuasion and threats applied by the Reverend Miller and by Whitley Stokes, the two college representatives presiding at the commencement:

> ... after hearing the arguments advanced in support of the position by Mr Miller and Mr Stokes, and after a declaration of Mr Millar that if the oath were insisted on, he would in consequence of the power invested in him, break up the Assembly, the Vice Chancellor yielded.[130]

The story may have been exaggerated or even fabricated. It was, after all, preceded by the dubious phrase "we hear". But if FitzGibbon did indeed raise this objection, he displayed not only a persistent malice, but outright absurdity. He had, it is true, initially expressed objections to admitting Catholics to Trinity.[131] But once the bill was passed, he had himself altered the statutes of the College to allow them to be admitted and to take degrees.[132]

FitzGibbon's antagonists on the Catholic Committee matched FitzGibbon, provocation for provocation. Its business purportedly done, the Committee officially disbanded in April 1793; before doing so, its members fired a Parthian shot at the hated, FitzGibbon-dominated government, by openly coming out in support of the once shunned United Irishmen and their plan of Parliamentary reform.[133] In their address of thanks to the King, they pointedly neglected to mention Westmorland's name.[134] As provocatively, they voted £500 to Simon Butler, their United Irish advocate, who had been fined precisely that amount by FitzGibbon for libeling the House of Lords and its hated Secret Committee.[135] In August, Keogh, Sweetman, McCormick and other leading members of the defunct committee took advantage of a social occasion to vent their contempt for the Lord Chancellor. They gave a public dinner to honour their leading supporters. The guests included Moira and Leinster, both of whom had firmly incorporated Catholic rights into their program of Whig opposition. Moira, expressing his own well-known sentiments toward the man who had publicly dressed him down three years before, as well as the sympathies of his Catholic hosts, proposed a toast to "the memory of Lord Chancellor Jefferies, may those who would imitate his policies take warning by his fate". Not surprisingly, this was a great crowd pleaser, meeting with "loud and repeated applause".[136] They made their discontent known through private as well as public channels. In July, Richard Burke, still operating under the pathetic delusion that he was acting for the Catholics, sent Dundas a letter from a Limerick correspondent. This gentleman blamed continuing unrest and discontent squarely on FitzGibbon:

> I don't think the country will ever be quiet while the Chancellor retains the power and weight he does at present.[137]

Burke added complaints of his own in a second letter:

> The Chancellor and his associates seem to have no other view than to defeat in all their beneficial consequences the measures taken in favour of the Catholics and in the next place to revenge themselves upon all who were instrumental in them.[138]

Burke's comments were characteristically over-charged, but they did have a large measure of truth. Moreover, many members of the English government itself, and not merely Catholics and their associates, seem to have had the same opinion of FitzGibbon's activities. Probably his harshest critic was the English chancellor, Lord Loughborough. Loughborough especially disliked the report of the Secret Committee.

Like Sweetman, he considered it a deliberate and none too convincing effort to defame the Catholics, "who are indirectly supposed to have contributed to the existence of the disorders".[139] Loughborough's use of the word "supposed" shows what little weight he attached to FitzGibbon's conclusions. FitzGibbon may have encountered renewed hostility and resentment on the part of the faithless, beloved Pitt as well.

During a parliamentary recess in April, he had traveled to England to consult on trade legislation. He almost certainly favored Pitt with a private version of his great parliamentary speech and warned again of Catholic treachery and treason. Shortly after his return to Ireland in May, he pursued the same theme in a long letter. In it, he gave Pitt a detailed account of the latest seditious activities of the Catholic Committee, including their resolution in favour of Parliamentary reform, and their vote of money to Simon Butler. He also presented their payment of £1,500 to Wolfe Tone as further proof "that their ultimate object is to separate this country from Great Britain".[140]

FitzGibbon and Tone already had a brief and not very friendly acquaintance. Tone had expressed reservations about FitzGibbon as early as 1789, and FitzGibbon, for his part, had good reason to dislike Tone's politics and his cavalier attitude toward his profession.[141] Apparently, the two were relations by marriage: Tone's long-suffering wife was a remote cousin of FitzGibbon's, and Marianne Elliot suggests that FitzGibbon shared the horror of Matilda Tone's family at her impulsive marriage.[142] But political considerations probably played a far greater part in the denunciation to Pitt. The English government had dismissed FitzGibbon's claims of a Catholic Committee-Defender conspiracy led by John Sweetman. To vindicate himself and his claims of Popish disaffection, he seized on the links between the Catholic Committee and the United Irishmen in the person of Tone.

FitzGibbon perhaps deserved credit for recognizing Tone's leadership ability, but his portrait of the man was characteristically distorted. Tone became, in the letter to Pitt, not only the evil genius of the Catholic Committee, but the sole founder and leader of the United Irishmen. Rather dubiously, considering his own modest, shabby genteel ancestry and his family relationship to the man, FitzGibbon held Tone's antecedent's as well as his politics up to contempt:

> They [the Committee] have voted fifteen hundred pounds to Mr. Tone, who is their cabinet minister and Advisor – who first proposed an alliance between the Puritans and Catholics, whose great object will be explained to you by the paper which I have the honour to enclose to you much better than any comment of mine upon the Subject – This Gentleman has been called to our Bar. He is the Son of a Bankrupt Tradesman and has the Merit of being the Founder of the Society of United Irishmen – He was also the original projector of the Catholic Convention, drew up the circular letter issued in the course of last summer in

> the name of Mr Edward Byrne, and composes most of the seditious and treasonable libels which are put forth by the Society of United Irishmen.[143]

Mr Tone, in short, was a bad, busy man, who was single-handedly responsible for both Catholic and Republican agitation in Ireland. As proof of his treasonable intentions, FitzGibbon enclosed a copy of the first declaration of the Society of United Irishmen, and in indiscreet letter of Tone's, dating from 1791, expressing his sense of the evils of the English connection.[144]

It was a standard FitzGibbon production, yet there was an underlying tone of hesitancy, even of abjection: "I am confident you will forgive me for troubling you upon a Subject on which I had the honour of some Communication with you when I was last at London".[145] The very fact that he felt compelled to pursue the matter suggests that Pitt, either openly or implicitly, had shown dissatisfaction with FitzGibbon's actions and demeanor toward the Catholics. As Pitt's own conduct in 1801 suggests, he remained fundamentally unconvinced by FitzGibbon's arguments.

Possibly as a result of this dissatisfaction, FitzGibbon went through the motions of complying with the hateful relief act. Throughout the summer and early autumn of 1793, he appointed a scattering of Catholic magistrates.[146] In so doing, he earned the cautious praise of the *Dublin Evening Post,* which saw signs of a change of heart in this half-hearted posturing.[147] He also went out of his way to show public cordiality toward safe, reliable Catholics. For example, when young Lord Southwell appeared in the Court of Chancery to take the oaths required by the new act, FitzGibbon "was particular in his politeness and attention to him".[148] After 1793, an unaccustomed nuance appeared in his public remarks on the Catholic issue. He never abandoned his belief in the fundamental incompatibility of Catholic rights and a Protestant state, and his private remarks remained as bloodcurdling as ever.[149] But he avoided portraying the Catholics, without, exception as ferocious, savage bigots, beyond hope or beyond redemption. Instead, he portrayed them as harmless, a-political dolts, perfectly content until the Whigs, the United Irishmen and the atheists, freethinkers and republicans of the Catholic Committee stirred up trouble.[150] The great coronation oath argument was a positive godsend, as it allowed FitzGibbon to elevate resistance to Catholic claims to a question of abstract, immutable law. However slight and minor, these acts of grace and favor suggest an awareness that the open bullying and intimidation he had so freely practiced toward Catholics throughout his career were no longer acceptable to those whose opinion he valued most.

15

The United Irish Challenge, 1791–93

I

The year 1793 brought a cruel abundance of crises, political and economic, to the Westmorland administration. In May 1793, a commercial panic struck the economy. Two of the greatest mercantile concerns and most extensive employers, Comerford and O'Brien and Cope and Binns, stopped payment, with the consequence that "numbers of manufacturers" were "turned out of employment".[1] The prospect of masses of unemployed turned loose in an already politically inflamed capital city inspired a brief display of unity between the government and the opposition. When the Privy Council met to consider the situation, members who habitually opposed the government and rarely attended, to wit, Grattan, Conolly and the Duke of Leinster, showed both their faces and a rare degree of co-operation.[2] The Privy Council report, released on 8 May, called for the release of £200,000 by the Bank of Ireland to restore confidence and to replace currency withdrawn in the initial stages of the crisis.[3] The Bank complied with this suggestion the very next day, and some measure of calm eventually returned.[4]

Westmorland admitted his own uncertainty about the causes of the panic, though he speculated that it originated in cyclical economic stagnation, in the hardships imposed by the embargo, in the uncertainty created by the political agitations of the past year, and in sheer mass panic among businessmen and financiers:

> I cannot pretend to fix on ye precise cause of ye present mischief, whether from unwise speculation, from ye stagnation of credit in England, from ye want of market, from ye embarrassments of ye war ... or from ye general distrust which ye political agitations of ye year threw on all ... dealings, I think but from ye general operation of these different causes.[5]

FitzGibbon inevitably took a major part in compiling and writing the report. He did not display Westmorland's diffidence about assigning causes for the panic. Far more than Westmorland, the report of the Privy Council blamed political agitation in Dublin and in Belfast for the economic panic.[6] FitzGibbon would naturally have favored this conclusion and he would have given it particular emphasis. He never had much of a mind for economic subtleties; above all, he saw the report as yet another way to discredit his enemies on the Catholic Committee and to a lesser extent the Presbyterians in their den of iniquity, Belfast. By deserting their proper sphere, trade, and dabbling in politics, they had plunged the country into economic as well as civil ruin. He repeated this same theory in later parliamentary speeches.[7] It was a charge much favored by Protestant reactionaries. John Foster had made use of it earlier in his own comprehensive and damning speech against the emancipation bill.[8]

II

The year 1793 confronted Westmorland not only with novel economic troubles, but with the accustomed political ones. Elements of the Volunteers continued to combine the practice of arms with the practice of political agitation, particularly in Belfast. As always, Westmorland watched anxiously for any sign of an alliance between radical Volunteers and radical Catholics. Early in November 1792, he entertained the hope, widely entertained by the English government, that sectarian animosity, particularly on the part of northern Presbyterian volunteers, would prevent such a catastrophe:

> By other accounts which I have, these republicans are far from agreed respecting Catholic Emancipation ... I believe more bigoted (pardon ye word) Protestants do not exist and their army is [set?] against ye Papists.[9]

A spy's report submitted on 30 November suggested that on the contrary, some of the newer elements within the Volunteers welcomed both Catholic emancipation and Catholic recruits to their ranks. According to this report, a new corps was forming in Dublin with the exclusive intention of agitating for both emancipation and parliamentary reform. Recruits swore an oath declaring that they would not lay down their arms until both were granted.[10] The new corps' external trappings were as subversive as its political agenda. It took as its model the French National Guard, and its very name, the National Battalion, evoked the citizen army of the revolutionary government. Even the uniforms were an exercise in sartorial provocation. The buttons were embossed with the national symbol of Ireland, but the English crown, which usually surmounted it, was conspicuously, defiantly absent.[11]

In spite of the new unit's blatant radicalism, Westmorland expressed some reservations about proceeding against it. The "old Volunteers", might take offense, not because they favored the aims of the new corps, but because the suppression of one corps might lead to the suppression of all.[12] Nonetheless, five days after receiving the spy's report, Westmorland issued a proclamation forbidding the array of the new Volunteer unit.[13] His dread of an armed, avowedly radical, non-sectarian force, ultimately outweighed his fears about the sensibilities of the "old Volunteers". Since most of them were Protestants, Westmorland hoped that class and sectarian interest would outweigh any lingering *esprit de corps*.

The new corps did not accept its demise passively. After a prudent period of dormancy, small bands attached to the "National Battalion" attempted to parade and drill. The maneuvers consisted mainly of marching to Dublin Bay and firing off rounds of ammunition. After one such incident on 20 January, Westmorland and the Dublin magistrates agreed on a plan to thwart further maneuvers and thus to demonstrate the government's determination. The showdown took place little more than a week later, on 28 January. The Lord Mayor, Alderman Warren, and the chief commissioner of police met a detachment of the National Battalion marching off for a second round of seaside target practice. The battalion did not immediately obey the order to disperse. According to Hobart, who provided an account to the Home Office in London, they deliberated for five hours before choosing compliance over defiance.[14]

This incident gave the final impetus to long-mediated legislative measures to restrain volunteering. In February, the government introduced and carried the so-called gunpowder act, which forbade the private acquisition or internal movement of gunpowder, artillery and other arms and ammunition by private subjects.[15] Henceforth, only the regular army could acquire and transport large quantities of arms and ammunition. The act's effects were obvious. The Volunteers could no longer arm themselves on the massive scale of professional armies. If they choose to appear in array, they could now do so only with sporting guns or pistols, the only weapons which the act allowed to civilians.

The militia bill, introduced into Parliament on 8 March, made even this inferior version of the citizen's army impossible.[16] The concurrent Catholic legislation made it impossible to confine the militia exclusively to Protestants, as had been the intention of the Dublin government as recently as the winter of 1792. Instead, the ranks of the militia were to be filled by all able-bodied men, regardless of religion, chosen from their parishes by lot. Parish priests took on a central role, drawing up and posting lists of all men in their respective parishes who were eligible for militia duty.

FitzGibbon's role in this particular item of legislation was comparatively minor. Lord Hillsborough, a kindred political spirit, took the chief responsibility for framing the bill.[17] As has been noted earlier, FitzGibbon confined himself to an unsuccessful attempt to deny Catholics commissions. He need not have bothered. The choice of officers fell to Protestant gentry, still resentful of Catholic agitation and concessions. With some exceptions, the most startling being John Foster in Louth, most of them took revenge on Keogh and the Catholic Committee for their political success by selecting only Protestant officers.[18]

The legislation passed with comparative unanimity and ease. Even the Whigs welcomed the end of potentially revolutionary citizens' forces.[19] But the new act, which aimed at defusing Volunteer military radicalism, had quite the contrary effect: it ignited a popular uprising unsurpassed in scale and violence. In May, Westmorland, declaring himself "beyond measure mortified", reported to Dundas a growing resistance to militia enrollment. Although he stated, "I shall be very happy if in a day or two I can send ye accounts of this mutinous spirit being subdued", he seemed prepared for the worst. He requested Dundas to "send us what recruits you can".[20] Events confirmed his pessimism. By mid-summer, resistance to militia enrollment had spread throughout Ulster, (particularly Presbyterian Down), Connaught, Munster and even hitherto placid Leinster.[21] Everywhere the riots were characterized by an unprecedented level of violence. Thomas Bartlett has argued that the militia disturbances represented a break with past public disorders. In the past, a "moral economy" had prevailed: in other words, past rioters had usually recognized and respected certain traditional limits when they resorted to violence. This moral economy broke down completely in 1793. Bartlett summarizes his own argument best: "Earlier disturbances had perhaps been characterised by a desire 'to avoid the effusion of blood'; but from 1793 all restraint was abandoned".[22]

Westmorland, his mind as always bearing FitzGibbon's characteristic stamp, was at first inclined to blame the inveterate discontents of the Catholic "old inhabitants".[23] But the rioters were as inclined to terrorize their own. They attacked priests who attempted to comply with the law, and in Westmeath they insulted and harassed "Mr O'Reilly", one of the few Catholics entrusted with a militia commission.[24] Denis Browne, an MP for Mayo, saw a more recent influence than atavistic grievances: the revolutionary philosophy of the United Irishmen, which, he claimed, had spread to the countryside via shopkeepers. These men, Browne claimed, traveled to Dublin to stock their shops and returned, not only with their accustomed merchandise, but with a supply of seditious literature, notably *The Rights of Man.*[25] The rioters do seem to have had some knowledge of the political ferment in the capital. Those who taunted Mr Reilly, for example, told him that they would have done worse by Lord Westmeath had he been present.[26] They apparently resented Westmeath's conduct toward Simon Butler during the latter's trial earlier that year for libeling the Lords Committee of Secrecy. Westmeath had acted with particular malice and vigor against Butler.[27] Others blamed the oppression and arrogance of government rather than the agitation of the United Irishmen or the Catholic Committee. Richard Burke wrote a long letter to this effect to an oblivious Dundas.[28] The nuisance, the poor compensation and the fears of many conscripts that they would be compelled to serve abroad also stirred unrest. The ideas and rhetoric which trickled into the countryside from Dublin gave their local grievances a novel vehicle for expression.

FitzGibbon, not surprisingly, had a great deal to say on the subject. His own county of Limerick saw one of the most violent episodes of the summer, the sack of the town of Ballyorgan by rioters trying to rescue their jailed fellows.[29] Westmorland, as has been observed, was the beneficiary of one of his early theories on the origins of the riots. FitzGibbon later seems to have adopted Denis Browne's notions concerning the ill-effects of seditious literature. In a speech made in July 1793, he made something of the same claim, though he blamed, not shopkeepers, but evil minded urban incendiaries, who ventured into the countryside and left seditious pamphlets and handbills to poison the minds of the peasantry.[30] FitzGibbon in turn received his share of blame for the outbreaks of violence. An anonymous correspondent of Richard

Burke's, possibly a Limerick Catholic with scores of his own to settle, attributed the riots in the main to FitzGibbon's tyranny : "... I can't think the country will every be quiet while the Chancellor retains the power and weight he has at present."[31]

The riots eventually abated toward the end of the summer, though FitzGibbon's rhetorical exertions had nothing to do with the restoration of peace. Some hasty ameliorative legislation, assurances that the militia would serve strictly as a home force, and above all, the relentless application of force by the regular army suppressed the rioters. The riots suggested to a terrified government the terrifying ease with which order and authority could break down in Ireland. They became all the more determined to eliminate perceived threats to both.

III

In government reports and in the government imagination, the United Irishmen appeared as the first cause of all the unrest and all the rebellion besetting the country. At their instigation, Defenders stole arms and met by night, Catholics abandoned their counting houses for republican politics, and the Volunteers got notions of armed revolution. Their skill at writing and disseminating seditious literature assumed heroic and fearful proportions in the minds of FitzGibbon, among many others.

Their actions in late 1792 and in 1793 certainly befitted a radical organization bent on agitation and confrontation. In January 1793, William Drennan proposed a plan of Parliamentary reform which drastically extended the franchise and which barely acknowledged any role at all for English authority or administration. Drennan merely stated that under his revamped plan of government, "All matters and things relating to the well governing of this kingdom which are properly cognizable in the Privy Council, shall be signed as such as advise and consent to the same."[32] He never defined which matters were "properly cognizable", but they were probably few and insignificant. Their practical tactics were on a par with their theories. They proposed a convention on the late Catholic model to cast their proposals into legislative form and to petition for their adoption.[33] In addition to anticipating a better government to come, the United Irishmen kept up their attacks on the bad one currently in place. During the fiscal crisis of May 1793, Hamilton Rowan allegedly printed a distributed a broadside blaming the loss of work and money on the British war with France.[34] The implication was that Ireland should declare a separate peace, and free herself from British diplomatic as well as economic tyranny. Yet the government refrained from taking direct measures against the United Irishmen. It chose to rely instead on indirect intimidation and on indirect legislation.

Belfast, the capital city of United Irish sedition, became the chief object of baleful official attention. The Lords' Committee Report made as many dishonorable mentions of Belfast and of the United Irishmen as it did of Dublin and its committee of Defender-inciting Catholic businessmen. The report alluded to the menacing behavior of the Northern volunteers and of their chaplains. Prayers, the report alleged, "have been offered up at Belfast, from the Pulpit for the success of [French] arms, in the presence of Military Associations which have been newly levied and arrayed in that Town".[35] The pulpits were obviously Presbyterian, the mother-church of all republicanism and disaffection.

Matters escalated, notwithstanding the public denunciations of the House of Lords. In March an altercation broke out between some citizens of Belfast and a detachment of soldiers who took it upon themselves to deface public portraits of Benjamin Franklin, General Dumouriez and other French and American revolutionary heroes. In spite of indignant complaints about military brutality and the arbitrary destruction of property, the government chose not to inquire too closely into the matter. They took the word of the duty officer that his soldiers, while perhaps somewhat excessive in their measures, were high-spirited loyal lads driven by a sense of indignation at such blatant sedition.[36] On a small scale, the government was already resorting to "vigor beyond the law." Along with private encouragement of military force, Westmorland and the council issued a proclamation which repeated, frequently word for word, the various charges against Belfast in the Lords' Committee, and which called upon the citizens "to abstain" from distributing and reading seditious literature, drilling "by day and night", etc. Hobart even went so far as to suggest playing off the proverbial Northern passion for gain against Northern habits of sedition:

> [The] violent spirit of the North might be somewhat compos'd by a hint from any of their London Correspondents that the agitation of the North must necessarily affect their credit [and?] ultimately be highly injurious to their Linen Manufacture.[37]

Finally, legislation against the Catholics could serve a double purpose. The convention act thwarted potentially conventioneering Presbyterian and United Irish reformers as well as further Catholic Back Lane parliaments.

FitzGibbon certainly would have given his approval to extraordinary military vigor applied to the citizens of Belfast. Through the Secret Committee Report and the Convention Act, he could openly display his antagonism for United Irishmen and especially Northern, Presbyterian United Irishmen. FitzGibbon's nature being what it was, his political antagonism also found expression in personal vendettas against individual United Irishmen.

His pursuit of Wolfe Tone continued. Having made a private denunciation of him to Pitt in May, he proceeded to make a public one in open Parliament in July. During the debates on the Convention bill on 10 July, he brandished a private letter written by "a gentleman who wears a bar gown, one of the leading members of the worthy Society of United Irishmen".[38] The gentleman wearing the bar gown was none other than Tone; the letter in question was the same that FitzGibbon had copied and sent to Pitt as proof of Tone's early inclinations toward rebellion, republicanism, and separation from England. FitzGibbon completed the identification by alluding to the £1,000 awarded to Tone by the Catholic Convention, and he implied that Tone, in company with like-minded associates, already had plans to overthrow the government:

> I have not a doubt that the moment the allied armies retreated last year from France, a serious design was entertained to rebel against Great Britain and to from a republic connected with France.[39]

Using the sympathetic pages of the *Dublin Evening Post*, Tone angrily refuted the claims made in FitzGibbon's Catilinarian oration.[40] His readership in the *Dublin Evening Post* probably believed his claim that he was the innocent victim of ministerial malice, but FitzGibbon remained unconvinced and undeterred. Within that week he had proceeded to other game, in the persons of the Sheares brothers, John and Henry.[41]

On 18 July, less than a week after dispatching Wolfe Tone, he denounced the Sheares brothers as Jacobin agents:

> There were in this city two persons who were members of the French Jacobin Club, and who, his Lordship believed, were in the pay of that society, to foment sedition.[42]

While FitzGibbon did not mention either brother by name, he gave broad hints of their identity to his auditors in the House: "One of their names appeared at the head of a printed paper published last month by the United Irishmen, to which society they also belonged."[43]

Henry Sheares lost no time in making a refutation and a denunciation of his own. Rather than limit himself to the columns of a newspaper, as had Wolfe Tone, he chose a more inflammatory and efficient means of agitation, a handbill. In it, he denied that he or his brother were Jacobins or in the pay of the French Jacobin Club. He also divulged that he had written a private letter to FitzGibbon, calling on him to retract the claims he had made in the House of Lords. When he received no reply, he deemed it "a duty I owe to myself, to the Society to which I belong and to the Public in general, to lay the circumstances of this transaction before the nation".[44] In fact, the Sheares brothers were enthusiastically Jacobin in their sympathies, whatever their formal relations with the club itself. Daniel O'Connell, then a schoolboy refugee, supposedly witnessed a gruesome manifestation of their true political views. He claimed that while making the cross-Channel voyage with the two brothers, he saw them exultantly displaying a handkerchief dipped in the blood of the King of France.[45] Nothing further came of FitzGibbon's own encounter with the Sheares brothers. It seems to have ended as so many of FitzGibbon's quarrels did, in undignified anti-climax.

FitzGibbon ran into more serious trouble when he took on Simon Butler. Butler, a younger son of Lord Mountgarret and a barrister, was articulate, ambitious and above all, well-born. The advocates of brotherhood and political equality were not immune to the feverish snobbery of 18th-century Ireland, or to the glamour of the Butler *nomen*. Drawing on his training as a barrister, Butler had compiled the so-called *Digest of the Popery Laws*, a comprehensive list of all laws against Catholics still in effect in 1792. His work, which became something of a bestseller, revealed the number and the petty, galling nature of the laws in force.

His later exercises in propaganda received a somewhat less favorable reception. With the collaboration of Oliver Bond, Butler drew up and published a denunciation of the Committee of Secrecy. Their pamphlet questioned the right of the Committee to summon witnesses at all, and criticized its "inquisitorial" methods of interrogation.[46] The Committee naturally would have attracted the propagandistic ire of the United Irishmen. John Sweetman, who was both a prominent member of the Catholic Committee and an early initiate into the brotherhood, had, after all, suffered the humiliating public exposure of his private correspondence. As inevitably, the House of Lords retaliated against Butler and Bond for the attack on its authority and dignity.

FitzGibbon, the prime mover of the Secret Committee, was certainly the prime mover of this action as well. During the trial itself, he showed something like moderation. FitzGibbon originally proposed a fine of £50 and a term of three months in Newgate prison.[47] His colleagues on the secret committee demanded a more draconian penalty of £500 and a prison term of six months. Their view and their sentence prevailed. Although he tried to moderate his colleagues' zeal in the matter of assigning a penalty, he gave free rein to his own habits of rhetorical excess when pronouncing sentence. Largely ignoring Bond, he gave Butler a brisk dressing-down before the assembled peers:

> "you, Simon Butler, cannot plead ignorance in extenuation, your noble birth, your education and the honorable profession to which you belong, his Majesty's gown which you wear and to which you now stand as a disgrace, gave you the advantages of knowledge and are strong circumstances of aggravation of your guilt."[48]

This particular speech was perfectly in keeping with FitzGibbon's past rhetorical traditions and with his most deeply rooted political prejudices. Nothing infuriated him more than members of the Protestant elite who deserted their own interests in favour of popularity, or worse in favour of visionary political schemes. Butler was another, more dangerous, specimen of the aristocratic irresponsibility that created the Regency crisis and the Whig Club.

If FitzGibbon had hoped to instill in Simon Butler a salutary sense of caution and shame, he badly underestimated his antagonist. However radical his political opinions, Butler fully retained his aristocratic pride and his aristocratic habits. Eschewing the journalistic weapons of his middle-class colleagues, Tone and Sheares, he chose to avenge his honour by challenging FitzGibbon. Of course, he could not act on his resolution immediately. His imprisonment caused an unavoidable delay. FitzGibbon's absence from Dublin through the early part of autumn further thwarted Butler from issuing a challenge. Finally, on 4 October, FitzGibbon returned to Dublin to be with his wife, who was in the final stages of pregnancy. One week later, perhaps delaying out of polite respect for the happy event in the Lord Chancellor's household, Butler took the first step to defend his honor:

> My Lord, Having a matter to communicate to your Lordship through the medium of a third person, I request to know whether a Gentleman on my behalf may have the honour of a private interview with your Lordship.[49]

FitzGibbon fully understood the meaning of the letter and responded in the same spirit:

> Sir, If you have any matter to communicate to me, and chuse that the communication shall be made through the medium of a third person, I will see any Gentleman whom you may send to me tomorrow at twelve o'clock.[50]

Hamilton Rowan, the man designated by Butler as his second, duly turned up at No. 6 Ely Place. There, Hamilton Rowan presented his friend's grievances:

> My friend Mr Butler has been the occasion of my waiting on your Lordship. It is in your Lordship's recollection that Mr Butler, having been sentenced to imprisonment and fine by the House of Lords, your Lordship, in pronouncing the sentence of the House, made use of expressions toward him which must have been very offensive to the feelings of any gentleman. Mr Butler conceives that in using such expressions, you were not delivering the sense of the House, but making a spontaneous attack upon him.[51]

FitzGibbon's response showed no trace either of trepidation or of regret. On the contrary, he admitted to everything and apologized for nothing:

> Mr Hamilton, when I passed sentence on Mr.Butler and Mr Oliver Bond, I did not more than, as Chancellor, I felt to be my duty. I made use of the words "that he could not plead ignorance, that his noble birth and profession, to which he was a disgrace, had aggravated the crime."[52]

The remaining dialogue of this little black comedy offered variants on this initial exchange. Hamilton Rowan, the soul of garrulous politeness, pleaded the insult and injury to Simon Butler. FitzGibbon, terse, grim and obdurate, maintained the justice of his comments. Indeed, he declared that were the "matter to be done again", he would speak and act the same, though he did add the slight qualifier "perhaps". The interview ended with FitzGibbon telling Rowan that he and Butler could do as they pleased, and abide the consequences: "As to what you are to do, that remains with yourself to determine, you know best, you know my situation."[53]

While not overly bright, Rowan did not need any more hints that FitzGibbon was not about to treat the challenge as a private gentleman. If Butler persisted, he intended to retaliate as Lord Chancellor and subject his late United Irishman antagonist to further legal penalties for threatening the King's peace as well as the King's servant and conscience in the person of FitzGibbon. Rowan, in turn, pleaded with Butler to drop the matter; Butler, who was as intelligent as he was spirited, yielded to persuasion.[54] Clearly, he was not to have the satisfaction of taking pot-shots of gentlemanly outrage at FitzGibbon, and having recently emerged from prison, he was not anxious to return. FitzGibbon had no further encounters with Butler. Debts, as well as political harassment compelled Butler to retire to Edinburgh, where he died in 1797.

Madden and other nationalist historians have made it an article of faith that the United Irishmen were pure-hearted, pure-minded reformers who were driven into rebellion by the harassment and brutality of FitzGibbon and his coterie of reactionaries and captive viceroys. Outside the realm of myth, it is difficult to sort out precisely when the United Irishmen adopted the course of armed revolution, though such a change probably took place sooner than their hagiographers preferred to believe. But there were never any doubts in FitzGibbon's mind; he believed from the start that the ends of the United Irishmen were to subvert the Protestant establishment in Church and State and to break the connection with England. And indeed, given FitzGibbon's peculiar mentality and his past political habits, he could have reacted to the United Irishmen in no other way. Acutely sensitive to the inherent instability of the government in Ireland, he dreaded change and agitation in any form whatever Volunteer plans for parliamentary reform or Whig notions of parliamentary independence. The avowed United Irish political program, however laudable, could only have inspired dread, loathing and legal retaliation from FitzGibbon. As he so clearly saw, English rule depended on economic subservience, on sectarian exclusivity, and on a small, much bribed and pampered, political elite. The United Irishmen from their inception avowed their opposition to these keystones of English rule. In FitzGibbon's mind, they were revolutionary in intention regardless of when they became so in fact: hence the harassment and intimidation of individual United Irishmen; hence the tireless efforts to link the United Irishmen with treason, with republicanism, with intrigues with France.

IV

The Jackson affair offered FitzGibbon and his government a perfect opportunity to give weight to their claims about the United Irishmen. Jackson was an English clergyman who succumbed to the new revolutionary faith of *liberté, egalité and fraternité*. During a sojourn in France, he had evidently made some contacts with the French government, and had agreed to report on the degree of revolutionary potential in England and in Ireland. Unfortunately, Jackson's discretion did not equal his enthusiasm. After some desultory travels in England, he was en route to Ireland when he fell in with one George Cockayne, an attorney. Jackson favored his traveling companion with a full account of his mission. He made a serious error in his choice of confidantes. Cockayne informed the Home Office, and received instructions to remain with Jackson, with the purpose of reporting on his actions and his contacts in Ireland. Unaware that he now was traveling in company with a government spy, Jackson arrived in Dublin. There he encountered Hamilton Rowan and Wolfe Tone. After his adventure with FitzGibbon and Simon Butler, Rowan had ended up in prison for printing and distributing seditious writings. Undeterred by his present circumstances, he freely confided to Jackson the promising state of discontent and rebellion in Ireland. Tone, equally undeterred by his experience with FitzGibbon, favored Jackson with a memorandum which essentially paraphrased the letter which had received so much exposure the previous summer. Jackson, of course enthusiastically introduced his charming and informative Irish acquaintances to Cockayne, and repeated their comments, written and spoken, on the potentially revolutionary state of Ireland. Cockayne, in turn reported everything to the English government, which promptly passed the information on to Dublin Castle.[55]

By May 1794, the Irish government felt confident enough about the weight of evidence against Jackson to arrest him. He was formally arraigned on a charge of treason on 23 May, but the trial was put off until November. The end of the legal term was fast approaching, leaving little time for the procedures required to plead the indictment and to summon witnesses (to wit Cockayne, who had scuttled back to England.)[56] During the hiatus the government faced some nerve-wracking difficulties in preparing its case, mainly because Cockayne, out of fear or out of shame at the unsavory role of star witness and informant, started having convenient lapses of memory. In the case of Tone, for example, he claimed that he could not give "positive testimony" about his conduct. He had, or so he claimed, "only caught the substance [of Tone's conversations with Jackson] by Hints and accidental words".[57] In June, Cockayne, claiming that his memory needed refreshing, asked to see copies of the letters he had sent to Pitt. Jackson's lawyers quickly seized on Cockayne's unpromising character as a witness. Sylvester Douglas, who succeeded Hobart as Westmorland's chief secretary, reported that there were "attempts making to get at facts, which if not anticipated and explained might tend to discredit the characters of the principal witnesses against Jackson".[58] A conviction for perjury in Cockayne's past was presumably one of these facts which required anticipation and explanation.[59] Nonetheless, Cockayne, however seedy and uncooperative, was the linchpin of the government's case against Jackson. They helpfully provided him with copies of his past correspondence and they defended his character as best they could. Westmorland described the position of the government with his blend of muddy prose and occasional flashes of shrewdness: "... with how bad an appearance of evidence, we should go into court, not a Person in Court but would attribute ye whole scheme to a snare and ye government would be sadly disgraced."[60]

The conduct of the principal defendants helped relieve the government of some embarrassment. Their conduct gave a very strong appearance of guilt. Rowan escaped from prison and fled first to France, and then to a discontented exile in the United States. Tone agreed to divulge his own role in the affair, in return for immunity and exile. As for Jackson, committed suicide shortly after the commencement of his trial in January 1795. The rumor persisted that his wife had brought poison to him, allowing him to evade conviction and a more public death. Mrs Jackson herself seems to have suffered no repercussions.[61]

FitzGibbon had dealings with other subordinate players in the affair. Throughout he seems to have displayed considerable moderation. The Rowans, husband and wife, in particular benefited. He took on the role of legal and financial advisor to Mrs Hamilton Rowan, especially in the matter of mitigating her husband's legal status. The lady was a persistent, and sometimes rather pesky, supplicant. Some years later, FitzGibbon, good-naturedly, if rather wearily, referred to her as "my almost daily oratrix".[62] She even made a descent on FitzGibbon at Mount Shannon, with no other apparent purpose but to keep up the pressure on him.[63] FitzGibbon's mass of responsibilities, legal and political, as well as the pressure of events, apparently delayed action on the matter for some years. Only in 1799 did he manage to draft an appeal on Rowan's behalf, not for a full pardon, but for some mitigation of his exile. Rowan found the realities of republican life in the United States appallingly dull and coarse, accustomed as he was to the aristocratic pleasures of Dublin. He begged to be allowed to return, if not to Ireland, then to some country in Europe, where he would have better access to civilization and to his family. FitzGibbon could see "no objection to allowing [Rowan] to quit America" and he agreed to provide assurances to Rowan "that if he should be intercepted by a British cruizer [*sic*] on his passage that he shall not be brought home and hanged".[64] FitzGibbon explained his own kindness to the Rowans, husband and wife, with the observation that Rowan "certainly has some merit in not being so abandoned as some of his colleagues".[65]

He was similarly moderate toward his antagonist Tone. Family pressure helped somewhat in his case. Tone was friendly with Marcus Beresford, a younger son of John the commissioner of revenue, and by all accounts a pleasant young man. Beresford wrote a letter to FitzGibbon pleading on his friend's behalf.[66] Acting largely on young Beresford's suggestion, FitzGibbon and Westmorland framed an agreement with Tone, whereby he could go into exile in return for disclosing all the details of his involvement with Jackson.[67] There wasn't much to tell, as FitzGibbon himself appears to have recognized. Westmorland, no doubt after consultation with FitzGibbon, reported that the Crown had only a slight case against Tone.[68] Through the arrangement of a confession in return for exile, they could get rid of an able malcontent, without an inconclusive or dubious trial.

FitzGibbon's conduct toward Rowan and Tone set the tone for his later treatment of United Irish prisoners. Except in very blatant cases of treason, he generally preferred to bargain for information rather than enforce the full penalty of the law. A cynical sense of the grudge-creating power of Irish history, rather than any overflowing kindheartedness, may have accounted for his habits of moderation. He preferred to send would-be revolutionaries into penurious and discredited exile, rather than add them to the long list of national saints and martyrs.

Shortly after the arrest and indictment of Jackson, the government finally took measures to "disperse" the society of United Irishmen and to seize their papers. It was a comparatively easy business to accomplish. The government's long-time informant Collins provided public testimony to the aldermen, which allowed the government to frame a warrant. Collins was suitably pensioned off, and the government retreated into comparative unconcern.[69] Another government informant, however, reported that the Sheares brothers were continuing to play host to meetings of the United Irishmen. At one such gathering in July, they allegedly entertained members of the hard-pressed Scottish societies.[70]

16

The Fitzwilliam Business

I

In spite of the turmoil aroused by Catholics, Defenders, United Irishmen, and rioting militia protesters, the government had not lost sight of those more established agitators, the Whig opposition. They dreaded the potential for trouble from the Whigs and from the Shannon interest, temporarily in "exile" because of Lord Shannon's stand on the regency question. The government especially dreaded the Whig/Shannon reaction to the Catholic relief bill, and especially the possibility that the Whigs would court the high Protestant party by adopting a staunchly anti-Catholic posture. While the Duke of Leinster had expressed his favorable sentiments early on, the other factions within the party, such as the Ponsonbys, were notoriously anti-Catholic.[1] During the deliberations of the Whig Club in 1791, the Ponsonbys had opposed a measure introduced by Napper Tandy, calling for the equality of all Irishmen.[2] In addition, the government was concerned for an impending bill on East Indian trade, which in return for a greater measure of Irish participation in Indian trade, confirmed the monopoly of the East India Company. Trade contention had always been a Whig specialty.[3]

To the administration's relief, the Ponsonbys chose to throw their support behind the relief bill, although Lord Shannon remained a true blue die-hard.[4] The curious action of Thomas Conolly suggests the reason for the sudden and startling change of heart on the part of many hitherto indifferent or antagonistic Whigs. Conolly voted against the bill, not because it gave concessions to the Catholics, but because it did not give *enough* concessions. He also expressed his hope that the Catholics would join in the movement for Parliamentary reform.[5] It was clear from his remarks that the Whigs, having suffered an eclipse as popular champions by the United Irishmen and other radical competition, had belatedly joined the race for the Catholic. As the Volunteers and the United Irishmen had long since learned, Catholic numbers could give a new lease on life to otherwise oft-defeated causes, such as parliamentary reform.

George Ponsonby more explicitly articulated the hope of the Whigs that by outdoing government concessions, they could dissolve any Catholic loyalties to government and win them over to the opposition. As Hobart reported to Nepean:

> The great point made by opposition, Mr George Ponsonby particularly, was to impute a change of sentiment in the Irish Parliament to what he termed base English influence and recommending the adoption of the Catholics into the constitution as a means of strengthening Ireland and weakening the influence of Great Britain.[6]

Hobart expressed hope that the Whigs would receive their just deserts for such shameless political opportunism:

> I am happy to say that the force of it was much diminished by the conviction that no man in the country was more averse to the Catholics than the gentleman who press'd the House to grant everything to them, and that his conduct upon the most interesting question that could rise in the country was solely directed by resentment against the government. He will not easily be forgiven by the Protestants and he will certainly be despised by the Catholics.

At the same time, Edward Cooke suggested that had there been enough high Protestant feeling on the subject, Ponsonby would have been willing to revert to the more traditional stance of his family.[7]

Nonetheless, the government could not afford entirely to despise the Whigs. They could still contribute their troublesome share to the general atmosphere of agitation, particularly on issues of trade and the conduct of the war against France. The Westmorland government wanted above all to eliminate the whole *raison d'être* for opposition, and to unite all parties in parliament against the French revolutionary government and against aspiring revolutionists in Ireland. The government particularly hoped to eliminate perpetual Whig troublemaking over "corruption", a term which covered a multitude of sins from the disbursement of pensions and places to the presence of officeholders and other government beneficiaries in parliament.

Throughout the 1780s, the opposition had seized on the venerable issue of corruption to harass the government and to aggrandize itself. In 1786, Forbes introduced another bill to disqualify placemen from sitting in parliament. The arguments fell into the usual pattern: The opposition maintained that the presence of government officers and pension holders in Parliament compromised its independence and created a despotism of greed. Those who stood to lose their seats, in response, indignantly defended their integrity and made counter-accusations of partisan vindictiveness and envy. In addition, the bill arbitrarily deprived them of their rights as subjects and as qualified men of property without due course of law. FitzGibbon remained true to form. With his usual deftness and an unusual wit, he suggested that the proponents of the bill would not display quite the same scorn of official lucre, were they in a position to receive it.[9]

The outcome followed Irish political tradition on these matters as well: Forbes' bill met with defeat. The government's superior powers of the purse always permitted it to maintain a majority of its beneficiaries in Parliament. Habits of inertia and reaction did the rest. Nonetheless, the introduction of bill to unseat placemen and to limit pensions became and annual exercise for the opposition.[10] The attempts to raise this issue in 1789 already have received attention.

In the winter of 1793, the government announced its intention to introduce a series of bills intended to placate the various critics of corruption, whether genuinely idealistic, like Forbes or chronically disappointed, like the Ponsonbys. In June 1793, Parnell brought forward the long-awaited result.[11] His responsibility bill suspended the hereditary revenue, and established a civil list, which encompassed the customs and barracks offices. The moneys for maintaining the civil list, to the sum of £269,000, were to accrue after payments were made on the national debt. In addition, the bill abolished the treasurer and vice treasurerships; instead the bill placed the Treasury under the authority of a Board of Commissioners. The Commissioners were to issue money only for the expenses of the civil list or for other purposes stipulated by Parliament, upon presentation of a royal warrant. A second bill limited expenditure on pensions, while a third prohibited some office-holders from sitting in Parliament, though revenue officers, the chief bugbears of the opposition, remained firmly eligible.[12]

The bills passed handily, though habits of opposition died hard. There were quibbles about the allegedly excessive sums of money allowed for pensions. Forbes, who had long made government expense and responsibility his pet issues, took the lead. He wanted some offices, notably, those attached to the customs, removed from the civil list and placed under direct parliamentary review, where their expenses could be further reduced, if need be. He also wanted the sum allotted for the concordatum reduced from £10,000 to £5,000. Hobart resisted Forbes' first proposal, but agreed to the second, to create unanimity and to preclude any further troublemaking on this issue.[13]

The prospect of obtaining their heart's desire made the Whigs happily compliant when the much dreaded East India bill came up for parliamentary review, shortly before the final readings of the place, responsibility and pension bills. After much negotiation, the Irish government had managed to secure provisions for an East India warehouse in Cork, and for twice yearly calls by ships bound for India. In return, the bill confirmed the monopoly of the East India company.[14] Westmorland reported with evident relief that the bill passed through committee "unanimously and with a Degree of Chearfulness and Liberality which I must say does very great honour to the House of Commons".[15] Although the government officially insisted that no thoughts of a *quid pro quo* had influenced this action, the liberalization of the navigation acts by the English parliament in the prior session considerably sweetened tempers.[16] Westmorland also observed the lack of opposition on the part of the "Mercantile Interest", which further reduced any incentive to parliamentary grandstanding on the issue.[17]

Probably most gratifying in the government's eyes was the reaction of Grattan, who had long made opposition to various pieces of trade legislation a staple. With his unerring instinct for the dramatic and the erratic, he not only supported the East

India bill, he called for a revival of the once detested commercial propositions of 1785. He cited the adjustment of the navigation act, the proposed establishment of the Irish civil list and the current settlement of East Indian trade as the reasons for his amazing change of heart. He "also pointed out that under Eden's treaty of 1787, French goods enjoyed more favorable terms than Irish in the English market.[18] His reasoning was rather curious, as trade with France was virtually at a standstill. But the Irish government had no desire to quibble with Grattan's faulty logic on the subject. Although they rejected his request to combine adoption of the East India bill with a consideration of new propositions, they were delighted that Grattan had raised the subject. As Hobart stated the matter, the Whigs handed the government a perfect opportunity to settle long-standing trade disputes. He predicted that the government would enjoy any "credit and popularity" ensuing from a commercial settlement, while Grattan and the Whigs "must be answerable for that part of the unpopularity which might attend it".[19] The attending unpopularity presumably would come from "the friends of protecting duties," and according to Hobart's reasoning, the Whigs would suffer the more because they had hitherto raised so much opposition.[20]

The opening months of 1794 saw an unprecedented outpouring of mutual admiration on both sides. In February of that year, Edward Cooke reported to Evan Nepean that Shannon and Grattan had been reconciled to the government. Only a small and disreputable rump remained: Curran, Duquerry, Egan and Parsons, whom Cooke described as "the disciple of Flood's with much of his policy and little of his ability." He also alluded to the long standing antagonism between Parsons and Grattan.[21] Grattan's old dislike for Parsons and his new support for government became apparent during debates on the war with France. During the course of the debate, Parsons called for a review of all past treaties of the English government with foreign powers. According to Cooke, he intended first to assert some sort of equal partnership for Ireland in foreign policy and secondly "to make Grattan unpopular".[22] Not surprisingly Grattan took the lead in opposing this motion. According to another dispatch, this time from Sylvester Douglas, he spoke "with great power", no doubt the power of anger and dislike, against this particular proposal.

> He [Grattan] called it an artificial motion, which under pretence of calling for papers solicited the Discussion of the propriety of the war.[23]

He then reminded Parsons of "that principle which had been unanimously approved by the House on the first day of the session, viz: that this Kingdom would stand or fall with Great Britain".[24] In short, he reminded Parsons that if he truly had doubts about the war, he had missed his opportunity to speak, and he must now hold his peace, if not forever, at least until the next session.

Edward Cooke hoped that with careful management and flattery from Pitt himself, Grattan could add his luster of mass popularity to the government:

> What should be made of this conjunction? My first opinion is that Grattan is

> the most important character in Ireland and that attaching him to Mr Pitt's government would be essential. This is difficult. He is very high minded and resentful and suspicious. He is however very steady and honourable and will act up to his professions. He has great sway over the public mind and he must play such a part as not to lose his authority. He wants not, perhaps wants not to take, Situation: he would stipulate for measures if any compliment were shown to him, he would take it immediately from Mr Pitt. In the uncertainty of events, his conduct here might be decisive and therefore he should be early thought of. Government is strong in numbers. They want not aristocratical addition. They want the chief of the people.[25]

All was not sunshine and happiness. Grattan continued to pursue the issue of new commercial propositions, much against the wishes of government, which wanted above all to avoid major items of legislation, even those which might be of benefit.[26] Forbes continued to call for further reductions in government expense, for the disenfranchisement of more placeholders and for greater parliamentary control over certain offices.[27] Lord Shannon, in spite of the court paid to him, and in spite of his new place as a treasury commissioner, remained resentful over Catholic emancipation. In a letter to Westmorland, written in December 1793, Shannon made this sulky rejoinder to a request for his opinion on the militia: "... indeed, before I can be prepared to give an answer to any question from Government, I should, with all due respect, first, by permission to ask what support are the Protestants of Ireland to expect from Administration after the experience of the last session of Parliament?"[28]

In spite of desertions by their old regency crisis associates, the Ponsonbys continued to make trouble. During the debates on Parsons' motion, George Ponsonby made the startling declaration that Ireland existed in a "federal" union with Great Britain, and therefore had an independent right to examine any treaties of alliance with foreign powers. He did not try to carry his unusual constitutional theories into effect, preferring instead to support Grattan.[29] He also dragged in a bill for parliamentary reform, which government wielded its majority to postpone until 1 August.[30] Finally, Ponsonby applied for leave to act as Jackson's counsel, which, as king's counsel he was required to do before he could represent an accused traitor.[31] By choosing to oppose the government in an inflammatory political trial, Ponsonby certainly continued his habits of provocation. In accounting for Ponsonby's erratic behavior during the debates over treaties, Cooke displayed again his astuteness and his mordant wit:

> It must be remembered that winds having been averse, he had not at that Time received the ultimate decision of the Duke of Portland and his connections in England.[32]

At the time, Cooke was merely poking cynical fun at George Ponsonby's political tergiversations. Unwittingly, he also pinpointed the fatal flaw that would destroy any hope of a rapprochement between the government and the Whig opposition.

FitzGibbon's own relations with the Whigs underwent similar fluctuations during the period between 1792–4. By 1792, he appears to have been on friendly dining and visiting terms with the Duke of Leinster, George Ponsonby and their respective relations. Relations with George Ponsonby soured during the session of 1792, when Ponsonby revealed FitzGibbon's efforts to detach him from the Round Robin. FitzGibbon was understandably "much incensed" over this public revelation of private negotiations. Westmorland could see some benefits accruing from FitzGibbon's mortification: "... it [Ponsonby's speech] will have the good effect of breaking up an appearance of friendship between him and the Ponsonbys which created great jealousy to many people."[33] But in March 1793, FitzGibbon transcended his usual vindictiveness and made personal overtures, not only to the Ponsonbys, but to the long-alienated Grattan. No doubt he felt that in the current crisis of authority, all Protestants, whatever their past differences, should join in resisting any further change and in restoring order. According to Westmorland, "Grattan wd. not meet with ye chancellor".[34] He would not relinquish either his grudge against FitzGibbon, or his fervor for Catholic relief. George Ponsonby's later conduct shows that FitzGibbon was equally unsuccessful in any appeals he may have made to his erstwhile dinner party intimate.

In his turn, FitzGibbon seems to have relapsed into profound cynicism about the possibility of ever placating the Whigs. His memoranda on the place and responsibility bills perhaps reflected this disenchantment. He criticized the pension bill for encroaching on the King's prerogative to grant pensions, while the clumsy drafting of the responsibility bill affronted his professional fastidiousness.[35] The bill, he complained, arbitrarily set up a civil list while failing to disavow past laws which had granted the king hereditary revenues. He also insisted on a very narrow interpretation of the powers of the new treasurers. They could not refuse any request for payment made under royal warrant, FitzGibbon insisted, unless the king's government attempted to withdraw money "in any manner not strictly warranted by law". Moreover, the commissioners of the treasury had no authority over the lord-lieutenant, who could demand any sum of money necessary to carry out the duties of his office.[36] His comments were of a piece with his passion for legal precision and his equal passion for inviolate precedent. But it is doubtful he would have liked any responsibility or pension bill, however impeccably framed. He probably looked upon these bills as he did on the Catholic bill; they were ill-advised gestures of appeasement which could only increase rather than silence unrest.

II

An event that seemed to apotheosize the end of Whig-government discords instead revived them. In 1794, that branch of the English Whigs under the direction of the Duke of Portland broke with Charles James Fox over the latter's continued opposition to the war with France. The defection of such a substantial part of the opposition party was nonetheless a mixed blessing. On one hand, it had the obvious benefit of bringing votes and electoral interests to Pitt's government. On the other hand, Pitt had to make some provision for the influx of ex-Whigs. In particular the Portland faction had their sights set on Ireland: specifically, Portland wanted Ireland for his nephew, Lord Fitzwilliam. His grace was still smarting over his ignominious departure from that country over a decade before; he had moreover, close familial and political ties with members of the Irish opposition, especially with the *gens* Ponsonby, who never could get over their sense that the management of Ireland rightly belonged to them. The mutual sense of resentment and lost opportunity following the Regency debacle had further strengthened ties between the English and Irish oppositions. In short, to strengthen the stability of the new coalition in England, Pitt was faced with the unpleasant prospect of handing Ireland over to the very people who had inveterately opposed his past men and measures in that country.

Nor had Portland been innocently dormant since 1789. On the contrary, as recently as 1792, he had been fishing in the muddy waters of Irish politics. The Catholic Committee, in the person of Edward Byrne, had made some overtures to Portland. Evidently Byrne and his fellow committeemen, like Westmorland, had feared the possibility of the Whigs playing the Protestant card. Nothing seems to have come of these negotiations. Byrne gave Portland a highly selective list of Catholic demands. Some, such as the right to serve as magistrates and as jurors, later appeared on the Catholic petition; others, such as a request for publicly funded seminaries, never appeared; yet others, notably the franchise, Edward Byrne tactfully avoided mentioning at all. His prudence was well justified. Portland remained tepidly favorable at best to the demands Byrne did see fit to mention: they seemed to him "reasonably salutary and beneficial". Nonetheless, he emphatically opposed permitting Catholics to vote. In Portland's view the franchise could only "create more than alleviate" discontent.[37] There do not seem to have been any further contacts, *sub rosa* or otherwise, between the Catholic Committee and the Whigs, English or Irish. Although Portland expressed his intention to communicate his thoughts to George Ponsonby, his cautious views on Catholic emancipation, fundamentally no different from Westmorland's, obviously had no influence on his Irish kinsman and colleague. Nonetheless, these contacts with Irish parties, however fleeting, showed a disturbing habit of mind among the Whigs on both sides of the water. They saw themselves as a shadow government, waiting only for the proper moment to come into their own.

Westmorland certainly took this view of the Portland Whigs. As soon as he got wind of the coalition and the ensuing negotiations for office, he bombarded Pitt with epistolary warnings about the danger of giving the government of Ireland to a family and to a party so closely connected to the Irish opposition and so prone to past intrigue. Such a move could only revive partisan wrangling just when it seemed on the wane:

> If ye expectation of his [Fitzwilliam] coming is held out at all, ye mischief to your government is evident and from ye different expectations, this kingdom will be in a most uncertain and dangerous state. No man will dare oppose himself to ye vengeance of ye dictators of that party, the Ponsonbys, or attend to ye injunctions of an imagined expiring government. Catholics, reformers ... every Politician will mount his hobby ... how cd you admit such people to your councils without security for their good behavior?[38]

More letters to the same effect followed, throughout the summer and autumn of 1794. In July, Westmorland requested Pitt not to allow Portland to receive any communication on Irish matters, except official dispatches.[39] In October, Pitt received this reproach and this advice on the proper management of Ireland:

> This kingdom wants troops and a strong government, not a party game and speculative measures. – It was quiet till these gentlemen thought proper to disturb it.[40]

No doubt old Ireland hands, who had grudges of a 1782 vintage against Portland and his party, cultivated such fears in Westmorland. Given his past history , FitzGibbon certainly would have been chief among them.

But Westmorland, and the established servants of government did have legitimate reason for concern. Fitzwilliam's own private correspondence revealed vast, indeed high-handed, schemes to change the face of Irish government. Above all he had ambitious plans for the Catholics. Not for him his uncle's tepidness on the subject of Catholic rights: Fitzwilliam was convinced that only the removal of all remaining political restrictions on the Catholics could assure stability and loyalty in Ireland.

His chief preceptors on this particular issue were Edmund Burke, who had a long standing and passionate dedication to the subject, and Dr O'Beirne. O'Beirne had abandoned Catholic for Protestant holy orders, and for the time being, he had abandoned his clerical career altogether for service as Portland's private secretary. Westmorland looked upon O'Beirne as Fitzwilliam's evil *eminence grise* and described him to Pitt as "a Popish recusant and political runner of no very good moral character".[41] No evidence exists to suggest that O'Beirne was immoral in any strict sense of the word, and his conversion to Protestantism seems to have been perfectly sincere. His moral faults probably lay in his extreme sympathy for the political aspirations of his former co-religionists, and in his success in instilling the same sympathy in Lord Fitzwilliam.

In addition to the removal of all remaining Catholic disabilities, Fitzwilliam committed himself to the removal of certain office-holders who either threatened his premier policy or who were, in his judgment, "corrupt". In particular, he signaled out FitzGibbon as the premier Protestant reactionary and John Beresford as the avatar of corruption.[42]

John Beresford had received unfavorable attention before this time, though in an encoded form. When the parliamentary opposition made attacks on the extravagance of the customs and revenue boards were, they were, in effect, attacking John Beresford. The Catholic Committee later adopted this same tack to discredit a notorious opponent and a notorious connection of the hated FitzGibbon. Beresford was hated, not only because he held high and lucrative office, but because many members of his family did. They were represented in the Church in the person of William Beresford, John Beresford's brother and FitzGibbon's brother-in law. His two sons, Marcus and John Claudius also enjoyed lucrative positions. John Claudius's many offices included one that sounded very pleasurable as well as profitable, taster of wines.

But the accusations of Beresford rapacity appear exaggerated. The truth seems to have been more mundane and obvious: they were a large family and they were loyal to government. It naturally followed that they would hold a large number of offices. In so doing they were the natural rivals of the equally large, office hungry Ponsonby clan and their collaterals. This simple, stark arithmetic of power lay behind all the cries of corruption. George Ponsonby's brother William admitted as much, shortly after Fitzwilliam's arrival in Ireland. Admittedly, Edward Cooke, who recorded this anecdote for Westmorland's benefit, was scarcely a detached observer, but if the story is at all true, wine, as well as power, went to "Billy's" head, leading to this *in vino veritas* revelation:

> The Ponsonbys are all powerful and Billy cannot contain himself. The other day at Lord Shannon's he got pretty drunk ... and burst out. He said he had long been in despair, floating on the surface, buffeted about and almost ready to sink, but at last he was successful, he had got the Power of the country and by g-d he would use it.
>
> On Friday at Parnell's he burst out again. Parnell had run out on the folly and cruelty of dismissing Beresford and had expatiated on his Integrity and diligence and knowledge and temper etc. Yes, says Billy, I admit it all. I know Beresford to be a very honourable man and a good officer and in all my private dealings with him he has been fair and honest but if I had allowed him to remain at the Revenue Board how could I have got the power of the country.[43]

Fitzwilliam was not as nakedly opportunistic as the Ponsonbys. His motives for attacking the Beresfords were at once loftier and more chilling. He had convinced himself, on the basis of highly biased views of Edmund Burke and of the Ponsonbys, that the Beresfords were harpies of corruption. Signs of trouble came even before Fitzwilliam set fatal foot in Ireland. In March 1794, during the comparative period of harmony between Whigs and government, Forbes tried to introduce another series of improvements on the government's manner of managing and disbursing money. After calling for the abolition of the offices of Receiver-General and Paymaster General, Forbes raised objections to John Beresford's presence on the newly created Treasury Board. Supposedly his tenure in this office conflicted with his position of as Commissioner of Customs. The attack quickly faltered. Beresford pointed out that he had not sought the position on the Treasury Board; he had been appointed. Sylvester Douglas observed that Beresford was only one of six Treasury Commissioners, and one of nine on the Revenue Board. Therefore, he scarcely exercised undue influence in either office. Parnell in the meantime, made the first of many defenses of Beresford's character. This initial attack ended quickly. Forbes withdrew the bill and his remarks.[44] But as the rumors of Fitzwilliam's appointment spread, it could scarcely have escaped Beresford's attention that he was a marked man.

According to O'Beirne, Beresford traveled to England shortly after the official announcement of Fitzwilliam's appointment, in September. Ostensibly he was attempting to settle the terms of a lease on a copper mine, but according to O'Beirne, he also wanted to appeal to Pitt for protection from "persecution".[45] Later, in November 1794, O'Beirne made claims that the "Faction", presumably meaning Beresford, FitzGibbon and other old government hands, had "fled to the K— with their complaints and their fears, their past services and their threatened persecutions".[46] O'Beirne was as prejudiced an observer on his side as Cooke was on his. But in light of the King's later decisive role in the downfall of Fitzwilliam, it does seem plausible that FitzGibbon and Beresford, among others, made tentative approaches to the King. Nonetheless, only later did this particular avenue of appeal take on importance. In the meantime, Westmorland continued to send minatory letters from Ireland. No doubt FitzGibbon contributed many ideas and even phrases to these productions.

In the midst of all this recrimination and agitation, Pitt tried to maintain a measure of equity and balance. He stood by Fitzwilliam's appointment out of loyalty to his new Portland allies. At the same time, he assured his old supporters in Ireland that they need not fear any drastic changes, either in their positions or in the policy of government in Ireland. At a series of meetings in October 1794, Pitt, William Windham, Portland and W.W Grenville established what they thought were universally agreed upon guidelines for Fitzwilliam's conduct in Ireland. Pitt later wrote a soothing account of these meetings to Lord Westmorland: any rumors of a viceregal revolution in men and measures were more the result of "Indiscretion, both in the principles and their Irish Connections, than of any settled Plan". His own experience had convinced him that "our new friends", far from acting the part of wild-eyed incendiaries, were, in their conduct "perfectly cordial and satisfactory and , under all the misfortunes abroad, they seem thoroughly inclined to take fairly their full share of the Difficulties of the Crisis and to persevere in all the unprecedented efforts which it requires." On a less cajoling note, Pitt emphasized his need for the Portland Whigs to bolster his beleaguered war policies: "Under these circumstances, I feel that to force them is a Breach, if it can be avoided with Honor, is to expose the Public and the King's service to an additional Risk which ... cannot be justified, and I trust on Reflection you will concur with me in that opinion." In other words, as a reward for their good behavior on the matter of the war, the dearest wish of the Portland Whigs would be fulfilled and Fitzwilliam was going to Ireland; Westmorland had no choice but to resign himself to that fact. In closing, Pitt repeated his promises that the status quo would remain intact: he had, or so it seemed, persuaded Fitzwilliam to surrender "all Idea of a new System of Measures or new Principles of Government in Ireland, as well of any separate and exclusive right in the department of Ireland different from any other in the King's service". This pledge clearly encompassed Catholic measures. In addition, Fitzwilliam agreed that "Lord FitzGibbon and all supporters of government should not be displaced, on the Change, nor while they continue to act fairly in support of such a system as shall be approved here." Finally, Fitzwilliam was not to assume office until "adequate provision", meaning an office greater than or equal to his current one, had been made for Westmorland himself.[47]

If Pitt thought the matter had ended there, he badly underestimated Fitzwilliam's obstinacy or the junto's determination not to give ground. Although nothing more seems to have been said on the subject of Beresford, Fitzwilliam retained the extraordinary notion that Pitt had given his tacit consent to his old friend's dismissal. According to his own later and dubious account, he had mentioned his intention to dismiss Beresford to Pitt, and had received no explicit objection.[48] If Pitt indeed was silent, as Fitzwilliam claimed, it was no doubt because he hoped to avoid a subject, which he thought had already been settled in quite a different way. FitzGibbon remained an open subject of contention well into November 1794 which suggests that Fitzwilliam had not relinquished his Catholic projects, either, whatever his disclaimers to Pitt. He was still determined to get rid of their most notorious and obdurate opponent. On this point, Pitt remained adamant, even to the point of threatening to revoke Lord Fitzwilliam's appointment, "which in some views would be the best [course] of all".[49] No personal love or loyalty directed Pitt's actions in this case. Retaining FitzGibbon served above all as a gesture of conciliation and continuity. To remove him would be dangerous and impolitic because it would cast aspersions on past governments, and it would give the impression of a revolution in men and measures.[50] There is a possibility that Pitt would have liked above all for FitzGibbon to retire quietly and of his own free will, with suitable remuneration. In December of 1794, shortly before his departure for Ireland, Fitzwilliam received the following ambiguous letter from Portland:

> Lord Westmorland has sent over recommendations of peerages, but the only one he pressed or seems to care about is an Earldom for FitzGibbon. Pitt showed me Ld. W.'s letter and said it might probably tend to facilitate other matters.[51]

What the "other matters" may have been remains unclear. Pitt may have been suggesting that the appointments of former members of the English and Irish opposition might go over better if a notable member of the old order received a gaudy new title. Or he may have hoped that a new title might sweeten FitzGibbon's temper, and make him either more cooperative, or more willing to make a voluntary departure.

Whatever Pitt's ultimate desires or intentions, O'Beirne expressed considerable foreboding about FitzGibbon's continued presence in government: "It was from the

Dint of that quarter that I chiefly apprehended danger and to that I shall chiefly ascribe the final failure of the hopes I had conceived for this ill-fated country, should that be the issue of the business."[52]

III

Fitzwilliam duly arrived in Ireland in January 1795. In one of his first dispatches, he claimed that he faced irresistible pressures from the Catholics to remove any and all disabilities:

> I tremble about the Roman Catholicks, I mean about keeping them quiet for the session because I find the question already in agitation and a [Committee] appointed to bring forward a petition for a repeal of the penal and restrictive laws.[53]

As always, Fitzwilliam's reality was not that of other men. It did not take into account the fact that his confidante O'Beirne, in union with Grattan, had deliberately whipped up Catholic expectation.

The Catholics had kept up a measure of activity even after the supposed final concessions of 1793. According to a spy's report, a group of Catholics met at the home of one "Dr Mcnavan" (doubtless a Castle variation on the name of William James MacNeven), who according to report, aspired to the discredited Keogh's place as leader of the Catholics. It was also possible that MacNeven, a United Irishman, hoped to keep the radical spirit alive among the Catholics. No sustained plan of action resulted, but this outcome by no means reflected either quiescence or contentment.[54]

On the contrary, if a letter of John Keogh to Dundas is any indication, a mood of bitter resentment seemed to prevail among politicized Catholics. Keogh wrote in response to a bizarre letter purporting to be from Evan Nepean, which hinted at further Catholic relief and which requested a meeting with Keogh, Byrne and "some other intelligent Gentlemen of weight in that Party."[55] Demonstrating his near-legendary cunning and caution, Keogh recognized the letter as a forgery and forwarded it to Nepean, with promises to help the government trace the author. At the same time, he favored Nepean with an account of Catholic fortunes since passage of the relief act. According to Keogh the "contrivances and tricks" of the "enemies" of the Catholics, kept them from enjoying the benefits and privileges of the acts of 1792 and 1793. He signaled out the Corporation of Dublin for particular dishonorable mention. Keogh also complained about the high proportion of militia officers drawn from the ranks of "Grand Juries who voted for our perpetual slavery", and he alluded with barely concealed rage to John Foster's prosecutions in Louth.[56] Of course, Keogh did not speak for all Catholics. He undoubtedly suffered particular disillusion because he had the misfortune to live in Dublin, home of the obdurate corporation, and perhaps because he had unduly grandiose expectations for himself. But to judge from later events, many Catholics, while quiescent for the time being, were by no means placated or content.

Certainly Grattan met with an enthusiastic response when he returned from a meeting with O'Beirne in London bearing tidings of the great things Lord Fitzwilliam was prepared to do for Catholics. According to Grattan, the Catholics only needed to make their wishes known, through petitions, and the new Whig government was prepared to grant their every wish.[57] The Catholics took him at his word. They had successfully put pressure on the reluctant Westmorland administration; they seemed virtually guaranteed success with this new, far more sympathetic and enthusiastic administration. Less than a week after his arrival, on 15 January, Fitzwilliam received the desired petition from the Catholics.[58] He made a great play of caution: "I have endeavored to keep clear of any engagements whatever", but a dispatch dated that same day revealed a man clearly set on granting the plea of the petition.

The upsurge of Defender violence in Meath, Westmeath, Longford and Cavan gave Fitzwilliam another pretext to pursue his much desired scheme. In response, he pressed for the formation of yeomanry corps, similar to those currently in array in England. Fitzwilliam intended that "the better orders of the people" regardless of religion, should comprise the yeomanry; but he claimed to have some apprehensions about putting arms in the hands of Catholics without at the same time granting them full political rights. In his letter to Portland, he fully revealed both his absolute *a priori* convictions, and his purported fears of Catholic disaffection:

> Convinced as we are of the Necessity as well as the fitness of the Measure taking place at no distant period, to attempt to defer it is to incur the certain inconvenience of rendering the Catholics useless at least, if not dangerous, of making them unwilling to act for external defence, unsafe to have committed to their hands the means of restoring Law, Order, and tranquillity, which can only be restored by means of a strong Police universally established under the Mask of a Yeomanry Cavalry, about which, as I stated before, there is not to be found a second opinion, provided relief to the Catholics precedes it.[59]

In the meantime, the anti-Fitzwilliam forces alternated between busy defiance and despair. In April 1795, an intimate of Lord Downshire, one John Pollock, gave a gloating account of a uniform, united Protestant resistance to Lord Fitzwilliam. According to Pollock, all the leading Protestants, FitzGibbon, Shannon, and Speaker Foster, stood prepared to make a bold resistance. Under their leadership "perfect discipline was established" and a majority of 120 had pledged to oppose any relief bill introduced by Grattan.[60] But Pollock was writing in triumphal retrospect. The reality suggests instead that members of the junto faced an uncertain future as long as Fitzwilliam was lord-lieutenant. Cooke, writing closer to events, took note of the resistance of Hillsborough, Shannon and the Speaker, but he added "I never saw an instance that Government would not carry a single Measure if there was no general opposition and of that I see no probability."[61] According to Fitzwilliam, even FitzGibbon admitted that "if it was my intention to give support to the petition, there was not a doubt of its being easily carried."[62] The unease of FitzGibbon, Cooke and others about the parliamentary outcome of debate of the Catholic question derived from the narrow belief, immortally articulated by Edmund Burke himself, that the loyalties of members of parliament could be bought and sold by the dispensers of patronage. They could only hope that the resentment engendered by Fitzwilliam's actions among loyal supporters of the status quo would eventually prevail even over the power and patronage of government.

Back in London, Fitzwilliam's uncle and colleague was expressing his shock that the whole issue was even being bruited. He was unconvinced by Fitzwilliam's axiom that a yeomanry made up of contented, fully emancipated Catholics equaled security for Ireland. A good old fashioned augmentation of the navy and of the regulars seemed to Portland at least as effective, with this advantage: "I understand that the increase of the Army Establishment and the grant to the Navy stand clearly and distinctly upon separate ground and in no respect whatever depend upon any measure connected with any changes, by which the political situation of the Roman Catholics can be affected."[63] Portland did not rule out further concessions altogether, but he begged Fitzwilliam to consider other, less drastic ways of winning over the Roman Catholics. Specifically, he alluded to the prospective seminaries "that have been so long in contemplation and are now as I conceive in considerable forwardness." As another possible crowd-pleasing measure, he proposed state support of the Catholic clergy, "by which they would in some degree be removed from the state of dependence in which they are kept by even the lowest order of their parishioners [and the removal from people of the burden of maintaining the clergy]."[64] In high Home Officese, an oracular language at which Portland excelled, he summed up the desired policy of the English government: stick to minor concessions and hold out the prospect of bigger ones in the eternal near future:

> ... by these means you might have gained an opportunity sufficient to digest and concert the measures which will be necessary to enable you to gratify the wishes of the Roman Catholics and to secure to them in common with their fellow subjects of every other denomination the most essential and permanent advantage.[65]

Unfortunately, in addition to stirring up the Catholics, Fitzwilliam continued to pursue his vendetta against John Beresford. He not only dismissed Beresford, he dismissed Edward Cooke from his position as undersecretary. In spite of this blow, Cooke kept up his correspondence with Westmorland, who then forwarded his letters to Pitt with the comment, "in two words, a complete Revolution".[66] The removal of the two premier members of the old governing junto contributed as much, if not more, to Fitzwilliam's undoing. He, or more accurately, his allies had raised both Catholic and Whig expectations in Ireland; at the same time, he rendered himself incapable of meeting those expectations. His actions created a solid and fatal cohesion between the English government, alarmed at Fitzwilliam's precipitance, and the angry, revenge-minded members of the old junto.

Counter-revolution was swift in coming: on 23 February, Portland informed Fitzwilliam: "I have the King's commands to inform your Excellency that it having been represented to HM that circumstances may possibly arise which may satisfy you that the welfare of HM's service requires that you shd withdraw yourself from the Admin. of the Govt. of his Kingdom of Ireland."[67] Fitzwilliam received his *congee* with a surpassing gracelessness and petulance. His lofty sense of himself and of his own infallibility had suffered a jarring and unaccustomed blow. His first impulse was to appoint the usual Lords Justices, Foster, FitzGibbon and the Primate, and to bolt. With great difficulty FitzGibbon, in company with Foster and the Primate, prevailed on him to stay in Ireland until the appointment of his successor. The news of the recall had aroused furious reaction in Dublin, at least among disappointed Catholics and Whigs, and FitzGibbon warned Fitzwilliam of efforts to "extend the Mischief to every part of the country". Such circumstances, he continued, "render it peculiarly necessary to preserve the Executive Government in its full strength, which certainly cannot be effected if it be committed to the Lords Justices".[68] Fitzwilliam reluctantly agreed, but his conduct during the interim seemed calculated to undermine the strength of the incoming executive government. He wrote up an apologia for his administration, which in essence portrayed him as a fearless champion of reform and religious toleration, destroyed by entrenched jobbers in the Castle and by bad faith at Westminster. He employed various Castle clerks to make fifty copies of this production, which he then distributed among his friends and supporters.[69] Later, he published it in the form of letters to Lord Carlisle. In his headlong indiscretion, or perhaps, in a petulant desire to create mischief for his successor, he published an excerpt from one of Portland's confidential memoranda, which seemed to imply plans within the British cabinet to use the Catholic issue to win support for a union.[70] Of course, it was by no means a new idea; as has been noted, Pitt himself had originally proposed such a conjunction of measures three years before. But Fitzwilliam's letter caused rage and panic, not only because it indiscreetly revealed a fond, but secret hope, but because it gave a false impression of the English cabinet's original intentions, which from the start had been to preserve the status quo, not to engage in any ambitious constitutional alterations.

Nor did Fitzwilliam's manner of departure merit the encomium, "he nothing common did or mean upon that memorable scene". He snubbed Pelham, the new chief secretary, at a levee, and dithered between leaving discreetly or with éclat.[71] FitzGibbon who had a particular interest in playing down popular upheaval, urged a quiet departure, and as an inducement, he had offered Fitzwilliam the use of his house in Blackrock. From there he could make a quiet departure in the vice-regal yacht. Fitzwilliam, at first agreed, then abruptly changed his mind in favour of a more public departure. FitzGibbon's own account gave the impression that Fitzwilliam was sadly disappointed in his hopes of a vast outpouring of public sympathy:

> Everything was perfectly quiet. Not even a Hiss from the Mob in the Streets addressed to any of the Men who followed him. At the College a set of fellows who had been planted there took his Horse from his coach and drew him from thence to the Pidgeon House – Much to the Annoyance of Lady Fitzwilliam, who I was told, [went] into Histericks. After he had got into the Boat which conveyed him to the Yacht, he waved his Hat and bowed most graciously to the [Navies?] who had [conveyed] him to the Pidgeon House and so the ceremony ended.[72]

FitzGibbon's letter suggests that reality, like beauty, is in the eye of the beholder. Accounts in the radical press and from other, less biased observers contradict his claims of apathy and idle curiosity on the part of the mob. Indeed, FitzGibbon's admission that there was a mob, hissing or not, suggests a considerable depth of popular feeling.

In his dealings with Fitzwilliam, FitzGibbon made no pretense of his opposition to "Popish projects". In Fitzwilliam's own words "entered fully and earnestly, but with perfect temper, on the subject [of further concessions] and stated strongly his alarms and the grounds of them".[73] Not only was Fitzwilliam unconvinced by the chancellor's arguments, they "entre nous tended exceedingly to confirm my own genuine opinion, for I never felt less led to doubt my own opinion but by an able statement on the other side than this."[74] According to John Pollock, who favored Westmorland with the happy, triumphal account of Fitzwilliam's fall, FitzGibbon had been at the forefront of the dedicated Protestants who had allegedly formed together to oppose Lord Fitzwilliam in Parliament. In Pollock's version of events, FitzGibbon, in conjunction with Speaker Foster, had wrung from Fitzwilliam a pledge that concessions to Catholics would not be a measure of government, and that every man had the right to act as he saw fit on the issue. Having won this concession, they then recruited their parliamentary phalanx of 120 Protestants good and true to oppose the issue.[75] Pollock's claim is dubious. No where in his own candid accounts to Westmorland or to Auckland does FitzGibbon mention such a Protestant coalition. It is a mark of FitzGibbon's own uncertainty on the subject that he broached the idea of a union to Fitzwilliam. In his own later account of their transactions to Lord Westmorland, he stated that in the course of a conversation with Fitzwilliam on his "Popish projects" "... I stated to him distinctly my opinion that a union with the Parliament of England was the only Measure which could give Great Britain a chance of preserving this country as a member of empire." He then made the dubious and rather self-important claim that Fitzwilliam had then passed his opinion on to Portland, who in turn gave the "private and confidential intimation which Lord Fitzwilliam has thought fit to publish to the world", meaning Portland's own hints of an eventual union. FitzGibbon insisted to Westmorland that he had made an important qualification to this suggestion: "I told him, however, that till Great Britain was at peace and we had a strong army in Ireland, it would be impossible to carry out such a measure."[76] But the very fact that FitzGibbon raised the subject during a conversation about "Popish projects" suggests that he admitted at least the possibility of Lord Fitzwilliam getting his way; he fell back on the scheme of a union as the last remaining hope for Protestant supremacy in Ireland. In other words, he was prepared to concede in 1795 what he bitterly contested in 1801, Catholic emancipation in conjunction with a union.[77]

FitzGibbon later suffered much opprobrium for allegedly poisoning the mind of the king against Lord Fitzwilliam and against further concessions to the Catholics. It is true that, in conjunction with his crony Auckland, he convinced the King that admitting the Catholics to Parliament and to office would violate his coronation oath. According to the argument as set forth by FitzGibbon, such an action would amount to a virtual repeal of the Acts of Supremacy and of Uniformity and of the Bill of Rights, the legal foundations of the established church of England and of Ireland. To do so would violate his coronation oath, which included a promise before God to uphold the Protestant Church as by law established. Unions being much on his mind, FitzGibbon also drew in the Act of Union with Scotland. In those articles, too, the English crown was obliged to "maintain the Protestant religion as by Law Established in England, Ireland and Berwick upon Tweed." The implication, as FitzGibbon drew it, was grim and apocalyptic: "... a repeal of the Test Act or the Act of Supremacy or the Act of Uniformity in favour of the Papists would in my opinion be a breach of the Articles of Union."

The argument made a number of dubious assumptions: that forms of government, or at least the form of government established at the Revolution, were fixed forever and that changing circumstances, political expediency and mere common sense could never alter them. It also presupposed that the ecclesiastical privileges of the Church of England and Ireland necessarily depended on the political monopoly of its adherents. It would indeed have been problematic to allow Catholic members of an Irish, an English or a united Parliament to adjudicate or frame statues involving the established church. But the coronation oath argument rested on the curious assumption that it was beyond the ingenuity of either the Irish or the English parliament to impose restrictions on the power of Catholic or indeed any non-conformist legislators, to alter or affect the Church's position. Moreover, it could be argued that the king had already breached his oath by assenting to the act of 1793. After all, Catholics could as easily undermine the Church by voting in Protestant members willing to attack the sacrosanct Acts of Uniformity and Supremacy.

Whatever its flaws and absurdities, the coronation oath argument was admirably suited to ensnare George III's dim mind and over-sensitive conscience. It was simple, it was high-toned, and it allowed the king to indulge his own natural stubbornness by upholding the supposed political will of God as set forth by the parliaments of 1689 and 1708. Moreover, as Anthony Malcomson has suggested, the King was already opposed to extending further rights to Catholics.[78] The coronation oath argument, however dubious, provided him with a much desired pretext for digging in his heels. It became a fortieth article to George III. He used it to resist Catholic concessions until his own final descent into madness. His despicable son would later fall back on it, without the old king's misguided integrity or success. In short, the coronation oath argument effectively stalled final concessions to the Catholics for over thirty years.

While it must be acknowledged that FitzGibbon articulated the coronation oath argument and that he did communicate it to the king, he probably did not originate it. That sort of elaborate ratiocination was not his style. Hitherto he had relied on the simple, blood and thunder imagery of Papist revanche and massacre. John Foster, in many ways a more effective practical politician, had presented a version of it in his speech on the Catholic bill of 1793.[79] Charles Agar of Cashel also took a keen interest in this line of thought, and he may have been responsible for one of its first public appearances in the *Freeman's Journal* of 10 October 1792. That edition included a paragraph claiming that the king would violate his coronation oath if he agreed to the Catholic franchise. Agar had protégés at the *Freeman's* and it is possible that he suggested the idea, or that he wrote the paragraph himself.[80] In addition, he seems to have been developing the argument on his own, if an elaborate sketch in his private papers is any indication; it is heavily scored and marked over, which suggests a man laboriously collecting his thoughts, not copying from another source.[81] Despite their uneasy relations, FitzGibbon may well have consulted with Agar to refine and reinforce his own ideas on the subject.

Nonetheless, where he fell short in theoretical originality, FitzGibbon certainly excelled in the mechanics of intrigue. He set up an elaborate network to communicate his borrowed ideas, making use, not only of Auckland, but of a very willing John Beresford and of Lord Loughborough, the English lord chancellor.[82] It is important to emphasize, not only his plagiarism, but his timing: FitzGibbon seems to have done much of this meddling with the King's conscience *after* Fitzwilliam's departure. Both Portland and Pelham, some weeks after Fitzwilliam's recall, made exasperated note of FitzGibbon's communications with the King.[83] Fitzwilliam, who had wanted so badly to dismiss FitzGibbon, would assuredly have been the first to complain had he suspected any such closet intrigue on the part of the lord chancellor.

On the whole, FitzGibbon seems to have tried to maintain reasonably civil and straightforward relations with Fitzwilliam, as indeed, he would. As a lover of office he was hardly likely to put it at risk. Fitzwilliam did not return the favour. To his mind, FitzGibbon's position as chancellor was all the more galling, as he could not take direct initiative in getting rid of him. In consequence, he resorted to more indirect means of undermining FitzGibbon's reputation and his powers. Most significantly, he took issue with FitzGibbon's manner of appointing magistrates, a major area of patronage for the lord chancellor, as this position, while comparatively lowly, bestowed great influence and prestige. Fitzwilliam's claim that FitzGibbon "takes the casual Recommendation of any man who is so good as to give it" was a crude attempt to get rid of FitzGibbon on other political grounds, apart from the Catholic issue.[84]

In addition, Fitzwilliam seems to have encouraged old enemies of FitzGibbon in the press and at the bar to act as his proxies. An editorial in the *Hibernian*, which portrayed FitzGibbon as a pimp, a lecher and a sadist, who delighted in the flogging and hanging of the hapless poor, was so crude and embarrassing that Fitzwilliam felt obliged to make a public disavowal and apology to FitzGibbon.[85] But according to Cooke he did offer his patronage to one Hoare, "who had written the abusive Pamphlets against the Chancellor", as well as to a man whom FitzGibbon had refused to make King's Counsel.[86]

In the renewed partisan warfare that followed, all ambiguity, all evidence in FitzGibbon's favour disappeared from consideration. Fitzwilliam became the upright hapless victim of an evil junto led by FitzGibbon and the Beresfords. The popular press lapsed into frightened quiescence after the brief renaissance of scurrility under Fitzwilliam, but the twenty-year propaganda war against FitzGibbon still raged in the form of ephemeral broadsides. One such production took the form of a parody of the creed:

> I believe in the Holy Earl of Clare, in the Holy Orange Lodges, in the Communion of Commissioners, in the forgiveness of sins by acts of indemnity, in the Resurrection of the Protestant Ascendancy and Jobbing Everlasting Amen.[87]

Another neatly distilled every possible propaganda point against FitzGibbon, from his low, turn-coat Popish ancestry, to his supposed pimping for Westmorland, to the supposed unchastity of Anne FitzGibbon.[88]

The popular feeling against FitzGibbon took a more violent turn on the day Lord Camden arrived in Ireland. As he was returning from the reception and ceremonies at the Castle, a mob armed with paving stones attacked his carriage. Although he tried to protect himself with the purse containing the great seal, a stone struck his forehead.[89] FitzGibbon himself later claimed that he had only narrowly escaped death.[90] His enemies, on the other hand, tended to minimize the damage. According to Charlemont, FitzGibbon had suffered a minor graze from some "blackguard" boys who were taunting him.[91] The truth seems to have been neither a melodramatic escape from near death nor a minor street comedy. Camden, a sympathetic, but reasonably detached witness, records that FitzGibbon did suffer an injury from the mob, but the wound was not of such magnitude that he was unable to attend a levee the following day.[92] A man by the name of O'Brien was later arrested for participating in the riot, and some attempt was made to identify him as FitzGibbon's attacker. Rather than retire in lofty dignity and let the law take its course, FitzGibbon, displaying again his habits of self-dramatization and vindictiveness, personally interrogated the man. To judge by his own account, he resorted to subtle intimidation to extract a confession from O'Brien; he told O'Brien that he had received information from one of the Aldermen which strongly suggested his guilt and which would lead to his "infallible conviction." O'Brien insisted on his innocence, and at his trial FitzGibbon had to admit that he could not "from his knowledge, say the traverser was one of the rioters".[93] Habits of legal scrupulousness prevailed ultimately prevailed over his habits of vindictiveness.

17

Repression and Rebellion, 1795–8

I

The new government was in a delicate position. It faced not only restive, bitter Catholics and a newly revived opposition, but suspicious, truculent Protestants. The strategy of the government took to form of re-asserting the status quo. First and foremost, the new administration went to work to defeat the Catholic bill. Even with the drastic shift in government weight and prestige, it was a closer vote than Camden would have liked. He apologized to Portland about the large margin of votes in favour of Catholic emancipation, and attributed this residue of support to past promises.[1] At the same time, Camden's administration, in keeping with its instructions, tried to coat this pill of rejection with a show of generosity and moderation in other matters. The government hurried through the bill establishing Maynooth on the heels of the rejection of the Catholic bill.[2] Camden also cajoled Foster and FitzGibbon into abandoning resolutions which they wanted to introduce into their respective legislative fiefs of Commons and the Lords. The resolutions in question asserted the eternal inviolability of the Protestant Establishment in Church and State and the perfect state of freedom which Catholics presently enjoyed.[3] Camden certainly wanted to maintain the Protestant establishment, if not forever, at least so long as it served the interests of the government in London. But he shrank from the arrogant triumphalism implicit in FitzGibbon's and Foster's resolutions. Fortunately for him, Foster and FitzGibbon felt secure enough in victory to dispense with embarrassing celebratory displays. With the Whig opposition, Camden and Pelham adopted a similar stance of evasion and conciliation. After engineering the defeat of Grattan's Catholic bill, they met other opposition initiatives with either silence or with strategic retreat. Efforts to discuss Fitzwilliam's recall, or the subject of the union all met with resolute silence on the part of the government.[4] In a similar spirit, the new administration made no attempt to block the repeal of the police act, once such a source of contention, or to interfere with the inquiries into the Commission on Wide Streets, the aim of which was to discredit John Beresford, by establishing his alleged dishonesty in the awarding of building contracts.[5] The government even went so far as to confirm the Duke of Leinster in the office of Clerk of the Hanaper, asking only his neutrality on the momentous questions.[6] As they pursued this combined program of retraction and resilience, Camden, Pelham, as well as various other government men such as Lees wrote reassuringly to London about the peaceful apathy which pervaded the country.[7] Self-interest and wishful thinking more than objectivity characterized their correspondence.

The avowed aim of the new government was to restore the mystique of the English government as a force, which preserved the political monopoly of Anglicans, but in all other respects maintained impartiality and fairness to all religious parties. Unfortunately, the Camden administration quickly replicated the dismal pattern of all its predecessors: it was headed by a well-meaning but limited young aristocrat dominated intellectually and emotionally by FitzGibbon. Within a month after his arrival, he, like Westmorland before him, was pressing the government to grant FitzGibbon an advance in the peerage. The further progress of FitzGibbon in the peerage signified not only the re-establishment of the old power group, but a public display of appreciation for the services of its members.

Camden displayed some diffidence on the subject; he seemed aware that FitzGibbon was, to say the least, a controversial figure, and any display of favour to him might undermine the government's desire to soothe the wounded, agitated feelings of Whigs and Catholics.[8] But he argued that the measure was perfectly in keeping with FitzGibbon's "high professional character" and with the government's policy of equity. Yelverton, who was notoriously favorable to the Catholics, was in line for a peerage. It seemed only just "that a mark of the King's favour should be shown at the same time to a person who has always pursued a different line upon these Questions".[9] The Protestants, Camden argued further, "are in want of every encouragement, for in consequence of what has passed for the last two years and of my discouraging it [FitzGibbon's and Foster's resolutions] they are hardly yet persuaded government is in earnest upon this measure" [the prevention of future Catholic concessions] Moreover, FitzGibbon's sufferings at the hands of the mob made him a worthy object of consideration.[10] After some delay, the English government granted Camden and presumably FitzGibbon their dearest wish. FitzGibbon acquired the title by which he became most notorious, the Earl of Clare.

His accession to a higher grade of the peerage was marked with dinners at Ely Place and summer invitations to Mount Shannon. In effect the beginning of the Camden administration marked the plenitude of his power. The Whigs and Catholics were in disarray, and the resurgence of the Defenders and of the United Irishmen, while disturbing, seemed as yet amenable to the usual tactics of repression. In short, there appeared to be no significant challenges either to his power or to the power of the Protestant oligarchy.

Nonetheless, FitzGibbon's hegemony did not go unchallenged, even at its apogee. There were voices of doubt and resentment, both in Dublin and in London. The most surprising and unexpected of the doubtful voices belonged to the chief secretary, Pelham. He was not entirely antagonistic to FitzGibbon. He added his voice to Camden's in requesting a further elevation in the peerage.[11] But unlike Camden, he did occasionally venture a criticism of FitzGibbon. As noted before, FitzGibbon's communications with the king on constitutional law exasperated him because he more than anyone else took seriously the mission of the Camden administration to remain above sect and above faction.[12] He did not want Castle men drawing the King into their party quarrels, any more than he wanted the Catholics and Whigs to exploit their various partisan ties.

This same distaste for factional antagonism made Pelham seriously propose the dismissal of Beresford. Again, no personal vindictiveness prompted this suggestion. On the contrary, his own brother was married to Beresford's niece. But to his mind, Beresford, whatever his personal or public merits, had become such a focus of partisan hatred that in the interests of peace, if not of strict justice, he should be dismissed with suitably handsome remuneration.[13] Whether Pelham ever raised the issue of the closet communications with FitzGibbon himself remains unknown. Apparently he either refrained or he framed his objections with masterful tact, as no denigration of Pelham appears in FitzGibbon's surviving correspondence.

On a more serious level, efforts to remove FitzGibbon from power revived in 1797. The initiative came from a predictable quarter: one French Laurence, who was an intimate of Edmund Burke. Laurence contacted Fitzwilliam who of course agreed that FitzGibbon's objectionable presence in government was at the bottom of Irish discontent.[14] But Laurence did not confine himself to the usual partisan suspects in pursuing this scheme to oust FitzGibbon. He also contacted William Windham, an English MP, much admired for his integrity and independence. According to French, some extracts from FitzGibbon's no-popery speech of 1793 convinced Windham of "the impossibility of doing anything through the present men in Ireland". Laurence went further afield and sounded Lord Carlisle and Sir Walter James, a relative of Camden himself.[15] Even these otherwise sympathetic men thought it desirable to remove FitzGibbon, if such was the price of peace in Ireland. This admission was particularly startling in Carlisle, since, by his own admission, he looked upon FitzGibbon as a *protégé*.[16] Nonetheless, Laurence's initiative came to nothing, for the same reason that had stood FitzGibbon in good stead throughout his career: there were no suitable alternatives, only a much traveled mediocre careerist, Serjeant Adair.[17] Burke, who had so many reasons to detest FitzGibbon, admitted as much. Burke also made the amazing admission that FitzGibbon, as a bigot and a reactionary, was in fact, "less mischievous" than Foster.[18]

II

It is not necessary for the purposes of this work to give a full account of the complex horrors of the late 1790s. Other, better historians have already covered that ground capably and thoroughly. The biographer of FitzGibbon has a comparatively simple task: relating his actions as the government's architect of repression and his speeches as the government's apologist of repression. Admittedly there is little or no direct documentary proof of FitzGibbon's role, if only because decisions at the Castle seem often to have been made in casual conversation, rather than through written memoranda. But framing acts of repression had consumed the chief part of FitzGibbon's career as a politician: he had set the pattern with the Police and the Whiteboy acts of the 1780s. It would have been extraordinary indeed if he had *not* taken the brutal initiative in the measures taken against the Defenders and the revolutionary, conspiratorial version of the United Irishmen which took shape after 1795. Moreover, the mere fact that he dominated Camden, as he had dominated Camden's equally good-natured and limited predecessors Westmorland and Rutland, lends credence to an overwhelming influence on policy.

Camden's papers contain a positive piece of evidence suggesting FitzGibbon's central role in the campaign of repression: a draft of a proclamation aimed at the Defenders in Connaught, which heralded Lord Carhampton's campaign in that district. The draft of the proclamation, framed by another of FitzGibbon's *protégés*, Attorney-General Wolfe, was certainly harsh enough. It gave the commanding officers the authority by an "immediate and effectual Exertion of Troops ... to suppress the Tumults" In other words, the disturbed areas of Connaught were laid wide open to unlimited force by the military. In anticipation of one of the provisions of the Insurrection Act, it called upon all "his Majesty's loving subjects" to "keep themselves, their Children, Servants and Apprentices within their Dwellings during at Night". Any individual who was absent, with the exception of those "called forth to assist in preserving the Peace ... may justly incur the Suspicion of being engaged in these dangerous associations." In other words, the proclamation made the assumption that all the inhabitants of Connaught were guilty of Defenderism, unless they proved their innocence each night by staying under lock and key at home.[19] FitzGibbon made some characteristic editorial changes, deleting excess verbiage in the opening preamble. He also strengthened Wolfe's implication that the inhabitants of the disturbed areas of Connaught would ultimately be held accountable *in toto* for Defender disturbances. Wolfe's original draft read that the inhabitants of Connaught, if discovered abroad at night, "may expose themselves to the Mischiefs which the further Continuance of such tumultuous proceedings may bring upon the guilty". FitzGibbon substituted "dangers" for "mischiefs" and emphasized that continued disturbances "must involve the Inhabitants of the Districts in which they have unhappily prevailed." Above all, he inserted the word "traitorous" in all phrases referring to Defender activities. Where Wolfe had defined the Defenders' conduct merely as "lawless proceedings", FitzGibbon rendered them "traitorous and lawless proceedings". Again, where Wolfe alluded to "dangerous associations"[20] FitzGibbon referred to them as "dangerous, traitorous associations". The warning was clear: unless the inhabitants of Connaught either desisted from or avoided Defender activities, they suffer, not the usual punishments for disorderly conduct, whipping, fines and imprisonment, but death or transportation as traitors. Moreover, the military would not be overly precise about distinguishing the guilty from the innocent. Carhampton fully took advantage of the license which this proclamation gave to him. With grim euphemism, the government later referred to his campaign of devastation as "vigor beyond the law".

In a cover letter which he sent with his annotations, FitzGibbon was blunt to the point of ingenuousness in accounting for the changes: "... to justify such a proceeding certainly it ought to appear that Treason is the main object of the Rioters – upon this principle it is that I have introduced into the draft the word "Traitorous" in more places than one."[21] He added, "If such a proclamation is followed up by military Execution in the disturbed districts, I have strong hopes that the unfortunate wretches who have been levied to disturb the public peace will be terrified into submission." All the familiar elements of FitzGibbon's past policy were encapsulated in these remarks: the assumption that the lower orders were too stupid and indolent to undertake a major rebellion on their own – they were necessarily "levied" by disaffected better elements – and the conviction that a consistent policy of terror would restore peace. The same spirit infuses the retrospective acts of indemnity, which protected both magistrates and soldiers from suits or complaints resulting from excessive force, and similar provisions for indemnity in the insurrection act. It is almost certain that FitzGibbon played the same part in framing these acts that he did in drafting the proclamation: clarifying, solidifying and above all, increasing the quotient of terror.

In addition to his legislative activities, FitzGibbon displayed an active interest in reports about lawlessness, and in one case at least, involved himself directly. He corresponded extensively with the re-instated Edward Cooke on the subject of a certain corporal Bourke or Burke. Bourke, a Limerick militiaman, had evidently come under the influence of the United Irishmen while stationed in the North. They had tried to use him as an agent to promote republicanism and desertion among his comrades. FitzGibbon offered to help Cooke entrap Bourke and obtain evidence from him. He was well qualified to do so, having a personal acquaintance with Bourke's family.[22] His motive was obvious. He wanted to protect his home county from the United Irish/Ulster bacillus. On a more squalid and pathetic level, he also intervened to see that one John Treacy, of Loughur, County Limerick, received his due reward for giving information against one Patrick Keating, who had evidently been administering oaths, though whether they were United Irish or Defender is unclear.[23] Like Peachum, FitzGibbon clearly believed that it was important to pay spies promptly.

Not surprisingly, considering his already mordant attitude toward Ulster, FitzGibbon regularly received Castle reports on the state of the North.[24] The news was not encouraging. In December 1796, he informed Agar that the "rebels in the North are in my poor opinion more formidable than ever." The insurrection act, which had been passed at the beginning of that year, had momentarily "warned" the northern rebels into "a deceitful tranquillity", but they retained large stockpiles of arms. FitzGibbon, sarcastically commented that the northern magistrates "wisely" refrained from confiscating these arms because "they say that the people remain quiet".[25] His own sense that the apparent peace of the north represented a lull before a well-armed storm undoubtedly prompted him to press for the forced disarming of Ulster, a policy for which he claimed credit in open parliament.[26] There is no reason to doubt his claim. It was characteristic, both of his policy and of his general attitude toward Ulster. No doubt he regretted that a similar policy had not been initiated in 1783 or 1784.

FitzGibbon even appears to have managed his own personal network of informers; at any rate, he had enough contacts in the shadowy world of professional spies to recommend an agent to the English government. The man seems to have performed satisfactorily; certainly Portland thought highly of his abilities and planned to use him on future missions.[27]

No evidence of suspicious conduct or disaffection was too trivial or absurd for FitzGibbon's interest. Two incidents, one involving an itinerant priest and another involving a Portuguese masquerading as a Turk, resemble absurdist *opera buffa*. He came upon the priest on the turnpike road while traveling to Mount Shannon in the early autumn of 1796. He was an old Frenchman of destitute appearance, and FitzGibbon, apparently out of pity, "asked him a few question in his own language." As FitzGibbon related the incident, the turnpike keeper happened to overhear what may have been a very halting, mutually uncomprehending exchange and helpfully offered the information that the old man spoke both English and Irish. His suspicions aroused, FitzGibbon proceeded to "interrogate the gentleman somewhat particularly", which probably meant that he shifted from abrupt kindliness to the manner that so terrified Chancery barristers. During this interrogation, it transpired the man had come from Belfast, but he remained otherwise evasive: "He would not say where he had lived during that time, nor how or by what route he had come from Belfast." Other helpful bystanders, no doubt attracted by another self-created FitzGibbonesque drama, provided the information that the mysterious man had only recently celebrated mass for them in the English and Irish language. Finally the man did admit to some knowledge of English, which, according to FitzGibbon, he spoke "very intelligibly". His reticence, his past residence in Belfast, his evasiveness about his linguistic skills and possibly his status as a priest all prompted FitzGibbon to commit him to the gaol. In typical FitzGibbon fashion, he combined harshness with kindness, giving his prisoner "a few shillings for his present subsistence". He then gave Mr. Holmes (the local magistrate) instructions to confine the man until he gave "full satisfaction that he was really what he appeared to be, a miserable decrepid [*sic*] old beggar".[28] The ultimate fate of the old priest remains unknown. FitzGibbon made no other recorded mention of him, nor did Camden. It would appear that he sufficiently proved his misery and decrepitude to Mr Holmes and went on his mysterious way. The whole action smacks of slightly absurd excess. FitzGibbon seemed incapable of entertaining the possibility that anyone, much less a Frenchman and a priest, could live in Belfast in perfect innocence. He also failed to consider that the French and the

Republicans might have preferred to employ more sophisticated and less obtrusive spies than old mendicant priests. Finally, he never considered the effects of his own terrifying mien, which even today makes viewing his later portraits an unnerving experience. The old man may well have been contradictory and reticent because he was terrified out of his wits by FitzGibbon, not because he was concealing guilty knowledge.

The episode of the Turk was as trivial and silly, but FitzGibbon acted with the same deadly earnestness. The man was a Portuguese who adopted an ingenious confidence scheme. In FitzGibbon's own words, "he was a mere impostor who, by letting his beard grow, and putting on a Turkish habit, meant to impose on the credulity of the natives", presumably by telling fortunes and doing minor magic tricks.[29] His suspicious appearance and questionably activities apparently led to his arrest in Nenagh, which in FitzGibbon's correspondence for this time appears to have been a hard town for misfits and outcasts.[30] For reasons obscure, he was removed from Nenagh and brought to Limerick City for interrogation. Manifesting again his extraordinary energy and his still more extraordinary habit of busy minuteness, FitzGibbon personally attended the interrogation. Since Portuguese was not numbered among FitzGibbon's linguistic accomplishments, two Limerick merchants undertook to interrogate the man.[31] FitzGibbon then ordered him to be returned to prison in Nenagh, along with instructions to the worthy Mr Holmes "to have an eye to him" as well as to his female companion, who was arrested and imprisoned with him.[32] Mr Holmes apparently decided he was essentially a harmless scoundrel and released the *faux* Turk along with his paramour. The man was soon arrested again in County Clare, not far from Mount Shannon. A laborer had informed the local magistrate that the Turk had prophesied that the French were coming to Ireland. FitzGibbon reported to Cooke that he was planning to ride over to the magistrate's house to "see that the Turk is safe", that is safely imprisoned.[33]

FitzGibbon himself eventually came to the same conclusion as Holmes: the Turk was a harmless vagabond and trickster. He dismissed a report forwarded by Cooke that the man carried "instruments for drawing maps", noting that the Turk had nothing of the kind in his possession in Limerick. He also behaved in an unlikely fashion for a spy. According to FitzGibbon he "studiously attracted the Notice of every person whom he met" (Indeed, Turkish attire would have that effect in County Limerick.) Moreover he was "very fond of whiskey and has been seen very frequently beastly drunk", not a useful habit in a profession requiring discretion. FitzGibbon pointed out that if the attorney-general wanted to pursue the matter, he could prosecute the Turk as a vagabond or deport him under the alien act, which regulated foreign nationals resident in Ireland. Like so many of FitzGibbon's adventures, this one ends in frustrating obscurity. What transpired next and what became of the Turk and his companion remain unanswered questions.

Though slight in itself, the tale of the Turks reveals FitzGibbon's relentless energy and his readiness to pursue subversion and disorder, even at the expense of his considerable stores of innate pride and common sense. There is a certain quality of *infra dig* in the spectacle of the Lord High Chancellor of Ireland acting the part of police magistrate, especially when the subject was so innately petty and pathetic. That a man so acutely conscious of his own dignity would participate in such a scene suggests FitzGibbon's profound suspiciousness and fear at this time.

FitzGibbon also took a minute interest in military matters. His letters from the period 1795–98, especially to Auckland, are full of critiques of various naval and military officers. In the aftermath of the failed invasion at Bantry Bay, he criticized "my friend" Admiral Colpoys for allowing the bulk of the French fleet to escape capture.[34] (Nonetheless, while he allowed himself the liberty of attacking Colpoys in private, he dutifully defended the actions of the British fleet when the subject came up for indignant comment in the House of Lords.)[35] The military too came in for harsh criticism. He dismissed Lieutenant-General Edward Smith, who commanded a detachment at Limerick, as a "gothick" and as a "mad Methodist". Another, Major-General Amherst, "utters more treason than any United Irishman." (Amherst may have suggested that the Irish lower orders had good reason to rebel, a sentiment common to many British officers, among them Sir John Moore).[36] Although FitzGibbon reckoned the Irish militia a fine body of men, he condemned the negligence of their officers.[37]

The premier military *bête noir* was assuredly Ralph Abercromby, who had ventured to criticize the military operations with the famous phrase that the army had "rendered itself formidable to all but the enemy". FitzGibbon's indignation knew no bounds; given his own personal advocacy of strong military exertion, he would have had little tolerance for any suggestions of moderation or limits to force. His anger against Abercromby was no doubt further encouraged by the reaction of Lord Abercorn. By this time, Abercorn had abandoned his flirtation with Catholic radicalism and had become an adoring intimate of FitzGibbon. As the presiding colonel of the Tyrone militia, he took Abercromby's remark as a personal insult and threw over his command. Afterwards, he favored FitzGibbon, as well as Camden, with a flood of indignant comments about the insult to his honor and to his name.[38] FitzGibbon in the meantime favored Auckland with his own denunciations of Abercromby; among other things he referred to him as a "Scotch beast".[39] Abercromby soon paid the price for his blunt epigram. In the face of reactionary uproar, he resigned his command and was replaced by General Lake. Lake promptly adopted techniques more to the taste of FitzGibbon and his compeers.

FitzGibbon's interest in the state of the military was understandable. However harsh and comprehensive his legislation, he clearly recognized that Protestant domination and Protestant security ultimately depended on military force. Moreover, many of his remarks and judgments were quite sound. For example, he esteemed General Dalrymple, one of the most steady and capable officers in the regular forces in Ireland.[40] But it is possible that an element of frustration played into this interest. FitzGibbon seems to have liked the company of military men, quite apart from his rational concerns as a statesmen. Like his arch-enemy, Tone, he may have had inclination toward the military life, but abandoned these aspirations under paternal pressure. This speculation is not entirely fanciful. He certainly had the makings of a fine military officer: immense personal courage, decisiveness, ruthlessness and, at least in his youth, dashing good looks.

FitzGibbon's possible intervention in the Armagh disturbances of 1795–1796 offers a novel complexity in the otherwise dismal monotony of the pre-rebellion years. Indeed the nature of the struggle created an exquisite dilemma for FitzGibbon and for the government. The resurgence of Defender – Peep Day conflicts in 1795 had culminated in the defeat of the Defenders at Battle of the Diamond; the victors, were, to say the least ungenerous in victory. A wholesale campaign of expelling Catholics, whether or not they had any ties to the Defenders, ensued. The appearance of the allusive placard "To Hell or Connaught" frequently preceded the forced expulsion. The government naturally took an interest in these events. A good many Defenders were indeed going to Connaught, bringing their turbulent philosophy and their resentments to a barely pacified area.[41] To make matters worse, the Orange order had emerged, a more overtly political body with an ideology of extreme loyalty in opposition to the revolutionary millenarianism of the Defenders. The connivance of some sympathetic gentry in Armagh and the skillful propaganda of the United Irishmen convinced a growing number of poorer Catholics in Armagh and elsewhere that the government was not merely indifferent to their fate, but actively encouraging the Orangemen in their depredations. It was a belief which the Camden administration devoutly wished to eradicate, if only to avoid adding further recruits to the ranks of the United Irishmen and the Defenders. In fairness, there was a genuine desire on the part of Camden, at least, to act justly and to put an end to the attacks on the Catholics. His correspondence breathes an anxiety to prove in Armagh, if not elsewhere, that while his administration opposed Catholic emancipation, it was not unfriendly to Catholics.[42]

The government's response was an evenhandedness at once macabre and ludicrous. Attorney General Wolfe traveled to Armagh in person for the spring assizes of 1796. There, he "selected from a great number of cases before me two of the same nature and both of capital crimes, one in which two defenders were charged, the other in which three Orangemen were charged with taking arms by force out of dwelling houses".[43] The two Defenders, and two of the three Orangemen were convicted and condemned to death. Isaac Corry, who accompanied Wolfe to the Armagh assize, was full of optimism that the spectacle of judicial murder inflicted on Orangemen and Defenders alike would restore the loyalty and affection of the lower orders for the government:

> The circumstance of an equal number of each body being convicted at the outset, tho' at other times of little moment is at this period probably not without

> considerable effect. The Mob will take the equality of number as a more indisputable proof of the equality of justice than any other that could be given to them.[44]

In addition to judicial theater, the government also passed an act which allowed victims of sectarian attacks to apply for compensation.[45]

As was the case of all measures by the Camden administration, whether coercive or conciliatory, those directed toward Armagh failed. The violence reached a new peak in the summer of 1796, after Wolfe's essay in evenhanded punishment. Even Cooke, that hardened, cynical soul, was shaken by the violence in Armagh: his letter to Gosford on the subject was uncharacteristically fervid:

> My Lord-lieutenant learns with the utmost regret that the outrages still continue in the County of Armagh, that those persons who style themselves Orange Boys are persecuting the lower orders of the Catholics with great cruelty, burning and posting their houses and threatening the lives of those who employ them. Your Lordship will see the necessity of checking at once these disgraceful proceedings, of giving full protection to every description of his majesty's subjects, and of bringing to immediate punishment those who shall violate the law.[46]

The sequel to the story is dismally familiar. The United Irishmen and the Defenders flourished, whilst the Orangemen entered the ranks of the militia and the yeomanry in increasing numbers.[47] With the mounting tide of rebellion, all too many frightened gentry and hard-pressed military officers were prepared to welcome men who at least were dependably loyal, however squalid and brutal their origins and past behavior. Simultaneously, Orangeism attracted adherents from the gentry and aristocracy. Even some of their past critics in the government adopted a more favorable attitude, notably Edward Cooke. In June 1798, Cooke rather prematurely congratulated the government for the quiet in the North, and attributed this unexpected state of affairs to "the Popish tinge" of the rebellion in Wexford. He also credited the "formidable" force of the Orange yeomanry for keeping order.[48]

A letter from General Dalrymple shows how closely and how early FitzGibbon watched the situation in Armagh. In August 1795, Dalrymple, who was stationed in Armagh, made a report to Pelham on the situation in that county. He painted a sorry picture of frightened Catholics preparing to take flight to America or Connaught and indolent, if not actively Orange, magistrates. He even complained that the government was insufficiently aware of the seriousness of the situation: "All this I have stated many times to the government, but no answers have I received. At this moment almost all are absent and business sleeps." According to Dalrymple, only one figure of note in government seemed prepared to listen to him and to recognize the dangers of the upheavals in Armagh:

> Lord Clare was with me, is master of the subject, and sees the confined state I am in, laws exist, but their explanation and execution are in the hands of those who approve not of them.[49]

FitzGibbon more than anyone else would have found the situation in Armagh disturbing. The reports of indolent or partial magistrates affronted his most cherished belief that the gentry should protect the poor and maintain order. The fact that the attacks were on Catholics also touched a nerve. Much as he feared and hated them, he piqued himself on the lofty administration of equal justice and equal protection to them. It was obvious from Dalrymple's reports that Catholics in Armagh were getting neither equal justice nor equal protection. Also, FitzGibbon more than anyone else would have recognized the explosive implications of Catholics getting driven off their lands with the Cromwellian benediction "Hell or Connaught". No one was more troubled by Catholic resentment over past dispossession. No one would have wanted more to put an end to lawless dispossession in an area already marked by the plantations of the seventeenth century. No one would have dreaded more the effect such dispossession would have had on United Irish strength in the north. Finally, although the troubles of 1795 took place largely in Anglican areas of Armagh, the Presbyterians bore the brunt of the blame in FitzGibbon's eyes. His prejudices against them naturally inclined him to portray them as habitual rebels. In this respect, or so he believed, they were as bad, if not worse, than the Papists. Moreover, he had long feared an alliance between Catholics and Presbyterians. To sabotage such a dread development, he seized any pretext, however dubious, to present the Presbyterians as the natural persecutors and enemies of Catholics. This mordant and highly distorted view was revealed most clearly in his famous speech to Lord Moira, where he blamed the Presbyterians for setting off the original Peep Day–Defender quarrels. At the same time, he minimized the equal provocations of the Catholic Defenders, again portraying them as the helpless dupes of the United Irishmen.[50] His absorbing interest in Armagh and his close association with Wolfe make it virtually certain that he suggested the double hanging strategy. No doubt he took particular pleasure in recommending the salutary execution of Presbyterians. In short, if disturbances persisted, it was not because of lack of zeal or secret favour for the Orangemen on his part.

FitzGibbon does not seem to have warmed toward Orangeism even in its respectable and Anglican manifestations. An exchange during his visitation at Trinity College Dublin is revealing. The subject of Orange societies came up when Whitley Stokes made the claim that a lodge existed in the college, and that the oath contained expressions of hostility, and indeed of murderous intent toward Catholics. One Moore, a student who claimed membership in an Orange Lodge, made the contrary claim that "There is nothing of hostility against the Roman Catholics in their oath. Its principal object is to express their loyalty and attachment to the constitution".[51] A copy of the oath provided by a Sizar Smith seemed to confirm Moore's testimony. The oath simply required prospective Orangemen to swear that they were not Roman Catholics.[52] Both Moore and Smith also added that there were no Orange Lodges within the college, though students did belong to extra-mural branches, either in Dublin or in the North. FitzGibbon waxed indignant at Stokes for his implications about the murderous nature of the Orange oath. In response to Smith's rather dubious claim that the Orangemen made it a point to "entertain no animosity toward any man on account of his religious opinion", FitzGibbon made the smug and equally dubious observation, "This is the great distinction of the Established Church." He added "It was exceedingly improper in Dr Stokes to make the observation he did yesterday to the contrary respecting the Orangemen, unless he was well-founded".[54] However, when another helpful Orange witness, Blacker, tried to provide a justification for his organization, FitzGibbon abruptly cut him short.

> *Blacker*: "It [the Orange Society] was founded for self-defence."
>
> *Vice-Chancellor*: It is unnecessary here to enter into any account of the origin of such institutions. If you consider yourselves as associates only in a learned seminary, you will be learned men, you will be religious men, you will be great men.[55]

When Blacker in response avowed on behalf of his fellow Orangemen that they were "resolved never to meet within the walls of the College, and to obey the statues in every respect, as far as we can", FitzGibbon laconically replied, "You are perfectly right."[56] Toward Moore, the other College Orangeman, he was still more explicit in his distaste: "However proper it may be to express your sentiments of loyalty, any association united by an oath is highly improper."[57] In short, FitzGibbon had no quarrel as such with basic Orange principles. They were his own. But he disliked the semi-conspiratorial feature of the oath, however loyal and peaceable; it smacked too much of the methods of the United Irishmen, the Defenders, and the prototypes of the Orangemen, the Peep Day boys. If he defended the oath against the implications of Dr Stokes, it was mainly because the United Irishmen had made such a huge propaganda success by making similar claims about the murderous agenda of Orangemen. The visitation at Trinity offered him a last-ditch opportunity publicly to refute such fatally persuasive claims.

An exchange between Portland and Camden in the spring of 1798 more indirectly suggests FitzGibbon's coolness toward the Orange organization. In March 1798, Portland reported to Camden that he had learned of the formation of an Orange Society in Ulster, consisting of 170,000 and purporting to defend "the King and our happy constitution." Under ordinary circumstances he would have been suspicious of such organizations, and of the fact that they were bound by a secret oath. Nonetheless, under the present circumstances, Portland thought it might be useful to harness this loyal force and use it to restore order in the South, if need be. The orderly deployment of Orangemen, he continued, would set a good example and serve as an inspiration to the well-disposed. Portland ended with these comments: "If this spirit shall have gone forth and can be managed and directed in the way which I have suggested for your Excellency, I shall most sincerely congratulate you upon it and consider it as one of the happiest and most fortunate events which has happened in the course of your administration."[58] Portland evidently seemed unaware that large numbers of Orangemen had already enlisted in militia and yeoman units. Similarly, he did not seem to recognize that the presence of avowed Orangemen in the forces of order served as a terror and a discouragement to Catholics. It was perhaps happier and more fortunate that Camden responded as he did:

> altho' it is possible they may be useful, if the disorders in this country should take a still more serious turn, at present any encouragement of them much encreases the jealousy of the Catholics; and I should therefore think it unwise to give open encouragement to their Party ...[59]

Nonetheless, Camden added that it was "inexpedient" to suppress the Orangemen altogether, and he was perfectly happy to continue the unofficial array of Orangemen by encouraging their enlistment in regiments either of the regular army or of the militia.[60] Considering FitzGibbon's influence over Camden, it is difficult to believe that he did not have a hand in this response. It is particularly significant that Camden ended this letter with comments on the disaffection of even the most loyal Roman Catholics, who "wait with some hope that a Revolution in Ireland will restore them to those possessions and that consequence they have lost."[61] These remarks are so characteristic of FitzGibbon that they suggest a recent discussion on the subjects of Catholics and Orangemen. FitzGibbon was probably less concerned than Camden about offending Roman Catholics. Like Portland, the presence of an autonomous armed body bound by oath troubled him. But unlike Portland, he was not prepared to ignore their potential for disorder and subversion. Possibly, he saw disturbing parallels with the Volunteers. The Volunteers had started out in precisely the same way, as an organization of Protestants bound to defend the country and constitution from the French and from the Papists. His instincts for order and precedent, and his past troubles with the Volunteers, would naturally have inclined him to dislike the Orange organization. He preferred to pursue the Orange political agenda through the established organs of government, and to route Orange zeal into the existing armed services.

Throughout the pre-rebellion years, FitzGibbon continued to act in his accustomed capacity as the premier apologist for government. There was one curious exception: his silence during the debates on the Insurrection Act. Why FitzGibbon felt obliged to hold his peace about an act that was undoubtedly his creation is a mystery. In the past, he had positively relished affronting the sensibilities of Whigs, Catholics and other opponents. He may simply have felt that the act had enough support in the House of Lords to pass without any rhetorical effort from him. f such was his instinct, he certainly was right to follow it. The Insurrection Act passed through the Lords with near-unanimity and with the most feeble opposition.[62]

III

As was often the case in FitzGibbon's political career, the intrigues of the Whigs inspired his most notable efforts. The recall of Fitzwilliam had restored them to their usual position of marginal futility. Grattan, Ponsonby and their small parliamentary coterie, continued to pursue their chosen agenda of Catholic emancipation and parliamentary reform, with predictable failure and growing discredit. Many once sympathetic Protestants associated both with the terrifying specter of a United Irish secular and democratic republic, complete with redistributed land.

The situation of the English opposition, under the leadership of Fox, was equally desperate. Pitt's government still held firm, in spite of military setbacks and financial troubles. The disturbed state of Ireland offered them, as it had in the past, a means of embarrassing a government from which they were frustratingly and seemingly permanently excluded. In March 1797, Moira in the Lords and Fox in the Commons introduced resolutions calling on the King to "remedy the discontents which unhappily prevailed in his majesty's kingdom of Ireland" (Moira's words) and "to adopt such healing and lenient measures as may appear to his majesty's wisdom best calculated to restore tranquillity and to conciliate the affections of all descriptions of his majesty's subjects in that kingdom to his majesty's person and government" (Fox's words).[63] Fox also defined the proposed"healing and lenient measures" as Catholic emancipation and parliamentary reform. The resolutions suffered inevitable and lopsided rejection. Few members of either house wanted to get embroiled in the thankless morass of Ireland. They readily grasped at the excuse offered by Pitt in the Commons and Grenville in the Lords, that it did not behoove the English parliament to intervene in the affairs of a sister kingdom.[64]

The following year, in February 1798, Lord Moira took measures to answer the plea of Irish autonomy. He raised the subject again in the Irish Parliament, where he also had a seat. There he denounced the system of "coercion and severity ... by which this kingdom is ruled." He then introduced yet another variant on his resolution of the previous year: "His Lordship, after commenting at much length on the efficacy of union in the present contest against France and the attainment of that union through the concession of Catholic emancipation and parliamentary reform, moved that an humble address be presented to his excellency the lord lieutenant recommending the adoption of conciliatory measures in place of those extraordinary powers which he had exercised and which Parliament had invested him."[65]

FitzGibbon inevitably rose to respond. It was but one more battle in his endless war with the Whigs on both "sides of the water". Indeed, he had been preparing for this encounter for a long time. He apparently anticipated some trouble from the Whigs even before Fox and Moira introduced their resolutions in the English Parliament. In January 1797, during the opening of parliament, he alluded to the irresponsible opportunism of the Whigs and assigned to them a large share of blame for the present disorders:

> It was not, his Lordship said, to the petty traitors of the land alone, that a French invasion was to be ascribed and with which we have been threatened originated – it was the to the folly of the better kind of people in this country adopting an interest in British party politics, that we owe the treason of the United Irishmen, the subverting sympathy and the daring hopes of France – What have we to do with the parties which agitate British politics? What is it to us whether Mr Pitt or Mr Fox leads the Administration of England, let us confine our cares to our own country and labour to maintain indissoluble that connection with the sister Kingdom which Heaven has pronounced upon by every natural and social relation, and which I trust Heaven will forever preserve.
>
> For a number of years, continued his Lordship, the members of a disappointed opposition have endeavored to wound the administration by representing this country as discontented, through detracting from the strength and reputation of one part of the empire in proportion as they calumniated the other, this was echoed by their friends here and at length gave birth to a species of legislators, who more artful and more wicked, would have made these *political hypochondriacs* subservient to the ruin of the country.[66]

In many respects, FitzGibbon was as disingenuous in his comments on Irish party politics as he was pompous in his appeals to Heaven. (Pious sentiments clearly did not come naturally to him.) From the start of his public career, he was as involved in party intrigues as any Whig, English or Irish. It mattered a great deal to him personally whether Mr Pitt or Mr Fox was at the head of administration, because Mr Fox would have had no compunctions about dismissing him. As thin were his appeals to Irish autonomy. Less than three weeks before, in a letter to Auckland dated 22 December 1796, FitzGibbon had declared "I have long been of opinion that an union with the Parliament of England can alone save us".[67] But whatever his prevarications, he aimed at one ruthless, open purpose: to portray the Whigs in both England and Ireland as aiders and abettors of treason, if they ventured to criticize the campaign of repression, in whatever Parliament.

If he was indeed engaging in a preemptive strike against the Whigs, he not only failed, he suffered a measure of rhetorical defamation in return. In defending his resolution, Fox made the claim that "a regular system was then devised for enslaving Ireland". He then alluded to FitzGibbon as one of the devisors, and cited some remarks which FitzGibbon had allegedly made during the regency crisis: "A person of high consideration was known to say, that half a million of money had been expended to quell an opposition in Ireland and that as much more must be expended to bring the legislature of that country to a proper temper."[68] In actuality, or at least in the *Parliamentary Report*, FitzGibbon had made a grim jest rather than a corrupt threat. In the debate of 25 February 1789, Brownlow had expressed a fear that Buckingham, would follow the precedent of Lord Townshend and prorogue Parliament prematurely to prevent passage of the proposed short-money bill. FitzGibbon had confirmed that Townshend had indeed issued an early prorogation, and when Parliament next met, a majority "voted him an address of thanks, which address cost this nation half a million of money." Presumably the £500,000 had been the sum required, in pensions and offices, to create the desired majority for government. FitzGibbon then stated, *not* that Buckingham's administration was planning to spend a similar amount of money, as Fox suggested, but that he hoped "to God that I shall never again see half a million of the people's money employed to procure an address from their representatives."[69] Fox's misrepresentation badly rankled. FitzGibbon even went so far as to write a reproachful note to Fox, which he requested Lord Henry Fitzgerald to deliver. This letter seems to have disappeared, but if his accompanying letter of explanation to Lord Henry is any indication, the tone combined aggrievement with avowals of his own honesty, priggish lectures on the fairness which one gentleman owes to another, and warnings about the dangers of such misrepresentations to the security of Ireland:

> Will you excuse the liberty I take with you in requesting that you will be the bearer of the letter with which I trouble you. I have sent it to you under a flying seal that you may see it contains nothing unbecoming me to write, nor unpleasant, as I hope to you to communicate to your friend and kinsman, and therefore, when you have read it I shall thank you to close the seal then give it to Mr Fox.
>
> My reason for troubling you is that, if explanation can be necessary for my writing to him upon the subject, you know me well enough to be enabled to satisfy him that I am neither such a fool or madman as to mean him offense or to proceed in the discreet spirit of my country to express anything like anger at what has passed. I do not think it is in his nature wantonly to injure or insult any man, much less one who is placed in the defenceless situation in which I stand. In this instance, he has certainly been misled into a statement highly injurious and dishonourable to me and most utterly untrue. All that I desire or expect of him is that in future, when he makes allusions so very personal to me, and in terms which cannot be mistaken, that he will have the goodness first to assure himself of the accuracy of his information.
>
> I might have hoped reasonably that my name would not have been held up as the avowed profligate who had publicly recommended a system of enslaving the Irish parliament, when I am conscious to myself that I never harboured, much less inculcated such an idea. If Mr Fox knew me, he would know that I hate jobbing and jobbers and if he will look back on my political life, he will find it hard to fix upon me any one act of jobbing or corruption. I have heretofore endeavored to preserve the connection between Great Britain and Ireland. How long their best friends may be enabled to preserve it I cannot say.[70]

What response Fox made, if any, is unknown. But the personal attack on him by Fox gave a new urgency to his response to Lord Moira. He knew that he had come to symbolize the forces of brutality and oppression. In defending the policies of government, he defended himself.

FitzGibbon's speech in answer to Lord Moira ranks in greatness with his speech on the Catholic bill of 1793 and his speech on the Act of Union of 1800. Certainly it was an eloquent and comprehensive apology. His basic argument was stark and brutal: the social order was collapsing and only the most stringent measures could restore peace. If the government failed to perform its most fundamental duty of providing security, then it would be responsible for far greater bloodshed that any currently taking place. In alluding to the disarmament of Ulster, for example, he declared:

> The Minister who issues such an order is deeply responsible for the act; if he does it wantonly and on light grounds he is highly criminal; but if the occasion demands such an exertion of authority for the preservation of the state, the Minister who withholds it is responsible for all the evil which may arise from such an act of timidity.[71]

FitzGibbon then took it upon himself to trace the origins of the present discontents. Elaborating on the theme which he had set forth in January 1797, he blamed the present rebellion squarely on the disruptive activities of the opposition in both England and Ireland over the past twenty years:

> It has long been the fashion of this country to drown the voice of truth and justice by noise and clamour and loud and confident assertion; and since the since the separation of America from the British empire, where the noble Lord well knows some British politicians had successfully played a game of embarrassment against Lord North's administration, they had been pleased to turn their attention to Ireland as a theater of political warfare, and to lend their best countenance and support to every motley faction which has reared its head in this country to disturb the public peace for the most selfish and mischievous purposes.[72]

In other words, Whig factionalism had led to United Irish treason. The allusion to the activities of Moira's Whig associates during the American war was a particularly acute *ad hominem* dig: Moira was a distinguished veteran of that conflict. FitzGibbon would return to the uncomfortable subject of the American war again.

Having made the claim that the Whigs had set an example of disaffection, he held them up as proof of the failure of any policy of conciliation. He ran down the list of concessions that the British government had already made to meet opposition discontent: the opening of the West Indian trade in 1779, the constitutional concessions of 1782 and the renunciation act of 1783. In this particular re-telling of Irish history, FitzGibbon presented the rejection of the commercial propositions as the quintessential act of Whig factional perversity: not only did the generous concessions of the past fail to satisfy them, they wantonly rejected the substantial privileges which the English government had offered in a spirit of generosity and conciliation:

> This offer [the propositions] was wisely rejected by the Irish House of Commons, under a silly deception put upon the people of Ireland, who were taught to believe that the offer thus made to them was an insidious artifice of the British Minister to revive the legislative authority of the British Parliament, which had been so recently and unequivocally renounced; and under this gross and palpable deception, were the solid interests of Great Britain and Ireland, their mutual peace and harmony of indissoluble connection sacrificed in the House of Commons of Ireland on the altar of British and Irish faction.[73]

The Regency Crisis marked the culmination of Whig folly, and, FitzGibbon claimed, the fatal point at which selfish factionalism paved the way for outright treason:

> I pass by the events of that disastrous period and shall only say that the intemperate, illegal and precipitate conduct of the Irish House of Commons upon that critical and momentous occasion, has, in my opinion, in all its consequences, shaken to its foundation our boasted Constitution and eminently contributed to bring this country into its present dangerous and alarming situation.[74]

From the Whig Club, it was only a short step to the evils of the United Irishmen. As FitzGibbon related the history of the 1790s, the United Irishmen were a more fatal and effective version of the Whig Club. They had succeeded where the Whigs had often failed and created a universal anarch of violence and disaffection throughout Ireland. They had started with the Catholics. In 1793, FitzGibbon had chosen to portray them as bloodthirsty fanatics acting as the willing tools of the Pope and their priests. By 1798, he had learned the limitations of such rhetoric and he chose instead to portray them as essentially loyal, peaceable souls, willingly submitting to the steady direction of their gentry and aristocracy. Then the United Irishmen and their minions on the Catholic Committee intervened:

> The first object of this Jacobin institution was, to detach the Catholics of Ireland from a committee composed of the principal noblemen and gentlemen of their communion and to place them under the management of a Directory composed of men of a very different description. They saw that so long as the great body of Catholics were directed by men of rank and fortune and approved loyalty, their allegiance had remained unquestioned and that under such influence, it would be a vain attempt to shake it.[75]

FitzGibbon then repeated the old charges of the Secret Committee of 1793: the new Catholic "Directory", having destroyed the influence of the nobility and gentry, incited their poorer co-religionists to "associate under the title of Defenders." FitzGibbon was a bit more coy in framing these charges than he was in 1793, but it was clear from his remarks that he remained absolutely and inviolably convinced that the Defenders were the *enrages* of the Catholic Committee and of the Committee's ultimate masters, the United Irishmen:

> I will not say that this system of robbery and outrage which was struck out for an ignorant and deluded populace was first devised by the Catholic Directory: But your Lordships are in possession of full proof that some of the unfortunate men who were capitally indicted as Defenders in the Summer of 1792 were patronized and protected by them and that considerable sums of money were paid out of their stock purse to defray the expense attending the trials of some persons who were then convicted in the county of Louth.[76]

The "full proof" was, of course, the infamous letters of John Sweetman, who by 1798 was every bit of the revolutionist FitzGibbon had more dubiously claimed in 1793.

Having aroused the disaffection of the Catholics to a satisfactory pitch, the United Irishmen corrupted the Dissenters by appealing to their favorite cause, parliamentary reform.[77] They also encouraged both Catholics and Dissenters to engage in volunteering.[78] Through these various activities, the United Irishmen had succeeded well and thoroughly in importing all the terrors of the French Revolution into Ireland.[79]

In the face of such a determined and ruthless revolutionary conspiracy, FitzGibbon maintained, any suggestion of conciliation was ludicrous. He provided a highly colored picture of rebel murder and atrocity, dwelling in particular on the assassination of magistrates. It is pointless to relate all of his anecdotal evidence. It served above all to buttress another of his central arguments: mere reform was not about to satisfy men bent on the destruction of all government and order. Only vigorous force could prevent the dreaded aims which the United Irishmen had cherished from the beginning: separation from England and a democratic secular republic, which to FitzGibbon was tantamount to unthinkable anarchy.

He also maintained that the government, in exercising its necessary duties to restore order, had behaved with all possible restraint and moderation. In a statement that must have surprised many inhabitants of Ulster, he declared that Lake, in carrying out the disarming campaign, had acted "will all the moderation, ability and discretion which have always marked his character as a gentleman and an officer".[80] In what became one of the most notorious passages of his speech, FitzGibbon defended the picketing of a blacksmith, who under the influence of that excruciating torture, revealed the location of a store of pikes.[81] FitzGibbon admitted the cruelty of such methods, but argued that it would have been crueler to allow the pike to fall into the hands of "banditti" who would have used them on their peaceful, law-abiding neighbors:

> Let me here request of the noble Lord to reflect on the number of probable murders which were prevented by this act of military severity and appeal to his candour and good sense, whether the injury done to society in putting Mr Shaw [the pike making blacksmith in question] on the picket is in any degree to be put in competition with the injury which must have arisen in leaving two hundred pikes of his manufacture in the hands of the rebels and assassins of that disturbed district? I deplore as sincerely as the noble lord can do these

> necessary acts of severity, but the Executive Government was reduced to the painful alternative of using the force entrusted to it in defense of the King's peaceable and well-affected subjects of tamely giving them up to the fury of a fierce and savage democracy.[82]

FitzGibbon also resorted to clever *ad hominem* attacks to underline his point about the brutal, determined nature of the rebellion and the necessity of force. He alluded to Moira's own harsh actions in South Carolina during the American war; in particular, FitzGibbon revived the unhappy memory of Moira's summary execution of Isaac Haynes, an American officer who in violation of his parole had encouraged guerrilla activities.[83] The point was, of course, that Moira had not always been an advocate of mercy and gentleness in the face of rebellion. He also made the claim that Ballinahinch, the main town on Moira's estate, "may vie in treason with the town of Belfast".[84] In short, if Moira spent less time dabbling in Whig intrigue and more time on his estate, he would see the extent of the rebellion and the necessity of force.

FitzGibbon strove mightily to prove that the government's acts of repression were not only moderate and necessary, but absolutely even-handed. He dwelt with particular force on the sensitive subject of Armagh, which Moira had also raised in his denunciation of the Irish government. To him in particular, any implication that the government had encouraged the actions of the Orangemen was absolutely intolerable. His description of the events of 1795 and 1796 reduced them to a matter of United Irish intrigue and Orange excess. According to FitzGibbon, the violence in Armagh, was the result of the

> wicked machinations of the Irish Brotherhood, and with unblushing effrontery represented by them as a government persecution instituted against the Northern Catholics. I will state the short history of this religious quarrel, and the noble lord will see the grievous indiscretion into which he has been betrayed upon this head of his accusation against the Irish government. Many years since, the Protestants in a mountainous district of the County of Armagh, associated under the appellation of Peep Day boys to disarm their Catholic neighbors who associated for their common defense under the title of Defenders. This feud however was soon composed and for years there was not a revival of it; but when the general system of robbing Protestants of their arms was established by the Irish Union, and the lower orders of Catholics, assuming their old appellation of Defenders, undertook this service, the Protestants formed under the appellation of Orangemen to protect themselves, and got the better of the Catholics; in so doing, they did commit many very grievous excesses, which I lament as much as the noble lord.[85]

If he blamed the United Irishmen for reviving the conflicts between Peep Day boys and Defenders, he put as great a share of blame on the gentry of Armagh, and in particular on the magistrates of that county, for keeping sectarian antagonism alive for their own electioneering purposes. In short, the bloodshed in Armagh was the fault of the United Irishmen, the magistrates, over-reacting Protestants and credulous Catholics, the fault of everyone *but* the government, which had tried throughout to restore order and to administer justice fairly.

Not only were the measures Moira proposed, Catholic emancipation and parliamentary reform, ineffectual in the face of widespread disorder, they were dubious in and of themselves. With regard to Catholic emancipation, FitzGibbon again maintained his judicious good manners and refrained from the excesses of 1793. He confined himself to constitutional abstractions: "... the altar was the pillar of the throne"; to undermine the Act of Supremacy and the other statutes which maintained the political monopoly of the Established Church would undermine the state itself. These acts could hardly be construed as harming the interests of Catholics; they already enjoyed the most perfect protection for their lives, liberty and property. The laws maintaining the establishment in church and state "bind us all indifferently". FitzGibbon did venture on the old ground of the dangers of allowing Catholics to exercise power in a Protestant state; nonetheless he framed these arguments with startling and effusive flattery for the Catholics themselves, at least in one account of his speech:

> No man in this country or out of it can entertain a higher respect for the Catholics of Ireland than I do – From this respect partly proceeds the fear that I would feel to admit them to these offices. I know the firmness of their religious attachments and that no conscientious Catholic can take or observe these oaths.[87]

His position had not changed one jot from 1793, but if he succeeded in nothing else, Moira had forced him to play an unaccustomed role: the friend and admirer of the Catholics reluctantly forced by the clear dictates of the constitution to exclude them from parliament and office.

As for the demands for parliamentary reform, they were essentially pointless:

> ... experience has proved that in the midst of popular turbulence and in the convulsions of rancorous and violent party contests, the Irish Parliament as it is now constituted, is fully competent to all practical and beneficial purposes of government, that it is fully competent to protect this, which is the weaker country, against encroachment and to save the empire from dissolution by maintaining the constitutional connection of Ireland with the British Crown.[88]

As in 1797, FitzGibbon was not speaking in full candour. He had long since decided that the Irish Parliament was not competent to do anything, much less secure Ireland for the British Empire, and he was secretly anxious for its dissolution. But it would not have done, of course, to have revealed his own disaffected purposes. For purposes of the attack on Lord Moira, it suited him to play to part of constitutional champion, not only of the Church, but of the Irish parliament.

But FitzGibbon had not yet run out of arguments against Moira's proposals. Not only did his proposals violate their Protestant constitution, granting them at this particular point would teach the lower orders a dangerous lesson: if they threatened enough, they could get what they wanted: "If we are to make such a precedent for the encouragement of rebellion, I beg of the noble Lord to say, where are we to draw the line?[89]

Finally, he made a masterful reversal of Moira's central premise, that the government, and by implication, FitzGibbon himself, was brutal and tyrannical. Moira and his fellow Whigs were by no means acting out of disinterested compassion for the suffering people of Ireland. On the contrary, they were cynically exploiting the ignorance and credulity of the Irish to re-establish the aristocratic tyranny that Lord Townshend had broken:

> If the noble lord wishes to know the genuine source of ostensible Irish grievances, he will be enabled to trace it to some of his political friends and connections in Great Britain and Ireland. The genuine source of Irish complaint against British government is, that they will not second the ambitious views of some gentlemen who claim an exclusive right to the public mind and to monopolize to themselves and their dependents the power and patronage of the Crown. The genuine cause of complaint against the British Cabinet is, that they will not suffer these gentlemen to erect an aristocratic power in Ireland which shall enable them to dictate to the Crown and the People, which shall enable them to direct and control the administration of Great Britain, by making the country of this government impracticable by any but their political friends and allies.[90]

In other words, the true champions of liberty and of the people of Ireland were in fact the King's ministers, and by implication of course, FitzGibbon. They were trying under the most difficult circumstances to restore order and to provide security to the law-abiding. The Whigs' seductive promises of Catholic emancipation and parliamentary reform masked their schemes to re-instate their own party tyranny.

Moira's answer was brief, if only because it would have been difficult indeed for even the most ready orator to have responded to such a flood of refutation, ridicule, and outright denunciation. He either had not seen FitzGibbon's letter to Fox or he had not been convinced by it, since he alluded once again to the famous remark about the £500,000.[91] FitzGibbon almost gleefully seized on Moira's comment, not only to establish his innocence, but his gentlemanly credentials as an Oxford scholar: "As to the transactions in Lord Townshend's time, he could have spoken of them merely from report as at the time they took place he was at the University of Oxford."[92]

FitzGibbon took great pride in his response to Moira, and he honored Pitt, Auckland and other of his English and Irish intimates with published copies.[93] In actuality, the speech probably did little to change opinions either way. He no doubt gave great assurance to fellow reactionaries who thought the United Irishmen, and the Catholics, whether Committee men or Defenders, should be hanged before they succeeded in guillotining or assassinating Protestant men of property. It appears to have had no effect whatsoever on the Whigs. On the contrary, if Lady Holland's journal is any indication, FitzGibbon's speech confirmed their own conviction of his shameless bloodlust. The Speech of the Honorable John, Earl of Clare, Lord High Chancellor of Ireland etc., etc. was known in fashionable Whig circles, simply as the "rope speech".[94]

FitzGibbon probably could have cared less what Lady Holland or any or her political or social intimates thought. But he could not maintain this air of lofty indifference when it became apparent that he had offended the premier Whig, the Prince of Wales. In ridiculing Moira's claims that he had publicly addressed his tenants and instilled in them a salutary sense of loyalty, FitzGibbon suggested that Moira had instilled, not loyalty to the king and constitution, but Whig partisan loyalty to the prince:

> he [Moira] says that he explained to his tenants in the town and its vicinity the horrors of republicanism, the many advantages of the Government and constitution under which they live, and above all, they he explained to them the splendid virtues of the heir apparent of the crown, that they all made to him the most unbounded professions of loyalty in which however, he would not have put implicit confidence if he had not observed the countenance of every man to whom he had addressed himself beam with joy and triumphant affection when he mention the name and the splendid virtues of his Royal Highness the Prince of Wales. Giving the noble lord full credit as a physignomist, I must conclude, if he will excuse me for a little professional pedantry, that the loyalty of his town of Ballinahinch is in *abeyance* during the life of his present majesty.[95]

It was a typical FitzGibbon *jeu d'esprit,* brutal and graceless. Unfortunately it could be taken, not only as a gibe at Lord Moira, but as an insult to the Prince. FitzGibbon inadvertently suggested not only that the Prince, as well as his Whig intimates, hoped to benefit from Irish disorder. In the wake of his supposed triumph over Lord Moira, FitzGibbon found himself in the humiliating position of offering apologies and explanations to the Prince through the good offices of Lord Abercorn.[96] Unfortunately, the Prince, upon receiving this communication, chose to consult Lord Moira, who was an intimate boon companion, but not a very detached or favorable judge. Not surprisingly, Moira made very harsh comments about Lord Clare's letter, his character and his veracity. While not magnanimous, Moira's sentiments were perhaps understandable: FitzGibbon had after all recently portrayed him a partisan intrigante. He did, nonetheless, encourage the Prince to make a non-committal, if not a conciliatory reply. He wisely saw that neither the Prince nor the Whigs could afford another imbroglio with a man who, however despicable, retained a large measure of power and influence and who had a positive genius for embarrassing them all.[97]

FitzGibbon himself seemed far more aware of his vulnerability than of his strength, to judge by the letter itself. Although he wrote with angry bravado to

Auckland, complaining of the Prince's blind reliance on Moira, he did not forget that the King, while malleable, was also frail and aging.[98] He could not afford to alienate Prince, if only because he could suddenly change from Lord Moira's dupe to the King of England. His letter, consequently was exceedingly long, and exceedingly abject, not to say cringing:

> But above all, I felt and earnest and anxious desire to relieve myself from the pressure of an imputation which lay heavy upon me, that I had been so lost to all sense of duty and decorum as to mention the name of your Royal Highness with levity and disrespect in the House of Lords of Ireland. Your Royal Highness will I hope believe me to speak with the genuine sentiments of my heart when I assure you that abstracted from every personal feeling for your Highness, I would cut out my tongue if it could give utterance to the feeling of disrespect for the family of my King. If I know myself, ingratitude is not among the vices of my nature, and surely I must be a monster of ingratitude if I were capable of treating your Highness with levity or disrespect in public or in private. I can never forget the unmerited attention with which I have been honored by your Royal Highness from the first day when I had the honor of being presented to you, and it will be the pride of my life to prove to the world that I feel most sensibly the duty by which I am bound to you.[99]

The letter makes for sad reading, if only because it suggests a fundamental lack of self-respect in FitzGibbon. Clearly, he shrank from no act, however degrading to himself or to others, to preserve his power from the most remote threats, including threats from his own blunders.

On a lesser level publicly, but on a very serious level privately, he also offended his dear friend Lady Louisa Conolly. In giving an account of the rebellious savagery of the lower orders, he observed that even Lady Louisa Conolly, in spite of her many acts of benevolence, was living in a state of virtual siege at Castletown.[100] Lady Louisa's servants and tenants evidently took this as a slight on their loyalty and she in turn wrote to FitzGibbon, defending their conduct. His letter of response illuminated FitzGibbon's kindlier qualities. He assured Lady Louisa that his remarks about her servants had been misrepresented, and he had never intended to cast aspersions on them. He then requested her "in my name [to] set their minds at perfect ease on this subject". He closed with singularly gracious and eloquent expressions of esteem: "Be assured that I never can think or speak of you without affectionate admiration and that I am with the truest respect and regard always your Ladyship's faithful humble servant."[101]

As for the content, as opposed to the effect of the speech, it would be possible perhaps to fault FitzGibbon for over-simplification. The United Irishmen, while certainly as active and as well-organized as he suggested, may not have been at the bottom of every rural outrage in the 1790s. Though they certainly saw the advantages of an alliance with the Defenders, FitzGibbon's claim that the Defenders were little more than subordinate auxiliaries of the United Irishmen from the start is open to question. While fundamentally correct about the government's role in the Armagh business, as has been noted, he was not always judicious or careful in assigning blame. For his own cynical and prejudiced purposes, he let the Defenders off too lightly, and laid too great an onus of blame on both the Presbyterians and the United Irishmen. Even his portrayal of the Whigs is open to dispute. They were reckless and eager for office; they had indeed set an example of contentiousness and extra-parliamentary agitation that the United Irishmen and the Catholic Committee imitated with dangerous effect. They were indeed naive to believe that Catholic emancipation or limited parliamentary reform would have satisfied the radical aspirations of the 1790s. But FitzGibbon himself was as partisan as any Whig, as ruthless in grasping power as they were in seeking it, and as unscrupulous in promoting his own private agenda of a union. He also disregarded the genuine, if frequently wrongheaded and disastrous, idealism of Whigs such as Fitzwilliam and Grattan. Moira himself could scarcely be dismissed merely as a hypocrite and opportunist with a short memory. Toward the end of his life he governed India with great competence and benevolence. But however easy it may be to quibble with FitzGibbon's interpretation of history, it is impossible to doubt his insight, his striking, if sometimes maladroit, turn of phrase and above all, his brave consistency. He never backed down and he never wavered, no matter how formidable his enemies, whether aristocratic Whigs, Catholics, or United Irishmen.

As for the policy which he defended at such great length, it is pointless to tax FitzGibbon with brutality. He was the avenging angel of the British Empire, locked in eternal conflict with the forces of republican darkness, Catholic, United Irish, Defender, French and American. Any means, from mock hanging to martial law, were worth the end, the preservation of British and Protestant civilization in Ireland. There was no room in his moral universe for the possibility that violence and repression can easily consume and corrupt the ends they are supposed to preserve. Nor could he admit the possibility that the Whigs, the United Irishmen, or the Defenders had legitimate causes for grievance. His rule was necessarily right. FitzGibbon was trapped not only by his own moral arrogance, but by the assumptions of his time. Pitt and his successor Liverpool were every bit as ruthless in their response to discontent, and Camden looked longingly at the harsh measures allowed by Scottish law.102 It was simply a given that sedition and rebellion merited only the responses of coercion and force. It was left to the Whigs of the early 19th century to prove their point that judicious reform can silence discontent while leaving the structure of power fundamentally intact.

If it is foolish to have expected FitzGibbon to have transcended his personality and time, it is as foolish to claim, as Whig historians later did, that he engineered his policies of repression with the deliberate intention of encouraging a rebellion and with it an excuse for union.[103] His entire career was marked by a terror of disorder, by a sense of Irish history as a relentless and bloody cycle, with 1641 just a revolution away. He wanted a union as a protection against further upheaval; he would never have encouraged upheaval to obtain a union.

IV

Up to the outbreak of the rebellion, FitzGibbon continued his personal campaign against Jacobinism and republicanism. In April, in company with Patrick Duigenan, he made his visitation to TCD. There he hectored a succession of cowed or defiant collegians into admitting their own or others' involvement in United Irish activities. In the process, he subjected his captive student audiences to a variety of his opinions on matters ranging from the insidious evils of necessitarianism to the value of evening lectures as a means of keeping impressionable youths out of mischief. His *modus operandi* was characteristic: he was lenient toward students who admitted to involvement in the United Irishmen, and more important, identified others. Toward those who chose to keep their counsel, or those, like Emmet, who defiantly refused to appear for interrogation, FitzGibbon was relentless. Not only did he order their expulsion, he announced his intention of writing to the chancellors of Oxford and Cambridge, providing a list of the student expelled and preventing the miscreants from infecting English seats of learning with their evil principles. It was a characteristic piece of over-reaction on FitzGibbon's part. It is doubtful that many of the students in question had the inclination or the religious background for Oxford or Cambridge.

The visit ended in the expulsion of 19 students. They ranged in age from 13 to 21; the greater number of them, seven in all, were sons of farmers; the next largest group consisted of the sons of "private gentlemen", followed in number by the offspring of merchants. The most notorious expellee, Robert Emmet, was the premier exception: he was the son of a physician. Religious affiliation was listed for only six of the students: five Roman Catholics and one Protestant. Nonetheless, it did not necessarily follow that students for whom no religion was listed were Protestants. George Keogh, the son of John of Catholic Committee fame, obviously was Roman Catholic, though no religious affiliation was listed by his name. To go by the very unsound criteria of name, family background and county of origin, the total of expelled students possibly came to ten Protestants and nine Roman Catholics. In effect, the students were typical of the United Irishmen as a whole, middling to well-to-do as far as income went, and fairly evenly divided between Catholics and Protestants.[104]

FitzGibbon thought the students he expelled were a very bad lot. (His own term for them was "pestilent".)[105] Yet it is impossible not to recognize and admire their bravery. Those who refused their co-operation stood firm before threats, questions and verbal bullying that had broken more mature men in the courts and in parliament. At one point, FitzGibbon took it upon himself to remind John Browne of Belfast, "You know the consequences, Sir, of your refusal." Browne responded with true northern forthrightness, "If the consequence was instant death, I would not take the oath."[106] George Keogh, who gave his age as fifteen, maintained his silence even when FitzGibbon gave him this sententious warning: "Think what must become of you in manhood, when at fifteen years old you have secrets in your breast which you are ashamed or afraid to reveal."[107] Little George was no doubt acting out of a contempt instilled by his father, not out of fear or shame.

FitzGibbon in contrast appeared throughout as a pompous bully, and sometimes as a ridiculous one. One Dogherty not only refused to reveal the name of a student who tried to recruit him to the United Irishmen, he also deprived FitzGibbon and Duigenan of the satisfaction of expelling him: "I am resolved to quit this country. I have no friend here. I will go to America." To which FitzGibbon responded, "You will never get forward there without money", a statement that as easily could have applied to Ireland as to money-worshipping America.[108] Probably the best that can be said in FitzGibbon's defense is that he was occasionally more moderate and conciliatory than Patrick Duigenan. For example, over Duigenan's strenuous objections, he permitted one student to keep his counsel about the names of his United Irish acquaintance, on the grounds that they were well known already.[109] He even had the grace, however briefly, to express his admiration for Dogherty's bearing, as well as regret at the necessity of expelling him.

But FitzGibbon went after bigger game than mere adolescent dabblers in rebellion. He expended much interrogatory energy on Whitley Stokes, a distinguished junior fellow and physician. He had already suffered FitzGibbon's attentions in 1797, when he testified before another Committee of Secrecy on the activities of the United Irishmen. Stokes had indiscreetly joined the United Irishmen at their foundation. According to his own account, he had left the society in 1792 and since that time had been "strictly a neutral man".[110] But FitzGibbon as well as his confederate attacked Stokes for keeping up contact with such United Irish unregenerates as Richard McCormick and Thomas Russell. Not only his personal, but his financial contacts with the society came under scrutiny. "Stokes at first balked at Duigenan's query, "Did you ever subscribe money to the funds of the Society of United Irishmen" :

> *Dr Stokes*: I cannot answer that question. I am not obliged to answer questions that may criminate myself.
>
> *Dr Duigenan*: Sir, you are bound by your statutes to answer every question which your Visitors shall propose to you.
>
> *Dr Stokes*: The oath ex officio is taken away by the act of King Charles II.
>
> *Dr Duigenan*: That act holds only in England.
>
> *Dr Stokes*: Lord Yelverton's act re-enacts in this country all English acts relative to oaths, but [*sic*] the act of Charles II relates to oaths. Therefore it is of force in Ireland.[111]

FitzGibbon intervened to warn Stokes that if he refused to answer questions, "it is our business to remove you". However, showing more tact and skill at cross-examination than Duigenan, he rephrased the question:

> Have you any objections to say whether you advanced any money to the United Irishmen since the year '92?[112]

Stokes was able to make the emphatic response: "I certainly did not since the year '92." Unfortunately, Stokes was a bit hazy in his chronology: toward the end of the visitation, it was established that Stoke had contributed to the prison expenses of Oliver Bond and Simon Butler in 1793. Not only was the date incorrect, Stokes' charity had gone to a cause guaranteed to antagonize FitzGibbon.[113]

Nonetheless, Stokes managed the amazing feat of convincing FitzGibbon that his contacts with United Irishmen after 1792 were on the whole brief and innocuous: he had contacted McCormick only to explain some testimony which he had given to the Committee of Secrecy, and he had acted as Russell's physician, not as his fellow conspirator. The warm testimony of Stokes' colleagues, as well as his activity in organizing a college yeomanry corps also stood him in good stead. If Stokes balked at answering questions, gentlemanly distaste for the role of informer, however inconsequential the information, as well as distaste for the tone of the proceedings themselves accounted for his reluctance, not guilty knowledge.[114] But he paid a high price for his moral fastidiousness, as well as for his early enthusiasm. FitzGibbon allowed him to retain his fellowship, but he placed harsh restrictions on his future advancement:

> We have, therefore, determined that he shall have no pupils, nor be raised to the board of senior fellows for the space of three years. We have fixed on that period, that when we come down to our next triennial visitation, we may see whether he has abjured all intercourse with these traitorous associations and wiped himself clean as a person countenancing a system of treason for the subversion of the established government of this country.[115]

Stokes survived this ignominy to enjoy a distinguished career, and his son later made an even greater name for himself as a physician. But the impression remains that Stokes was punished less for his indiscretion than to set an example to the other tutors and fellows of the university. FitzGibbon, in effect, expected them to operate as unpaid spies, on the watch for any future indiscretion in their students, when they were not engaging in salutary evening lectures and assigning additional translations of Longinus and Tacitus, FitzGibbon's other recommendations for keeping young minds out of mischief.[116] If they were reticent or reluctant as was Stokes, their careers would suffer like his.

The newspapers, even the erstwhile opposition ones, reported that FitzGibbon left Trinity in triumph, cheered on by the purged and loyal student body.[117] No doubt, it represented a great triumph indeed to break any United Irish organization in Trinity, however rudimentary it appeared to be. Not only was Trinity the premier center of learning in the country and the school where future public men were formed, it was physically strategic. With some foresight, FitzGibbon recognized the danger of a band of collegiate United Irishmen seizing control of buildings so close to the Parliament and the Castle. But in light of the deluge that broke out less than a month later, the great purge of Trinity took on an air of theatrical futility.

During the rebellion itself, FitzGibbon, like most members of the government, was confined to Dublin. Since the business of repression now lay exclusively with the military, and not with parliament or the courts, he was largely relegated to the role of correspondent and commentator. Auckland was the chief recipient of his accounts, though the problematic Malone correspondence contains some fugitive letters on the subject as well. As was his wont, he acted the armchair general and criticized Walpole's incompetence.[118] And of course, he gave a full account of the sectarian atrocities committed by the Catholic rebels in Wexford.[119] Yet there is a curious quality of detachment in FitzGibbon's letters on the subject of events in Wexford, along with an absence of the rhetorical excess that sometimes marked his speeches on Catholic issues. He seemed to recognize that he had no need to resort to any device beyond simple narrative: the brutality of the rebels in Wexford proved his point about Catholic inveteracy and savagery as years of speechmaking never could.

V

Given FitzGibbon's own past attitudes, he ought to have been at odds with the Marquis of Cornwallis, who arrived in July to replace the exhausted and discredited Camden. For one thing, Cornwallis did not fit the usual pattern of Pitt's viceroys, that is to say he was not an ignorant, inexperienced and intellectually modest young aristocrat. He was on the contrary, a mature and experienced man with a distinguished civil and military career. He endured service in the American war of independence, and most Americans remember him only as the losing general at the battle of Yorktown. But American myopia and self-importance aside, his career in India as governor-general of Bengal is probably of far more significance. There, he won military victories over a far more formidable foe than General Washington, Sultan Tipoo of Mysore. He also promulgated an ambitious land reform scheme in Bengal, which was humane in conception, if not always practical in application. As early as 1797, Pitt had considered sending him to that other troubled pole of empire, Ireland, but Cornwallis had refused, mainly because he disagreed with the central premise of Irish policy at the time, the denial of further political rights to the Catholics. He felt that without "very great concessions little if at all short of what is termed Catholic Emancipation", military coercion was futile. The demands of 1798 put these disagreements in abeyance: nothing seemed more suited to the circumstances of rebellious Ireland than a lord-lieutenant who was also a capable soldier. In addition to his military experience, he brought qualities which had been absent from Irish government for many years: firmness, humanity, moderation and independence of mind.

From the start he made it clear that he would not tolerate sectarian triumphalism or gratuitous attacks on Catholics. In both his official and his private correspondence, he insisted on attributing the rebellion to Jacobinism, rather than Catholicism, as had become the habit of the more rabid loyalists.[121] His determined fair-mindedness inevitably enraged many loyalists, some of whom took to calling him "Croppy-Wallis".[122] Others attributed his leniency towards Catholics to concupiscence: according to one malicious loyalist gossip: "Corny is snug at the Park [Phoenix Park] and ... he has a *Papist* girl."[123]

FitzGibbon might have been expected to join, if not lead, the ranks of loyalist detractors. Yet by July, Cornwallis had come to the startling conclusion that FitzGibbon was "the most moderate and right-minded man among us".[124] Still more extraordinary was this letter, which Cornwallis directed to Portland in September 1798:

> The principal personages here who have been in the habit of directing the councils of the Lord-lieutenants, are perfectly well-intentioned and entirely attached and devoted to the British connection, but they are blinded by their passions and prejudices, talk of nothing but strong measures, and arrogate to themselves the exclusive knowledge of a country of which from their own mode of governing it, they have in my opinion proved themselves totally ignorant.
>
> To these men I have shown all the civility and kindness in my power and have done for them all the ordinary favours which they have asked, but I am afraid that they are not satisfied with me, because I have not thrown myself blindly into their hands. With the Chancellor, who can with patience listen to the words *Papist* and *Moderation* , I have inevitably talked on all public points which have occurred ...[125]

Much of what Cornwallis said of these unnamed "principal personages" could as easily have applied to FitzGibbon in his past career. He had been no stranger to passions and prejudices, his speech to Lord Moira had been a long series of variations on the theme of strong measures, and he too had frequently piqued himself on his superior knowledge of Ireland. And yet Cornwallis arrived in Ireland to find a soul mate of moderation and magnanimity.

In part, FitzGibbon's usual habit of ingratiating himself with the lord-lieutenant shaped the persona that he presented to Cornwallis. Unlike cruder, less intelligent reactionaries, FitzGibbon saw from the start that Cornwallis had come to conciliate, not to aid and abet the Protestants in their campaign of revenge against Catholic rebels. To retain his hegemony at the Castle, he adopted the same language of moderation. But it would be profoundly unjust and inaccurate to attribute his actions solely to his exquisite instincts for getting and keeping power. He also acted out of habits of mind that had existed long before he came into contact with Lord Cornwallis. In the first place, his view of the lower orders as the hapless stupid tools of "intelligent treason", while a degrading oversimplification, nonetheless disposed him to mercy. He always preferred to blame and to retaliate against their leaders. Secondly, FitzGibbon felt himself in a position to afford mercy. He was convinced that after the rebellion, which to borrow Cooke's phrase, was largely of a "Popish complexion", the English government would never again seriously entertain either Catholic emancipation or any other reform that could undermine Protestant supremacy. Better still, the rebellion gave new credibility to his own secret radical agenda, the dissolution of the Irish parliament and union with Great Britain. Thirdly, FitzGibbon's keen sense of Irish Catholic historical memory may have inclined him to exercise moderation in the aftermath of the rebellion. The arbitrary and frequently unjust acts of retaliation following the rebellion of 1641, to his mind, had created a permanent sense of grievance that had contributed in large part to the rebellion of 1798. He wanted to avoid adding to the cumulative weight of historical resentment and thus to avoid future rebellion.

Such considerations prompted him to co-operate fully in a legislative campaign of amnesty. He enthusiastically cooperated in framing the so-called act of grace, which gave a free pardon to those rebels who surrendered their weapons and took an oath of allegiance. This act of grace was not comprehensive; if nothing else, such sweeping generosity would have outraged loyalists. In the initial stages of the legislation, FitzGibbon had left blanks in the clause for exceptions. The intention was to allow the beneficial provisions of the act of grace to go into effect as soon as possible, while allowing various magistrates, military officers and others with more extensive local knowledge to suggest exceptions.[126] But the English cabinet and in particular FitzGibbon's English counterpart, Loughborough, objected to giving assent to an incompletely drafted bill.[127] In response to these criticisms, FitzGibbon, presumably in consultation with Castlereagh, Cornwallis's chief secretary, Cornwallis himself, Cooke and Wolfe, added general categories of those exempt from pardon. Exceptions encompassed persons guilty of murder or conspiracy to murder soldiers, yeomen who either deserted or administered United Irish oaths, those having "direct communication or correspondence with the enemy", and those United Irishmen who had served as members of the executive, provincial and county committees, as well as those holding the rank of captain. Members of this last class of exception were offered the opportunity to surrender themselves by a certain date and go into exile, rather than face trial and execution. Much correspondence was expended on the inclusion of United Irish captains in the list of exceptions to the general amnesty. Cornwallis took an almost apologetic tone as he explained to Portland why men who held what appeared to be a comparatively modest rank were excepted: "... I should not have inserted those who in the general organization of the conspiracy, received only the appointment of captains and who in most of the counties were men of very little consideration, if I had not understood that in some few counties these Captains were the leaders in the Mischief, and the most powerful agitators of treason."[128] But far more important than all this activity spent on determining exceptions is the reason behind it: Cornwallis and FitzGibbon wanted to present the parliament with a *fait accompli* in the form of a few broad categories of exemption. They dreaded above all the prospect of the Irish Parliament, in a revenge-minded fury, drawing up long and detailed lists of exceptions, based on the prejudices or private feuds of individual members. The strategy seemed to work: the act did pass with comparatively few rumblings, as both Cornwallis, and FitzGibbon himself had hoped.

Although the government expressed its intention to punish the ringleaders of the rebellion, their most singular act of mercy affected men of a very high rank indeed: the United Irish leaders in Leinster, notably Thomas Addis Emmet and William James MacNeven. They had not had the opportunity to participate in the various rebellions that broke out in the spring of 1798. In March of that year, the government had arrested them and seized their papers.[129] Insofar as FitzGibbon was concerned, the arrests resulted in one of the more colorful and violent scenes in a life littered with assaults on his carriage and house, duels and challenges to duels. After the arrests of Emmet, MacNeven and their confederates, FitzGibbon again confronted that commonplace of his political life, an angry mob, while en route to a meeting of the Privy Council at the Castle. He displayed great bravery, and on a less edifying level, his full repertory of coarse language. Apparently, the display of a pistol rather than his inventive expletives eventually dispersed the crowd.[130]

The business of putting down rebellion in the field delayed any legal measures against the "Directory", but by July, the government had set into motion the grim machinery of prosecution. Oliver Bond, FitzGibbon's erstwhile judicial victim of 1793, was found guilty of treason and condemned to death in company with William Michael Byrne, adored by the United Irish hagiographers, Madden and Teeling, for his youthful courage and gallantry, condemned by the government for collecting arms in anticipation of a French invasion.[131] The condemnation of Bond in particular unnerved some of his fellow members of the United Irish directory. The 19th-century hagiographers attributed the subsequent actions of the state prisoners to comradely feeling for Bond and pity for his wife and children.[132] Such considerations may have played a part, but more important perhaps, Bond's condemnation alerted the state prisoners to the government's earnestness and to their own danger. In an effort to avert the executions of Bond and Byrne and to prevent further prosecutions and death sentences, the prisoners approached the government with a proposal: in return for their testimony about their revolutionary and diplomatic activities, they would go into voluntary exile. In addition, their testimony was to have certain limits. They would testify only to their own actions; they would not implicate or testify about others. William James MacNeven was especially anxious to initiate such negotiations, as there was much evidence of his negotiations with the French, another major category of hangable United Irish offense.[133] Arthur O'Connor was reportedly more reluctant, but he could afford the luxury of defiance.[134] He had already escaped the clutches of English justice at Maidstone, and the Irish government had far less of a case against him.

Cornwallis and Castlereagh were initially willing to consider the proposal. Nonetheless, their premier apostle of clemency and moderation, FitzGibbon, was at Mount Shannon, convalescing from his latest bout of ill health. In his absence, there was "no other of our political friends who was likely to have temper to hear even the statement of the question I sent"[135] A consultation with a group of law officers and judges, among them Carleton, Kilwarden, the Attorney and the Solicitor General and the prime serjeant, did not provide the sort of judicial detachment which Cornwallis had apparently expected. The response of Chief Baron Carleton, whom Cornwallis described as "a cool and temperate man", was highly influenced by the political climate and highly unfavorable: he "gave his opinion in the most decided manner against listening to the proposal, and declared that it would have such an effect on the publick mind, and that he did not believe if Byrne and Oliver Bond were not executed, that it would be impossible to condemn another man for high treason".[136] He also added his conviction that some to the state prisoners who had signed the proposal, particularly MacNeven, could conceivably be convicted, while the others "might be liable to pains and penalties by proceedings against them in Parliament". According to Cornwallis, "Kilwarden and the Attorney General spoke to the same effect".[137] In the face of so much overwhelming judicial opposition, Cornwallis backed down and rejected the proposal. Byrne, slated for execution first, was hanged immediately afterwards.

FitzGibbon's reappearance in town revived negotiations and brought a new respite for Bond, the remaining candidate for the gallows. He of course favored the plan. He had no pity for the state prisoners as he did, in a fitful, condescending way, for the rebels in the field. On the contrary, he held them all in the utmost contempt. It would appear that he particularly despised MacNeven. In a letter to Auckland, he sneered at MacNeven's apprehensions as his own trial and probable execution approached.[138] But FitzGibbon's historical sense came to the rescue of the state prisoners, as it had come to the rescue of more obscure participants in rebellion. He had no wish to create martyrs, even of the reluctant Dr MacNeven. Martyrs kept alive the spirit of resentment and disaffection, and inspired further rebellion in honor of their sacred memory. More important, FitzGibbon welcomed the opportunity to obtain testimony from the prisoners themselves. He anticipated using their admissions of negotiations with the French and of other revolutionary activity not only to discredit the United Irishmen, but to protect the government form the accusations of liberal Protestants that its harsh measures had been unjustified. He could associate Catholic emancipation and parliamentary reform, the two great forces of unrest of the past two decades, with Jacobinism, atheism, bloodshed and chaos. Thus, he could confirm the prevailing order forever.

FitzGibbon's influence over-rode that of his colleagues Kilwarden and Carleton. At his urging the government again entered into negotiation with the prisoners and agreed to their conditions, testimony about their own activities in return for their permanent exile in any country not at war with the King of England. As Kilwarden had predicted, many loyalists were infuriated that high-ranking United Irishmen had cheated the gallows with government connivance.[139] FitzGibbon nonetheless held firm to his conviction that the deferred pleasures of public discredit were preferable to the immediate pleasures of violent judicial revenge.

Disappointed loyalists could at least take some satisfaction in Bond's fate. As a result of the successful negotiations with the government, he avoided the fate of his young companion Byrne. But he celebrated his deliverance with such enthusiastic excess that he died a few days after his reprieve.[140]

The state prisoners fulfilled their end of the bargain by testifying before committees of secrecy in both the House of Commons and the House of Lords. One such show had already taken place, in 1797, prompted by the discovery of a cache of United Irish papers. The resulting report, which FitzGibbon had of course drafted, had already established the government line: the United Irishmen were revolutionary conspirators bent on overthrowing the government, effecting a separation from England and establishing a republic with the aid of the ambitious, godless French. The appeals to Catholic emancipation and parliamentary reform were simply empty slogans used to dupe the ignorant and credulous to join their treasonous ranks.[141] The Secret Committees that sat in the autumn of 1798 had no other purpose but to re-assert the same premises. They differed from the Committee of 1797 only in having the cooperation of high-ranking United Irish witnesses. The state prisoners, for their part, also had motives other than the mere recitation of whom they had seen in Paris and how they had obtained arms: they hoped to portray themselves to the public in both England and in Ireland as honest, well-intentioned reformers, driven into rebellion by the cruelty and excess of the government.

FitzGibbon played his part in this rather empty farce in his usual style. As he did at the Trinity visitation, he reveled in the role of compleat polymath. For example, FitzGibbon seized the opportunity to demonstrate again his much self-vaunted knowledge of the Irish Catholic lower orders as well as a smattering of the Irish language. In an effort to show that the lower classes were not necessarily violent bigots, Dr MacNeven observed that they hated Protestantism only because they associated it with the English conqueror, not because they had any theological objections as such. When MacNeven, a native Irish speaker, pointed out that the Irish word for both Protestant and Englishman was *Sassanach*, FitzGibbon quickly confirmed the truth of his observation, something presumably that few of the other noble lords on the committee could have done.[142]

In the midst of these diversions, FitzGibbon never lost sight of his fixed purpose, which was to bring as much discredit as possible on the United Irishmen and their dangerously seductive program. He set the tone of his interrogation by asking MacNeven whether the common Irish cared "so much as a drop of ink from this pen" for Catholic emancipation and parliamentary reform. MacNeven admitted that many did not, but he emphasized that just as many of the poorer Irish had access to newspapers, and had formed both an understanding and an opinion on both issues.[143]

FitzGibbon of course disregarded the finer nuances of MacNeven's response and in his final report he repeated once again the old verity:

> As to Catholic Emancipation (as it is called) it was *admitted* by them all to have been a mere Pretence from the first Establishment of the Irish Union ...[144]

The hapless MacNeven's testimony provided FitzGibbon with another opportunity for misrepresentation and distortion. At one point, MacNeven tried to explain the opposition of the United Irishmen to all Church establishments. He would, he declared, "as soon see the 'Mahometan' religion established as the Catholic".[145] In writing up his report, FitzGibbon willfully took this to mean that MacNeven was bent on destroying, not *religious establishments* but *religion itself*, Catholic as well as Protestant.[146] MacNeven, in fact was a dutiful Catholic; years later, his elaborate requiem mass enthralled and delighted New York City.[147] But FitzGibbon succeeded in portraying MacNeven as a bloodthirsty infidel, and himself, for one brief amazing moment, as the defender of the Catholic religion.

The final printed versions of the reports infuriated the prisoners. Their feelings were perhaps understandable, though they surely must have recognized that a report on the United Irishmen authored by FitzGibbon would hardly be a model of balance, nuance and fair-mindedness. Anger led to indiscretion: the chief witnesses published an advertisement denouncing the reports of the secret committees and denying their validity.[148] Much outraged letter-writing on the part of various government functionaries ensued, as well as some threats to proceed with trials and hangings in the wake of this display of bad faith on the part of the prisoners.[149] In the end, the government took the less drastic course of re-convening the committees of secrecy in both houses.[150] The prisoners were then called upon to specify those points they considered false or misleading. Their objections turned out to be few and minor. O'Connor quibbled about the date of his initial negotiations with the French, while MacNeven, already identified by FitzGibbon as a Catholic infidel, denied that it had ever been his intention to pay debts to France by selling the lands of the established church.[151] This episode did little to increase enlightenment on the subject of the United Irishmen and much to sour tempers on both sides. It became the overriding wish of the government to get rid of the lot.

In this wish, the Irish government was thwarted. Cooke, Castlereagh and the other Castle habitus had assumed that the prisoners would retire in obscurity and discredit to America. They had not reckoned on the vagaries of American foreign policy. The United States was preparing to go to war with France in the wake of a diplomatic insult. Consequently, the American minister to England, Rufus King, adamantly refused to accept the United Irish state prisoners because of their past intrigues with France. To King's nervous, Francophobic mind, the Irish state prisoners could as easily side with the French against the American government.[152] The Irish government had no choice but to comply with King's wishes. Faced as he was with overcrowded prisons, Castlereagh did express some irritation at King's inconvenient fastidiousness:

> It is perfectly natural that America should be very jealous of receiving Irish convicts but unless she prohibits emigration from this country altogether, she will infallibly receive United Irishmen and the majority of our prisoners are not more dangerous than the general class of American settlers.[153]

The bulk of the state prisoners were simply released once Loyalist passions had died down. Nonetheless, the most prominent and notorious prisoners, including O'Connor, MacNeven and Emmet, remained in custody until 1802. MacNeven and Emmet eventually settled in the United States, once the tide of Francophobia and xenophobia had abated. There, they took a belated but no less satisfying revenge on King. Emmet successfully mobilized Irish voters to defeat King in his bid for the New York Assembly in 1808.[154]

FitzGibbon also had dealings with various individual rebels and alleged rebels, in addition to his *en masse* actions toward prominent United Irishmen and their anonymous followers. In some cases, he was openly vindictive, as only FitzGibbon could be. The Auckland correspondence contains an instance so grisly that Auckland's fastidious Victorian descendant edited it out of the 19th century published version. FitzGibbon simply could not understand why, after Wolfe Tone's sadly botched suicide attempt, the provost marshal could not haul him off and hang him anyway, severed throat and all.[155] There is little that can be said in FitzGibbon's defense. He was no doubt angry that a man to whom he had shown clemency used his life and liberty to engage in arch-rebellion. Nor was he alone in expressing a belief that Wolfe Tone should hang, whatever his self-inflicted wounds. Some of the officers who oversaw Tone's imprisonment were similarly disgruntled.[156] At any rate, Tone's death, was fully as agonizing as FitzGibbon would have wished, even without the hangman's intervention.[157]

FitzGibbon also received blame from Francis Plowden for allegedly persecuting Francis Arthur, a wealthy Limerick Catholic. Arthur, a yeomanry officer, was accused among other things, of receiving letters from Lord Edward Fitzgerald, of storing arms and of enrolling United Irishmen in western Limerick. The chief witness against him was a man called Maum, but according to Plowden, there were more powerful men behind him, FitzGibbon among them. Plowden made claims of an animus against Arthur for political, religious and personal reasons:

> With that gentleman [Arthur] Lord Clare was personally acquainted, and no man better knew the extent and weight of Mr Arthur's property and influence in the country. His Lordship's interests had felt the power of their opposition, his pride had been galled by the contraction of his arbitrary despotism, from the liberal and constitutional principles of a man of independence. Thenceforth he was a marked object of proscription and persecution. He had moreover, given private displeasure to his Lordship and was a Roman Catholic. The ministers of public terror were let loose upon him and by their ingenuity of torturing have exhibited in their native colors, the spirit and tactics of the system.[158]

Plowden also made the lurid suggestion that the notorious Judkin Fitzgerald of Tipperary had a hand in Arthur's troubles. According to Plowden Maum, already convicted for various acts of rebellion, was on his way to Botany Bay when he was stopped and brought before Fitzgerald. "In what particular manner he was tampered with cannot be traced further than that the [name] ... of Arthur [was] then suggested to him, ... of whom it appears he had not the least knowledge. It appears also that some assurance was given to him by the High Sheriff of the County of Tipperary (Thomas Judkin Fitzgerald) which made him perceive an interest in convicting some persons, under the description of accomplices with him."[159]

Plowden's lurid melodrama aside, the case against Arthur does appear to have been rather flimsy. Maum made the claim that Lord Edward Fitzgerald entrusted him with letters for Arthur; he claimed further that Lord Edward had named Arthur as a particular intimate. Nonetheless, the only evidence that Arthur had even received such letters came from two military officers, Captain Brand and Lieutenant-Colonel Cockerell. They claimed to have heard from a certain Joseph Anderson that he had pointed out Arthur's house to Maum, so that he could deliver the letters. These claims Anderson denied: "The witness is positive that Maum did not ask him to point out Mr Arthur's House."[160] Nor could the assembled court-martial obtain any evidence of the more violent acts alleged against Arthur, collecting arms and recruiting United Irishmen, apart from hearsay repeated by the same Joseph Anderson. He was no doubt anxious to make up for his earlier failure as star witness by offering other, safely unprovable allegations.[161] The court-martial could not convict Arthur of treason and hang him, but at the same time, it could not entirely repudiate evidence offered by high-ranking officers. Consequently, it entered the verdict that he was "guilty in part of the crime laid to his charge", presumably that he had received correspondence from Fitzgerald. In the absence of evidence capable of sustaining a capital charge, the court-martial ordered him to pay a fine of £5,000 "in to the Treasury for the use of his Majesty" after which he was to be transported for life.[162]

The evidence suggests that General Morrison, who commanded the army stationed in Limerick, was absolutely convinced that Arthur was deeply involved in treason and was a dangerous man. Morrison does not seem to have been an inordinately bloodthirsty or violent man. In summarizing the Arthur case to Castlereagh, he added, that in conducting the courts-martial, he had tried to extend "lenity, Forgiveness and even Tenderness ... to the deluded".[163] But he insisted that Maum had prevaricated about the key point of the whole trial, his inquiries for directions to Arthur's house. He also insisted that Arthur had "*endeavored* to prove an alibi", the implication being that he had tried to devise or create an alibi where none had existed. Morrison's letter also contains the only evidence of FitzGibbon's involvement in the case: "... in regard to his character, I have understood him to be a most dangerous man and as I am a stranger in the country, will only refer his excellency to the Lord Chancellor and Gen'l Massey (now in Dublin) whose country residences are in this neighborhood."[164] In other words, FitzGibbon, when asked by Morrison, had described Arthur as a dangerous character. FitzGibbon did behave with supreme irresponsibility in making such an assessment of Arthur. He seems to have forgotten that he was Lord Chancellor, with a tremendous amount of influence and a responsibility to behave with equity both in and out of his court. By indulging in this bit of private character assassination, he not only harmed Arthur, he abused his office. Nonetheless, this indiscreet display of personal animus does not amount to a deliberate plot by FitzGibbon to frame Arthur as Plowden suggested.

The aftermath of Arthur's case seems to suggest that on the contrary FitzGibbon may actually have intervened to mitigate the terms of Arthur's sentence. Again the evidence is slight and indirect. Arthur appealed his sentence, and Castlereagh made the following summary of his case as the government viewed it:

> In addition to my official letter of this day, I must be permitted privately to mention to you that the proceedings of the Court Martial on Mr Arthur are not transmitted in such a form as can enable my Lord Lieutenant to make an adequate judgment on the case. No treasonable matter is alleged against Mr Arthur, but Mr Maume's [sic] deposing that Lord Edward had told him Arthur was one of his confidentials, which is mere hearsay evidence and is inadmissible. The mere delivery of letters is not treasonable without proof of the tenor of the letters – and Mr Arthur's offering Mr Maume [*sic*] money in consequence of Ld Edward's letter is not treasonable unless it be proved that Arthur knew that Maume was employed in treasonable practices by Lord Edward and that the money was given for these purposes. All these circumstances justify suspicion but do not prove guilt.[165]

In light of the absence of convincing evidence, the government reduced Arthur's sentence from transportation to temporary banishment. He was simply to absent himself from Ireland for the duration of the rebellion. He was also obliged to pay the massive fine decreed by the court martial.[166] The analysis of the evidence against Arthur suggests a professional competence far beyond anything Castlereagh, no lawyer, could have managed on his own. It seems likely, if not certain, that he consulted a knowledgeable professional man who moreover knew intimately the circumstances and people of Limerick. Only one person in the Irish government could have fit that description.

Moreover, Arthur's trial and sentence took place at the end of June and the beginning of July, shortly after Cornwallis's arrival. He would surely not have commented on FitzGibbon's moderation and right-mindedness if he had arrived in Ireland to find the lord high chancellor actively pursuing a legal vendetta against a prominent Limerick Catholic. If FitzGibbon did indeed help to frame the opinion which Castlereagh relayed to Morrison, such an action would surely have contributed to Cornwallis's initial high opinion of him.

FitzGibbon may indeed have detested Arthur; he may indeed have put in a bad word for him with General Morrison, at some time in the past. But the nature of the government communications suggests that once Arthur was convicted and sentenced, FitzGibbon recognized the fundamental legal unsoundness of this action and intervened to help, rather than harm, Arthur. If he stayed discreetly in the background, he may have done so to avoid embarrassing Morrison, who had formed his own opinion of Arthur from FitzGibbon's own observations.

Finally, James Roche once again serves as a witness in FitzGibbon's favor. As a prominent member of the Limerick merchant community, he surely knew Francis Arthur very well. Yet he declared, without any exception or reservation, that FitzGibbon had saved many people, now very respectable, "from the lash and the halter", in spite of the undeniable guilt of some of them.[167] Roche was very old and possibly mildly senile when he penned his charming, if rambling memoirs. But even in his dotage, he could not have forgotten the tribulations of a rich and noted member of his own community. Still less would he have forgotten FitzGibbon's part in them, if any. The fact that he made no comment about Arthur suggests that Roche numbered him among those FitzGibbon had intervened to save.

One charge of cruelty against a fallen rebel even Grattan the younger found hard to swallow, though of course, he felt obliged to include the charge in his father's memoirs. Evidently there were claims that FitzGibbon had proceeded in "great state" in his carriage to watch the execution of Dr Esmonde, who was hanged from the Carlisle Bridge with grisly incompetence. Grattan the younger made the observation that FitzGibbon was probably caught in the crush of observers while on his way from the Four Courts and was perforce, a witness of the spectacle.[168] FitzGibbon had taken some interest in Dr Esmonde, if only because he served as such a useful example of the cruelty and rebellion ingrained the "old inhabitants" of all ranks. In one of his epistolary commentaries on the rebellion, he made a point of mentioning to Auckland that Esmonde was a Roman Catholic with an income of £1,000 a year.[169] But whether FitzGibbon would have gone out of his way to see this particular rebellious Catholic "old inhabitant" dispatched is certainly open to doubt.

Along with the well-documented example of his harshness to Tone, and the more dubious instances of alleged cruelty to Arthur and Esmonde, FitzGibbon engaged in highly visible acts of mercy. Roche claimed that before the rebellion FitzGibbon had met with the Sheares brothers to warn them about the dangers of dabbling in revolution, with no success and with mutual anger and frustration.[170] The brothers were captured and condemned to death for, among other actions, inciting troops to desert. Sir Jonah Barrington continued the melodramatic saga of the Sheares brothers with the story of his own appeal to FitzGibbon to permit a stay of execution. According to this tale, FitzGibbon read a letter from Henry Sheares, and offered the comment, "What a coward he is!" Nonetheless, he agreed to obtain a respite for Henry, though he insisted "John Sheares cannot be spared." FitzGibbon does not seem to have pursued the matter any further than to offer his half-hearted and contemptuous cooperation. Barrington, according to his own account, spent a hair-raising and futile day racing about the corridors of the Castle, trying to obtain the necessary documents to spare Henry's life. He arrived at the prison to find the executioner severing the head of his old college friend and holding it aloft with the ritual proclamation, "Here is the head of a traitor."[171]

FitzGibbon's role in Lady Louisa Conolly's final interview with Lord Edward Fitzgerald was perhaps his most notable act of grace. Years later, Sir Charles Napier, a nephew of Lady Louisa, who inherited all the political prejudices of his Fitzgerald relations, gave this grudging but candid account of FitzGibbon's conduct in a letter to Madden:

> I abhor Lord Clare ... but truth is truth and [he] behaved like a man of feeling and generosity on that occasion.[172]

He did so by allowing Lady Louisa to visit her nephew's deathbed, a request refused by all the other major figures of government. FitzGibbon himself initially had refused any requests by family members to see Lord Edward, but when Lady Louisa, accompanied by her niece Sarah Napier, appeared on his doorstep at night to press her case once more, he was unable to resist her dramatic and pathetic appeal. He called for his own carriage and accompanied Lady Louisa to Newgate. There he waited for three hours, the duration of Lady Louisa's hard won final interview, which ended in Lord Edward's death. Reportedly, the sight of Lady Louisa encountering her doomed nephew brought tears to FitzGibbon's eyes.[173] His tears were a mark of his grief for Lady Louisa, no doubt, but they also may have been a sign that the carnage of the 1790s could sicken and weary even Lord Clare.

FitzGibbon later suffered much blame from the younger Grattan for following this act of grace and pity with an act of attainder against Lord Edward. Infected by the melodrama which inevitably seemed to surround the affairs of Lord Edward, as well as by his own pious antagonism for FitzGibbon, young Grattan painted a picture of the chancellor overriding all legal objections and forcing the attainder through the House of Lords.[174] The Fitzgerald family inevitably took the view that the attainder represented an act of gratuitous judicial cruelty against their beloved black sheep. Recruiting Charles James Fox and other prominent relations, they appealed to Pitt, to Cornwallis and to the King, on the grounds that Lord Edward could not suffer attainder, since he had not lived to stand trial.[175] The appeals failed and the attainder passed. But young Grattan, in attacking FitzGibbon for this act of cruelty to Lord Edward's family, naturally failed to take into account FitzGibbon's awkward position at the time. In the face of much opposition, he had already agreed to clemency for a group of notorious rebels. He simply could not afford to defy loyalist opinion any further, in spite of his love for Lady Louisa, his sorrow over Lord Edward's misspent career and his feeling for the Fitzgerald family. The government needed to make an example of at least one prominent rebel to placate loyalist opinion. Also, the younger Grattan failed to mention that FitzGibbon had made arrangements to sell Lord Edward's meager property to his step-father, Ogilvy, at a nominal price.[176] Ogilvy was then to hold the property in trust for Lord Edward's children. FitzGibbon also seems to have had every intention of reversing the attainder at some time in the more peaceful future. His own sudden death prevented him from taking this much desired step. Owing mainly to the law's delay and not to any lingering malevolence against Lord Edward, the attainder remained in effect until 1819.

Table 1 Students Expelled from Trinity, 21 April 1798

Name	*Father's profession*	*Age at admission*	*Where born*	*Religion*
Thomas Robinson	Merchant	20	County Dublin	**Protestant**
Thomas Corbett	Not given	Not given	Not given	Protestant*
William Corbett	Farmer	13?	County Cork	Protestant*
David Shea	Farmer	16	County Limerick	Roman Catholic*
John Carrol	Farmer	21	County Limerick	**Roman Catholic**
Dacre Hamilton	Private gentleman	15	Dublin	Protestant*
Arthur Newport	Merchant	15	Waterford	Protestant*
John Browne	Merchant	16	County Antrim	Protestant*
Peter McLoughlin	Farmer	15	County Mayo	Roman Catholic*
George Keogh	Private gentleman	13	County Dublin	Roman Catholic**
Bernard Killian	Farmer	24	County Fermanagh	Protestant*
Edmund Barry	Farmer	19	County Cork	Roman Catholic*
Thomas Bennett	Merchant	18	Cork City	Protestant*
Robert Emmett	Physician	15	Dublin	Protestant**
James Thomas Flinn	Merchant	22	Dublin	**Roman Catholic**
Michael Ferral	Farmer	19	County Longford	**Roman Catholic**
John Pennefather Lamphier	Private gentleman	18	County Tipperary	Protestant*
Patrick Fitzgerald	Private gentleman	15	County Kerry	**Roman Catholic**
Martin John Ferrall	Private gentleman	21	County Cork	**Roman Catholic**

Bold text in the right hand column indicates that religion was recorded for student. A single asterisk indicates my guess as to student's religion, based on the often unreliable criteria of name or place of origin. A double asterisk indicates that the student's religion was not recorded, but it is known from other sources. I again must thank Dr Anthony Malcomson and the staff at PRONI for providing me with a copy of the register of expelled students

18

The Act of Union and After, 1798–1802

I

The rebellion finally gave Pitt the pretext he had long been seeking to make a public introduction of the idea of a union. He assumed that there was enough mutual hatred between the various religious factions and enough general disillusionment with the political structure in general to render the idea of union a matter of indifference, if not of outright rejoicing. Protestants would find themselves in a safe majority, while Catholics and Presbyterians presumably would find domination from Westminster less irksome than the contemptible familiarity of domination from Dublin. Accordingly, in the autumn of 1798, Pitt summoned the leading members of the Irish government to London to discuss the idea. FitzGibbon, of course, was among the first to make the journey to London.[1]

His support for the union probably garnered for FitzGibbon his greatest degree of infamy in the eyes of generations of nationalist memoirists and historians. Yet he played a comparatively minor role in the actual passage of the great act. Because the House of Lords was a secure government preserve, he was not obliged to engage in a great campaign of corruption, *à la* Castlereagh. Nonetheless, there were some struggles, notably a short-lived contretemps over the status and number of Irish peers in the Union House of Lords.[2] The government also suffered the unexpected and unpleasant surprise of Lord Downshire's defection on the question.[3] Nonetheless, the smaller numbers in the House of Lords made it easier for the government to manage discontents and to minimize the effects of disaffection. FitzGibbon sponsored a petition in his home county of Limerick: predictably FitzGibbons and Furnells numbered heavily among the signatories.[4] He also bore most of the expenses for this outpouring of loyal, unionist sentiment in Limerick. In 1802, the printer was dunning his estate for the as yet unpaid costs of making copies of the petition.[5] FitzGibbon did have some procedural disagreements with the government's approach to the union. He would have preferred to have made use of parliamentary commissioners to negotiate the terms of union, after the pattern of the Scottish Act of Union, rather than a forced bill.[6] While a rabid and eager unionist, he also had some qualms about pursuing the matter in a time of war.[7] But whatever his doubts about timing and method, there is no question that he welcomed the measure, that it had been the desire of his heart since 1793, that he saw no choice between union and the chaos of government by a weak feckless Protestant elite, perpetually endangered by Popish "projects" and Presbyterian Jacobins.

The matter of Popish projects accounted for most of the drama and complication in this episode of FitzGibbon's life. From the start, there was a fundamental misunderstanding between FitzGibbon and the English government about the nature of the union. To FitzGibbon the union was no more and no less than a means to secure Protestant supremacy forever. The incorporation of Ireland into the United Kingdom would secure a solid Protestant majority, which majority was unlikely ever to pass an act of emancipation. The English government was not so consistent or so rigid. Most English statesmen with any influence over Irish affairs, seem to have accepted the likelihood that the remaining Catholic disabilities would eventually be removed. They saw the union not as a means of permanently deferring Catholic emancipation, but as a necessary condition for passing such an act with safety to the Protestant interest in Ireland. Pitt and Westmorland had both taken such a view of the union as early as 1792, and even Pelham flirted with the notion of some sort of a "final settlement" of the Catholic issue, with or without a union.[8] Certainly Cornwallis, Castlereagh, and Edward Cooke thought that emancipation would eventually follow a union, though they were unwilling initially to unite the two issues.[9] A union along Protestant lines was to take place before any discussion of emancipation. Emancipation following quickly on the heels of a Catholic rebellion could have angered Irish Protestants and, by making them more recalcitrant toward the union, could have impeded its progress.

It would appear that FitzGibbon's colleagues in government prudently concealed their true sentiments about the relationship between the union and Catholic emancipation. Nonetheless, to tax Cornwallis, Castlereagh, and Cooke with deceit would be an exaggeration. Probably they hoped that once the union passed, FitzGibbon, like other Protestant diehards, would abandon his morbid fears of the Irish Catholics and comply with a final emancipation bill. Nor was such a belief entirely fanciful. FitzGibbon after all had supported the bill of 1793, which was passed under far more dangerous and turbulent circumstances. Moreover, FitzGibbon's public demeanor toward the Catholics between 1795 and 1798 had been, at least by his standards, remarkably polite and moderate. For example, in 1796 he had expressed his hope to Frederick Trench that "Catholic gentlemen of good principles" would raise yeomanry units. He went on to add that the true struggle was not between Catholic and Protestant, but between "good order and protection" and "Anarchy and Plunder".[10] In a similar spirit, he defended the officers of the newly revived Irish Brigades from aspersions cast on their loyalty and their religion by Lord Blayney.[11] There was also his moderate conduct in the aftermath of the rebellion, which had convinced Cornwallis of FitzGibbon's fundamental "right-mindedness". In private, of course, FitzGibbon's comments remained more in character. At the same time that he was making encouraging noises to Frederick Trench about Catholic yeomen, he was implying to Lord Camden that the chief purpose of the yeomanry was indeed to keep a close watch on the Catholics.[12] As for his defense of the Irish Brigades, it was a comparatively cheap gesture of good will. The Duc de FitzJames and the Comte Walsh de Serrant were not interested in equal political rights or a reform of parliament. Moreover, the brigades were in fact deeply resented by the majority of Irish Catholics. Poorer Catholics looked upon the officers as émigré crimps, while Catholic gentlemen resented that fact no similar commands had been offered to them.[13] In short, FitzGibbon was as antagonistic as ever toward Catholics. He had simply acquired a modest degree of prudence in venting his prejudices. Even during the initial negotiations about the union, he had continued to play the part of moderate man of good will. There was, for example this amazing account by George Canning of his encounter with FitzGibbon in London in 1798:

> Chapter 1: Lord Clare's arrival in London. Lord C. himself very reasonable. Confesses he fears nothing himself from the Catholics having everything but it is impossible to carry the point in Ireland.[14]

His claim of indifference on the subject of Catholic emancipation was, to put it bluntly, a lie, as his own behavior after the union amply proves. He no doubt felt he could afford to make such remarks because he would never be called upon to prove his sincerity. In short, if FitzGibbon was "deceived" on the subject of Catholic concessions, he had no one to blame but himself. He had engaged in considerable deceit himself, giving his colleagues in government the distinct impression that he was not the bigoted die-hard of the past, but a moderate and pragmatic man, who could be persuaded of the necessity of emancipation when the time was ripe.

FitzGibbon's conduct over the Maynooth bill of 1799 exploded this particular delusion. A bill confirming a new grant to the college had passed through the Commons with comparative ease, and the Irish government expected simply as a matter of course that there would be virtually no debate on it in the Lords. Instead, FitzGibbon proposed throwing out the bill. In so doing, he made a ferocious speech denouncing the institution of Maynooth as "a useless expense to the public". He criticized the application of past grants, and he complained about the government's lack of power over the institution itself. He also cast aspersions on the caliber of students at Maynooth. Because education at Maynooth was provided at government expense, it attracted mainly "youth of a middle class"; these eleemosynary young men lowered the tone of the place. As a result, "the parents of ... a higher distinction would not send their children there." Presumably the uncouth middle class charity pupils lost a civilizing influence in the guise of their wealthy, well-born co-religionists. Most devastating of all, FitzGibbon seized the opportunity to remind his fellow lords of the conduct of many Catholic priests during the rebellion. Instead of warning their flocks about the evils of treason and inculcating proper sentiments of loyalty, they had remained either indifferent, or they had actively participated in the rebellion. As an example, he signaled out Thomas Hussey, the Roman Catholic bishop of Waterford and, more important, the president of Maynooth. FitzGibbon described him as "the author of a diabolical pamphlet that went to commit Catholics against Protestants an to create rebellion in the county". FitzGibbon's portrayal of Maynooth's president as a Popish firebrand "went to commit" his fellow peers against any grant for the college. By a resounding minority, they threw out the bill.[15]

His arguments against the Maynooth bill were tactless and often illogical. Thanks to his sweeping claims of financial chicanery, FitzGibbon managed the considerable feat of provoking the spirit and the anger of Lord Kenmare. His fellow lay trustees were as indignant at FitzGibbon's implications of mismanagement and hastened to vindicate their conduct.[16] Clearly, they were not placated by FitzGibbon's suggestion that their offspring would exercise a civilizing influence on their fellow classmates of a lesser "distinction". Considering the reactionary politics of the Catholic gentry and aristocracy, and their alienation from their poorer co-religionists, it is highly doubtful there could have been much refining and liberalizing contact between the sons of the grandees and their less exalted classmates at Maynooth.

As for FitzGibbon's allusions to the conduct of some priests during the rebellion, they had little relevance to the subject at hand, and, in the case of Hussey, they were grossly unfair. Hussey was an unlovely man in many respects: temperamental, hot tempered, and unpopular with the government and with some of his fellow Catholic bishops.[17] But he was also a distinguished scholar, who had earned the respect of no less a man than Doctor Johnson. Moreover, to portray Hussey, of all people, as a Popish rebel, was flagrantly absurd. Hussey had tirelessly opposed Jacobinism and was horrified by the United Irishmen. He offended mainly by demanding respect for the consciences and religious sensibilities of Catholics, in stark contrast with his more pliant predecessors. Notably, he had acted on behalf of soldiers who were forced to attend serves in Protestant churches. The "diabolical pamphlet" in question had simply pointed out that the Protestant temporal powers had no right to interfere with Catholic theological teaching or religious discipline, a distinction acknowledged by the act establishing Maynooth. And FitzGibbon was hardly in a position to condemn Hussey for sectarian hate-mongering; his own pronouncements in the subject of religion were at least as inflammatory, if not more so.[18] Above all, Hussey's occasional acts of tactlessness and the activities of the rebel priests scarcely proved that the college had failed in its mission to produce loyal Catholic clergy. After all, both Hussey and his opposite number, John Murphy, had been educated in Spain.

FitzGibbon's behavior was as baffling as it was astonishing. Hitherto, a chilly neglect had characterized his attitude toward Maynooth. It is true that in the initial stages of the college's establishment, FitzGibbon had made some hostile rumblings to Beresford on the subject: he suggested that the government support for Maynooth possibly represented yet another violation of the almighty Coronation Oath.[19] Nevertheless, he did not pursue this line of argument further. Calculated acquiescence to Camden and Portland, who saw Maynooth as an essential sop to hostile Catholic opinion, and satisfaction at the more essential success of defeating Catholic emancipation probably accounted for his restraint. Initial hostility gave way to contemptuous indifference. Although the act establishing Maynooth appointed him one of the trustees, FitzGibbon showed a marked lack of interest in the duties of his position. For example, he failed to attend a meeting concerned with the crucial business of selecting a site for the school.[20] Of course, a busy man like FitzGibbon could hardly be expected to concern himself with day to day minutiae. But for a man who had expressed such morbid suspicions of the Catholic clergy in the past, he showed a remarkably offhanded attitude to an institution run by and for that class of men.

His action clashed not only with his past behavior as a trustee, but with his loyalties as a servant of government. Cornwallis wanted above all to ensure either Catholic support for or at least Catholic indifference to the union. The Maynooth grant was an essential part of this placatory strategy, as FitzGibbon surely must have known. The grant also was extremely unpopular with many Protestants who wanted either an outright abolition of the college or a severe reform of its governing policy.[21] Open denunciations of Maynooth from a man of FitzGibbon's stature encouraged the college's enemies and humiliated the government.

Concern about a new "Popish Project" of the English government's may have overwhelmed FitzGibbon's usual loyalties and roused him from his wonted languor toward Maynooth. In the winter of 1799, the English government was seriously considering a state subsidy for the Catholic clergy in return for a measure of control over ecclesiastical appointments in the British Isles.[22] Toward this end, Robert Hobart, the former chief secretary, entered into negotiations with the Vatican and with the Irish and English Catholic clergy. Sir John Cox Hippesley, an expatriate resident in Rome and a self-appointed expert on Vatican affairs, acted as the go-between. These negotiations had nothing whatsoever to do with the bedeviling issues of emancipation. The English government was simply interested in gaining more influence over the Catholic clergy and in turn more effectively using them as agents of political and social control in Ireland. But a Catholic clergy under the control of government, dutifully inculcating sentiments of loyalty to King and Constitution in return for a subsidy, could effectively undermine claims of the subversive nature of the Roman Catholic Church, one of the premier arguments against emancipation.

Their close friendship makes it very likely that Hobart informed FitzGibbon about his activities. FitzGibbon was far too shrewd not to see the full implication of these contacts with Rome. No doubt to his mind, negotiations for clerical subsidies could lead all too easily to negotiations for further political rights for the laity. FitzGibbon probably had no desire to intervene directly to put an end to the business. His experiences in 1793 and in 1795 would have taught him the risks of aggressive meddling. Moreover, open opposition would have embarrassed friend Hobart. Instead, he may have resorted to legislative theatrics, casting himself as the Protestant avenger of extravagance and dishonesty and the Maynooth board of trustees as Popish wastrels and ingrates. By throwing out the bill, he may have hoped to demonstrate the unpopularity of any support for the Irish Catholic clergy, whether middle class seminarians or parish priests. This spectacle of Irish Protestant outrage would, in turn, discourage any further rapprochement between London and the Vatican.

Whatever his motives, FitzGibbon paid a high price for his actions. Cornwallis, predictably furious, berated FitzGibbon as though he were a clumsy subaltern. In particular, he reproached FitzGibbon for encouraging extreme reactionaries who were "so blinded by their Protestant zeal as to exult exceedingly in the justice of the punishment which they conceived to be hereby inflicted on the Catholics for their late offenses".[23] The fact that Cornwallis was probably the first lord-lieutenant ever to cross FitzGibbon is not the only point of interest. Cornwallis had thought of FitzGibbon as his most staunch ally against "Protestant zeal"; by rejecting the Maynooth bill FitzGibbon had betrayed their common principles. FitzGibbon in his turn blustered: he had been grossly misquoted by the newspapers. In the speech as he had actually delivered it, he had "distinctly and repeatedly" maintained the necessity for a "well-regulated academy" for Roman Catholics.[24]

Cornwallis was perfectly unmoved by FitzGibbon's tribulations with the press. He insisted that FitzGibbon make an immediate public declaration of his and the government's support for Maynooth. FitzGibbon duly took the next opportunity in open Parliament to declare that the rejection of the Maynooth bill did not mean the demise of the college:

> His Lordship stated that it had erroneously gone abroad that the House of Lords wished to overthrow the entire establishment. Nothing had fallen from him to warrant such an opinion. He thought the institution a useful one and under proper control and management of great national consequence.[25]

In the meantime, Castlereagh scrambled to undo the damage of FitzGibbon's action. FitzGibbon believed, or had claimed to believe, that the bill could simply be returned to the Commons for further debate. Whatever his true understanding of legislative procedure, he made an extraordinary blunder for a parliament man of over twenty years' standing. Bills could not be returned from the Lords for further consideration once they had passed in the House of Commons. The government staged its own parliamentary drama, this time for the benefit of the Catholics. Castlereagh went through the charade of trying to introduce a new bill, with the sole intention of reassuring the Catholic public of the government's continued support for Maynooth.[26] After encouraging the House of Commons to reaffirm the grant to Maynooth at the earliest allowable opportunity, Castlereagh arranged for an emergency loan from funds granted for the lord-lieutenant's expenses.

As a result of this episode, the Catholic clergy and the institution of Maynooth became the chief targets of FitzGibbon's hatred for Irish Catholicism. As his speech of 1793 indicated, he had always looked upon the ecclesiastical institutions of the Church with hostility. But this particular hostility had been overshadowed by his loathing for the Jacobin atheist merchants on the Dublin Catholic Committee. After 1799, priests and Maynooth became the lightening rod for FitzGibbon's feelings of anger at the humiliation he had suffered at Cornwallis's hands. FitzGibbon had received a jarring reminder that Cornwallis was not as malleable as past viceroys. He was a mature and experienced statesman who was not afraid to control and discipline subordinates, even FitzGibbon himself. That he had exerted authority over FitzGibbon on the matter of the Catholics added to his humiliation. FitzGibbon considered himself the premier government expert on Catholics and their evil ways. In addition, he was determined never to allow a recurrence of the dreadful events of 1793 when his known opinion was so blatantly disregarded. Cornwallis's action reminded him that the English government, not he, ultimately determined Catholic policy, for better or for worse. FitzGibbon retaliated for his humiliation in the usual manner, epistolary backbiting and legislation. In a letter to Camden, dated 7 May 1799, he blamed the priests for the continuing unrest in Ireland; he then blamed the government, and by implication Cornwallis himself, for not keeping the alleged clerical terrorists in line:

> The system of the United Irishmen seems to have given way in a great degree to the revival of Defenderism, which I am confident is universally encouraged by the Papist clergy. Will the British government ever learn the necessity for assuming a tone of Authority over that body of Men? At present we seem to counteract their system of terror only but the most scrupulous and punctilious ceremony in everything which may affect their passions and prejudices. The truth is they have for some time been dealt with as with the predominant power of the state, and if they are dealt by in the same manner much longer, they will certainly become predominant.[27]

He himself assumed a tone of authority in the form of an act altering the governing structure of Maynooth College. In the original act, the lord chancellor and the senior judges had acted as trustees, along with the Catholic bishops and leading members of the Catholic aristocracy and gentry. FitzGibbon transformed the judges into visitors. In effect, the judges were no longer the Protestant firsts among equals, acting in co-operation with the Catholic senior hierarchy and gentry; they were now to exercise a supervisory, authoritarian role over their Catholic subordinates.[28] These visitors were to make triennial inspections of Maynooth, the first taking place within twelve months of the act's inception. The lord-lieutenant also acquired more control over the personnel and governance of Maynooth. In the original act, he reviewed the by-laws of the college, and he had the authority to reject or revise any not directly concerned with the exercise, discipline and teaching of the Roman Catholic religion. FitzGibbon's revised act gave the lord-lieutenant the additional rights to appoint the president of Maynooth and to order other visitations at his discretion. At the same time, the act left wide areas of latitude to the Catholics involved with Maynooth. As was the case with the original act, the government could not interfere with bylaws related to religious teaching, practice or discipline. FitzGibbon also elevated three Roman Catholics to the exalted position of visitor: Troy, the Catholic archbishop of Dublin, O'Reilly of Drogheda and Lord Fingall. They alone had any visitorial authority over matters affecting religion.[29] In short, the act left the Catholics in control of the one area that mattered the most to them, the teaching and practice of their religion. Troy took a dismissive, almost cynical, view of the whole exercise. In his opinion, FitzGibbon, having made loud and public threats to bring Maynooth to heel, had to come up with something to maintain his credibility. The result was a handful of minor changes in the college's regulations.[30]

II

Apart from the aberration of Maynooth, FitzGibbon worked harmoniously enough with Cornwallis on the union. As always, whenever a major government issue was at stake, FitzGibbon spoke. His speech on the union was unquestionably his greatest rhetorical achievement.[31] In a succession of powerful images, he offered a profoundly nihilistic vision of Ireland and of Irish history. All the familiar stock figures from his past speeches made an appearance, draped in phrases of grim, somber eloquence. The Catholics, of course, loomed large in his rhetorical landscape. With that strange combination of loathing and shrewdness which characterized his perceptions, FitzGibbon portrayed them both as savages and as tragic victims. He attributed their addiction to errors of Popery to natural savagery and ignorance, as was his wont, but he also blamed the tactical errors of the English reformers for the failure of Protestantism to take hold in Ireland. In keeping with his own views of religion as a political, rather than a theological, system of control, FitzGibbon suggested that it would have been better to have allowed the Irish to retain the customs and practices of Catholicism in return for renouncing the authority of the Pope. Imposing Protestant ritual and Protestant theology by force served not only to create "hypocrites and martyrs", it also served to create a nation of rebels.[32] Resentment of English ecclesiastical authority led all too quickly to resentment of English political authority. In what is probably the most perceptive explanation for Irish sectarian conflict, FitzGibbon portrayed Irish Catholicism not as a religion, but as an endemic rallying point for forces of resistance against the alien English ruler:

> it is a melancholy truth that ... all have clung to the Popish religion as a common bond of union and an heredity pledge of animosity to British settlers and the British nation.[33]

Having established the tragic antagonism between savage, rebellious Irish Catholics and misguided English Protestant zealots, FitzGibbon once again unfolded a story, which he had told countless times in speeches from his earliest political career. Repeated Irish Catholic rebellion had ended in repeated defeat, the seizure of rebel lands, and the settlement of English Protestants on alienated Catholic estates. Unconsciously or not, FitzGibbon took revenge for years of taunts at his own dispossessed Catholic ancestry by portraying the English settlers, many of whose descendants comprised his audience, not as standard bearers of Protestant enlightenment and civilization, but as rapacious freebooters. He reserved his most telling denigration for the Cromwellian settlers, who combined greed with two other characteristics much loathed by FitzGibbon, Protestant heterodoxy and political radicalism:

> And thus a new colony of new settlers composed of all the various sects which then infested England – Independents, Anabaptists, Seceders, Brownists, Socinians, Millenarians and Dissenters of every description, many of the infected with the leaven of democracy – poured in Ireland and were put into possession of the ancient inheritance of its inhabitants.[34]

His obvious contempt was not much mitigated by his disclaimer of respect:

> I speak with great personal respect of these men when I state that a very considerable portion of the opulence and power of the kingdom of Ireland centers at this day in the descendants of this motley collection of English adventurers.[35]

The centuries of sectarian warfare had ended in an impasse. The Protestants had conquered the land, but not the Irish Catholics. The country remained in a state of endemic civil war, which no concession and no gesture of conciliation could still. Only the military power and protection of England kept further rebellion in check. In what is perhaps his most memorable rhetorical turn of phrase, FitzGibbon presented a nightmare of Irish history from which there was no waking:

> What then was the situation of the Revolution and what is it at this day? The whole power and property of this country has been conferred by successive monarchs of England upon an English colony, composed of three sets of English adventurers who poured into this country at the termination of three successive rebellions. Confiscation is their common title; and from their first settlement they have been hemmed in on every side by the old inhabitants of this island, brooding over their discontents in sullen indignation ...What then was the security of the English settlers for their physical existence at the Revolution? and what is the security of their descendants at this day? The powerful and commanding protection of Great Britain. If by any fatality it fails you are at the mercy of the old inhabitants of the island.[36]

Along with obdurate, revenge-minded Catholics, FitzGibbon also blamed feckless, irresponsible Irish Protestants, another stock collective character of his rhetoric. He once again launched into the old familiar tale of foolish aspirations and foolish defiance, of misguided, kindly English concession leading to still more unreasonable demands. He once again made claims of an irresistible progression from the Volunteers, to the Whig Club, to the United Irishmen, to the Catholic rebels of Wexford. To underscore his claim, FitzGibbon made veiled accusations that Henry Grattan had treasonable contacts with the United Irishmen, notably Samuel Nielson.[37] Unquestionably FitzGibbon displayed dubious morality and still more dubious legality in making such claims. While the belief that Grattan was up to his neck in treason prevailed widely in government circles, nothing had ever been established beyond the fact that he had some indiscreet interviews with Samuel Nielson.[38] But the absolute truth of his claims mattered not a whit to FitzGibbon. Grattan's dubious conduct provided him with an irresistible rhetorical opportunity: the premier champion of Irish Protestant Whiggery plotting treason with his spiritual sons, the United Irishmen.

Given the unrelenting bleakness of his historical vision, FitzGibbon displayed a curiously child-like optimism in his discussion of the union. In the rhetorical universe of his speech, it served as the irresistible *deus ex machina* in the bloody tragedy of Irish history. Wise and firm English rule would protect Protestants and Catholics alike from anarchy. On the vexed subject of emancipation, FitzGibbon dutifully hewed to the official Cornwallis line, that the subject could be discussed with safely only in the calm dispassionate atmosphere of a union parliament:

> If the Catholics or Ireland are not satisfied with the indulgence which they have already experienced and are determined to press their demands of an unqualified repeal of the Test Laws and the Act of Supremacy, let them be discussed upon their solid merits in the imperial Parliament, where the question will not be influenced by passion and prejudice.[39]

Nonetheless, he gave a hint of his own sentiments, and incidentally, indulged in covert rhetorical revenge against his new hate figures, the Roman Catholic clergy and their stronghold, Maynooth:

> My unaltered opinion is, that so long as human nature and the Popish religion continue to be what I know they are, a conscientious Popish ecclesiastic never will become a well attached subject to a Protestant state and that the Popish clergy must always have a commanding influence on every member of that communion.[40]

But if, as he implied, the union would put to an end forever the hope of emancipation, it would also force Irish Protestants to stop their self-destructive habits of political contention and turn their attention to their true responsibilities as landlords. As he had in the distant days of the Tenantry Bill of 1780, FitzGibbon scolded his fellow Protestants and landlords on their neglect and carelessness

> I wish to withdraw the higher orders of my countrymen from the narrow and corrupt sphere of Irish politics and direct their attention to objects of national importance, to teach them to improve the internal energies and extend the resources of their country, to encourage manufacturing, skill and ingenuity and open useful channels for commercial enterprise and above all, seriously to exert

> their best endeavors to tame and civilize the lower orders of the people...to relieve their wants and correct their excesses; unless you will civilise your people, it is vain to look for tranquillity or contentment.[41]

He also indulged in wildly fantastic promises of English capital pouring into a newly tamed and civilized Ireland, claims that the more clear-headed anti-unionist, Foster, effectively questioned, and that later history resoundingly refuted.[42] Above all, he made the still more exalted and dubious claims of a new era of wise, steady English rule, in spite of the past policy mistakes which he had so tellingly noted at the beginning of his speech. He even went so far as to make the claim that he would willingly trust Ireland to the direction of an English Parliament, even if there was not a single Irish member in it.[43] FitzGibbon of course, could easily make such a declaration, since he had an assured place in the union parliament. In 1799, he had been awarded the English title, Lord FitzGibbon of Sidbury.[44]

In the end, bribes and promises of peerages and offices probably carried more weight with FitzGibbon's fellow peers than his superb, if flawed speech. Nor did his speech elicit much public reaction. Grattan, of course, responded with a pamphlet defending his good name and retelling the same dismal history from the perspective of an embattled Whig.[45] Cornwallis was highly complimentary, as was Edward Cooke, though he did take some exception to FitzGibbon's remark aspersing the loyalty of Catholic priests.[46] Unlike FitzGibbon, who saw the union as the premier measure of repressing Catholic political agitation once and for all, Cooke was anxious to maintain dubious Catholic loyalties for his and for the government's secret agenda. But such was the chill on public opinion in the aftermath of the rebellion, that his "besotted nation" comments of 1785 garnered more controversy than this more complete and detailed denunciation of Ireland and the Irish.

III

Oddly enough for someone who in the past had repeatedly expressed such contempt for public opinion, FitzGibbon also tried his hand at attracting wider support for the union. The result was a pamphlet entitled *No Union, but Unite and Fall!* which he wrote under the pseudonym "Paddy Whack". This attempt at rhetorical bonhomie took the form of an epistle from "Paddy Whack" to his mother "Sheelagh." Paddy works as a labourer in England and as an occasional assistant for a doctor. In the course of their association, the doctor, conveniently Scottish, enlightens Paddy about the many benefits of a political union with England. With assorted "arraghs", "by Jazuses" and other stage Irish sound-effects, Paddy proceeds to repeat these arguments to his mother. Rather awkwardly, FitzGibbon also introduced the metaphor of the union as a marriage. Apparently honest John Bull has offered Sheelagh his hand in marriage. Paddy's pro-union arguments are meant to encourage Sheelagh to accept this eligible offer.

FitzGibbon used this metaphor to promote one simple, indeed, simplistic argument: Ireland was inferior culturally as well as physically. She required the security of a union with England to save herself from the external threat of France and from the internal ills of poverty and anarchy. To underscore his point, FitzGibbon dwelt at length on the alleged miseries of ancient Ireland, and in particular its arbitrary, capricious brehon law.

If brehon law was the paradigm of Irish barbarism, James I represented the triumph of English civilization. According to FitzGibbon, James broke the power of the brehons and introduced the universal rule of the common law into Ireland. James also furthered English civilization with the plantation of Ulster, which introduced a whole population of sober, industrious settlers into Ireland.[47] (This sentiment represented a startling departure from FitzGibbon's usual view of Ulstermen, particularly the Presbyterians, as inveterate rebels and republicans.)[48] Unfortunately, later rulers of Ireland were unable or unwilling to continue James's work and eventually, Ireland fell under the control of a corrupt aristocracy and parliament. FitzGibbon attacked at length the factionalism that made Ireland virtually ungovernable.[49]

The Union, so FitzGibbon argued, would break the power of this contentious oligarchy. The political stability conferred by Union would encourage future settlement by the "liberal English merchant", and the equally liberal English manufacturer and farmer. These eligible immigrants would introduce both English capital and English values: among them thrift, sobriety and diligence. They also would introduce their benevolent employment practices.[50] His claims probably would have astonished most English workers, beset by hostile labour legislation and falling wages.

The arguments presented in *No Union!* are not particularly interesting. Many of them received a far more subtle and powerful presentation in his great pro-Union speech to the Irish House of Lords. Nor would anyone consult "No Union!" for historical scholarship. As shall be seen, FitzGibbon shamelessly distorted history. Yet this embarrassing bit of ephemera does raise one intriguing and baffling question: who in the world was he addressing?

FitzGibbon may have been trying to address the "lower orders," *à la* Hannah More. If so, he may have adopted the persona of Paddy to establish a rapport with his audience. One can only hope that FitzGibbon did not consider Paddy a realistic portrayal of a common Irish laborer. Even he must have been aware of the stage convention and its elements of exaggeration. However, he may have assumed that his audience would look beyond the comic exaggerations and find in Paddy a recognizable and sympathetic figure. If so, he should have examined more closely the works of Miss More: she eschewed any flourishes of dialect and stuck to plain, blunt and easily readable language. A minimally literate reader certainly would have had trouble deciphering FitzGibbon's stage Irish demotic, however amusing or ingratiating.

In the same vein, FitzGibbon's promises of high wages and kindlier treatment from the prospective English employers may have represented, not patent delusion, but a sincere appeal to the concerns of the lower orders, as he understood them. As he made clear during his interrogation of Dr McNeven in 1798, FitzGibbon never could believe that the mass of poor Irish either understood or cared about Catholic emancipation or parliamentary reform. They wanted only comfort and the security of honest work.[51]

Finally, FitzGibbon may have tried to placate the largely Catholic sensibilities of the lower orders by minimizing or evading their greatest historical traumas. His transformation of republican Ulster into a bastion of British civility already has received attention. He gave the impression that Ulster was an unpopulated desert until the plantation and that no such thing as a displacement of original inhabitants ever took place. As for Cromwell, FitzGibbon eliminated him from his historical narrative as completely as Cromwell himself had eliminated the defenders of Drogheda.[52]

Nevertheless, there are problems viewing *No Union! but Unite and Fall*, as an address to the Irish lower orders. For one thing, FitzGibbon had never deigned to address them before this time. Indeed, he usually thought that reason was wasted on the "barbarians". They were too hopelessly mired in bigotry and bitter historical memory. His proto-revisionism also has an ambiguous quality. He must have known how specious his history would have appeared to the average Catholic Irish. His own father was a hardened opportunist who coolly shed the Catholicism of his youth with hardly a backward glance; yet even old FitzGibbon nourished a visceral and sometimes indiscreet loathing for King William.[53] Moreover, FitzGibbon regarded the Catholics as the chief opponents of union.[54] Given this perception, it seems unlikely that he would have gone out of his way to appeal to an audience he fundamentally despised and feared.

The younger Henry Grattan gives a possible clue to FitzGibbon's motives for writing this pamphlet. In one of his many poison pen portraits of FitzGibbon, Grattan stated that he "was not a bad flatterer".[55] Indeed, flattery may have been the ultimate reason for *No Union! but Unite and Fall!* FitzGibbon was not trying to persuade the Irish to accept the Union, he was attempting to flatter the English into taking more responsibility for the civilization of Ireland after the Union.

To charm and cajole them, he adopted the guise of Paddy, a childish brute who, nontheless, was amenable to kindness and good government. By glossing over past atrocities, FitzGibbon may have hoped to placate English self-complacency. By appealing to the past glories of King James and the Ulster plantation he may have been reminding his English readers of what had already been accomplished in Ireland. By appealing to the present glories of English benevolence and industry, he may have hoped to inspire his readers to emulate the Jacobean example.

He amused, cajoled and flattered to no purpose. As FitzGibbon was to learn all too shortly, most English politicians had little interest in Ireland, apart from maintaining her political quiescence and economic subordination. There was no need for "liberal" English manufacturers to locate in Ireland. They could get plenty of low-wage Irish and, indeed, English labour in factory boom towns like Manchester. In short, whatever his knowledge of Ireland, FitzGibbon was singularly ignorant of the ethos that even then was emerging from Manchester and that would have such malignant repercussions in Ireland during the famine. He obviously did not anticipate the likes of Charles Edward Trevelyan, who in R.F. Foster's words "intimated that the Famine was the design of a benevolent Malthusian God who sought to relieve overpopulation by natural disaster."[56]

IV

FitzGibbon was spared knowledge of these Victorian horrors. Nonetheless he did live to suffer the shattering disillusionment of the Catholic emancipation crisis, which ended in the resignations of Pitt in England and Cornwallis and Castlereagh in Ireland. It is impossible to exaggerate his rage, his bafflement, his sense of betrayal and his despair. Probably Edward Cooke gives the best indication of FitzGibbon's state of mind following the revelations of Pitt's and Cornwallis's true sympathies on the bedeviling subject. He wrote to Castlereagh:

> I received a rather warm letter last night from the Chancellor. He is hurt at your not having consulted with him. I wrote for answers and I send you the copy...

Cooke affected to treat the whole matter lightly. He requested Castlereagh to return the copy of his letter to Lord Clare, "with your best thanks, for I can assure you the copying of it has bored me much more than the mailing can bore you".[57] In other words, Lord Clare and his temper were tiresome and petty matters. But Cooke's postscript revealed that he was more nervous than he let on. He requested Castlereagh to avoid mentioning that he had knowledge of the letter.[58] FitzGibbon's formidable rage would wax exponentially if he knew that Cooke was showing copies of their correspondence to Castlereagh. With the latter gentleman FitzGibbon would not deign either to write or to speak. As for Cornwallis, FitzGibbon made this assessment of the man he had once admired so extravagantly:

> That preposterous old Mule who has just quitted the government of Ireland did more mischief here than he could repair if he were to live to the end of the new century.[59]

But nothing could compare to his rage against the proposed beneficiaries of emancipation, the Irish Catholics themselves. In a letter to Lord Shannon, a receptive auditor indeed, FitzGibbon inveighed against the madness, the stupidity and the sheer evil of "rebel schemes of emancipation". In particular, he dwelt on the Catholic capacity for sectarian cruelty and republican revanche. He assured Lord Shannon that if the rebel schemes for emancipation had passed, both of them would have been hanging from lampposts.[60]

FitzGibbon closed his letter to Lord Shannon ended with a sort of embittered bravado. In spite of the stupidity and irresponsibility of Pitt, Cornwallis, and the other ministerial traitors, their schemes for Catholic emancipation would never succeed. The forces of the established church would stand firm, and the King would oppose, as would *"all of his sons"* (FitzGibbon's emphasis). FitzGibbon could no doubt make such assurances, having done his work so well with the king, though he was on slightly more shaky ground with respect to *all* the sons. Sussex and Kent tended to be rather liberal on the subject, when they thought of it, and the fickle Prince of Wales was again wooing Mrs Fitzherbert at this time. But FitzGibbon's assessments of the royal family are secondary. More important is the sense of dread and failure beneath these assurances to Lord Shannon. The union, rather than destroying forever the hope of emancipation, only gave the subject a new lease on life. The Catholics had been left, willfully or otherwise, with the impression that emancipation would soon follow the union. They would never let the subject rest. FitzGibbon no doubt suspected that the English government would eventually succumb, as they did in 1793, if only out of weariness. In effect, he had failed, even though the forces of emancipation had lost office. Worse, he had received crushing proof that 1793 was no mere aberration. In spite of his services and his loyalty, the English government would willingly sacrifice his known opinions and his feelings if it suited their larger imperial purpose.

V

His first major appearance in the union House of Lords, a debate over the extension of martial law in Ireland, was a tired revival of the Lord Moira drama of 1798. The protagonists, the antagonists and the speeches were familiar. Moira and Fitzwilliam took the lead in protesting the measure's constitutional impropriety, excessive harshness and hasty introduction. These arguments, introduced by these men, provoked a predictable response from FitzGibbon. He insisted, on the contrary that martial law was absolutely necessary, given the innate savagery and obduracy of the Irish and their addiction to rebellion. Although this speech was later re-printed in the *Annual Review*, it was not one of FitzGibbon's better efforts. Absent was one of the salient features of the great speeches of 1798 and 1800, the insight, however partisan and distorted, into the causes of Irish discontent. FitzGibbon resorted instead to the simple-minded and highly dubious claim that the rebellion resulted from sheer perversity, and not from any legitimate motive, however mistaken:

> It did not, as some former rebellions had done, proceed from misplaced loyalty, religious zeal, or party difference, all principle had been subverted, every laudable feeling stifled and suppressed, and no other object cherished than a rivalship in domestic treason, relentless murder and cowardly assassination.[61]

Always one for the telling anecdote, FitzGibbon alluded to the murder of his steward, Mr Allen, an incident which had taken place in 1799. Several of FitzGibbon's household servants, including a man who had been in service to the family since old FitzGibbon's time, were convicted and hanged for the crime. FitzGibbon declared to his fellow peers that the unfortunate man was murdered "merely because he was an Englishman".[62] No doubt the crime was shocking, and no doubt it was profoundly disillusioning to find that old family retainers were guilty. But the sad truth was that FitzGibbon was as guilty of cynical misrepresentation. In his initial accounts of the murder, FitzGibbon, having no pressing political reason to lie, attributed the crime, not to fanatic Irish nationalism but to mere greed. A number of his servants were participating in a combination to keep local milk prices at an artificially high level; they made midnight raids on farmers who refused to cooperate and beat them. The steward, accidentally discovered them while they were preparing for one such expedition, and they killed him in a panicked effort to prevent him from revealing their activities to their formidable master.[63] In short, the servants in question do not seem to have had any premeditated designs against Allen as an Englishman; on the contrary, they acted only to preserve their places , and of course, to avoid prosecution and conviction. But in his disillusion and anger, FitzGibbon willfully distorted this sad, commonplace crime, creating for himself and for his like-minded auditors a useful paradigm for the irredeemable savagery of the Irish. FitzGibbon, the skilled and cynical barrister, no doubt well knew what chills this sort of a remark would sent down the spines of backwoods peers and squires in England. He also added the claim that Allen's murder set off a major rebellion in Limerick, which hitherto had "remained quiet during the early part of the rebellion." The murder of Allen was to have been the beginning of a mass killing of local gentry and aristocracy. FitzGibbon himself, or so he claimed, headed the list of the prospective targets of assassination. The ringleader, the treacherous servant of long-standing, allegedly confessed to a priest "that a list of twenty had been made, whom it was resolved to murder, and that his master [i.e. FitzGibbon] was of the number, whom, to use their own phrase, he had sworn to *sweep*, in one of his evening walks around his farm".[64] FitzGibbon was quick to assure his auditors that the native Irishry had no reason to hate him or to wish for his demise:

> He was the only person who gave employment and bread to the poor in that neighborhood, and without him they must be reduced to the greatest wretchedness.[65]

There could, therefore be only one motive for their designs, "merely a pure love of blood".[66] FitzGibbon, who had aimed his remarks at Lord Fitzwilliam in particular, pointedly alluded both to his status as an absentee landlord and to his alleged naivet about Irish affairs:

> If the noble Earl ... could find time to visit his estates in the county of Wicklow, he would see that these representations were not exaggerated. He would there behold nothing but traces of desolation, and signs of the renewal of these horrors.[67]

Having transmogrified his steward's murder into a cross between Beaumarchais and de Sade, and having satisfactorily belittled Lord Fitzwilliam, the ignorant absentee, FitzGibbon went on at length to prove that martial law, far from imposing a tyranny on the country, was in fact not as effective as it could be. Conniving attorneys regularly subverted the judgments of military tribunals by filing writs of habeas corpus and attempting to transfer jurisdiction of cases to the royal courts, which were actually open. FitzGibbon alluded to the case of Wolfe Tone, to illustrate his point.

> Theobald Wolfe Tone, whose name made a conspicuous figure in the secret committee, had been taken in arms in a French ship of war, and condemned by a military tribunal. The Court of King's Bench was then sitting, however, under a military guard, and a worthy limb of the law discovered that it could not be open without being compelled to interfere. He therefore applied for a write of *Habeas Corpus* which of course was granted. The consequence was that Mr. Tone had an opportunity to cut his throat with a razor and to disappoint the justice of the country. Immediately after, the petty solicitors flocked to Dublin from every part of the kingdom and procuring writs of *Habeas Corpus*, prevented the trial of the rebels.[68]

Clearly Tone's death still rankled, though FitzGibbon refrained in this instance from expressing his sentiments that a man with a severed throat could conceivably hang.

He ended with a few more anecdotes about Irish savagery, and he defended himself from a charge widely circulated since 1798 and repeated in particular by Moira, that he was an advocate of torture. He reiterated the tale of the pike-making blacksmith who after some momentary discomfort on a picket, divulged the hiding place of his productions. He made the same defense that he had made to Lord Moira in 1798: "he would say that it should be maturely considered whether society would suffer most from the murder of two or three hundred loyal and well-disposed men, which was probably thus prevented, or from a rebel blacksmith being placed half a minute on the picquet [*sic*]?"[69]

The young Grattan later claimed that this particular production inspired universal disgust among the honest, straightforward and humane English. They found FitzGibbon's fawning demeanor toward them and his brutality toward his own countrymen alike disgusting. Nor did he enjoy his customary rhetorical dominance in the union House of Lords. Even a comparatively insignificant figure, Lord Caernarvon, "*pinioned*" FitzGibbon in the House, or so the younger Grattan phrased it.[70] There were some elements of truth in this assessment. Wilberforce, a far more reliable witness, reported that Pitt, an auditor at the debate, left the audience in disgust during FitzGibbon's speech.[71] But Pitt had always disliked FitzGibbon, a dislike no doubt confirmed by a forced and turbulent personal interview with FitzGibbon following the Catholic emancipation crisis.[72] On the other hand, Westmorland and Grenville, FitzGibbon's friends from his days at the Castle, far from exhibiting disgust, strongly supported him, and one English peer, Lord Mulgrave, declared that FitzGibbon had fully convinced him of the need for martial law. Mulgrave was probably not the only one. In spite of his exaggerations and his shameless lies, FitzGibbon probably convinced a goodly number of English Tories that Ireland was a bloody maelstrom of Popery and rebellion. Lord Caernarvon did indeed give a very spirited speech which included number of sarcastic allusions to FitzGibbon and his servant problems, but he did not, unfortunately, *pinion* the votes to defeat the bill to extend martial law.[74] On the contrary, it passed resoundingly.

Nonetheless, in spite of his inimitable combination of high Victorian moralizing and anti-unionist *schadenfreude*, the younger Grattan was at least partially right. FitzGibbon, who had risen so spectacularly and so effortlessly for the passed seventeen years, had indeed reached the limits of his power. In spite of his loyal service in Ireland, his tireless efforts on behalf of the union and his like-minded views, FitzGibbon did not receive a position in Addington's new no-Popery cabinet, the next logical step in his advancement. The reason for his exclusion was so patently ironic that it bordered on the ludicrous. FitzGibbon was simply too notoriously anti-Catholic, or so Addington informed Lord Glenbervie:

> ... efforts had been made to place Lord Clare in this Cabinet and I [Glenbervie] said I had clearly seen that to be his aim. [Addington] said it would be declaring too strongly to the Irish Catholics that the power which had been employed against them was only transferred to London.[75]

In other words, anti-Catholicism, which had hitherto served FitzGibbon so well, now became the chief cause of his failure in England. FitzGibbon's knack for influencing others, another key to his past advancement, played against him as well. Addington feared FitzGibbon's potentially disruptive influence over Hobart, who did obtain cabinet office.[76]

To compound the irony, FitzGibbon seemed utterly unaware of the reason for his exclusion. On the contrary, if the debate over Taylor's divorce bill is any indication, FitzGibbon angled for a place in Addington's government by resorting to precisely those tactics that had led to his initial exclusion: a rabid, and indeed rather inappropriate display of anti-Popery.

The bill itself originated in a squalid sentimental comedy involving the eponymous Mr Taylor, his wife and a young clergyman who had seduced and impregnated her. Mr Taylor, not surprisingly, sued for divorce, and when the bill came up for debate, several bishops and lay lords chose to include a provision forbidding the marriage, not only of the guilty pair, but of any adulterous clergyman and his paramour.

FitzGibbon opposed the clause, and in so doing, he presented the view that the Church, while an essential prop of the state, was nonetheless subservient to the secular power of the common law. Any jurisdiction which the Church of England exercised over marriage was solely owing to an accident of statute law at the Reformation. Even when the Church declared a marriage invalid, only the intervention of secular authority in the guise of a parliamentary statute effectively ended the union. In short, marriage was exclusively a civil contract over which the Church had no binding authority.

FitzGibbon combined this crudely Erastian disquisition with an attack on the "strange corruptions of the Romish Church and the impure practices of it, of the tyrannous authority and dominion the See of Rome assumed, and the gross impositions it laid on the minds of men, contending among other absurd pretensions, for the infallibility of the church as undeniably arising from the infallibility of the Pope".[78] Precisely what relation His Holiness's impositions and pretensions had to the subject at hand is unclear. FitzGibbon may have been venting spleen left over from the great Catholic emancipation debacle. He may also have included this rhetorical flourish to remind Addington of his anti-Popish credentials and of his ideological worthiness of a place in the cabinet.

FitzGibbon's unexalted view of the Church as the humble tool of the state no doubt offended a good many high churchmen. More important, this speech probably confirmed the decision to exclude him from the cabinet. Certainly Eldon, FitzGibbon's fellow chancellor and fellow anti-Catholic, found his views dubious and subjected him to a condescending correction on points of law and of Church doctrine:

> The Lord Chancellor left the woolsack to speak to the law points mentioned by his noble and learned friend, who, he said though he perhaps pursued his studies and inquiries into the decision of the Law Courts, and laws themselves with better advantage than he had, yet he undoubtedly had not quite so long an experience of both as he had possessed ... With regard to marriage being a civil contract, it undoubtedly was a civil contract, but his noble and learned Friend must recollect that it was in the whole view of it, and even in the ritual itself, declared to be a divine ordinance, and had ever been so considered by the Ministers of the Church of England and by all polemical writers.[79]

FitzGibbon, of course, brooked no contradiction, even from a superior firmly in cabinet office:

> Lord Clare said a few words also in explanation, but adhered to his opinion that marriage was ever since the reformation a civil contract and nothing more.[80]

But except to exert his authority in Irish affairs he never spoke at length after this debate. Perhaps he prudently avoided speaking because of an unfamiliarity with larger English and imperial political issues. Yet he may also have recognized that Eldon had humiliated him, and he maintained a general reticence out of mortification.

According to the younger Grattan, FitzGibbon loitered disconsolately in London after the closing of parliament, still hoping vainly for English office.[81] There may have been a more uxorious reason for FitzGibbon's continued stay in London. It was, after all, the height of the London season and he had his fashion-mad wife *en suite*, not a lady to brook a premature return to newly provincialized Dublin. Moreover, FitzGibbon was a very astute and very proud man. He would have recognized a lost cause when he saw one, though he never seems to have recognized the true reason for his failure.

Whatever his reasons or his schemes, a dangerous riding accident inadvertently prolonged FitzGibbon's stay in London more than even he might have desired. According to the fullest and most reliable accounts, FitzGibbon had been exercising his horse in Hyde Park. When he took his mount to a pond to give it water, it suddenly bolted.[82] The newspapers of the time delicately avoided mentioning the exact nature of his injuries, but appears that he suffered a strangury, the result of blows to his groin and genitals from the pommel of his saddle. FitzGibbon did survive the accident, and more miraculously, he survived the surgery which his doctors performed to relieve his condition. But he was bed-ridden for two months and was only able to return to Ireland in July. The otherwise intelligent and fair account of FitzGibbon which appeared in the *Dictionary of National Biography* later attributed FitzGibbon's death to this accident. In fact, by August, FitzGibbon was reporting to Auckland that he was fully recovered and , no doubt a great relief to this avid horseman and hunter, he was able to "ride nearly as well as ever".[83] FitzGibbon did indeed die very shortly after the accident, but overwork or drink probably did him in, not his high strung horse.

VI

If FitzGibbon had hoped to make up for his disappointment in England by exercising his accustomed authority in Ireland he was quickly disappointed. Cornwallis's successor Hardwicke had received due warning from no less a personage than the King to avoid domination by FitzGibbon:

> The King recommends the Lords Primate and the Chancellor as men that will not deceive the Lord-Lieutenant, but he should not deal with the openness necessary if he did not hint that the latter may be a useful instrument in the Earl of Hardwicke's hands, but if not attended to may attempt to guide, which can neither be expedient nor creditable.[84]

Unlike Addington, George had little concern about the sensibilities of Irish Roman Catholics. With the curious, fitful acuity of the simple-minded, George saw FitzGibbon's habits of domination, not his political/religious opinions as a threat to the stability and the reputation of government. In this assessment he was remarkably prescient.

In spite of the King's warning, Hardwicke initially was anxious for FitzGibbon's recovery and eager for his presence and his advice.[85] Unfortunately, his good intentions and his hopes of a harmonious working relationship with FitzGibbon were alike disappointed. FitzGibbon returned from England a restless and disillusioned man. Whatever self-consoling explanations he had given himself, the fact remained that he had failed to advance in England, and he was firmly confined to a position which, as a result of the union, was much diminished in responsibility and prestige. Moreover, he was still smarting over the flouting of his opinion and his authority on the vexed issue of Catholic emancipation. Given FitzGibbon's suspicious and prickly mood, only abject deference and absolute submission to his direction would have placated him. Unfortunately, Hardwicke had too much a sense of duty and dignity to allow FitzGibbon to act as *de facto* lord lieutenant. Nor was the new chief secretary, Charles Abbott, more amenable. He had too much self-importance and too much self-will. FitzGibbon was soon engaged in a series of undignified squabbles with both and in particular with Abbott. Hardwicke he merely despised as a weak dupe. Arguably, he detested Abbott more than Wolfe Tone, John Sweetman or any of his multiplicity of past antagonists.

FitzGibbon did have some reason for his antagonism. Abbott was an authentically obnoxious individual: self-satisfied, self-important, domineering and busily fretful over minutiae. Nonetheless, he was a genuinely dedicated and genuinely intent on providing fair and efficient administration. Nor was he necessarily the worst English official character with whom FitzGibbon had dealings. He was no more fretful than Thomas Orde and no more grating in his manner than Lord Buckingham. But conduct which FitzGibbon had tolerated in his dizzying rise to power, he found unbearable in the wake of his baffling failure and frustration following the union. He raged endlessly about Abbott in letters to his extraordinarily patient confidante, Auckland. Abbott, he declared, "... is without competition the most arrogant, presumptuous, empty prig I have ever met with or heard of."[86] But Abbott rankled less than the gnawing sense that he had lost his grip on Irish policy and on power. The final stage of his career was an increasingly desperate and pathetic fight to preserve what influence yet remained. Abbott's obnoxious manner was a subordinate *causus belli*.

Hardwicke and Abbott inadvertently increased the provocation with their tactless, though well-meant, interventions in two particularly sensitive areas for FitzGibbon: Limerick and law. The administration of martial law was at the bottom of the matter of Limerick. During the rebellion and in the period of unrest immediately following, FitzGibbon had convinced Cornwallis to waive the requisite review of court martial sentences passed on offenders in Limerick. Cornwallis, no doubt convinced that his right-minded chancellor would not request such a drastic measure without good reason had agreed. Hardwicke, a humane man, had requested Sir James Duff, the commander in that district, again to refer any sentences from courts martial in Limerick to the lord-lieutenant for confirmation. At the same time, he kept this particular order confidential. He thought that if word of his proposed lenity spread, it might actually encourage an upsurge of violence. In short, martial law was to be mitigated, but the fear of its full severity was to remain in the minds and hearts of the populace of Limerick. For his proposal to have any effect, Hardwicke was necessarily obliged to keep it a secret even from the premier magnate of Limerick and premier advocate of strict courts martial, FitzGibbon himself. Unfortunately for Hardwicke, FitzGibbon, ever cunning and astute, did learn about the new policy and promptly revealed both the order and his fury at it. Inevitably, he attributed the order, not to Hardwicke's humanity, but to Abbott's malignant meddling:

> This power has been revoked within the last week by Mr Abbott, without the slightest communication with me, although it is notorious that the power was given to Sir Jas. Duff at my recommendation, and that it has done more to restore quiet in this country than any measure taken since the Disturbance broke out.[87]

Indeed, the plan to modify martial law in Limerick had all the earmarks of the Catholic emancipation infamy: an act of indulgence performed in secrecy. Hardwicke, for his part, was mortified at FitzGibbon's display of temper and at his indiscretion.

In matters legal, two issues caused affront and much aggricul correspondence: the choice of a successor to Baron Metge, who had recently resigned from the Court of Exchequer, and the reprieve of Sir Harry Hayes. In the matter of Metge, FitzGibbon took offense, not at the lack of consultation, but at the manner in which Hardwicke sought his opinion on a possible successor. Hardwicke, no doubt acting from motives of efficiency, requested FitzGibbon to submit three candidates whom he considered most suitable to succeed Metge. FitzGibbon interpreted Hardwicke's gesture as another insidious move to increase Abbot's domination rather than as an honest effort to solicit his opinion:

> ... I received a letter from him [Hardwicke] to desire that I would return to him three persons for his scrutiny and selection or rather for the scrutiny and selection of Mr. Abbott. Feeling that his excellency meant to give me precisely that degree of credit which is extended to a sheriff going out of office, I did in very peremptory terms refuse to make the return which he required of me as degrading to the situation which I hold.[88]

To have satisfied FitzGibbon's irritable sense of punctilio, Hardwicke was obliged either to accept his recommendation without "a scrutiny of it by any man" [meaning Abbott] or to submit his own candidates to FitzGibbon for comment and recommendation. Poor Hardwicke was doomed never to get it right about FitzGibbon. In an effort to placate FitzGibbon, Hardwicke had promised to send any recommendation he might make directly to the King. In so doing, he provoked this polite, but critical response from Pelham, the former chief secretary and now a member of Addington's administration:

> Your excellency's conduct toward the chancellor on the subject of Baron Metge's resignation, must be highly gratifying to him and certainly such as his high professional character, professional experience and attachment to the interests of Great Britain and Ireland justly entitle him to; at the same time you

> will forgive me if I observe that it appears to me that it might have been sufficient if your Excellency had asked him for his opinion without pledging yourself to forward his recommendation to his majesty.[89]

No doubt as a result of FitzGibbon's activities in 1795, Pelham shared the conviction of the King and the prime minister that FitzGibbon had exercised too much dominance for too long in Ireland. Nonetheless, the letter showed an amazing obtuseness toward Hardwicke's miserable situation. Hardwicke knew all too well how little gratification FitzGibbon found in any conduct of his, least of all his conduct on the matter of Baron Metge's successor

FitzGibbon himself gave the best account of the case of Sir Henry Hayes and of his own cause for grievance in this particular instance:

> Sir Henry Hayes and Murphy were indicted and tried on the same statute, for carrying off a woman by force with intent to marry her. Murphy succeeded in ravishing his lady ... Sir Henry Hayes attempted to ravish his, but did not succeed because the cock would not fight. He was at length brought to trial, found guilty and respited by Mr Day upon a silly doubt in his mind on a point of law ... Poor Murphy has been hanged and Sir Henry Hayes has been pardoned...Certainly if every any crime deserved capital punishment in a civilized society, Mr Murphy's and Sir Henry's did merit it. But it will be difficult to persuade the lower orders of the people that equal justice has been administered to rich and poor.[90]

His indignation that his opinion was again was ignored, and no doubt in his laudable desire to assure that equal justice was meted out to rich and poor, caused him to overlook several essential points. In the first place, the recommendation of the jury, not a "silly doubt" had influenced Justice Day.[91] Probably the most telling point in Hayes' favour was the fact that his cock had not fought, to borrow FitzGibbon's own inimitable turn of phrase. He had more ever made every effort to treat his victim, Miss Pike, kindly during her enforced captivity, and she had eventually returned to her father *virgo intacta.*[92] Murphy on the other hand, was hanged, not because he was poorer than Sir Henry Hayes, as FitzGibbon suggested, but because he was more potent.

FitzGibbon's festering sense of grievance sometimes took an absurd and childish turn. For example, in a brief note to Abbott concerning a candidate for Judge Advocate of the courts martial, FitzGibbon declared the man's fitness for the post. He then addressed his note to Mr. Charles Abbott, Chief Secretary, and he followed this title with a long line of et ceterae, creating a veritable hieroglyph of contempt.[93] Clearly dignity in adversity was not one of FitzGibbon's more notable virtues.

FitzGibbon also continued to bombard Auckland, Hobart and his other remaining friends in England with indignant accounts of his slights and mistreatment. Hobart and Auckland were suitably distressed by these highly colored letters, but there was little they could do apart from making an occasional protest.[94] Hardwicke in the meantime did not remain passive. He wrote long frustrated letters to Addington, complaining of FitzGibbon's unreasonableness, uncooperativeness and indiscretion.[95]

With a neat irony redolent alike of Greek tragedy and of second rate fiction, the Catholics were the unwitting instruments of FitzGibbon's final undoing. His always formidable loathing for Catholics waxed as his influence waned, and his letters of 1801 were full of sulfurous references to their bigotry, cruelty and general bad principles.[96] He could not retaliate against the English government for the betrayal of the principles of the union, but he could retaliate against the Catholics with petty harassment and with frequent assertions of dominance. Indeed, the Catholic menace gave his flagging political career its one remaining *raison d'être*. In one of his restless, miserable letters to Auckland, he expressed his intention to postpone any return to England, unless, of course, there was a resurgence of "Popery projects", in which case he would bestir himself sooner.[97]

A second Maynooth crisis of FitzGibbon's own making revealed to him that he could no longer exercise his accustomed power even over the Catholics. The crisis originated in the clumsy framing of the original act of 1795, which had established Maynooth. Unquestionably, Maynooth had come into existence to provide a safe reliable supply of Catholic priests trained under government control and at government expense. Portland and Camden certainly stated that aim very clearly in their various dispatches on the subject.[98] But the actual wording of the bill never explicitly stated that Maynooth was, in effect, a government sponsored seminary. It simply declared that Maynooth was a school for the better education of Papists, and it set aside the previous laws which prohibited Catholics from establishing schools exclusively for members of their own denomination.[99] The reasons for this statutory coyness are unclear. Possibly, Camden, Pelham and Portland wanted to avoid offending the high Protestant party by explicitly declaring intentions which might give an impression either of establishing Roman Catholicism or of putting it on an equal footing with the Church of Ireland.

They may temporarily have placated feelings in 1795, but they laid the ground for FitzGibbon's cavil and meddling after 1799, when he abruptly seized on the notion that Maynooth was to educate not only the Catholic clergy, but the laity. His renewed concern about this issue resulted in part from a new phase of his loathing for Catholics; the objects at this stage were country or hedge schoolmasters, who FitzGibbon claimed, had been prominent in the rebellion. Those who had not been hanged or shot had re-established their schools, which were, to use FitzGibbon's own lurid phrase, "seminaries of treason." The clergy encouraged these schools by threatening to ex-communicate any parents who sent their children to any school not directed by a Catholic. In most country districts, Catholic schools were necessarily rebel schools.[100] By opening Maynooth to lay students, FitzGibbon no doubt hoped to educate at least a handful of lay Catholics under safe government control. But

FitzGibbon involved himself in Maynooth above all because he wanted to assert his control over Catholic issues in general. Maynooth, which had already been the cause of much frustration and humiliation, no doubt had a certain symbolic significance.[101]

FitzGibbon had hinted at his views as early as 1799; in making his apologies and excuses to Lord Cornwallis, he referred to it not as a clerical seminary but as an "academy" for Roman Catholics in general.[102] Nonetheless, the lay school does not seem to have come into existence until late 1800 or 1801. The circumstances behind its inception are sketchy and obscure. By his own admission, FitzGibbon himself was a prime mover, persuading Archbishop Troy to set aside moneys for an expansion for lay pupils.[103] He may also have enlisted the aid of Lord Fingall, one of the Catholic visitors. If he did indeed employ Fingall as his ally and as his mouthpiece, he chose well. Fingall was amiable and impeccably subservient to government. He was also limited intellectually, making it all the easier for the more cunning and astute FitzGibbon to establish his dominance. Above all, Fingall had a schoolboy son. There is a good likelihood that FitzGibbon, who had no mean talent for flattery and ingratiation, persuaded Fingall that young Lord Killeen would have a good influence on the uncouth seminarians at Maynooth. The school may have had other proponents acting on entirely different motives. But by the autumn of 1801, Lord Fingall's son was duly enrolled as a lay student at Maynooth. And FitzGibbon who up to this point had never had any but the most remote contact with the Catholic gentry or aristocracy, was suddenly on very cordial terms with Lord Fingall. Fingall had invited FitzGibbon to his house in London, and FitzGibbon for his part sent an extraordinary note to Fingall, giving him virtual *carte blanche* to appoint magistrates in County Meath, a sensitive, much disturbed area.

> I shall always be happy to attend to any recommendation from you, and write by this post to Mr Dwyer, my secretary to sent me down a warrant for Mr Johnson's appointment to the commission of the peace and in future, you have only to send any recommendation you may wish to forward to me to Mr Dwyer and the appointment shall take place of course.[104]

Of course, FitzGibbon could safely make such a gesture. Lord Fingall, who had massacred a detachment of rebels on Tara Hill, could be counted on to recommend safely reactionary magistrates. But the letter certainly represented a startling turnaround in their relations. The same Lord Fingall, when Lord Killeen, had made hostile comments in 1787 about the malign intentions of Attorney-General FitzGibbon.[105] For his part, FitzGibbon had expressed considerable displeasure with Lord Fingall for attempting to reverse his attainder in the English courts and the English House of Lords in 1794.[106] FitzGibbon's schemes for Maynooth may have accounted for this sudden change in their relationship from remote hostility to mutually flattering cordiality.

Nonetheless, FitzGibbon had not seen fit to inform his fellow visitors, Lords Kilwarden, Norbury and Avonmore, of his new conception of Maynooth. They had no knowledge of the school's existence until a visitation which took place in the autumn of 1801. They had completed a tour of the existing seminary and while amicably strolling in the garden with the director, they happened to see a new building in the process of construction. When they asked its purpose, the director informed them that the building was to serve as a dormitory for lay students. Kilwarden, Norbury and Avonmore, who never mistook Maynooth for anything other than a government-controlled seminary, immediately informed the director that the presence of a lay school deviated from the original purpose of the foundation. They requested him to stop any further outlay on the school until the government could consider the matter. The three judges then consulted with Hardwicke, who agreed with them that a school for the laity at Maynooth would interfere with the eleemosynary aims of that institution. He also feared that it would discourage enrollment at Trinity and with it any irenic contact between Catholic and Protestant boys. While Hardwicke gave no order to dissolve the school outright, he confirmed the directive of Kilwarden, Norbury and Avonmore to suspend any further outlay or enrollment.[107]

When he got wind of the government's actions, Fingall immediately sought out his patron FitzGibbon. Either poor dim Fingall got the purport of the order wrong, or FitzGibbon willfully chose to misunderstand. At any rate, FitzGibbon descended on Lord Hardwicke in another display of indignation, demanding to know why the government was arbitrarily closing the lay school and dispersing the pupils, Lord Fingall's son among them. Hardwicke patiently explained that the school was to be phased out gradually, not disbanded and he presumably explained the opinion of FitzGibbon's fellow visitors. Hardwicke apparently believed that this latest skirmish with FitzGibbon was over. At any rate, FitzGibbon seemed placated, and Lord Fingall, ever pliant, assured Hardwicke and Abbott that he would enroll his son in an English school.[108]

Unfortunately, Hardwicke underestimated FitzGibbon's determination and his desperation. In December, FitzGibbon was again meddling in affairs at Maynooth. Having lost control of Lord Fingall, he turned his powers of persuasion and intimidation on Dr Troy. According to Troy, FitzGibbon summoned him specifically to complain about the imminent demise of the lay school:

> The Chancellor sent for me and asked me how things were going on at Maynooth. I told him no alteration had taken place. He said it was the most absurd and extravagant thing that ever entered the mind of man to prevent laymen being educated at the College and that every country schoolmaster might teach and why not those who were better qualified and under the control of Government?[109]

Troy responded to this onslaught with an appeal to another authority:

> My Lord, I understood that it was Lord Kilwarden who made the representation to Government against the establishment of the school.

To which FitzGibbon responded with this extraordinary re-interpretation of recent transactions:

> No such thing ... I have asked Lord Kilwarden about it and he told me that in conversation with Lord Hardwicke he had mentioned his visitation to the College and how very much to his satisfaction he found everything there and that he noticed the school merely as a matter of conversation, without in any degree complaining of it.

According to his own later account of the conversation, Troy took this remark to be an unmistakable directive to continue the lay school. FitzGibbon reinforced this impression with his peremptory remarks of dismissal:

> The Chancellor desired me to write down to Maynooth to go on just as usual and to take no notice. I accordingly wrote to Dr Dunn and I thought the matter was over and we should hear no more about it.

Troy was to hear more than he ever cared to about the subject. Dr Dunn, understandably confused by this flat contradiction of a previous government order, apparently wrote to Hardwicke for an explanation. Troy received a summons to the Castle, where he repeated his particular version of events to Hardwicke and Abbott. Four days later, on 21 December, FitzGibbon was requested to call on Lord Hardwicke. Hardwicke and Abbott then presented him with a copy of Troy's affidavit, and asked him to explain what was, to all appearances, an attempt to suborn Troy and to subvert a government directive.

It is impossible not to admire FitzGibbon's bravado and resourcefulness in the face of this humiliating confrontation. He blustered: "This old gentleman has very much misunderstood and misrepresented me." He prevaricated, insisting that he had merely repeated the established government line on the lay school: "That in regard to the order which had been sent, I had understood from the lord lieutenant that no money was to be laid out nor any change made till the determination of government should be signified to him on the subject." Skillfully applying the time honored precept that the best defense is a good assault, he launched into a rambling and varied denunciation of Maynooth, former chief secretary Pelham, Bishop Troy, Bishop Caulfield of Wexford and the savage, bloody-minded Catholics in general. It was a waste of public money, he declare, to maintain "a monastery for the education of Two Hundred priests at the expense of £8,000 per annum"; he would far rather "send them back to Salamanca", which presumably to his mind was a cheaper solution. FitzGibbon blamed Maynooth's transformation into an £8,000 per annum monastery on Pelham and Troy. They had intrigued behind the backs of the visitors and the other trustees to pervert the original character of Maynooth, which he insisted, had always been intended as a mixed institution. (Thus did FitzGibbon settle scores with Troy for informing on him, however reluctantly.) With a relevance known only to his own enraged, humiliated mind, FitzGibbon also launched into a denunciation of

Troy's pastoral brother Caulfield, who had recently written a pamphlet defending himself from Sir Richard Musgrave's charges of complicity in the late rebellion. FitzGibbon's full comments do not appear in the record of this particular conversation, but he probably expressed a conviction that Caulfield was a liar and that Sir Richard's allegations were correct. He made ominous noises about reviving the penal laws against priests, presumably to prevent them from writing pamphlets and from interfering, however inadvertently, in his grand conception of Catholic education. Finally, he insisted that the Catholics were still engaged in a systematic campaign of sectarian murder, particularly in Kildare, though again, only FitzGibbon knew the relevance of this information to the subject of Maynooth.[110]

Hardwicke remained perfectly unmoved by FitzGibbon's diatribe. With great patience and no doubt with great weariness, Hardwicke reminded FitzGibbon that whatever the precise intentions of Maynooth, the education of priests in Ireland under government control was certainly its premier, if not exclusive intent. He also emphasized again that neither he nor anyone in government had intended to dissolve the lay school abruptly and arbitrarily. He had merely requested further consultation on the subject and no further outlay of funds. As for FitzGibbon's claims about continuing Catholic atrocities, Hardwicke, duly investigated and found that most of the crimes to which FitzGibbon had alluded had taken place over 18 months before. Moreover, FitzGibbon himself had apparently not been unduly worried about Catholic savagery and rebellion. He had fully agreed to a plan to try any as yet imprisoned offenders in a specially commissioned civil court, rather than by the more drastic and severe court martial. Hardwicke was too kind and too magnanimous to mention the obvious conclusion: if Catholic murderers still stalked abroad in Kildare, FitzGibbon's own lenity was at least partially responsible.[111]

There were other flagrant absurdities and inconsistencies which, if he took notice of them, Hardwicke refrained from mentioning. There was, for example, FitzGibbon's apparently willful obliviousness to the opinion, not only of Hardwicke, but of his fellow trustees. Even his close friend Kilwarden opposed any introduction of a lay school at Maynooth. Hardwicke also tactfully passed over FitzGibbon's bullying of Dr Troy and his gross misrepresentation of Troy's role. Far from intriguing in secret to turn Maynooth into a monastery, Troy had, in fact, cooperated with FitzGibbon until it became clear that the government wished otherwise. The wretched man was perfectly indifferent on the subject of lay pupils. He was sick unto death of the whole subject, and anxious to extricate himself from the miserable position in which he found himself, bullied by the Earl of Clare on one side and rebuked by the lord-lieutenant on the other. Hardwicke also refrained from observing that FitzGibbon had missed an opportunity to clarify the status of Maynooth in 1800, when he revised the nature and duties of the governing board. (On the other hand, knowing the sentiments of the other judges, FitzGibbon may simply have allowed the opportunity to slip, preferring instead to bully or flatter the Catholic visitors in secret to get his way.) Above all, Hardwicke refrained from pointing out that FitzGibbon had lied. His disclaimers and his largely pointless denunciations of Catholic villainy could not conceal his indisputable attempt to coerce Dr Troy into keeping the lay school in existence, in direct contradiction of the known opinion of the government. Quite apart from the unlikelihood that Troy would have either the malice or the hardihood to slander FitzGibbon, his entire account, down to the chancellor's characteristic turns of phrase, rings true.

The interview ended on a characteristic note of inconclusiveness and placation. Hardwicke asked FitzGibbon to submit a memorandum on Maynooth. FitzGibbon then departed for what must have been a dismal Christmas at Mount Shannon. FitzGibbon sent off a memorandum on Maynooth to Hardwicke a week after the ill-fated interview at the Castle. It said nothing of particular novelty or interest. He merely reiterated his claims that Troy and the other Catholic bishops had secretly perverted the true character of Maynooth, and he made the obvious statement that it was essential to come to some kind of agreement about the future direction of the school.[112]

Hardwicke, in the meantime, sent another exasperated letter to Addington on the vexed subject of FitzGibbon:

> He [FitzGibbon] seems to me, with a great share of cleverness and vivacity, to be very deficient in consistency and precision in his ideas.[113]

He also made this startling statement, given the exhaustive anti-Popish diatribe which FitzGibbon had delivered not a week before:

> It would be curious if after all that has passed Lord Clare should be attempting to acquire popularity with the Catholics at the expense of government.[114]

It is difficult to know just which Catholics FitzGibbon had been attempting to court. Certainly Bishop Troy had no reason to love the thought of a lay school or to love FitzGibbon for so high-handedly sponsoring it. FitzGibbon's patronage of Lord Fingall may have prompted this remark. If so, Hardwicke had no reason to fear that Lord Fingall would join in a confederacy with FitzGibbon. No doubt it was very flattering to receive calls, friendly letters and a share of County Meath patronage from the lord chancellor. But once Fingall understood the government's sentiments, he promptly abandoned FitzGibbon and the lay school. However dim and pliant he was, Fingall knew where power and authority ultimately rested.

But however correct Hardwicke may have been about FitzGibbon's "vivacity" and his inconsistency on the subject of Maynooth, he overlooked FitzGibbon's over-riding and very consistent motive for setting off the whole contretemps, his own devastating sense of insignificance and marginality. In the course of his last interview with Hardwicke, FitzGibbon made this poignant *cri de coeur*:

> ... he had for sixteen or seventeen years been the scapegoat of English government ... and that he felt that summary order upon the subject [of the lay school] ought not to have been given without his consent.[115]

It is perhaps the final irony of the whole business that FitzGibbon's view did prevail. The lay school at Maynooth remained in existence until 1817. In addition, the loathsome Abbott was soon transferred from Ireland to England where he assumed the post of Speaker of the House of Commons. But FitzGibbon did not live to see these triumphs. He died a little more than a month after the interview with Hardwicke.

FitzGibbon's final illness was sudden in its onset and mysterious in its nature. On 11 January 1802, he reported to Auckland that his nose had bled for almost 13 hours and that he was feeling extremely weak and debilitated.[116] At the urging of his doctors in Limerick, he went to Dublin for further consultation on his condition, as soon as he had the strength to travel. His friend Auckland urged him to come to London, in the belief that English doctors were superior to any in either Dublin or in Limerick. FitzGibbon himself seemed to think that he was at least strong enough to last out the end of the current chancery term in March, at which time he planned to resign his office and travel to the south of France to convalesce. But after a week or so of trying to conduct Chancery business with uneven results, Hardwicke, genuinely concerned for FitzGibbon's well-being, decided to ask for his immediate resignation. FitzGibbon was spared what would have been a final, if well-intentioned, humiliation. Edema and congestive heart failure set in before Hardwicke could formally request the seals. FitzGibbon sank into a coma and died on 28 January 1802.

The suddenness of his illness is startling. It is true that FitzGibbon's letters were full of accounts of various illness. He seems in particular to have been prone to gout, as were many of his contemporaries.[117] But as striking was his amazing physical resilience. He quickly recovered from an accident that would have incapacitated many others. Moreover, he was a vigorous active man who loved riding, hunting and other outdoor sports. He also had an extraordinary capacity for hard work. In short, he had a remarkable constitution that had weathered many worse crises, both emotional and physical. Mentally, he was still ready to do battle with Hardwicke, Abbot, Troy and all the legions of Popery. It is certainly possible that his constitution simply gave out after a lifetime of hard living, burdensome work and emotional turbulence. But FitzGibbon's wife inadvertently raised another possibility. In one of her many letters lamenting her fast approaching widowhood and destitution, she stated that her husband was dying of a "liver complaint".[118] FitzGibbon's symptoms, massive bleeding, edema and congestive heart failure, all characterize one liver complaint in particular, cirrhosis. To put the matter bluntly, there is at least a possibility that FitzGibbon drank himself to death. He was a notorious drinker, even in an age when over-indulgence was a given of gentlemanly life. He may have hit the bottle particularly hard after the Maynooth incident and surpassed even his own amazing capacity. If he was indeed suffering from cirrhosis, his doctors were singularly ignorant of it. They allowed him to drink Madeira and water to the very end.[119]

Whether he died of exhaustion or of a more squalid illness, there is no question of his courage, stoicism and dignity in the face of death. The pettiness and rage that characterized the final months of his life dissolved. He accepted the grim verdict of his doctors with calm, and probably with some relief. He then methodically set about completing what he could of unfinished chancery business. The end was an agonizing process of slow suffocation, but he never complained.[120]

Plowden later portrayed FitzGibbon's deathbed as a scene of frenzied religious devotion and attempted apostasy:

> After Lord Clare understood (as his friends reported of him) that his cause was helpless, he gave his mind to devotion and three times on the same day partook of the holy sacrament from the hand of his brother-in-law the Archbishop of Tuam. In the latter part of his illness, he is said to have expressed a wish to be attended by a Catholic priest, which was not complied with.[121]

No doubt it was immensely satisfying to Plowden, a Catholic, to imagine the Earl of Clare crying out vainly for a priest in his final desolate hours. But this bit of hearsay is probably groundless. At most FitzGibbon, like many rabid anti-Catholics, had a sneaking and morbid fascination with the ritual splendors of Popery. But his calm and his presence of mind on his deathbed make it unlikely that he attempted a sudden and radical rejection of his long-held political and religious opinions. If he had deathbed doubts, he probably would have suppressed them. The case of Lord Dunboyne had recently entered the docket of the chancery court. FitzGibbon was too worldly a man, too cautious a lawyer and too conscientious a husband and father to follow Lord Dunboyne's dangerous example. Pace Plowden, FitzGibbon probably died convinced that the Church of Ireland was the surest path to advancement in Heaven, just as it had been the surest path to political and social advancement on earth.

Official accounts of the funeral in government newspapers gave the impression of a grand and somber occasion, marked by dignified mourning for a departed statesman and judge.[122] The reality was a grotesque public carnival. Both Lord Cloncurry and Thomas Parsons recalled the crowds milling around the house at Ely Place, yelling execrations and cheering when the coffin emerged for the funeral procession.[123] Years later, another witness reported that passersby had pelted the coffin with dead cats, an insulting alluding to an alleged claim of FitzGibbon's that he would render the Catholics as tame as cats (or variously, geld cats).[124] None of the other observers remarked on this singular incident. Chance, rather than crude deliberate mockery, may have accounted for this story. Possibly the mob pelted the hearse and coffin with debris which happened to include one or more dead cats. Even in the safety of the churchyard of St Peters, FitzGibbon's remains suffered another, if inadvertent indignity. Water suddenly filled the grave as FitzGibbon's coffin was lowered, engulfing the remains with mud.[125] In 1983, his remains were again disturbed. St Peter's was demolished, and the bodies in the churchyard were removed to Mount Jerome, where they were buried in a mass grave. FitzGibbon's remains were included in the anonymous heap.

A poignant entry in the *Dublin Evening Post* reveals the terrible evanescence of both his fame and his infamy. It reported briefly and without comment that his grand carriage, once the subject of so much praise and blame had been sold to a Russian nobleman.[126] All the trappings of rank and power had disappeared, leaving only his enigmatic character to baffle and divide later historians as sharply as it did his contemporaries.

19

Epilogue

The aftermath of FitzGibbon's death had all the hallmarks of his life: cruel irony, macabre comedy, and inutterable sadness. Whatever mourning there was for FitzGibbon took second place to various feuds over wills and maintenance The turmoil began even as he lay on his miserable death bed.

His final break with his sister Arabella was to be a long-standing source of rancor that lasted until the 1820s. An obscure quarrel over the sale of some of her son's property appears to have exhausted both FitzGibbon's patience and his affection for his sister. The details of the transaction are maddeningly few, and those few come from that maddeningly untrustworthy source, Grattan's *Memoirs*. Acting in some sort of a fiduciary capacity, possibly as a guardian or trustee, FitzGibbon had purchased land from the Jefferyes' estate. He probably acted with Arabella Jefferyes' consent in yet another attempt to relieve her chronic money troubles. Arabella's only son apparently learned of the sale upon attaining his majority and objected. Young Jefferyes either felt that his uncle had not paid a fair price for the property or he simply wanted the property itself. If the latter reconstruction of events is correct, young Jefferyes doubtless lacked the financial wherewithal to refund the entire price of purchase to his uncle. He may have offered only a fraction of the price and complained about depreciation or he may have offered nothing on the grounds that the sale was wrong to begin with. Arabella took her son's part. In the general obscurity and confusion of the case, her reasons present the greatest conundrum. The long bankruptcy that was her life again offers the most likely explanation. She may have concluded that she had sacrificed a steady source of income in the form of an estate for a lump sum of money that had disappeared all too quickly. Like her brother, she had a flexible sense of reality that always put her in the right. She no doubt rearranged the past to support the belief that her brother had taken advantage of a struggling widow and her son. Albinia Fremantle also sided with her brother and mother. She may have felt that they had a legitimate grievance, or she may simply have had a grudge against her uncle for his failure to get her husband promoted.[1] Mrs Jefferyes' two other daughters, the appalling Lady Cahir and Lady Westmeath, do not seem to have become involved in the matter. Their private concerns probably spared them. Lady Cahir was just entering into a life of married bliss. Lady Westmeath was in the process of ending her very unblissful marriage, and venturing into a second. Apart from the distractions of love and marriage, they probably would have taken their uncle's part. Lady Cahir and her captive husband were on visiting terms with their formidable uncle, and Lady Westmeath may have been estranged from her mother altogether.[2]

The precise chronology of these events poses another unsolvable riddle. It is only certain that the issue of the alienated estate did not emerge before 1791. FitzGibbon would not have rescued Arabella from eviction or tried to obtain a promotion for Albinia's husband had they accused him of bad faith.

Whatever the origins of the quarrel, it seems to have remained *en famille* during FitzGibbon's lifetime. At any rate there was no public mention of it in the newspapers, which even in the repressive 1790s would have made some allusion to so spectacular a family quarrel. Arabella and her children may not even have realized how much they had alienated their formidable relation. If so, FitzGibbon's will quickly enlightened them, in no uncertain terms. He disinherited Arabella, Albinia Fremantle and young Jefferyes in terms that he usually reserved for rebellious Catholics, United Irishmen and the opposition in general.

> And I do hereby request of the guardians of my dear children never to suffer them during their minority to have any intercourse with the said Arabella Jefferyes or George her son, or Albinia her daughter. I have by sad and long experience found them all to be utterly destitute of every principle of truth, justice or gratitude.[3]

In spite of the Protestant pieties of the preamble and in spite of his affectionate references to his wife, his children and other relations still in his good graces, the will had one over-riding and bitter purpose: to prevent the perfidious Jefferyes from ever entering into possession of any part of his estate. FitzGibbon clearly anticipated the possibility that he would die soon and that his children would die young. He was a sickly man and a hated one, which rendered him vulnerable to disease or assassination. Three brothers and two daughters had died young, so he well knew the frailties of minor children. He listed a formidable array of claimants who were to take precedence over the objectionable Jefferyes should his children die before attaining their majority. They included the two sisters still in favor, Elizabeth Beresford and Elinor Trant, and their sons, the two good Jefferyes nieces, Lady Cahir and Lady Westmeath, and their sons, his two cousins Thomas FitzGibbon and Thomas Gibbon FitzGibbon and their sons. Barring an extraordinary demographic catastrophe, Arabella and her two errant children had no hope of ever coming into possession of any part of the estate. (FitzGibbon did not however, chose to visit the sins of fathers, mothers and grandmothers on successive generations. His will permitted the children of Albinia Fremantle and George Jefferyes to inherit in the absence of all other claimants.)[4]

FitzGibbon underestimated his sister's habits of litigation. She promptly filed a suit to break the will.[5] In addition, Arabella and her son filed a suit in the court of chancery to reclaim the disputed estate. According to the younger Grattan, Lord

Chancellor Manners declared the sale void in 1817, though he acknowledged that his predecessor had paid a fair price for the estate. In keeping with the *leitmotif* of the memoirs, the younger Grattan attributed a fierce anti-Union speech to the younger Jefferyes when he received the verdict:

> When Jeffreys [*sic*] came out of court, he openly addressed some of the lawyers in the hall and said that his uncle had never done a single act that procured him the esteem or thanks of his countrymen. "I," exclaimed he, "opposed him on the Union. I have a piece of plate voted to me for the part I then took, and I afterwards saw Lord Clare die, repenting of his conduct on that very question."[7]

The implication was, of course, that young Jefferyes' dedication to the Irish nation, and not his disputes over real estate, had earned him the enmity of his uncle. The claim is dubious, as is Jefferyes' purported speech. FitzGibbon may well have resented Jefferyes' opposition to the Union, but he probably resented far more his perceived greed, ingratitude and treachery. Indeed, given FitzGibbon's feelings, young Jefferyes probably never went near his uncle's busy and dramatic deathbed.

The dispute dragged on until 1826. The existing evidence suggests that the second earl agreed to pay monetary damages. Jefferyes and Clare then carried on another desultory legal argument over the precise sum. Lord Clare finally settled with his cousin for £1,700.[8]

Arabella had no apparent part in these final transactions, which suggests that her turbulent life had come to an end. In her final years she verged on insanity, if she did not actually slip into it altogether. In 1807, she wrote an extraordinary letter either to the chief secretary or to the personal secretary of the Duke of Richmond, then lord-lieutenant. Following the suit of her sister-in-law, she claimed a pension for herself because she had served the Protestant government by saving Lord Clare's life in 1795. She described in great detail how a rampaging mob of "Papists" had pursued her brother from College Green to his house in Ely Place. There, the Popish mob started preparations to break down the door, drag Lord Clare from his house, and hang him from the nearest lamppost.He might have died and the government might have lost a valued servant, but for the resourcefulness of Arabella herself. She claimed that she appeared on the scene disguised as a kitchen maid. She diverted the crowd from the house by spreading a rumor to the effect that "a rigiment of Hos is galloping down here to hus – oh yea, yea where will we go?" The mob, in her version of events, believed her and went scurrying off to the Customs House. To impress on her interlocutor her remarkable heroism, she concluded, "thus I saved Lord Clare's life at the risk of being town limb from limb if I had been recognized by any of them." Arabella based her claims on her family's services to government, as well as her own. From 1762, she declared, her husband "constantly supported government. Her two sons-in-law, to whom she referred with no little infelicity as "two of the oldest peers in Ireland", were both firm supporters of "the protestant interest and his majesty's government". Finally, Arabella offered her expertise on the Catholic issue. The claims of French emissaries were a ghostly echo of her alienated and dead brother, while the oblique allusions to tithes were the faded last gap of "Lady" Jefferyes, the Whiteboys' friend.

> I could, I think, give you some very useful information relative to the state of the south of Ireland – where I am well persuaded that French emissaries are placed to pervert the minds and morals of poor oppressed wretches whose grievances are intolerable and who now only look to the Roman Catholic Committee for a redress of them ... if Government redress'd their grievances and left them in the peaceable possession of their potatoe gardens, and the milch of their cows, these two millions of poor creatures would consider themselves affluent and happy.[9]

Her tale was, of course, a pathetic tissue of lies and delusions. None of the newspaper accounts of the riots of 1795 give any mention of a dramatic rescue by a lady disguised as a kitchen-maid. Even if she had made this dramatic quick change, her absurd stage Irish accent would have exposed her immediately. Poor stage-struck Arabella was writing a good part for herself in a play which was never performed. Whatever may have been the case with her pliant creation Lord Cahir, she could not claim Lord Westmeath either as a son-in-law or as a political supporter. He had divorced her daughter with great publicity over ten years before, and he ardently supported Catholic Emancipation.[10] As for her assessments of the Irish peasantry, she seems not to have learned any lessons from her experiences with the Whiteboys. She never could realize that her beloved cottiers had political and economic aspirations quite independent of her direction, Mr Keogh's or the agents of the French. The letter does not appear to have reached the Duke of Richmond' s secretary. Some companion or relative had the pity and the kindness to intercept it.[11]

His wife, "the disconsolate widow", as Lord Shannon sarcastically termed her, was also a discontented legatee. FitzGibbon kept his wife in style during his lifetime, but in his will he could provide only a modest £1,100 per annum. Obedience to paternal dictates, rather than any deathbed resentment toward his wife dictated this particular bequest to his wife. According to Anne FitzGibbon herself, a provision in old John FitzGibbon's will limited her widow's portion to this amount. While an annual income of £1,100 may have been perfectly adequate when she married Mr FitzGibbon, the Honorable Attorney General, her standing and circumstances had changed considerably since that time. Anne FitzGibbon immediately perceived that £1,100 per annum could not support her dignity as Countess of Clare and as the widow of the lord chancellor of Ireland. While her husband slipped into coma and death, she dashed off letters of appeal to FitzGibbon's friend, the former viceroy Lord Westmorland. These missives played on the same basic themes: she was on the verge of destitution; to maintain herself as became Lord Clare's widow, she deserved at least as large a pension as Lady Lifford. There may have been a certain chilly self-absorption in her frantic production of begging letters as her husband approached his death. But Anne FitzGibbon had been a sheltered beauty all her life. She could not support herself in any meaningful or appropriate way, unlike energetic middle class ladies like Henrietta Battier or Mary Anne McCracken. Her social position and her lack of education prevented her. She really had no other recourse but to get the most generous maintenance for herself that she possibly could.

Anne FitzGibbon had no qualms about dunning prime ministers as well as viceroys for her due. In 1816, she subjected Lord Liverpool to complaints about her poverty: "He [her son] is looked upon to be a rich man, when, alas, it is quite otherwise."[13] Her claims must have seemed somewhat unconvincing. Her son, the second earl of Clare had the financial wherewithal to make frequent trips to Italy and to undertake a substantial expansion of the house at Mount Shannon. Nonetheless, her persistence, if not her persuasiveness paid off, and she did receive her pension. Still unsatisfied, she promptly undertook another letter writing campaign to obtain a second one. Unfortunately, she failed in this particular endeavor.[14]

In her quest for a place on the Irish Civil List, Anne FitzGibbon at least deserves credit for family feeling. She also pressed the claims of FitzGibbon's cousin Thomas for a revenue office. Allegedly, her husband had expressed a wish to provide for Thomas FitzGibbon.[15] Out of respect for the late chancellor's dying wish, or perhaps out of a desire to avoid yet another spate of correspondence from the grieving widow, the Irish government duly appointed Thomas FitzGibbon to the post of collector of customs for the port of Limerick.[16] Anne FitzGibbon also requested a concordatum for Thomas's sister Mary Anne.[17] The reasons for this particular demand are unclear. Certainly Lord Clare's widow was not fulfilling any deathbed promises. Mary Anne FitzGibbon was a convert to Roman Catholicism.[18]

Apart from her various legal tangles, Anne FitzGibbon's widowhood appears to have been pleasant and placid enough. She played cards with Mrs. Fitzherbert at Brighton, graced the London season and engaged in visits to various English and Irish country houses. Maria Edgeworth encountered Anne FitzGibbon on one such visit in 1822, and in a letter, she offered a savage pen portrait of an aging belle: garrulous, silly and narcissistic:

> Lady Clare is a painted – made up – vulgar thoroughgoing woman of the world ... Her ladyship pressed me to visit her in Ireland, but I never desire to see her again.[19]

In her distaste for Anne FitzGibbon's conversation and cosmetics, Miss Edgeworth overlooked the kindness of her invitation, and possibly, the loneliness that might have prompted this once radiant beauty to seek out even her priggish, censorious company. Her hopes, pleasures and plans finally ended in 1844. She is buried in Kensal Green, far from the husband who brought her eminence and love as well as turmoil.

Both FitzGibbon and his wife were unquestionably devoted parents, whatever their vicissitudes as a couple. There were five children, three girls and two boys. The two eldest girls, Isabella Mary Anne, born in 1787, and Louisa, born in 1790, died of smallpox in 1791. Isabella Mary Anne's death particularly devastated FitzGibbon. FitzGibbon touchingly described his own grief in a letter to a Limerick associate who had suffered a similar loss. His thoughtfulness and sympathy reveal a side of FitzGibbon's character too easily overlooked:

> I do not like to hear you talk in so desponding a style of your health. I can see plainly that your spirits are much affected, and so long as the mind is agitated, your bodily health will necessarily be impaired ... I feel from experience how cruel a blow the loss of a favorite child is, but, still, a little reflection has taught me the necessity of bearing the misfortune with fortitude. Surely you have every reason to induce you to summon up resolution to enable you to encounter your present melancholy. If you will do so, a little time will calm the uneasiness of a mind which now occasions your want of health.[21]

As much as his busy schedule allowed, FitzGibbon was affectionate and attentive toward his surviving children. The collection of books which he purchased from Denis Daly's estate in 1792 included a number of titles clearly intended for children, including La Rochfoucauld's *Fables*.[22] In 1798, he took time from the momentous activity of that year to accompany his two little boys when they went off to school in England.[23]

What kind of relationship he would have had with his children as adults remains an eternal unanswered question. Their mother was their sole parental influence for most of their lives. Her affection and devotion are beyond dispute, but she was also very demanding and possessive, especially toward her daughter. This girl, named for her late sister Isabella Mary Anne, seems to have been cast early on in the role of companion to her dazzling and fashionable mother. The hypercritical Miss Edgeworth acknowledged that she was a handsome girl and she a decent marriage portion of £10,000, but she never managed to establish a life independent of her mother.[24] Extraordinary devotion, or perhaps an exhausted will, held her fast. By the time her mother died in 1844, Lady Isabella Mary Anne FitzGibbon was approaching fifty, an age when she had little hope of marrying and no hope of children. Legal wrangles troubled the final years of her sad and otherwise dull life. She filed suit in Chancery against her niece, Lady Louisa FitzGibbon, and Lady Louisa's husband, because of their failure to pay legacies from her father and her elder brother the second earl of Clare. She died in 1873, before any resolution of the suit.[25]

While the lives of FitzGibbon's two sons were not as thwarted, they never displayed their father's brilliance or force of character. The second Earl of Clare, also named John FitzGibbon, gained a modest literary fame as one of the objects of Byron's romantic friendship. The two attended Harrow together, and Clare inspired one of Byron's juvenile efforts, addressed to "The Friend of my Youth". Byron remained infatuated with his boyhood friend. He later declared to Thomas Moore that he loved Lord Clare more than "any (male) thing in the whole world".[26] (Such sentiments must have been distasteful to Moore, who had endured an interview during the first Lord Clare's Trinity visitation. In his memoirs, he portrayed the late Lord Chancellor as a monster of blustering arrogance.)[27] Clare does not seem to have reciprocated this feeling with the same ardor. Some years after their schoolboy idyll, he postponed a visit to his old Harrow admirer to go shopping with his mother. Byron accused his friend of neglect and cruelty, but he failed to take into account the all powerful will of Lady Clare.[28]

In politics, he took the mother's line, rather than the father's on Catholic Emancipation. A surviving letter suggests that like many liberal-minded landlords, he came to the resigned conclusion that Catholic Emancipation was certainly preferable to O'Connellite upheaval:

> It is clear the people neither mind the magistrates nor their priests when they act in opposition to their wishes.[29]

In this same spirit, he voted for Catholic Emancipation in 1829. Yet in the disenchanted aftermath, when relations between Catholics and Protestants deteriorated, he maintained a liberal attitude. Unlike many landlords, he managed to maintain the political loyalties of his tenants, an indication of judicious management, no doubt, but also of his liberality on sectarian questions.[30]

Apart from the practicalities of politics, he does not seem to have had any of his father's violent abhorrence for Roman Catholics and Roman Catholicism. Travel, something his father rarely did, may have had its purported broadening effects in his case. The second earl of Clare seems to have loved Rome, which he visited frequently. He also married a Catholic, a daughter of Lord Gwydyr, whom he met in Rome.[31] The marriage was disastrously and mysteriously short-lived, and his wife retired to a convent.[32]

On the matter of England's relationship with Ireland, the second Earl was very much his father's son. He articulated his ideas on the subject most completely in a letter to Lord Farnham, written in 1847. Farnham had requested Clare's opinion on proposals to organize an Irish party to press for more relief during the great famine. Clare refused to participate because he felt such a party would create unnecessary dissension. While not denying the horrifying magnitude of the crisis, he insisted that co-operation with England, not the formation of an Irish special interest group, offered the surest means of addressing it:

> at this awful crisis, we should not I think do anything which can be construed into a distrust of our rulers or of their ability to serve us. The question to be submitted to Par[liamen]t is not purely an Irish question. The interests of England are fully as much concerned in it, as we are inseparably united to the greater and richer country. I am convinced it is the inclination as well as the duty of England to assist us in extricating us from our present difficulties. The evil must be probed to the bottom and by the blessing of providence, the united councils of both countries will save us from the horrors of famine now, and will prevent their recurring in future.[33]

As for his career in public service, he attained neither his father's eminence nor his notoriety. His service as governor-general of the Bombay presidency from 1830 to 1834 marked its pinnacle.[34] The second earl spend the greater part of his time coping with lawsuits and financial disarray in his estate. His efforts were largely ineffectual. To judge from his lawyer's voluminous correspondence, he lost track of large sums of money, including a £5,000 loan and scrip worth £2,000.[35] The final stage of his life resembled one of the more melancholy scenes in Joseph Sheridan Le Fanu's fiction. He died in London in 1851. According to his sister's brief in Chancery, his personal assets could not cover his outstanding debts:

> The personal estate of ... John, Earl of Clare not specifically bequested situate in England consisted of a small cash balance at Messrs Coutts and Co, the Bankers of the said testator, and of a small sum of money in his writing desk and purse.[36]

No doubt the famine contributed to the already heavy encumbrances and losses affecting the estate. The second earl's assets consisted mainly of arrears in rent from estates in Limerick and Tipperary.[37]

Robert Hobart, the second son and third Earl, was as sad and as futile a figure. His mother's cultivation of the popular Catholic interest reaped for him the dividend of a seat for County Limerick.[38] As member for Limerick, he followed the new family line and supported Catholic Emancipation. A pronounced streak of shallowness and fecklessness characterized much of his public and private conduct. One colleague complained of his habit of avoiding crucial votes out of personal pique.[39] He certainly did not marry with his father's astuteness. He eloped with a married woman, a certain Diana Crosbie Moore, *née* Woodcock. In keeping with the ruthless double standards of the time, Mrs FitzGibbon was roundly snubbed by county society. In one of his few acts of political exertion, Richard FitzGibbon enlisted his brother's help to petition for a living for one of his wife's few champions, the local clergyman. Their efforts profoundly irritated William Lamb, then serving as chief secretary:

> Lord Clare and Mr FitzGibbon want a living for Mr Westhorp, whose principal merit is that his is the only family in the county of Limerick that will receive Mrs FitzGibbon. Tho' I have the greatest toleration and even partiality for ladies of that description, yet I cannot go so far as to say that associating with them in compliance with the wishes of a patron is the best possible recommendation for a clergyman ... that damned little man milliner Clare – he knows I promised him nothing: but like all Irishmen, if you put one single civil word in your communication with them, they immediately construe it as a promise, and charge you with a breach of faith if they don't get what they have asked.[40]

Lazy and reckless though he was, Richard FitzGibbon did have the redeeming merit of kindness. During the famine, he generously assisted emigrants, and in the process, he further diminished the already encumbered and cash poor FitzGibbon family fortune. Like his brother, he remained liberal on sectarian matters. While serving as lord-lieutenant of County Limerick, Richard FitzGibbon drew criticism for filling the post of deputy-lieutenant exclusively with Catholics.[41]

Richard FitzGibbon succeeded his brother as Earl of Clare, but the honor soon became an empty one. The male line came to a starkly dramatic end when his only son died in the fabled charge of the Light Brigade. When the third earl died shortly afterwards in 1862, Mount Shannon came into the possession of his eldest daughter, Louisa, and her husband, who had assumed the name FitzGibbon. Lady Louisa's extravagance hastened the ruin which her uncle's incapacity and her father's generosity had set into motion. Her sons finally sold the estate in 1888. The last of the resident FitzGibbon line polluted at least one shade at Mount Shannon by turning Roman Catholic. The fully fitted oratory described in the auction catalogue was Lady Louisa's final improvement. Like her aunt, the mysterious second Lady Clare, she retired to a convent.[42]

It is, of course, impossible to know precisely what direction FitzGibbon's career would have taken had he lived. Probably, he would have remained in eclipse during the Duke of Bedford's administration, and enjoyed something of a revival of influence during the triumvirate of Richmond, Manners and Saurin. But it is doubtful that FitzGibbon would have had a second chance at a larger career in England. George Canning's perceptive and graceful epitaph for FitzGibbon acknowledged him as a true friend of the English interest, but one who, by nature and temperament, no longer could serve that interest adequately:

> He was a man amongst all his countrymen the most suited to his time. Perhaps the time is past when his character was of the kind to be most beneficial, and that in the feeling of gratitude, as we look back and compare the past and the present, we may be authorized to sink some portion of our regret.[43]

In and of itself, his massive unpopularity in Ireland need not have hampered FitzGibbon's prospects in England. Of greater harm was the fact that most of the ranking and influential men in English government had come to perceive him as an over-bearing troublemaker. Certainly his actions and demeanor toward Lord Hardwicke would have confirmed such a reputation. It seems most likely that FitzGibbon would have ended up like Duigenan, a marginal and slightly ridiculous figure.

His vision of Ireland as an integral part of the Protestant British empire survives in an embattled form, though it would be interesting to know what FitzGibbon would have made of the fact that Ulster Presbyterians man the last bastion of unionism. Of course, in the part of Ireland he most loved, after his fashion, his ideas met with complete rejection, and the thing he most dreaded did occur: for better or for worse southern Ireland became an independent Catholic state. In fact, during the war of independence, the republican forces in Limerick made two dramatic, physical gestures of renunciation and contempt: they burned Mount Shannon, even though it had long since passed into the ownership of an American speculator, and they blew up a statue of FitzGibbon's grandson, the Crimea hero. Yet much to FitzGibbon's credit was ignored in this ferocious campaign of oblivion. Unfortunately, FitzGibbon lived at a time when his own fragile social identity and the imperial order were under constant challenge. In his various struggles, his most ruthless and harsh qualities dominated his public persona. Had FitzGibbon lived in more stable political times, his unquestionable virtues, his passionate sense of justice, his compassion for the poor and his untiring dedication to his public duties, might have been more prominent and of greater benefit to Ireland. And to serve Ireland always was FitzGibbon's aim, however destructive his social and religious hatreds, however wrong-headed and brutal his measures and methods.

Bibliography

MANUSCRIPT SOURCES

GREAT BRITAIN AND NORTHERN IRELAND

Belfast: Public Record Office of Northern Ireland

Aldborough Papers
Abercorn Papers
Castlereagh Papers
Downshire Papers
Gosford Papers
Normanton Papers
Rosse Papers

Kent: County Archives

Camden Papers (also on microfilm in the library of Trinity College Dublin)

London: British Library

Sir William Betham, Genealogical Collections, III, p. 66 , BM Add MS 23,686, (also on microfilm in the National Library of Ireland)

London: Public Record Office

Home Office Papers (NLI microfilm)
State Papers (NLI microfilm)
Chatham Papers (NLI microfilm)

Sheffield Public Library

Fitzwilliam Papers (NLI microfilm)

University of Keele

Sneyd Muniments

IRELAND

Dublin: National Library of Ireland

Bolton Papers
Bennett Papers
Fingall Papers
FitzGibbon Papers
Gormanston Papers (since removed from the collection)

Heffernan Papers
Leinster Papers
Dublin: National Library of Ireland (continued)
Melville Papers
Trench Papers (microfilm)
Sydney Papers
Trinity College Dublin
Hutchinson Papers
Madden Papers
Sirr Papers
Dublin: Irish State Paper Office
Westmorland Papers
Rebellion Papers
Dublin: National Archives of Ireland
Chancery documents concerning the FitzGibbon estate (MS 6192)

PUBLISHED MANUSCRIPTS

Aspects of Irish Social History 1750–1800, Belfast: Public Record Office of Northern Ireland, 1969

The Convert Rolls, Eileen O'Byrne, ed., Dublin: 1981

Historical Manuscripts Commission publications:

The Manuscripts of the Earl of Carlisle, Report 15, Appendix VI, London: 1897

The Manuscripts and Correspondence of James, First Earl of Charlemont, Report 13, Appendix VIII, 2 volumes, London: 1889,

The Manuscripts of the Earl of Donoughmore Report 12, Appendix IX, London: 1891

The Manuscripts of J.B. Fortescue, preserved at Dropmore, Report 13, Appendix III, 10 volumes, London: 1892

The Manuscripts of Lord Kenyon, Report 14, Appendix III, London: 1894

The Manuscripts of the Duke of Rutland, preserved at Belvoir Castle, Report 14, Appendix I

The Manuscripts of P. V. Smith, Report 12, Appendix IX, London: 1891

The Irish Parliament: 1775, William Hunt, ed., London, Dublin: 1907

The Kenmare Manuscripts, M. McLysaught, ed., Dublin: Irish Manuscripts Commission, 1942

King's Inn Admission Papers, E. Keane, P.B. Phair, T.U. Sadleir, eds., Dublin: 1982

Peep O'Day Boys and Defenders: Selected Documents on the County Armagh Disturbances 1784–96, David W. Miller, ed., Belfast: Public Record Office of Northern Ireland, 1990

Registry of Deeds, Dublin, P. Beryl Eustace, ed., Dublin: 1956

NEWSPAPERS AND PAMPHLETS

NEWSPAPERS

Dublin Evening Post

Faulkner's Dublin Journal

Freeman's Journal

Hibernian Journal

Limerick Chronicle

Morning Post or Dublin Courant

Volunteer Evening Post

Volunteer Journal or Weekly Advertiser

Volunteers Journal or Evening Herald

PAMPHLETS BY SUBJECT

FITZGIBBON

Character of the Late Earl of Clare

Lessons to a Young Lord Chancellor

Jerome Alley, *The Judge, or an Estimate of the importance of the judicial character, occasioned by the death of the late Lord Clare, Lord Chancellor of Ireland*, London: 1803

Henrietta Battier, *The Gibbonade*, Dublin: 1794

WHITEBOYS AND TITHES

The Mirror or Cursory Observations on the Licentious Pamphlets of Theophilus, etc., Dublin: 1787

Remarks on the Justification of the Tenets of the Papists, lately published by Dr James Butler, Dublin: 1787

James Butler, *A Letter from the Most Reverend Doctor Butler, Titular Archbishop of Cashel to the Right Honorable Lord Viscount Kenmare*, Kilkenny: 1787

Patrick Duigenan [Theophilus]*An Address to the Nobility and Gentry of the Church of Ireland as by Law Established*, (Dublin: 1786)

Daniel Thomas, *Observations on the Pamphlets published by the Bishop of Cloyne*, Dublin: 1787

Dominic Trant, *Considerations on the Present Disturbances in Munster*, Dublin: 1787

Richard Woodward, *The Present State of the Church of Ireland*, Dublin: 1787

THE CATHOLIC QUESTION

An Address from the General Committee of the Roman Catholics to their Protestant Fellow Subjects and to the Public in General, Dublin: 1792

Defense of the Subcommittee of the Catholics of Ireland from the Imputations attempted to be thrown on that body particularly from the charge of supporting the Defenders: published by Order of the Subcommittee, Dublin: 1793

The Speech of Edward Sweetman, Captain of a Late Independent Company at a Meeting of the Freeholders of the County of Wexford convened by the Sheriff in September of 1792 to take into consideration Mr Edward Byrne's letter, recommending a plan of delegation to the Catholics of Ireland in order to prepare a humble petition to the legislature; (Dublin, 1792)

John Sweetman, *A refutation of the Charges attempted to be made against the Secretary for the Subcommittee of the Catholics of Ireland,* Dublin: 1793

THE FITZWILLIAM CONTROVERSY

The Conclusion to the Strictures on the Earl Fitzwilliam's Letters to the Earl of Carlisle, London: 1795

Earl Fitzwilliam, *A letter from Earl Fitzwilliam, recently retired from this country to the Earl of Carlisle*, Dublin, London: 1795

THE ACT OF UNION

A Proposal for Uniting the Kingdoms of Great Britain and Ireland, London: 1751

The Anti-Union, Dublin: 1798–1799

R. Bentley, *Observations upon the state of public affairs in the year 1799*

John FitzGibbon [Paddy Whack], *No Union! but Unite and Fall!* London: 1799

Henry Maxwell, *An Essay Towards an [sic] Union of Ireland with England,* Dublin: 1704

J.L. de Lolme, *An essay Containing a Few Strictures on the Union of Scotland with England, and on the Present Situation in Ireland* , London: 1787

MISCELLANEOUS

The Ante-Union Pamphlets, 1788–1799

PARLIAMENTARY DEBATES, REPORTS AND SPEECHES

Cavendish Parliamentary Diaries

Debates Relative to the Affairs of Ireland, Dublin: 1763

William Woodfall, *An Impartial Report of the Debates that occur in the two houses of Parliament in the course of the first session of the Parliament of the United Kingdom of Great Britain and Ireland,* London: 1801

Journal of the House of Lords (Ireland)

Parliamentary Register (1781–89)

House of Lords (Ireland), *Report from the Committee of Secrecy of the House of Lords in Ireland as Reported by the Right Honorable John, Earl of Clare, Lord High Chancellor, 30 August 1798*

The Speech of the Right Honorable John, Lord Baron FitzGibbon, Lord High Chancellor of Ireland, Delivered in the House of Peers on the Second Reading of the Bill for the relief of His Majesty's Roman Catholic Subjects, 13 March 1793, Dublin: 1798; London and Dublin: 1813

The Speech of the Right Honorable John, Earl of Clare, Lord High Chancellor of Ireland, on a motion made by the Earl of Moira, Monday, 19 February 1798, Dublin: 1798

Speech of the Right Honorable John, Earl of Clare, Lord High Chancellor of Ireland in the House of Lords of Ireland on a Motion made by him on Monday, 10 February 1800, Dublin: 1800

Statutes at Large, passed in the Parliaments held in Ireland

PUBLISHED LAW REPORTS

William Ridgeway, *Reports of Cases upon Appeals of Writes of Error in the High Court of Parliament in Ireland since the Restoration of the Appellate Jurisdiction*, 3 vols., Dublin: 1795

—,*A Report of the Proceedings in cases of High Treason at a Special Commission of Oyer and Terminer held in and for the County and City of Dublin in the month of July, 1798* (Dublin, 1798)

Schoales and Lefroy, *Reports of Cases Argued and Determined in the High Court of Chancery during the Time of Lord Redesdale*, Dublin: 1810

Hughes, *The Practice of the Court of Chancery in Ireland*, Dublin: 1837

PUBLISHED LETTERS AND MEMOIRS

Journal and Correspondence of William, Lord Auckland, His Grace the Bishop of Bath and Wells, ed., 4 vols., London: 1862

Sir Jonah Barrington, *Personal sketches of his own time,* 2 vols. London: 1827

—,*Historical Anecdotes of the Legislative Union between Great Britain and Ireland,* 2 vols., London: 1835

—, *The Rise and Fall of the Irish Nation*, New York: 1835 (pirated American version of the above)

Correspondence of the Right Honorable John Beresford, William Beresford, ed., 2 vols., London: 1854

Correspondence of Edmund Burke, Holden Furber, et. al., eds., 9 vols., Chicago: University of Chicago Press, 1958–1970

Memoirs and Correspondence of Lord Castlereagh, Lord Londonderry, ed. 12 vols., London: 1848–9

Lord Cloncurry, *Personal Reflections of his Life and Times*, Dublin: 1850

Charles, First Marquis Cornwallis, *Correspondence*, Charles Ross, ed., 3 vols., London: 1859

Maria Edgeworth, Letters from England 1813–1844, Christina Colvin, ed., Oxford: 1971

Thomas Moore, *The Life and Death of Lord Edward Fitzgerald,* London: 1832

The Later Correspondence of George III, A. Aspinall, ed., 5 vols., Cambridge: 1968

The Correspondence of George, Prince of Wales, A. Aspinall, ed., 8 vols., Cambridge: 1965

Henry Grattan, *Memoirs of the Life and Times of the Right Honorable Henry Grattan*, 5 vols., London: 1849
The Retrospections of Dorothea Herbert 1770–1806, L.M. Cullen, ed., Dublin: 1988
Correspondence of Emily, Duchess of Leinster, Brian Fitzgerald, ed., 3 vols., Dublin: 1953
James Roche, *Critical and Miscellaneous Essays by an Octogenarian*, 2 vols., Cork: 1851
Lord Shannon's Letters to His Son: A Calendar of Letters Written by the Second Earl of Shannon to his son Viscount Boyle 1790–1802, Esther Hewitt, ed., Belfast: 1982
Charles Hamilton Teeling, *History of the Irish Rebellion of 1798 & Sequel to the History of the Irish Rebellion of 1798*, Dublin: 1972 (reprint)
Life of Theobald Wolfe Tone, William Theobald Wolfe Tone, ed., 2 vols., Washington, DC: 1826

MONOGRAPHS AND GENERAL HISTORIES (before 1950)

Caesar Litton Falkiner, *Studies in Irish History and Biography*, London: 1903
John Ferrar, *History of Limerick*, Limerick: 1787
J.A. Froude, *The English in Ireland in the Eighteenth Century*, 3 vols. New York: 1881
William Edward Hartpole Lecky, *A History of Ireland in the Eighteenth Century*, 5 vols. London: 1892
R.R. Madden, *The United Irishmen, Their Lives and Times*, London: 1843; London and Dublin: 1862
Sir Richard Musgrave, *Memoirs of the Different Rebellions in Ireland*, Dublin: 1802
J.F. O'Flanagan, *Lives of the Lord Chancellors of Ireland*, 2 vols., London: 1870
Francis Peter Plowden, A Historical Review of the State of Ireland, 5 vols., London: 1805
A History of Ireland from its Union with Great Britain, January 1801 to October 1810, 3 vols., Dublin: 1810

MONGRAPHS AND GENERAL HISTORIES (since 1950)

Thomas Bartlett and T. W. Hayton, *Penal Era and Golden Age: Essays in Irish History 1690–1800*, Belfast: 1979
Thomas Bartlett, *The Fall and Rise of the Irish Nation: The Catholic Question 1690–1830* Dublin: 1992
Geoffrey Bolton, *The Passing of the Irish Act of Union: A Study in Parliamentary Politics*, London: 1966
Patrick Corish, *Maynooth College 1795–1995* Dublin, 1995
L.M. Cullen, *An Economic History of Ireland since 1600*, 2nd edition, London: 1987
J.W. Derry, *The Regency Crisis and the Whigs*, Cambridge: 1963
John Ehrman, *The Younger Pitt, London*: London: 1969

Marianne Elliot, *Partners in Revolution: The United Irishmen and France*, New Haven and London: 1982
Wolfe Tone: Prophet of Irish Independence, New Haven: 1989
R.F. Foster, *Modern Ireland 1600–1972*, London: 1989
Constantine FitzGibbon, *Miss Finnegan's Fault*, London and New York: 1953
Eliot Fitzgibbon, *Earl of Clare: Mainspring of the Union*, London: 1960
K. Theodore Hoppen, *Landlords, Politics and Rural Society*, Oxford: 1984
Brian Inglis, *Freedom of the Press in Ireland*, Studies in Irish History, Vol. IV, T.W. Moody, R. Dudley Edwards, J.C. Beckett, eds., London: 1979
Edith Mary Johnston, *Great Britain and Ireland, 1760–1800: A Study in Political Administration*, Edinburgh: 1963
Peter Jupp, *British and Irish Elections, 1784–1831*, London and New York: 1973
James Kelly, *Prelude to Union: Anglo-Irish Politics in the 1780s*, Cork: 1992
—, *That Damn'd Thing called Honour*: Dueling in Ireland 1570–1860, Cork: 1995
Oliver MacDonagh, *The Hereditary Bondsman: Daniel O'Connell 1775–1829*, New York: 1988
A.P.W. Malcomson, *John Foster: The Politics of the Anglo-Irish Ascendancy*, Oxford: 1978
W.J. McCormack, *The Dublin Paper War of 1786–1788: A Bibliographical and Critical Inquiry*, Dublin, 1993
—, *The Pamphlet Debate on the Union between Great Britain and Ireland, 1797–1800*, Dublin, forthcoming.
R.B. McDowell, *Ireland in the Age of Imperialism and Revolution 1760–1801*, London and Oxford: 1979
Gerard O'Brien, *Anglo-Irish Politics and Social Conflict in the Age of Grattan and Pitt,* Dublin: 1987
Maurice O'Connell, *Irish Politics and Social Conflict in the Age of the American Revolution*, Philadelphia and London: 1965
James A. Reynolds, *The Catholic Emancipation Crisis in Ireland, 1823–29*, New Haven: 1954
Hereward Senior, *Orangeism in Ireland and Britain 1795–1836*, London: 1966
Stella Tillyard, *Aristocrats,* New York: 1994
Maureen Wall, *Catholic Ireland in the Eighteenth Century*, Gerard O'Brien and Tom Dunne, eds., Dublin: 1989

ARTICLES

"Lord Clare", Gallery of Illustrious Irishmen, XVI, *Dublin University Magazine*, vol. xxx, p. 670 ff.
"Mrs Jeffreys of Blarney Castle", *Journal of the Cork Historical and Archaeological Society*, 2nd Series, Vol. I, 1895, pp. 83–5

Thomas Bartlett, "An End to Moral Economy: the Irish Militia Disturbances of 1793", *Past and Present*, 99, (May 1983), pp. 41–64.

J.C. Beckett, "Anglo-Irish Relations in the Later Eighteenth Century", *Irish Historical Studies*, 14 (1964–65), pp. 20–38

Maurice Bric, "The Tithe System in Eighteenth Century Ireland", *Proceedings of the Royal Irish Academy*, Vol. 86, C, Number 7, (1986), pp. 271–88

L.M. Cullen, "Late eighteenth century politicization in Ireland: problems in its study and its French links", *Culture et Practiques Politiques en France et en Irelande XVIe-XVIIIe Siecle: Actes du Colloque de Marseilles 28 septembre-2 octobre, 1988*, pp. 137–45

J.S. Donnelly, Jr., "The Rightboy Movement", *Studia Hibernica*, 17–18 (1977–8), pp. 120–202

Marianne Elliot, "The Origins and Transformation of Early Irish Republicanism", *International Review of Social History*, 23 (1978), pp. 405–28

Peter Jupp, "Earl Temple's Viceroyalty and the Question of Renunciation", *Irish Historical Studies*, 17 (1971), pp. 499–520

James Kelly, "The Irish Trade Dispute with Portugal", *Studia Hibernica*, no. 25 (1989–90), pp. 1–45

Denis Kennedy, "The Irish Whigs: Administrative Reform and Responsible Government 1782–1800", *Eire Ireland*, 8 (1973), pp. 55–69

R.B. McDowell, "Some FitzGibbon Letters from the Sneyd Muniments in the John Rylands Library" *John Rylands Library Bulletin* , vol. 34, no. 2, pp. 296–312,

—,"The Fitzwilliam Episode, *Irish Historical Studies*, 16 (1966), pp. 115–30

—,"Ireland in the Eighteenth-Century British Empire", *Irish Historical Studies*, 9 (1974), pp. 49–63

Maureen Wall, "The Rise of a Catholic Middle Class in Eighteenth-Century Ireland", *Irish Historical Studies*, 6 (1958), pp. 91–116

Notes

CHAPTER 1

1 *Volunteers' Journal/Evening Herald*, 1 November 1784 2 PRONI, Normanton Papers, T3710/C29/45, p. 2; see also *Hibernian Journal*, 14 January 1795, "To a certain lord": "You cannot, it is true, plead much of public merits to the present administration [Lord Fitzwilliams], and still less can you expect to be instrumental to the private gratification of the present Viceroy. The unfashionable virtues of Lord Fitzwilliam will not extract from you, my Lord, those very gentle and very humble submissions which your noble spirit was flattered in stooping to pay to the tender frailties of his predecessor." 3 Trinity College Dublin, Madden Papers, f518. 4 Sir Jonah Barrington, *The Rise and Fall of the Irish Nation* (New York, 1845), p. 34. 5 See for example, *The Memoirs of the Life and Times of the Right Honorable Henry Grattan* (London, 1849), iii, pp. 397 and 430. Neither of FitzGibbon's own sons wrote a similar pious memoir in defense of their father, though the second Earl of Clare did chose to defend the family honor in a less literary fashion. He challenged young Grattan to a duel for some remarks the latter had made about Lord Clare the elder. The two do not seem to have had any contact after this encounter. See, James Kelly, *That Damnd Thing called Honour: Dueling in Ireland 1570–1860* (Cork, 1995), p. 264. 6 William Edward Hartpole Lecky, *A History of Ireland in the Eighteenth Century*, 5 vols. (London, 1892), ii, p. 419. 7 J.F. O'Flanagan, *Lives of the Lord Chancellors of Ireland*, 2 vols. (London, 1870). 8 C.L. Falkiner, *Studies in Irish History* (London, 1902), p. 122. 9 Falkiner, pp. 138–9. 10 Sir Richard Musgrave, *Memoirs of the Different Rebellions in Ireland* (Dublin, 1802), pp. 117–18. Sir Richard also may have been answering those of FitzGibbon's enemies who sneered at his low birth and rapid rise from obscurity. 11 *Dublin University Magazine*, vol. xxx, pp. 670ff. 12 J.A. Froude, *The English in Ireland in the Eighteenth Century* (New York, 1881), 3 vols., iii, p. 51. 13 Quoted in Falkiner, pp. 106–7, footnote. 14 James Roche, *Critical and Miscellaneous Essays by an Octogenarian*, 2 vols. (Cork, 1851), ii, pp. 113–14. 15 Ibid. 16 London, Research Publishing Co., 1960. 17 It does not appear that Mr Eliot Fitzgibbon is in any way descended from the Earl of Clare, in spite of their common surname. If there were any relationship, however remote, Mr Fitzgibbon almost certainly would have claimed it in his work. 18 *Miss Finnegan's Fault* (London, 1953), p. 102. 19 Constantine FitzGibbon made this amazing extrapolation from an anecdote in J.F. Flanagan's *Lives of the Irish Lord Chancellors*. Flanagan simply reported that Clare, out of a desire to avoid ostentatious displays of piety, avoided his parish church and took communion at a more remote location. Flanagan attributed this story to no less a source than Nathaniel Hawthorne. I have not been able to locate any allusion whatsoever to Clare in my edition of Hawthorne's collected works. Flanagan may have confused him with some other American author. Perhaps the collected works of Ralph Waldo Emerson bear investigation. It would be interesting to know what Emerson, the apotheosis of American optimism, would have made of a character like Clare. 20 The nature of the surviving evidence also has thwarted these and other fine historians. Apart from letters and government memoranda that he wrote to others, no personal papers of Clare's survive, in the form of journals

or correspondence, that might have given presented his point of view or explained his motivation more fully. Clare was a busy many and one not given much to introspection, so he may not have kept a journal in the first place. Neither of his sons followed the example of the younger Grattan and attempted a pietistic memoir. As has been noted, the second earl seemed to think that the dueling pistol was mightier than the pen. As for that very revealing source of evidence, letters from others, a dying Clare ordered the destruction of all his personal and political correspondence (Falkiner, p. 102)

CHAPTER 2

1 *The Rise and Fall of the Irish Nation*, p. 33. 2 *HMC Charlemont*, i, pp. 108–9. 3 Henrietta Battier (Peter Pindar), *The Gibbonade or Political Reviewer* (Dublin, 1794), 1st number, p. 7; 3rd number p. 12. 4 Sir William Betham, *Genealogical Collections*, iii, p. 66 (BM Add MS 23,686); "... Of the genealogical deduction of the Earl of Clare's family, I have no knowledge further back than to his grandfather [*sic*] John FitzGibbon, Esq., Representative in Parliament for Newcastle, born in 1708 ...'. 5 Sir Richard Musgrave, *Memoirs of the Different Rebellions in Ireland* (Dublin, 1802), pp. 117–18; "The exalted sphere to which he has been raised, and the honors conferred on him by our gracious sovereign prove the superior excellence of a mixed government, where the monarch selects men like him distinguished for wisdom, abilities and virtue to fill the principle departments of state." 6 Reprinted in Constantine FitzGibbon, *Miss Finnegan's Fault*, pp. 80–3. Although this letter is supposedly in the Chief Herald's office, I have not been able to find any trace of it. 7 Hugh Kearney, *Strafford in Ireland 1633–41: A Study in Absolutism* (Cambridge, 1959, 1989), p. 76. 8 P. Beryl Eustace, ed., *Registry of Deeds, Dublin* (Dublin, 1956), i, p. 20, No. 46. 9 FitzGibbon, op. cit. 10 O'Flanagan, ii, p. 157 . 11 Henry F. Mageah, ed., *Register of Admissions to the Honorable Society of the Middle Temple*, i, p. 301, "John FitzGibbon, son and heir of Thomas F. of Ballysheeda, Limerick, Ireland, gent". 12 *Registry of Deeds / Abstracts of Wills*, i, pp. 209–10, No. 487. 13 Ibid. 14 *Roche*, ii, p. 39; *O'Flanagan*, ii, pp. 157. 15 E. Keane, P.B. Phair, T.U. Sadleir, eds., *Kings Inn Admission Papers* (Dublin, 1982), p. 168; Eileen O'Byrne, ed., *The Convert Rolls* (Dublin, 1981), p. 103. 16 *Convert Rolls*, p. 103; "Indented articles of intermarriage between Barbara Lynch, daughter of Pierse Lynch and Gibbon FitzGibbon", Dublin: National Library of Ireland MS D6597–6612. The marriage articles are dated 25 October 1765. If it was indeed his intention to make a good marriage, Gibbon did only modestly well. Her father settled £800 on the couple and in return, Gibbon agreed to pay Barbara an annuity of £120. In addition, their children were to share an inheritance of £1,600. Barbara may not even have been a Protestant heiress. A Barbara Lynch conformed on 10 November 1765. She was identified as "now of Dublin". Barbara was originally from Galway and she and her new husband may have established residence in Dublin as a step toward her conformity. Nonetheless, they seem to have made Limerick their permanent home. On such precarious evidence it is impossible to establish any positive correspondence between Gibbon's bride and the Barbara Lynch listed in the convert rolls (Convert Rolls, p. 166). 17 *O'Flanagan*, ii, pp. 158–9, footnote 2. 18 Quoted in John Ferrar's *History of Limerick* (Limerick, 1787), p. 383. 19 *O'Flanagan*, ii, p. 158. 20 See Dublin: National Archives of Ireland, MS M6192 for the full extent of his holdings. 21 *Burke's Irish Family Records* (London, 1976), entry under Grove-Annesley family, p. 27. 22 *Freeman' Journal*, 21–22 March 1786, Postscript for 21 March 1786. "This lady possessed the most benevolent heart. The poor found in her a liberal patroness and as she lived universally respected and admired, so she is now as universally lamented in her death." It is doubtful that FitzGibbon had any part in this production. It is probably the work of his good-hearted and literary-minded brother-in-law Dominic Trant with whom Mrs. FitzGibbon passed her final years. FitzGibbon himself never seems to have acknowledged her existence, at least in any public pronouncement. He seems to have been very much his father's child.

23 *Burke's Family History*, op. cit., p. 431 This pedigree is very thorough and helpful, though there are some errors: most notably FitzGibbons mother's name is given as Minchin. In actuality, one of Elinor Grove's sisters married a man by the name of Minchin. 24 Quoted in Falkiner, p. 105 Falkiner believed that Malone referred to John FitzGibbon. More confusingly, there is no date to indicate whether the letter was written when John FitzGibbon was at Oxford. I myself am inclined to think that the letter referred to Ion. Admittedly FitzGibbon loved fashionable clothes and took a great interest in his own appearance, but he never could be accused of delicacy of manner. From his earliest young manhood, FitzGibbon was forceful, arrogant and overbearing. The boy described in this letter seems on the contrary poignantly insecure and frightened of making a bad impression, qualities much more in keeping with the "mild and easy temper" described by Roche. 25 The sons, Thomas and John, are mentioned in a legal document of 1742 ("Deed between John and Elinor FitzGibbon and Arthur Blennerhasset and Arabella Groves", NLI MS D6597–6612). Ion is listed in the *Alumni Dublinesis*, but he does not appear in the catalogue of Oxford alumni. This circumstance leads me to infer that he died shortly after his twenty-first birthday. 26 John Ferrar, *History of Limerick* (Limerick, 1787), p. 364. 27 *Grattan*, i, p. 192. 28 Holden Furber, ed., *The Correspondence of Edmund Burke*, vii (Cambridge, Chicago, 1970), p. 192. A common association with William Gerard Hamilton, as well as their family connection, may have brought Burke and the elder FitzGibbon together. (Burke was Hamilton's client secretary.) These contacts with the elder FitzGibbon almost certainly contributed to Burke's obsession with FitzGibbon the younger. The son departed spectacularly from the sympathy and hopes for the Catholics that old FitzGibbon and Burke had expressed in their private conversations. 29 Henrietta Battier, *The Gibbonade*, 1st number (Dublin, 1794), p. 2; Mrs. Battier displays a firm belief in the myth of Old FitzGibbon's Jesuit education as well as the casual anti-Semitism of her time: Quick from St Omer's at preferment's name / The eleemosynary student came / Forsook his beads and in the Temple grew / At once a lawyer, Protestant and Jew." 30 E. MacLysaght (ed.), *The Kenmare Manuscripts* (Dublin, 1942), pp. 73–5, 288–315. 31 William Gerard Hamilton to John Hely Hutchinson, 29 January 1763, Trinity College Dublin, Hutchinson Papers, C/1/16. 32 *Burke Correspondence*, i, pp. 275–6. 33 *Roche*, ii, pp. 116–17. 34 Hamilton to Hutchinson, 4 December 1762, Hutchinson Papers, C/1/13. 35 *Debates Relative to the Affairs of Ireland* (Dublin, 1763), pp. 208–21. 36 *Hibernian Chronicle*, 30 November–4 December 1775, debate of 30 November 1775. 37 William Hunt ed., *The Irish Parliament: 1775* (London, Dublin, 1907), p. 20. 38 William Theobald Wolfe Tone, ed., *Life of Theobald Wolfe Tone*, i, (Washington, DC, 1826) p. 138. 39 Public Record Office of Northern Ireland (PRONI), Belfast, T3244/11/1. 40 *Roche*, ii , p. 36; O'Flanagan II, p. 160. 41 *Grattan*, ii, p. 42; *Alumni Dublinesis*, p. 287; *Alumni Oxoniensis*, ii, p. 467; *Kings Inn Admission Papers*, p. 168. 42 Barrington, p. 33; *Dublin University Magazine*, xxx , p. 675; *O'Flanagan*, ii, p. 161–3. 43 According to *Watson's Almanac*, FitzGibbon did not move to his own house at 6 Ely Place until early in 1784. 44 Ridgeway, *Reports of Cases upon Appeals of Writs of Error in the High Court of Parliament in Ireland since the Restoration of the Appellate Jurisdiction*, iii. (Dublin, 1795) pp. 106–203. 45 See for example, *PR*, ix, p. 129–30. 46 William Beresford, ed., Correspondence of the Right Honorable John Beresford II (London, 1854) pp. 104–5. 47 See, for example, the amazing comments in his vitriolic speech of 1793 against the Catholic bill; *The Speech of the Late Rt. Hon. John, Earl of Clare, Lord High Chancellor of Ireland, Delivered in the Irish House of Peers on the Second Reading of the Bill for the Relief of His Majesty's Roman Catholic Subjects in Ireland, 13 March 1793* (London, 1813), p. 3. 48 Lord de Rosse to Lord Redesdale, 9 May 1822, PRONI, Rosse Papers, d/20. My thanks to Kevin Whelan, who very kindly sent me a copy of this particular letter. 49 This very striking turn of phrase appears in his speech in support of the Act of Union; *The Speech of the Right Honorable John, Earl of Clare, Lord High Chancellor of Ireland on a motion made by him on Monday, 10 February 1800* (Dublin, London, 1800) p. 22. 50 Sir Edward Newenham to Sir John Gay Alleyne, 29 September, 1784, Public Record Office, London, Chatham Papers, 30/8/329; *Dublin Evening Post*, 4 December 1783; Postscript for same date, 2 or 11 January

1795. (The microfilm that I used was extremely indistinct and I could not determine the date clearly.). 51 Act of Union Speech, p. 22. 52 Lord Westmorland to William Pitt, 11 January 1793, NLI, MS 886. 53 J. Ridgeway, op. cit.; FitzGibbon to William Eden, 22 August 1785, University of Keele, Sneyd Muniments The Sneyd Muniments, consisting of letters from FitzGibbon to William Eden, is perhaps the largest collection of FitzGibbon's surviving letters. These letters are now in the library of the University of Keele. A close friend of the second earl of Clare, Ralph Sneyd, came into possession of FitzGibbon's letters to Eden after the second earl's death. Sneyd's family, in turn, eventually donated them to John Rylands Library. R.B. McDowell did an interesting and perceptive overview of these letters in the *John Rylands Library Bulletin*, vol. 34, No. 2, pp. 296–312, "Some FitzGibbon Letters from the Sneyd Muniments in the John Rylands Library". The letters were moved to Keele after this article appeared. C.L. Falkiner also published a collection of FitzGibbons letters to Eden in an appendix to his biographical study. Falkiner, pp. 141–54. The copies of these letters that were so generously given to me by the Keele librarian in 1985 were uncatalogued. I have since learned that copies of these letters also are available in the Public Record Office of Northern Ireland. These copies are catalogued with the meticulousness so characteristic of that institution.54 For his relations with his wife, see A. Aspinall (ed.), *The Later Correspondence of George III*, iv, p. 8, no. 2584, footnote. He was a very kind and attentive guardian to his young cousin Thomas FitzGibbon, later a persistent and tiresome suitor for an excise office. For the circumstances of FitzGibbon's guardianship see NLI MS 7866; for Thomas FitzGibbon's pursuit of office, see ISPO, Westmorland Papers, Carton 1/ff141, 142, 144. 55 FitzGibbon to Eden, 10 January 1786 in Falkiner, p. 145; FitzGibbon to Roger Cashin, 21 November 1801. This letter is in a private collection. I must acknowledge the kindness and generosity of Dr Malcomson for bringing this letter to my attention; FitzGibbon to General Morrison, 29 June 1798, NLI, MS 7333. 56 See, for example, Lord Fitzwilliam's very grudging acknowledgment, as repeated by Edmund Burke; Burke to Captain Emperor John Alexander Woodford, 31 May, 1797, R.B. McDowell and John A. Woods, (eds.), *The Correspondence of Edmund Burke*, ix (Cambridge, Chicago, 1970), p. 363. 57 FitzGibbon to Roger Cashin, 15 May, 1794, NLI, MS8343/9. 58 *Falkiner*, p. 148. 59 Daniel Hayes, whose verse was quoted earlier, preferred the gamy revels of the Limerick Hell Fire Club to the staid drudgery of the London bar. His taste for the bizarre eventually transmogrified his poetic voice, and lofty classical odes gave way to bloodcurdling gothic brooding. One of his later poems, a translation of a tribute to the blessings of Trappist monasticism, is grisly and morbid even by the standards of the contemporary graveyard school (*Epistle from the Abbé de Rance to a Friend, written at the Abbey of La Trappe*, Paraphrased from Mons. Berthe by Daniel Hayes, Esq., Dublin, 1792 reprint). Another relation, Margaret Blennerhasset, was the lone female member of the Hell Fire Club, a dubious contribution to the cause of women's equality (*Burke's Irish Family Records*, p. 136). Even old FitzGibbon may have been affected. Although in public he gave the impression of a handsome, suave, self-possessed man of the world, a prescription dating from 1753 reveals that he suffered from "nervous colic" (NLI, MS 8343/5). This condition may have been a temporary reaction to by now unknowable stresses. On the other hand, "nervous colic" could have been a chronic ailment for a man, driven not only by his struggles to get ahead, but by an innate emotional instability. His cool charm may have given way, at least on occasion, to sudden nervous rages. His youngest child may have picked up violent extremes of temperament, as well as legal learning, from his father.

CHAPTER 3

1 Grattan, ii, p. 269; *Hibernian Journal* , 24–9 November 1775, House of Commons debate, 23 November 1775. (The microfilm of this particular paper is badly smudged; consequently my reading of the date may be wrong.) 2 O'Connell, illustrations between pp. 128–9. 3 See for example London, Public Record Office, State Papers (SP) 63/464/111, a petition of the Citizens of

Dublin, transmitted 25 February, 1779; 63/464/315, Buckinghamshire to Weymouth, 29 April 1779, and 63/464/318, resolutions printed in the Hibernian Journal, 28 April 1779. 4 SP 63/461/328–31, Buckinghamshire to Weymouth, 12 December 1778. 5 SP/63/464/318, op. cit. 6 See, for example, SP 64/465/9; Buckinghamshire alludes with relief to the anger and betrayal which the American alliance with France aroused in the Presbyterians, a disillusion which made them less of a threat to the internal security of Ireland: "I am well assured they [the Presbyterians] have lost entirely, or at least in great measure their penchant for the American cause; they are disgusted with the Americans for their alliance with France and rejecting the late offers of government: I believe the American flag would cause as great an alarm as the French." (Buckinghamshire to Weymouth, 24 May 1779; Buckinghamshire's obvious relief suggests his deep fears of pro-American sympathies in Ulster). 7 SP 63/461/328–31, Buckinghamshire to Weymouth, 12 December 1778. 8 See, SP 63/464/361–2 Buckinghamshire alludes to the politicization of the Volunteers in a letter to Weymouth dated 23 May 1779: "this arises from the insinuations that are daily circulated in the Publick Prints, that the Idea of their numbers may conduce to the attainment of political advantages to their country." See, also SP 63/467/28–29 (Buckinghamshire to Weymouth, 14 October 1779), on his own unsuccessful attempts to prevent the Volunteers from appearing in force in Dublin and standing in parade formation while the Lords and Commons brought their opening addresses to the Castle. 9 SP 63/464/361–2, Buckinghamshire to Weymouth, 23 May 1779. 10 That circumstance rendered at least some service by providing the spurious excuse for not giving effect to the intent of the militia bill. 11 See, for example, SP 63/459/217–20 and 63/459/276–81, which elucidate Buckinghamshire's scramble to get money for the most minimal defense establishment; See, also SP/460/37–9, Buckinghamshire to Weymouth, 30 April 1778, which opens on this foreboding note: "It is with great Concern that I am reduced to the Necessity of laying before your Lordship the miserable state of his Majesty's Treasury here"; SP 63/465/267; Buckinghamshire to Weymouth, 12 July 1779: "I have repeatedly mentioned how very necessary it was to give some satisfaction to the Kingdom upon Commercial Points ..." 12 See, SP 63/467/101–2 Buckinghamshire to Weymouth, 8 November, 1779: "... it is too much in addition to be fretted hourly with inadmissible soliciting to labour ineffectually to conciliate the jealousies of impracticable politicians and to be obliged frequently to [suffer] suspicions of a duplicity of conduct to which my heart has ever been a stranger." See, also, John Beresford to John Robinson, 22 November, 1779: "You seem to fear that confusion may be the consequence of removing the present government. I cannot answer that it may not; but I will positively say that if they (Buckinghamshire and Chief Secretary Heron) stay much longer, it will not be possible for their successors to recover the ground ... You want and able Chief Governor and Secretary, in whom gentlemen will have confidence" (*Beresford*, i, p. 88). 13 See, SP 63/459/59–62 for an example of Grattan's early political activity. His resolutions of 2 June 1778 are a compendium of patriot grievances. 14 See for example, *Hutchinson Papers*, C/1/11, C/1/13, C/1/19, C/1/20. 15 The bulk of my biographical information about the provost comes from that as yet invaluable source, *Dictionary of National Biography*, ix, p. 377; see, also, Hutchinson's own defense of his career, political and academic; Hutchinson Papers, C/1/116. 16 Again, I have relied on the DNB VI: pp. 143–4 for my information about Duigenan. 17 Hutchinson Papers, C/1/116. 18 *Hibernian Chronicle*, 15–19 May 1777, *Dublin News* for 10 May 1777. 19 Ibid., 12–15 May 1777. 20 Ibid., 12–15 May 1777; *Grattan* , i: pp. 279–80; *Hutchinson Papers*, C/1/119. 21 *Grattan*, i, op. cit. 22 *Hibernian Chronicle*, 13–17 November 1777; proceedings of the King's Bench, 7 November 1777.

23 FitzGibbon's efforts on behalf of Duigenan marked the beginning of an association that would continue sporadically throughout his life. Nonetheless, their common opposition to Hutchinson and their later political agreement drew them together far more than any particular liking, at least on FitzGibbon's part. On the contrary, he appears to have had little respect for Duigenan's judgment (Dublin: ISPO, 620/18/8; FitzGibbon to Pelham [no date] 1797). This letter alludes to Duigenan's unreasonableness over a much favored case in the Admiralty Courts. Among other

unfavorable comments on Duigenan's temper, FitzGibbon added, "I very much fear the Bear will not be tamed." FitzGibbon may also have recoiled from a man who caricatured his darkest self. **24** *Grattan*, i, p. 280. **25** *Hibernian Chronicle*, 2–6 April 1778, Dublin news for 31 March 1778; Grattan, op. cit. **26** PRONI, Macartney Papers, D572/7/32. **27** *Cavendish Parliamentary Diaries*, vi, Part 9, p. 267. In the 1770s and early 1780s, before the publication of the Parliamentary Register, Sir Henry Cavendish took extensive notes on the debates in the Irish Parliament. The original manuscript of these notes are in the Library of Congress, in the United States, and are on microfilm in the National Library of Ireland. **28** Ibid. **29** James Butler's many trials and tribulations with suspicious Protestants and an equally suspicious Vatican are elucidated in his private papers, which are on microfilm in the National Library of Ireland (special list 170, uncatalogued). The originals are deposited in the archives of the Diocese of Cashel in Thurles. **30** SP 63/459/111–16, rough copy of Popery bill, 1778. **31** *Dublin Evening Post*, 6 August 1778, Postscript for same date "We hear it from good authority that a certain gentleman, the father of the Popery bill, is under such apprehensions for the safety of his person, that he never ventures abroad, without being attended by several servants, armed with blunderbusses and pistols." **32** SP63/458/227, Buckinghamshire to Weymouth, 10 December 1777, and 63/459/109–10, Buckinghamshire to Weymouth, 4 March 1778. **33** The military considerations behind the bill are suggested in SP 63/459/111–16, which hints at the unheard of possibility of allowing Catholics, in the event of an invasion to have license to take up arms. The bill by implication would render them sufficiently loyal and trustworthy to allow for such an extremity! The ever present anxieties about Popish disaffection and Popish aid and sympathy for France can be seen in SP 63/460/82–4; J. Irwine's plan of defense for Munster, dated 3 April 1778; SP 63/460/326; Lord Amherst to Lord Weymouth, 8 July 1778 and SP 63/460/328, anonymous source to Buckinghamshire, 17 June 1778. **34** *Dublin Evening Post*, 6 August 1778. **35** *Cavendish*, vi, Part 13, p. 166, debate of 4 August 1778. See again, the remarks of the ineffable Ogle, *Cavendish*, vi, Part 11, pp. 70–3, debate of 16 June 1778. **36** *Cavendish*, vi, Part 11, p. 237, debate of 16 June 1778* **37** Sir Edward Newenham actually introduced the clause, and he emphatically denied that he was trying to harm or jeopardize the Catholic bill; *Cavendish*, vi, Part 11, p. 22, debate of 16 June 1778; there is no particular reason to disbelieve him. Unlike Ogle, he does not seem to have been actively antagonistic to the bill, and as a prominent popular politician, he would naturally have been an enthusiast for the Presbyterians. For an excellent collection of documents on Presbyterian political mobilization in the 1770s see *Aspects of Irish Social History 1750–1800* (PRONI: Belfast, 1969), pp. 34–46 and 155–65; Buckinghamshire later made the claim that many members were actually relieved when the Test Act rider was removed from the Catholic bill; they had voted more out of fear of the Presbyterians, rather than love for their liberties. For the motives of Shannon and Ely, see SP 63/460/263–4, Buckinghamshire to Weymouth, 18 June 1778; for the general fear of Presbyterians on the part of many government members, see SP 63/460/259–60, Heron to Sir Stanier Porten, 17 June 1778. **39** *Grattan*, i, p. 289. **40** *Cavendish*, vi, Part 13, p. 252, debate of 4 August 1778. **41** *Cavendish*, vi, Part 13, p. 247, debate of 4 August 1778. **42** Ibid., vi , Part 13, pp. 258–9, debate of 4 August 1778. **43** See for example his remarks to his good friend William Eden in a letter dated 28 August 1784, when he was safely established as attorney general. Sneyd Muniments. **44** *Cavendish*, vi, Part 11, p. 305, debate of 16 June 1778. **45** Ibid., vi, Part 11, pp. 301–8. **46** *Dublin Evening Post*, 6 August 1778. **47** *Cavendish*, vi, Pt 13, p. 249, debate of 4 August 1778. **48** Ibid., p. 255. **49** Ibid., pp. 45–7. **50** See Fosters remarks, *Cavendish*, vi, Part 13, pp. 47–50, debate of 3 August 1778 and Scott's comments, same debate, pp. 88–95. **51** Ibid., p. 116. **52** Ibid., p. 118. **53** The entirety of this particular drama appears in *Cavendish*, vii, Part 15, pp. 97–102 , debates of 20 and 22 November 1779. **54** Ibid. **55** Ibid. **56** Ibid. **57** *Hibernian Journal*, 22–4 November 1779. **58** A full and of course, glorifying account of this particular campaign appears in *Grattan*, ii, pp. 3–9. **59** SP 63/467/101–2, Buckinghamshire to Weymouth, 8 November 1779. **60** *Beresford*, i, p. 68. **61** The supposed unholy alliance of FitzGibbon and Beresford received particular emphasis during the Fitzwilliam administration. See, for example, the *Hibernian Journal*, 14 January 1795 ("To a certain lord") which suggests FitzGibbon's alliance with "that sink of pollution the Customs House". O'Beirne, Fitzwilliam's political confidante, also played up the alliance of corruption. See Sheffield Library, Fitzwilliam MS, [uncatalogued] O'Beirne to Fitzwilliam, 6 September 1794. **62** *Beresford*, i, p. 63. **63** Ibid., i, p. 68. **64** SP 63/467/139–42, Buckinghamshire to Weymouth, 26 November 1779. **65** SP 63/467/198–9, Buckinghamshire to Hillsborough, 2 December 1779. **66** *Cavendish*, vii, Part 15, pp. 138–40, debate of 23 November, 1779. **67** *Beresford*, i, p.105–8. **68** Ibid., p. 103, 105–8. **69** Ibid. **70** O'Connell, pp. 272, 276. **71** See, for example, the *Hibernian Journal*, 2–5 June 1780, "To John F_____n, Esq."; this long philippic against FitzGibbon, the first of many speaks of the bill as "the Redemption of the Bulk of the Nation from the worst of Slavery and the extreme of Wretchedness" and "the mercenary views of a few Landlords who would hold their tenantry in perpetual vassalage and make a Russian transfer of the Life of the Subject along with the property": O'Connell, op. cit. **72** Scott actually introduced the heads of the bill on 15 May 1780; *Cavendish*, viii, Part 17, pp. 34–47 **73** *Cavendish*, viii, Part 17, pp. 47–50; Part 19, debate of 13 June 1780, p. 123, 152–3. **74** *Cavendish*, viii, Part 19, p. 225, debate of 11 August 1780. **75** See David Dickson, "Middlemen", in *Penal Era and Golden Age: Essays in Irish History, 1690–1800* (Belfast, 1979), pp. 162–85. **76** SP 63/469/95–6, Buckinghamshire to Hillsborough, 20 April 1780, *Dublin Evening Post*, 20 April, 1780; Yelverton's motions on the subject were defeated on 27 April 1780; SP63/469/124, Buckinghamshire to Hillsborough, 27 April 1780; the majority against was a hair-raising 25. **77** *Dublin Evening Post*, 20 April 1780; House of Commons debate, 19 April 1780. **78** *Grattan*, ii, pp. 37–8. **79** *Dublin Evening Post*, 20 April 1780, House of Commons debate of 19 April 1780. **80** Ibid. **81** Ibid. **82** SP 63/469/101–3, Buckinghamshire to Hillsborough, 19 April, 1780; 63/469/195–8, Buckinghamshire to Hillsborough, 8 May 1780; 63/469/264–5, Same to Same, 24 May 1780; 63/469/284–6, Buckinghamshire to Heron, 28 May 1780. **83** SP 63/469/147–8, Buckinghamshire to Hillsborough, 29 April 1780. **84** SP 63/469/130, Same to Same, 26 April 1780. **85** SP 63/469/195–8 op. cit. **86** SP 63/470/236, Heron to Sir Stanier Porten, 9 August 1780. **87** 63/470/267–8, Buckinghamshire to Hillsborough, 17 August 1780. **88** Ibid. **89** *Cavendish*, viii, Part 19, debate of 12 August 1780, pp. 249–50. **90** SP 63/469/253–5, Heron to John Robinson, 20 May 1780; SP 63/469/256–7, Same to Same, 18 May 1780. **91** SP 63/469/253, op. cit.; *Cavendish*, viii, Part 17, pp. 71–106. **92** *Cavendish*, viii, Part 17, debate of 19 May 1780, pp. 295–7. **93** *Hibernian Journal*, 2–5 June1780, "To John F_____n". **94** *Dublin Evening Post*, 25 April 1780, Postscript for same date. **95** *Dublin Evening Post*, 30 March 1780. **96** See, for example the *Freeman's Journal*, 12–15 August 1780; House of Commons debate, 11 August, 1780 which in an account of the tenantry Bill debate stated that "Petulant Jack was silenced". See also, the *Dublin Evening Post*, for 10 October 1780. The *Volunteers' Journal* seems to have favored the variation "Jack Fitzpetulant"; see, 21 November and 5 December 1783 (in Dublin news of same dates) and 24 December 1783 (Dublin news of 23 December 1783); it also made much use of the variation "Fitzprig"; see, 18 October 1784 (Postscript of same date); the *Dublin Evening Post* also made use of this mutation of FitzGibbon, e.g. 5 and 26 October, 1784 (Postscript for same dates). **97** *Dublin Evening Post*, 27 January 1781, "Maw-worm's epitaphs ... continued". **98** Ibid., 10 May 1781 "Metempsychosis: A vision"

CHAPTER 4

1 SP63/476/134–8, Carlisle to Hillsborough, 15 September 1781. **2** Ibid. **3** Ibid. **4** Ibid. **5** HMC Carlisle, p. 510. **6** *HMC Charlemont*, i, p. 148. **7** Edward Gibbon, *Memoirs of My Life* (London, 1991), pp. 204–5. **8** For a much fuller account of the trade dispute with Portugal than this study can offer, see James Kelly, "The Irish Trade Dispute with Portugal", *Studia Hibernica*, vol. xxv, (1989–90), 1–45. 9 SP63/474/72–3, Carlisle to Hillsborough, 30 January 1781; SP63/477/9–10, Carlisle to Hillsborough, 29 October 1781. 10 SP 63/476/40–3, Hillsborough to Carlisle, 10 September 1781. 11 *Cavendish*, ix, Part 21, pp. 4–22, debate of 1 November, 1781; for comments on "Disrespectful expressions made in Irish Parl", see, SP 63/476/275–9, Hillsborough to Carlisle, 21 October 1781. 12 SP 63/476/275–9. 13 *Parliamentary Register* (1781–2), debate of 29 October 1781, p. 16. 14 Ibid., p. 26. 15 Ibid. 16 *PR* (1781–2), pp. 210–11. 17 Ibid., p. 212. 18 Ibid. 19 Ibid., p. 215. 20 Ibid., p. 222. 21 Ibid., p. 226. 22 SP 63/480/162–6. 23 *PR* (1781–82), p. 95. 24 Ibid. 25 Ibid. 26 Ibid. 27 *PR* (1781–2), p. 9. 28 Ibid. 29 SP 63/476/227–9, Carlisle to Hillsborough, 10 October 1781. 30 *PR* (1781–2), p. 7. 31 Ibid. 32 SP 63/477/76–7, Carlisle to Hillsborough, 10 November 1781. 33 SP 63/480/10–13, Carlisle to Hillsborough, 29 December 1781. 34 SP 63/480/290–5, Carlisle to Hillsborough, 3 March 1782; SP 63/480/296–300, Same to Same, 3 March 1782. 35 *PR* (1781–82), p. 179. 36 Ibid. 37 SP 63/480/12–15. 38 SP63/480/296–300, Carlisle to Hillsborough, 3 March 1782. 39 Ibid. "I have been since informed and have good Reason to believe that Mr Flood and Mr Grattan, not only by their conversation, but by letters to the country are exerting themselves with many others to obtain addresses from the Volunteer Corps and from the Grand Juries at the ensuing Assizes ..." 40 SP63/480/224. 41 SP 63/480/296–300; London, Public Records Office, Home Office Papers (HO) 100/1/119–20. 42 HO 100/1/3–6; Carlisle to Hillsborough, 26 March 1782. 43 *HMC Carlisle*, p. 510. 44 SP 63/480/290–5. 45 SP63/480/296–300. 46 Ibid. 47 *Statutes at Large Passed in the Parliaments Held in Ireland*, xii, pp., 237–42; 388–90. 48 SP63/480/84–90. 49 SP 63/480/251–3 Carlisle to Hillsborough, 23 February 1782. 50 Ibid. 51 SP 63/480/288, Carlisle to Hillsborough, 23 February 1782. 52 See, for example ,SP 63/465/179, Buckinghamshire to Weymouth, 28 June 1779; 63/465/283–293, Report of the Commissioners of Revenue on the State of Ireland, which notes the loyalty of Catholics, and indeed the whole country during "a late alarm in the South"; 63/466/9–10, Weymouth to Buckinghamshire; Weymouth repeats a scare rumor of priests coming from continent to stir up discontent, but adds "the zeal which the Roman Catholicks of Ireland have shown leaves no reason to doubt of their Loyalty"; 63/467/3, Buckinghamshire to Weymouth, 3 October 1779. 53 *Grattan*, ii, p. 205. 54 *PR* (1781–2), p. 205. 55 Ibid. 56 *PR* (1782), p. 250: "He [FitzGibbon] explained with great professional ability, the nature of the privileges that were going to be granted; and concluded that thought it would be improper to allow papists to become proprietors of boroughs, there was no good reason why they should not possess estates in counties or any Protestant tenants holding under them should not exercise a right of voting for members of Parliament." 57 *PR* (1781–2), p.238. 58 Ibid. 59 *PR* (1781–2), pp. 241–2. 60 SP 63/480/22–3, heads of Gardiner's bill. 61 A pen portrait of FitzGibbon that appeared in Walker's *Hibernian Magazine* in August 1789, portrayed this bizarre action in heroic terms: 'In the senate his services have been inestimable – at a time when a just and liberal policy induced the legislature to unbind the heavy burdens of the Roman Catholics, and to bid that long oppressed people to go free; generosity which is seldom guided by discretion, had hurried the House of Commons so eagerly into the business, that in unchaining the Roman Catholics, they incautiously loosened every link that secures the landed property of Ireland –this instantly appeared to the sagacious and penetrating mind of Lord FitzGibbon, he pointed out the danger and stopped them on the very brink –a profound and awful silence took place, the house seemed terrified at its own conduct the then Attorney General compared the situation of the house to an army panic struck – the proceedings were instantly stopped till proper cautionary measures were taken (p. 394). If Mr Walsh's actions are any indication, this "profound and awful silence" was not general. It was broken, at least occasionally, by a profound and awful irritation at an action that gave the appearance of tiresome legal hairsplitting by an attention-grabbing young man. 62 *Cavendish*, ix, part 24, debate of 20 February 1782, p. 141. 63 *PR* (1781–2), p. 305. 64 Ibid. 65 *Dublin Evening Post*, 2 March 1782; House of Commons debate, 1 March 1782. These more conciliatory remarks do not appear in the

Parliamentary Reports. **66** *HMC Carlisle*, pp. 615–16, 617. **67** HO 100/1/74–82, Portland to Shelburne, 16 April 1782. **68** HO 100/1/74-82, *Grattan*, ii, pp. 272–3, pp. 293–4. **69** HO 100/1/74–82. **70** *HMC Carlisle*, p. 632. **71** HO 1/100/153-6, Portland to Shelburne, 27 April 1782. **72** *HMC Carlisle*, p. 620. **73** HO 100/1//74–82, Portland to Shelburne, 16 April 1782. "I must not, however pressed in time, omit to acquaint your Lordship that I found there was a design of moving the thanks of both Houses to Lord Carlisle and Mr Eden, and that the latter was to be recommended to the King for some distinguished mark of His Majesty's royal favour. I observed that unusual as I believed it to be, I should not wish the friends of my administration here to oppose the motion of thanks to Lord Carlisle provided it contained nothing that could be construed into a suspicion of doubt of the good intentions of his majesty's present servants; but that considering Mr Eden's late behavior, I hoped they would resist any attempt to reward or even to thank him." The attempt could only have originated with FitzGibbon. He was Eden's greatest Irish intimate and he was certainly disappointed in and resentful of Portland. **74** Ibid., *HMC Carlisle*, p. 629. **75** Ibid. **76** *PR* (1781–2), pp. 339–40. **77** SP63/480/395; Carlisle did make oblique hints, however, that he would not be sorry to see the Declaratory Act repealed. In a letter pleading for the prompt return of Yelverton's bill re-enacting English statutes, he ended with this remark: "It is not for me to determine whether (?) the total extirpation of it [the Declaratory Act] would not be an act of as sound policy as it would be of unexpected generosity." (Carlisle to Hillsborough, 12 March 1782, SP 63/480/350). **78** *O'Flanagan*, ii, p. 167. **79** Ibid. **80** *HMC Carlisle*, p. 629. **81** HO 100/1/133–9, Portland to Shelburne, 24 April 1782; 100/1/142–6, Shelburne to Portland, 29 April 1782; 100/1/149, Shelburne (?) to Portland, 3 May 1782; HO 100/1/166–7, Portland to Shelburne, 5 May 1782. **82** *Grattan*, ii, p. 303; HO 1/100/290, Portland to Shelburne, 29 May 1782. **83** *HMC Carlisle*, pp. 629–30. **84** *Grattan*, ii, pp. 350–1. **85** Ibid. **86** *HMC Carlisle*, op. cit. **87** For an example of how Grattans reputation had sunk, see the *Dublin Evening* Post for 28 December 1782 (Hampden to Henry Grattan, Esq.). According to this editorial, Grattan was less enthusiastic and active in promoting the rights of Catholics than FitzGibbon. No mention, of course, was made of Flood's manifest lack of enthusiasm for the bill. **88** *PR* (1781–2), p. 430. **89** Ibid. **90** *Cobbett's Parliamentary History*, xxiii, pp. 147–52. **91** HO 100/3/235–40, Townshend to Temple, 26 October 1782; HO 100/3/247–8, Same to Same, 4 November 1782. **92** HO 100/2/300–5, Temple to Townshend, 15 April 1782. **93** 100/8/89–93, Temple to Townshend, 15 January 1783; 100/8/96–8, Townshend to Temple, 19 January 1783; HO 100/8/175–6, Townshend to Temple, 19 January 1783. **94** PR (1781–2), p. 348. **95** Ibid., p. 439. **96** Ibid. **97** HO100/2/63, Portland to Shelburne, 8 June 1782. **98** *PR* (1781-2), p. 439. **99** HO 100/2/246; HO 100/2/268–9, Portland to Shelburne, 23 July 1782. **100** *PR* (1781–2), p. 444. **101** HO 100/2/290, Portland to Townshend, 27 July 1782. **102** HO 100/2/244 Townshend to Portland, 24 July 1782. **103** FitzGibbon to Temple, 31 October 1783, BM Add MS 40179/f.96. **104** HO 100/9/157, Temple to North, 3 June 1783; HO 100/9/163, Windham to Nepean, 5 June 1783. **105** HO 100/9/279, 25 July 1783, Northington to North. **106** *Dublin Evening Post*, 18 May 1782. **107** Dublin, Irish Public Records Office, MS6192; the document in question includes a Chancery brief filed 19 May 1864, which alluded to old FitzGibbon's contacts with Silver Oliver on p. 2. **108** Mrs. Morgan John O'Connell, *The Last Colonel of the Irish Brigade* (London, 1892), pp. 304–12. **109** *Dublin Evening Post*, 2 September 1783, "Dublin, Election Intelligence". **110** Ibid., 9 September 1783. **111** *Falkiner*, pp. 141, 143. **112** Ibid., p. 141. **113** PRONI, Normanton MSS, T3719/C17/28 "It [FitzGibbon's experience during the election] has effectively corrected a very dangerous vice in my nature – I shall now at least keep mankind at arms length till I know them." FitzGibbon to Agar, 10 September 1783. **114** *Dublin Evening Post*, 9 September 1783, "Dublin, Election Intelligence". **115** *Volunteers' Journal*, 14 November 1783, House of Commons debate, 12 November 1783. **116** *PR* (1784), p. 216. **117** Oliver Macdonough, *The Inspector General: Sir Jeremiah Fitzpatreick and Social Reform 1783–1802* (London, 1981), pp. 132–9. **118** HO 100/1/282–5, Portland to Shelburne, 23 May 1782; *Grattan*, iii, p. 200. **119** *Falkiner*, p. 141. **120** *Grattan*, iii, p. 112. 121 Ibid., p. 134. 122 PRO 100/10/304. 123 *Grattan*, iii, p. 202. 124 *HMC Charlemont*, i, p. 108, footnote. 125 *Falkiner*, p. 141. 126 PRO 100/10/302–3. 127 *Volunteers' Journal*, 21 November, 1783. 128 *Dublin Evening Post*, 10 April 1784; 29 May 1784, 14 September 1784, Postscript for those dates. 129 *Volunteers' Journal*, 21 November 1783. 130 *Dublin Evening Post*, 20 November 1783. 131 Ibid., 27 January 1784, Postscript for same date. 132 *Volunteers' Journal*, 5 December 1783. 133 *Dublin Evening Post*, 1 January 1784. 134 *Volunteers' Journal*, 5 December 1783. 135 *Dublin Evening Post*, 2 December 1783, Postscript for same date. 136 *Volunteer's Journal*, 15 October 1784 "To the Attorney General" by J.T.: "This opinion, Sir, [his comment against the Volunteers] has excited some degree of surprise in the kingdom. Had it been delivered by a lowly descended upstart, who disgraced a dignified station with drunkenness, debauchery and every other vicious propensity derived from his base origins – our wonder would cease; but the world knows, Sir, you do not come under this description."

CHAPTER 5

1 Bolton Papers, 16,350/3. 2 Ibid. 3 Ibid. 4 *HMC Charlemont*, i, 123–6. 5 *Dublin Evening Post*, 22 November 1783: "To the Roman Catholic Committee". 6 *Kenmare*, p. 80. 7 Bolton, 16,350/9. 8 Bolton, 16,350/3. 9 HO 100/1/266–71, Portland to Shelburne, 18 May 1782. 10 Ibid. 11 HO 100/3/253–4, Temple to Townshend, 8 November 1782. 12 HO 100/12/125–30, Rutland to Sydney, 27 February 1784. 13 The debates on the bill appear in PR (1784), pp. 122–30. 14 HO 100/13/159–60, Rutland to Sydney, 21 June 1784; Same to Same, 30 June 1784 100/13/167–9. 15 *PR* (1784), pp. 141–2; HO 100/12/272–3. 16 HO 100/12/268–70, Orde to Nepean, 7 April, 1784; HO 100/12/393–7, copy of petition against Wide Streets Act, with Rutlands comments. 17 HO 100/12/291–2,100/12/293–5, 100/12/300–8. 18 Brian Inglis, Freedom of the Press in Ireland, (London, 1979), pp. 42, 45. 19 *Volunteers' Journal*, 5 April 1784. 20 NLI, Sydney Papers, 51/C/8, Sydney to Rutland, 1 May 1784. 21 HO 100/12/300-8. 22 Inglis, pp. 38–40, 43. Three years later, in 1787, Eden, then in Paris to negotiate the Anglo-French trade agreement, wrote to FitzGibbon and requested a copy of the Irish press act. One of the French ministers, Montmorin, was considering implementing a similar measure. FitzGibbon, always happy to help a brother reactionary, provided Eden with the information that Montmorin had requested. In his letter he made the astonishing claim that he had prosecuted only two printers for libel under the act. (Magee's hair powder comment presumably was one of those instances.) He did express some qualms about how the French government might use the act. He had, after all, frequently expressed his abhorrence of Popish despotism and now he was lending his assistance to the premier Popish, despotic regime in Europe: "I do not see that it [the act] can ever be made an improper use of – whether that will necessarily follow should the French government be enabled to establish similar regulations, I will not take upon me to determine." (Sneyd Muniments, FitzGibbon to Eden, 18 November 1787). 23 Ibid. p. 22; *Volunteer Evening Post*, pp. 34–7, 39, 44,50; *Freeman's Journal*, pp. 35–8, 46; *Faulkner's Dublin Journal*, pp. 57–60. 24 Sneyd Muniments, FitzGibbon to Eden, 29 August 1784. 25 Inglis, pp. 25–7. 26 *Dublin Evening Post*, 5 October 1784; in this issue Orde is referred to as "Aguecheek"; in the issue of 28 October 1784, the anonymous writer thoughtfully suggests that one of Rutlands cast-off mistresses might serve as a good wife for FitzGibbon "if there be no objection to a young, amorous, saucy companion." (Postscript "ADVERTISMENT EXTRAORDINARY"). 27 *Dublin Evening Post*, 25 May 1784, Postscript for same date. 28 HO 100/13/67. 29 HO 100/14/37–9, Orde to Nepean, 4 August 1784; 100/14/48–9, Sydney to Rutland, 11 August 1784. 30 HO 100/14/85–6, Rutland to Sydney, 25 August 1784. 31 *Grattan*, iii, pp. 207–9. 32 Very possibly the fact that the most prominent seditious journalist, Matthew Carey, was a Roman Catholic may have led the government to see legions of seditious Papist hacks. The proprietors of the other major opposition prints, the

Dublin Evening Post and the *Hibernian Journal*, were Protestant. 33 Bolton 16,350/65. 34 Sir Patrick made these offending remarks in December of 1783; see *Volunteers' Journal*, 12 December 1783 ("The True-Born Irishman"). For an example of the deep suspicion surrounding him, see Sydney Papers, 51/C/20, Rutland to Sydney, 7 October 1784: "As to Sir Patrick Bellew, I believe he carries his ideas of mischief as far as any Catholick in Ireland." But Rutland had to admit that he had no solid proof of anything apart from indiscretion. He could only promise Sydney that his spies would keep a close watch on Bellew. 35 Sydney Papers, 51/C/20, Rutland to Sydney, 7 October 1784. 36 See, for example, Baron Hamiltons accounts of his high-handed, but failed attempts to obtain a Catholic address: Bolton 16,350/27,47, 49; see also, Bolton 16,350 for Lord Dunsany's more tactful efforts to persuade his kinsman, Lord Fingall. 37 For an account of Kenmares efforts and their failure see *Volunteer Evening Post*, 8–11 May 1784, Postscript for 11 May 1784. The government expected more out of poor Kenmare than he could reasonably deliver. Long before the famous break in 1792, he appears to have been despised by more assertive and spirited Catholics. See the *Volunteers' Journal*, 21 November 1783, which gave an account of the burning of an effigy of Kenmare. The effigy bore a placard which read "Bear your sufferings a hundred years more and your Protestant neighbors will pity you" (*Dublin News*, 21 November 1783). 38 Bolton, 16, 350/16. 39 Bolton 16,350/57. 40 Bolton 16,350/42. 41 Thomas Bartlett, *The Fall and Rise of the Irish Nation: The Catholic Question 1690–1830* (Dublin, 1992) pp. 109–13. 42 The *Freeman's Journal*, which was both pro-government and pro-Catholic, particularly enjoyed mocking Sir Edward. See, for example, the edition of 23–6 July 1791. The article in question, dated 25 July 1791, accused Sir Edward of taking part in a Bastille Day riot. "An action, it is said, is intended to be brought against him by several persons who had their windows broken, which may prove of more serious consequence to him, than the *exploit* of St Doulough's well." 43 Bolton 16,350/21 Tandy to ? 2 October 1784 "I have a scheme in Hands which I think will effectually secure the support of the whole Nation, no less than an Expectation of getting the Roman Catholics to renounce their Pretensions to a Right of Suffrage, many of them see they are the only obstacle to our Union and I think I shall succeed." 44 *PR* (1783), p. 238. 45 HO 100/10/314–17. 46 Mr Vernon of Clontarf, already mentioned, was one of these correspondents, as was the Archbishop of Armagh. In fairness to Rutland, at least, his fundamental kindness and good nature occasionally led him to express some doubts about some of his more extreme informants. See for example his comments on one of the Archbishop's letters, *HMC Rutland*, iv, p. 141, Rutland to Sydney, 7 October 1784. Nonetheless, even during his occasional fits of moderation Rutland never fully relinquished his policy of intimidation. It was in this same letter, that he suggested threatening the Catholics with the revocation of the rights and privileges granted in 1782 if they failed to return to a suitably a-political, obsequious demeanor. 47 Bolton 16,355/10–12, Orde to William Pitt, 25 August 1784. 48 Sneyd Muniments, FitzGibbon to Eden, 28 August 1784. 49 Bolton 16,350/64; "The Attorney General has promised me a visit." Hamilton to Orde, 18 October 1784. 50 In his letter to Sydney, Rutland assures him that if it were found necessary to revoke the legislation of 1782, there were "persons of respect and independence in both houses who would willingly undertake such an office." (Sydney MS, 51/C/20) FitzGibbon undoubtedly was foremost in volunteering his services in such a contingency. For later threats of this kind from FitzGibbon, see BM Add MS 35,771/f135–8; "Substance of a conversation between Lord Hardwicke and Lord Clare" on the subject of Maynooth It should be noted that this kind of legislative blackmail was not exclusive to FitzGibbon. Other reactionary Protestants had a fondness for it. 51 Bolton, 15,958/2; the *Volunteers' Journal* took a more mordant view of this transaction and saw the Limerick response to the requisition as further proof of FitzGibbon's corrupting influence. A letter to "the Right Honorable Hugh Massey" accused the erstwhile popular hero of Limerick of acting as the "paltry tool of the man he despises, I mean the A______y G_____l". *Volunteers' Journal/Evening Herald* 15 September 1784, "To the Right Honourable Hugh Massey" by "Sempronius". 52 Ibid. 53 *Volunteers' Journal/Evening Herald*, 2 August 1784, Postscript for same date. 54 *Volunteers'*

Journal/Evening Herald, 20 September 1784; the petition was dated 18 September 1784. 55 *Grattan*, iii, p. 208. 56 *Volunteers' Journal/Evening Herald*, edition of 20 September 1784, Dublin news for 20 September 1784. 57 *Volunteers' Journal/Evening Herald*, 22 September 1784; HO 100/14/102, Rutland to Sydney, 20 September 1784. 58 The reporting paper was the *Volunteers' Journal/Evening Herald*, edition of 29 September 1784, *Dublin News* for 28 September 1784. 59 *Volunteers' Journal/Evening Herald*, edition of 4 October 1784, *Dublin News* for 2 October 1784; *Volunteers' Journal/Evening Herald*, edition of 11 October 1784, *Dublin News* for 9 October 1784. 60 HO 100/14/111 Sydney to Rutland, 25 September 1784. *Volunteers' Journal/Evening Herald*; 27 September 1784; Postscript for same date. 61 Bolton 16,350/45. 62 Bolton, 16,350/44; Carleton to Orde, 18 October 1784. 63 HO100/14/238–9. 64 *PR* (1785), pp. 406–7. 65 *Volunteers' Journal/Evening Herald*; 8 November 1784; "To John Fitzpetulant". 66 See for example, the same publication for 1 November 1784, which ingeniously compared FitzGibbon to Lucifer. This entry also described the Dublin aggregate meeting summoned by Reilly as "the people assembled in a legal and constitutional manner to deliberate on the most advisable mode for a reform of that corrupt representation, which supported the various measures of a tyrannical government and the unjustifiable views of an overbearing aristocracy." 67 The ineffable *Volunteer Evening Post* offers a contrary example in the edition of 5–7 October 1784, which praises FitzGibbon's "legal knowledge and undaunted conduct". 68 Bolton, 16358/1 Orde to Pitt, 4 October 1784; on Bradstreet's scruples see Bolton 16,350/62, Carleton to Orde, no date. 69 Bolton 16,350/64; FitzGibbon to Orde, 11 December 1784. 70 *Grattan*, iii, p. 213; there is a slight discrepancy in the accounts of Reilly's punishment. An account in *Freemans*, stated that Reilly was merely fined a mark and then released. *Freeman's Journal*, 2–4 December, 1784, Postscript dated 2 December, 1784. 71 HO 100/4/154–5; see also, the reprint in the *Dublin Evening Post*, 16 October 1784, ("CITY OF DUBLIN MEETING"). 72 This adjuration can be found in *Faulkner's Dublin Journal*, 5–8 February 1785; "To the People of Ireland". 73 *Volunteer Evening Post*, 2–4 December, 1784; Postscript for 4 December, 1784. 74 *Grattan*, iii, pp. 221–3. 75 *Volunteer Journal* or *Weekly Advertiser*; 13 March 1786; *Dublin News* for 8 March 1786 (This periodical was published in Cork and took the same anti-government editorial stance as its Dublin namesake.) 76 Reynolds died in a duel with a neighbor shortly after his legal victory, and FitzGibbon then had the responsibility of prosecuting his murderer. FitzGibbon's legal, if not personal enmity carried into the next generation. In 1795, in his capacity as Lord Chancellor, he removed Reynolds' son and namesake from the rolls of the magistracy, because of his alleged leniency toward accused Defenders. Undoubtedly moved by his late father's as well as his own grudge against FitzGibbon, Reynolds composed a savage letter which touched on FitzGibbon's every vulnerability, from low birth to the sensitive subject of his Catholic/Jesuit ancestry. FitzGibbon's enemies avidly copied and circulated copies of the letter, no doubt because Reynolds spoke for many gentlemen of his class who felt wronged, slighted or passed over by the arrogant son of an ex-Jesuit. For an account of FitzGibbon's proceeding against Keon, the antagonist in Reynold's fatal duel, see the *Volunteer Evening Post*, 23–6 June 1787, Postscript for 23 June 1787; Reynold's letter was widely circulated and copied, even by individuals who worked closely with FitzGibbon in government. Charles Agar, the bishop of Cashel kept a copy (PRONI T3719/C29/45/ p. 1); Lord Aldborough, the victim of a legal battle with FitzGibbon also retained a copy (PRONI T3300/13/18/1). 77 *Dublin Evening Post*, 9 November 1784, Postscript for same date FitzGibbon's alleged preference for hair powder over gun powder surfaced again in the radical press; see *Morning Post/Dublin Courant*, 6 December, 1794; Postscript for same date, *Volunteer Journal* or *Weekly Advertiser* (later the *Independent Gazette*); 3 February 1785, *Dublin News* for 31 January 1785, *Volunteer Journal* or *Weekly Advertiser* 10 February 1785, *Dublin News* for same date; *Faulkner's Dublin Journal*, 5–8 February 1785; according to *Faulkner's* the paragraphs of 9 November 1784 "were pronounced and declared a contempt of that court [the Kings Bench]". 78 HO 100/12/125-30; Rutland to Sydney, 27 February 1784; Bolton, 15,958/2 "Sheriff ready to convene county, but so far no request from freeholders. Leinster leading interest. Lord Mayo ... and gentlemen of property not friends to innovation." 79 Bolton, 16,350/11, no date. 80 Sneyd Muniments, FitzGibbon to Eden, 29 August 1784. 81 HO 100/14/209–10; Cooke to Nepean, 30 October 1784. 82 *PR* (1785), i, p. 62. 83 Ibid., pp. 370 Brownlow bore the burden of introducing the measure. Lord Charles was indisposed on the day it was to have been introduced. The English opposition also got into the act, a foreshadowing of their actions in 1785 and 1789. At the same time, Lord Surrey attacked attachments in the English House of Commons. *Volunteer Journal (Cork)*, 10 February 1785. 84 Ibid., p. 406–7. 85 Ibid. p. 405: "Let no puny babbler presume to blast with vile unhanded calumny the reputation of the judges of the land." 86 *Grattan*, iii, p. 220. 87 Ibid. p. 410. 88 Sydney, 51/C/23 Rutland to Sydney, 22 November 1784, "I am more and more sanguine as to the success of my favorite project, the Establishment of a National Protestant Militia". 89 Ibid., p. 297. 90 *PR* (1785), ii, p. 284. 91 Ibid., pp. 288–9. 92 Gerard O'Brien, *Anglo-Irish Politics in the Age of Grattan and Pitt* (Dublin, 1987), p. 152.

CHAPTER 6

1 Bolton, 16,350/3. 2 For a much more detailed study of this whole question see James Kelly, *Prelude to Union: Anglo-Irish Politics in the 1780s* (Cork, 1992). Based on my own exposure to the author's exhaustive knowledge of the subject, I am confident that this work will be a definitive source for many years to come. 3 See for example *Beresford*, i, pp.268–98 for some examples of the feverish, detailed work that all of the principles put into the propositions. 4 John Ehrman, *The Younger Pitt* (London, 1969), pp. 205–9. 5 Ibid., p. 210. 6 There are many and dismal examples of this sort of rhetoric. See for example PR (1785) II, p. 48 "perish the empire! Live the Constitution!" and p. 326. 7 *PR* (1785), ii, pp. 445–6. 8 Sneyd Muniments, FitzGibbon to Eden, 22 August 1785. 9 *PR* (1785), ii, p. 379 . 10 Ibid., pp. 377–8. 11 Ibid., pp. 447–8, *Grattan*, iii, p. 266. 12 *PR* (1785), ii , p. 468. 13 Their exchange must have been very colorful indeed because the *Parliamentary Register* did not record it in full, but discreetly stated: "A warm altercation took place between the Attorney General and Mr Curran, but as it was personal and did not apply to the subject in the debate, we think it improper to give it in this work." *PR* (1785), ii, p. 472. 14 *Grattan*, iii, p. 270 Bitterly as FitzGibbon detested Curran, he at least acknowledged his enemy's social standing by consenting to meet with him. FitzGibbon would not even deign to answer a challenge from Napper Tandy, considering him too lowly for a gentlemanly death by dueling pistol. See James Kelly, *That Damnd Thing Called Honour*, op. cit., p. 264. 15 *Froude*, ii, p. 485, *DNB*, vii, p. 156. 16 *PR* (1785), ii, p. 382. 17 See Bolton, 15,839/1 for a discussion of the status of the Navigation Acts in Ireland prior to Hawkesbury's legislation. 18 Ehrman, pp. 339–41. 19 BM Add. MS. 38221, f267–8, FitzGibbon to Hawkesbury, 10 March 1787. (My thanks to Dr Anthony Malcomson for bringing this and other documents on the Navigation Acts to my attention.) 20 Ibid. 21 Ibid. 22 BM Add MS 38309, f144, Hawkesbury to FitzGibbon, 19 March 1787. 23 BM Add MS 38221, f317, FitzGibbon to Hawkesbury, 2 April 1787. 24 *PR* (1787) pp. 380–81. 25 Ibid. 382–4. 26 Ibid., p. 384. 27 *PR* (1787), pp. 380–1, "My sentiments are, Irish equality and British shipping."

CHAPTER 7

1 Bolton, 15,926/333. 2 Ibid. 3 "An Act for the better execution of the Law within Dublin and certain parts thereto"; *Irish Statutes*, iii, pp. 734–62. 4 Ibid. 5 Bolton, 15,928/4. 6 See for example, Grattan's remarks, *PR* (1786), p. 330, 340–1 where he alludes to "armed patrols". 7 Sir Edward Newenham made the sweeping and rather irrelevant claim that freedom of elections in the city and county of Dublin were destroyed forever by the act: *PR* (1786), p. 327. 8 Ibid., p. 337.

9 Ibid., pp. 341–2. 10 Ibid. 11 *PR* (1789), p. 394. 12 The Puritanism of the Americans or the bad example they had set for Ireland in rebelling successfully against British rule seem the only likely explanations for his curious antipathy to a people with whom he seems to have had no contact whatsoever: *PR* (1789), p. 398. 13 The most complete and interesting account of Fitzgerald's life and career appears in HO 100/18/85–6, in a letter to the Duke of Rutland dated 27 February 1786. The author is unknown. 14 SP 63/459/119, Buckinghamshire to Weymouth, 7 March 1778. 15 HO 100/18/85-6. 16 Ibid. The account that follows of McDonnell's murder is taken largely from this document. 17 Ibid. 18 *Dublin Evening Post*, edition of 8 June 1786; Postscript for 8 June 1786. 19 *Dublin Evening Post*, 13 June 1786; Postscript for same date. 20 *HMC Rutland*, iv, p. 290. 21 *Dublin Evening Post*, 22 June 1786, Postscript for same date. 22 Oddly, the *Dublin Evening Post*, usually FitzGibbon's greatest journalistic nemesis, contained an informative and sympathetic explanation of the statute and of its use in the Fitzgerald trial. "Juridicus", 29 June 1786. 23 *Dublin Evening Post*, 22 June 1786, Postscript for same date. 24 *Dublin Evening Post*, 15 June 1786; "Extract of a letter from Castlebar". The comments about Brecknock's Jewishness appear to have been false as well as cruel. On the scaffold Brecknock espoused a highly individualistic, millenarian form of Christianity. He recited the Lord's prayer in Greek and declared that he "had drove the Devil from every pore in his body and that he knew he should live a thousand years with Christ." *Dublin Evening Post*, 17 June 1786; Postscript for same date; "Sentence and Execution of George Robert Fitzgerald, Esq., Brecknock and Fulton." 25 *HMC Rutland*, iv, p. 313. 26 PRONI, Aldborough Papers, T3300/13/16/1. 27 *HMC Rutland*, iv, p. 313. 28 *Dublin Evening Post*, 13 June 1786. 29 Ibid. 30 *Dublin Evening Post*, 20 June 1786; for the jury challenges see *Dublin Evening Post*, 15 June 1786, "Castlebar Intelligence". 31 *Dublin Evening Post*, 27 June 1786, "To the Proprietors of the Dublin Evening Post" by "Fitzpatrick". 32 Ibid. 33 *Dublin Evening Post*, 24 June 1786, Dublin news for same date. 34 HO 100/16/3-4 Rutland to Sydney, 28 December, 1784. 35 For a highly colored account of Whiteboy activities and their effect on the clergy, see, a petition to the Duke of Rutland from the beneficed clergy of the Diocese of Cork and Ross; Bolton 15,809; see, also, "Some Accounts of the Proceedings of the Whiteboys and of the Conduct of their Abettors", John Barter Bennett's account of the rise of the Whiteboys in Cork. Bennett wrote this account in 1787 and updated it 1803; NLI, MS 4161 J. S. Donnelly, Jr, who has done invaluable and comprehensive work on Irish agrarian movements, has provided a useful summary and analysis of Bennett's work. See "A Contemporary Account of the Rightboy Movement: The John Barter Bennett Manuscript", *Journal of the Cork Historical and Archaeological Society*, lxxxviii, 247 (1983), pp. 1–50. For an authoritative modern assessment of the Rightboys, see J.S. Donnelly, Jr, "The Rightboy Movement", *Studia Hibernica*, 17–18, (1977–8), pp. 120–202; for another excellent study, see Maurice Bric, "The Tithe System in Eighteenth Century Ireland", *Proceedings of the Royal Irish Academy*, Vol. 86, C, No. 7, (1986), pp. 271–88. 36 There were hundreds of these dismal screeds, which to any humane secular sensibility, are by turns boring, intellectually dishonest and infuriating. Probably the most palatable and comprehensive was Richard Woodward's *The Present State of the Church of Ireland* (Dublin, 1787). 37 Orde himself made this point in his characteristically detailed memorandum on the subject. Bolton, 15,959. To be precise, it is point number 3 out of 44. 38 Woodward, pp. 93–4. 39 Bennett, pp 40–1 (1803 addendum); Bolton, 16,350/81. 40 Bennett, p. 43 (1803 addendum). 41 Bennett, pp. 32–3 (1803 addendum). 42 Ibid., p. 45 (1803 addendum). 43 For an account of Luttrell's progress, see HO 100/18/387–9; Rutland to Orde, 27 October, 1786. 44 *PR*(1787), p. 59. 45 *Freeman's Journal*, 1–4 July 1786; "For the Freeman's *Journal* to the Right Honourable A____ G____". 46 Bolton, 15, 959, op. cit.; 16,355/94–5 Orde to Pitt, 17 February 1787. 47 Bolton 16,355/94–5; see also Sydney's response on the subject HO 100/18/278, 6 September 1786; Sydney pointed out to Rutland that an attack on the clergy constituted an attack on the entire Protestant establishment, though he did point out that the clergy could prudently consider ways to modify their exactions of tithes. 48 *Irish Statutes*, xiv, pp. 165–70 "An Act to Prevent Tumultuous Risings and Assemblies and for the more Effectual Punishment of

Persons Guilty of Outrage, Riot, and Illegal Combination and of Administering and Taking Unlawful Oaths". **49** Bolton 16,355/94–5; HO 100/20/113–14 Orde to Nepean, 14 February 1787, "... no objections of weight were made to any parts of the Bill but such as we had agreed in the morning to omit or alter." **50** *PR* (1787), p. 232. **51** Ibid., p. 185. **52** Biblical exegesis does not appear to have been one of FitzGibbon's many talents. Jesus merely drove the moneylenders from the Temple. He did not shut the Temple's doors, nor did He order magistrates to demolish it. Had FitzGibbon searched a little more closely, he would have found a far more a propos remark in Matthew 24:1–3, "I tell you this: not a single stone here will be left in its place; every one of them will be thrown down". **53** Ibid., p. 191. **54** *Freeman's Journal*, 1–3 March 1787, *Dublin News* for 2 March 1787. **55** Bolton 16,355/94–5, Orde to Pitt, 17 February 1787. The government also may have feared public resentment. Of course Orde, Rutland and their Castle advisors usually had no patience with popular unrest and little compunction about repressing it; but even they must have sensed that FitzGibbon's zeal had betrayed him into bad judgment, even political stupidity. Far from terrorizing middlemen, Whiteboys or both, the chapel wrecking clause could as easily provoke them into further agitation. Moreover, the Castle men surely saw the implications of Henry Grattan's successful fight against the clause: Catholics might turn to the opposition for patronage and protection, which would make them even less amenable to government than they already were. Certainly the *Dublin Evening Post* encouraged such a development. A paragraph praising Henry Grattan for defense of chapels also admonished Catholics to remember "with warm gratitude the successful combat this gentleman gave to this clause" (*Dublin Evening Post*, 27 February 1787, Postscript for same date). Fears of exacerbated Catholic discontent and a Catholic/Whig alliance may have accounted for two extraordinary attempts to salvage FitzGibbon's reputation for humanity, once such a propaganda selling point. The *Volunteer Evening Post*, the most obsequious of the government newspapers, undertook the task. The first attempt to rehabilitate FitzGibbon was a revolting combination of moral perversity and sycophancy: ... indeed, nothing shows the moderation and goodness of heart of the Attorney General more than his behavior on this occasion [withdrawing the clause]; as certainly, (had he chose) he might have had the bill passed in the very form that he first introduced it; but that was never his original design – he just brought it in as it then stood, merely in terrorem (*Volunteer Evening Post*, 27 February 1787). Apart from the fact that legislative sadism hardly showed "moderation and goodness of heart", FitzGibbon's jounalistic flatterer ignored his own avowed intention to enforce the chapel wrecking clause if necessary. The Catholic public, never favorable to FitzGibbon anyway, probably remained unconvinced. In October of 1787, the *Volunteer Evening Post* printed another flattering pen portrait of FitzGibbon.; this time as the benevolent and tolerant landlord: "The Right Hon. the Attorney General has diffused general happiness among the tenants of his Limerick estate, where though many of those people called middlemen bid high rents for several tracts of land, yet he with an exalted generosity refused their offers and gave leases on moderate and advantageous terms, indiscriminately to Protestants and Roman Catholics alike." (*Volunteer Evening Post*, 18–20 October 1787, Postscript for 20 October 1787). Of course, two vaguely apologetic paragraphs could not dispel the mutual suspicions between the Catholics and the Rutland administration. Still less could the captive writers of the *Volunteer Evening Post* turn FitzGibbon into the kindly, scrupulously fair patron of the Catholics. Indeed, the chapel wrecking clause continued to rankle, if the deliberations of the 1792 "Back Lane" parliament are any indication. Edward Sweetman made this thundering denunciation of FitzGibbon and his legislation: "What ... are we to spare [this man] who made it his public and profligate boast that he would prostrate the chapels of the Catholics? ... He is the calumniator of the people, and therefore, he has our hatred and contempt. Loyalty itself becomes stupidity and vice where there is no protection, and are we to tender a gratuitous submission to men who have held us in fetters and in mockery and in scorn?" (Tone, *Life*, i, p. 85). Above all, if the paragraphs were indeed written to forstall an alliance between the Catholics and the opposition, they proved unnecessary. Not until 1793 did the Whig opposition show any sustained interest in Catholic issues.

56 See *PR* (1788) pp. 193–232 for the full text of Grattan's amazing tour de force. 57 *PR* (1788), pp. 234–5. 58 Bolton, 15,883/9 FitzGibbon to Orde, 15 September 1787. 59 *PR* (1788), p. 237. 60 HO 100/23/139–40; this letter is dated 21 March 1788. 61 See, for example, Bolton 15,938 1–2; 15,935/1. 62 *Irish Statutes*, xiv, pp. 338–45, "An Act for the Better Execution of the Law and the Preservation of the Peace within the Counties at Large"; for a draft of the bill see Bolton 15,941/1. 63 Bolton 15,941/1, op. cit. 64 See *PR* (1787) pp. 460–1 (Mr Conolly on the role of lawyers) p. 438, 439 (Mr Alexander on the peaceableness of Ulster); see also pp. 433, 435–6. 65 HO 100/21/226–7, 10 August 1787, Rutland to Sydney. 66 Ibid.; for FitzGibbon's equivocal role, see *Lord Shannon's Letters to his son Viscount Boyle, 1790–1802* (Belfast (PRONI), 1982) p. lxvi. 67 Ibid.

CHAPTER 8

1 A complete view of Orde's educational schemes appears in Bolton, 15,888/1; for his narrowly sectarian aims, see 16,355/94–5 Orde to Pitt, 17 February 1787 "I take for granted that you will approve of all measures which may tend to establish with more firmness and security the Ascendancy of Protestants." 2 Bolton 15,883/9 FitzGibbon to Orde, 15 September 1787. 3 *Freeman's Journal*, edition of 7–10 June 1788, Postscript for 7 June, 1788. 4 *Dublin Evening Post*, 3 May, 1788, "Law Intelligence", 31 May 1788, "Law Intelligence". 5 *Dublin Evening Post*, 8 May 1788, "Court of Kings Bench". 6 *Dublin Evening Post*, 10 May 1788, Postscript for same date. 7 Ibid., 10 June 1788, "Kings Bench". 8 Ibid., 17 June 1788, *Dublin News*. 9 See *PR* (1788), p. 393, for an example of Griffith's interest, not only in the police act, but in prison reform. 10 PRONI, Downshire Papers, D607/B/195 FitzGibbon to Hillsborough, 17 August 1786. 11 *Dublin Evening Post*, 3 April 1788, Dublin news for same date. 12 See *Hibernian Journal*, 15 July 1795, "Commission Intelligence" for 10 July 1795; Sneyd Muniments, FitzGibbon to Auckland, 11 January 1800. 13 HO 100/27/181–2. 14 HO 100/52/56–8, Westmorland to Dundas, 16 May 1794. 15 HO 100/18/235–6 The opinion denying a writ of error to reverse Gormanstons attainder was dated 19 April 1786. See HO100/18/234–5 for Gormanston's petition. 16 Thomas Bartlett, *The Fall and Rise of the Irish Nation: The Catholic Question 1690–1830* (Dublin, 1992), p. 112. 17 See speech in *Cavendish*, vi, Pt. 11, pp. 301–8 "They are the great Popish families of Ireland who have set their faces against this clause (the gavel act) to prevent the accumulation of property in the hands of a man descended from the lineal descendent of a great Popish family, but the man who would take benefit under this law are not in a situation to wish to aggrandize any one of the family." 18 The arch-Catholic brother of Lord Gormanston, Jenico Preston the elder, who was to have legal quarrels of his own with FitzGibbon, blamed the dilatoriness of Irish lawyers for the family's difficulties. Jenico Preston to Jenico, Lord Gormanston, 18 October 1798. (This letter was in the National Library of Ireland, under the catalogue designation 13,756/3. The Gormanston papers have since been removed from the National Library.) 19 NLI, Fingall Papers, 8022/10. 20 HO 100/21/173 (Lord Lifford's brief, dated 14 June 1787); for legal doubts about Catholic guardians, see Fingall Papers, 8022/10. Lord Killeen to unknown correspondent (Sir Patrick Bellew?), January 1787 (no day given). 21 Gormanston Papers, 13,756/1, Jenico Preston to Jenico, Lord Gormanston, March 1791 [no day given]: "They [FitzGibbon and Portland] both openly declared their determination to breed you a Protestant." 22 Fingall Papers, 8022/10 Killeen to Sir Patrick Bellew, January 1787 [no day given]. 23 Ibid., 1 January 1787 John Preston to Lord Killeen; 2 January 1787 same to same. 24 Ibid. 25 *PR* (1787), pp. 366–7. 26 *Dublin Evening Post*, 17 March 1787; House of Commons debates, 16 March 1787. 27 *PR* (1787), p. 517. 28 Fingall Papers, 8022/10, C.J. Dixon to Lord Killeen, 26 December, 1786. 29 Ibid., Lord Killeen to Sir Patrick Bellew, Januar, 1787 [no day given]. 30 Gormanston Papers, 13,764/3, FitzGibbon to William Cruise, 3 January 1787. 31 Ibid. 32 Fingall Papers, 8022/10, John Preston to Lord

Killeen, 1 January 1787; Preston mentions that one William Cruise was among those served with one of Lady Gormanston's writs of habeas corpus. 33 Ibid., Killeen to Sir Patrick Bellew, op. cit. 34 This is FitzGibbon's indignant quote. See *Freeman's Journal*, 11–13 February 1790, House of Lords debates, 11 February 1790. FitzGibbon, it should be noted, hardly showed much respect for the elder Jenico's office either. In the initial debates on the matter of young Jenico, in 1787, he had contemptuously referred to the uncle as a person 'stiling [sic] himself Chancellor to the Prince Bishop of Liege": *PR* (1787), p. 368. 35 Sir Edward alluded to little Jenico's guard in his parliamentary speech on the subject. 36 There was for example his letter of admonition of March 1791 (no day given), (Gormanston Papers 13,756/1). Mr Preston always feared that Lady Gormanston and the Duke of Portland might use his own tactics: he warned young Jenico not to be so imprudent as to venture into England "While you are in Ireland and in your Catholick guardians' hands, there is a Law to protect you against her and her [dear] Duke of Portland, but once you get to England, then you have no protection whatsoever against them." 37 Fingall Papers 8022/10. 38 See Carhampton's defense of Jenico the elder: *Freeman's Journal*, 11–13 February, 1790, Parliamentary Report, House of Lords debate, 11 February 1790. 39 *Hibernian Journal*, 12 April,1790; Postscript for 9 April, 1790. 40 Gormanston Papers 13,756/1. 41 They finally met in the latter part of March, 1791, but by 10 April, Lady Gormanston had returned to England, and there were, apparently, no further communications between mother and long-estranged son. 42 *Burke's Peerage and Baronetage* (1967) Gormanston family and collaterals. 43 See the version of the speech in the *Hibernian Journal*, 19 February 1790, House of Lords debates, 18 February 1790: "As to the minor in question, he said it was not so much his being bred a Catholic, but his being educated at such a place as Liege, where he must imbibe principles respecting government and constitution very different from what is held by the liberal in this question." 44 Gormanston Papers,13,757/8, John Preston to Jenico, Lord Gormanston, 17 August 1800. 45 Ibid. 46 Gormanston Papers 13,756/3, Jenico Preston to Jenico, Lord Gormanston, 20 August 1800; "As to the chancellor, I should imagine that he was glad of an opportunity to make you some amends for his past behavior and I am glad that he behaved to you as he did on this occasion." 47 *Freeman's Journal*, 11–13 February 1790, Parliamentary Report, House of Lords debates, 11 February 1790. This clause was successfully incorporated into the final act; see *Irish Statutes*, xv, pp. 233–5. 48 Ibid.; for Curran's objections see *Freeman's Journal*, 20–3 February 1790. 49 Gormanston Papers, 13,756/3, He remarked at length on the dangers of "democratick" sympathies among the Catholics in the letter to his nephew in his letter of 18 October 1798. In fact, he urged Jenico to reverse the outlawry to prove that he harbored no such evil principles. 50 The elder Jenico's later letters were all addressed from a small cottage in that principality. 51 *HMC Rutland*, iii, p. 303, Rutland to Orde, 23 May 1786; Bolton, 15,923. 52 Ibid., p. 320, Rutland to Orde, July 1786 [no day given]. 53 Bolton, 15,923. 54 *HMC Rutland*, iii, p. 304, Orde to Rutland, 31 May 1786. 55 Ibid., p. 307, Rutland to Orde, 8 June 1786. *HMC Rutland*, iii, p. 309. Henrietta Battier, *The Gibbonade*, 1st number, (Dublin, 1794), p. 23. See, for example, *Dublin Evening Post*, 11 September 1788. Supposedly, her "elegant and brilliant dress" at a drawing room at St James had the effect of convincing "the English ladies that taste and fashion are perfectly intimate with their sister country." 56 10 June 1788, Postscript for same date. 57 16 October 1788, Postscript for same date. 58 8 January 1795. 59 For FitzGibbon's own account of his reception from these worthies, see PRONI, Pretyman/Chatham Papers, T326/1/6958/550, FitzGibbon to Buckingham, 6 October, 1788; while Thurlow's reception was "flattering", FitzGibbon had this to say about Pitt: "What Mr Pitt's sentiments upon the subject may be, I have not a conjecture, as he never in any degree opened himself to me further than in general terms of his personal good opinion of me."

CHAPTER 9

1 *HMC Fortescue*, i, pp. 331–2, Buckingham to William Wyndham Grenville, 24 May, 1788. **2** Ibid., p. 346, Buckingham to Grenville, 17 July 1788. **3** *HMC Fortescue*, i, p. 332, 24 May 1788. **4** Ibid. **5** *PR* (1788), pp. 5–10. **6** *HMC Fortescue*, i, p. 298. **7** *PR* (1788), p. 9. **8** *PR* (1788), p. 67. **9** *PR* (1788) pp. 268–9 "I am very closely and have been very early attached to them." **10** *PR* (1788), p. 249. **11** Ibid. **12** *PR* (1788), p. 250. **13** *PR* (1788), pp. 334–5. **14** *PR* (1788), pp. 353–73. **15** *PR* (1788), p. 382. **16** Ibid., pp. 393–4. **17** Ibid., p. 272. **18** Ibid. These were John O'Neil's words. **19** Ibid., pp. 275–9. **20** Ibid., p. 313. **21** Ibid. **22** Ibid. **23** Ibid., pp. 320–1. **24** *HMC Fortescue*, i, p. 307, Buckingham to Grenville, 29 February, 1788. **25** Ibid. **26** *PR* (1788), pp. 431–2. **27** *HMC Fortescue*, i, p. 309, Buckingham to Grenville, 16 March 1788. **28** Ibid. **29** *PR* (1788), p. 434. **30** Ibid., p. 437. **31** *HMC Fortescue*, i, p. 309. **32** *HMC Fortescue*, i, p. 311, Buckingham to Grenville, p. 311; p. 316, Buckingham to Grenville, 26 March 1788; p. 319–20, Buckingham to Grenville, 11 April 1788. **33** Ibid., p. 323, Buckingham to Leinster, 18 April 1788. **34** Ibid., p. 327, Buckingham to Grenville, 13 May 1788; p. 331, Same to Same, 24 May 1788. **35** Ibid., pp. 325–7, Buckingham to Grenville, 13 May 1788. **36** Ibid., p. 336. **37** 13 May 1788. **38** *Fortescue*, i, p. 327, Buckingham to Grenville, 13 May 1788. **39** Ibid., p. 359, 18 October 1788, Buckingham to Grenville. **40** Ibid., p 309, Buckingham to Grenville, 2 March 1788. **41** Ibid., p. 324, Buckingham to Grenville, 25 April 1788. **42** Ibid., pp. 329–30, S. Bernard to W.W. Grenville, 19 May 1788. **43** J.W. Derry, *The Regency Crisis and the Whigs* (Cambridge, 1963), pp. 13–20. **44** *HMC Fortescue*, i , p. 362, 11 November 1788, Buckingham to Grenville. **45** Ibid. **46** Ibid., p. 370, Buckingham to Grenville, 15 November 1788. **47** Ibid., p. 396, Buckingham to Grenville, 3 January 1789. **48** Ibid., p. 390, Buckingham to Grenville, 22 December1788. **49** Ibid., p. 365, Buckingham to Grenville, 12 November 1788. **50** Ibid., pp. 390–1, Buckingham to Grenville, 22 December 1788. **51** Ibid., p. 385, Buckingham to Grenville, 13 December1788. **52** Ibid., p. 389, 18 December 1788. **53** Ibid., p. 398, Buckingham to Grenville, 15 January 1789. **54** Ibid., p. 372, 18 November 1788. **55** Ibid., p. 375, Buckingham to Grenville, 23 November 1788. **56** Ibid. **57** Ibid., p. 372, Buckingham to Grenville, 18 November 1788. **58** Ibid. **59** Ibid., p. 377, Buckingham to Grenville, 1 December 1788. **60** Ibid., p. 381, 8 December 1788. **61** Ibid., same letter, p. 383. **62** Ibid., p. 406, Buckingham to Grenville, 5 February 1789. **63** Ibid., p. 368, Buckingham to Grenville, 15 November 1788. **64** Ibid., p. 383, Buckingham to Grenville, 8 December 1788. **65** Ibid., p. 400, Buckingham to Grenville, 15 January 1789. **66** Ibid., p. 383. **67** Ibid., p. 385, Buckingham to Grenville, 13 December 1788. **68** Ibid., p. 401, Buckingham to Grenville, 25 January 1788. **69** Ibid. **70** Ibid., p. 396, Buckingham to Grenville, 3 January 1789. **71** Ibid., p. 397, Buckingham to Grenville, 10 January 1789. **72** Ibid., p. 402, Buckingham to Grenville, 25 January 1789. **73** Ibid., p. 394, Buckingham to Grenville, 3 January 1789. **74** Ibid., p. 386, Buckingham to Grenville, 13 December 1789. **75** Ibid., p. 400, Buckingham to Grenville, 15 January 1789. **76** Ibid., p. 406, Buckingham to Grenville, 5 February 1789. **77** Ibid., p. 407, same letter. **78** *PR* (1789), p. 7. **79** Ibid. **80** Ibid., p. 23. **81** I bid., p. 36. **82** *HMC Fortescue*, i, p. 409, Barnard to Grenville, 7 February 1789. **83** *PR* (1789), p. 28. **84** Ibid., p. 35. **85** Ibid., p. 36. **86** Ibid., p. 37. **87** Ibid., pp. 46–84. **88** Ibid., p. 84, "Mr Fitzherbert informed the House that by His excellency's command, he had to lay before them the resolutions agreed to by both Houses of the British Parliament." **89** Ibid., p. 95. **90** Ibid., p. 116. **91** *HMC Fortescue*, i, p. 416. **92** *PR* (1789), p. 120. **93** Ibid., p. 128. **94** Ibid., p. 145. **95** *HMC Fortescue*, i, p. 433, Buckingham to Grenville, 14 March 1789. **96** Ibid., p. 410, Buckingham to Grenville, 8 February 1789. **97** Ibid., p. 412, Buckingham to Grenville, 14 February 1789. **98** Ibid. p. 413, same letter. **99** Ibid., p. 425, Buckingham to Grenville, 2 March 1788. **100** Ibid. p. 426, Buckingham to Grenville, 4 March 1789. **101** *Grattan*, iii, p. 363. **102** *PR* (1789), pp. 53–4. **103** Ibid., p. 10. **104** Ibid., p. 29. **105** Ibid., p. 49. **106** Ibid., p. 75. **107** Ibid., p. 78. **108** Ibid., pp. 129–30. **109** Ibid., p. 129. **110** Ibid., p. 50. **111** See for example *Grattan*, iv, p.347

"The question men should have asked was not 'Why was Mr. Sheares upon the gallows?' but 'Why was not Lord Clare along with him?' " **112** *PR* (1789), p. 130. **113** Ibid., pp. 53–4. **114** Ibid. **115** *Grattan*, iii, p. 383-4. **116** *HMC Fortescue*, i, p. 419 Buckingham to Grenville, 21 February 1788. **117** Ibid., p. 423, Buckingham to Grenville, 25 February 1789; p. 434, Same to Same, 21 March 1789. **118** *PR* (1789), p. 192. **119** *HMC Fortescue*, i, pp. 423–4, 25 February 1789. **120** *Dublin Evening Post*, 9 April 1789. **121** *HMC Fortescue*, i, p. 426, Buckingham to Grenville, 4 March 1789. **122** Ibid., p. 440, Buckingham to Grenville, 28 March 1789. **123** Ibid.; W.B. Ponsonby was Postmaster General. His brother George, who was Counsel to the Commissioners, was also dismissed; *Grattan*, iii:, p. 389. **124** *HMC Fortescue*, i, p. 458, 460. **125** Ibid., p. 441, Buckingham to Grenville, 31 March 1789. **126** Ibid., p. 436, Buckingham to Grenville, 25 March 1789. **127** Ibid., pp. 441; p. 443, Buckingham to Grenville, 3 April, 1789; Buckingham's maddening habit of changing his mind creates some confusion in his correspondence. In a latter dated from the same day, he declares that he will force Ely to surrender the post office. Since he made no formal applications to dismiss Ely, he must have reverted to the original course of FitzGibbon-induced moderation, p. 435. **128** Ibid., p. 435, Buckingham to Grenville, 22 March 1789. **129** Ibid., p. 441. **130** Ibid., p. 443. **131** Ibid., p. 441. **132** Ibid., p. 442; p. 464, Buckingham to Grenville, 6 May, 1789; p. 469, Same to Same, 13 May, 1789. **133** Ibid., p. 464. **134** Ibid., p. 465. **135** *Lord Shannon's Letters to his Son*, pp. lxxxviii-lxxxix. **136** *HMC Fortescue*, i, p. 410, Buckingham to Grenville, 7 February 1789. **137** *PR* (1789), p. 179. **138** Ibid., p. 181; Brownlow articulated this particular line of reasoning. **139** Ibid., p. 182. **140** Ibid., pp. 353–7. **141** Ibid., pp. 253–4. **142** Ibid., 256–7. **143** Ibid., 258–9. **144** Ibid., 268. **145** Ibid., pp. 297–8. **146** Ibid., p. 278. **147** Ibid., pp. 299–300. **148** *HMC Fortescue*, i, p. 433, Buckingham to Grenville, 14 March 1789. **149** Ibid., p. 429, Buckingham to Grenville, 12 March 1789. **150** Ibid., p. 432, Buckingham to Grenville, 12 March 1789. **151** Ibid., p. 434, Buckingham to Grenville, 21 March 1789. **152** Ibid. **153** Ibid., p. 430 Buckingham to Grenville, 12 March 1789. **154** Ibid., p. 462, Buckingham to Grenville, 1 May 1789. **155** *PR* (1789), pp. 442–64. **156** *HMC Fortescue*, i, p. 462. **157** *Grattan*, iii, pp. 433–8. **158** Ibid., iii, pp. 440–1: "It was, however, said their proceedings were the result of faction concerted at meetings and clubs (Lord Clare's speech in the House of Lords) and taverns, and a low species of language was resorted to and applied to them by the party who had excluded them from power and 'whose joy, like their revenge on this occasion knew neither decency nor moderation'." **159** Ibid., p. 430. **160** *HMC Fortescue*, i, p. 461, Buckingham to Grenville, 28 April 1789. **161** Ibid., p. 462. **162** Ibid., p. 463, Buckingham to Grenville, 6 May 1789. **163** Ibid., p. 467, Buckingham to Grenville, 13 May 1789. **164** Ibid. **165** Ibid., p. 468, same letter. **166** Ibid. **167** Ibid., p. 480, Buckingham to Grenville, 17 June 1789. **168** *Faulkner's Dublin Journal*, 5 May 1789. **169** *Dublin Evening Post*, 2 May 1789. **170** *Hibernian Journal*, 1 May 1789. **171** Ibid. **172** *Hibernian Journal*, 1 December 1789. **173** *Freeman's Journal*, 23 June 1789.

CHAPTER 10

1 Jerome Alley, *The Judge, or an Estimate of the importance of the judicial character, occasioned by the death of the late Lord Clare, Lord Chancellor of Ireland* (London, 1803), p. 35. **2** *The Speech of Edward Sweetman, Captain of a Late Independent Company at a Meeting of the Freeholders of the County of Wexford convened by the Sheriff in September of 1792 to take into consideration Mr Edward Byrne's letter, recommending a plan of delegation to the Catholics of Ireland in order to prepare a humble petition to the legislature* (Dublin, 1792), p. 5. **3** *Morning Post* or *Dublin* Courant, 25 March 1794. **4** *Morning Post* or *Dublin Courant*, 12 April 1794. **5** *Morning Post*, 18 December 1794. **6** *Dublin Evening Post*, 13 February 1802; later reprinted as a pamphlet entitled *The Character of the Late Earl of Clare* (Dublin, 1802). **7** *O'Flanagan*, ii, p. 280. **8** C.L. Falkiner, *Studies in Irish History and Biography*, mainly of the 18th Century (London, 1902), p. 123, 139. **9** *Morning Post*; 13 March 1794. **10** PRONI, Aldborough Papers, T3300/13/16/4. **11** Sir Jonah Barrington, *Historical*

Anecdotes of the Legislative Union between Great Britain and Ireland, ii, (London,1835), p. 286. 12 Sir Jonah Barrington, *Personal Sketches of his Own Time*, i (London, 1827), p. 367. 13 *Barrington*, i, p. 368. 14 *Roche*, ii, p. 113. 15 *Freeman's Journal*, 9 February,1797; House of Lords debates, 7 February, 1797. 16 *Freeman's Journal*, 3–5 November 1789, "Postscript" for 3 November 1789. 17 *O'Flanagan*, ii, p. 281. 18 *Schoales and Lefroy*,Reports of Cases Argued and Determined in the High Court of Chancery during the Time of Lord Redesdale, (Dublin, 1810), ii, p. 704; the entire case can be found in *Schoales and Lefroy*, ii:, pp. 690-720. 19 *Dublin Evening Post*, 16 March 1790. 20 Hughes, *The Practice of the Court of Chancery in Ireland* (Dublin,1837), p. 1. 21 Ibid., p. 20. 22 *Dublin Evening Post*, 13 February 1802. 23 *Schoales and Lefroy*, i, p. 117. 24 *Schoales and Lefroy*, i , pp. 120–22. 25 *Schoales and Lefroy*, ii, p. 724; for account of entire case, see pp. 721–31. 26 Aldborough Papers, 1330/13/16/4. 27 See for example, *Ridgeway*, iii, pp. 376–430, *Inchiquin v. Burnell*. 28 *Freeman's Journal*, 7 February 1797; House of Lords debates, 6 February, 1797. 29 *Dublin Evening Post*, 9 July 1796. 30 *Hibernian Journal*, 31 August 1791; *Dublin News* for 30 August 1791. 31 *Hibernian Journal*, 13 November 1789, "Postscript" for 11 November 1789. 32 *Dublin Evening Post*, 5 December 1789. 33 *Ridgeway*, iii, p. 62. 34 Hughes, pp. 429–30. 35 NLI, FitzGibbon Papers, 8343/7, Richard Pepper Arden to FitzGibbon, 21 November 1800. 36 *O'Flanagan*, ii, p. 271. 37 Ibid. 38 *Dublin Evening Post*, 6 May 1802. 39 *O'Flanagan*, ii, p. 205. 40 *Ridgeway*, iii, p. 56. 41 Ibid., pp. 24–79. 42 *Hibernian Journal*, 13 November 1789; "Postscript" for 11 November 1789. 43 *Dublin Evening Post*, 31 December 1789. 44 *Ridgeway*, ii, pp. 504–33 offers a complete narrative of the case. 45 *Ridgeway*, ii, p. 533. 46 *Ridgeway*, ii, p. 528. 47 *Freeman's Journal*, 2–4 March 1790, House of Lords debate, 1 March 1790; *Ridgeway*, ii:, pp.147–75; *Ridgeway* does not record FitzGibbon's opinion. 48 *Freeman's Journal*, op. cit.; *Ridgeway*, ii, pp. 147–75. 49 *Schoales and Lefroy*, ii, p. 611, footnote (b). 50 Ibid. 51 *Schoales and Lefroy*, ii:, p. 611. 52 Ibid. ii, pp. 73–109; ii, pp. 607–41. 53 *Ridgeway*, ii, pp. 410–11; 427; narrative of entire case, iii, pp. 345–434. 54 *Ridgeway*, ii: p. 317; narrative of entire case II, pp. 310–32. 55 *Ridgeway*, ii, pp. 590–1; narrative of entire case, ii, pp. 557–623. 56 *Ridgeway*, ii, p. 501; narrative of entire case, ii, pp. 445–503. 57 *O'Flanagan*, ii, p. 243; for O'Flanagan's own highly charged version of the case, see ii, pp. 235-45. 58 *Hibernian Journal*, 2 December 1789; *Dublin News* for 1 December 1789. 59 *Ridgeway*, iii , pp. 106–13. 60 Ibid., pp. 114–15, 170. 61 Ibid., p. 115. 62 Again FitzGibbon did not specifically mention *Fauconberg v. Birch*, though his reasoning was clearly in the same spirit. He drew on the precedent of *Bowes v. Shrewsbury*, which directly addressed the issue of Catholic property trusts. (Ridgeway, iii, pp. 184–6). Nonetheless, FitzGibbon did turn a blind eye to Thomas Redington's acquisition of Kilcornan through the agency of his other Protestant brother, Nicholas. 63 *Ridgeway*, iii, pp. 187–8. 64 Ibid., p. 199. 65 Ibid. 66 Ibid. 67 Ibid., p. 191, 193. 68 Ibid., p. 199. 69 Ibid., p. 197. 70 The complete narrative of this very complex case can be found in *Ridgeway*, iii, pp. 106–203. 71 Hughes, p. 223. 72 HO 100/32/f180–3. 73 *Ridgeway*, ii, pp. 263–4; 74 *Ridgeway*, iii, pp. 263–4; for a complete narrative see pp. 205–66. 75 *Dublin Evening Post*, 3 October 1789.

76 *Dublin Evening Post*, 13 October 1789. 77 An excellent and thorough account of Magee's ill-fated legal battle with Clonmell and Higgins appears in Brian Inglis's *Freedom of the Press in Ireland*, pp. 55–6 and 75–9; Inglis makes the very plausible suggestion of FitzGibbon' s motives for dismissing the case on p. 77. 78 Privy Council Papers (PC), 1/13/44. 79 He was probably Stephen Radcliff, who was called to the bar in 1752, and who served as judge of the Prerogative Court until 1792. 80 PC 1/13/44. 81 HO 100/56/f25—6. 82 PC 1/13/144. 83 Ibid. 84 HO 100/56/f25-6. 85 *O'Flanagan*, ii, pp. 208–11. 86 PRONI, 3244/11/1 (FitzGibbons will). 87 HO 100/70/f363–4. 88 Ibid. 89 *Ridgeway*, iii, pp. 202–3. 90 Hibernian Journal, 10 May 1799. 91 Ibid., 10 July 1799. 92 *Freeman's Journal*, 17 January 1797; House of Lords debates, 16 January, 1797. 93 *Journal of the House of Lords (Ireland)*, vii, pp. 493–4. 94 *Freeman's Journal*, 21 January 1797; House of Lords debates, 20 January, 1797. 95 Ibid. 96 Ibid. 97 Aldborough Papers,T3300/13/16/4 and T3300/13/15/4; I have not been able to locate a copy of

the actual print. I have extrapolated the contents from rough drafts of speeches in the Aldborough papers and from his lordship's own descriptions of the offending print in the same collection. **98** *Freeman's Journal*, 9 February, 1797; House of Lords debates, 6 February, 1797. **99** Ibid. **100** Ibid. **101** *Freeman's Journal*, 9 February, 1797;House of Lords debates, 7 February, 1797. **102** Ibid.; see also Aldborough Papers, T3300/13/15/3 for accusations concerning Roman Catholic magistrates. **103** *Freeman's Journal*, 9 February 1797; House of Lords debates, 7 February 1797. **104** Ibid. **105** *Journal of the House of Lords (Ireland)*, vii, pp. 509–10. **106** Ibid., p. 515. **107** Aldborough Papers, T3300/13/14/4; one of the peers in question was Yelverton. Though the others were not specifically named, they may have included Agar and Dillon, both of whom Aldborough later consulted as mediators; JHL, vii, p. 516. **108** PRONI, Powerscourt Papers, T3244/8; Aldborough Papers, T3300/13/14/12. **109** *Freeman's Journal*, 4 July 1797. **110** Powerscourt Papers, T3244/8/1. **111** Ibid. **112** Aldborough Papers, T3300/13/14/5. **113** Ibid. Yelverton's statement is curious, considering his cordial relationship with FitzGibbon in the 1780s. Their differing politics on the Catholic question no doubt caused a coolness, but Yelverton was a fellow judge and a firm government man in other respects. FitzGibbon certainly would have given him a respectful hearing at least. It seems more likely that Yelverton simply wanted to avoid the whole volatile mess, an unheroic, but understandable decision. **114** Aldborough Papers, 3300/13/16. **115** Ibid. **116** Ibid. **117** Aldborough Papers, T3300/13/18/1 and 3300/13/18/2. **118** Aldborough Papers, T3300/13/15/3. **119** Aldborough, T3300/13/14/12. **120** Ibid. **121** Ibid. **122** *Freeman's Journal*, 14 February 1797; House of Lords debates, 12 February, 1797. **123** Aldborough Papers, T3300/13/15/8. **124** *HMC Emly*, p. 199. **125** Ibid. **126** Powerscourt Papers, 3244/8/1, FitzGibbon to Lord Powerscourt, 12 January 1798. **127** *HMC Emly*, p. 199. **128** Aldborough Papers, T3300/13/15/8. **129** Barrington, *Personal Sketches*, i, pp. 369–71; Knaresborough, still on his personal quest to hang, had returned from transportation in 1798. **130** Aldborough Papers, T3244/8/2. **131** Ethel M. Richardson, *Long Forgotten Days* (London, 1928), p. 320. **132** Barrington, *Personal Sketches*, i, pp. 359–60; Richardson, pp. 317–27. **133** Aldborough Papers, T3300/13/14/19. **134** Aldborough's own personal euphemism. See Richardson, p. 320. **135** Aldborough Papers, T3300/13/14/25. **136** Aldborough Papers, T3300/13/12/2 and 3. **137** Aldborough Papers, T3300/13/14/1. **138** Aldborough Papers, T3300/13/12/7. **139** Aldborough Papers, T3300/13/12/7. **140** Aldborough, T3300/13/12/12. **141** Aldborough, T3300/13/12/9. Beresford was applying to Eardley for a map of his estate on 22 March 1796, just over a week after Eardley's estate was decreed to McCausland. Aldborough, T3300/13/12/8 On 14 March 1797 Beresford came into formal possession. I can only assume from this very confused appearance of a common interest in the same estate at the same time, that McCausland either carried out the bids on behalf of Beresford, or he sold the estate to Beresford soon after coming into possession of it. **142** *Freeman's Journal*, 9 February 1797; House of Lords debates, 6 February 1797.

CHAPTER 11

1 See, for example, the *Dublin Evening Post*, 4 March 1784; in a mock Last Will and Testament FitzGibbon bequeaths, among other things, "my cranky phaeton and my four wildest and unruly horses". For a more complimentary picture of FitzGibbon as a smart figure in a phaeton see the same publication for 4 May 1784. **2** *Dublin Evening Post*, 20 June 1789. **3** An advance description of the carriage appears in the *Dublin Evening Post*, 24 July 1790. The description was apparently based on reports from the workshop in London. **4** *Dublin Evening Post*, 6 November 1790. **5** Ibid., 9 November 1790. **6** Dublin Evening Post, 20 July, 1790; *Hibernian Journal*, 22 September 1790. **7** *Freeman's Journal*, 6 November, 1790: "... Voiture of the first elegance of construction, and the most magnificent of execution ..."; *Faulkner's Dublin Journal*, 21 September 1790: "The Chancellor's state coach is the admiration of every man of science who has seen it." **8** *Freeman's*

Journal, 23–25 September 1790: "Let Irishmen profit by the example and not grumble, when a good example is brought to their doors for profit and improvement." **9** The Mount Shannon auction catalogue of 1888, which is now in possession of the Georgian society, stated that the "Drawing and Morning Rooms Furniture is mostly Louis Quatorze carved, gilt and covered ..." In yet another attack on his failure to buy Irish, the *Morning Post/Dublin Courant* attacked FitzGibbon for importing his furniture from an English dealer. The same article attributed Italian, rather French tastes to FitzGibbon. According to the *Morning Post*, FitzGibbon had asked his English friends to recommend an ebeniste and they "feeling the dignity of the man, apply in turn to their Italian friends, and thus he is accommodated". (4 November 1794, *Dublin News* of same date) For obscure reasons, the *Morning Post* considered Italian furniture uniquely undignified. **10** *Falkiner*, p. 146–7, FitzGibbon to Eden, 26 August 1786; 27 October 1787. **11** *Lord Shannon's Letters to his Son*, p. 219. **12** The auction catalogue states that "There are also some replicas from the Dresden gallery ... most of these have been nearly a century in the FitzGibbon Family at Mount Shannon." I am assuming these paintings were copied from the Elector of Saxony's collection, since he would have been the premier patron of art in Dresden. How FitzGibbon ended up with paintings from Dresden is an interesting question. If they had been in the family for "nearly a century" as of 1888, it is doubtful that the second earl purchased them. Moreover, his own tastes ran to things Italian, to judge by his travels. To my knowledge he never spent any time in Germany, though he may have passed through on his way to his beloved Rome. Dr Malcomson, who has kindly enhanced my own very limited knowledge in this area, offers the most convincing explanation for the presence of these copies. Eden's brother was the British envoy to Dresden from 1783 to 1791 and he may have arranged to have these copies made for FitzGibbon. **13** Sneyd Muniments, no date (autumn, 1798?). **14** *Dublin Evening Post*, 9 November 1784, Postscript for same date. **15** *Morning Post/Dublin Courant*, 6 December 1794, Dublin news for same date. **16** *Dublin Evening Post*, 10 May 1781, op. cit. **17** Sir James Prior, *Life of Malone* (London, 1860), pp. 138–9. **18** Dr Malcomson, not the author, undertook this painstaking, if unsuccessful search. **19** It is difficult to document a negativity, but I have checked copies of *Watson's Almanac* from 1780–1802, and did not find FitzGibbon's name on any of the subscription lists. **20** PRONI, T2910. **21** Sneyd Muniments; for the "Hotch" dictée error see his letter of 2 January 1797; for the "Seve" blunder, see 25 August 1787; Dr Malcomson has suggested that in fairness, I should at least make allowances for FitzGibbon's frequent state of intoxication. He may have made these errors when he was drunk and when sober he may have been perfectly capable of writing good, accurate French. **22** Kent County Archives, Camden MS (TCD microfilm C/183/7), FitzGibbon to Camden, 3 September 1796. **23** See his exchange with Dr. MacNeven during the meetings of the Secret Committee; Richard R. Madden, *The United Irishmen: Their Lives and Times* (London, Dublin, 1860), p. 223. **24** *O'Flanagan*, ii, p. 251: "It has been asserted by your Lordship that I took bail for several persons under the denomination of defenders ... It has been represented that one of the parties houghed a cow and hung a threatening notice on one of her horns; had he houghed your Lordship and hung a threatening notice on one of your horns, I would have acted in the same manner." **25** *The Gibbonade*, 3rd number (Dublin, 1794), p. 12. "Nay Jacky Gingerbread who holds in shade / Immortal Pope – yet reads the Gibbonade / Yes, Jacky reads me with that special grace / With which he sometimes meets – his lady's face." **26** An unfavorable legal decision from FitzGibbon, as well as radical conviction, may have prompted Mrs Battier's masterful political satire. Her earlier works are worthy, but unremarkable, comprising for the most part odes to various friends and intimates, as well as stringently orthodox Anglican religious poetry. They also offer the few bits of biographical information that exist about her. She evidently had a long, protracted suit in both the King's Bench and in Chancery. In a poem entitled "Lines Addressed to Mr. Samuel Whyte of Grafton Street" she alludes to "Our injured cause, so overwhelmed with blame/It lay like Chancery when FitzGibbon came". Mrs Battier may have been indulging in a poetic fancy, using Lifford's Chancery court as a metaphor for the laws delay. Or she may actually have had a case pending, and she had hopes of a quick and fair decision from FitzGibbon. Obviously, these hopes were disappointed. The ode to Mr Whyte appeared in a collection entitled *The Fugitive Pieces: A Collection of Miscellaneous Poems, the genuine productions of a Lady never before published* (Dublin, 1791), p. 199; Ironically, FitzGibbon subscribed to this collection, generosity he must have regretted bitterly. **27** *The Later Correspondence of George III*, iv, p. 8, letter 2584 (footnote). **28** *Lord Shannon's Letters to his Son*, pp. 218, 219; with undoubted sarcasm, Shannon also referred to Anne FitzGibbon as the "disconsolate widow", p. 216. **29** *Dublin Evening Post*, 27 September 1788, Postscript for same date. **30** At least, Mrs. Fitzherbert remained on intimate enough terms with Lady Clare and her children to receive news of the second Earl of Clares marriage. See Anita Leslie, *Mrs. Fitzherbert* (New York, 1960), p. 194. **31** A. Aspinall, ed., *The Correspondence of George, Prince of Wales III* (Cambridge, 1965), p. 423, letter 1343. **32** Ibid., v, p. 336, letter 2136. **33** See Constantine FitzGibbon, pp. 95–6; The ineffable Buck also wrote his memoirs, which were edited by Sir Edward Sullivan and published in London in 1906. **34** PRONI, T3244/11/1; FitzGibbon almost always refers to her as his "dear" wife, never merely as his wife or as Lady Clare. **35** Sneyd Muniments, FitzGibbon to Auckland, 17 June 1800. **36** *Later Correspondence of George III*, iv, p. 8, letter 2584 (footnote): "He was a buck, a sportsman, a hard rider and drinker, a man of gallantry though a decided cuckold and a man of spirit, though a submissive cuckold." **37** Lucyle Werkmeister, *A Newspaper History of England 1792–1793* (Lincoln, Nebraska, USA, 1967), p. 32. **38** National Library of Ireland, Leinster Papers, MS 631, Lady Clare to the Duchess of Leinster, 4 February 1794. **39** Brian Fitzgerald, ed., *Correspondence of Emily, Duchess of Leinster*, ii, (Dublin, 1953), pp. 334–5. **40** Earl of Ilchester, ed., *Lady Holland's Journal*, i, (London, 1909) p. 131. **41** Valentine, Lord Cloncurry, *Personal Recollections of the Life and Times* (Dublin, 1849), p. 125. **42** Peter Jupp, *British and Irish Elections, 1784–1831* (London, New York, 1973), p. 167. **43** Francis Edwards Catalogue, March 1982, item 137d 1041. **44** "Mrs Jeffreys of Blarney Castle", *Journal of the Cork Historical and Archaeological Society*, 1895, Second Series, Vol. I, p. 83; the spellings of that simple, homely name are many and varied in the surviving documents. I have chosen to go with the baroque, rather pretentious "Jefferyes" because that is how FitzGibbon rendered the name in his will. **45** Ibid., p. 84. **46** *Falkiner*, p. 143. **47** PRONI, Midleton Papers, 1248/15/f7, Reverend Charles Broderick to FitzGibbon, 21 April 1790. **48** HO 100/31/252, Westmorland to Dundas, 5 August 1791. **49** "Mrs. Jeffreys of Blarney Castle", p. 82. **50** L.M. Cullen, ed., *The Retrospections of Dorothea Herbert, 1770–1806* (Dublin, 1988), pp. 308–9. **51** For Arabellas feelings on Catholics who would presume to political equality, see NLI MS 13,992, where she refers to Keogh and the other members of the Catholic committee as "upstart, purseproud Brawlers. Arabella, like most ambitious social upstarts, naturally hated her own kind. **52** NLI, Scully Papers, 27/537/f4049; Dennis Scully's notes on an anti-Catholic petition of 1813: "Lord Cahir is an union peer, has always given his proxy to any Government and against the Catholics. He was the unit by whom the Marquess of Wellesleys motion in favor of Emancipation was defeated in 1812." Lord Cahir did make one brief show of independence from his formidable in-laws. He briefly considered opposing the Union, but he may have been engaging in a ploy to get something from government. (PRONI, Castlereagh Papers, 3030/545, Cahir to Castlereagh, 19 January 1799). **53** Dorothea Herbert's invaluable *Retrospections* certainly gives the impression of an insufferable and tiresome woman: "She was a beautiful little Creature, wild with Spirits and very Affable, but she cursed and swore tremendously", p. 315. One cannot help but pity poor Lord Cahir and wonder if he wouldnt have been better off as a free, happy member of the Parisian canaille. Not coincidentally, perhaps, he died quite young, in 1819, no doubt worn out by his life of marital happiness. **54** Anita Leslie, *Mrs. Fitzherbert* (New York, 1960), pp. 181, 196. **55** Mark Bence Jones, *A Guide to Irish Country Houses* (London, 1988), p. 53. **56** Dorothea Herbert, *Retrospections*, p. 309. **57** Cloncurry, pp. 123–4. **58** Ibid. **59** Ibid. **60** NLI MS 2564; the Hayes Catalogue states that this little book of household accounts was kept by Dominic Trant; while he made some entries, the book seems to have been largely in her keeping. **61** The book of household expenses cited above lists some legacies made by Mrs FitzGibbon to one of the Trants' footmen, which can only mean that he had been of particular service to the old woman while she was in residence. **62** See the *Dublin Evening Post*, 21 May 1789 for an account of one of her performances. **63** She refers uncharitably to all of FitzGibbon's sisters as "amiable she-bears/Who with legitimacy, all inherit/Their fathers piety – and their brothers spirit." The interpretation is plain: the FitzGibbon sisters were amoral and immoral termagants. *The Gibbonade*, 1st number, (Dublin, 1794), p. 2. **64** PRONI T 3244/11/1. **65** *Lord Shannon's Letters to his Son*, p. 216. **66** See *Faulkner's Dublin Journal*, 2 February 1802, "The Earl of Clare". **67** Limerick City Library, Vere Hunt Correspondence, the particular fragment also is not dated. **68** Normanton Papers, T3719/C21/31, Trant to Agar, 16 August 1787. **69** Ibid. T3719/C21/29, Agar to Orde, 1 August 1787; Same to Same 11 August, 1787. **70** Ibid., T3719/C14/16, Trant to Agar, 21 March 1780. **71** *Hibernian Journal*, Edition of 23 June 1790, Postscript for 22 June. Trant died at Cahir. Possibly he was called in to settle the troubled business of the Cahir estate, and he, however unintentionally or unwillingly, sparked Arabella's interest in the business. **72** See, for example, the charming letter quoted in Mrs Morgan John O'Connell, *The Last Colonel of the Irish Brigade*, i, pp. 311–12; it is addressed to Maurice OConnell and dated 28 May 1783: "I hear with great pleasure from Mr Francis Spottswood that you had completely triumphed over the very ungenerous attempt made to distress you, your Brother and your Kinsman and that the gentleman who had been imposed upon by the artifices of a very paltry and contemptible and lying informer, became in time sensible of his error and made the proper acknowledgment of his mistake ... May I request that you will be so good as to present my most sincere compliments to the good ladies of your family and to assure them that I do not forget their very kind attentions to me during those two very agreeable days I had the pleasure of spending last October at Derrinane? If I were permitted by the troublesome business of the world, I would scale mountains much more rugged than those of Dunkeran to repeat so pleasing a visit." **73** Ibid., pp. 316–35. **74** Normanton Papers, T3719/C2415, Trant to Agar, 29 May 1790. **75** NLI, Townshend Papers, MS 394/f74, Lord Westmorland to Lord Melville, 15 July 1797; FitzGibbon used the good offices of a former lord-lieutenant and (of course) his good friend Lord Westmorland, who actually undertook the negotiations with Lord Melville. Some delay ensued because of uncertainties whether young Trant would go to Madras, where there were immediate vacancies, or to Bengal, which was the plum of Indian presidencies. Much to Elinors gratification, the boy ended up in Bengal. **76** Wellesley Papers, BM Add. MS 37, 308/ff 283–5; FitzGibbon to Lord Wellesley, 9 March 1800. **77** NLI, MS 7866. **78** Ibid. **79** *Limerick Chronicle*, 14 September 1799. **80** NLI, Heffernan/Considine Papers, (uncatalogued), FitzGibbon to William Heffernan, 20 September, 1797. **81** NLI, FitzGibbon Papers, MS 8343/14. **82** Ibid. **83** *Limerick Chronicle*, 14 September, 1799. **84** *Alumni Dublinesis*, p. 287; he was enrolled 3 October, 1796; Kings Inn Admission Papers, p. 168; he was admitted Hilary term 1799. **85** *Irish Marriages*, i, (London, 1897), p. 157. **86** Ibid. **87** NLI MS 8343/6. **88** *Watson's Almanac* (1792), p. 122. **89** Kings Inn Admission Papers, p. 168. **90** Kings Inn Admission Papers, p. 168, *Alumni Dublinesis*, p. 287. **91** PRONI, T3244/11/1. **92** For more information about Arabella's dispute with her brother, see Chapter 19, pp. 388–90. **93** *Registry of Deeds*, i, p. 209; Jeremiah Hayes refers to his nephew Patrick Furnell, which can only mean that he is the son of one of his sisters. **94** *Convert Rolls*, p. 129 **95** Limerick Archives, DeVere Hunt Papers, Letter book 2, No. 24, FitzGibbon to Hunt, 14 March, 1784. **96** *Registry of Deeds*, i, pp. 209–10. **97** *Lecky*, ii, p.419. **98** PRONI, De Ros Papers, D638/132, 28 March, 1797. **99** The newspapers of the time are littered with accounts of FitzGibbon's entertainments. The *Freeman's Journal* was particularly gushing. There is, for example, this example "The Lord Chancellor's house and living takes now the lead in the first line of fashion. If it will be granted that his revenue is great, his expenditure is princely ..." (edition of 9–12 January 1790, *Dublin News* for 9 January 1790). For a list of guests at a specific party, see the same invaluable journal, edition of 9 April 1795, *Dublin News* for 7 April 1795. The guest list included the usual government types: Camden, Shannon and Waterford, as well as Foster, who probably did not make too many appearances at Ely Place as a rule, and none after 1799 or so. In fairness, the *Dublin Evening Post* could swoon just as much. See the 12 June 1790 edition of that paper for a breathless account of a petit souper (sic) for Lord and Lady Westmorland and "a select set of about twenty." According to this squib, the company were "most elegantly entertained". **100** NLI, Leinster Papers, MS 631, Anne FitzGibbon, Lady Clare to the Duchess of Leinster, 4 February 1794. Westmorland commented with some disapproval on FitzGibbon's association with Ponsonby; he described it as an 'appearance of friendship ... which created great jealousy to many people", Westmorland Papers, Carton 1/f58 Westmorland to Dundas (?), 10 March 1792. FitzGibbon had evidently gone out of his way in the aftermath of the Regency Crisis to negotiate with George Ponsonby and bring him back to the government fold. Ponsonby's indiscreet revelation of these contacts caused something of a breech. As for the Duchess of Leinster, these pleasant visits might well have come to an abrupt end if she could have seen FitzGibbon's cruel letter to Eden relating her adultery with George Ogilvie, the man who was to become her second husband. The letter in question (Sneyd Muniments, 22 August 1785) was written in the wake of the failure of the commercial propositions, when FitzGibbon was in a particularly foul mood even for him. But why he would signal out the poor duchess is baffling. Her son had opposed the propositions, but no more than any other member of his party. Possibly his close ties to Fox and the other English Whigs made him, and his stepfather Ogilvie, the epitomes of opposition troublemaking. For a more empathetic account of the Duchess of Leinster's liaison and later marriage with Ogilvie, see Stella Tillyard, *Aristocrats* (New York, 1994), pp. 223, 226, 268–70 and 274–83. Not surprisingly, there was no welcome for radicalism in politics or in fashion at 6 Ely Place, as Lucy Fitzgerald, the Duchesss daughter discovered: "Apl. 18 We went to town for a ball at Lady Clare's. I had my hair turned close up, was reckoned democratic and was not danced with", Tillyard, p. 334. **101** PRONI, Normanton Papers, T3719/C29/45, p. 2. **102** *Hibernian Journal*, 14 January 1795, "To a certain lord". **103** *Volunteer Evening Post*, 12–14 April 1785, "For the *Volunteer Evening Post* Report of the Proceedings of the Inquest appointed by his most REDOUBTABLE MAJESTY KING HACKBALL. To enquire into the real character his Majesty's most declared and dangerous enemy JOHN FITZGIBBON, Attorney General to a person stiled King of Great Britain and Ireland". Sneyd Muniments, FitzGibbon to Auckland, 17 June 1800

CHAPTER 12

1 *HMC Fortescue*, i, p. 480, Lady Buckingham (writing on Buckingham's behalf) to W.W. Grenville, 13 June 1789; HO 100/27/170, Buckingham to Grenville, 26 June 1789. **2** Ibid., p. 545, Robert Hobart to W.W. Grenville, 1 December 1789. **3** HO 100/27/216-19, 27 July 1789, Sydney or Grenville (unclear in document) to Buckingham. **4** BM Add. MS 40180/f138–9, FitzGibbon to Buckingham, 20 July 1789. **5** *HMC Fortescue*, i, pp. 539–40, Grenville to Thurlow, 17 November 1789; p. 542, Thurlow to Grenville, ? November, 1789; pp. 542–3, Grenville to Hobart, 25 November 1789. **6** Ibid., p. 540. **7** Ibid., p. 540, Grenville to Thurlow, 18 November 1789. **8** Ibid., Thurlow to Grenville, same date. **9** Ibid., pp. 542–3. **10** Ibid., p. 544. **11** Ibid., p. 544. **12** Ibid. **13** Ibid., p. 546; R. Hobart to Grenville, 1 December 1789; entire letter pp. 544–6. **14** Ibid., p. 547, FitzGibbon to Grenville, 2 December 1789; entire letter pp. 546-8. **15** Ibid., p. 548. **16** Ibid. **17** Ibid. **18** Ibid., p. 548–9, Grenville to FitzGibbon, 2 December,1789. **19** bid., p. 550, Grenville to Westmorland, 5 December, 1789; pp. 550–1, Grenville to Hobart, same date. **20** Ibid., p. 550. **21** Ibid., p. 551, Thurlow to Grenville, 6 December 1789. **22** Ibid., p. 554, FitzGibbon to Grenville, 14 December, 1789. **23** Ibid., p. 551, Hobart to Grenville, 9 December, 1789. **24** Ibid., pp. 552–3, Grenville to FitzGibbon, 9 December 1789. **25** Ibid., p. 554, FitzGibbon to Grenville, 14 December 1789. **26** Ibid. Presumably FitzGibbon meant 1783. **27** Ibid., p. 555. **28** Ibid., p. 554. **29** HO 100/31/252 Westmorland to Dundas (?), 5 August, 1791; "If the Chancellor of England had a nephew in ye Army, no government who were [*sic*] obliged to consult him daily wd chuse to put [on?] him what he might term a slight but wd be happy I believe to embrace an opportunity of keeping him in good humour". **30** HO 100/43/319, Westmorland to Dundas, 24 May 1793. **31** See for example, Westmorland Papers, Carton 1/f114, FitzGibbon to Westmorland, 25 March 1795. **32** The *Dublin Evening Post*, alluded to their close relationship frequently, referring to the nefarious combination of "Lord Jacky", "Major Bobsy" [Hobart] and "Cooking Ned" [Edward Cooke]. See 13 November 1792 and 20 November 1792; See also Sneyd Muniments, 22 June 1799 for continue friendly contacts after Hobart's departure from government. **33** While I never have found any explicit statement to this effect, I suspect that uneasy memories of the embarrassingly outspoken and independent Midleton had much to do with the reluctance to appoint another Irishman to the Seals. For more information about Midleton, see *DNB*, ii, pp. 1291–2. **34** *Freeman's Journal*, 6–9 February 1790, House of Lords debates, 8 February 1790. **35** Ibid. 9–11, 11–13 March 1790; House of Lords debates, 9 and 10 March 1790. **36** Ibid., 25–27 February, 1790, House of Lords debates, 25 February 1790. **37** Ibid., 6–9 March 1790, House of Lords debates, 6 March 1790. **38** Ibid., 6–8 April 1790, House of Lords debates, 5 April 1790. **39** My thanks to Professor L.M. Cullen for bringing this detail to my attention. Of course, none of the accounts of the dispute, either in the contemporary newspapers, or in the younger Grattan's memoirs, took any notice of this motive. **40** *Irish Statutes*, vii, "An Act for Better Regulating the Corporation of the City of Dublin", Clause IX, p. 753. **41** *Freeman's Journal*, 13–15, 1790, "Postscript" for 16 April 1790; there is also the younger Grattan's account, *Grattan*, iv, pp. 1–7. **42** *Freeman's Journal*, 17–20 April 1790. **43** Ibid., 24–27 April 1790. **44** *Dublin Evening Post*, 13 May 1790. **45** Ibid.; *Freeman's Journal*, 13–15 May 1790. **46** *Freeman's Journal*, 13–15 May 1790. **47** *Freeman's Journal*, 2—28 May 1790. **48** Ibid. **49** Ibid., 8–10 June, 1790. **50** Ibid., 24–26 June, 1790; 10–13 July, 1790; the election took place on 24 June and the hearing before the privy council on 10 July 1790 **51** *Grattan*, iv, p. 6. **52** Ibid., p. 7. **53** Ibid. **54** Ibid. **55** Ibid. **56** Ibid. **57** *Freeman's Journal*, 13–15 July 1790; the meeting took place on 13 July 1790. **58** Ibid., 15–17 July 1790. **59** Ibid. **60** Ibid. **61** Ibid., 20–23 July 1790; *Dublin News* for 21 July 1790. **62** Ibid. **63** *Grattan*, iv, p. 8. **64** Ibid. **65** *Freeman's Journal*, 27–29 July 1790, House of Lords debates, 24 July 1790; all subsequent quotes from the speech are from this same source. **66** Or so Sir Edward Newenham claimed. He claimed at a subsequent meeting "I have in my hand a kind of pamphlet, published in Faulkners Journal [*sic*]". See *Freeman's Journal*, 3–5 August 1790. Actually, the speech appeared in all the major Dublin prints in one form or another. For the quote from the *Freemans Journal*, see 29–31 July 1790, *Dublin News* for 29 July 1790. **67** *Freeman's Journal*, 27–29 July 1790, House of Lords debates, 24 July 1790. **68** Ibid.; See also *Irish Statutes* vii, p. 752: "And be it enacted by the authority aforesaid, That the name of every person who shall hereafter be elected by the lord mayor and aldermen of the said city or the usual quorum of them to serve in the office of place of lord mayor to the said city, shall be returned to them by the commons of the common council of the said city for their approbation; without which approbation such person shall not be capable of serving in the office or place of lord mayor ..." **69** *Freeman's Journal*, 29–31 July 1790, *Dublin News*, 29 July 1790. **70** Ibid., 3–5 August 1790. **71** Ibid. **72** *Grattan*, iv, pp. 9–18. **73** Ibid., p. 10. **74** Ibid., pp. 11–12. **75** Ibid., p. 12. **76** Ibid., p. 13. **77** Ibid., p. 14. **78** Ibid., pp. 15–16. **79** Ibid., p. 10. **80** Ibid., p. 17. **81** Ibid., p. 25, Grattan to Rev. Edward Berwick, 3 September 1790. **82** Ibid. **83** Grattan also seems to have asked Berwick to ask the advice of Charlemont, also no great friend of FitzGibbon. **84** *HMC Donoughmore*, p. 324, Lord Donoughmore to John Hely Hutchinson, 2 October 1790. **85** *Freeman's Journal*, 7–9 December 1790. **86** *HMC Kenyon*, p. 531.

CHAPTER 13

1 Falkiner, p. 149 **2** *Freeman's Journal*, 20–22 July 1790, "Postscript" for 20 July 1790; 20–23 July 1790, *Dublin News* for 21 July 1790. **3** Ibid., 22–24 July 1790. **4** Ibid. **5** Dublin: ISPO,

Westmorland Papers, Carton 1/f8. 6 ISPO, Westmorland Papers, Carton 1/f8. 7 *Freeman's Journal*, 14–16 April 1791, news item dated 14 April 1791. 8 *Freeman's Journal*, 19–21 July 1791, item dated 24 June 1791. 9 See L.M. Cullen, "Late eighteenth century politicization in Ireland: problems in its study and its french links", pp.137–45 in *Culture et Pratiques Politiques en France et en Irelande XVI e-XVIIIe Siecle: Actes du Colloque de Marseille 28 septembre–2 octobre, 1988*; see also David W. Miller, ed., *Peep O'Day Boys and Defenders: Selected Documents on the County Armagh Disturbances: 1784–96* (PRONI: Belfast, 1990). 10 *HMC Charlemont*, ii, p. 105, FitzGibbon to Charlemont, 16 July 1789. 11 *Faulkner's Dublin Journal* reported this more sympathetic news item on 6 May 1789. This item was perfectly in keeping with *Faulkner's* fundamentally hostile attitude; it gave an impression of sectarian harmony, which in turn strengthened the implication, much emphasized by reactionaries within government and without, that Catholics had no reason to look for further rights. 12 *Freeman's Journal*, 3–5 August 1790, essay by "Ormonde"; see also 17–19 August 1790, essay by "Plain Truth". 13 *Freeman's Journal*, 24–27, 1790, *Dublin News*, 24 July 1790. 14 Ibid., 31 July–3 August 1790. 15 ISPO, Westmorland Papers, Carton 1/f8, op. cit. 16 Ibid. 17 R. Madden, *The United Irishmen, Their Lives and Times* (Dublin, 1857), p. 223. 18 London, Public Records Office, Chatham Papers, 30/8/26, Westmorland to Pitt, 12 October 1790. 19 Westmorland Papers, Carton 1/f12. 20 Westmorland Papers, Letter Book, Westmorland to Pitt, 5 March 1791. 21 Ibid., Letter Book, Westmorland to Pitt, 7 March 1791. 22 Ibid. (in the letter book incorrectly dates this letter 1792. Internal evidence suggests 1791, especially the allusion to the political activities of English Catholics to gain relief: "The Catholics insist to obtain further privilidges [*sic*] (which they understand they are to be given in England by ye agitation of that Question ...". 23 *HMC PV Smith*, p. 367. 24 Westmorland Papers, Letter Book, 7 March 1791, op. cit. 25 Dublin: ISPO, Rebellion Papers, 620/19/23. 26 Westmorland Papers, Letter Book, 12 August 1791. 27 *Grattan*, iv, p. 41. 28 Rebellion Papers, 620/19/24: "The Whig Club is not a transfusion from the People. We do not thoroughly understand that Club and they do not feel for us." 29 Westmorland, Letter Book, Grenville to Westmorland, 24 March, 1791; "Fox is to move to extend the provisions to all Catholics". 30 *Grattan*, iv, p. 41, op. cit. 31 Westmorland Papers, Letter Book. 32 Rebellion Papers, 620/19/28. 33 Westmorland Papers, Letter Book, Dundas to Westmorland, 6 October 1791. 34 Marianne Elliot, *Wolfe Tone: Prophet of Irish Independence* (New Haven, 1990), pp. 154–55. 35 Westmorland Papers, Letter Book, Dundas to Westmorland, 6 October 1791. 36 Westmorland Papers, Letter Book, Westmorland to Dundas, 11 October 1791. 37 Ibid. 38 Westmorland Papers, Carton 1/f25, Pitt to Westmorland, 22 December 1791. 39 Ibid., Carton 1/f27. 40 Ibid., Carton 1/f41, Westmorland to Dundas, 11 January 1792: "... if the suspicion shall be confirmed (a suspicion too much strengthened by your Dispatch and the ... questionable language and situation of Mr [Richard] Burke) that the British Govt. means to take up the Catholics and play what is called a Catholic Game ... a stand will be taken by ye Protestants without distinction against ye government in their own Defence. No administration will be able to conduct His Majesty's business without expressly stipulating a different policy and His Majestys government will be laid at the feet of those aristocratic following which are at present in [opposition] to it." 41 Westmorland Papers, Carton 1/f42, Westmorland to Dundas, 14 January 1792: "Mr Burke has written a most impertinent letter demanding a categorical (?) answer from government; he is ye agent of ye most violent set of agitators, his Language has been most imprudent and he's done much mischief here"; see also, Letter Book, Westmorland to Dundas, 17 December 1791. 42 A complete text of this petition appears in *Grattan*, iv, p. 42. 43 Westmorland Papers, Carton 1/f196; See also *An Address from the General Committee of the Roman Catholics to their Protestant Fellow Subjects and to the Public in General* (Dublin, 1792), which offered a justification of the purge. 44 20–22 December 1791, *Dublin News* for 20 December 1791, op. cit. 45 For allusions to "Democratic Catholics" see Westmorland Papers, Westmorland to Dundas, 12 December 1791; for allusions to "Clubs of Brotherhood" see the same letter and Carton 1/f57, Westmorland to Dundas, 28 November 1791. 46 Westmorland

Papers, Carton 1/f42, Westmorland to Dundas, 14 January 1792. **47** Westmorland Papers, Carton 1/f42. **48** Westmorland Papers, Letter Book, Westmorland to Hobart, 17 December 1791. **49** Westmorland Papers, Carton 1/f41, Westmorland to Dundas, 11 January 1792. **50** Ibid. **51** Ibid. **52** Ibid. **53** Ibid. **54** Ibid. **55** Westmorland Papers, Carton 1/f42, Westmorland to Dundas, 14 January 1792. **56** Westmorland Papers, Carton 1/f43, Dundas to Westmorland, 16 January 1792. **57** Ibid. **58** Westmorland Papers, Carton 1/f46, Westmorland to Dundas, 21 January 1792. **59** Ibid. **60** Westmorland Papers, Letterbook, Westmorland to Pitt, 24 February, 1792. **61** The debate appears in full in *A report of the Debates in both Houses of Parliament on the Roman Catholic Bill* (Dublin, 1792). **62** Westmorland Papers, Letter Book, Westmorland to Dundas, 21 February 1792. **63** *Report of the Debates in both Houses of Parliament on the Roman Catholic Bill* (Dublin, 1792), p. 245. **64** *Dublin Evening Post*, 6 March 1792, House of Lords debates, 3 March 1792. **65** Ibid. **66** *Freeman's Journal*, 20–21 March 1792, House of Lords debates, 21 March 1792. **67** *Dublin Evening Post*, 22 March 1792, House of Lords debates, 21 March, 1792. **68** *Dublin Evening Post*, 22 March 1792, Postscript for same date. **69** *Hibernian Journal*, 26 September 1792, "To the Lord High Chancellor of Ireland". **70** *Faulkner's Dublin Journal*, 12–14 April 1792, *Dublin News*, 14 April 1792. **71** *Dublin Evening Post*, 22 March 1792; the *Dublin Evening Post* expressed the ironic hope that his "speedy falling off may not evince his having commenced the champion of freedom from party motives, rather than a sincere regard for constitutional principles." **72** *Faulkner's Dublin Journal*, 16–19 June 1792, *Dublin News* for 19 June 1792, "Combination". **73** *Morning Post* or *Dublin Courant*, 10 July 1792. **74** Rebellion Papers, 620/19/114, report dated 30 December 1792.

CHAPTER 14

1 Westmorland Papers, Carton 1/f55. **2** Westmorland of course immediately blamed Richard Burke. See Westmorland Papers, Carton 1/f56, Westmorland to Dundas, 7 June 1792: "It is likewise possible that this paper, like all ye other Papers ye Committee have produced, may have no effect on ye minds of ye Catholics and that ye country people may continue as little moved by this agitation as by ye other [measures] of ye same gentlemen with ye assistance of Mr Rcd. Burke may have attempted." FitzGibbon, for his part, attributed the idea to Tone. See his letter to Pitt, dated 14 May, 1793 (PRO, Chatham Papers, 30/8/327,f843): "He was also the original projector of the Catholic Convention." Tone himself attributed the idea to Myles Keon of Roscommon (*Tone*, i, p. 62). If Keon was indeed the father of the convention, his role represented an ironic turn of events indeed; he had been one of the more obsequious Catholics in 1784 and had tried, unsuccessfully, to organize a loyal petition from the Catholics of Connaught. See Bolton MS, 16,350/62, Mile Keon to Thomas Orde, 2 November 1784. **3** Bolton MS, 16,350/23 (dated 2 July 1784) and 16,350/24 (dated 28 September, 1784). **4** Westmorland Papers, Carton 1/f55. **5** Westmorland Papers, Carton 1/f61, Westmorland to Dundas, 2 May 1792. **6** Westmorland Papers, Carton 1/f55. **7** For instances of the pressures on Burke see, Dublin, National Library of Ireland, Melville Papers, MS 54a/f57, Edward Byrne to Richard Burke, 28 May 1792 and f/60 Burke to Dundas, 5 June 1792. **8** Westmorland Papers, Carton 1/f56, Westmorland to Dundas, 7 June 1792. **9** Ibid. **10** Ibid. **11** Ibid. **12** For the entire text of the resolutions see the *Dublin Evening Post*, 25 August 1792, "County Limerick meeting 21 August 1792". **13** *Hibernian Journal*, Edition of 29 August 1792, Postscript for 27 August 1792, "Intelligence Extraordinary" by "Tasso". **14** Westmorland Papers, Carton 1/ f57, Hobart to Westmorland, 25 June 1792. **15** Westmorland Papers, Carton 1/ f62, Westmorland to Dundas, 19 September 1792; Carton 1/f69, same to same, 18 November 1792. **16** Elliot, p. 184. **17** Ibid., p. 185; see also *Proceedings at the Catholic Meeting of Dublin Convened 31 October 1792, with the letter of the Corporation of Dublin to the Protestants of Ireland* (Dublin, 1792) which contains a full text of the resolutions and the Catholic response. **18** Westmorland Papers, Carton 1/f69, 18 November 1792. **19** Ibid. **20** Ibid. **21** Ibid. **22** Ibid. **23** Ibid.

24 Ibid. 25 Ibid. 26 Westmorland Papers, Carton 1/f71. 27 Ibid. 28 Ibid. 29 Dublin: National Library of Ireland, MS 886, Westmorland to Pitt, 28 November 1792. 30 Ibid. 31 Ibid. 32 Ibid. 33 Ibid. 34 Westmorland, Letter Book, Westmorland to Pitt, 14 December, 1792. 35 Ibid. 36 Ibid. 37 Tone, *Life*, i, p. 77. 38 Elliot, p. 196; Westmorland Papers, Letter Book, Westmorland to Pitt, 10 December, 1792. 39 Westmorland Papers, Carton 1/f79, Westmorland to Pitt, 7 December 1792; Tone, *Life*, i, p. 77. 40 Westmorland, Letter Book, Westmorland to Pitt, 14 December 1792; Carton 1/f79 Westmorland to Pitt, 7 December 1792, Elliot, p. 198. 41 Westmorland Papers, Carton 1/f79, Westmorland to Pitt, 7 December 1792. 42 It was ordered printed by authority of the convention on 7 December 1792 and eventually published in January 1793. 43 Tone, *Life*, i, p. 85. 44 Ibid. 45 Maureen Wall, "The Catholics and the Establishment, 1782–93", in Gerard O'Brien, ed., *Catholic Ireland in the Eighteenth Century: Collected Essays of Maureen Wall* (Dublin, 1989), p. 159. 46 *Morning Post* or *Dublin Courant*, 8 September 1792. 47 For the entirety of this dispatch, see Westmorland Papers, Carton 1/f87, Dundas to Westmorland, simply dated, January 1793; his cover letter for the dispatch is dated 3 January 1793 (Carton 1/f86). 48 Ibid. 49 Ibid. 50 For a full text of the bill, see *A Collection of Statutes which have been enacted during the Reign of his present majesty for the Relief of English and Irish Catholics, and a short account of the disabilities to which they are still subject* (London, 1812), pp. 134–5. 51 NLI MS 886, Westmorland to Pitt, 11 January 1793. 52 Ibid. 53 Westmorland Papers, Letter Book, Westmorland to Dundas. 54 *Freeman's Journal*, 10–15 January 1793; , House of Lords debates, 10 January 1793. 55 Ibid. 56 Ibid. 57 Ibid. 58 Ibid. 59 NLI MS 886, Westmorland to Pitt, 11 January 1793. 60 NLI, Melville Papers, 54A/f74, "Memorandum of the Conversation which passed with Mr Dundas at Wimbledon on the 21st and 22nd of January 1793 in the presence of Mr Pitt. 61 For the rather abortive negotiations with Abercorn, see M. Elliot, pp. 187-88,201–2; see, also, HO 100/43/15, Cooke to Nepean, 26 February 1793 and HO 100/43/21–3, Hobart to Nepean, 26 February, 1793. 62 *Freeman's Journal*, 14–16 March 1793, House of Lords debates, 13 March 1793. 63 For their remarks and the full debate see the *Freemans Journal*, 14–16 March 1793, 13 March 1793. 64 PRONI, T3244/11/1. 65 PRONI, T3247/2139. 66 Sneyd Muniments, FitzGibbon to Auckland, 11 January 1797. 67 Kent County Archives, Camden Papers, C/0183, FitzGibbon to Camden, 28 August 1798 (These papers are available on microfilm in the Trinity College Library.) 68 Act of Union Speech, (1800 print) p. 17. 69 *The Speech of the Right Honorable John, Lord Baron FitzGibbon, Lord High Chancellor of Ireland, Delivered in the House of Peers on the Second Reading of the Bill for the Relief of His Majesty's Roman Catholic Subjects* (Dublin, 1798), p. 31. 70 Ibid., p. 3. 71 The quoted phrase appears on p. 21; on evil intentions of old Irish see pp. 37–8. 72 p. 6. 73 Ibid. 74 p. 13. 75 Ibid. 76 p. 28. 77 pp. 23–6. 78 p. 31 79 *On the Duties of Christian* (Dublin, 1793), p. 96; for the supremely unenthusiastic response, see Elliot, p. 204. 80 FitzGibbon, *Speech on Catholic Bill of 1793*, p. 31. 81 FitzGibbon, *Speech on Catholic Bill of 1793*, p. 39. 82 Madden, p. 223. 83 Ibid., p. 20. 84 Ibid., p. 36. 85 Ibid., pp. 21–2. 86 Elliot, p. 207. 87 *Freeman's Journal*, 14–16 March 1793, House of Lords debates, 13 March, 1793. 88 Ibid. 89 Ibid. 90 *Freeman's Journal*, 2–4 April 1793, Postscript for 2 April 1793. 91 *Burke Correspondence*. 92 The turn of phrase appeared somewhat later, in an editorial in the *Dublin Evening Post*, dated 8 January 1795. 93 HO 100/43/127, Westmorland to Dundas, 21 March 1793. 94 *Freeman's Journal*, 16–19 March 1793, House of Lords debates, 15 March 1793. 95 Ibid. 96 *Dublin Evening Post*, 14 February 1793, House of Lords debates, 11 February 1793. 97 Westmorland Papers, Carton 1/f88, Report of the Committee of Secrecy dated 5 February 1793. 98 Ibid. 99 Ibid. 100 Ibid. 101 Ibid. 102 Ibid. 103 Ibid. 104 *Dublin Evening Post*, 28 March 1793, House of Lords debates, 25 March 1793. 105 Ibid. 106 Ibid. 107 *Defence of the Sub-committee of the Catholics of Ireland from the Imputations attempted to be thrown on that body, particularly from the charge of supporting the Defenders* (Dublin, 1793), p. 1. 108 Ibid., p. 3. 109 Ibid., pp. 3–4. 110 Ibid., p. 4. 111 Ibid., pp. 6–7. 112 Ibid., p. 7. 113 Ibid. 114 Ibid. 115 Ibid., p. 8. 116 Ibid. 117 Ibid. 118 Ibid., p. 9. 119 Ibid., pp. 10–11. 120 Ibid. 121 John Sweetman, *A*

Refutation of the charges attempted to be made against the Secretary for the Sub-committee of the Catholics of Ireland (Dublin, 1793), p. 2; for his account of his dealings with Nugent see pp. 2–6. **122** Ibid., p. 8. **123** Ibid. **124** See his regurgitation of the same charges in *The Speech of the Right Honorable John, Earl of Clare, Lord High Chancellor of Ireland, on a motion made by the Earl of Moira, February 19, 1798* (Dublin, London, 1798), pp. 18–19. **125** *Irish Statutes*, xvi, p. 794. **126** *Dublin Evening Post*, 13 July 1793, House of Lords debates, 11 July 1793. **127** Ibid. **128** Westmorland Papers, Carton 1/f69, 18 November 1792. **129** *Dublin Evening Post*, 28 March, 1793, House of Lords debates, 25 March 1793. **130** *Dublin Evening Post*, 1 August 1793, *Dublin News* for same date. **131** *Freeman's Journal*, 16–19 March 1793, House of Lords debates, 15 March 1793 "... although it would be highly indecent for any House of Parliament to meddle with the charter of the present Trinity College, which by the will of the founder was established peculiarly for Protestants, yet his idea was that any future College to be founded should not be for Catholics exclusively, but open both to them and Protestants and to admit indiscriminately fellows and professors of both religions." **132** HO 100/44/240 Westmorland to Dundas, 11 July 1793; for the clause itself see HO 100/44/263. **133** HO 100/43/238, Sackville Hamilton to Hobart, 25 April 1793. **134** HO 100/43/234–5, Sackville Hamilton to Hobart, 22 April 1793. **135** HO 100/43/238. **136** *Dublin Evening Post*, 24 August 1793, "CATHOLIC DINNER", 20 August 1793. **137** HO 100/46/75, [unknown] to Richard Burke, 18 July, 1793. **138** NLI, Melville Papers, 54A/f80,Richard Burke to Dundas, 21 July 1793. **139** HO 100/43/97–8; endorsed note dated 16 March 1793 on the subject of Hobarts dispatch of 12 March 1793. **140** Chatham Papers, 30/8/327/f843, FitzGibbon to Pitt, 14 May 1793. **141** Tone, *Life*, i, p. 138: "FitzGibbon's want of temper and undoubted partiality will let in his resentments and his affections to bias his decisions." **142** Elliot, p. 69. **143** Chatham Papers, 30/8/327. **144** Ibid. **145** Ibid. **146** They included Harvey Hay in Wexford *(Dublin Evening Post*, 18 July 1793, Postscript for same date); James Scully of Tipperary (*Dublin Evening Post*, 25 July 1793); Edward Bellew of Louth (*Dublin Evening Post*, 8 August 1793, *Dublin News* for same date); and Hugh O'Beirne of Leitrim (*Dublin Evening Post*, 14 December 1793) I am listing only those men who were explicitly named as Roman Catholics or, in the case of O'Beirne, can be assumed to be Roman Catholics by the highly unreliable criterion of name. There may have been others buried in the newspaper columns that I missed, or assumed, again by the highly unreliable criterion of name, to be Protestant. **147** *Dublin Evening Post*, 25 July 1793: "FOR THE DUBLIN EVENING POST". **148** *Morning Post* or *Dublin Courant*, 5 September 1793, Dublin news for 4 September 1793. **149** See for example his remarks to Lord Camden in a letter dated 7 September, 1796, where he suggests that the government should keep an especially close eye on the Catholics in the event of any invasion attempts by the French (Camden Papers, C/183/8). **150** His speech to Lord Moira contained a classic example of his new public rhetoric on the Catholic issue. See pp. 18–19

CHAPTER 15

1 HO 100/43/284–6, Westmorland to Dundas (?), 7 May 1793. **2** Ibid., see also HO 100/43/294–6, Privy Council memorandum dated 8 May 1793. **3** HO 100/43/294–6. **4** HO 100/43/299, Westmorland to Dundas, 9 May 1793. **5** HO 100/43/284-6. **6** HO 100/43/294–6: "The evil first began to show itself in November last and it arose principally, if not entirely from the distressed situation of the Kingdom and the Fears which were then entertained of its Tranquillity being interrupted ... In the town of Belfast in particular the prospect of a local tumult there induced a sudden withdrawal of Deposits from the Banks there and had given an almost universal check to credit." **7** *Freeman's Journal*, 13 July 1793, House of Lords debates, "Everyone saw the mischievous consequences that had arisen to this country, by the injury that public credit experienced from the sedition propagated through the nation by a petty congress that existed in this metropolis." **8** *An Accurate Report of the Speech of the Right Honorable John Foster, Speaker of the House of*

Commons (Dublin, 1793) p. 29. 9 Westmorland Papers, Carton 1/f68, Westmorland to Pitt, 3 November 1792. 10 Rebellion Papers, 620/19/112, spy's report dated 29 November 1792. 11 Ibid. 12 Westmorland Papers, Carton 1/f76, Westmorland to Pitt, 1 December 1792. 13 Westmorland Papers, Carton 1/f77, Westmorland to Pitt, 4 December 1792. 14 HO 100/42/214–15, Hobart to Nepean, 28 January 1793. 15 HO 100/43/9; the act received the royal assent on 26 February 1793. 16 HO 100/43/71–3 Hobart to Nepean, 8 March 1793. 17 Ibid. 18 *Dublin Evening Post*, 5 September 1793, "DUBLIN CASTLE" 19 HO 100/43/87, Hobart to Nepean, 9 March 1793; HO 100/43/117–19, Same to Same, 19 March 1793. 20 HO 100/43/319, Westmorland to Dundas, 24 May 1793. 21 HO 100/43/323–8; this document, which bears no date, is an account, by county, of the disturbances. 22 *The Fall and Rise of the Irish Nation: The Catholic Question 1690–1830* (Dublin: 1992), p. 182; my summary of Bartlett's original and insightful argument is necessarily cursory. For his complete study of the militia disturbances, see Thomas Bartlett, "An End to Moral Economy: the Irish Militia Disturbances of 1793", *Past and Present*, 99, (May 1983), pp. 41–64. 23 HO 100/43/319, op. cit. 24 HO 100/43/323-8. 25 HO 100/44/115–19; this document consists of memoranda on the disturbances, submitted by various magistrates and anonymous sources. Denis Brownes memorandum is dated 6 June, 1793. 26 HO 100/43/323–8. 27 Ibid. 28 Melville Papers, 54A/f80, Richard Burke to Dundas, 21 July 1793. 29 HO 100/44/287, Westmorland to Dundas, 18 July, 1793. 30 *Dublin Evening Post*, 20 July 1793, House of Lords debates, 18 July 1793. 31 HO 100/46/75 ? to Richard Burke, 18 July 1793 32 Rebellion Papers, 620/20/1. 33 Ibid., "Let the national convention draw up 1st a DECLARATION OF RIGHTS personal, political, religious, national, and 2ndly, a PETITION OF RIGHT from the People of Ireland and the king of Ireland." 34 HO 100/44/15, Cooke to Nepean, 29 May, 1793 and 100/44/17. 35 Westmorland Papers, Carton 1/f 88. 36 HO 100/43/89–90, Hobart to Nepean, 12 March 1793; HO 100/43/103, General Whyte to Cooke, 17 March 1793. 37 HO 100/43/67, Hobart to Nepean, 6 March 1793. 38 *Freeman's Journal*, 13 July 1793, House of Lords debates, 10 July 1793. 39 Ibid. 40 Elliot, pp. 227–8. 41 The Sheares brothers were the sons of a Cork banker. John, the younger, was apparently the more intelligent and forceful of the two. Notwithstanding their differences in temperament, they were devoted to each other and to revolutionary ideas, which they had imbibed during a sojourn in France. FitzGibbon had an early and intimate acquaintance with the two brothers. O'Flanagan, whose biography of FitzGibbon is embellished with charming, if sometimes questionable, anecdotes, claimed that FitzGibbon and Henry Sheares had both courted the same young lady. She chose Henry Sheares over FitzGibbon, then a "young briefless barrister". (*O'Flanagan*, ii, p. 217). It is by now impossible to determine the truth of this poignant bit of sentimental comedy. If FitzGibbon was indeed disappointed in love, the experience does not seem to have wounded him very deeply; up to and even after his marriage, he seems to have found plenty of amorous consolation. Moreover, he could easily have found other opportunities to become acquainted with the Sheares brothers in the social milieu of 18th century Ireland. FitzGibbon attended TCD at roughly the same time as the Sheares brothers, and they shared a common acquaintance with the Roche family. (*O'Flanagan*, ii, p. 219) It is true that FitzGibbon took an inordinate amount of interest in the Sheares brothers, and a romantic might conjecture or hope that memories of his lost love inspired him to look after the well-being of her widower and her brother-in-law. But FitzGibbon may simply have wanted to save Henry Sheares, and incidentally his brother, for their own sakes. The elder Sheares in particular seems to have had a feckless charm that appealed to the protective instincts of a good many people, including the elder Mr Roche and Jonah Barrington. Whatever the foundation for this curious relationship, FitzGibbon's conduct toward the two brothers in the summer of 1793 displayed no marks of sentiment. 42 *Freeman's Journal*, 20 July 1793, House of Lords debates, 18 July 1793. 43 Ibid. 44 Rebellion Papers, 620/20/23. 45 Oliver MacDonagh, *The Hereditary Bondsman: Daniel O'Connell 1775–1829* (New York, 1988), p. 26. 46 HO 100/43/42, Hobart to Nepean, 1 March 1793. 47 HO 100/43/42, Hobart to Nepean, 1 March, 1793. 48 Rebellion Papers, 620/20/28.

49 Ibid. **50** Ibid. **51** Ibid. **52** Ibid. **53** Ibid. **54** *O'Flanagan*, ii, p. 216–17; according to O'Flanagan's account, one of FitzGibbon's social intimates, one Colonel Murray, passed on a hint to Rowan of the risk he was running. Rowan undoubtedly passed this intimation on to Butler. **55** HO 100/46/148–9, Spy's report to Dundas (?), 10 April 1794; see also Elliot, pp. 239–45. **56** HO 100/52/138-9, S. Hamilton to Evan Nepean, 3 July 1794. **57** HO 100/52/46–7, Westmorland to Dundas, 12 May 1794. **58** HO 100/52/230, S. Douglas to John King, 23 October 1794. **59** HO 100/52/232–3, King (?) to Douglas, 24 October 1794. **60** HO 100/52/46–7, Westmorland to Dundas, 12 May 1794. **61** *Beresford*, ii, p. 29, Marcus Beresford to John Beresford, 2 May 1794; HO 100/57/229, Pelham to J. King, 30 April 1795. Those two superb writers, Somerville and Ross, tell a charming story involving FitzGibbon, Jackson's beautiful widow and a feckless young barrister by the name of Richard Guinness. Jacksons widow was apparently quite a femme fatale and under the influence of her persuasive charm, Guinness agreed to act as chief mourner at Jacksons funeral. This action almost destroyed his legal career until FitzGibbon intervened. He allowed Guinness to appear in Chancery, a resounding indication that the Lord Chancellor of Ireland was convinced of the young man's fundamental soundness and loyalty. In the course of his kindly conversation with Guinness, FitzGibbon referred to Mrs. Jackson, no doubt with the appreciation of a true connoisseur of such things, as "a handsome jade". This anecdote appears in *An Incorruptible Irishman, being an account of Chief Justice Charles Kendal Bushe and his wife Nancy Crampton and their times, 1763–1843* (London, 1932) pp. 87–8. **62** *Rebellion Papers*, 620/47/41, FitzGibbon to Cooke, 13 August 1799. **63** Chatham Correspondence, 30/8/256, Westmorland to Pitt, 21 October 1794. **64** *Rebellion Papers*, 620/47/41. **65** Ibid. **66** *Beresford*, ii, pp. 29–31, Marcus Beresford to John Beresford, 7 May 1794. **67** Young Beresford seems to have been Tone's chief negotiator with the government. The agreement with Tone appears to have been taken from suggestions outlined in his letter to his father of 7 May 1794, cited above. **68** HO 100/52/46–7, Westmorland to Dundas, 12 May 1794. **69** HO 100/52/72–3 Cooke to Nepean, 26 May 1794. **70** HO 100/52/159, S. Hamilton to Nepean, 14 July 1794.

CHAPTER 16

1 Westmorland Papers, Carton 1/f42, Westmorland to Dundas, 14 January 1792. **2** HO 100/34/35, Westmorland to Pitt, 1 January 1792. **3** Westmorland Papers, Carton 1, f79, Westmorland to Pitt, 7 December 1792; Carton 1, f78, Westmorland to Dundas, 5 December 1792. **4** HO 100/43/21–3, Hobart to Nepean, 23 February 1793. **5** HO 100/42/246, Hobart to Nepean, 5 February 1793. **6** HO 100/43/21–3, op. cit. **7** HO 100/43/15, Cooke to Nepean, 26 February, 1793. **8** PR (1786) 275–314. **9** Ibid. pp. 291–2. **10** Ibid., p. 314. **11** HO 100/43/71–3, Hobart to Nepean, 8 March 1793; HO 100/44/125–7, Hobart to Nepean, 11 June 1793. **12** For the provisions of these various bills, see HO 100/44/125–7, Hobart to Nepean, 11 June 1793; HO 100/44/227–9, Hobart to Nepean, 11 July 1793 and HO 100/45/166–7, Hobart to George Rose, 29 November 1793. **13** HO 100/44/227–9, Hobart to Nepean, 11 July 1793. **14** HO 100/44/172–3, Hobart to Dundas, 21 June 1793. **15** HO 100/44/268–9, Westmorland to Dundas, 5 July 1793. **16** Ibid. **17** Ibid. **18** Ibid. **19** HO 100/44/214–17, Hobart to Nepean, 7 July 1793. **20** Ibid. **21** HO 100/46/161–4, Cooke to Nepean, 7 February 1794. **22** Ibid. **23** HO 100/51/159–60, Sylvester Douglas to Nepean, 5 February 1794. **24** Ibid. **25** HO 100/46/161–4, op. cit. **26** HO 100/51/192–3, Sylvester Douglas to Nepean, 17 February 1794. **27** HO 100/51/244–9, Douglas to Nepean, 11 March 1794. **28** NLI, MS 886, Shannon to Westmorland, 14 December 1793. **29** HO 100/46/161–4. **30** HO 100/51/227–9, Sylvester Douglas to Nepean, 5 March 1794. **31** HO 100/52/82-3, Sackville Hamilton to Sylvester Douglas, 2 June 1794. **32** HO 100/46/161–4. **33** Westmorland Papers, Carton 1/f58, Westmorland to Pitt(?), 10 March 1792. **34** Chatham Correspondence, 30/8/191, Westmorland to Pitt, ? March 1793. **35** For his comments on the pension bill see NLI, Melville Papers, 54/3, FitzGibbon to Dundas,

January–April (?), 1793. **36** The comments on the Responsibility Bill appear in a memorandum from FitzGibbon to Westmorland, dated 7 April, 1794. (Edinburgh: Advocates Library, Glenbervie Letterbooks, pp. 40–5). **37** Sheffield Public Library, Fitzwilliam Privacy (uncatalogued, NLI microfilm p. 5642), Portland to Fitzwilliam, 17 October 1792. **38** Chatham Papers, 30/8/218, Westmorland to Pitt, 1 April 1794. **39** Chatham Papers, 30/8/248, Westmorland to Pitt, 18 July 1794. **40** Chatham Papers, 30/8/271, Westmorland to Pitt, 23 October 1794. **41** Chatham Papers, 30/8/278, Westmorland to Pitt, 30 November 1794. **42** See for example Fitzwilliam Papers, O'Beirne to Fitzwilliam, 1 November 1794. **43** Westmorland Papers, Carton 1/f132, Cooke to Westmorland, 18 January 1795. **44** HO 100/51/244, Douglas to Nepean, 11 March 1794. **45** Fitzwilliam Papers, O'Beirne to Fitzwilliam, 6 September 1794. **46** Ibid., O'Beirne to Fitzwilliam, 1 November 1794. **47** Chatham Papers, 30/8/325, Pitt to Westmorland, 19 November 1794. **48** HO 100/56/270–1, Fitzwilliam to Portland, 13 February 1795. **49** Chatham Papers, 30/8/325, Pitt to Westmorland, 19 November 1794. **50** Pitt articulated these sentiments with particular clarity in a letter to Westmorland dated 19 October, 1794 (Chatham Papers, 19 October 1794). **51** Fitzwilliam Papers, Portland to Fitzwilliam, 4 December 1794. **52** Fitzwilliam Papers, O'Beirne to Fitzwilliam, 1 November 1794. **53** HO 100/46/259–60, Fitzwilliam to Portland (?), 8 January 1795. **54** HO 100/51/201–2, S. Douglas to Nepean, 20 February 1794; HO 100/51/225, Douglas to Dundas, 1 March 1794. **55** HO 100/46/152, Nepean to Keogh (purportedly), 28 March 1794. **56** HO 100/46/154–7, Keogh to Nepean, 15 April 1794. **57** The evidence for Grattan's incitement comes, admittedly, from two highly biased sources: see Westmorland Papers, Carton 1/f115, Cooke to Westmorland, 11 March 1795 and Sneyd Muniments, FitzGibbon to Auckland, 25 March 1795; but the fact that Grattan took management of the "Catholic business" suggests the truth of claims made by FitzGibbon and Cooke (HO 100/56/222-28, Fitzwilliam to Portland, February ? 1795). **58** HO 100/46/259–60, Fitzwilliam to Portland (?), 15 February 1795. **59** HO 100/46/264–7, Fitzwilliam to Portland, 15 February 1795. **60** Westmorland Papers, Carton 1/f111, John Pollock to Westmorland, 15 April 1795. **61** Westmorland Papers, Carton 1/f133, Cooke to Westmorland, 23 January 1795. **62** HO 100/46/268–70, Fitzwilliam to Portland, 28 January 1795. **63** HO 100/46/237–42, memorandum dated February 1795, unsigned, but probably Portland. **64** Ibid. **65** Ibid. **66** Chatham Papers, 30/8/324–5, Westmorland to Pitt, 15 February 1795. **67** HO 100/56/290–1, Portland to Fitzwilliam, 23 February 1793. **68** Fitzwilliam Papers, FitzGibbon to Fitzwilliam, 7 March 1795. **69** Westmorland Papers, Carton 1/f114, FitzGibbon to Westmorland, 25 March 1795; the published apologia appeared under the title, *A Letter from Earl Fitzwilliam, recently retired from this county, to the Earl of Carlisle* (Dublin and London, 1795). **70** Ibid.; for the discussions of a union between Fitzwilliam and Portland see HO 100/56/292–7, Fitzwilliam to Portland, 20 February 1795; in this dispatch, Fitzwilliam queries Portland on why he would delay concessions and suggests that a union would be the only possible pretext. He adds "... doubtless the end is most desirable and perhaps the safety of the two kingdoms may finally depend on its attainment, but are the means wished such as are justifiable or such as any man would wish to risk in hopes of attaining the end – through such a medium I look for a union I am ready to grant, but it is not the union of Ireland with Great Britain, but with France ..." **71** HO 100/56/467–9, Pelham to Camden, (?) March 1795; Westmorland Papers, Carton 1/f114, FitzGibbon to Westmorland, 25 March 1795. **72** Westmorland Papers, Carton 1/f114, op. cit. **73** HO 100/46/268–70, Fitzwilliam to Portland, 28 January 1795. **74** Ibid. **75** Westmorland Papers, Carton 1/f111, Pollock to Westmorland, 15 April 795. **76** Westmorland Papers, Carton 1/f114. **77** Sneyd Muniments, FitzGibbon to Auckland, 25 March 1795. **78** A.P.W. Malcomson, *John Foster: the Politics of the Anglo-Irish Ascendancy* (Oxford, 1978), p. 425. **79** *An Accurate Report of the Speech of the Right Honorable John Foster, Speaker of the House of Commons* (Dublin, 1793), p. 18. **80** My evidence of Agar's connection with the Freeman's is admittedly retrospective. During the Aldborough affair, the printer of the *Freeman's*, one Robert Ross, appealed to him to answer Aldborough's frivolous charges of libel and misrepresentation. (Normanton Papers, PRONI/T3719/631/10). But the very fact that Ross would have contacted Agar suggests friendship or patronage of some standing. **81** PRONI, Normanton Papers, T3719/C29/6; Cashel to Westmorland, 2 March 1795 (draft); for a fair copy of same, see T3719/C29/7. **82** For an excellent account of FitzGibbon's use of English contacts to spread the gospel of the coronation oath see Malcomson, pp. 424–7. **83** BM Add MS 33101/f2159/12, P[Portland] to Pelham, 12 March 1795: "I cannot but inform you for the purpose of putting you on your guard that we have learnt from the most unquestionable authority that a correspondence has been carried out, or at least letters have been written by Lord FitzGibbon to the King (to whom they have been delivered by Lord Westmorland) with a view and with more effect than could be wished to prejudice his mind and to alarm his conscience against the concession to the Catholics." For Pelham's response, dated 30 March 1795, see HO 100/57/37–8: "The different correspondences that subsist between individuals in this country and in England is beyond all belief." **84** HO 100/46/263, Fitzwilliam to Portland, 10 January 1795. **85** The editorial, entitled "To a certain Lord", appeared on 14 January 1795; for Fitzwilliam's apologies, conveyed through O'Beirne, see Chatham Papers, 30/8/110, Beresford to Auckland, 19 January 1795. **86** Westmorland Papers, Carton 1/f127, Cooke to Westmorland, 13 January 1795. **87** ISPO, Miscellaneous Papers, IA-80–6. **88** Normanton Papers, T3719/C29/45, p. 2; however much they may have agreed on the issue of Protestant supremacy, it would appear that Cashel detested FitzGibbon, since he kept a copy, not only of this poem, but of George Nugent Reynolds' famous philippic. (T3719/C29/45, p. 1) No doubt after aggravating Privy Council meetings with FitzGibbon, his Lordship perused these in his private hours with much pleasure. **89** HO 100/57/41-44, Camden to Portland, 1 April 1795; HO 100/57/45–6, Pelham to King, 1 April 1795. **90** *Beresford*, ii, p. 103, FitzGibbon to John Beresford, 18 April 1795. **91** *HMC Charlemont*, ii, p. 259, Charlemont to Haliday, 2 April 1795. **92** HO 100/57/41–4, Camden to Portland, 1 April 1795. Camden did, however, repeat FitzGibbon's claim that if the stone had not come in a "slanting direction" the would might have been fatal. **93** An account of OBrien's trial and of FitzGibbon's testimony appears in the *Hibernian Journal*, 15 July 1795, Commission intelligence for 10 July 1795.

CHAPTER 17

1 HO 100/57/249, Camden to Portland, 5 May 1795. **2** HO 100/57/123–6, Camden to Portland, 14 April 1795; HO 100/57/127 (list of trustees of college); HO 100/57/129 (draft of Maynooth bill). **3** The evidence on the point of the resolutions is maddeningly contradictory. Camden submitted the proposed resolutions to Portland for his approval, and initially seemed dubious, but willing to allow them to be moved and discussed. (See HO 100/57/148–9, Camden to Portland, April 1795; for the resolutions themselves see HO 100/57/150–1). But he soon changed his mind, if the evidence of his letter of 4 May 1795 is any indication. He alludes to "my discouraging the resolutions" (HO 100/57/245–6) Pelham was certainly favorable the resolutions. He seemed to think they were essential to end years of enhanced expectation among the Catholics as well as to calm the fears of Protestants. HO 100/57/152–3, Pelham to Portland, 20 April 1795. **4** HO 100/57/169–70, Camden to Portland, 22 April 1795. **5** HO/100/57/21–8, Pelham to Portland, 30 March 1795; HO 100/57/57–7, Portland to Camden, April 1795. **6** HO 100/58/63–4, Camden to Portland, June, 1795. **7** See, for example, HO 100/57/247–8 and 249, Camden to Portland, 5 May 1795; Pelham made the slightly more pessimistic comment "The force that is in this country keeps it quiet, tho' it does not prevent occasional meetings and swearings of Brothers and defenders, not do I think that anything will secure the peace of the country but some continued and regular system for the better administration of justice." HO 100/58/99–100, Pelham to Portland, 28 June 1795; for Lees' comments see NLI, Townshend Papers, 394/170/23, Lees to Townshend, 9 May 1795, "All in Peace and Order here.". **8** HO 100/57/243-4 Pelham reported Camdens feelings to Portland, 3 May 1795. **9** HO 100/57245–6, Camden to Portland, 4 May

1795. **10** Ibid. **11** HO 100/57/243–4, op. cit. **12** HO 100/57/37–8, Pelham to Portland, 30 March 1795, op. cit. **13** HO 100/56/467–9, Pelham to Portland, [written shortly after Pelham's arrival in late March 1795 and dated simply Tuesday night]. **14** *Burke*, xi, pp. 349–53. **15** Ibid., p. 350. **16** Ibid., pp. 297, 350. **17** Ibid. **18** Ibid., p. 355. FitzGibbon never seems to have come to a similar grudging respect for his long-time adversary. He spoke with considerable contempt of Burke in his letters to Auckland. In a letter dated 23 March 1798, he felt obliged to apologize for a burst of marginal obscenity in a copy of one of Burkes pamphlets which he forwarded on to Auckland. (*Auckland*, iii, p. 394) In fairness to FitzGibbon, he always appeared at his most unlovely in his letters to Auckland. More creditable, kindly sentiments may have appeared in his lost correspondence. **19** Camden Papers, C/0183/2/2. **20** Ibid. **21** Camden Papers, C183/2/1, FitzGibbon to Camden, 10 August 1795. **22** Rebellion Papers, 620/24/155, FitzGibbon to Cooke, 29 August 1796. **23** Rebellion Papers, 620/30/161, John Treacy to FitzGibbon 21 April 1797; this folio also contains a report of the Privy Council dated 25 May 1797, recommending that Treacy be paid £100. **24** Rebellion Papers, 620/51/260; no date (1797?) FitzGibbon to Camden: "The enclosed is a copy of a Northern Treasonable Dispatch, which has been just put in my hands. The Gentleman who gives it to me says that no time should be lost in apprehending the persons named and that on searching the house of those whose names are marked, great quantities of arms and ammunition will be found." **25** PRONI, Normanton Papers, C30/1, FitzGibbon to Agar, 16 December 1796. **26** *Freeman's Journal*, 21 March 1797, House of Lords debates, 20 March 1797. **27** HO 100/75/325–7, Portland to Camden, 27 March 1798. **28** The whole of this episode may be found in the Camden Papers (microfilm C/0183/7), FitzGibbon to Camden, 3 September 1796. **29** Irish State Paper Office, Misc. letters, 620/18/8, 19 September 1796. **30** Ibid. **31** Ibid., FitzGibbon to Cooke, 18 September 1796; Camden Papers, C/0183/11, FitzGibbon to Camden, 22 September 1796. **32** ISPO, Misc. Letters, 620/18/8; FitzGibbon to Cooke, 18 September, 1796. **33** Ibid., FitzGibbon to Cooke, 19 September, 1796. **34** Sneyd Muniments, FitzGibbon to Auckland, 2 January 1797. **35** *Freeman's Journal*, 19 February 1797, House of Lords debates, 17 January 1797. **36** Sneyd Muniments, FitzGibbon to Auckland, 11 January 1797. **37** Ibid., Same to Same, 2 January 1797. **38** For this absurdly self-important man's reaction or perhaps more accurately, over-reaction, see, for example, PRONI, Abercorn Papers, T2541/1K16/94, Abercorn to FitzGibbon, 26 March 1796; he later retracted his resignation (Abercorn MS, D623/A/80/99, Abercorn to Camden, 1 May 1798). **39** *Auckland*, iii, p. 395. **40** Sneyd Muniments, FitzGibbon to Auckland, 11 January 1797. **41** HO 100/65/89, Camden to Portland, 28 October 1796. **42** See, for example, PRONI, Gosford Papers, D/1606/1/1/182, Camden to Gosford, 19 January 1795 and D1606/1/1/100B, Camden to Gosford, 7 November 1795. **43** Rebellion Papers, 620/23/62, Wolfe to Camden, 1 April, 1796. **44** Ibid., 620/23/61, Isaac Corry to Cooke, 1 April 1796. **45** HO 100/62/262–3, Camden to Portland, 13 October 1796. **46** PRONI, ------- ------, d1606/1/1/185A, Cooke to Gosford, 7 July 1796. **47** For appeals of United Irishmen to Catholics fearful of the Orangemen, see PRONI, Downshire Papers, D607/D/102, 16 July 1796, Lane to Downshire: "That a flame may end and will burst forth is surely to be apprehended. The emissaries of the United Irishmen are astir in every quarter. When they apply to Catholics, they give them the alternative of taking the oath and being protected or of being burnt out and sent to Hell or Connaught". In other words, they suggested that without the protection of the United Irishmen, they would be at the mercy of Orangemen. See also Rebellion Papers, 620/24/161, Pollock to Colonel Ross, 27 August 1797. For defenses of the Orangemen, see Rebellion Papers, 620/24/106, Thomas Knox to Pelham, 13 August 1796. **48** HO 100/77/21–2, Cooke to Wickham, 2 June 1798. **49** BM Add MS 33101/f2142, Dalrymple to Pelham, 9 August 1795. **50** *The Speech of the Right Honorable John, Earl of Clare, Lord High Chancellor of Ireland on a motion made by the Earl of Moira, Monday, February 19, 1798* (Dublin and London, 1798), pp. 23–4 (This speech will be referred to as "Moira" in later citations). **51** PRONI, T3247/2/f20, (this document is a transcript of the examinations conducted by FitzGibbon and

Duigenan at Trinity in April of 1798). **52** Ibid., f30. **53** Ibid., f31. **54** Ibid. **55** Ibid., f32. **56** Ibid. **57** Ibid., f20. **58** HO 100/75/285–7, Portland to Camden, 24 March 1798. **59** HO 100/75/331–4, Camden to Portland, 29 March 1798. **60** Ibid. **61** Ibid. **62** The debate on the Insurrection Act in the House of Lords appears in *Freeman's Journal*, 6 March 1796; the debate itself took place on 3 March 1796. **63** *Cobbett's Parliamentary History*, xxxiii, p. 127 (Moira), p. 155 (Fox). **64** Ibid.; for the entire text of the debate in the Lords, see pp. 127–39; for the debate in the Commons, see pp. 143–65. **65** *Freeman's Journal*, 20 February 1798, House of Lords debates, 19 March 1798. **66** Ibid., 17 January 1797; House of Lords' debates, 17 January 1797. **67** This letter appears in the Sneyd Muniments. **68** *Cobbett*, xxxiii, p. 143. **69** *PR* (1789), p. 181. **70** PRONI, De Ros Papers, D638/132, FitzGibbon to Lord Henry FitzGerald, 28 March, 1797. **71** *Moira*, p. 31. **72** Ibid., p. 4. **73** Ibid., p. 13. **74** Ibid., p, 17. **75** Ibid., p. 19. **76** Ibid., pp. 18–19. **77** Ibid., p. 19. **78** Ibid. **79** Ibid., p. 20. **80** Ibid., p. 33. **81** This particular torture was similar to the rack and involved tying the arms and legs of a prisoner to stakes, then pulling at the stakes simultaneously to tear muscles and tendons. **82** Ibid., pp. 39–40. **83** Ibid., p. 30. **84** Ibid., p. 33. **85** Ibid., pp. 23–4. **86** Ibid., p. 59–60. **87** This particular rhetorical flourish appears in the *Freeman's Journal*, 22 February 1798, House of Lords debates, 19 February 1798; FitzGibbon did not see fit, however, to be quite so elaborately complimentary in the published version of his speech. **88** *Moira*, p. 63. **89** Ibid. **90** *Moira*, pp. 66–7. **91** Ibid., p. 69. **92** Ibid. **93** He complained to Auckland of the "beastly blunders committed in the printing office"; *Auckland*, iii, p. 395, FitzGibbon to Auckland, 23 March 1798. **94** Elizabeth, Lady Holland, *Journals*, i, Earl of Ilchester, ed. (London, 1909), p. 131. **95** *Moira*, p. 33. **96** *Correspondence of George Prince of Wales*, iii, pp. 419–20. **97** Ibid., p. 423, (letter no. 1343), Moira to Colonel J. McMahon, 16 April 1798. **98** *Auckland*, iii, p. 395, FitzGibbon to Auckland, 23 March 1798. **99** *Correspondence of George, Prince of Wales*, iii, pp. 419–20 (letter 1340). **100** *Moira*, pp. 22–3. **101** PRONI, McPeake Papers, T3048/B, FitzGibbon to Lady Louisa Conolly, 3 March 1798. **102** HO 100/75/162–9, Camden to Portland, 6 March 1798: "[I] conceived it to be very fortunate that the Laws of that Kingdom [Scotland] are framed as to enable the Government to act with vigor". **103** The younger Grattan, of course, articulated this charge; see *Grattan*, iv, p. 349. **104** See the attached Appendix for a list of students expelled, their social backgrounds and their religious affiliation. **105** PRONI, Trinity Visitation, T3247/2/f76. **106** Ibid., f18. **107** Ibid. **108** Ibid., f62. **109** Ibid., f70–1. **110** Ibid., f13. **111** Ibid., f12. **112** Ibid. **113** Ibid., f77. **114** Tone's journal provides strong evidence of Stokes' dissociation from the later trends of the United Irish movement. He complained that Stokes was too afraid of bloodshed ever to act on his strongly radical convictions. *Tone*, i, p. 41. **115** Ibid., f78. **116** Ibid., f74–5; FitzGibbon's recommendation of Tacitus is odd, considering that great historian's republican sympathies and obvious contempt for imperial government. **117** *Faulkner's Dublin Journal*, 24 April 1798; *Dublin Evening Post*, 1 May 1798, "COLLEGE VISITATION", 20 April 1798. The poor *Dublin Evening Post*, once so exuberantly radical, was reduced to echoing the gushing comments of *Faulkner's Dublin Journal*. According to both newspapers, the Chancellor left Trinity "amidst the most general and heartfelt plaudits of the Students", grateful for his "very great moderation" and the "indulgence which he extended to the offending Students." **118** *Auckland*, iii, p. 436. **119** Ibid., p. 437; Prior, *Life of Malone*, pp. 249–50. **120** HO 100/69/379–83, Portland to Camden, 10 June 1797; Camden, in response, suggested that the demand for further concessions to the Catholics, was merely a ploy and that Cornwallis simply did not want to accept a subservient position. HO 100/69/412–17, Camden to Portland, 20 June 1797. **121** HO 100/77 200–1, 28 June 1798, Cornwallis to Portland, 28 June 1798. **122** PRONI, Downshire Papers, D607/F/502, Robert Ross to Lord Downshire, 29 October 1798. **123** Downshire Papers, D607/G/15, 12 January 1799, R. Johnson to Lord Downshire. **124** HO 100/66/350–1, Cornwallis to Portland, 26 July 1798. **125** HO 100/78/352–4, Cornwallis to Portland, 16 September 1798. **126** HO 100/77/315–16, Cornwallis to Portland, 30 July 1798. **127** HO 100/77/280–3, Wickham to Cooke, 23 July 1798; for Loughborough's comments on the bill see HO 100/79/213–3, Loughborough to FitzGibbon, 23 July 1798. **128** HO 100/77/315–16, Cornwallis to Portland, 30 July 1798; see, also, Castlereagh to Wickham, 30 July 1798. **129** HO 100/75/213–14, Camden to Portland, 12 March, 1798. **130** Thomas Moore, *The Life and Death of Lord Edward FitzGerald*, ii, (London, 1831), p. 26; extract from the journal of Lady Sarah Napier: "By this time I heard from the others that all Dublin was in consternation on Monday morning, that upon the papers [belonging to the Leinster United Irishmen] being carried to council, the Chancellor was sent for at the Courts to attend it, that he dashed out in a hurry and found a mob at the door, who abused him and he returned the abuse by cursing and swearing like a madman. He met Lord Westmeath, and they went into a shop and came out with pistols and the Chancellor thus went on foot to Council." **131** Charles Hamilton Teeling, *History of the Irish Rebellion of 1798 & Sequel to the History of the Irish Rebellion of 1798* (reprinted, Dublin, 1972), pp. 297–9; *Madden*, iv (4th series, second edition), pp. 161–3. In addition, transcripts of Bond's and Byrne's trials were published by Ridgeway: *A Report of the Proceedings in cases of High Treason at a Special Commission of Oyer and Terminer held in and for the County and City of Dublin in the month of July, 1798* (Dublin, 1798). **132** See, for example, Teeling's reference to "the humane intentions of his fellow prisoners", p. 299. **133** HO 100/66/350–1, Cornwallis to Portland, 26 July 1798: "... Dr MacNeven [*sic*] might possibly be convicted"; See, also, *Auckland*, iv, p. 38, FitzGibbon to Auckland, 1 August 1798. **134** HO 100/66/391–7. **135** Ibid. **136** Ibid. **137** Ibid. **138** See *Auckland*, iv, p. 38, 1 August 1798, "... [MacNeven] who was one of their ambassadors to the directory in the last summer, seems very apprehensive and with some reason, that if he is brought to trial he stands a fair chance of being convicted." MacNeven himself on the contrary developed an odd respect for FitzGibbon. Years later, he would contrast FitzGibbon's "warm" Irish sensibilities with the cold calculation of Castlereagh and Grattan. (Madden, p. 240) It is difficult to account for this extraordinary judgment, apart from MacNeven's possible desire to score off Grattan, not a popular figure with many United Irishmen. There is the possibility as well that FitzGibbon showed civility and a glimpse of his hearty charm to MacNeven in person, while skewering him in his private correspondence. **139** HO 100/66/355 Castlereagh to Wickham, 31 July 1798. **140** Teeling, p. 299. **141** The report of 1797, which was issued on 12 May 1797, can be found in HO 100/72/444–5. **142** Madden, p. 223. **143** Ibid., pp. 223–4. **144** *Journals of the House of Lords*, viii, p. 144. **145** Madden, p. 223. **146** *Journals of the House of Lords*, viii, p. 144 "... their plan of Reform and Revolution ... would have involved in it equally the destruction of the Protestant and Popish religion. The said [MacNeven] having distinctly acknowledged that the Intention was to abolish all Church Establishments and not to have any established religion, and that for his own Part, he would as soon establish the Mahometan as the Catholic Religion, though he was himself a Roman Catholic". **147** Madden, pp. 247–8. **148** HO 100/66/363–4. **149** HO 100/66/363 Castlereagh to Wickham,? August 1798 [No date]; HO 100/66/364–5, Pitt to Castlereagh, 1 September 1798. **150** HO 100/66/365–6 Castlereagh to Wickham, 5 September 1798. **151** HO 100/66/399–400, Minute of a conversation between Alexander Marsden and O'Connor, Emmet and MacNeven, 29 August 1798. **152** HO 100/66/369, King to Portland, 13 September 1798. **153** HO 100/66/377–8, Castlereagh to Wickham, 29 October, 1798. **154** For a truly superb example of Emmet's political invective against King during that election, see Charles R. King, ed., *Rufus King: His Life and Correspondence*, v, pp. 15–23. Emmet, among other things accused King of being an accessory in his brother Robert's death. **155** BM Add MS 34455/f38–9, FitzGibbon to Auckland, 26 November 1798, "... after he [Tone] was brought up to be tried by a military tribunal in Dublin upon what principle was his execution delayed from Saturday to Monday? Nay more, there was fully time to execute him on Monday, after it was known that an application would be made to the Kings Bench and before it was made. And what do you [*sic*] surgeon's mate that a man whose throat was cut could not die of hanging." The discreetly censored version of this letter appears in *Auckland* iv, pp. 70–2). **156** Elliot, p. 400. **157** Ibid., pp. 398–9. **158** Francis Plowden, *The History of Ireland from its Union with Great Britain in January*

1801 to October 1810, i, (Dublin, 1810), p. 122. 159 Plowden I, p. 283. 160 Rebellion Papers, 620/17/14; transcript of Francis Arthur's trial before a court martial, 23 June 1798 161 Ibid. 162 Ibid. 163 Rebellion Papers, 620/17/14, Morrison to Castlereagh, 26 June 1798. 164 Ibid. 165 Rebellion Papers, 620/18/9/3, Castlereagh to Portland, 27 June 1798. 166 Rebellion Papers, 620/39/22, Castlereagh to Morrison, 4 July 1798. 167 *Roche*, ii, p. 115. 168 *Grattan*, iii, p. 401, footnote. 169 *Auckland*, iv, p. 19, FitzGibbon to Auckland, 14 June 1798. 170 *Roche*, ii, p. 112. 171 Barrington, *Rise and Fall of the Irish Nation*, pp. 356–7. 172 Trinity College Dublin, Madden Papers, f415. 173 PRONI, McPeake Papers, T3048/B/51 Account of the death of Lord Edward FitzGerald, written by Emily Bunbury, daughter of Lady Sarah Napier, August 1832. 174 *Grattan*, v, p. 167. 175 *Moore*, ii, pp. 225–80. 176 Ibid., p. 281. 177 Ibid., pp. 281–2.

CHAPTER 18

1 HO 100/78/27–8, Cornwallis to Portland, 8 October, 1798. 2 Sneyd Muniments, FitzGibbon to Auckland, 16 March 1800. 3 Ibid., FitzGibbon to Auckland, 26 August, 1799. 4 *Limerick Chronicle*, 14 September 1799. 5 PRONI, Official Papers, T3245/5/OP/121/3, A. Watson to John Dwyer, February–March, 1802? 6 Malcomson, p. 389. 7 Ibid. 8 For Pelham's views see Rebellion Papers, 620/30/136 Pelham to the Bishop of Ossory; Pelham drafted two replies; the first, dated 23 May 1797 alluded to a "compact upon some known and acknowledged principle that might be intelligible to all that were concerned". He also suggested that the Pope be "made a party to the settlement"; in the letter which he actually sent, dated 26 May 1797, he alluded only to "some permanent settlement in Church and State ... that as far as human wisdom is capable of discerning such a measure, a system calculated to anticipate all future claims". 9 See, for example, Charles, Lord Cornwallis, *Correspondence*, iii, Charles Ross, ed., (London, 1859), p. 146 and p. 175. 10 NLI, Trench Papers (microfilm p. 4910, uncatalogued), FitzGibbon to Frederick Trench, 22 October 1796. 11 *Hibernian Journal*, 10 February 1797, House of Lords, 7 February, 1797. 12 Camden MS, C/0183/8, FitzGibbon to Camden, 7 September 1796; In discussing the claims of radical Catholics that the yeomanry corps were aimed at them, FitzGibbon had these words of wisdom to offer Camden: "I cannot but think that it will dangerous in the extreme to damp the ardor of those who may be depended upon, under an Apprehension that their zeal may become the subject of misrepresentation by the Catholicks, who, I will freely own to your excellency are in my opinion the body of all others in this country at the present moment, who ought to be watched most narrowly if a foreign enemy were to make a descent upon us." 13 On the reaction of the native Catholic gentry see HO 100/46/261–2, Fitzwilliam to Portland, 7 January 1795: "I hear the Roman Catholic gentlemen themselves are not pleased: they fancy they might themselves as well have been the Cols if Roman Catholic Regts were to be raised"; for lack of enthusiasm among the general Catholic populace see *Dublin Evening Post*, 13 October 1795, Postscript for same date. 14 BM Add MS 3784/273/f4; quoted in Peter Dixon, *Canning: Politician and Statesman* (London, 1963), p. 61. 15 This speech was of course widely reported in all the Dublin newspapers. I myself have relied on the version in the *Dublin Evening Post*, 18, 1799, House of Lords, 15 April 1799. 16 *Cornwallis*, iii, p. 92. 17 *Castlereagh*, ii, p. 284. 18 FitzGibbon already had an animus against Hussey, but initially he seems to have despised the bishop more as a minion and intimate of Edmund Burke than as a priest. Sneyd Muniments, FitzGibbon to Auckland, 19 May 1797; "This gentleman [Hussey] is a pet of Mr. Edmund Burke's and to him we are indebted amongst other favours conferred upon us for his presence in Ireland." FitzGibbon later adopted the more general hostility of Sir Richard Musgrave and other extreme Protestants. See Sneyd Muniments, FitzGibbon to Auckland, 23 May 1797; in this letter FitzGibbon again alludes to the "composition" of Dr Hussey and adds "It seems to be a good sample of the Moderation of the Popish Clergy in Ireland". 19 *Beresford*, ii, p. 73, FitzGibbon to Beresford, 14 February 1795. 20 Patrick Corish, *Maynooth College 1795–1995* (Dublin, 1995), p. 11. 21 Surprisingly, Fitzwilliam's former personal secretary

O'Beirne, now elevated to the dignity of Bishop of Meath, was among the severest critics of Maynooth. He went so far as to suggest that the Protestant Archbishop of Dublin be included on the board of trustees. O'Beirne had obviously come a long way from his enthusiastic support of Catholic rights. His suggestion shows not only a more suspicious attitude, but an amazing lack of astuteness. Nothing could have been more calculated to affront the so called "titular" bishops on the board or promote general suspicion and wrangling. It is doubtful that the Protestant archbishop would have had much knowledge of or sensitivity to the traditions of Catholic education. Fortunately, this particular suggestion was ignored. *Castlereagh*, ii, p. 284, O'Beirne to Castlereagh, 27 April 1799. **22** For a documents related to these negotiations see *Castlereagh*, ii, pp. 80–160. See in particular J.C. Hippesley's letter to Hobart, dated 10 February 1799 (pp. 104–20). **23** *Castlereagh*, ii, pp. 278–9, Cornwallis to Clare, 18 April 1799. **24** Ibid., p. 277. **25** *Dublin Evening Post*, 25 April 1799; House of Lords debates, 18 April 1799. **26** *Castlereagh*, ii, p. 279, Castlereagh to Portland, 26 April 1799. **27** Camden Correspondence, C/081/1, FitzGibbon to Camden, 7 May 1799. **28** *Cornwallis*, iii, pp. 374–5. **29** *Irish Statutes* (1800), "An Act for the better government of the Seminary established at Maynooth for the Education of Persons professing the Roman Catholic Religion, and for amending the Laws now in Force respecting the said Seminary", pp. 923–8. **30** Corish, pp. 24–5. **31** It should be noted that the structure and content of this great speech were not entirely original. FitzGibbon seems to have been strongly influenced by an essay by on J.L. de Lolme published in 1787 as an introduction to a reprint of Defoe's history of the Scottish union. De Lolme, a Swiss lawyer and minor gentleman, had emigrated to England. Following the example of Voltaire, he had become infatuated with his country of adoption, and he had written numerous pamphlets on the English government and constitution. His introduction to Defoes history included a long analysis of the history of Ireland, in which he attributed its current difficulties to the legacy of bigotry and hatred left by the Reformation. There can be no doubt that FitzGibbon read de Lolme. His speech in support of the act of union paraphrases de Lolme's account of the Reformation almost word for word. But it would be wrong to see FitzGibbon as a mere plagiarist. De Lolme only provided FitzGibbon with a structure for his speech and some wording; FitzGibbon brought a sensibility entirely his own to the speech: one of bleakness, foreboding, and a consuming loathing for the Irish, Catholic and Protestant. De Lolme, in contrast, was urbane and fair minded. In other words, they embraced the union for different reasons. De Lolme believed the union would elevate and improve the Irish. FitzGibbon saw it mainly as an instrument of imperial coercion. See J.L. de Lolme, *An essay Containing a Few Strictures on the Union of Scotland with England, and on the Present Situation in Ireland* (London, 1787). **32** *Act of Union*, pp. 8–9. **33** Ibid., p. 13. **34** Ibid., pp. 16–17. **35** Ibid. **36** Ibid., p. 22. **37** His entire speech is littered with such dark hints; see in particular pp. 31, 54 and 59–60. **38** Cornwallis, a man not given to paranoia, believed Grattan guilty of misprision; see HO 100/78/379–80, Cornwallis to Portland, 24 September 1798; for Grattan's own rather unconvincing claim that Neilson, in company with John Sweetman, stopped by Tinnehinch for a chance visit, see *Grattan*, iv, pp. 412–13. **39** *Act of Union*, pp. 69–70. **40** Ibid. **41** Ibid., p. 84. **42** Ibid., p. 74. **43** Ibid., p. 58. **44** For his coy gloating on this titular acquisition see once again the invaluable Sneyd Muniments, FitzGibbon to Auckland, undated but probably September 1799: "What you have mentioned from the warmth of your feelings for me would certainly be a very honorable and flattering mark of favour to me. But to that or any other object I shall never look at a time when the attainment of it can throw a difficulty in the way of Mr Pitt in his progress to the great object of settling this country. Whenever he feels the time to have come when such a mark of distinction can be conferred upon me, I should be much wanting if I were not to thank him for it as the most honorable reward that I could receive." **45** Henry Grattan, *An Answer to a Pamphlet Entitled the Speech of the Earl of Clare on the Subject of the Legislative Union between Great Britain and Ireland* (Cork, 1800). **46** *Cornwallis*, iii, p. 184. **47** *No Union! but Unite and Fall!* (London, 1799), pp. 16–17, 21. **48** *Freeman's Journal*, 21 March 1797, House of Lords debates, 20 March 1797.

49 Ibid. pp. 9–10. 50 Ibid., p. 34. 51 *No Union!*, p. 11. 52 Ibid., p. 39. 53 William Gerard Hamilton, then serving as private secretary to Lord Halifax, reported that he had won favour with Old FitzGibbon "who is a Papist" by abusing King William. William Gerard Hamilton to Hely Hutchinson, 29 January 1763 Trinity College Dublin, Hutchinson Papers, C/1/16. 54 See, for example, University of Keele, Sneyd Muniments, FitzGibbon to Auckland, 5 February 1799. In this letter, FitzGibbon alludes to alleged "cabals of the Catholicks, who have been very buzily [sic] employed since the opening of the session in Consultation with the Levelers [*sic*] of their own Sect and with Mr Geo. Ponsonby and his gang." 55 Henry Grattan, *Memoirs of the Life and Times of the Right Honorable Henry Grattan* (London, 1844–47), iii, p. 397. 56 R.F. Foster, *History of Modern Ireland* (London, New York, 1988), p. 326 (footnote). 57 PRONI, Castlereagh Papers, 3030/1597, Cooke to Castlereagh, 10 February 1801. 58 Ibid. 59 Sneyd Muniments, FitzGibbon to Auckland, 10 August 1801. 60 PRONI, Shannon Papers, 2707/A/2/2/156, FitzGibbon to Shannon, 13 February 1801. 61 *Woodfall's Parliamentary Reports* (1801), p. 539. 62 Ibid., p. 542. 63 For FitzGibbons initial, and true, account of Allen's murder, see Sneyd Muniments, FitzGibbon to Auckland, 17 June 1800. 64 *Woodfall*, p. 542. 65 Ibid. 66 Ibid. 67 Ibid. 68 *Woodfall*, pp. 540–1. 69 Ibid., p. 544. 70 *Grattan*, iii, p. 402. 71 Ibid. 72 See FitzGibbon's own allusions to their conversations in the letter to Lord Shannon previously cited. 73 For Lord Grenvilles supporting remarks see *Woodfall*, p. 552; for Westmorland, see pp. 559–60; Mulgraves remarks appear on p. 546. 74 *Woodfall*, pp. 552–7. 75 *The Later Correspondence of George III*, iii, p. 515 [footnote]. 76 Ibid. 77 *Woodfall*, pp. 76–7. 78 Ibid. 79 Ibid., p. 81. 80 Ibid. 81 *Grattan*, iii, p. 402. 82 The fullest account of his accident that I could find appears in the good old *Times*, 26 May 1801; the Times coyly stated that FitzGibbon had been "bruised in a manner to endanger his life." *Faulkner's Dublin Journal*, edited by the inimitable Gifford, used FitzGibbon's accident as an excuse to indulge in loyalist paranoia: "There needed little more than the malicious satisfaction at his Lordships danger, which was not even concealed by the enemies of the Empire, to convince us how precious his life must be to every man who has at heart the true interests of Ireland, as well as the general prosperity of our beloved Sovereign and his Dominion." (28 May, 1801). 83 Sneyd Muniments, 19 September 1801. 84 *Later Correspondence of George III*, iii, p. 530. 85 BM Add MS 35,771/f4–6, Hardwicke to Abbott, 8 June 1801: "... I rejoice too at the prospect of Lord Clare's recovery, for I was very apprehensive that though his life might have been saved by the skill of his surgeons and by his own firmness in submitting to a dangerous operation he would not entirely recover the effects of his unfortunate accident." 86 Sneyd Muniments, FitzGibbon to Auckland, 19 September 1801. 87 Sneyd Muniments, 19 September 1801; for Hardwickes motivation and justification for his actions see BM 35,771/f158–62. 88 Sneyd Muniments, 19 September 1801. 89 BM Add MS 33,114/f39, Pelham to Hardwicke, 22 September 1801. 90 Sneyd Muniments, 19 September 1801. 91 BM Add MS 45,031/f32, Hardwicke to FitzGibbon, 28 August 1801. 92 BM Add MS 45,031/f32, op. cit.; BM Add MS 33,114/f36–7, Kilwarden to Hardwicke, 15 September 1801. 93 Rebellion Papers, 620/59/15, FitzGibbon to Abbott, 29 August 1801. 94 For the responses of Auckland and Hobart see *Auckland*, iv, p. 144 and 146. 95 BM Add MS 35,771/f158–62, op. cit. 96 See, for example, his letter to Auckland dated 22 October 1801 and 17 November 1801 in the invaluable Sneyd Muniments. In that latter missive, FitzGibbon complained not only of general Popish disaffection, aided and abetted by the clergy, but of a "treasonable Protestant Committee of Irish Correspondence at Paris". 97 Sneyd Muniments, 22 October 1801. 98 See, for example, HO 100/57/123–6, Camden to Portland 14 April 1795; in this dispatch, Camden alludes to "seminaries for the education of Priests of the Roman Catholic persuasion"; see also HO100/46/301–9, a draft dated 26 March 1795; in this draft, Portland sets forth proposals not only to establish "Seminaries for the Education of Persons of the Catholic Persuasion who may be disposed to devote themselves to the profession of the Church" but to provide maintenance for the Roman Catholic clergy. 99 See HO100/57/129 for a draft of the bill. 100 Sneyd Muniments, 22 October 1801. 101 In spite of his morbid obsession

with Maynooth, FitzGibbon never seems to have set foot in the place. For example, he repeatedly criticized the vulgarity of the students, but was flabbergasted when he received direct proof of his claim from his friend Kilwarden, who was far more conscientious about his responsibilities and who thought that a mixture of lay and clerical students was the worst possible arrangement. When Kilwarden "told the chancellor of the nature of their examination of an hour at the visitation about St Augustine and Origen and their coarse vulgar jokes and manners at the dinner, Lord Clare seemed much surprised at it, and seemed not to know they were of such a description." In addition, FitzGibbon adamantly denied any possibility that wealthy well-born Catholics might prefer more prestigious Trinity to Maynooth. According to Abbot, the provost of Trinity had informed him that "There were many sons of opulent Catholics and their numbers of this class increased ... the Chancellor did not admit it, and ought to be put in full and unquestionable possession of the fact." FitzGibbon's ignorance about Trinity is all the more surprising because he was vice-chancellor and in a perfect position to know about the growing presence of Catholics. *Cornwallis*, iii, p. 371. **102** *Castlereagh*, ii, p. 277. **103** BM Add MS 35,771/f135–8; "Substance of a conversation between Lord Hardwicke and Lord Clare" on the subject of Maynooth. **104** NLI, Fingall Papers, 8023/6, FitzGibbon to Fingall, 1 October 1801; in this same letter FitzGibbon expresses regret that he could not call on Fingall in London, which suggests a standing invitation of some sort. **105** NLI, Fingall Papers, 8022/10, Fingall (then Lord Killeen) to Patrick Bellew, January 1787. **106** HO 100/52/56–8, Westmorland to Dundas, 16 May 1794. **107** For details of the lay school contretemps, see Cornwallis, iii, p. 365–7 and Charles Abbott, Lord Colchester, Diary and Correspondence (London, 1861), iii, pp. 335–6. **108** *Cornwallis*, iii, pp. 366, 367; see also FitzGibbon's hasty allusions to Fingall's appeals and to his previous conversations with Hardwicke: BM Add MS 35,771/f135–8. **109** BM Add MS 35,771/f134; the other quotations from Dr Troy appear in this same manuscript which was a memorandum or dictation taken either by Abbott or by Alexander Marsden. **110** BM Add MS 35,771/f135–8; this manuscript consists of a transcript of Lord Clare's remarks, interspersed with Hardwicke's weary qualifications and explanations; for Abbott's blunter expressions of skepticism, see Colchester, i, p. 334; Abbott wrote on his copy of FitzGibbon's version "Query – if there was a doubt, why did he not send Dr Troy to His Excellency or to his Secretary ... for an explanation?" **111** Ibid. **112** *Cornwallis*, iii, pp. 371–2. **113** Ibid., p. 368. **114** Ibid., p. 368. **115** BM Add MS 35,771/f135–8. **116** Sneyd Muniments. **117** Examples of FitzGibbon's bouts of illness are legion. See in particular his letter of 10 September 1796 to Camden (Camden Papers, C/0183/9) where he complains of gout and nervous exhaustion and he makes the claim that for the past several months he had not been free of illness for more than a few days. At the same time, he declared his willingness to come to Dublin if needed, which suggests that FitzGibbon never allowed illness to stand in the way of his exercise of power. **118** Westmorland Papers, Carton 1/f140, Lady Clare to Westmorland, 26 January 1802 **119** *Freeman's Journal*, 30 January 1802 "THE EARL OF CLARE". **120** Ibid.; while undoubtedly a biased source, there seems no reason to believe that he didnt meet his death calmly. In a sense, he had nothing left to do but to curse, if not God, the English government and die. **121** *Plowden*, i, p. 121, footnote. The *Freeman's Journal* also reported that FitzGibbon received the sacrament three times on his deathbed, though of course, no mention was made of his requests for a priest (edition of 4 February 1802, *Dublin News* for 3 February 1802). **122** See the account in the *Freeman's Journal*, 2 February 1802, which makes the implausible claim that "An unfeigned sorrow, decent and dignified, pervaded every countenance, which spoke at once the feelings of the living and the worth of the dead." (The Earl of Clare). **123** *Cloncurry*, pp. 123–4; PRONI, Rosse Papers, T3498/D/5/41, Thomas C. Parsons to Parsons, 1 February 1802. **124** TCD, Madden Papers, f518, narrative of William Fisher. **125** Ibid. **126** *Dublin Evening Post*, 11 September 1802, Postscript for same date. **127** *Falkiner*, p. 140.

CHAPTER 19

1 I am extrapolating much from this very sketchy account given by young Grattan in a footnote, no less: "His nephew Jefferyes had instituted a suit in the Court of Chancery respecting his estate, of which Lord Clare was trustee and which he had bought. Lord Chancellor Manners (in 1817) set aside the sale and decreed the estate to Jefferyes. It was, however, admitted that it had been sold for its full value", *Grattan*, iii, pp. 402–3. 2 NLI, De Vesci Papers, (microfilm p. 6799) FitzGibbon to Lord De Vesci, 29 December 1796: "Last night I had a note from Lord Cahir which he sent by express after me, to say that the whole of the French Fleet, one ship excepted had been taken by Lord Bridport.'" It can only be assumed that FitzGibbon had stopped at Cahir Castle or had stayed overnight before proceeding on to Limerick. As for Arabella's relations with her other daughter, it certainly seems odd that eleven years after their divorce, she could not remember that Lord Westmeath was no longer her son-in-law. Only a prolonged separation between mother and daughter could have allowed Arabella to maintain this willful delusion. Possibly, Arabella was unhappy that her daughter had divorced "one of the oldest peers in Ireland", to use her own rather maladroit phrase. See, also, the tantalizing letter in the Abercorn Papers (PRONI, 623/A/81/3) 11 November 1800. Abercorn declined to give an opinion on a family quarrel over which the former Lady Westmeath and current Mrs. Bradshaw had consulted him, though he expressed sympathy for "... the circumstances and feelings which distress you." The quarrel could have involved Mrs. Bradshaw's volatile mother. 3 PRONI, T3244/11/1. 4 Ibid. 5 *Lord Shannon's Letters to his Son*, p. 217. 6 *Grattan*, pp. 402–3. 7 Ibid. 8 NLI, FitzGibbon Papers, MS 8343/3. 9 NLI MS 13,992. 10 See his brief but highly favorable comments when the controversial bill of 1793 was introduced into the House of Lords, *Freeman's Journal*, 14–16 March 1793, House of Lords debate, 13 March 1793; for their divorce see *Burke's Peerage* (1847), p. 1037; see also Wolfe Tone's contemptuous reference to Westmeath as "that contemptible cuckold", *Tone*, ii, p. 223. 11 The letter is copied in a very fine hand, but it does not seem ever to have been sent. 12 ISPO, Westmorland Papers, Carton 1/f140, Lady Clare to Lord Westmorland, 26 January 1802; f142, Same to Same, 27 February 1802, f143 Same to Same, 8 February 1802, f144, Same to Same, 1 March 1802. 13 Peel Papers, BM Add. MS 38263/f81–2, Lady Clare to Lord Liverpool, 14 July 1816. 14 She alludes to her first pension, which was £700 per annum in the previously cited letter to Lord Liverpool. For the refusal of a second, see BM Add. MS 38263/f90–1, Lady Clare to Lord Liverpool, 21 July 1816, which is a letter of protest at his decision to decline her request. 15 Westmorland, Carton 1, f143, f144; the negotiations for a provision for Cousin Thomas were still in process as late as 1805. See Add MS. 38241/f274–5 Lady Clare to Lord Hawkesbury, 29 November 1805. 16 A legal document dated 17 January 1819 names Thomas as a Collector of Excise. See *Registry of Deeds/Abstracts of Wills*, ii, p. 328, document 513. 17 Peel Papers, BM Add MS 42,050/f236–7, Lady Clare to Peel, 24 December 1815. 18 Maurice O'Connell, ed., *The Correspondence of Daniel O'Connell*, ii, p. 504, letter 1045. 19 Christina Colvin, ed., Maria Edgeworth, *Letters from England 1813–1844* (Oxford, 1971), p. 393. 20 Lady Sarah alludes to the recent deaths of these children in her letter to the Duchess of Leinster; *The Correspondence of Emily, Duchess of Leinster*, ii, op. cit. 21 NLI, Miscellaneous Papers, MS 10756/T3244/313, FitzGibbon to Stephen Dixon, 15 October 1791. 22 PRONI, T 2910, Catalogue of works from the library of Denis Daly, purchased by FitzGibbon in May 1792. 23 Sneyd Muniments, FitzGibbon to Eden (Auckland), 21 September 1798; "I have been settled here quietly since the prorogation of our Parliament with the intermission only of four days which I gave up to escort my little boys to Dublin on their return to Sanbury (??)". 24 *Edgeworth*, p. 393; PRONI, T3244/11/1 (op. cit.). 25 Dublin, National Archives of Ireland, MS5192. 26 Leslie A. Marchand, *Byron: A Biography*, iii, (New York, 1957), p. 1001 . 27 Thomas Moore, *Memoirs, Journal and Correspondence*, i, (London, 1853), p. 64: "There sat the formidable FitzGibbon, whose name I had never heard connected but with domineering insolence and cruelty." Yet Moore did include some kindlier memories of FitzGibbon.

Some time later, he attended a dinner where he and FitzGibbon were the only guests, aside from members of the hosts immediate family. Moore wrote: "Of course, the presence of such a man as Lord Clare was not very likely to untie my tongue, but in the course of dinner, he, with very marked kindness, asked me to drink a glass of wine with him. I met him once afterwards in the streets when he took off his had to me and these two circumstances, slight as they were in themselves, yet following so closely upon my trying scene before him in the Visitation Hall, were somewhat creditable, I think, to both parties. *Moore*, i, p. 71. **28** *Marchand*, i, pp. 179–80. **29** James A. Reynolds, *The Catholic Emancipation Crisis in Ireland, 1823–29* (New Haven, 1954), p. 53. **30** K. Theodore Hoppen, *Landlords, Politics and Rural Society* (Oxford, 1984), p. 160. **31** *Burke's Peerage* (1847), p. 211; the second Lady Clare does not appear to have come from a Catholic family. She may have been a convert. Burke, op. cit. pp. 1049–52. **32** FitzGibbon, pp. 67, 72. **33** PRONI, Leinster Papers, D3078/3/34/4. **34** *DNB*, vii, p. 159. **35** NLI, FitzGibbon Papers, 8343/14. **36** Dublin, National Archives of Ireland, MS167. **37** Ibid. **38** He also owed a sinecure to his father's influence. In one of his rare exercises of patronage to a family member, FitzGibbon bestowed the office of Usher in Chancery on his schoolboy son. See Chapter 11, p. 26. **39** *History of Parliament Trust,. The History of Parliament, The House of Commons, 1790–1820*, iii (London, 1986), pp. 758–9. **40** David Cecil, Melbourne, (London, 1965), p. 235. **41** NLI, FitzGibbon Papers, 8343/14, ? Dickson to Richard FitzGibbon, (no date). "My dear colonel, It has been much observed upon that your only Deputies in this city were two Roman Catholics and no Protestant, one of whom should have resigned before he took the part he did , in politics. I should therefore feel very much obliged if your would have the kindness to nominate me to one if it does not interfere with your own arrangements." **42** FitzGibbon, pp. 67, 72. **43** *Falkiner* p. 140.

Index